The Gaffer's Handbook

To my mother and father

The Gaffer's Handbook

Film lighting practices, equipment and electrical distribution

Harry C. Box

Edited by Brian Fitt

Focal Press

OXFORD AUCKLAND BOSTON JOHANNESBURG MELBOURNE NEW DELHI

Focal Press
An imprint of Butterworth-Heinemann
Linacre House, Jordan Hill, Oxford OX2 8DP
225 Wildwood Avenue, Woburn, MA 01801-2041
A division of Reed Educational and Professional Publishing Ltd

A member of the Reed Elsevier plc group

First published in the United States of America as *Set Lighting Technician's Handbook* 1993
Second edition 1997
First published in Great Britain 1999

British Library Cataloguing in Publication Data
Box, Harry C.
The gaffer's handbook: film lighting practices, equipment and electrical distribution. – European ed.
1. Cinematography – Lighting
I. Title II. Fitt, Brian
778.5'2343

Library of Congress Cataloguing in Publication Data
Box, Harry C.
The gaffer's handbook: film lighting practices, equipment and electrical distribution/Harry C. Box; edited by Brian Fitt.
p. cm
Previously published under title: Set lighting technician's handbook.
Includes index.
ISBN 0 240 51523 4
1. Cinematography – Lighting – Handbooks, manuals, etc. I. Fitt, Brian.
II. Box, Harry C. Set lighting technician's handbook.
III. Title.
TR891.B68 98–35044
778.5'343–dc21 CIP

ISBN 0 240 51523 4

Typeset by Avocet Typeset, Brill, Aylesbury, Bucks
Printed and bound in Great Britain by Biddles Ltd, Guildford and King's Lynn

Contents

List of tables

Preface

Terminology

Imagine that your mother visits you on the set. You introduce her to the gaffer, who seems like a nice fellow, that is, until he starts giving orders: ‘Hang a baby. Kill the midget and have two blondes standing by for the martini.’

The set lighting profession uses volumes of peculiar-sounding technical terms. In this book, terms are defined the first time they are used, and can also be found in the glossary. You will find, however, that the same equipment has different names from country to country, city to city and studio lot to studio lot. An *Obie* light is called a *basher* in England. In Jamaica a *scrim* is known as a *strainer*, while here we often simply call it *wire*. A *wall sled* is called a *Grumpy* at Paramount Studio (the name that people around the lot bestowed on its inventor). There are even a few common terms that are difficult to use in polite conversation.

People who work in rental houses will act as if you are out of your mind if you call something by a different name than that with which they are familiar. This can be frustrating when working out of town with a new rental house.

To make matters even more unpredictable, terms change over time and are constantly being invented and evolving. I’ve adopted the terms that, in my experience, are most universally used, but you will no doubt run across many other names that do not appear here.

The correct terms for the head of the camera and lighting departments are Director of Photography or Cinematographer. To some, the abbreviation DP is objectionable for various reasons (DP also stands for Displaced Person, the label given refugees after the Second World War). Having acknowledged this fact, I am going to go ahead and use DP anyway as a matter of convenience in writing and reading. Readers should be aware, however, that for many Directors of Photography, the use of the abbreviation in conversation does not show proper respect for the title.

Acknowledgements

I am indebted to many individuals for their generous contributions to this book: Darryl Murchison, whose discussions during the early stages of writing helped set the book on course; Michael Skinner, who generously shared his expertise helping me unravel the vagaries of the NEC; Doug Pentek, Earl Gilbert, Larry Parker, Cyrus Yavneh, Russ Brandt, Dean Bray, Frieder Hochheim, Herb Breitling, Michael

Kaiping, Scott Toland and Jon Bart, all of whom read and improved sections of the book; Richard Mula and Pete Romano, who shed much light on the subject of underwater lighting; Frank 'The Dinosaur' Valdez and Gary Scalzo, who lent their expertise to the section on rigging; and Vance Trussell, whose suggestions and ongoing interest and encouragement were invaluable to me.

I also gratefully acknowledge the many manufacturers who provided technical information, photographs, and illustrations. The manufacturers are listed in Appendix G. I also thank Doug Pentec and Carly Barber of Hollywood Rental and Robert Guzman of Concept Lighting for the use of their rental equipment in creating the artwork.

I would like to extend a special note of thanks to the illustrators, Shawn Murphy and Lisa Cyr, who may well have been inking drawings on their wedding night in order to make the publication deadline.

My very greatest thanks, love and appreciation go to Joan Box for her loving attention to my split infinitives and for her unending support.

Finally, thanks to my family, to Dana, and to other close friends for their support in the writing of this book.

Additional acknowledgements for the second edition

There is a great deal of new material in the second edition and more people to acknowledge for their contributions to its research. I would like to thank Eric King, who shared his expertise on HMIs and electronic ballasts. I owe a debt of gratitude to Chris Barratt, without whose generosity and vast experience I could not have created the new section on generator troubleshooting. I also thank Bernie Kret at Strand, who helped with the new section on electronic dimmers. I lastly would like to praise the talents of John Huey, who created additional artwork for the second edition.

Editor's comments

It was once said that the British and Americans are two nations separated by a common language, this is sometimes even more so when describing electrical equipment and lighting. With the free movement of technicians in the film and TV industries between continents many of the terms have been accepted into more general use. Although, I must admit, I found 'suicide pins' an interesting idea.

Much of Harry's book describes the practices relating to the Hollywood-based film industry, however, the principles he discusses with regard to electrical distribution and safety are just as relevant anywhere in the world. As we tend to deal with higher voltages in Europe we have to be doubly careful!

The chapters which discuss all the operational problems are particularly relevant to anybody working either in film or on TV location work. Although the book describes American equipment most items or their equivalents are available in Europe. Much of the lighting equipment in use today evolved from the original designs of Mole-Richardson of Hollywood. 'Moles' also had a factory in England and operations throughout Europe in the post-Second World War era, and if you look closely you can see the 'sons and daughters of MR' in many of today's designs.

The film industry works very much on 'light as you go along', which necessitates vast quantities of equipment being available just in case, whereas TV studios either keep to the fairly standard rigging arrangements or plan equipment levels to a much tighter budget. Location work in both film and television tends to be done in the same way, although the budget for a Bruce Willis film will be somewhat larger than that for *Inspector Morse* or *Pride and Prejudice*.

I have tried to avoid making too many changes to the original text so that the reader may get a better understanding of American film practices and their terminology.

The accepted term for light sources in Europe is 'luminaire', however the film industry calls the same thing 'lights' 'lamps' 'fixtures', or 'heads'. Theatre electricians may talk about 'instruments' or 'luminaires'. To avoid any confusion between luminaires and the lamps contained within I have gone along with Harry's terminology, calling them lights in many cases. I have, however, tried to avoid the term 'lamp' being used to describe a luminaire as this can be most confusing. The glossary describes only luminaires and lamps with cross-referencing when needed.

The term 'HMI' is generally used these days to describe discharge lights, rather like 'Hoover' describes every modern vacuum cleaner. I have tried to reflect the fact that there are many discharge lamps made by several manufacturers and, hopefully, have avoided too many 'HMIs'.

May I say that I really enjoyed reading Harry's book and I hope the changes made for this European edition have contributed to your better understanding of the material.

In conclusion, I would also make the observation that there is not enough training in the lighting industry and publications such as this go a long way to putting the matter right. I hope all students of lighting, whether they are past their sell by date like me or just beginning, will find the book as interesting as I did.

Brian Fitt

1

Set basics: your first barbecue

The technical aspects of film-making – film stocks, cameras, lighting, sound, effects – all involve a myriad of small details that, taken as a whole, seem impossibly complex. As with any craft, to become a master requires years of experience and exposure to many different situations. It has been my experience, however, that no single piece of equipment or procedure or technique is really complicated; there is no single thing that cannot be explained and understood in less than ten minutes. Making films is the artful application of millions of relatively simple details. This book helps with some of those details, describing procedures that save time and promote safety, clarifying aspects of the craft that are confusing and often misunderstood, and supplying a wealth of information about the hundreds of gadgets of which lighting technicians are so fond.

Starting with the basics, we begin with a summary of the role of the lighting crew on a film set.

Job descriptions of the lighting crew

The electric, grip and camera departments fall under the direction of the *director of photography* (DP). The *gaffer* and *key grip* are the DP's lieutenants. The gaffer is the head of the electric department, and is in charge of the lighting crew. The gaffer's crew consists of the *assistant chief lighting technician*, known as the *best boy electric* or *second electrician*. Under the best boy are the set *electricians*, also called *lamp operators* or *third electricians*.

Director of photography

Q: How many directors does it take to screw in a light bulb?
A: One. No, two. No, no one . . .

The director of photography (DP) is the director's right hand; he or she is the one who helps the director make all the hard decisions.

It is the DP's responsibility to create on film what the director and he or she have envisioned for each scene, to evoke the proper time, place and atmosphere with the lighting, and to help choose the camera angles that will be most effective in telling the story. He or she chooses the lighting sources, balancing realism against the dramatic potential of more stylized effects, as called for by the script and the director. The DP has a say in the design and colour of the sets and the wardrobe and in the selection of locations. He or she helps the director decide how each scene is to be covered and what overlap the various camera angles will provide for the editor. In choosing the camera angles, the DP must maintain proper screen direction (a responsibility shared with the script supervisor) and lighting continuity between setups. The DP usually shoots tests prior to the beginning of photography. He or she may experiment with various lighting effects, with different gel colours, with a special lab process or different filter combinations – looking for a combination of effects that will accomplish the special requirements of the script. The DP may also conduct his or her own research prior to production to ensure accuracy and authenticity of a period and to inspire ideas for the cinematography.

The DP holds a position of immense responsibility, creatively and financially. A producer depends on the DP not only for the photographic quality of the film, but also for maintaining the production schedule. The DP always faces conflicts, in meeting both his or her own aspirations for the photography and meeting the demands of the film's schedule and budget. The lighting crew fights the DP's battles on the front lines. Their ability to light the set quickly and efficiently directly affects the DP's ability to produce good work and maintain the production schedule.

Gaffer

The gaffer is the *chief lighting technician* (CLT). He or she works directly with the DP to implement the lighting plan and help achieve the photographic look of the film. The DP, gaffer and key grip attend preproduction meetings together and scout the locations where filming is to take place. They discuss the DP's approach to each scene and determine what lighting preparations and equipment are required.

On the set, the gaffer is responsible for the execution of the lighting scheme, the organization and operation of the lighting crew. The DP typically expresses his or her goals as to the mood and the motivating sources of light for the scene, and the f-stop at which he or she wants to shoot. The DP and the gaffer discuss the lighting. The DP may have specific lamps in mind or may leave it to the gaffer to translate general ideas into specifics. The gaffer then instructs the crew, and sees to the exact placement and focus of each light to accomplish the DP's instructions. Typically once the gaffer has executed the lighting the DP will 'sweeten' to taste, with a few adjustments.

The gaffer must have a very strong eye for lighting and a solid knowledge of which lights to use to create any desired effect. As the lighting starts to come together, the gaffer functions as the director of photography's second pair of eyes. The gaffer is always on the lookout for problems – inadequate light, overexposure, hot spots, ugly shadows, and so on. Together the director of photography and gaffer look for ways to make the scene look more interesting. A first-rate gaffer has a critical eye for the balance of light and shade, the modelling of facial features and the separation of foreground from middle ground and background. The gaffer, carrying light meters on a belt, often stands next to the DP at the camera to view and measure the light hitting the subject and consult with him or her on issues of fill ratio and balance of exposure.

A very important part of the gaffer's job is organizing and running the operation. He or she must constantly be cycling through the many tasks at hand, pushing forward the progress of each project, keeping an eye on the performance of the lighting crew, thinking ahead so that power and lights are readily at hand for each shot and forestalling delay by maintaining constant vigilance over every possible need.

The gaffer should never have to leave the immediate area in which the action is being filmed. He or she must rely on the crew to be near at hand to make lighting adjustments and to run for equipment when it is needed. If, during filming, it is necessary to clear the set, the grips and electricians remain just outside the set, near the door, during the takes. Because the lighting crew is always under time pressure, an electrician who stays near the action, listens and thinks ahead can do a lot to help the gaffer improve the speed and efficiency of filming.

Best boy electric

The best boy electric is the gaffer's chief assistant. He or she is in charge of personnel and equipment for the electrical department: a vital role in the smooth running of the lighting crew. The best boy's duties include scouting the locations with the gaffer, making scouting notes and creating light plots with the gaffer when necessary, compiling the list of equipment needed, supervising the load-in (loading electrical equipment into the van at the rental house before the first day of production), organizing the equipment and supplies in the van, supervising equipment removal from and return to the van at each location, keeping track of inventory and damage, and supervising the load-out after the last day of production. At each location, the best boy plans the routing of the feeder cable and supervises the distribution of electrical power to the lights. In addition to the equipment inventory, the best boy keeps track of gels and expendables; co-ordinates equipment orders, returns, subrentals and special orders; and is in charge of hiring and laying off extra electricians when needed. The best boy supervises the electrical crew's start-up paperwork and time cards.

During filming, the best boy functions like a coach, rotating his or her crew into and out of play, making sure electricians are positioned where they are needed, ensuring that everyone doesn't wander off to graze at the craft service table or flirt with the make-up department – at least, not all at once. The best boy also repairs or exchanges broken equipment, changes burned-out lamps, maintains equipment and keeps the van organized for easy access to equipment.

The best boy is the first person an electrician goes to if he or she has a complaint. A chain of command operates on the set; an electrician should not speak directly with the production manager or the director. If necessary, the best boy will take up the issue with the gaffer. It is then the gaffer's responsibility to fight for the needs of the electrical crew. There are always enough opinions on a set. It is preferable that the lighting crew be noticed for their good work, not for their remarks.

Most important, the best boy is the emissary of the electrical department, communicating and negotiating with other departments, with the fire marshal, and with rental houses and other equipment suppliers. A best boy who maintains good relations with each department can get co-operation when it is needed. For example, when the best boy needs to put a light on the roof of a building, the locations team must make the necessary contacts to secure that spot. When the best boy needs some extra equipment delivered quickly, his or her relationship with the transportation department and the contact at the rental house comes into play. The best boy's diplomacy is key.

Electricians

Electricians are affectionately known as *sparkies*, or in the USA *juicers*, *set lighting technicians* or *lamp operators*. The electrician's primary responsibility is placing and focusing lights and setting flags according to the wishes of the gaffer. At each location, the electricians unload and reload the lighting equipment from the vans, run cabling and run the distribution of electrical power for the lights. They may be asked also to provide power for other departments – hair, make-up, camera, sound – however, the transportation department usually provides power for all vehicles. On the set, electricians are responsible for safely securing lights and stands during use; manipulating the intensity, direction, colour and quality of light; wiring practical lamps (such as table lamps and wall sconces), switches and wall outlets on constructed sets; and anticipating the needs of the gaffer so that equipment is at hand when needed.

An experienced lamp operator handles the equipment with deft speed and smoothness, an economy of movement that comes with familiarity. His or her focused concentration is on two things: the activities of the lighting crew and the behaviour of the light. He or she is constantly attentive to the gaffer and DP, and to fellow electricians who might need a hand. Simultaneously, the electrician is aware of the light falling, blasting, leaking and spilling on to the faces and the surfaces around the set. Through the exchange of a few words, hand signals or by clairvoyance, the electrician grasps the gaffer's intention and manipulates the lamp to create the desired effect.

I should add that film electricians are very rarely licensed journeymen or master electricians. They are not qualified to wire buildings or work on power lines. Their job is lighting films.

Grip department

Q: How many grips does it take to screw in a light bulb?
A: Grips don't change light bulbs. That's electric.

The grip is primarily responsible for laying and levelling dolly track, rigging and operating various types of camera dollies, cranes, platforms and scaffolds. The department is usually made up of the camera grip who is assisted by a rigger, a chippie (carpenter) and one or more grips. The camera grip or dolly grip is in charge of operating the dollies and cranes: laying and levelling dolly track, moving the camera smoothly to exact marks and with precise timing, and booming the camera up and down. Camera grips also rig support for the camera when it is placed in unusual places, such as on the bonnet of a car.

In the USA the division of labour between grips and electricians is slightly different. In America the grip department is made up of the key grip (who runs the department), best boy grip (who administrates), the dolly grip and company grips. In addition to operating the dollies and cranes, the grip department is responsible for all non-electrical aspects of lighting – setting flags, flying large frames overhead and operating shiny boards. When lights are hung from an overhead grid, rigged to the set wall or rigged to a telescoping arm (condor), the grips will generally rig the support for it.

The company

A film crew is composed of freelance artists, technicians, and administrators who are brought together by the production company when the production is ready to be mounted. The producer and director select the department heads: the DP, production designer, sound mixer, editor and so on. Each department head usually brings his or her own staff on to the production. The DP recommends a gaffer, camera grip, camera operator and camera assistants with whom he or she prefers to work. The gaffer, in turn, recommends electricians he or she knows and trusts.

Each production brings new faces, new locations, and new circumstances, and yet you can count on certain constants in relationships between electricians and the other departments.

Production staff

The crew is officially hired by the producer. Although the gaffer usually brings electricians on to the crew, once an electrician is offered a job, it is the producer with whom he signs the deal memo or contract. Pay cheques are handled by the accounting department or by a payroll company.

The duties of the unit production manager (UPM) include preparing the script breakdown and production schedule, establishing and controlling the budget, supervising the selection of locations, overseeing daily production decisions such as authorizing overtime and making schedule changes due to weather – and managing all the off-set logistics including housing, meals, transportation, permits, security and insurance.

The production co-ordinator assists the production manager. His or her duties include booking the crew and cast, booking and returning equipment, ordering expendables and supplies, making deals for locations and services, monitoring petty cash, distributing production information to the various departments, co-ordinating and distributing the shooting schedule and keeping the budget. The production manager and production co-ordinator work out of the production office, making frequent visits to the set.

Assistant directors

The assistant director (1st AD) runs the set. He or she co-ordinates the actions of every department and the cast, plans the day's schedule, approves the call sheet (which is usually prepared by a second assistant director), keeps everyone informed about the shots and plans ahead to minimize the amount of time used for each setup. The AD must stay informed of any potential delays or problems and facilitate, co-ordinate and motivate the actions of the crew, solving problems before they occur. He or she is responsible for keeping the production moving and on schedule on an hour to hour basis.

The ADs are responsible for co-ordinating the actions of all the departments. For example, if an electrician needed some furniture moved in order to place a light and the set decorator was nowhere in sight, the 1st or 2nd AD would take the matter in hand.

The AD staff take care of the actors: co-ordinating their schedules, ushering them through make-up and wardrobe and to and from the set. The AD also directs the background action, supervises crowd control, and determines safety precautions during stunts or complicated setups. The AD calls out 'Rolling' just before the cameras roll and 'Cut' after the director calls 'Cut.' It is the nature of the job that the AD has to tell everybody what to do all the time. One shouldn't hold it against him or her, though; a good AD can make the difference between a 12-hour day and a 16-hour day.

The AD is aided by a 2nd AD, who in turn is helped by 2nd 2nd ADs and a squad of production assistants (PAs). You can usually enlist the help of a PA for any odd job that presents itself; just ask first to be sure that the 2nd ADs can spare the PA.

Script supervisor

Details such as the hand in which an actor holds his beer, at what point in the scene he puts out his cigarette, whether his shirtsleeves are rolled up or not are observed and noted by the script supervisor. For this reason it is vital for him or her to be able to see the action on every take; if you stand in his or her way, you risk being jabbed by a sharp little pencil. The script supervisor also keeps track of the scene and take numbers, lenses used, shot scale, movement, eye-line direction, good takes, flawed takes (and reason), line changes (including add libs and mistakes) etc. The gaffer will sometimes have the best boy take detailed notes on the placement of the lights especially if the scene may be replicated at another time. The script supervisor can provide the best boy with the applicable scene numbers for his or her notes.

Camera department

The camera department is made up of the DP, camera operator, 1st Assistant, 2nd Assistant and a loader. The first camera assistant (1st AC) is responsible for keeping the camera in focus, making lens changes, threading the film, and maintaining the camera. The 1st AC never leaves the camera's side.

From time to time the 1st AC calls on the lighting crew to help get rid of stray light hitting the lens. (When a light shines directly into the lens, it causes a flare on the image.) The AC and the grips watch for 'hits' during setup and rehearsal.

The 2nd AC and loader aid the 1st AC with lens changes, magazine changes, film loading and paperwork. Almost all camera equipment runs on batteries, but a 2nd AC will need power to run a video monitor or to charge batteries. When a director is using a video monitor it quickly becomes habit to supply power to the monitor as soon as the camera is placed. Similarly a stinger should be supplied for the dolly at all times.

Sound department

The sound mixer oversees the recording of audio, monitors the sound levels, and is generally responsible for the quality of the sound recording. The sound mixer is the one person on the set who is lucky enough to perform his or her job from a sitting position. He or she can usually be found reading the paper at the sound cart.

The boom operator is the person who actually positions the microphone (mike) within range of the actors, either by holding it on a pole over their heads, by wiring them with radio mikes or by planting hidden microphones on the set. When a power cable must cross the microphone cable, it must be run under the microphone cable so it doesn't restrict the boom's movement.

The boom operator has to contend with shadows cast on to the actors and backgrounds by the microphone and boom pole. Boom operators are very good at analysing the lighting and sometimes have to go through all sorts of contortions to avoid casting shadows. Very often setting a topper on one or two lights eliminates shadows cast on to the back wall. Flat-on hard light from the direction of the camera tends to throw mike shadows on to the back wall. Snooting the light (see Chapter 3, section on Fresnels) so that it only lights the face, or raising it higher, so the light is angled downward, then topping the light, can eliminate the problem. Steep, top-down lighting tends to throw microphone shadows down across the actor's clothes. Sometimes the lighting is such that a boom microphone simply cannot be used, and the sound department must accommodate by using other methods.

The sound department has a vested interest in good placement of the generator. Even with baffles to deaden it, engine noise can still be a nuisance.

Ballasts and dimmers usually hum, and can become a concern for sound. Place them as far from the microphones as possible (preferably in another room or outside). (And if you wear a pager, don't forget to put it on silent (vibrate) mode.)

Dimming, light cues, and effects create line noise. It is best if the sound cart can be powered off separate utility power. All crew members must check with an electrician before plugging in their own electrical equipment; mistakenly plugging a monitor into a dimmer channel, for example, would provide an unexpected fireworks display.

Locations

A script might call for a city street, department store, hospital, church, factory, private residence, prison, airport terminal, office building, hotel lobby or post-apocalyptic tundra. Many settings can be more easily (and cheaply) filmed at an existing real site than recreated on the studio stage or lot. Whatever the case, the locations department finds, secures and co-ordinates the film's locations.

When on location any questions or problems pertaining to the building or grounds (such as access to locked rooms or access to circuit breaker panels) are handled by the building engineer through the locations co-ordinator. The locations co-ordinator obtains permission to place lights in unorthodox places – like on a roof. Care must be taken not to damage the floors, walls, garden. When a house has hardwood floors, for example, the grips and electricians can put rubber crutch tips on the legs of the stands and ask that layout board be put on the floors to protect them.

Transportation

The drivers are responsible for operating and maintaining all the production vehicles. In addition to the 'production van' (usually a 40 ft van which carries all the lights), transportation usually provides vehicles (with hydraulic lift gates), to the electric department. These are particularly useful on location when equipment needs to be shuttled to several sites in one day, or must be dispersed over a large area. Drivers may also be dispatched to make runs, to return equipment to or pick it up from suppliers. It is a good idea for the best boy to give the transportation co-ordinator as much advance warning as possible, as needs arise.

Art department

Q: How many art directors does it take to screw in a light bulb?
A: Does it have to be a light bulb? I've got a really nice candelabra we could use.

Construction builds the sets, *set dressing* decorates the set with items not handled by an actor, while the *props department* is responsible for anything that is handled by an actor. Wall lamps, practicals, 'oil' lanterns etc. are provided and placed by the set decorators. Wiring them is taken care of by an electrician. Employees of the set decorator move furniture.

Hair, make-up, wardrobe, stunts, special effects, first aid, craft service and catering are the remaining departments on the set with which electricians need to consult from time to time. It pays to stay on good terms with every department.

Block, light, rehearse, shoot

Progress on the set is measured in *setups*. A feature film crew may shoot twenty to thirty setups per day. The assistant director tries to schedule the shots so that all the shots in a scene in which the camera is looking in one direction, requiring one particular lighting setup, are shot together at one time. When possible, wider master shots are photographed first, establishing the lighting for the scene. Closer coverage, which usually requires refinements to the master setup, follows. Once coverage from one direction is complete, the AD calls 'Turning around', 'Moving on' or 'Next setup', and the camera is moved around to shoot the other way. The crew then relights the scene for the new camera angle. Once a scene is completed, the AD calls 'New deal', and the company clears out the set, and the director and actors block out the next scene on the schedule.

Although it is convenient when the shots can be scheduled in an efficient order for lighting, the AD may have other priorities. Shot order may be arranged to give precedence to, for example, a particularly difficult performance or a stunt that will destroy part of the set.

The standard procedure for filming each new scene has four steps: block, light, rehearse and shoot. First the director, DP and actors block the entire scene (plan the staging). During blocking rehearsal, the set is usually cleared so that the actors and director can work without distraction. The director and principal actors are called the *first team*. The DP, gaffer, and key grip watch the rehearsal to determine lighting needs and constraints. The 2nd AC marks the actors' positions with tape at their feet.

Once the scene has been blocked, the actors are sent to make-up, and the DP begins lighting. Often, the lighting crew has already roughed in some of the lights during a prelight. The actors are replaced by costumed stand-ins, who act as models for the gaffer and DP while the lights are placed. The *stand-ins* are known as the *second team*. The camera crew sometimes rehearses complicated camera moves using the stand-ins to avoid dulling the performances of the principal actors with technical rehearsals.

Once the lighting is in place, the AD calls the first team back to the set for final rehearsal. He calls 'Quiet please. Rehearsal's up'. The actors run through the scene with the camera and sound crew to iron out any remaining problems. The AC gets final focus marks; the dolly grip gets marks for the camera moves. After one or two rehearsals, the scene is ready to shoot.

Final rehearsals may take place while the electricians and grips are still adding final touches to the lighting. As a courtesy to the actors and director, everyone works quietly while the actors are on the set.

To save time between setups, electricians may begin lighting a new part of the set while the rest of the crew is filming, but before the camera rolls. When the AD calls 'Hold the work', he expects the work to stop immediately.

When it is time for cameras to roll, the AD calls 'Picture's up', followed by 'Roll sound'. Second ADs and set PAs, who are equipped with walkie-talkies, echo 'Rolling' in every part of the set. Everyone remains absolutely silent once 'Roll sound' is called. Be careful not to stand in an actor's eye-line. It distracts an actor to see a technician standing directly in his line of sight (staring blankly at him) while he or she is trying to perform. When the take is finished, the AD broadcasts 'That's a cut' on the walkie-talkie, at which time work can resume.

The AD makes other announcements, such as:

- 'Going again right away.' The electrical crew may not have time to resume work because a second take will be rolling immediately.
- 'Hold the roll.' There has been a momentary delay. It cues the sound mixer to stop rolling tape while the problem is fixed.
- 'That's lunch, one half hour.'
- 'Abby Singer is up.' The Abby Singer is the second to last shot of the day. It was named for (former) assistant director Abbey Singer, who always had 'just one more shot' after the last shot of the day.
- 'Martini is up.' The martini is the last shot of the day. (Your next shot will be out of a glass.)
- 'That's a wrap.' This announcement is made after the last shot of the day has been successfully completed. Electricians then begin wrapping: taking down the lights, coiling the cable and loading the van. When filming will resume in the same place on the following day and the equipment can simply be left where it is, it is a 'walk away'.
- 'MOS.' This phrase means that sound will not be recorded for the shot. The term comes from the early days of sound. It is an acronym for minus optical stripe.
- 'Fire in the hole!' This is announced before a shot in which there will be gunfire or explosions. Be prepared for a loud noise to follow.

2

Preproduction planning: lighting package, consumables and personal tools

Preproduction planning

One of the first responsibilities of the gaffer during preproduction is to prepare an equipment list (equipment and consumables lists are given in Appendices I and J). To come up with a complete equipment list, the gaffer needs to have clear ideas about how each scene will be lit. In scouting the locations and looking at the sets, the gaffer, key grip and DP are confronted with the particular challenges they'll need to address. The gaffer reads the script carefully, making notations and raising questions for the DP. He discusses scenes with the DP. The input of the director, production designer, and costume designer will often steer important lighting decisions.

Production meetings

At every stage of planning the gaffer is considering three things: equipment, personnel and time.

- **Equipment** What basic equipment will be needed to light the scenes? Which scenes will require special equipment (e.g., condor cranes, xenon spotlights and the like)? Will the transportation department need to furnish extra vehicles on particular days to move equipment from place to place?
- **Personnel** How many extra electricians will be needed to operate this special equipment, or to prerig or wrap-out cabling and equipment? Are there days on the schedule that are particularly difficult, or large locations that will require extra hands?
- **Time** What prerigging time will be required to achieve efficiency during shooting? What wrap time will be required? Can the shooting be realistically accomplished in the time allotted for it in the schedule? What workable solutions can the gaffer suggest to the assistant director and UPM?

Additionally, the DP and gaffer co-ordinate with the production designer to determine what special considerations should be given to the lighting in designing the sets. Designers are generally very conscious of lighting and will design the sets with windows in places that will make good lighting; however, looking over the designer's plans will forestall impediments to the lighting and may inspire ways to incorporate the DP's lighting ideas into the design.

During preproduction the DP and gaffer also discuss how to approach the material. What is the mood and style of the film? When will the shots be fairly conventional, and when will there be Steadicam shots that reveal every corner of a room, requiring that all lights be hung above or outside the set? What gel colours will be needed? What film stocks will be used? Will the lighting be at a low level or a high level? Each of these questions affects the equipment the gaffer will need.

Scouting locations

The director, assistant director and department heads scout each location in a group, discussing how the scenes will be played out. The DP and gaffer formulate a rough idea of how they will light each space. During the scout the DP, gaffer and key grip are constantly working out plans to adapt the space for lighting. Towers may need to be built outside the windows to support large lights. Wall spreaders or other lighting support may need to be rigged near the ceiling. Windows may need to be gelled or tented.

The best boy takes notes, which include: lighting plots, special rigging required and special equipment required. If the lighting is complex he or she may also want to make notes on the placement of windows and doors in each room, as well as wall sconces or chandeliers that may be seen on camera. If possible, he or she also notes the geography of the furniture and blocking of the actors. These notes will be invaluable during future discussions.

In addition to absorbing this information, the best boy needs to determine a location for the staging area and placement of the production van. He or she must carefully ascertain where the generator can be placed so as to be as close to the set as possible without causing sound problems, and how the feeder cables can be run to the set without entering into the shots. If a tie-in is a possibility, the best boy inspects the power boxes to determine their suitability. If house circuits may be used, he or she locates and examines the breaker box to determine its capacity and the layout of circuits. The best boy locates the light switches for sconces and house lights. He or she co-ordinates with the locations manager and the contact at the location to gain access to locked rooms, or to arrange for lights to be placed on neighbouring property or on the roof. The best boy must find the service entrance through which to bring in trolleys and equipment without encountering stairs. He or she must locate the elevators. If large numbers of fluorescent lights will be needed, he or she must get a count of the number of tubes to be ordered. In short, the best boy must fully think through the lighting needs at each location and prepare for all contingencies.

Once the locations have been scouted, the gaffer and best boy look over the production schedule; evaluate personnel, equipment and time requirements; and appraise the production department of their needs. It is helpful to create a calendar that outlines when extra workers and equipment will be required.

Equipment package

The load-in is the first day of work for an electrician on a feature film. It is the first day the electrician puts his or her hands on the lights.

The best boy supervises the check-out and load-in, making sure the order is correctly filled and that all the equipment is in full working order. The check-out must be extremely thorough. Even at the best rental houses, you cannot assume that all the equipment will be in perfect working order or leave the counting to someone else. At the completion of filming, any broken or missing items will be charged as 'lost and damaged'. There are an infinite number of ways circumstances can conspire to foul things up: Orders are often changed at the last minute, special equipment may be coming from more than one rental house, etc. Almost always a few items will require maintenance or be miscounted by the rental house, so count and check the equipment carefully.

Lights

Luminaires, lanterns, lights, units, heads, fixtures and fittings are all terms for film lights. Generally, many of the colloquial terms for lights will be used; such as '10K', 'Baby 2k' '1.2HMI'.

Each light should be tested at check-out. Take the time; you do not want to discover problems on the set when production is in full swing. Once you establish a routine for checking lights, it takes very little time to check all the items listed on the checklists in Tables 2.1 and 2.2.

Table 2.1 Checklist: tungsten (Fresnel and open-face) lights

- Check that each luminaire is complete. Each must have a full set of scrims, a scrim box or bag, and barn doors. Count scrims. A complete five-piece set includes two doubles, one single, one half-double, one half-single, and one gel frame (Figure 2.1).
- Barn doors. Check fit. Check for floppy doors. Most gaffers prefer four-leaf doors to two-leaf. Doors should be fitted with safety bond.
- Plug in each luminaire and turn it on to check the lamp and the switch. Make sure you have any needed connector adaptors. Wriggle the cord at the switch and luminaire housing to ferret out any intermittent discontinuity (a problem with power cord or lamp base contacts).
- Check spot/flood mechanism for smooth, full travel. Observe the beam as it changes. An uneven or odd-shaped beam is evidence of an improperly aligned lamp, or a bent or damaged reflector.
- With power off, open the luminaire and check the condition of the reflector. Especially with hot-burning luminaires such as baby-babies, or baby-juniors, the reflector can get cooked by prolonged use when tilted steeply downward. The reflector must be properly aligned, unbent, clean and in good condition.
- Inspect the lamp for blisters and bulges – evidence that the lamp has possibly been mishandled and burn-out is imminent.
- Check that the lens is clean and free of cracks. A little dust build-up on the lens will reduce the light output.
- Check that the locking handle works properly. The threads sometimes get stripped.
- Check that the tilt lock knuckle holds the luminaire firmly. The disks at the swivel point wear out and occasionally need to be replaced.

Table 2.2 Checklist: HMI

- Each unit should be complete with scrim set, barn doors, lens set (PARs only), two head feeder cables, ballast and power feeder cable (Figure 3.26). With units using large-size Socapex connectors, a junction box is also needed to connect the head feeders to one another.
- Barn doors. Check for floppy doors, bad fit, or missing barn door safety bond.
- Hook-up and turn on each luminaire using both head feeders. Inspect head cables for bent pins or connectors that are incorrectly mated, cuts in cable insulation, and loose cable strain relief collar at connector. Check READY and ON indicator lights on head and ballast.
- Allow several minutes to reach full output. Using a tri-stimulus colour temperature meter, measure the correlated colour temperature and green/magenta shift of each unit. Mark these measurements on a piece of white camera tape and tape it to the yoke of the luminaire. Also include the date and the unit number.
- Number each head, ballast, and lamp box so that the same head, lamp, and ballast are always used together.
- Check spot/flood mechanism for smooth, full travel. An uneven or odd-shaped beam is evidence of an improperly aligned lamp, or a bent or damaged reflector.
- Watch for unstable arcs. If in question, use a welder's glass to observe the lamp.
- You may want to check for earth faults and leakage current from the head and from the ballast. Current leaking to the lamp housing or ballast casing will give you a nasty shock if you become well grounded (such as when standing in wet grass). This is rarely a problem with new equipment, but often occurs with older, poorly maintained equipment. You can run into this problem if the wires in the head feeder cables are crossed, or if there is a short in the cable, the head, or the ballast. [*Note*: Although this problem may occur in America, UK Health and Safety Regulations, which require all equipment to be tested and to be in a safe condition before being used, should prevent this type of hazard.]
- You may also want to test the restrike capability of the luminaire by turning it off, and attempting a restrike after 15 seconds. If the luminaire will not restrike, try again once every 60 seconds to see how long you have to wait. *Note*: Repeated unsuccessful ignition attempts will discolour the inside of the lamp; don't overdo it.
- Inspect the lamp for blisters and bulges – evidence that burn-out is imminent.
- If the ballast uses a fuse, get a couple of spares.
- Check that the lens is clean and not cracked. If the lens is cracked it must be changed for an undamaged one. Dust on the lens will reduce the light output.
- Check that the locking handle works properly. The threads sometimes get stripped.
- Check that the tilt lock knuckle holds the luminaire firmly. The disks at the swivel point wear out and occasionally need to be replaced.

Stands

There are many different kinds of lighting stands, from short to very tall, from light-weight to heavy steel. All types of stands are covered in detail in Chapter 4. The stand check-out checklist in Table 2.3 enumerates the check-out procedure.

Electrical distribution system

Lighting a set can require heavy loads of electricity. When shooting on location, where necessary electrical service is not available, the production is powered by one

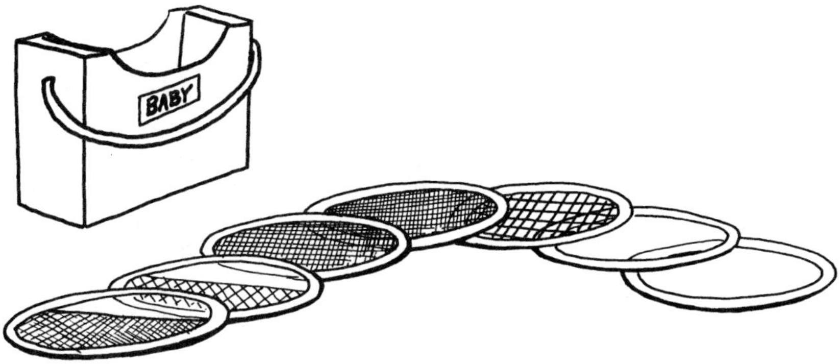

Figure 2.1 Complete scrim set with box. The set includes, from left to right, a half-double, half-single, 2 doubles, a single and a set of gel frames

or more generators that are designed to run quietly and produce the quantities of power needed. Electricity is fed to the lights through the distribution system. Electricity and distribution are covered in detail in Chapters 8, 9 and 10. The check-out checklist in Table 2.4 gives a brief description of the components of the distribution system, with some notes of things to watch for during the check-out.

Loading the production van

When shooting on location, the lighting crew works out of the production van, or grip truck. Depending on the size of the production, the vehicle may be anything from a cargo van to a 10-ton van, to a fully customized, 40-ft 18-wheeler. A fully equipped production van like the one shown in Figure 2.2 is complete with dual generators mounted on the tractor. The box comes equipped with shelving for the lights, brackets on the doors to hold stands, a large hydraulic lift gate, one or more side doors with stairs, interior lighting and a well-organized design. Smaller 5- and 10-ton vans have jockey boxes underneath both sides that carry cable and sandbags. Larger vans have doors along the length of the belly that can hold a substantial quantity of cable and distribution equipment.

Table 2.3 Checklist: stands

- Raise each stand to full extension. Check for binding and corrosion. Test each locking handle to ensure that the tubes will lock off safely.
- Inspect for bent or broken braces, or loose or missing brace bolts.
- Crank stands and motorized stands should be tested by raising and lowering the stand with a sand bag on the top. The weight is necessary to prevent the stand's inner mechanism from binding up when lowered.
- Pneumatic tyres should be fully inflated and should roll smoothly.
- Check that the wheel swivel locks, brace hinges, collars, and so on operate properly.

Table 2.4 Checklist: cable and distribution

- The main isolator is a high-amperage (200 or 400 A), fused switch box used as a main on/off switch for power to the set. Be sure that at least one spare fuse is included.
- Feeder cable. Heavy-gauge (4/0 or 2/0), single-conductor cable used to run power from the power source to the set. Check connectors for bent or broken ends. Inspect cable for cuts in the insulation showing exposed copper.
- Deuce boards. Fused remote switches which subdivide current into 200 A sub-circuits. Stock spare fuses.
- Heavy extension cables that carry power to various areas of the set and to high-amperage luminaires. Check for melted, overheated plastic on connectors. Check for bent or broken pins. Check for gashes in cable insulation.
- Distribution boxes, which plug into the larger feeder cable to provide a number of smaller outlets. Stock replacement fuses.
- Stingers. Extension cord. Used to carry power to medium and small luminaires (2,000 W and less). Check connectors for melted or blackened plastic. Test any suspicious looking ones.

[*Note*: The above checklist for distribution systems refers to American practices. In the UK, British Standard BS 5550 is the code of practice for location lighting for the entertainment industry. The UK distribution system will differ substantially from the American system, but the principles regarding safety are much the same.]

An *equipment trolley* (head cart) (Figure 2.3) is customized with large pneumatic tyres and sturdy shelves on to which a variety of the most commonly used lights are packed. The one shown in Figure 2.3 also carries a variety of stands (or gel rolls).

Trolleys, trucks and barrows provide convenience and mobility during shooting and expedite loading and unloading. You typically have at least two trolleys, one for tungsten units, for example, the other for HMIs. When the van travels, the trolleys are simply secured in the aisle. Lights are packed tightly and neatly on to the shelves of the trolleys, and on to the shelves of the van, grouped according to size. Once the lights are packed, the best boy labels the shelves show where each type of light is kept. It is helpful to include the number of lights on each shelf. This makes it easy to conduct an inventory quickly at the end of a day's shooting. Before the van travels, the lights are secured with rubber 'bungy' cords. Large lights, 5 kW and 10 kW Fresnels and large discharge sources, are kept on the floor of the truck along with the ballasts.

The electric crew typically also has a milk crate cart for stinger crates, practical bulbs and wiring devices, dimmers, a gel crate, consumables and rolls of gel (Figure 2.4).

One or more cable trucks (Figure 2.5) also are typically part of the equipment package. Cable trucks can be stowed in the aisle of the van during travel, convenient for keeping cable ready to be wheeled out. Similarly, a doorway dolly can be used (Figure 2.6).

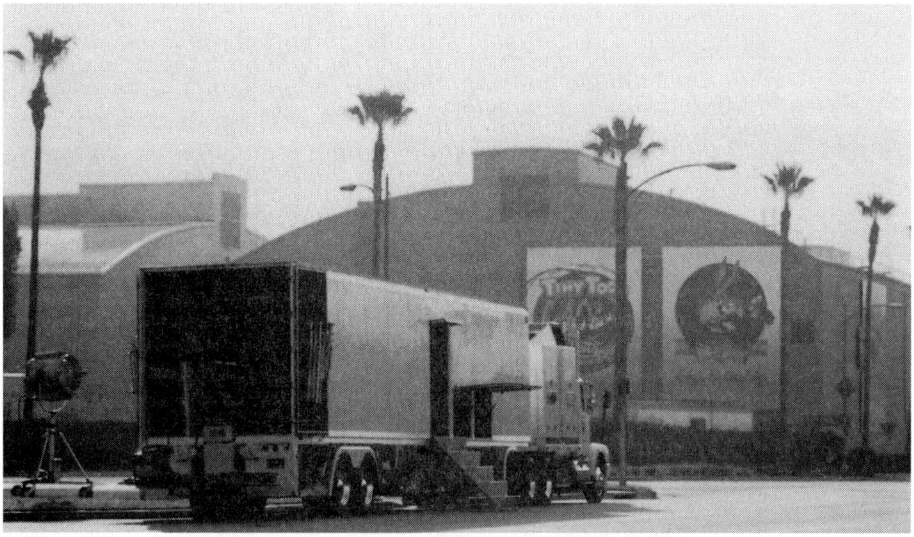

Figure 2.2 A 40-ft production van with two tractor-mounted generators. Note that stands are mounted to the rear doors. The small door on the side provides access to 12 kWs. (Photo courtesy of Hollywood Rental, Sun Valley, CA.)

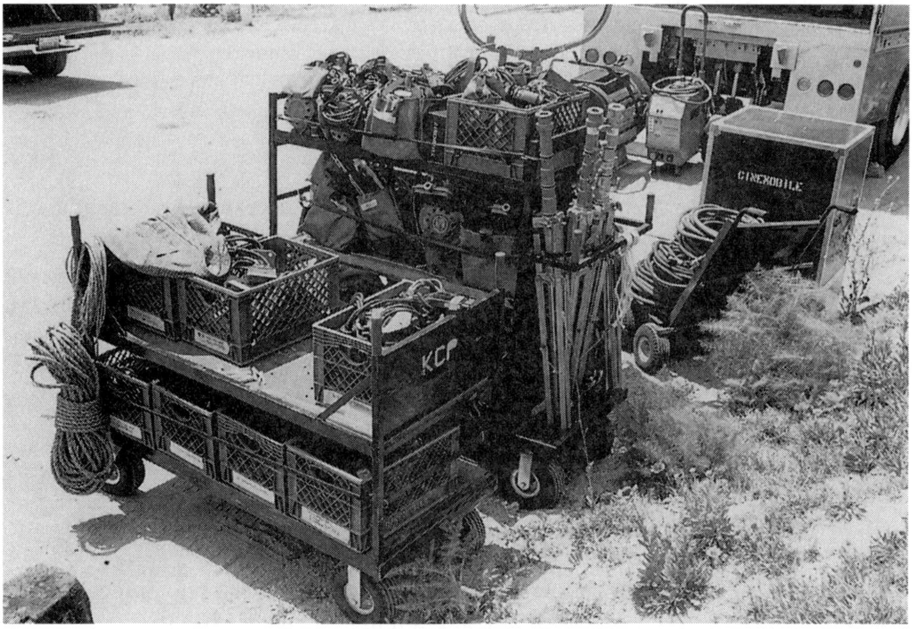

Figure 2.3 Pictured here are a 'tungsten trolley' (holding a crate of Peppers, and shelving for tweenies, babies, zip soft lights and baby juniors), a 'distro cart' containing crates of splitters and adaptors, and a cable truck (far right)

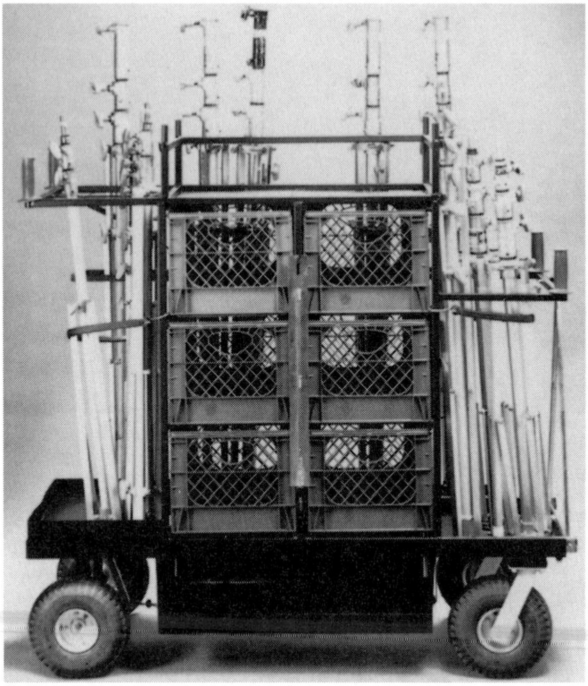

Figure 2.4 This trolley carries various types of stands. Milk crates contain hand dimmers, variacs, stingers, adaptors, practical bulbs and other electrical expendables. It may also hold rolls of gel and a milk crate of cut gel. (Courtesy of Backstage Studio Equipment, Sun Valley, CA.)

When packing the van, be sure you provide immediate access to equipment that is routinely needed. Don't bury your distribution boxes under cable or behind big lights. Put spare items such as fluorescent tubes, spare lamps, fuses, etc. on the top shelves, along with lights that are seldom called for. During night shooting, reserve a special spot for the items that will be packed away last, the work lights and associated cable and distribution.

The workbox, a wooden chest of drawers, is usually secured inside the van. It is used to store spare bulbs, electrical consumables, tools, paperwork and supplies.

Consumable supplies

Consumables (see also checklist in Appendix J) are supplies that are purchased and used up in the course of production. In addition to equipment inventory and check-out, the best boy and electricians use preparation days for organizing and prepping consumables, cutting gels for the lights, and completing any similar tasks to get everything ready for the first day of shooting.

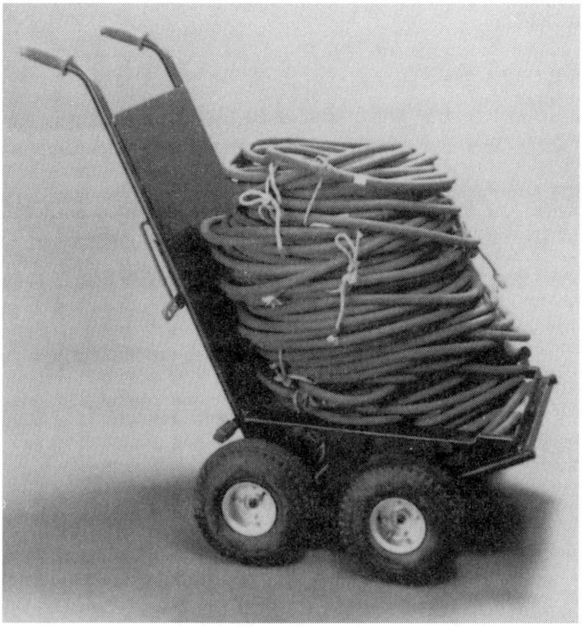

Figure 2.5 A cable truck is another method of moving cable from place to place. (Courtesy of Backstage Studio Equipment, Sun Valley, CA.)

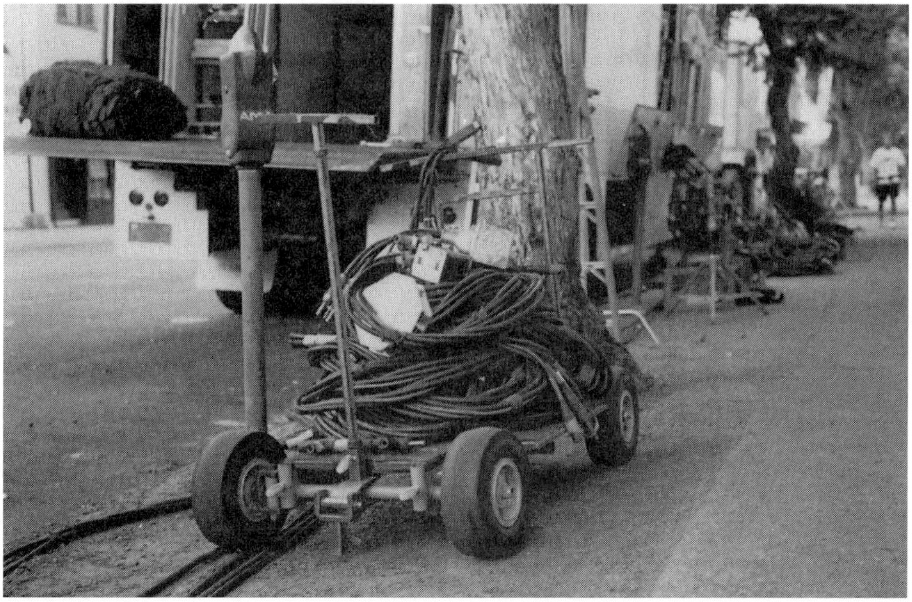

Figure 2.6 Cable or large lights are moved from place to place on a doorway dolly

Gels and diffusion

Gels are used for three purposes:

1. To correct the colour of one light source to match that of another (tungsten correction, daylight correction, carbon arc correction, and fluorescent correction gels).
2. To alter the colour of a source to create an effect (theatrical or effects gels).
3. To reduce the intensity of a source without altering its colour (neutral-density gels).

Diffusion media are white gels which soften light. Gels come in wide rolls and in sheets. They can be applied to lights or windows or put in frames that are placed in front of the light source.

Cuts of gel are kept in a crate or box, sectioned according to size and colour (Figure 2.7). This practice makes gel fast and easy on the set, and ultimately saves gel because less is wasted. Precut colour correction gel and diffusion in squares of 6 in., 8 in., 10 in., and 12 in., with some at 20 in. and 24 in. A 6-in. square fits inside the barn doors of units 1 kW or smaller. An 8-in. square fits the small Fresnels. The 10-in. and 12-in. sizes fit inside the doors of regular 2 kW Fresnels and outside the doors of lights that are 650 watts and smaller. (The larger cuts of gel fit on the outside of the doors of 2 kW Fresnels , 1200 W discharge sources and PAR lights.) Anything larger than 24 in. can be gelled using a frame.

The best way to cut gel from the roll is to use a template. Cut a 24 × 48 in. piece of ½ in. plywood and score it with grooves ¼ in. deep, making the grid pattern of 6-, 8-, 10- and 12-in. squares. The matte knife blade slices down the grooves and makes cutting gel very fast and easy. The smaller cuts can be made from the scraps left over from the larger cuts. Once the gel is cut and organized, the gel crate finds a home on the cart, where it will remain close at hand during shooting. Assorted rolls of gel may be kept on a trolley, and the remaining rolls are stored in boxes on the van.

Electrical consumables

A production may or may not require all of the items described here. During preparation these items are organized in the drawers of a work box, into crates on the milk crate cart, and into boxes on the shelves of the van. Label each drawer, crate and box with its contents. A large capacity tool box with drawers makes an excellent storage place for all the small consumable items. You can also keep gel swatch books, special tools and meters in the tool box. The tool box fits right on the milk crate cart (see Figure 2.7).

- **Black wrap** A durable, black foil used on the lights to control spill and to shape the beam. It is available in rolls of 12 in. (50 ft), 24 in., and 36 in. (25 ft). White wrap is also available.
- **Crocodile clips** Used to attach gels and diffusion to the lights. (In the USA wooden clothes pegs are used.)

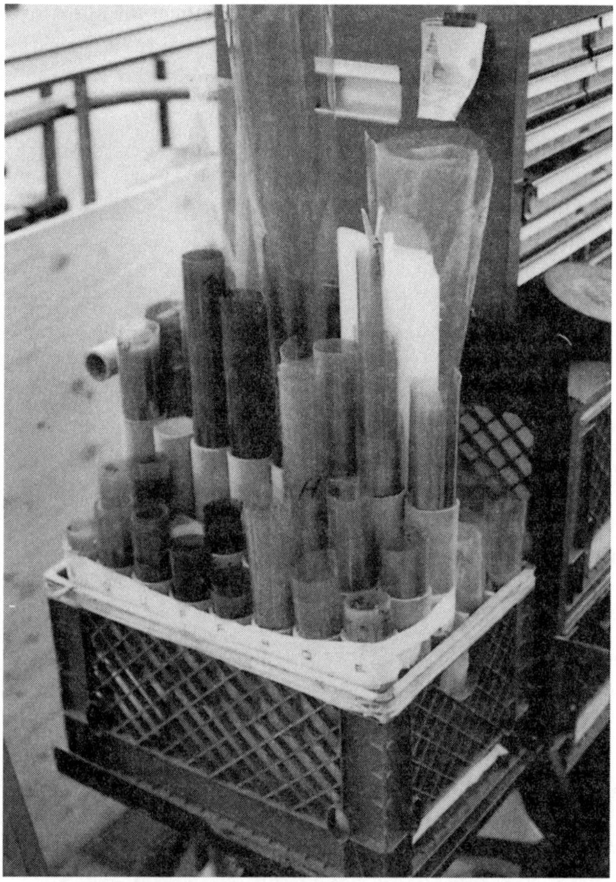

Figure 2.7 Cut gel and diffusion are marked with permanent marker and stored according to size and type in a sectioned milk crate

- **Rubber matting** Used to cover power cables where they cross doorways and other traffic areas. It comes in rolls 48 in. wide, up to 100 ft long.
- **Sash cord** White cotton rope used for tying cable to pipe, among other things. Commonly used weights are #6, #8, and #10.
- **Trick line and mason line** Weight #4, non-stretch rope. Trick line is black. Mason line is white. It comes in handy for odd jobs, such as making stinger tie-strings and power cord hangers.
- **Bungy cords and S-hooks** Black rubber Bungy cords come in various sizes and should be ordered to fit the shelves.
- **Connector strips** Used for plugging several low current light sources into one outlet.
- **Wire nuts** Insulated cap used to splice two bare wires together.
- **Dimmers** Household dimmers of 600 W and 1000 W are commonly used to dim small lights and practicals.

- **Sockets** Household lamp sockets are used to mount light bulbs in set pieces and soft boxes. Use porcelain sockets, as photo bulbs will melt a plastic socket.
- **In-line switches** When rigging practical lights in sets, it is sometimes handy to have a plug-in switch on the line.
- **Plug tops and sockets** The best boy stocks male and female connectors to replace the plugs and sockets when necessary (13 A, 15 A, 16 A).
- **3-core cable** The best boy may want to have rolls cable, which is handy for cabling special lights and devices.
- **Fuses** A selection of fuses for all types of equipment in use.
- **Phase tape** Tape used for insulating wire splices. It comes in a variety of colours (red, yellow, blue, black and green/yellow) and is handy for colour-coding cables and distribution boxes.
- **Gaffer tape** Heavy 2 in. fabric-based tape that rips cleanly in the direction of the weave. It is used to tape just about everything.
- **Paper tape** Tape that has less adhesion than gaffer tape. Black 2 in. paper tape is handy for masking light. It has less of a tendency to pull the paint off walls than gaffer tape.
- **White camera tape** 1 in. and 2 in. tape used for labelling equipment.
- **Snot tape** A sticky film that is handy for mounting gels in gel frames (3M transfer tape).
- **Best boy paint** White, heat-resistant paint used to repaint the reflective surfaces of soft lights without altering the colour of the light emitted.
- **Dulling spray** A spray applied to shiny surfaces to tone down reflective glints.
- **Streaks and tips** Coloured hair spray used to tone down or black out surfaces that are too bright. It is water soluble, washes off easily after filming, and comes in shades of auburn, beige, black, blond, brown, grey, pink, silver and white.
- **Practical lamps** For wall sconces, table lamps etc. in the set, household base bulbs. Typically a selection of wattages from 25 W up to 150 W is on hand.
- **Fluorescent** There are various types of cinematography-friendly commercial fluorescent tubes which replace fluorescent tubes in offices and commercial buildings where the existing fluorescent lights are not correct for photography. See Appendix E.
- **Spare flashlight bulbs** Replacement bulbs for electricians' flashlights.
- **Batteries** AA for flashlights and pagers. AAA for light meters. Disk batteries for DM73 voltage/continuity meter. 9 V for amp probe and light meters.
- **Cotter pins** Used when hanging lights to hold the spigot securely in a 'C' clamp or any other type of hanger.
- **Visqueen heavy plastic sheet** Used to protect equipment and electrical connections from rain, precipitation, dew, dust, and sand.
- **Crutch tips** Put on the legs of stands to protect floors. Sizes: ¾ in. for small stands, 1¼ in. for large stands.
- **Refracil** A heat-resistant cloth, similar to asbestos, that will not burn when a hot light is placed on it. It protects ceiling and wall surfaces from heat damage.
- **Bailing wire** Stiff wire, also called stovepipe wire. Can be used as a barn-door safety bond, although safety chains or wires are preferable.

- **Safety chain** Also called grip chain or sash chain. In addition to barn door safety, safety chain is used for such tasks as chaining the legs of a stand to a high platform.
- **Automatic tape gun (ATG)** A dispenser for snot tape. Used to attach gels to windows and gel frames.
- **Poly** Polystyrene ⅜, ½ or 1 in. thickness. Comes in 4 × 8 ft sheets. It is used to bounce light and gives off a softer and weaker light than foamcore.
- **J-lar tape** Clear 2 in. tape used to repair ripping gel and to stop gel from rattling in frames or on windows.
- **Chalk** Used to mark dolly marks on floor.
- **Duvetyn** Thick, black canvas-like cloth used for obstructing light in a multitude of applications, such as blacking-out and tenting windows and covering distracting objects.
- **Foamcore** An extremely lightweight bounce board made from ¼ in. foam reinforcement glued between two sheets of white, glossy card stock. Foamcore also comes with flat black on one side and is available in 4 × 8 ft sheets.
- **Hardware** Includes drywall screws for mounting wall plates, staples, pushpins, nails, bolts, nuts, and so on for general construction.
- **Timber** It is useful to stock lumber in a variety of sizes and forms. For example, 1 × 3 in. (batten) board is used to build soft boxes; 2 × 4 in. and 2 × 6 in. boards are used for wall spreaders. Plywood may be laid on the floor to make a 'dance floor' for smooth dolly moves.
- **Rope** Manila hemp (rough brown rope) in ¼ in., ⅜ in. and ½ in. thickness. Among the many uses, ¼ in. is used for tag line and guy wires.
- **Show card** Thick card stock, usually white on one side and black on the other, used to bounce light or to absorb it. Show cards come in a range of colours, including silver.
- **Silicone spray** A dry lubricant used on dolly track.
- **Brass rubbing paper** Tracing paper or Vellum 1000 H translucent paper used to white-out windows. Available in very wide rolls.

Preparations

- **Set box** The best boy will often prepare a set box, which is kept close to the action at all times, and contains all the commonly needed items: tape rolls, cord, power strips, dimmers and a supply of crocodile clips or clothespegs.
- **Tape rolls** Put together a selection of tape rolls on a loop of sash cord: one roll each of 2 in. gaffer tape, 2 in. black paper tape, and white camera tape. Snot tape should also be readily available. The phase tape rolls (all colours) go together on a separate rope.
- **Practical bulbs** Mark and organize practical bulbs so their wattage and type are easily readable. Label the boxes. Insert (foamcore) dividers in a couple of milk crates. Stock compartments with various types and wattage to keep near the set.
- **Home-made boxes** Home-made lighting lights, such as soft boxes, are wired by an electrician. Soft box construction is discussed in Chapter 6.

Tools and personal gear

Tool belt

Carry all the tools and supplies you will need on a tool belt (Figure 2.8). Include the following:

- **Leather work gloves** Cowhide or equivalent. Used for handling hot lights and dirty cable and hardware. Clip them on to your belt when you're not wearing them.
- **Crocodile clips/clothespegs** Keep a dozen or so on your belt. Figure 2.8 shows an inverted clothespeg, which is handy to pull hot scrims out of lights.
- **Screwdriver** Carry a flat-head screwdriver and a Phillips screwdriver or, better, a single screwdriver with a reversible tip: flat-head on one side, Phillips on the other.
- **Utility knife with retractable blade** For cutting gels, foamcore, rope, and so on.
- **Scissors** Small, sharp scissors are often handy for making more careful cuts of gels, etc.
- **Flashlight** Electricians frequently find themselves working in the dark. When dealing with electricity, you always need to see what you are doing. Small, rugged, focusing flashlights are very popular and easy to carry on your belt.
- **Permanent marker** For labelling gels, lights, connectors, cables and so forth.
- **Ball-point pen** For taking notes, filling out paperwork, taking down phone numbers, etc.

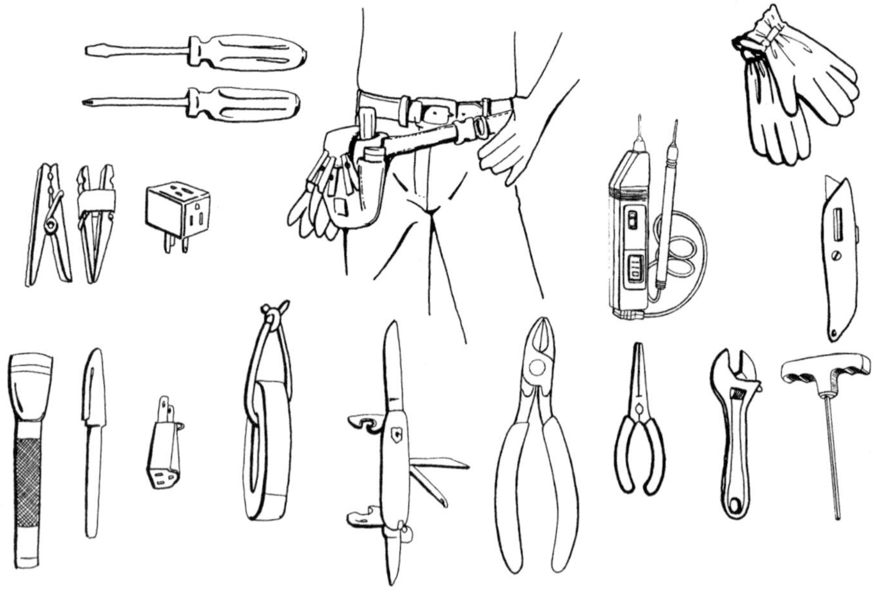

Figure 2.8 Tools

- **Gaffer tape** Loop sash cord through the tape, and attach it to your belt with a carabineer. If the roll is too bulky, you can make a 'tape cube'. Fold about 9 in. of tape on to itself, then continue to wind tape around until you have about 5 or 6 ft of it wound on to the strip. The tape cube can go in your back pocket.
- **Knife** A sharp knife with a retractable blade is useful for cutting rope, gel, card and foamcore.
- **Wire snips** Used primarily for cutting wire for practical lamps and making wire splices.
- **Crescent wrench** An adjustable wrench is used to adjust the friction of a luminaire yoke, tighten a pipe clamp, and perform countless other jobs. The jaws must be large enough to fit a ¾ in. bolt. You can find 6 in. crescent wrenches with an extra wide jaw, which are ideal. An 8 in. wrench is bulky, and a standard 6 in. crescent wrench is not quite big enough.
- **Speed wrench** Ratcheted wrench for securing sister-lugs on to bus bars.
- **Needle-nose pliers** Used for pulling hot scrims out of a light, small repairs, etc.
- **Voltmeter/continuity tester** Used to check line voltage (120 V, 220 V, 230 V, 240 V, 415 V) and to check for voltage drop. Used to locate broken connections in power cords. A continuity tester tests for burned-out bulbs and fuses.
- **Circuit tester** Plugs into a household outlet and tells you if the line is energized. Also indicates if the polarity and grounding are correct.
- **Line sensor** Hold this device near a wire or plug to determine if a wire has current flowing through it. The device senses the magnetic field.

Personal gear

Electricians get dirty; jeans, a T-shirt, and sneakers are normal apparel. Weather permitting, it is advisable to protect your legs and arms with long trousers and a shirt. Be prepared for the weather. In southern California you might need only sunscreen, a baseball hat, sunglasses, and a jacket and jeans for after sunset, but be prepared for all weather conditions. When shooting on location, bring full rainwear, boots, cold-weather jacket, hat and gloves, and a change of clothes in case you get wet. Also consider the terrain. Hiking boots or work boots are often desirable. You might want to keep the following personal gear in your duffel bag:

- sunscreen
- lip ointment
- mosquito repellent
- ear protection (disposable earplugs or head gear for when firearms are used)
- eye protection (goggles or safety glasses): the special effects department usually supplies eye protection to everyone who is needed near the action during explosions and stunts.

3

Luminaires

Luminaires come in all shapes and sizes. The design of the lantern, lamp, lens, reflector and accessories determines the nature of the beam, and provides some methods of controlling it. A lantern's beam characteristics, such as brightness, focusability, evenness, punch, softness, size, shape and colour, dictate its function in our lighting arsenal. Each type of lantern has specific advantages in certain applications, and there are tricks to using each. In this chapter we will concentrate on the most common types, Fresnels, softlights, open face, area lights, PARs, discharge sources and fluorescents. Chapter 11 describes ellipsoidal spotlights, par-cans, xenon lights, and more specialized and exotic luminaires.

Tungsten lights

The incandescent filament

Incandescent lanterns, commonly called *tungsten* lights, create light by running current through a tungsten filament until it glows, that is, until it is heated to incandescence. They can be powered by either AC or DC. Since tungsten filaments burn most efficiently at a colour temperature of 3,200 K (Kelvin degrees), tungsten-balanced colour motion picture films are designed to reproduce colours accurately when lit at 3,200 K colour temperature. Note that *colour temperature*, expressed in degrees Kelvin, is a measure of the colour output, not actual operating temperature. Daylight-balanced films are designed to reproduce colours accurately when lit with light having a colour temperature of 5,600 K, or daylight.

Tungsten light and daylight include every colour across the colour spectrum, and are therefore said to have a continuous spectrum. The graph of spectral power distribution (Figure 3.1) compares the distribution of energy across the spectrum of a tungsten source to that of daylight. Daylight is much stronger at the blue end of the spectrum, and tungsten light is much stronger at the red end. (Colour balance and colour correction are explained in detail in Chapter 6.)

Figure 3.1 Spectral power distribution graphs (SPD). These graphs illustrate the distribution of energy over colour spectrum for four primary light sources. Incandescent lamps are strong in the yellow orange and red, and weak in blue and violet. As colour temperature increases the curve shifts towards the blue spectral band.

In contrast, daylight is stronger on the blue end of the spectrum. Shown here are spectral distribution for: (A) clear noon sky (10,000 K), (B) clear north sky (7,000 K), (C) sun plus sky (6,500 K), (D) overcast sky (6,800 K), and (E) direct sun (5,600 K). Incandescent and daylight sources have continuous spectrum as shown by their smooth spectral distribution curves. HMI and fluorescent sources do not have a continuous spectrum. An HMI has a multiline spectrum (correlates to 5,500 K) which appears to the eye much the same as daylight. Note that generally the HMI graph has a similar distribution as line C or E on the daylight graph.

The fluorescent graph shows a standard cool white bulb (correlates to 4,500 K). Note that most of its energy comes from narrow peaks. The colour rendition of this bulb will be poor.

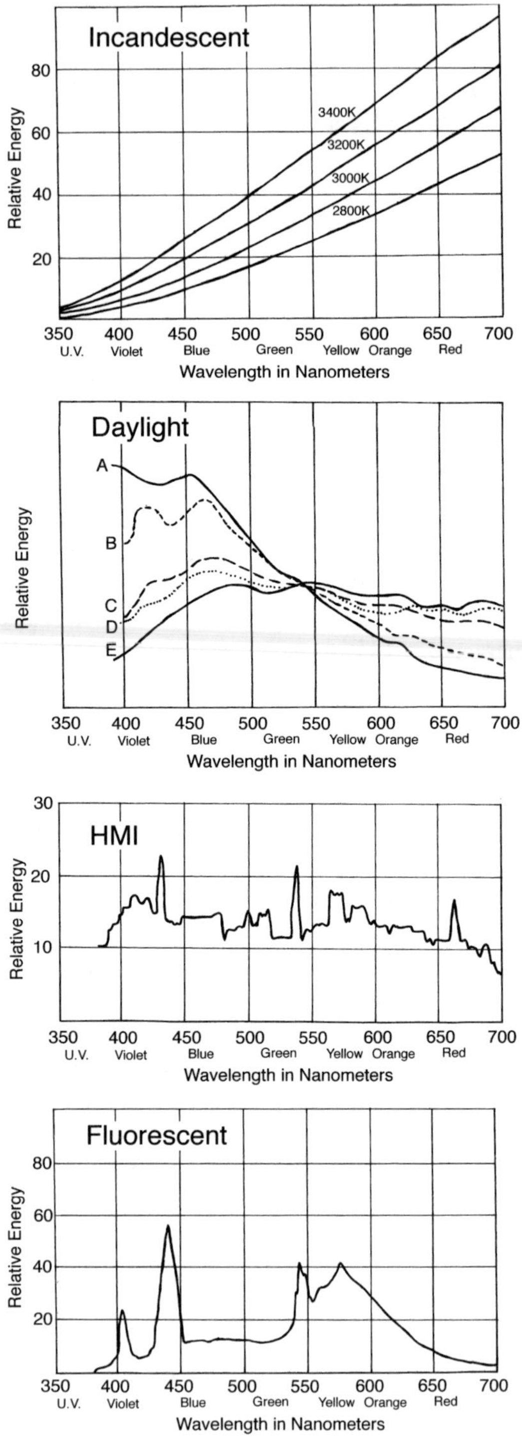

Tungsten halogen versus standard tungsten lamps

A *tungsten halogen* lamp is a type of incandescent lamp that contains special regenerative elements to prevent blackening on the sides of the lamp. The regenerative elements carry the evaporated tungsten, which is responsible for the blackening, back to the filament where it is reused, thereby increasing the life of the lamp. For the regenerative process, called the *halogen cycle*, to occur, a high temperature (at least 250°C) must be maintained inside the lamp, and for this reason tungsten halogen lamps tend to be compact and are made of quartz, which can withstand the high temperature. In the old days, large 10 kW lamps contained a cleaning agent that had to be manually swished around the inside of the lamp between uses to clean off the tungsten blackening.

The standard type of lamp used in each lantern is listed in Appendix E. There are often alternatives to the standard type: a lamp with a different wattage or colour temperature, or one that uses frosted instead of clear glass.

Fresnels

The *Fresnel* lantern (pronounced frenel) is designed to create a relatively even field of light with adjustable intensity and field size, making it a flexible light with which to work. For these reasons, it is the most commonly used lantern in film and television (Figure 3.2). Figure 3.3 illustrates the entire range of Fresnel sizes.

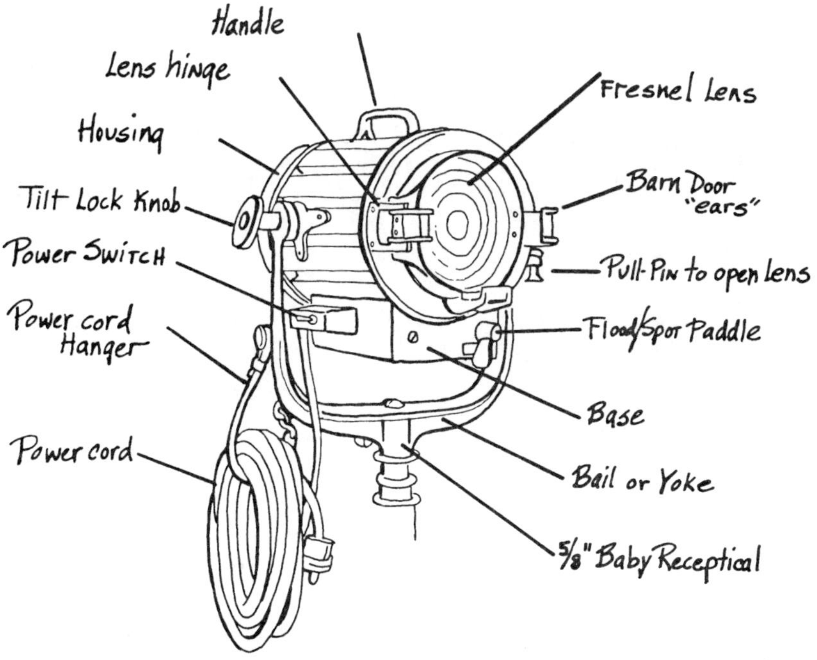

Figure 3.2 Anatomy of a Fresnel fixture

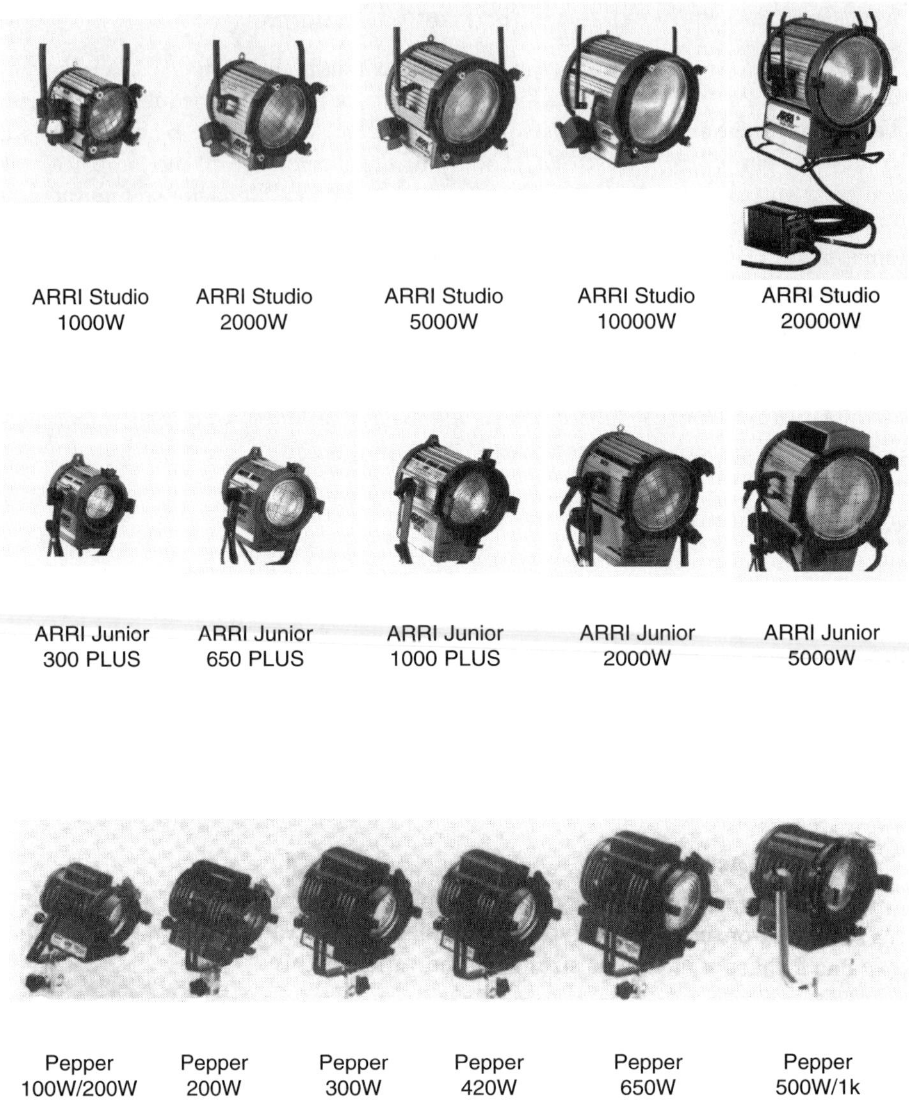

Figure 3.3 Fresnel lights

The lantern is named for its Fresnel lens, which bends the diverging rays of light emitted by the lamp into a controlled beam of light. The Fresnel lens has the same light-bending characteristics as a standard plano-convex lens, but the Fresnel's design compresses the convex curve into jagged steps (Figure 3.4), making it lighter and thinner so that it retains less heat and is less prone to cracking.

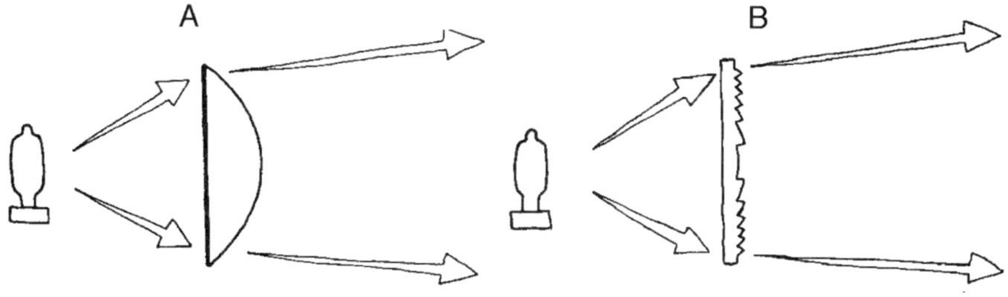

Figure 3.4 (A) A plano-convex lens. (B) A Fresnel lens

Inside the housing, the lamp and spherical reflector are mounted together and can be moved towards or away from the lens by an exterior adjustment knob. Moving the lamp and reflector toward the lens floods the beam, increasing its spread and decreasing its intensity (Figure 3.5A). Moving the lamp and reflector away from the lens spots the beam, making it narrower and more intense (Figure 3.5B). The adjustable focus makes it quick and easy to obtain the desired intensity or beam width.

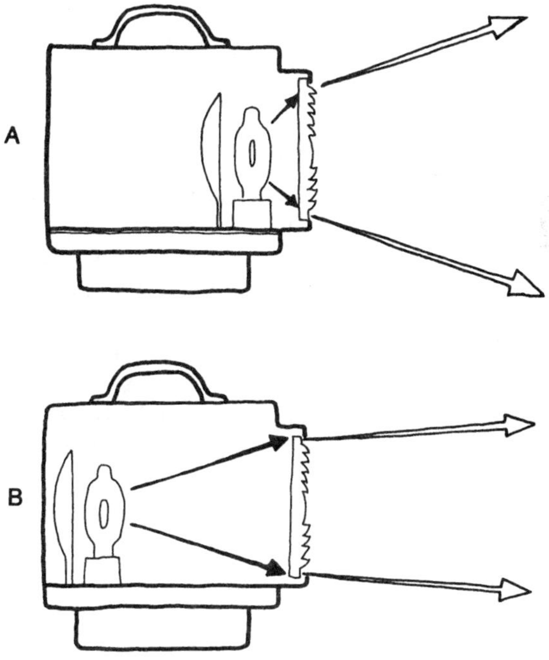

Figure 3.5 (A) A Fresnel lamp and reflector in flood position. Rays are refracted into a wide beam. (B) A Fresnel in spot position. The lamp and reflector are positioned so that the rays are concentrated into a tighter, more intense beam

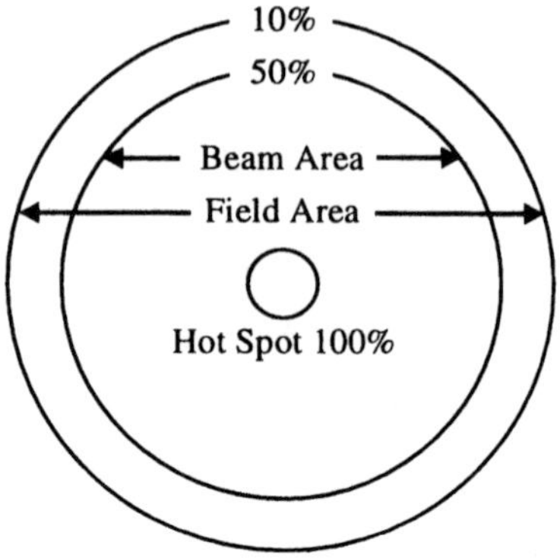

Figure 3.6 The field defines the usable light – the area of light in which the intensity is at least 10 per cent of the peak value. The beam is defined as the area of light in which the intensity is at least 50 per cent of the peak value. The *hot spot* is the brightest spot within the beam. The terms *field area* and *beam area* refer to the area of the field and beam respectively

Fresnel beam

To anticipate how the light will behave when an actor walks through it, the electrician must have a three-dimensional mental picture of the beam's shape and intensity, the manner in which intensity falls off towards the edges, and how varying the amount of spot or flood changes these characteristics. In describing the photometric qualities of a lantern, the terms *field* and *beam* are often used (Figure 3.6). A polar distribution graph (Figure 3.7) gives a clear picture of the shape of the beam intensity and how it changes from flood to spot.

At full flood the beam is relatively even across a 40° sweep, then falls off quickly towards the edges. Note that in full flood the beam has no central hot spot; the field is very even. As the lamp is spotted-in, the beam narrows and gets brighter in the centre, falling off rapidly on either side. At full spot the usable portion of the beam is narrow, about a 10° angle. The term *throw* refers to the distance from the lamp to the subject. A lamp in spot position has a greater throw; it will illuminate the subject to the same brightness at a much greater distance. Table A.14 in Appendix A gives the intensity at any distance for a variety of lanterns.

These are terms for the light manufacturer's sales literature; they rarely are mentioned on set, but in practice electricians use these concepts all the time. For example, let's say a large room is to be evenly lit using several lights spaced evenly along one wall of the room. In order to make the light intensity even across the whole room, the lamps are set at full flood, and the edge of the beam of each light is feathered into that of the next. The beams overlap slightly at the 50 per cent point, creating an even 100 per cent intensity across the entire space.

Photometric data provided by manufacturers denotes the range of spot and flood achieved by each light by giving the beam angle at the two ends of the range. A

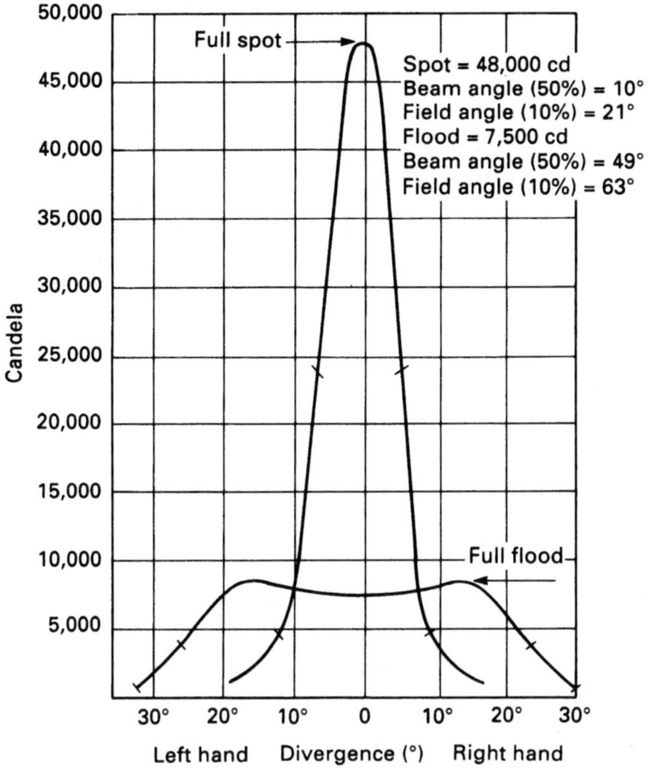

Figure 3.7 A polar distribution graph shows light intensity across the diameter of a field of light. The upper tick marks denote the beam angle (the 'working' light); the lower tick marks denote the field angle (the 'usable' light). In flood position the light offers virtually even intensity across the wide spread of the beam; in spot position beam intensity falls off rapidly outward from the central hot spot. Note: cd is an abbreviation for candela or candle power. It is a measure of brightness: cd = footcandles × (distance in ft)^2 or cd = lux × (distance in metres)^2

typical Fresnel has a range from about 10° to 45° or 50°. (Such data may also be expressed by giving the beam diameter and peak intensity, in foot-candles (FC), at various distances from the lantern.) Table A.13 in Appendix A gives the beam diameter at various distances for given beam angle.

The lamp and its installation

Lamps are referred to by designation code which are listed with other specifications in Appendices A and E.

Most larger Fresnels used in motion picture work have a bi-post lamp base. Smaller lamps have a bayonet base. Figure 3.8 shows how to open up various models of lights to get at the lamp.

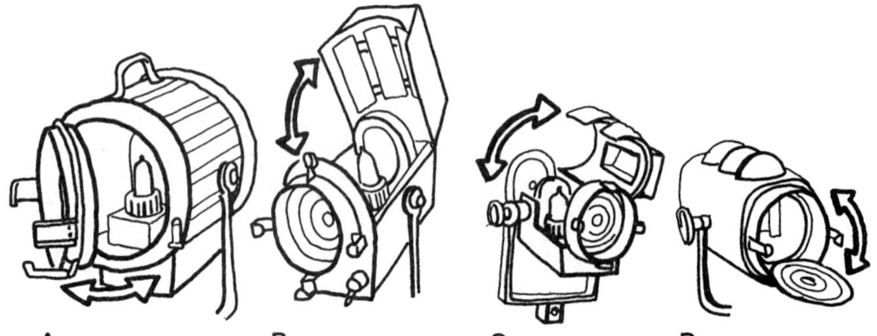

Figure 3.8 Four common ways to access the inside of a Fresnel fixture. (A) With most lights of 1,000 W and larger, the lens door swings open on a hinge. (B) On a baby-baby, the top of the housing swings back on a hinge at the back of the fixture. (C) The top of a pepper's housing swings open to one side. (D) The lens of a midget is held in place by a spring

On small units, the lamp simply plugs straight into the lamp base and is held in place by friction. When removing the lamp from this type of base, be careful not to break the glass off its porcelain base. Firmly grasp the porcelain base and wiggle the lamp out. Do not handle the glass. On lights of 2,000 W and larger, a screw in the lantern's lamp base tightens the base around the pins of the lamp. With this type of base, the lamp comes out freely when the thumb screw is loosened.

The position of the lamp relative to the reflector is critical to the proper operation of the light. The filament of the lamp sits precisely at the focal point of the reflector. Therefore, if the lamp is not seated properly, or the reflector is bent, the lamp's performance is drastically reduced.

Tilt angle

To ensure proper heat dissipation, manufacturers recommend that Fresnels be hung with the base down. Each type of lamp has a limit to the amount it can be tilted on its side without shortening the life of the lamp. For example, a 5 kW Fresnel lantern should burn with the lamp oriented within 45° to vertical. In addition to damaging the lamp, the compact-type 2,000 W light hung at an extreme downward tilt will melt the reflector. In practice, tilt angle is only a concern with lights that have large, expensive lamps. Small lights are hung in whatever manner is required.

Fresnel accessories

Each Fresnel should always be accompanied by barn doors and a set of scrims in a scrim box or scrim bag. A typical equipment package also includes snoots and at least one focal spot in various sizes to fit the various lights.

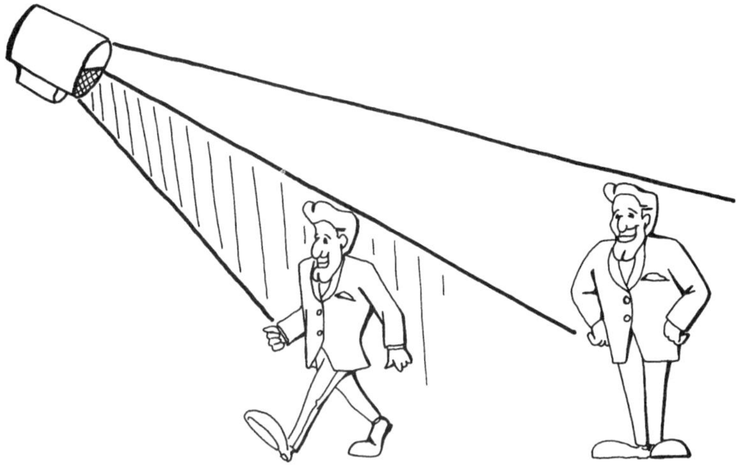

Figure 3.9 A bottom-half scrim is used to even out intensity as the subject moves closer to the light fixture

Scrims

A scrim is a stainless steel wire screen used to reduce the intensity of the light. A single scrim has a loose wire weave, is identified by its green ring frame and cuts the intensity of the light by approximately a half-stop. A double scrim has a tighter weave, is identified by its red ring frame, and cuts the light by approximately one full stop. A standard set of scrims includes a single, two doubles, a half-single, a half-double and a gel frame. Quarter scrims and graduated scrims are also available for some lanterns.

Half scrims affect just one-half of the beam. A bottom-half double can be used to even out the intensity of the light as the subject moves closer to the lantern (Figure 3.9). It reduces the light falling on objects close to the light, bringing the light level down to that of objects farther from the light.

A gel frame can be used to hold light gels or diffusion for short spans of time; however, because of the heat close to the lens, many lights will melt gels mounted in the gel frame. Similarly, hot scrims will melt the gel in a gel frame (and make a big gooey mess on the scrim). Therefore, gels and diffusion materials are often attached to the barn doors, where the heat is less intense.

Appendix A lists the appropriate scrim size for various lanterns.

Barn doors

Barn doors provide the most basic control over the placement of the edges of the beam of a Fresnel or open-face lantern. Because the doors are so close to the lantern, the cut-off is fairly soft (Figure 3.10).

Barn doors typically have two large leaves and two smaller triangular ones. When the bigger doors are horizontal, they are said to be 'Chinese'; when they are vertical, we call them 'English.' By closing the two large leaves into a narrow slit and folding the small leaves out of the way, you can make a narrow slash. The slash can be hor-

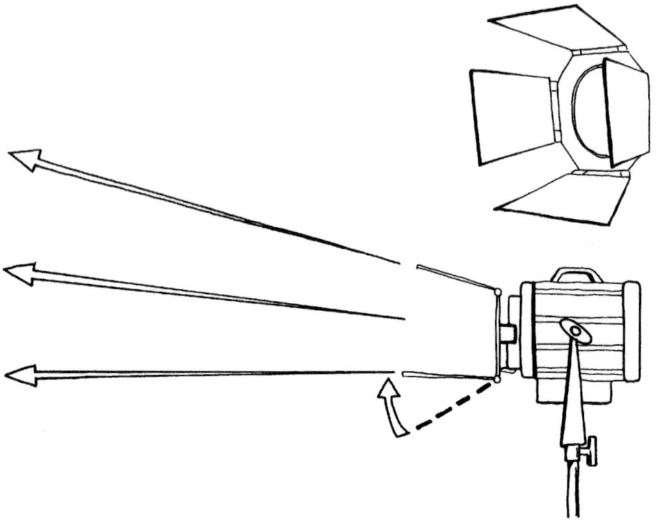

Figure 3.10 Barn doors contain the light, putting a straight edge on the beam

izontal, e.g. for an eye light, or alternatively, turned diagonally to make a slash across a background.

Snoot

When a very confined, narrow, circular beam is desired, replace the barn doors with a snoot. Snoots come in various sizes, from wide (called a top hat) to very narrow (stovepipe). Some snoots are fitted with four rings with different aperture sizes so that you can adjust the beam width (Figure 3.11).

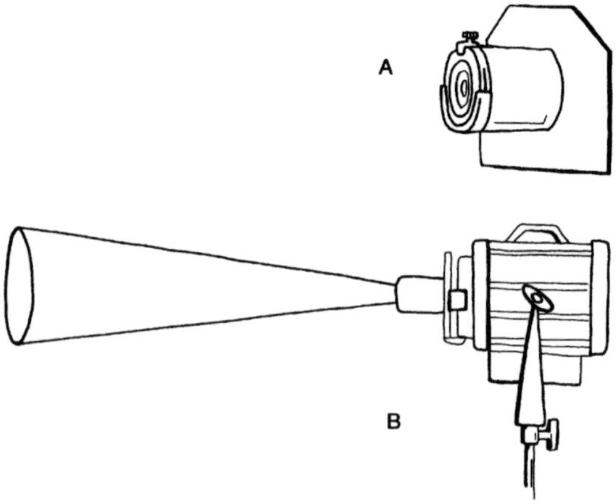

Figure 3.11 (A) A snoot with multiple aperture rings allows some flexibility in beam width. (B) A snoot confines the beam to a narrow circle

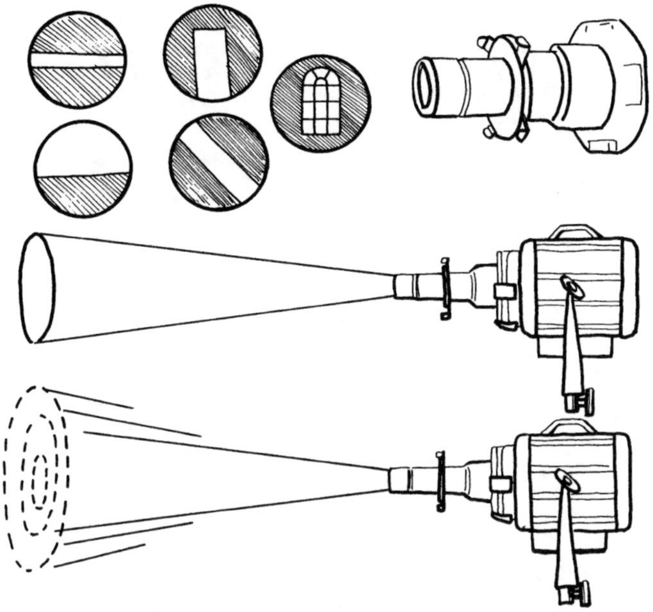

Figure 3.12 A focal spot. The four framing shutters can be pushed into the beam to form hard cuts in any shape: a narrow slit for an eye light, a rectangle to frame a doorway, a straight line cut, or a diagonal slash, for example. It can also project gobo patterns. The gobo fits into a slot on the barrel. The beam can be focused to create hard edges or defocused to soften them

Focal spot

A focal spot essentially changes a Fresnel into a spotlight. The focal spot lens assembly creates a narrow, bright, even circle. Like an ellipsoidal reflector spotlight, a focal spot has framing shutters. It accepts design patterns called gobos and mattes, which can be projected and focused on to the scene. It has interchangeable lens tubes, wide beam and narrow beam. It also comes with a gel ring to add colour gels (Figure 3.12).

Shutters

Shutters are like heavy-duty venetian blinds; they have rows of parallel slats that open and close. The shutter is mounted on the front of the light (Figure 3.13).

The shutter can be controlled to smoothly reduce the amount of light getting to the subject. Shutters are handy when the light level needs to change during a shot. Care must be taken to avoid projecting a venetian-blind pattern on the subject. Keep the light some distance from the subject, and use diffusion material between the two. Be watchful also for a vertical shift in the position of the beam as the shutters are closed. Shutters are frequently used to create a lightning effect; a sudden flash can be produced by opening and quickly closing the shutter. Use appropriate caution; the shutters will warp from the heat build-up if kept closed for too long.

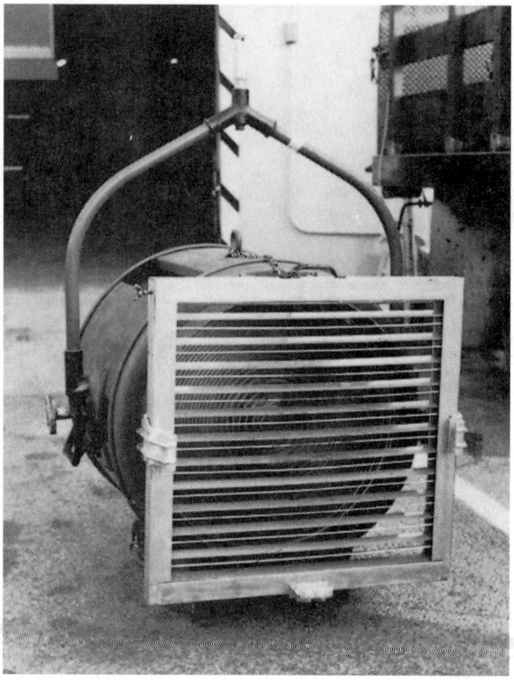

Figure 3.13 Shutters on a 10 kW Fresnel. (Equipment courtesy of Hollywood Rental, Sun Valley, CA.)

Dedolight

Strictly speaking, Dedolights, manufactured by Dedo Weigert Film, Munich, are not Fresnel lanterns. They are small, compact, 100 W and 150 W lanterns that use two specially designed lenses in an assembly that is more efficient than a Fresnel and that provides a hard, adjustable beam with exceptionally even light across the field (Figure 3.14).

The special lens assembly gives the lantern an unusually wide range of adjustment (from 40° in full flood to 2.5° in full spot) and unusual punch for long throw. A 100 W Dedolight has roughly the same light output as a 300 W Fresnel. The lights are so small, lightweight and unobtrusive that they can easily be hidden in the set.

The lights have various accessories, including barn doors, gel frames, lightweight mounting hardware, suction mounts, camera clamps and a focal-spot-like projection attachment. The projection attachment allows extremely precise control of the beam. It can be shuttered in on a beer label, for instance, providing a hard edge cut with no colour fringing or softness around the edges. For this reason, the lights are useful in tabletop setups and miniature work.

The 100 W Dedolights run on 12 V. The 150 W version runs on 24 V. The power supplies power three, four or five lights at a time. There are three power settings on the power supply for each light: high (3,300 K, maximum light output), medium (3,200 K, medium light output), and low (about 3,000 K, lower light output). The lights can also be powered directly off battery.

The Dedocool is a 250 W tungsten-balanced light designed for lighting small areas when a great deal of light is needed, for an extremely high shutter speed, for example. Used at close range, the light can provide 220,000 FC at 8 to 12 in., while giving off very little heat. Insects, plants, food, plastics, paper, and other such items that would be adversely affected by the heat of any other source of this intensity can be filmed using this light. A cooling fan at the back of the lantern is necessary to cool the lamp. The special power supply keeps the fan running for a short time after the light is turned off to cool the light. If the light is unplugged hot, damage to the fan can result.

Soft lights

Soft lights (Figure 3.15) are designed to produce soft, shadowless light. Instead of using a lens, the light from the long tubular lamps is directed into a concave reflector.

Because the light is indirect, bounced off a diffuse surface and exits through a relatively large aperture, the resulting light is soft and has a wide, even, uncontrolled

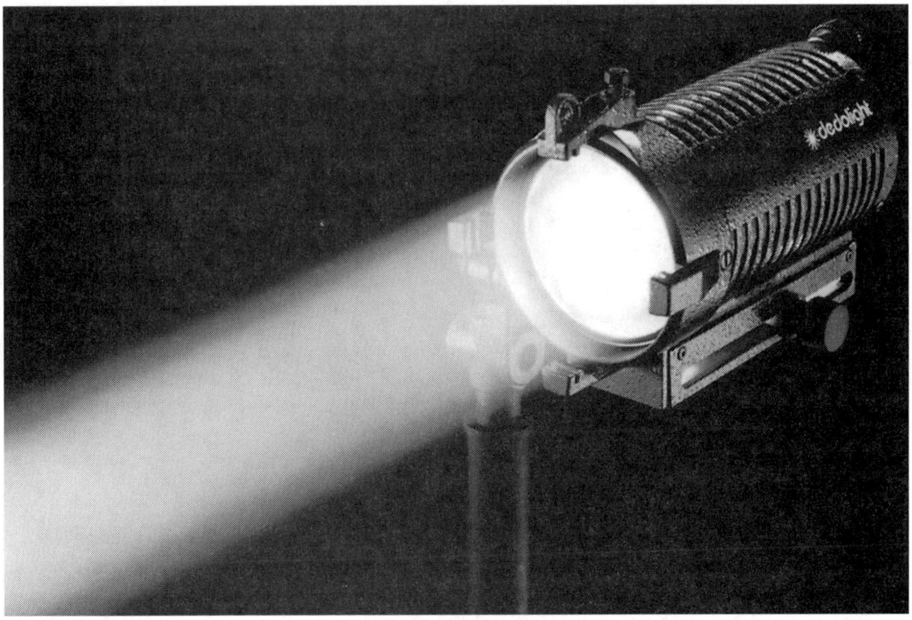

Figure 3.14 The refined beam of a 100 W Dedolight. (Photo courtesy of Dedotec USA, Inc., Lodi, NJ.)

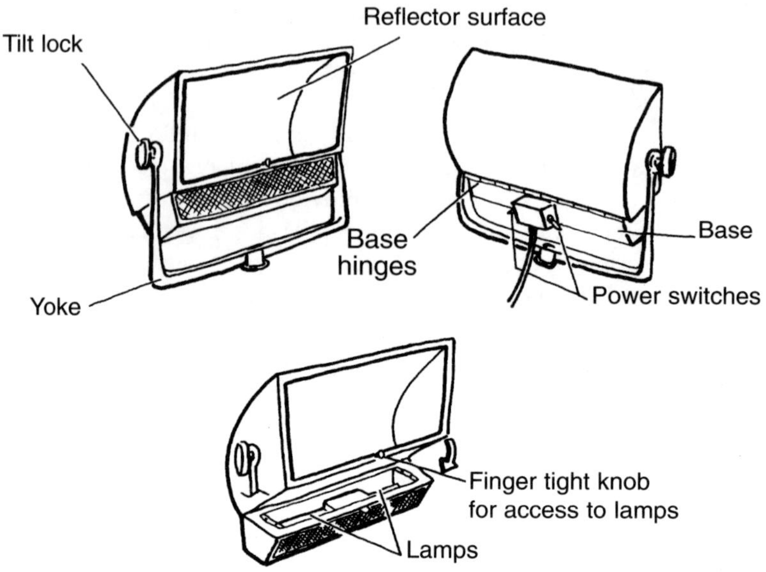

Figure 3.15 Anatomy of a 2 kW zip soft light. (Equipment courtesy of Hollywood Rental, Sun Valley, CA.)

spread. Soft lights are commonly used for fill. Table A.2 (Appendix A) provides soft light specifications.

Because soft lights use indirect light, they produce far less light per watt than Fresnels. Most soft lights have multiple lamps, each switched individually, making it easy to increase or reduce the light's intensity. Figure 3.16 shows the egg crate and

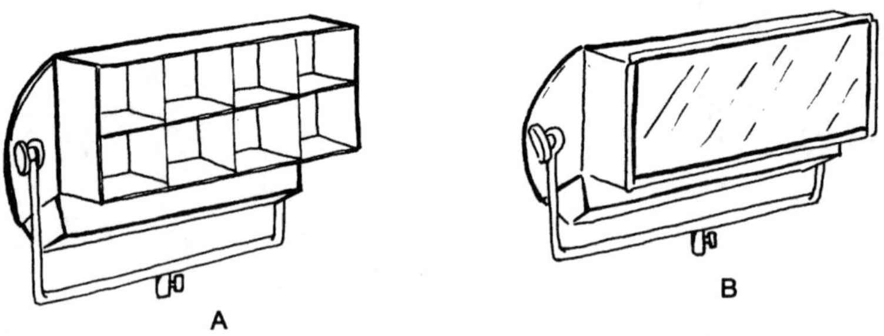

Figure 3.16 Soft light accessories: (A) Egg crate. This black, metal grid helps control spill and also reduces the overall intensity of the light. It is a good idea to keep an egg crate with each soft light because they are used frequently. (B) Diffuser frame (shown here placed on the front of the egg crate). This square gel frame fits in the front of the unit to hold coloured gel or diffusion. (Equipment courtesy of Hollywood Rental, Sun Valley, CA.)

snoot, which can also be used to contain and control soft light. Soft lights don't generally have scrims, but you can improvise by inserting a baby scrim between the base and the white reflector surface, sandwiched with the egg crate and held in place with a spring clip.

To maintain maximum intensity and proper colour temperature, the white reflector must periodically be cleaned or repainted. When repainting the interior surface, use best boy white paint. Best boy white reflects light without changing the colour of the light, and it withstands high temperatures. If regular white paint is used, it will appear off-colour.

To gain access to the lamps, loosen the finger screws that lock the basket to the reflector and hinge the base open. The lamps are double-ended and are held in place in a spring-loaded porcelain base. To install the lamp, insert one end and push back the spring until the other end can slide in.

Area lights

Scoop lights and sky pans

Scoops (Figure 3.17F) and sky pans (Figure 3.17H) are very simple lights that have been around since incandescent lights were first used in motion pictures. They

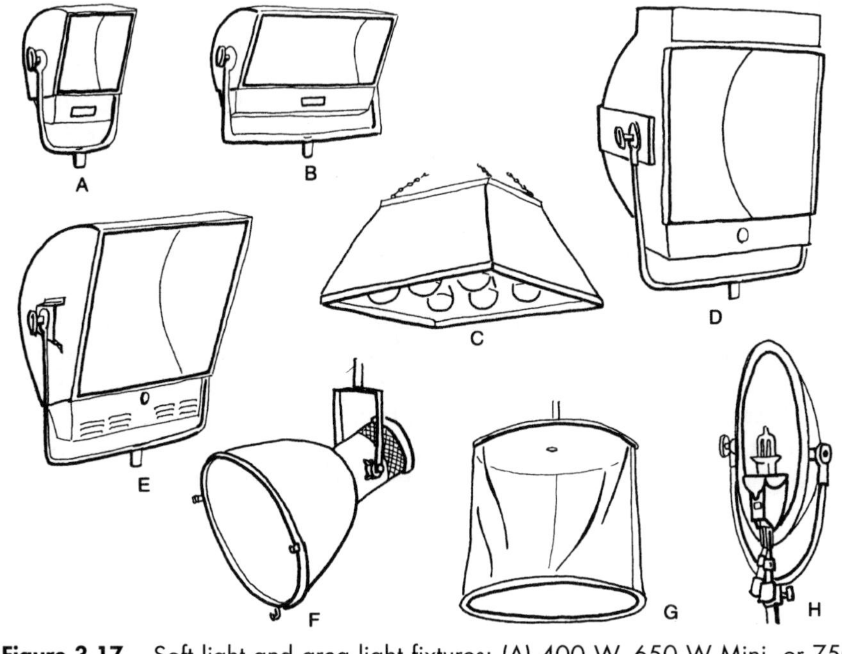

Figure 3.17 Soft light and area light fixtures: (A) 400 W, 650 W Mini, or 750 W Baby Soft light, (B) 2 kW Zip, (C) six-light chicken coop, (D) 8 kW Super Softlite with eight 1 kW globes, (E) 1 kW, 2 kW or 4 kW soft light, (F) scoop, (G) space light, (H) sky pan

consist of an exposed lamp mounted in a large white reflector. Scoops are 1 kW or 2 kW; sky pans can be 2 kW, 5 kW or 10 kW.

Sky pans are used for general illumination over a large area or for lighting scenic paintings, backdrops, or backings, which must be lit evenly from side to side and from top to bottom. The light can be made softer and more even by employing a frame of spun glass diffusion. The gel frame fits into a metal skirt that one attaches to the face of the light.

Chicken coops and space lights

The chicken coop (Figure 3.17C) hangs on a chain and uses six 1000 W silver bowl lamps. The lamps are silvered on the bottom to prevent direct hard light from shining downward. Chicken coops and space lights are commonly hung throughout a very large set to fill the space with a general soft overhead illumination. A space light (Figure 3.17G) consists of six 1 kW nook lights configured like spokes of a wagon wheel, pointing down into a silk cylinder. At the bottom is a round diffusion ring to which a diffusion material or gel can be clipped.

Cyc strips, ground rows and borders

A cyc strip is a row of open-face lights having a specially shaped reflector used to illuminate a cyclorama, or cyc, evenly from top to bottom and from side to side. Cyc strips come in either short strips of one, two, three or four lights or longer strips of six, eight, nine or twelve. The larger strips are wired in groups to provide three or four separate circuits for different coloured gels, with one circuit of several lights per colour (Figure 3.18).

A four-circuit cyc strip might have the three primary colours of light red, green and blue, and either a white circuit or a second blue circuit. (Blue gel absorbs more light than the other colours and is therefore weaker.) By mixing the primary colours using dimmers on each circuit, the cyc can be made any colour or can take on a gradation of colours from top to bottom.

Cyc strips are positioned on the floor, called a ground row, or in a trench below floor level, pointing up at the cyc, and they are hung from pipes or battens in front of or behind the cyc, pointing down at it. The angle of the strip and its distance from the cyc are critical for achieving even lighting from top to bottom.

Strips of PAR lights, called border lights, are also used to light cycs and curtains. PARs have a better throw and a tighter, more intense beam, which is sometimes needed on a very tall cyc to carry light into the centre of the cloth.

Open-face lights

As the name implies, open-face lights do not have a lens and are therefore slightly brighter per watt than a Fresnel. However, their light is less even, and they are harder to control (Figure 3.19). Two problems with all open-faced lights are hard shadows

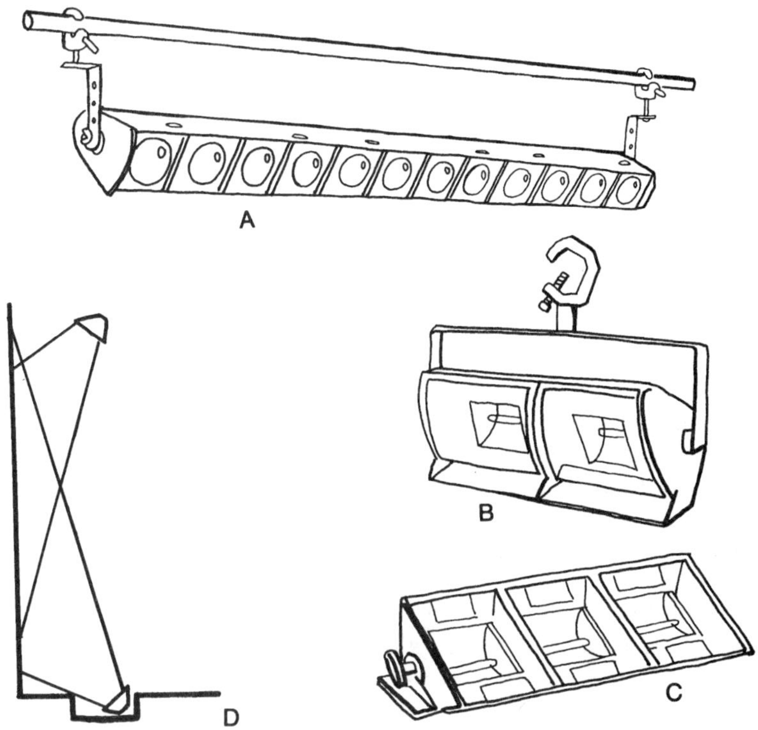

Figure 3.18 Cyc lighting: (A) a border light; (B) a two-light far cyc (also made in strips of many lights and in groups of four); (C) a ground row cyc strip (comes in strips of 1, 2, 3, 4, 6, 8, 9 and 12 or more lights); (D) the typical cyc lighting method lights the cyc evenly from top to bottom

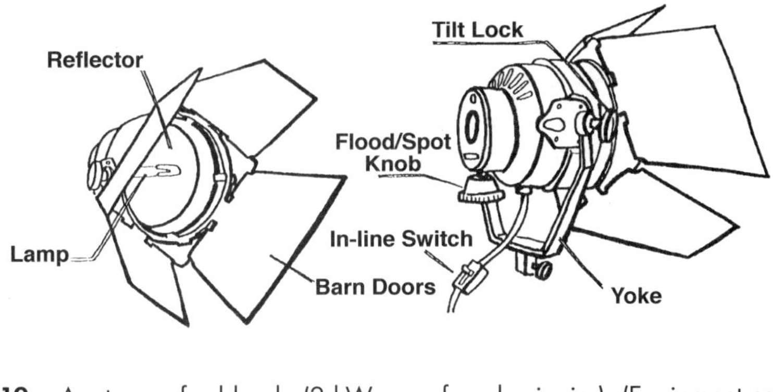

Figure 3.19 Anatomy of a blonde (2 kW open-face luminaire). (Equipment courtesy of Hollywood Rental, Sun Valley, CA.)

and the need to provide a safety glass or mesh to catch the quartz from the envelope in the event of the lamp shattering. The European standards require that particles of quartz 3 mm or more in size are retained in the housing in the event of the lamp exploding.

Open-face lanterns can be divided into three varieties: prime lanterns, broads and nook lights and portable lanterns. Figure 3.20 illustrates open-face lights with which an electrician must be familiar. Table A.3 (Appendix A) lists their specifications.

Prime lanterns

Prime open-face lanterns (Figures 3.20A and B) have a round face and an adjustable reflector for flood/spot control, and they come with barn doors and a scrim set. The flood/spot mechanism alters the lamp's position relative to the reflector. When the lamp is close to the reflector, the reflector sends out a wide beam; when the lamp is pulled away from the reflector, it reflects a narrower beam. They are durable lights with a relatively high intensity per watt, and they are much more controllable than broads and nook lights. They are also relatively lightweight; all sizes mount on a baby stud.

Open-face prime lanterns are often bounced into a white surface such as foamcore to create soft light. Note that open-face lights tend to burn very hot and can melt a foamcore bounce board or destroy a flag if it is placed too close to the light. Think twice before rigging a light close to set pieces, and allow ventilation above the lantern.

Broads and nook lights

Broads and nook lights (Figure 3.20F and G) consist of little more than a long, double-ended lamp and a curved or V-shaped silver reflector. Nook lights are small and light, and can be easily hidden in the set. Because broads and nook lights create raw, hard light, they tend to be used for jobs such as throwing light on a background or illuminating a soft box. They are also handy as work lights.

Light kits

Photo-flood lanterns

The Lowel K5, DeSisti Pinza, and other similar lanterns provides a regular lamp socket that can be fitted with a photoflood (or any other type of household lamp) of up to 500 W. Because K5 kits are lightweight and can be easily hung, clamped, dangled or taped to walls and ceilings, they are easy to rig. Fitted with R-40 mushroom floods and hoods (Figure 3.21), they can create nice pools of light from above.

Stick-up kits

A stick-up is a very small open-face light that can be taped or clipped into the smallest of places. It can be fitted with a 100 W or 200 W, 120 V bayonet base lamp or

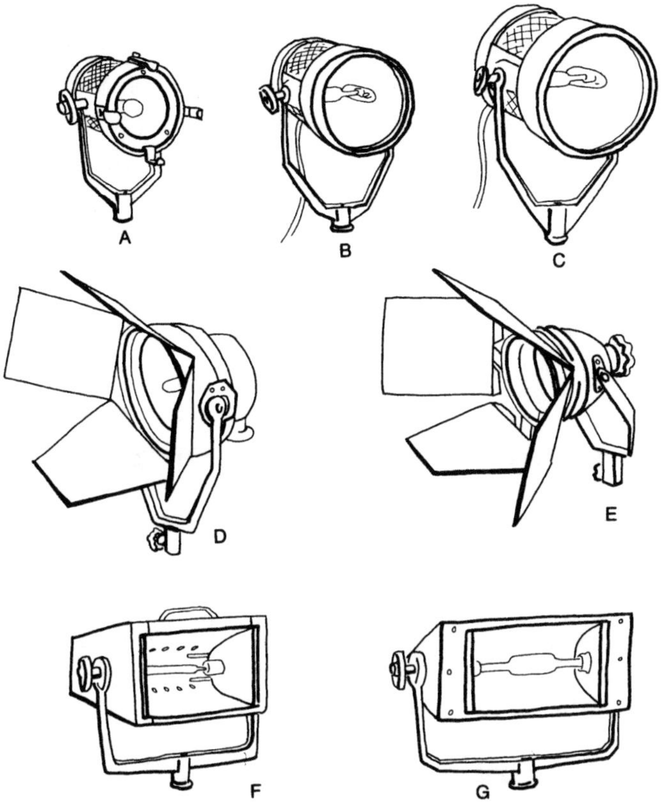

Figure 3.20 Open-face fixtures: (A) 650 W Teenie-Weenie, (B) 1 kW Mickey, (C) 2 kW Mighty, (D) 2 kW blonde, (E) 1 kW redhead, (F) 1 kW broad, (G) 1 kW or 2 kW nook light. (Equipment courtesy of Hollywood Rental, Sun Valley, CA.)

with a 100 W, 12 V lamp. The latter is ideal as a dome light in an automobile because it can run off the car battery (Figure 3.22).

Because a stick-up is so small and light, it can be taped in place or hung on push-pins. When the light is placed against a surface, insulate the surface with a double or triple layer of refracil heat-resistant cloth. You can wrap a piece of black wrap around the back of the lantern to act as barn doors.

Portable light kits

Portable open-face lights are normally used by small, mobile camera crews for documentary, industrial and promotional video and film work. The lights come in kits with a full complement of accessories, including adaptive, lightweight mounting hardware and lightweight stands. The units are small and usually draw 1,000 W or less (Figure 3.23).

Lightweight, portable soft lights are also available. Compact lanterns can illumi-

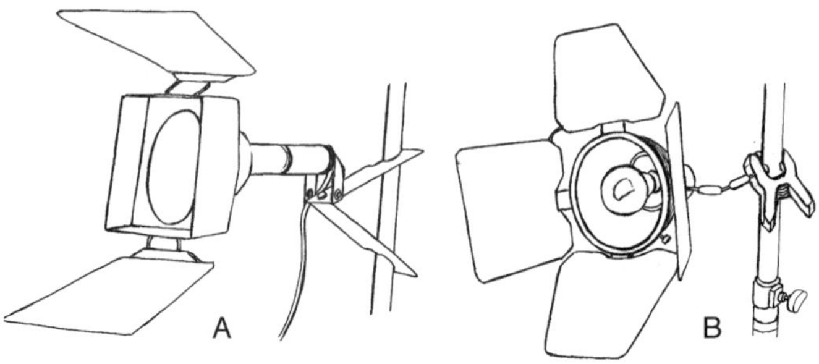

Figure 3.21 (A) Molite or Lowel K5 – an R-40 lamp with attachable barn doors, (B) a Pinza reflector lamp which takes photoflood lamps

nate only a limited area, but they can be useful to supplement heavier lighting equipment.

The quality of the light can be manipulated using gel frames to alter colour or to diffuse the light. Because the raw light from an open-face lantern is often hard and unattractive, cinematographers often seek to soften the source. Bouncing the units into silver umbrellas provides a large, yet lightweight, source of soft light.

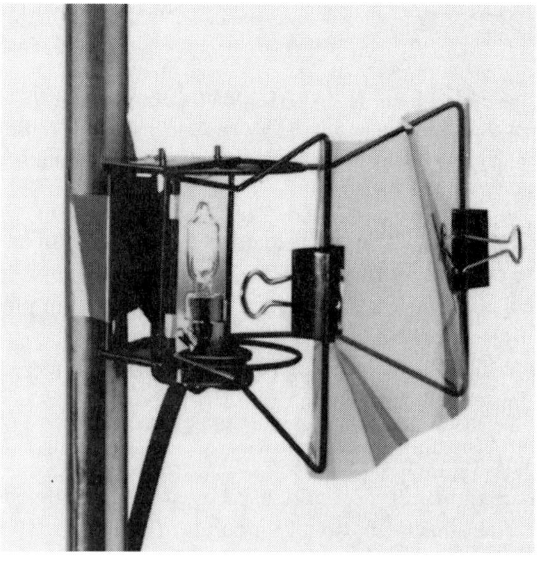

Figure 3.22 The stick-up illustrated is 3 in. tall, weighs 9 oz. with its 9 ft power cord. It comes with a wire frame for securing gel and diffusion. (Photo courtesy of Great American Market, Hollywood, CA.)

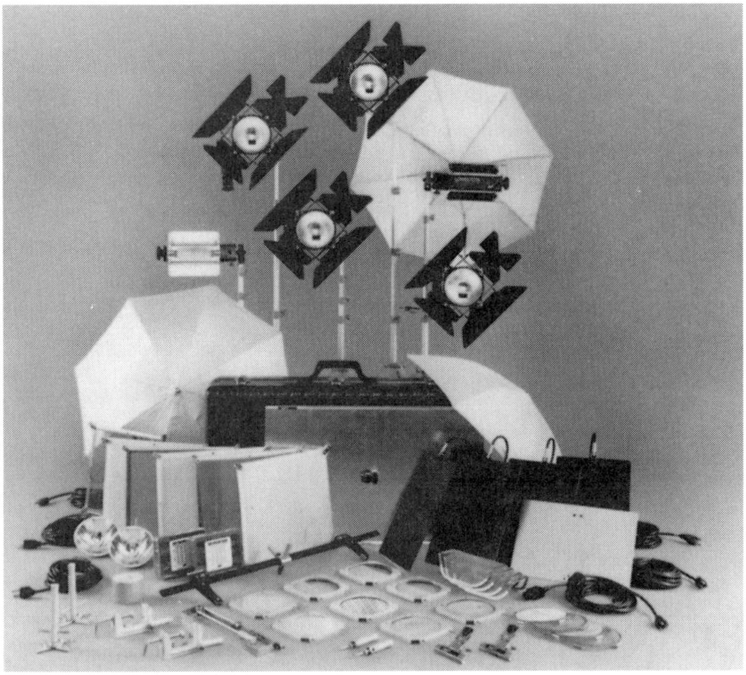

Figure 3.23 Lowel open-face lighting kit with accessories. The 'solo' kit shown includes two Toto lights, four Omni lights, scrims, special barn doors, silver umbrellas, flags with flexible shafts, scissor clamps, c-clamps, a space clamp (special furniture clamp), a door-top hanger, a cucaloris, diffusion glass, a spare lamp case, power cords and extensions, reflector boards, and white bounce boards, and more. (Photo courtesy of Lowel-Light Manufacturing, Inc., Brooklyn, NY.)

PAR lights

Parabolic aluminized reflector (PAR) lights are sealed-beam lamps. That is, the lamp, lens and reflector are one permanently sealed unit, like a car headlight (Figure 3.24).

PAR lamps are typically mounted in clusters of individually switched lamps, with one to as many as thirty-six lights to a cluster. 'Maxi-brutes' use 8 in. diameter PAR-64 lamps. 'Mini-brutes' use 4¼ in. PAR-36 lamps (Figure 3.25B). The lamps are capable of being adjusted, either individually or in groups, to give a crude form of 'spot/flood'. They are referred to by the number of lamps in the cluster: for example, a four-light, six-light (Figure 3.25C), or, most common, nine-light. (Table A.4 in Appendix A list the common types.) Lamps are made in various beam widths: wide flood, medium flood, narrow spot and very narrow spot. PAR lamps tend to have an elliptical beam rather than a circular one. A PAR lamp can be turned in its fixture to orient the beam as required. PAR lamps are also available with a dichroic reflector giving a 'daylight' colour temperature (about 4,000 K).

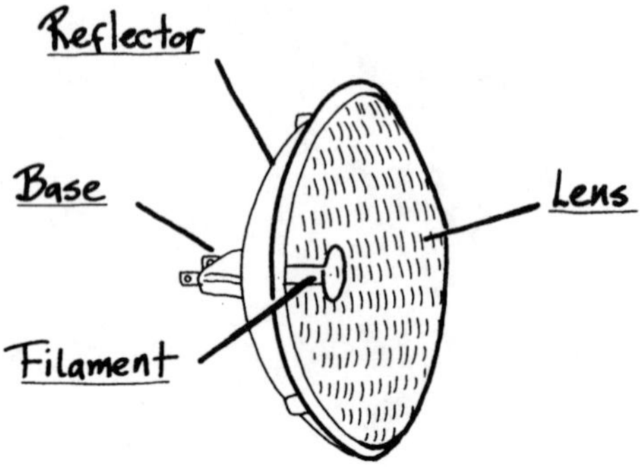

Figure 3.24 Anatomy of a PAR lamp

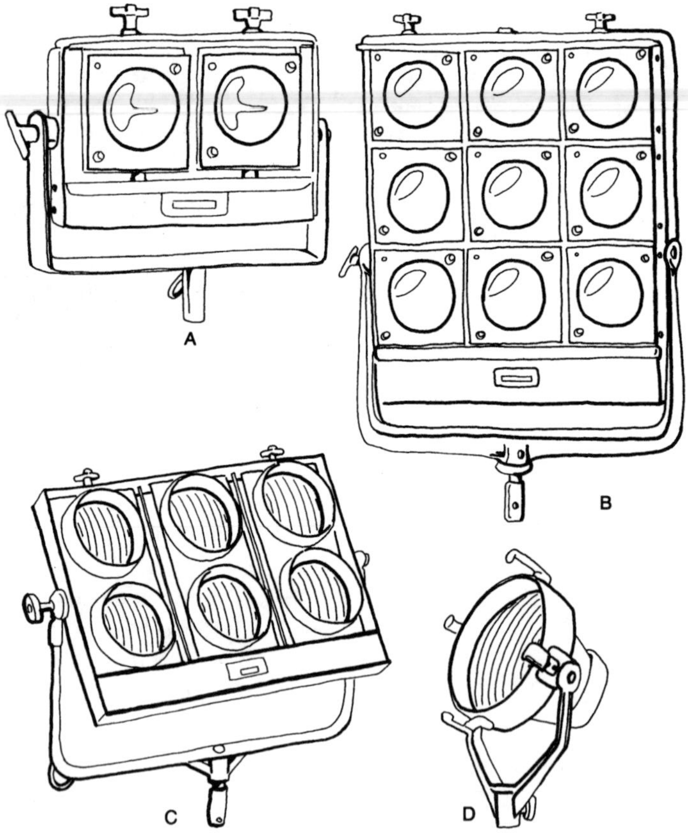

Figure 3.25 PAR fixtures: (A) two-light FAY (650 W per light); (B) 'Mini-brute' nine-light FAY (650 W per light); (C) six-light PAR (1 kW per light); (D) 1 kW PAR

PAR lights tend to burn very hot and can melt a foamcore bounce board or destroy a flag if it is placed too close to the light. Be careful when rigging a light close to set pieces, and be sure to allow ventilation above the lantern. These lamps have a lot of punch; they can throw fairly long distances or over a fairly wide area. The light they produce is very hard and unpleasant when used directly on faces.

Discharge lanterns (HMIs)

Lanterns employing discharge source lamps are a highly efficient source of daylight-balanced light (5,600 K or 6,000 K, depending on the lamp manufacturer). They are used when mixing with natural daylight. An HMI puts out about four times as much light as a tungsten light of the same wattage, 85 to 108 lumens per watt of electricity, compared to 26 lumens per watt for tungsten halogen lamps. This is partly because an incandescent lamp expends 80 per cent of its energy creating heat (infrared wavelengths), whereas HMIs convert that same percentage of its energy into usable illumination. As a result, HMIs operate at much cooler temperatures, making them more comfortable to work under and better for lighting temperature-sensitive subjects, such as animals and food (not to mention actors).

Discharge sources require a ballast connected between the AC power source and the lamp head. The component parts of a discharge source are the head, the head cable, the ballast and, in most cases, a separate ballast cable (Figure 3.26). Standard HMIs run on AC power only (a couple of notable exceptions are described later).

There are two types of ballasts: magnetic, which are standard, and electronic (also called square-wave or flicker-free), which are becoming increasingly common. With a magnetic ballast, the camera must be crystal-controlled and must be run at one of a number of specific frame rates. More about this shortly. There are five types of HMI lanterns: Fresnels, sealed beam PARs, single-ended (non-sealed-beam) PARs, soft lights and battery-powered sun guns. Specifications for HMI lanterns appear in Tables A.5, A.6, A.7 and A.8 in Appendix A.

HMI Fresnels

Small Fresnels of 200 W, 575 W, and 1,200 W are commonly used as interior direct light or bounce light when daylight colour balance is needed. They are equivalent in function to a tweenie, a baby and a junior respectively. These sizes have the advantage of plugging into a standard household outlet when necessary. Medium size HMI Fresnels of 2,500 W, 4,000 W, and 6,000 W are used in much the same manner as 5 kW and 10 kW tungsten units, to light large interiors, to double as sunlight, to provide fill on exteriors, or to provide key light and backlight on night exteriors.

Large HMI Fresnels, 12 kW and 18 kW, have replaced the carbon arc as the workhorse large light. A necessary part of almost any equipment package, the 12 kWs are used for fill on day exterior shots. To cover wide exterior night shots, they are often mounted to an 80 ft arm. Another common application is making sunlight effects

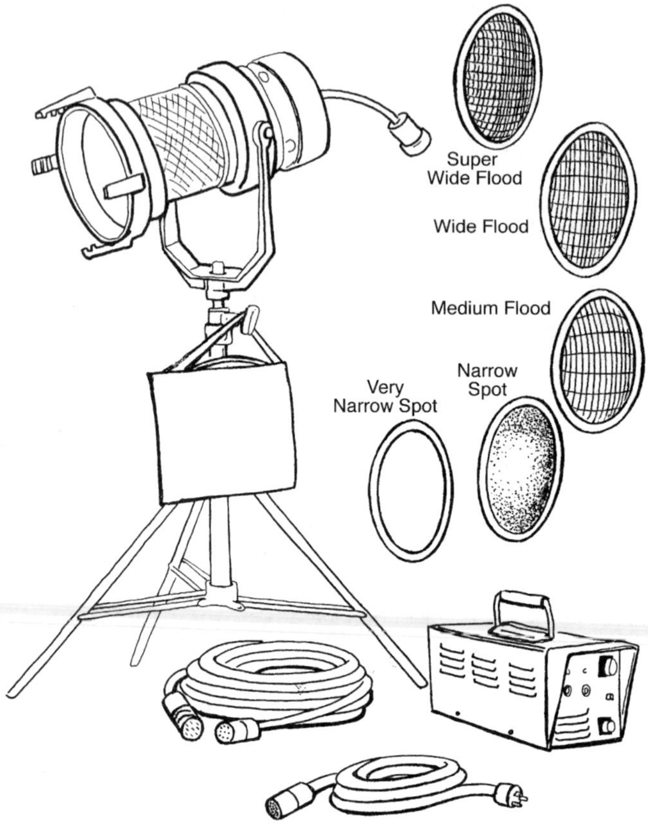

Figure 3.26 LTM 1200 discharge source PAR head, head cable, ballast cable, ballast, scrims, lens case and set of spreader lenses

through windows both on location and inside the studio. They may be put through diffusion or bounced to create a large, bright soft source.

HMI (sealed-beam) PARs

PAR lights are more efficient than Fresnels, and they deliver a strong punch of light with a long throw. It is possible to add spreader lenses in front of the sealed beam unit which will change the shape of the beam. See Figure 3.26 and Table A.6 (Appendix A). In this type of lantern the beam can only be adjusted by the addition of the separate lenses. The lamp itself cannot be moved in relation to the reflector and upon failure the whole unit comprising lamp and reflector has to be replaced.

Generally, the beam of an HMI PAR is elliptical, not circular. The shape varies with the lens used. The medium and wide flood lenses create a more oblong beam than the others. Take, for example, the LTM 1200 PAR. A narrow or very narrow lens gives about a 12° beam width and an 8° beam height. Medium and wide lenses create a much wider ellipse: Medium gives 22° × 9°, wide 53° × 22° (about 2½ times as wide as it is high). The pebbled lens (very wide flood) gives a circular beam with about a 64° spread. On some lanterns the entire housing can be rotated so that the oblong beam can be oriented to any angle. Alternately, you can simply rotate the lens.

HMI single-ended (non-sealed-beam) PARs

Single-ended PARs are similar in appearance to sealed-beam units. Instead of using a sealed-beam lamp they use a single-ended lamp mounted in a highly efficient parabolic reflector, thus enabling the lamp to be moved in relation to the reflector, giving a variable beam output. This focusing ability, coupled with interchangeable front lenses, gives a more flexible lantern. An ultraviolet-protective glass is mounted on the front of the unit for safety reasons. Lantern manufacturers provide a selection of spreader lenses (see Table A.6 in Appendix A).

Because the single-ended lamp is not mounted horizontally, (as most double-ended lamps), but on the optical axis of the reflector, taking advantage of the relatively small arc within the shapeof the parabolic reflector, single-ended HMI lanterns can deliver more light than a sealed-beam lantern. Advantages of single-ended units are a larger availability of lamps in various wattages and, upon failure, only the lamp has to be changed.

A 2,500 W PAR with a spot lens is so intense that a piece of wood 4 ft from the lantern will begin to smoke in a matter of minutes. With 4 kW and 6 kW PARs this sometimes gets to be a problem. PAR lights also work well as a bounce source to create soft light (but be sure to use wide or extra-wide lens or you'll melt or burn the bounce surface).

Again, the lenses affect both beam shape and angle. The very narrow and narrow spot lenses give a circular beam of 6° and 8°. The medium and wide flood lenses give a wide elliptical beam of 27° × 11°, and 60° × 25°, respectively. The super-wide flood gives a circular beam of about 54°. To turn an oblong beam, the operator rotates the lens.

HMI soft lights

As with incandescent soft lights, the lamp of an HMI soft light is aimed into a white concave reflector. The bounced light and large aperture create a soft, even field of daylight-balanced light. The HMI soft light, of course, produces much greater quantities of light than an incandescent (see Table A.8 in Appendix A).

HMI sun guns

A sun gun is a small (125 W, 200 W, 250 W or 400 W) light powered by a 30 V nickel-cadmium (ni-cad) battery, usually in the form of a battery belt (Figure 3.27, and Table A.7 in Appendix A).

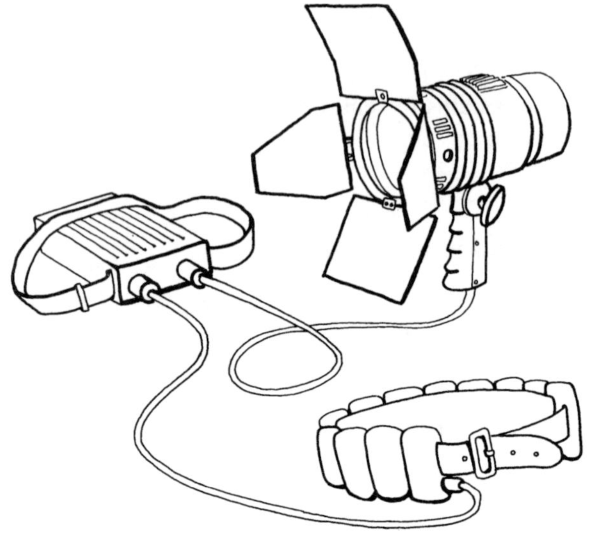

Figure 3.27 This discharge source sun gun takes a 250 W SE HMI lamp and has a colour temperature of 5,600 K. It operates on a 30 V battery belt and is adaptable to a 24 V car-type battery

The light has a hand grip as well as a mounting stud. Sun guns are sometimes employed in remote locations where power is not available, for example, in a cave in the mountains of Mexico, and in situations where the expediency of a battery-powered light takes priority, for example in a moving vehicle or on a moving elevator.

Although the 30 V ni-cad belt batteries are supposed to last as long as an hour, rented batteries rarely keep the light going for more than 20 to 25 minutes. When battery-powered lights are to be relied on over the course of a whole scene or a whole day, it is necessary to have many batteries on hand. They must be fully charged overnight (8 hours), and it helps to have them 'topped-up' again within an hour prior to use.

HMI operation

Setup

The ballast circuit breakers should be off or the ballast unplugged while connecting or disconnecting head cables. The breakers should remain off while plugging in the power (Figure 3.28).

Head cable connectors (Socapex or VEAM) have multiple pins and a threaded collar that screws on to their receptacle. Use the keyway to orient the plug into the socket. VEAM connectors for 575 W, 1,200 W, 2,500 W, and 4,000 W lanterns are nearly identical, except that the keyway and pins are oriented differently. To tell the

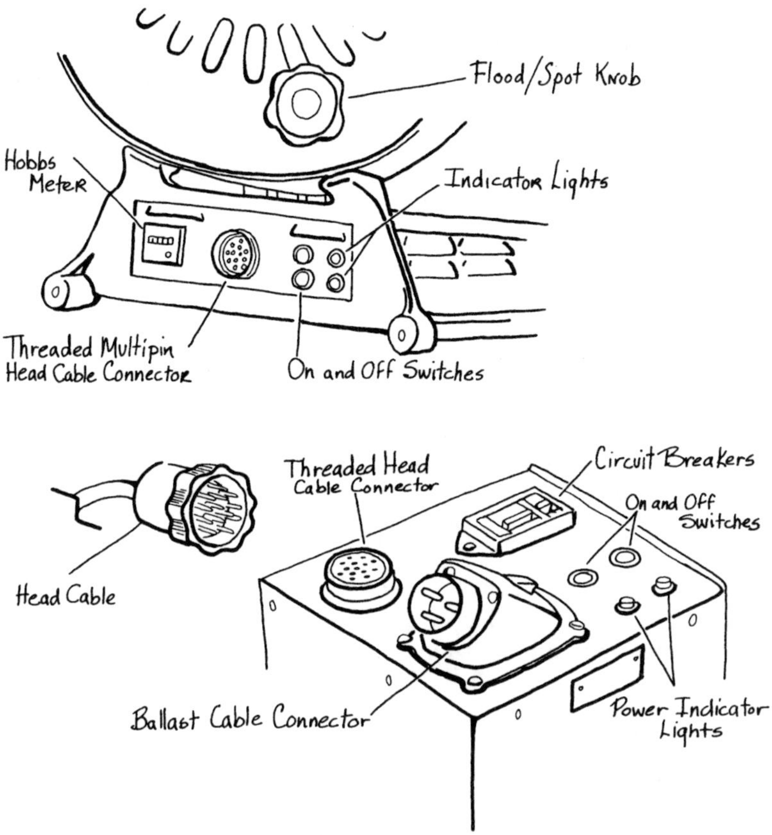

Figure 3.28 Anatomy of an HMI head and ballast. (Equipment courtesy of Hollywood Rental, Sun Valley, CA)

cables apart many manufacturers and rental houses colour code the connectors or cables as follows:

- Green 575 W
- Yellow 1,200 W
- Red 2,500 W
- Blue 4 kW.

Be sure to tie a tension relief so that the weight of the head cable does not pull on the connector, especially with larger lights that have heavy head cables.

Junction boxes

The large Socapex connectors used on some head feeders can only be connected to a panel-mounted receptacle and not to another head cable. A junction box (j-box) provides a means of connecting one head cable to another.

Striking the lamp

Once the head cable is connected to the head and ballast, plug in the ballast and switch on the circuit breakers. With 12 kW and 18 kW lamps, place the lamp in full spot position before pushing the ON switch. This backs the lamp away from the lens so that the lens does not crack from thermal shock. Also, in the (rare) event that the lamp explodes during warm-up, the chance of shattering the lens is minimized. When 12 kW lamps do explode, they often go within the first 5 or 10 minutes of ignition or reignition.

Before pushing the ON switch, call out 'Striking' to warn people that the light is about to be ignited. HMIs have ON/OFF switches on both the head and the ballast, and most models can be turned on and off from either place. When you press the ON switch, the ballast causes the high-voltage ignition on the head to operate, and this makes a buzzing sound.

The igniter circuit for standard lamps (not hot restrike) provides an ignition charge of 5,000 V to 17,000 V, depending on the size of the lamp. The ignition charge creates a brief arc between the electrodes in the lamp. Once the flow of electrons is initiated, the ballast brings the voltage down to the operating level and regulates the current.

Once ignition has taken place, the lantern will begin to emit light. From a cold state it takes 1 to 3 minutes for the substances in the lamp to vaporize. At the same time, lamp voltage, lamp current, luminous flux and colour temperature are all reaching their nominal values.

When a lamp is hot, gases inside the lamp are under greater pressure and high resistance is created between the electrodes. Much higher voltages (25,000 V to 65,000 V) are necessary to ionize the gap between the electrodes. The electronics of most newer ballasts take this into account and have better hot restrike performance. An old magnetic ballast may not have sufficient voltage to generate an arc until the lamp has cooled. In the case of 12 kW and 18 kW sources the ballast may not be able to produce sufficient voltage to accomplish a hot restrike, and you have to wait a couple of minutes for the lamp to cool before it will light again.

Hot restrike lamps have additives to reduce starting voltage and better insulation between pins in the case of single ended types. Special lamps are produced by the manufacturers for 'hot re-strike' operation. (See the lamp data in Appendix E7)

Ultraviolet emissions

All discharge source lamps produce light that has harmful amounts of ultraviolet (UV) radiation. Skin and retinal burns can result from direct exposure to the light. For this reason, a special housing and protective lens must be used. Ultraviolet rays are reduced to a safe level when the light passes through the glass lens or when the light is indirect, bouncing off the inside walls of the lantern, for example. Discharge sources always have a safety switch that shuts off the lamp if the lens door is opened or if the lens breaks. You can get a nasty burn very quickly by tampering with these safety features or by using broken or home-made equipment that doesn't have them.

A damaged or poorly made lantern that leaks direct UV radiation can, and has, caused skin burns, retinal burns, and even skin cancer. If prolonged proximity is unavoidable, as when operating a 12 kW in a condor, and you start to feel some burning on your skin, place a flag to block radiation from the lantern.

Mercury

Discharge source lamps contain very small amounts of mercury, which is poisonous. If a lamp breaks, take sensible precautions to prevent ingestion of toxic chemicals. Keep chemicals off your hands. Wash your hands. Dispose of broken and burned-out lamps in an appropriate place. Normally burned-out lamps must be returned to the rental house for inventory.

Troubleshooting

If a discharge source will not work, first double-check all the obvious possibilities. Are the ballast breakers turned on? Are the cables connected properly? Is a lamp installed? If the light still doesn't work, isolate the problem; is it the head cable, the head, the lamp, the ballast or the power? Isolating the problem requires a logical, methodical approach. If the problem is hidden, you may have to change out each component before you find the problem. In the worst case there is more than one faulty part conspiring to confuse things. You can eliminate possibilities by temporarily borrowing a ballast and head cables that are known to work; this will usually get you to the heart of the problem quickly.

Problems with the head

If the indicator light shows that there is power at the head but nothing happens when you press the 'ON' button, or if the lamphead shuts itself off when tilted down, it is likely that the lens door is slightly loose, allowing the UV protection micro-switch to shut off the unit. Check that the door is tightly closed, even when the light is tilted forward. You may need to adjust the rod on the micro-switch so that the switch engages. Once in a great while the micro-switch becomes overheated, breaks and must be replaced.

If the light makes a striking sound but will not take, the problem is most likely with the lamp, igniter circuit or internal cables. If the lamp is hot from prior use, it is very likely that the lamp simply needs a minute to cool before it will restrike.

As lamps gets older, they have more difficulty striking. As the electrodes wear away and the gap between them becomes wider; the igniter has to generate sufficient voltage to bridge the gap. You may have to try several times before the lamp takes. Wait 20 seconds between strikes. It is time to replace the lamp when its electrodes have worn down so far that the igniter can no longer induce an arc.

The most basic way of checking that the igniter is running is actually to look for a discharge in the lamp. If the igniter is working but the lamp cannot start because it is old or there is some problem with the ballast then there will be a glow in the lamp when the igniter runs.

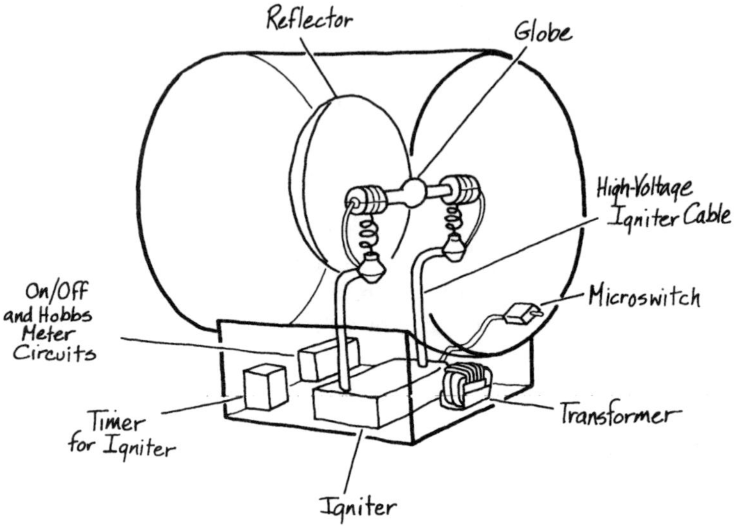

Figure 3.29 Interior anatomy of an HMI head

When using an electronic ballast, be wary about repeatedly attempting to strike a bad head. (See section headed 'Ballast electronics' in this chapter.)

With the larger lanterns (12 kW, 18 kW), if the head makes a loud buzz and arcing sound when you attempt to strike, but does not take, check the high-voltage cables and lamp cables. The lamp cables connect the lamp to terminals at the base of the lamp holders. The high-voltage (HV) igniter cables run from the base of the lamp holders to the igniter circuit in the base of the head (Figure 3.29).

If the lamp cables are hanging close to a metal part (such as the reflector), the start-up charge may arc. This deprives the lamp of the necessary start voltage and burns away the lamp cables over time. When installing the lamp, position lamp cables so they have plenty of clearance and will not arc to the reflector or lamp housing. If you find a lamp cable that is partially burned (blackened, fraying strands of cable), do not use that lamp until the lamp cables have been replaced.

Another cause of HV cable burnout is overheating. The cables can get jostled around and the terminal screws loosened, causing overheated contacts which eventually burn right through the igniter cables or lamp cables. Check and tighten the terminals each day when the lights are getting moved around a lot.

Problems with the ballast

Some magnetic 12 kW ballasts have a selector switch that must be set at the appropriate input voltage (208 V or 240 V). Improper input voltage selection can cause trouble in striking and operating the light. The Cinemill's ballast has an internal patch panel instead of a selector switch. To check or change the input voltage selection, remove the front panel of the ballast and repatch the plugs inside. Some ballasts are self-regulating, and require no adjustment to be used with 208 V or 240 V power.

Ballast hum is normal; none the less, it is the electrician's duty to remedy any annoyance to the sound mixer. It is best to place ballasts in a separate room from the start. When one ballast is particularly noisy, exchange it with a new one. In the meantime, placing sandbags above and below the ballast helps dampen vibration. Building a tent with furniture pads also helps, but do not block ventilation.

If a magnetic ballast starts to buzz, it can be a symptom of low input voltage. When operating on a low input voltage, the ballast has to draw more current to provide the needed voltage to the head. This can cause overheating and nuisance circuit breaker trips. Check the line voltage.

Problems with the head cable

If the indicator lights are on at the ballast and off at the head, and you get absolutely no response from the head when you try to strike it, the problem is most likely in the cable or the ballast. A bad contact in the head cable connector or damaged wire in the line are common culprits. Dirty connector pins may also be at fault, in which case the pins should be blown out with compressed air and cleaned with contact cleaner. Swap the head feeder for a new one to see if it is malfunctioning. (Note: The neon indicator lights in the head sometimes burn out. The light is often integral to the switch and it is an expensive part for the rental house to replace, so you cannot always count on them being in working order.)

When the head cables are checked out at the rental house, and periodically during shooting, check for missing screws on the strain-relief part of the connectors. If the strain-relief clamp comes loose, the connections inside can get pulled out and twisted. Also look for damaged insulation along the length of the cable. Treat head cables with care; avoid dragging them across pavements or throwing them on the ground because this can bend the connectors, making them impossible to connect. Never run head cables where heavy equipment and vehicles will run over them; this will damage the wires inside, causing endless headaches later on.

The pins and keyway are oriented differently for different sizes of HMIs and for the products of different manufacturers. Check that you are using the right head cable. The keyway orientation normally prevents you from using the wrong kind of connector, but if the connector is forced into place, it may appear to be connected. Again, colour-coding similar-looking head cables by wattage helps avoid this.

Problems with flicker

Flicker is one of the most aggravating problems you can have because it can occur from a number of different causes. Most commonly it is due to a bad connection in the distribution system, but sometimes it is due to a wandering arc in the lamp, improper voltage, bad power cable connection or faulty head cable. An intrepid and dauntless electrician is needed to track down the actual cause of the flicker.

First, let me stress that we are now talking about visible flicker. It is a common misconception that a visible 'flicker' in the light is cause for concern about the generator's frequency regulator. Electricians are generally aware that to avoid flicker

HMIs require a precisely regulated frequency rate; however, one must realize that this type of 'flicker' is a pulsation recorded on film only, it is not visible to the eye on set. (More about this horror later under 'Flicker-free solutions: square wave ballasts'.)

Visible, random, intermittent flicker is almost always caused by a bad connection in the distribution system, head feeder, or ballast feeder cable. In the worst case, a bad contact in the power feeder or distribution cable can cause the light to stop working altogether. Try to determine if more than one light is being affected. If so, what part of the distribution do they share? Are they on the same extension cable? Are they on the same phase? Check the neutral connections.

Check for loose-fitting pins and hot connectors and black pitting on the pins of the power feeders. Contact cleaner works miracles to restore dirty pins. When working in dirt, dust or sand over an extended time it is a good idea to give all the electrical connectors a cleaning every week or so. Blow out dirt with compressed air, and clean the pins and receptacles with contact cleaner.

A visible ongoing pulsation or a flutter in the light is evidence of a wandering or unstable arc in the lamp. Arc instability may be due to the non-horizontal orientation of the lamp or to a defective lamp. For example, some 1,200W PAR lamps develop a wandering arc when the inner lamp is positioned on a tilt. Arc instability may also be due to excess current on the electrodes, which points to faulty voltage regulation by the ballast or to improper input line voltage. Excess current wears down electrodes at an accelerated pace, ageing the lamp before its time. Before discarding a lamp as unstable, check it by using a different ballast.

The condition of the arc can be checked by viewing the lamp through a welding glass. Because of the other lights in use, a wandering or fluttering arc may not be apparent to the eye when looking at the subject on to which the light is falling, but it will register on film. The problem becomes clearly apparent when you observe the arc in the lamp. This is harder to do with Fresnels because you cannot see through the lens very clearly.

Note: Do not attempt to view the lamp directly under any circumstances.

Momentary spikes or flashes in a discharge source, other than during the warm-up period, may be an indication that the Hertz rate of the generator is jumping (magnetic ballasts only). The generator's frequency meter may not detect very short, erratic frequency pulses. Measure the current with a frequency meter that has a high sampling rate to determine if the governor in the generator is faulty.

Flicker-free solutions: square-wave ballasts

Standard magnetic ballasts

The light intensity of a discharge source increases and decreases 100 times per second (120 in the USA, Canada and Mexico) twice every AC cycle. This fluctuation is not visible to the eye but a steady pulsation will be captured on film if the camera is not in precise synchronization with the lights. To avoid capturing light pulsation on the filmed image, you must

1. Use a crystal-controlled camera.
2. Run the camera at one of a number of specific frame rates.
3. Use a line current that is maintained at exactly 50 Hz (60 Hz in North America).

The frame rate must divide evenly into 100 (120 in North America) in order for the film to receive the same amount of light in each exposure. Safe frame rates at any shutter angle are listed in Tables D.1 to D.4 (Appendix D). At any of these frame rates, the camera motor must be crystal-controlled. A wild or non-crystal-controlled camera cannot be used with magnetic HMI ballasts.

Standard ballasts will also create light pulsation on film if the AC frequency is not precisely controlled. The frequency for any AC power line can be checked by using an in-line frequency meter or by measuring the light's flicker rate with a photosensitive Cinecheck frequency meter pointed at the lamp-head itself (magnetic ballast only). Rental companies can supply a frequency meter with their equipment. Additionally, most generators have built-in frequency meters.

Three-head, three-phase solution

One way to get around the discharge source pulsation problem if you have an off-speed shot or a shot using a wild camera (and you only have magnetic ballasts) is to use three standard discharge source ballasts connected to three heads, each powered from a different phase of a three-phase source. Because the three phases peak a third of a cycle apart, when taken together the three lights have an actual frequency of 300 peaks per second (3 × 100). At this frequency, the camera should not detect the pulsation (Figure 3.30).

The lights must be bounced or mounted close together and placed far enough from the subject not to create separate shadows. The light created will be flicker-free at any normal frame rate. If filming at high speed for slow motion photography this solution will not be satisfactory and it will be necessary to use flicker-free ballasts.

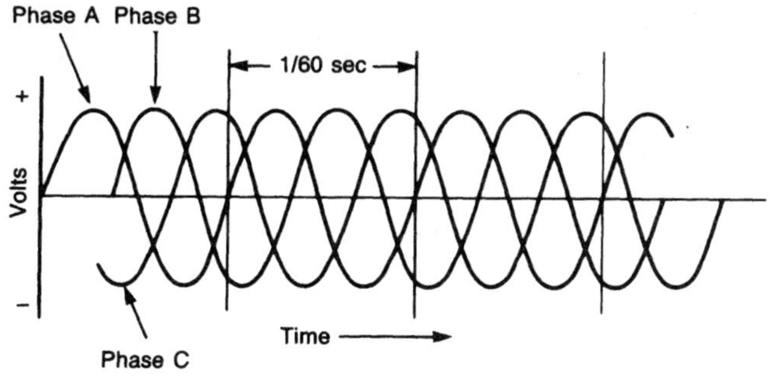

Figure 3.30 With three-phase power, the peak of each leg is a third of a cycle out of sync with the last, creating six peaks in each cycle. At 50 Hz, that amounts to 300 peaks per second, which is a high enough frequency to be flicker-free at any frame rate

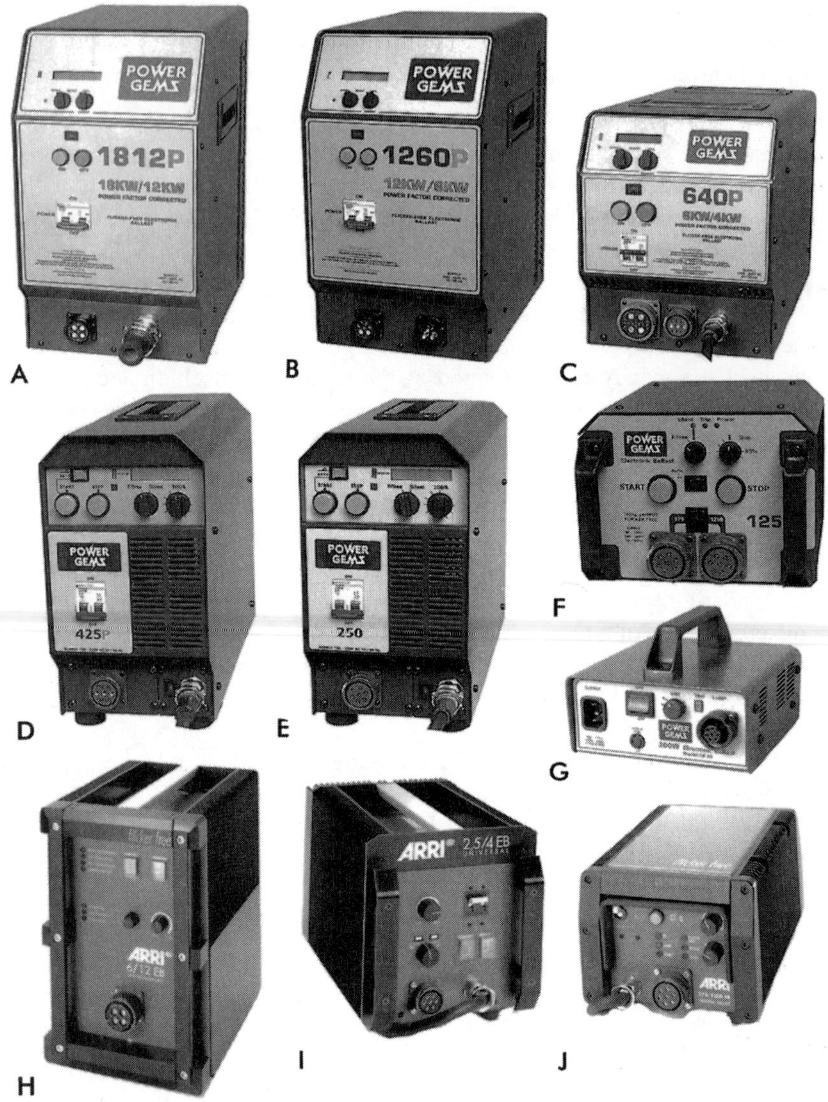

Figure 3.31 Electronic flicker-free ballasts. Power Gems and Arri ballasts are constant power ballasts. Most models are dual-wattage with auto-sensing. On Power Gems (A) 18 kW/12 kW, (B) 12 kW/6 kW, (C) 6 kW/4 kW, (D) 4 kW/2.5 kW, (E) 2,500/1,200 W controls include: Start and Stop momentary switches, breakers, dimmer pot, silent/flicker-free selection switch, and liquid crystal operation/ diagnostic display. The 1,200 W/575 W model (F) has a wattage selection switch and separate output connectors for 575 and 1,200 W lamps. G is a 200 W ballast. A–D above are power factor corrected models. Arri ballasts shown are (H) 12 kW/6 Wk, (I) 4 kW/2.5 kW, and (J) 1,200 W/575 W. Arri also makes electronic ballasts for their 200 W and 125 W fixtures, and an 18 kW/12 kW model. All European models include power-factor correction

Square-wave electronic ballasts

Square-wave ballasts eliminate the flicker problem. They allow you to film at any frame rate, at changing frame rates, and with a wild camera (Figure 3.31).

When filming an action sequence, explosion or a car crash, for example, some of the cameras will shoot at a high shutter speed, slow-motion. To give the DP the flexibility to choose any speed, the light output from the HMIs must be made constant.

A square-wave ballast maintains a virtually constant output of light over the whole AC cycle by squaring off the curves of the AC sine wave. The changeover period is so brief that the light is virtually continuous (Figure 3.32).

Unfortunately, the square wave causes the lamp, igniter and other parts of the head to make a high-pitched whistle. The head becomes a resonating chamber, amplifying the noise and projecting it out toward the set and the microphones. To make the ballasts quiet when recording dialogue, electronic ballasts are fitted with a switch to change between flicker-free operation and silent operation. In the silent mode, a special circuit electronically rounds off the sharp corners of the square wave, which eliminates the noise (Figure 3.32e).

In the silent mode, a square-wave ballast provides flicker-free light at frame rates up to about 34 frames per second (fps), and in flicker-free mode, up to 10,000 fps. Make sure that all ballasts are set to the same setting.

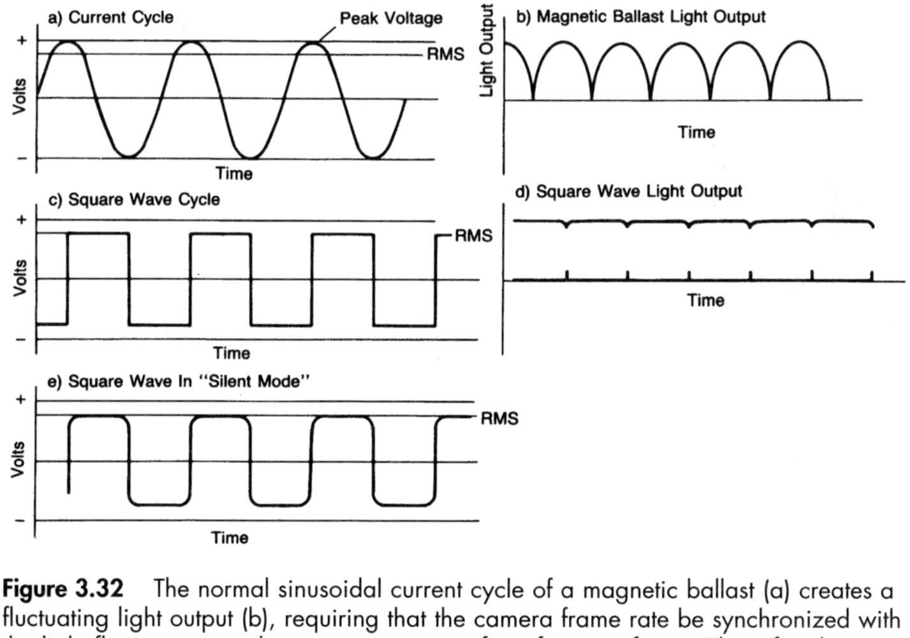

Figure 3.32 The normal sinusoidal current cycle of a magnetic ballast (a) creates a fluctuating light output (b), requiring that the camera frame rate be synchronized with the light fluctuations to obtain even exposure from frame to frame. The refined square-wave signal of an electronic ballast (c) creates virtually even light output (d), rendering the fixture flicker-free. The sharp corners of the normal square-wave signal create noise in the head. When operated in silent mode, the ballast electronically rounds off the corners of the square wave (e).

The shape of the lamp contributes to the intensity of the buzz. Globes with elliptical envelopes tend to be noticeably quieter than the square type. Wolfram, for example, makes the quieter rounded lamps (Figure 3.33). Head manufacturers and lamp manufacturers are both in the process of developing quiet igniter and lamp parts matched for use with electronic ballasts.

Square-wave ballasts completely process and regulate the input power, and as a result they offer additional advantages and features including:

- light weight; a lot less backache than their ship-anchor magnetic counterparts
- wide tolerance for voltage and Hertz rate discrepancies. Variation of up to ± 10 per cent in voltage or line frequency has no adverse effect on operation
- 'dimming' capability. By controlling current, the ballast can dim the lamp 50 per cent, or about one stop of light. At 50 per cent power, a lamp's colour temperature will be 75 K to 200 K higher (bluer) than normal
- increased light output (5 per cent)
- increased lamp life (as much as 20 per cent).

In addition, modern *constant power* electronic ballasts are able to regulate not just lamp current, but lamp power, enabling the ballast to compensate for changing lamp voltage as a lamp ages. Constant power means the lamp has stable, optimal colour temperature that remains uniform regardless of lamp age or line voltage. Constant power designs are also less prone to overheating than constant current ballasts. (A constant current ballast may output more than the rated power when connected to a higher than normal output voltage due to lamp variation or high-output cable loss. (i.e. the current remains constant but if the volts increase then VA becomes greater, and if R increases then I^2R becomes greater).)

The more sophisticated electronic ballasts (like those shown in Figure 3.31) incorporate self-diagnostic messages on a display or warning lights. After shutdown the display will identify the problem: an overheated power module, improper input

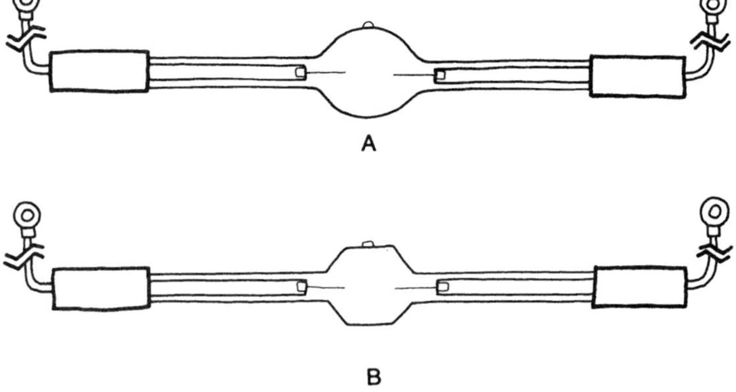

Figure 3.33 An elliptical lamp (A) is less noisy than the squarer design (B) when operated with a square-wave power source

voltage, a short in the output circuits, current on the ground wire, an incorrectly connected cable, everything but a readout of the gaffer's blood pressure. If the ballast shuts off, be sure to check the display before rebooting the ballast.

Power factor correction circuits

European electrical codes now require the use of power factor correction with mains power, (this still is not required in the USA).

Because of its heavily capacitive front-end components, with no power factor correction an electronic ballast puts current and voltage out of phase with one another. As a result, it typically has a power factor of 0.7 or less, meaning the ballast has to draw at least 30 per cent more power than it uses. Some types of rectifiers also create spike currents that can reach 2.5 times those of the equivalent sinusoidal waveform. This happens because the capacitors are only charging at the peak of the sine wave. This would create extremely high loads on the service or generator and could interfere with the generator's voltage regulator and even burn out the alternator. To contend with spike currents the generator would need to be oversized to at least twice the size of the load. Spikes would also affect other units running on the same service.

Also associated with low power factor and irregular waveform are the return currents on the neutral wire. With uncorrected square-wave ballasts, 65 to 80 per cent of the current does not cancel out between phases, even when all the phases are evenly loaded. This means that when operating a lot of large lights, the neutral wire will need to be doubled or even tripled to carry the additive current (see 'Power factor' in Chapter 8).

A power factor correction circuit realigns the waveform, and induces a smoother waveform. Power factor correction circuits successfully increase the power factor to as much as 0.98. The ballast uses power more efficiently and minimizes return current and line noise and also reduces heat, thereby increasing reliability.

Troubleshooting

The development of electronic ballasts with features such as constant power output, sophisticated diagnostic and protection circuits, and power factor correction is the result of years of ballast manufacturers struggling to master reliability. The older, simpler electronic ballasts are susceptible to blowing electronic parts. For example, repeated hot stabs can burn out the inrush resistor that protects the front-end rectifier bridge diodes and capacitors during start-up. The most common repairs to older electronic ballasts revolve around damage to input rectifiers, vented (blown) capacitors, open inrush resistors or blown power module fuses, all caused by high inrush current. To protect the inrush resistor, be sure to turn off the main ON/OFF switch or breaker after use, and make sure it is off before plugging in the power cord.

Another common repair on older ballasts is damage to the output transistors (IGBTs and FETs) caused by a short or arc path in the head or head cable. A shorted igniter circuit can burn out ballast after ballast. In some cases the ballast will continue to work even though internal parts are damaged. The result is that other parts overheat and short out, and the repair bill and turnaround time keep going up.

Newer ballasts include back-end protection circuits, a sensor shuts it off if it senses a short. This protects the ballast but it doesn't lower the blood pressure of the gaffer who is waiting for that light to come on. As a precondition to operation, sophisticated ballasts demand that the head and cables be in good condition, with no short circuits in the power feeds or to earth, and that they are properly earthed.

Once an electronic ballast craps out, there is seldom anything you can do but replace it. Nothing inside an electronic ballast is user-serviceable; you have to leave it to a qualified electronics technician. For this reason preventative steps become all the more important. There are many things electricians can do to prevent a failure. The main one is to treat the equipment like an electronic device. Electronic ballasts must be handled gently, and be thoroughly protected from heat, moisture, condensation, precipitation, dirt, sawdust and so on. They cannot be left baking on a hot beach or outside overnight in the dew. Magnetic ballasts are just about bullet proof, being made mostly of copper and iron. They can take all kinds of abuse, both physical and electrical, without failing. Electronic ballasts are made of circuit boards, relays, capacitors and transistors; and although they have rugged casings and use heavy, commercial-grade components, electronic ballasts cannot be treated like magnetic ballasts. The electrician must enter a solid-state frame of mind when handling this equipment.

Ballast electronics

A magnetic ballast is a very simple device. Input power is routed through the main breakers to a choke coil that is connected between the main input and the lamp. The coil may be tapped in several places to provide for various input voltages and to provide high start-up voltage. Capacitors are also included to compensate for the inductance of the coil, and to restore unity power factor. The coil provides the start-up charge for the igniter circuit, then acts as a choke, regulating current to the lamp once the light is burning. Power from the coil is routed to the main contactors (which are controlled by a low-voltage control circuit) and to the igniter circuit wire.

An electronic ballast (Figure 3.34) is more complicated. There are three primary stages to a square-wave ballast. The first stage, the DC intermediate circuit, converts power to DC. As a preliminary, power flows from the mains supply through the circuit breakers and earth leakage detection circuit to the RF mains filter. (The RF filter restricts the flow of noise back on to the supply service.) Contactors K1 and K2 and the start-up resistor form a circuit that charges the capacitors before the power electronics are activated at start-up. The input rectifier and capacitors then convert the current to DC, the input rectifier inverts the negative half of the AC cycle, and the capacitors level it out to one continuous positive DC voltage.

The second and third stages are referred to as the power electronics or power modules. The second stage is a step down or buck converter (HF-converter board and HF-choke) that draws a constant current from the DC intermediate stage, then precisely regulates current flow to the final power electronics. Actual current flow is constantly monitored by the control board and adjusted by controlling the high fre-

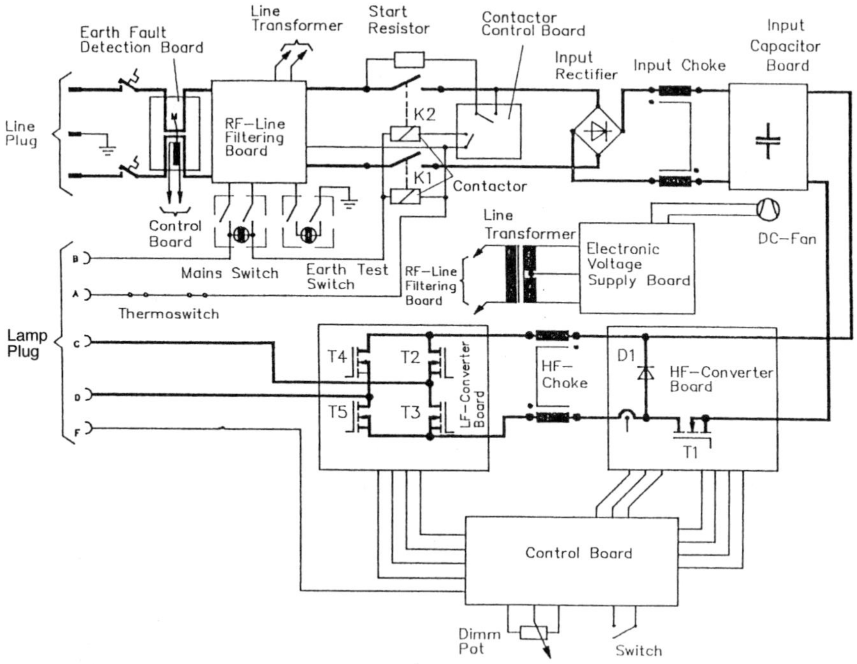

Figure 3.34 Block diagram of a 2,500 W electronic ballast (power factor correction circuits are not shown). (Courtesy Arri Lighting, New York and B & S Elektronische Gerate GmbH, Germany.)

quency (20 kHz) duty cycle of transistor T1. It is this circuit (T1, D1 and HF-choke) that allows a constant power ballast to maintain a lamp at optimum colour and output performance as lamp voltage increases with age.

The final stage (LF converter board) serves as an inverter, turning the DC current into an AC square wave using four specialized transistors (insulated gate bipolar transistors, or IGBTs). The IGBTs switch back and forth in pairs (T4 and T3, then T2 and T5), reversing the polarity at a frequency controlled by the control board. (Frequency is not referenced to the mains rate. Thus, an electronic ballast is not affected by a generator that is slightly off speed.) Power for the control boards is provided by a transformer and voltage supply board circuit.

Whether the ballast is electronic or magnetic, there are seven wires that run through the feeder cable from the ballast to the head (except in some Arri ballasts that get away with six). They are: two (thicker) power wires, VOH (voltage out hot) and VOR (voltage out return); an earth wire; the igniter's power line; and the control wires which go to the head ON/OFF system. These switches are integrated with the lens door safety switch, so that in the event of the lens door being open, the system will not operate.

In the head, VOH and VOR run directly to the terminals of the lamp. The earth wire is connected to the lamp housing. The igniter's power line and VOR are connected to the primary step-up transformer of the igniter circuit. This transformer steps voltage up to about 5000 V. From there current runs through a spark gap to a secondary transformer, which boosts voltage up to the starting voltage of the lamp, in the order of 25–65 kV. When the operator pushes the strike button two things happen: The contactors in the (magnetic) ballast are closed (in an electronic ballast the control board turns on the power control circuits – FETs and IGBTs – which apply voltage to VOR and VOH) and a 200 V to 350 V strike voltage is sent to the head on the igniter power line.

Taking it in extreme slow motion, the strike sequence happens as follows: The ignition voltage climbs from zero, increasing until the voltage potential is sufficient to bridge the spark gap. When a spark bridges the gap, a very high voltage start charge is delivered to the electrodes of the lamp from the secondary transformer. After 1 to 1.5 seconds a timer circuit removes igniter power from the circuit. Once the flow of electrons is initiated in the lamp, the ballast starts to hold back current. The lamp arc stabilizes and voltage rises to normal operating value.

The spark gap is set to deliver the proper strike voltage for the lamp. To some extent increasing the spark gap can improve hot restrike characteristics because it increases strike voltage; however, adjusting the spark gap involves special tools and an experienced technician, the parts are fragile and extremely small. Too narrow a gap will produce insufficient voltage to arc the lamp; with too wide a gap the voltage will not bridge the spark gap.

The lamp is turned off when the SAFE ON line is interrupted, either by the lens door micro-switch, or by the OFF button on the head or ballast. This opens the main contactors in a magnetic ballast or shuts off the power control circuits in an electronic ballast.

Discharge lamps

HMI (Mercury [Hg] medium-arc Iodide, Osram), HMI/SE (single-ended, Osram), MSR (medium source rare earth, single-ended, Philips), GEMI (General Electric metal iodide), CID (compact indium discharge, Thorn UK), CSI (compact source iodide, Thorn UK),[1] DAYMAX (made by ICL), and BRITE ARC (Sylvania) are trade names of lamps in the discharge source family registered by the various manufacturers. They all consist of two tungsten-coated electrodes surrounded by mercury vapour and other metal halides held in a quartz envelope. The flow of electrons switches electrons in the gas from one highly excited state to another, releasing energy in the form of visible and UV light. While the mercury is responsible for most of the light output, an optimal mix of halides of rare earth metals in the mercury vapour brings a balance of colour output. The result is a quasi-continuous multi-line spectrum, meaning that the colour is made up of narrow peaks of various wavelengths rather than a continuous spectrum, which closely resembles the make-up of daylight and renders colours faithfully on film. There are

1. CID and CSI are used in stadium lighting. CID (5500K) are also used in small sungun fixtures and have the same colour characteristics as HMI globes.

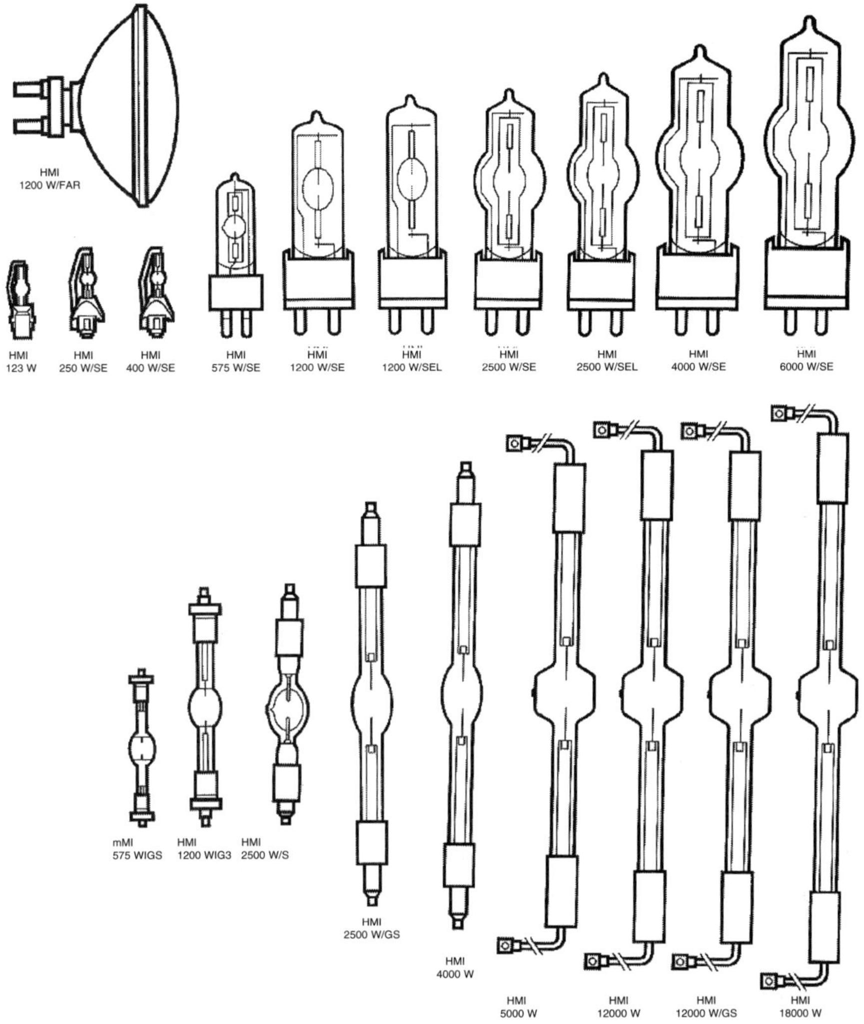

Figure 3.35 HMI lamps. (Courtesy of Osram Corp., Van Nuys, CA.)

three kinds of discharge source lamps: single-ended, double-ended, and PAR lamps (Figure 3.35).

Single-ended lamps

The design of single-ended (SE) lamps allows for greatly improved efficiency when mounted axially and used with a bright reflector, as in SE PAR lanterns. They are also used mounted vertically in newer models of Fresnel lanterns. Single-ended lamps of 575 W and larger can generally be burned in any orientation. The design and short overall length of SE lamps make it easy for them to restrike while hot.

Double-ended lamps

Fresnels and soft lights use double-ended lamps. The range of sizes is shown in Figure 3.35. Double-ended lamps of 4 kW and larger must be burned with their arc within 15° of horizontal; never tip these larger HMIs on their side.

PAR lamps

Some models must be operated in a horizontal orientation, others can operate in any orientation. The sealed lens/reflector envelope provides UV protection, but manufacturers recommend that an additional spreader lens be used as a second protection, in case the lens envelope breaks. Only some PAR lamps are made to extinguish automatically if the lens envelope is broken.

Relamping discharge source heads

Before relamping a light, be sure that the breakers are off, the lantern is unplugged and the lamp is completely cooled. Discharge source lamps build up internal pressure when in use. It is dangerous to handle them when hot; if broken, they will explode, sending shards of hot quartz in all directions.

The golden rule when relamping any lantern is never to touch the quartz envelope with your fingers and never to allow moisture or grease to come into contact with the lamp. Even a light smudge of finger grease will cause a hot spot on the quartz envelope, which weakens the quartz and causes the envelope to bubble during use. When the lamp loses its shape, the lamp's photometric and structural properties are compromised and the lamp could explode. Discharge lamps are too expensive to handle carelessly. At the time of writing, a 12 kW discharge lamp is priced at around $1,200! When a discharge lamp explodes, it shatters the lens and destroys the lamp holder and reflector, bringing the total loss to a staggering sum. Always handle lamps with a clean and dry rag, with clean cotton gloves (editor's gloves), or with the padding in which the lamp is packed. Make it a practice to clean the lamp once it is mounted in the lantern. Use a presaturated alcohol wipe or isopropyl alcohol and a clean lint-free tissue.

Double-ended discharge lamps have metal ends that are laid into the lamp holder. HMIs of 2,500 W and larger have clamps that close around the lamp ends and are tightened with a screw. Finger screws, Allen screws, nuts or standard screws are used. Discharge lamps of 6 kW, 12 kW and 18 kW have connection wires that have to be attached to terminal screws on the base of the lamp receiver. Lamps of 575 W and 1,200 W are held in a U-shaped receiver. Their ends are threaded and are tightened in place with knurled nuts. The 200 W lamp has a knife plug, a flat tab that slides into the connectors on the base and is locked in place with tightening screws.

Insert double-ended lamps into the lantern with the molybdenum ribbon horizontal so that it does not block light returning from the reflector (Figure 3.36).

Orient the nipple on the lamp upward or outward toward the lens, not downward or toward the reflector. The nipple should always be above the arc to prevent a cold spot from forming where chemicals in the lamp enclosure may condense and interfere with the burning cycle.

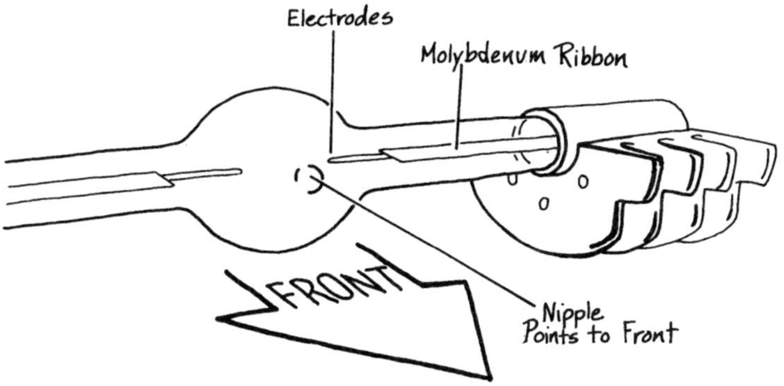

Figure 3.36 Proper installation of an HMI globe. Notice that the ribbon is horizontal and the nipple is oriented outward. (It may also be oriented upward.) Connections are tight. HMI globes should be cleaned with an alcohol-impregnated cloth as a part of daily maintenance. (Equipment courtesy of Hollywood Rental, Sun Valley, CA.)

Be sure the lamp's contact pins are tightly secured in place. Contamination in the contacts or a loose contact will impair proper cooling. A bad contact, evidenced by pitting and discolouration on the contact pins, causes premature lamp failure. A loose lamp may also vibrate.

With some SE PAR lanterns, it is impossible to install or remove the lamp without handling it by the glass. Great care must be taken to avoid breaking the glass where it attaches to its ceramic base. Wiggle the lamp gently along, not across, the axis of the pins; any stress across the axis can very easily snap the quartz. The better single-ended PAR lanterns provide a lamp release. When the knob is loosened, the lamp can be inserted and removed with ease.

Colour temperature

Factors that affect the colour output of HMIs are the type of lamp (5,600 K or 6,000 K), the number of hours the lamp has been used, lamp cooling and the regulation of the power by the ballast. It is good practice, especially with HMIs larger than 2,500 W, to match heads to ballasts and number and label both the head and the ballast with the colour temperature and the amount of green that the light emits. For example, a head and ballast would be labelled '1, 5,500 K, +2, 13/5/98.' This indicates ballast 1, which is matched to head 1, 5,500 K colour temperature, has a +2 CC of green on the date shown.

Lamp life

When a discharge lamp is brand new it will often show a very high colour temperature (10,000 K to 20,000 K). This is sometimes accompanied by some arc instability, causing flicker. You may want to 'burn-in' the lamp before filming starts, or colour correct the lamp. During the first couple hours of use, the colour temperature comes down quite quickly to the nominal value (5,600 K or 6,000 K) and the arc stabilizes. Thereafter the colour temperature changes over the life of the lamp at the rate of 0.5 K to 1 K per hour, depending on conditions. The colour temperature decreases because as the gap between electrodes increases, more voltage is required to maintain the arc, and as the voltage increases, the colour temperature decreases. For safety reasons, manufacturers recommend that lamps not be used for more than 125 per cent of their rated service life. As the lamp ages, changes in the quartz glass envelope make the lamp increasingly fragile.

Lamp cooling

You can overheat a lamp and cause damage to the reflector or lens by pointing the lights at an extreme up or down tilt. Also, if the light receives inadequate ventilation, the colour temperature will shift toward green and blue.

Carbon arc lights

From the very earliest days of motion pictures, carbon arc lights have been lighting movies (Figure 3.37). In their heyday there were quite a variety of arc fixtures from Fresnels of various sizes, to broads, ellipsoidal spotlights and follow spots (see Table A.9 in Appendix A). Pick out any movie in the Classics section of your video store and you will be watching a film lit with arcs. The silhouette of a Brute arc became a Hollywood icon. By the 1970s arc lights were being replaced by another type of high luminance daylight technology – the HMI. Discharge sources had clear advantages over arcs. Each arc light requires a full-time operator. The carbons must be constantly trimmed and changed every 20 to 30 minutes. The lights must be shut off whenever possible to save the carbons and prevent excess heating. The phrase, 'Lights, camera, action', comes from the days when the lights were turned on immediately before each take. Arcs are noisy and make smoke. With the general shift to a more thrifty and speedy mode of production, arcs are now rarely used. They sit in rows on the top shelves of the studios' lamp docks, dusty hulks, relics of a time gone by.

Still, arcs are by no means extinct. Every year there are at least a few films and commercials that haul out Brutes. In fact they seem to have even made a small comeback in the late 1990s. Why? Ask any gaffer or DP who has worked with them. The quality and colour of an arc is beautiful; no other source truly replicates it. Many gaffers consider them the nicest of all sources.

Operation

An arc light operates by maintaining an arc flame between the positive and negative carbon electrodes. As the arc flame burns the ends of the carbons away, a motor feeds the carbons so that the arc gap remains constant. The arc flame emanates from the pointed tip of the negative carbon, licking upward toward the cratered end of the positive carbon. As a result, the positive carbon burns away twice as fast as the negative.

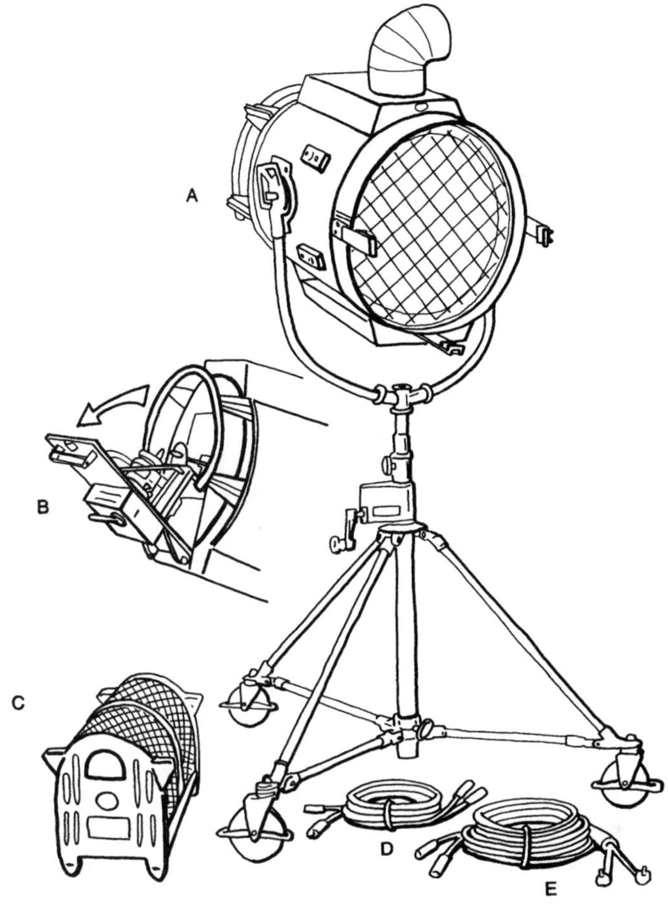

Figure 3.37 Components of a studio arc light: (A) Head with chimney attached. (B) Access to the carbons and internal mechanism is gained by folding out the back of the unit. (C) Power grid. (D) Head cable. (E) Grid cable with lug connectors. (Equipment courtesy of Mole-Richardson Co., Hollywood, CA.)

On average, a positive carbon will last about 30 minutes, depending on the length and type of the carbon. The positive carbon is constantly rotated by a motor so that its crater burns away symmetrically.

With a perfectly trimmed arc light, the feed motor maintains exact alignment of the positive and negative carbons as they burn away (Figure 3.38). The tip of the negative electrode should be pointed directly at the lower lip of the crater on the positive. The gap between them should be ¾ in. The positive carbon should protrude from the baffle plate about 1$\frac{7}{16}$ in. to 1½ in.

A rheostat controls the speed at which the positive carbon is fed and rotated. The arc light operator checks the alignment of the carbons during the operation by peering through one of several darkly tinted peepholes in the side of the housing. By

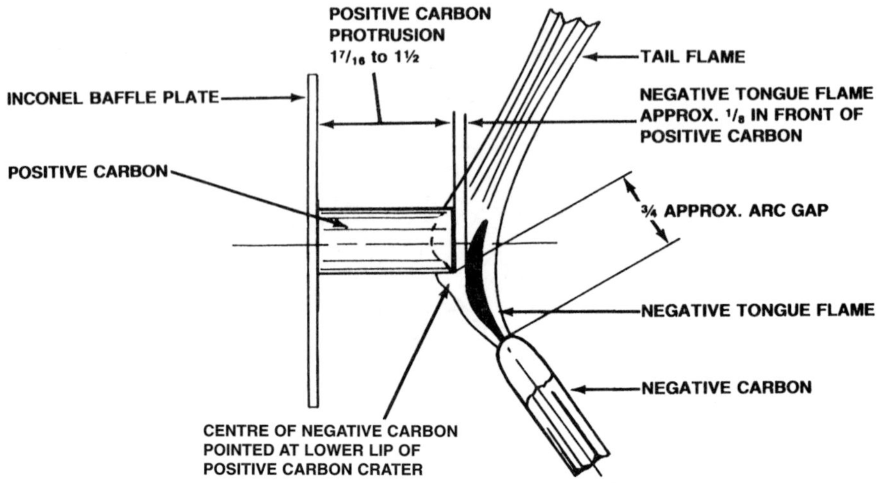

Figure 3.38 Ideal carbon arc flame. (Courtesy of Mole-Richardson Co., Hollywood, CA.)

checking the alignment and gap of the carbons from time to time, the operator can determine if the positive carbon is burning faster or slower than the feed rate. If the gap is getting bigger, the operator must increase the feed rate; if the gap is growing smaller, the operator must decrease the feed rate.

The alignment of each electrode is adjusted manually by turning one of two knobs on the back of the fixture. Turning the knob clockwise screws the electrode in; counterclockwise pulls it back. If the carbons burn themselves out of alignment, first realign them with the manual knobs, then adjust the feed rate to keep the carbons aligned. Do not attempt to use the feed rate to bring the carbons back into alignment.

Installing the electrodes

On the Litewate Brute, manufactured by Mole-Richardson Co., the entire carbon feed assembly is mounted to the back panel of the light. This panel hinges down and out to give access to the interior mechanics (Figure 3.39). In the event that the mechanism breaks down, the back panel can be replaced without exchanging the entire light. On older models, access to the inner workings is gained through a door on the side of the light.

When installing new electrodes, the power switch (Figure 3.40D) should be off. Determine whether the light is cool. If it is hot, you must use pliers to operate the internal levers.

For the following discussion letters in parentheses refer to Figure 3.39. The carbon holders are likely to be in the position where the last set of carbons were removed, that is, cranked in toward each other. Drop the negative carbon carriage (A) to the bottom position by pressing the dimpled release lever (Q). The lever disengages the carbon holder from the drive rod (C) and allows it to slide freely.

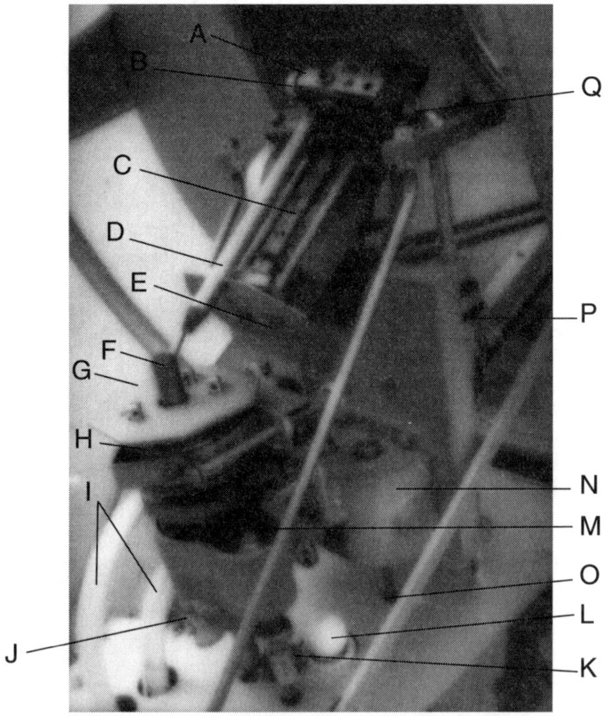

Figure 3.39 The carbon feed mechanism of a Litewate Brute Arc hinged out of the back of the light: (A) negative carbon carriage; (B) carbon roller; (C) negative drive rod; (D) negative carbon; (E) negative baffle plate; (F) positive carbon; (G) positive baffle plate; (H) positive brushes; (I) power leads; (J) carbon release lever; (K) manual handcrank shaft for positive carbon; (L) work light; (M) feed gear; (N) gear box; (O) manual handcrank shaft for negative carbon; (P) feed motor; (Q) dimpled release lever. (Photo by Rob Lewbel. Equipment courtesy of Mole-Richardson Co., Hollywood, CA.)

On the Litewate Brute, a spring-loaded lever on the negative carbon holder allows you to hold back the roller clamp (B) to install the carbon. On the Brute, the negative carbon is held by a thumb screw.

The positive carbon is held in place by the brushes (H). Rotate the cammed carbon release lever (J) to open the brushes to allow installation of the positive carbon. Before inserting the positive electrode, depress the striker lever to bring the negative electrode up into striking position. Slide the positive carbon in through the back panel until it touches the negative carbon. It should protrude from the baffle plate by 1½ in. and the butt end of the positive carbon will stick out of the back of the housing. Align the carbons so that the tip of the negative carbon touches the centre of the positive carbon. Release the striking lever. Clamp the positive carbon in place with the carbon release lever. Close the back of the housing or the access door. Note: Align the carbons so that the negative carbon touches the centre of the crater of the positive carbon, not the lower lip. If the negative carbon hits the lower lip during striking, it may shatter the edge of the crater, causing uneven burning for several minutes.

Powering an arc light

Arc lights run exclusively on DC power. Studios with DC feeds typically are modelled on the American system and use the same luminaries – a three-wire system with 120-V DC between phase and neutral, and 240-V DC across the phases. When using a 120-V DC power source, the arc light plugs into the grid, which supplies the light with its operating voltage of about 73 V from a 120-V DC source. Most studios outside Hollywood have been converted to AC. When only AC power is available a rectifier must be used instead of the grid. Most rectifiers operate off of three-phase AC power and provide 73-V DC to the light.

The polarity of the cables is critical to the operation of the light. Connecting the light with reversed polarity will cause the light to sputter and hiss during striking, and if left on for more than a few seconds, it will burn out the core of the negative carbon, and the tip of the positive carbon is likely to split or crack. Be sure that pos-

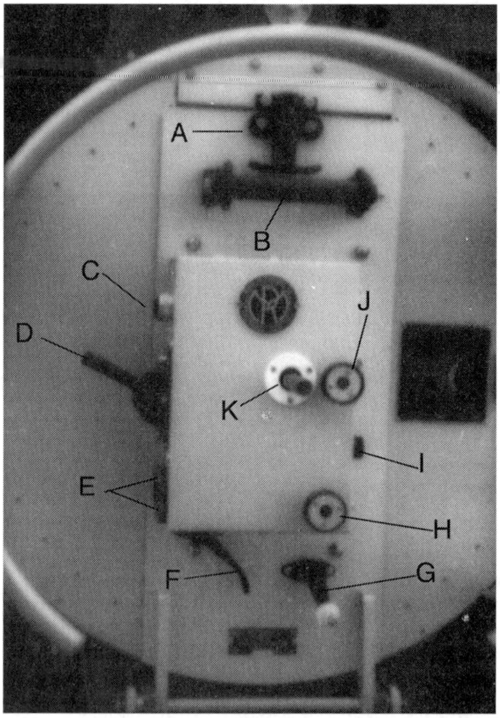

Figure 3.40 The back panel of a Litewate Brute Arc. A) spring-loaded door latch, B) handle, C) polarity indicator light, D) power switch, E) recessed power cable receptacles, F) striker lever, G) flood/spot crank, H) negative manual handcrank, I) feed rate rheostat, J) positive manual handcrank, K) butt end of positive carbon. Photo by Rob Lewbel. (Equipment courtesy of Mole-Richardson Co., Hollywood, CA.)

itive is connected to positive and that negative is connected to negative. If you are unsure about which is which and they are not identified with colour codes, check the connectors with a DC voltmeter before striking the light. A red warning light in the back panel of the fixture glows if the polarity is reversed, but the light is not always reliable (Figure 3.40C).

It is good practice to fire up the light to check for proper operations as soon as you have power. If there is any kind of problem, you will be able to fix it without holding up the entire production.

If the grid voltage is too high or too low, it will adversely affect the performance of the light. If the negative electrode becomes burned to a slender point, it is a signal that the voltage is too high and the carbons are burning too fast. If the negative carbon burns to a blunt end, the voltage is too low. In either case, the arc flame becomes unstable and can start to flicker.

Striking an arc light

For the following discussion letters in parentheses refer to Figure 3.40. When the carbons are properly aligned, trimming an arc light is as simple as turning the power switch on (D) (this energizes the electrodes and engages the feed motor), gently turning the striking lever (F) until the carbons momentarily touch, causing an arc and then immediately releasing the striking lever. When the negative carbon contacts the positive carbon, the arc flame will immediately ignite. Once the light is fired, check the arc flame through the peephole. Advance the positive carbon using the handcrank (J) so that the tip of the negative points directly at the lower lip of the crater on the positive about three half turns of the knob. Do not hold the striking lever down for too long because this can damage the carbons and the generator.

Striking partially used carbons

Every time you turn off an arc light, you should immediately check and realign the carbons so that they are ready for immediate restrike. When the gaffer asks for the lights again, it is too late to start realigning the carbons.

Realignment is simple. With the power switch off, back off the positive carbon with the handcrank. Press the striking lever to bring the negative carbon into striking position, then crank the positive carbon forward until the negative carbon touches it in the middle of the crater. Release the striking lever. Now you are ready to go as soon as the gaffer asks for light.

If you have to restrike without realigning the carbons, there is a good chance you will chip the edge of the crater, which can make the flame unstable. To fix a cracked positive carbon, turn up the rheostat (I) and even out the edge of the positive by burning it away. Once it is even again, return the rheostat to normal speed.

Daily maintenance and lubrication

For consistent, quiet operation, arc lights need to be lubricated three times daily: once at the start of the day, once after lunch and once at the end of the day. The lubrication holes are shown in Figure 3.41; however, it is better to remove the gear housing cover and lubricate these parts more carefully if time permits and the light

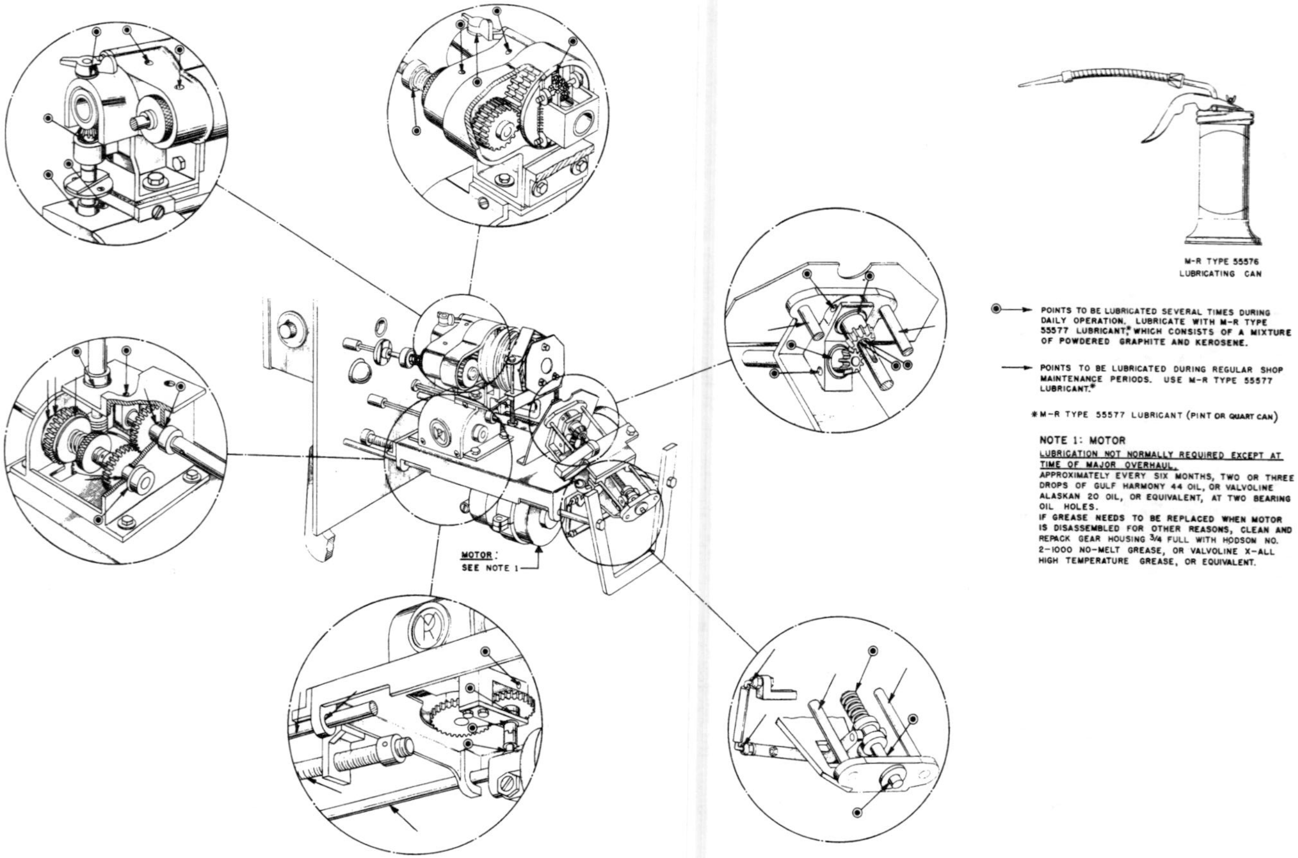

Figure 3.41 Carbon arc light lubrication holes. (Courtesy of Mole-Richardson Co., Hollywood, CA.)

is cool. Be careful not to get lubricant on the clutch because this will cause the clutch to slip and will make manual adjustment of the carbons difficult. Lubricate gears and all joints or places where there is metal-to-metal friction.

Arc lights are lubricated with a solution of finely powdered graphite and kerosene. The kerosene acts as a carrying agent to work the graphite into the gears and other moving parts. Heavy lubricants such as WD-40 and oil should not be used because the high temperature of the light will evaporate the liquid, leaving only a gummy residue that impedes the operation of the light. Once oil has worked its way in, the residue can only be cleaned out by taking apart every mechanical part of the gear and clutch assembly. If a graphite/kerosene solution is unavailable, diesel fuel also provides lubrication without gumming up the gears.

During use, fragments of carbon and smoke will dirty the inside of the lens. To clean the inside of the lens and the housing, access is gained by swinging open the floor of the housing. The floor is hinged and held in place by a pin at the bottom front of the light. Additional trays on the bottom of each side of the light hinge open for quick cleaning. During daily maintenance, the lens should be cleaned with household glass cleaner and the inside of the light should be blown out with compressed air. All debris and carbon chips should be emptied from the lamp trough.

Carbons and filtration

There are two types of carbons: white-flame carbons and yellow-flame carbons. Both carbons produce a light that is very high in UV frequencies and both must be filtered with gels to reduce the UV emissions to a usable level.

Unfiltered white-flame arcs have a colour temperature of approximately 6,200 K. A Y-1 gel filter corrects the colour to 5,700 K. Using both a Y-1 and an MT-2 gel on a white-flame arc corrects the colour temperature to between 3,200 K and 3,400 K.

Yellow-flame arcs naturally produce a light at approximately 4,100 K. A YF or YF-101 filter corrects the colour temperature to approximately 3,200 K. Yellow-flame carbons have a greater tendency to flicker than white-flame carbons and arc light operators often prefer to use a white-flame carbon and colour correction gel instead.

The following is a list of the different types of arc correction gels available, what they are used for and the various manufacturers' names for them:

- Y-1: Straw-coloured gel used with white-flame carbons to reduce UV and convert colour to daylight (GAM 1560, Y-1 L.C.T. Yellow; Lee 212, L.C.T. Yellow (Y-1); Mole Y-1; Rosco 3107, Tough Y-1.
- WF Green: preferred in Europe for same use as Y-1 (Rosco 3110, Tough WF Green; Lee 213, White Flame Green).
- MT2: Used with Y-1 to convert white flame arcs to 3,200 K. Also used as an amber conversion for HMI and CID lights (Rosco 3102, Tough MT2; Lee 232, Super Correction WF Green to Tungsten; GAM 1570, MT2).
- 1/2 MT2: Used with Y-1 to make a partial conversion to tungsten. Light looks slightly yellow to daylight film and slightly blue to tungsten film (Rosco 3115, Tough 1/2 MT2; Gam 1575, 1/2 MT2).

- 1/4 MT2: Used with Y-1 to warm the daylight balanced arc slightly (Rosco 3116, Tough 1/4 MT2).
- MTY: Combination Y-1 and MT2. Reduces UV and converts white flame arcs to 3,200 K (Rosco 3106, Tough MTY; GAM 1565, MTY).
- MT 54: A straw coloured gel used to warm the colour of white flame arc lights and HMIs (Rosco 3134, Tough MT 54).
- YF-101: Green gel used with yellow-flame carbons to reduce UV and correct to 3200K (Lee 230, Super Correction L.C.T. Yellow; Mole YF-101).
- UV Filter: An almost clear gel used to remove UV from arc and HMI sources (Rosco 3114, Tough UV Filter; Lee 226, UV; GAM 1510, UV Shield).

Fluorescent lights

Until relatively recently cinematographers regarded fluorescent lighting as a minefield of photographic headaches, virtually incompatible with motion picture photography. Fluorescents were associated with ghoulish green skin tones, poor colour rendering, anaemic light output, noisy humming ballasts and the same shutter speed restrictions that exist with magnetic ballasts.

It took the innovations of a determined gaffer and his best boy to overcome these obstacles. Freider Hochheim and Gary Swink designed luminaires, ballasts, and lamps tailored to the needs of film production. Their company, Kino Flo, Inc., continues to make ground-breaking advances in the photographic applications of fluorescent technology. Various manufacturers now offer stand-mounted fluorescent lanterns with high-frequency, flicker-free ballasts (Table A.10 in Appendix A), which operate with commercially available lamps. Kino Flo makes their own lamps, which are high output and colour correct (Table A.11 in Appendix A). Cinematographers have discovered the positive qualities of fluorescent lights: lightweight luminaires that put out soft, controllable light that wraps around the features and creates a pleasing eye light. They can easily be built into sets when a fluorescent environment is called for, but can also be used purely as a low profile, soft lighting instrument.

Fluorescent high-frequency ballasts

High-frequency ballasts bypass the problem of intensity fluctuation by converting the mains input frequency up to between 20,000 and 40,000 Hz. The period of time between the off and on pulse of each cycle is so short that the illuminating phosphors do not decay in light output. The phosphors are essentially flicker-free. When shooting on constructed sets, such ballasts are used for built-in fluorescent light fixtures. However, when filming in older locations, existing banks of fluorescents will usually not have electronic high-frequency ballasts, and therefore fewer shutter speeds and shutter angles can be used. Commercial electronic ballasts are becoming more common. In a modern installation, open up the fixture to check the ballast type.

Colour-corrected fluorescent tubes

When filming in a location with ceiling fluorescents, the lighting crew will typically replace all the existing fluorescent tubes with colour-corrected tubes.

In the UK and Europe, there are a wide range of fluorescent tubes available with very high colour rendering values. The most prominent of these are GE Northlite (5,500 K), Philips Col/95 (5,600 K), GE Nat Delux (3,600 K), and Philips Col/93 (3,200 K), which are used for critical colour work, and 'Artificial Daylight' which is a full spectrum tube, (including UV) which also meets critical colour rendering criteria. This latter tube can be used as an alternative to 'Northlight' if the UV content is not important. If an approximation to sunlight is required, 'Kolor-rite' offers a correlated colour temperature of 4,000 K with a very high colour rendering index. There is also a range of 'Polylux and Pluslux' lamps which provide very good colour rendering and are used where correlated colour temperatures of 2,700 K, 3,000 K, 3,500 K and 4,000 K are required. This latter group of lamps are usually referred to as 'Tri phosphor lamps' as the rare earth high output phosphors are similar to those originally adopted for colour television tube production.

Kino Flo

Kino Flo makes fluorescent lighting systems specifically for film production work, utilizing various types of lamps, luminaires, and ballasts (see Table A.11, Appendix A). Kino Flo tubes are specially designed to be used with Kino Flo high-output ballasts. The Kino Flo KF55 (5,500 K) and the KF32 (3,200 K) broad-spectrum fluorescent lamps are engineered to correspond to the spectral sensitivity curves of colour film emulsions. Kino Flo tubes mix wide-band and narrow-band phosphor crystals with rare earth elements. The phosphor blend displays a complete spectrum of light (Colour Rendering Index of 95) and no green spike when operated with Kino Flo high-output ballasts. Kino also offers a warmer tube, KF29 (2,900 K) which gives DPs the option of a warmer source for specific applications.

Kino Flo also supplies special green and blue tubes for lighting green and blue screens. Red, pink and yellow tubes are also available, which are great for decorating a set with neon-like lines of light. Kino Flo tubes are safety-coated to make the lamps more durable and to ensure that no glass fragments, mercury, or harmful phosphors will be released if the lamp should break. Table E.2 (Appendix E) lists all Kino Flo tubes and Figure E.1 (Appendix E) illustrates base types.

Kino Flo ballasts run at high frequency (25 kHz), resulting in flicker-free operation at any frame rate or shutter setting. The lights turn on instantly, even when cold, requiring no warm-up time. Kino Flos can be dimmed about one stop on a Variac dimmer. Kino Flo dimming ballasts can reduce output to 3 per cent without flicker. (You cannot use an electronic SCR dimmer or household resistance-type dimmer with a fluorescent light.) Kino Flo ballasts are lightweight and run silently.

Kino Flo 120V/240V systems

- **Portable luminaires** Kino Flo luminaires come in various configurations and

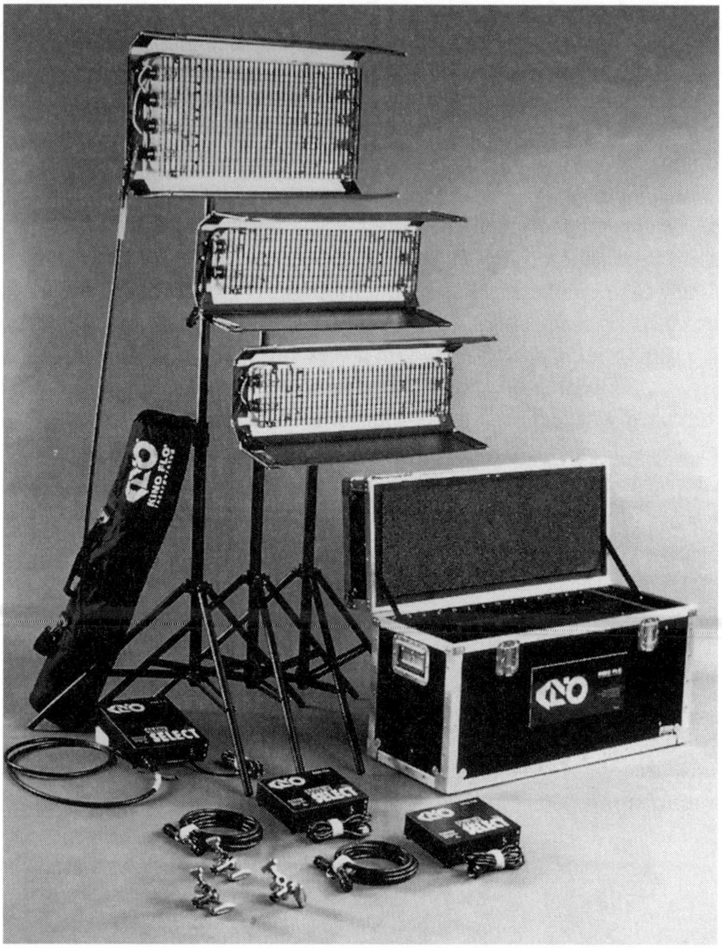

Figure 3.42 Kino Interview Kit illustrates the 2-ft four-bank, and double-bank fixtures with stands, mounting adaptors and travelling case. (Photo courtesy of Kino Flo, Inc., Sun Valley, CA.)

sizes: four-bank systems, double-bank systems, and single systems each have their own corresponding ballast and head cable (Figure 3.42). All luminaires come in 4-ft, 2-ft and 15-in. sizes. Each luminaire is equipped with a lightweight egg-crate louvre that controls the spread (and slightly reduces the intensity) of light. The luminaire has a snap-on mounting plate for attachment to a C-stand (Figure 3.43), but because they are lightweight, they can also be taped or stapled into place.

- **Wall-o-lite** The Wall-o-lite is an amazingly bright luminaire with ten 4-ft lamps and a built-in ballast (Figure 3.44). It puts out about as much light as a 2.5 kW HMI Fresnel bounced from a polystyrene screen. It has proved especially useful for lighting matte screens (green screens or blue screens). It creates a broad, even

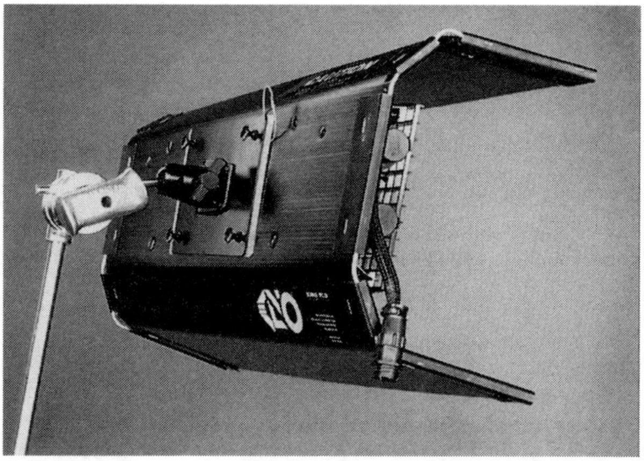

Figure 3.43 Kino mounting plate. (Photo courtesy of Kino Flo, Inc., Sun Valley, CA.)

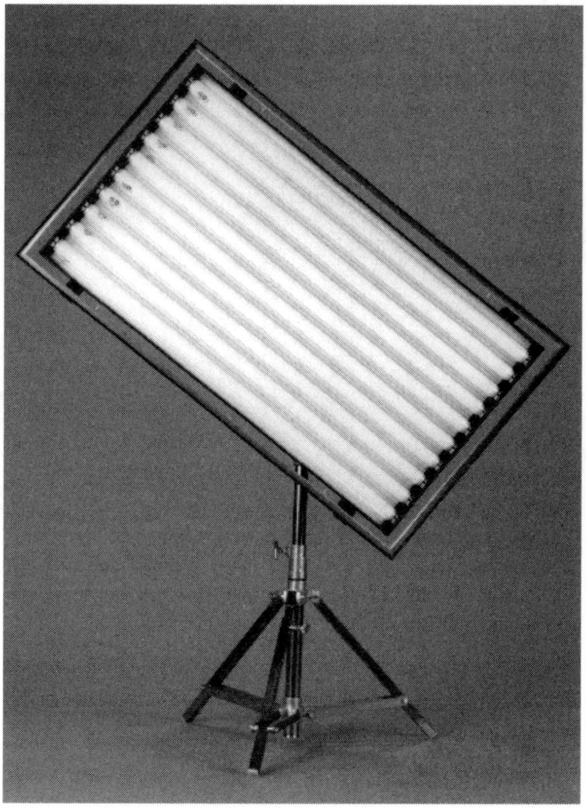

Figure 3.44 Kino wall-o-lite. (Photo courtesy of Kino Flo, Inc., Sun Valley, CA.)

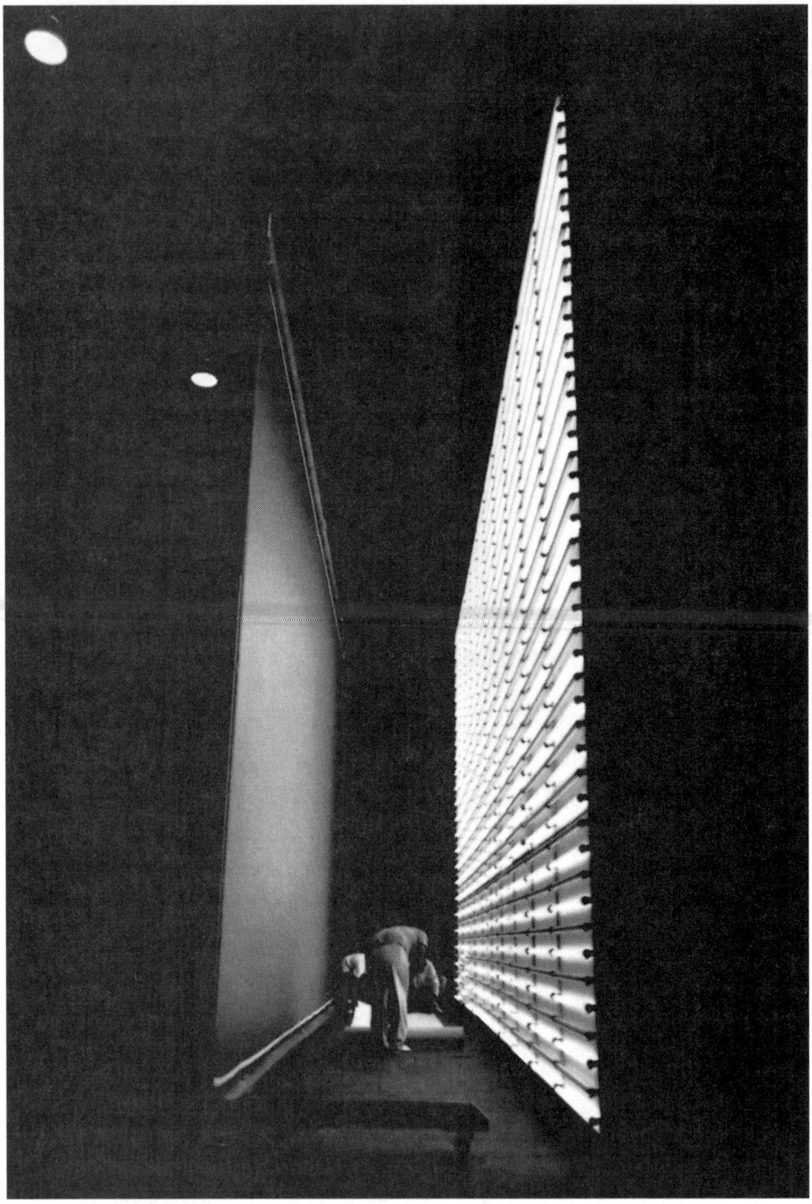

Figure 3.45 Kino rear-lit screen for matte photography. (Photo courtesy of Kino Flo, Inc. Sun Valley, CA.)

light, which is necessary for matte work. Kino Flo provides green (560 nanometres) or blue (420 nanometres) tubes that are extremely bright in a selected part of the spectrum and will fully saturate the matte colour. Up to 50 Wall-o-lite luminaires can be connected and controlled on a single three-position remote switch (10 lamps/OFF/5 lamps).

- **Big Foot luminaires** Kino also makes 8-ft and 6-ft luminaires that run on the high-output Mega-ballast. Double- and single-tube versions are available.
- **Studio Luminaires** The Kino Flo studio luminaires (Image 80, 40, and 20) are designed for studio applications and green and blue screen work. They are yoke-mounted with metal housings and built-in ballasts. They come in 8-tube (4 ft), 4-tube (4 ft) and 4-tube (2 ft) luminaires.
- **Trans-panel system** Figure 3.45 shows the Kino Flo trans-panel lighting system. This system of modular 12-tube panels creates a wall of even, bright light for back-lighting a translight or blue-screen. The system is powered from a master controller, which can control up to 44 panels. The controller can dim the panels up to four stops with no change in colour output. A translight hung as close as 3 ft in front of the panels will be evenly illuminated to about 640 FC. For blue screen work, an 8-ft separation is recommended. KF55 or Super Blue lamps are used to light a rear-transmission blue screen.

12V DC kits: 12-V Single, Mini-Flo and Micro-Flo

Kino Flo makes a variety of 12 V DC fixtures that can run on battery power or a 12 V transformer power supply (220 V or 120 V AC).

- **12-volt single** The 12 V single ballast can power T-12, T-10 or T-8 lamps, ranging in size from 15 in. up to 4 ft (Figure 3.46). In a car or elevator where AC power is not available, you can run any of the standard Kino luminaires from a 12 V DC battery. With the proper adaptor cables, you can power a standard four-bank luminaire from four 12 V ballasts. The 9-, or 15-in. lamps are ideal in a night-time car scene to give the appearance of dashboard light. The Kino Flo 12 V kit includes two 15-in. single-tube luminaires, dimmable ballasts, all the usual accessories, cigarette lighter connector and spring clamps to connect to a car battery.
- **Mini-Flo and Micro-Flo** The 12 V Mini-Flo system is a 9-in. lamp with a corresponding fixture, ballast, and head cable. The Micro-Flos are tiny 6-in. and 4-in. tubes, thinner than a pencil (either tungsten or daylight) (Figure 3.47). Their size makes them uniquely suited for many special applications, such as to light a face inside a space suit helmet. They are commonly used for tabletop and miniature photography.

Using Kino Flo luminaires

The component parts of each luminaire (fixture with barn doors, reflector, egg-crate louvre, lamp harness and tubes) can be disassembled and employed as needed (Figure 3.48): bare tubes (taped under a bar counter, for example), bare tubes taped to a reflector for greater light output, or the assembled luminaire with or without the egg-crate louvre, depending what takes priority, control of side spill or maximizing light output.

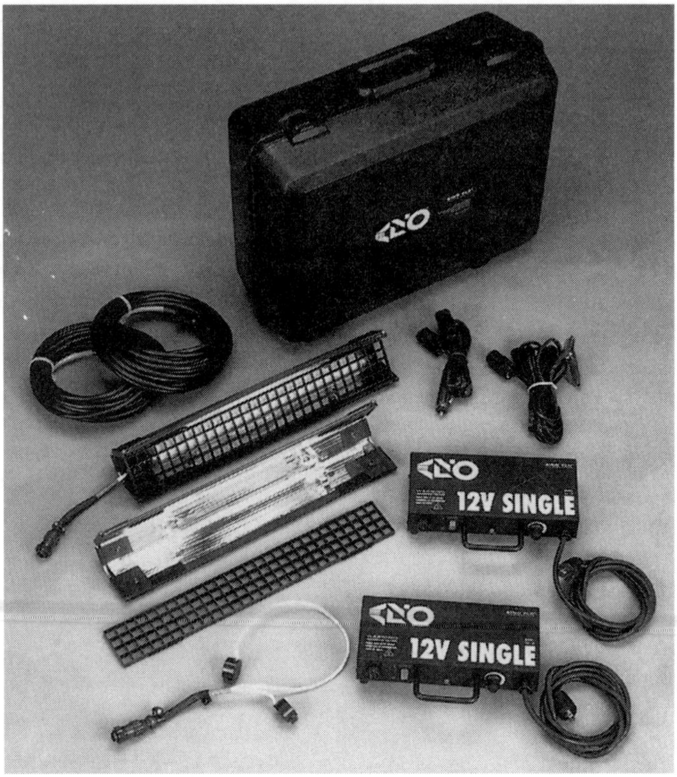

Figure 3.46 Kino 12 V DC single kit: 15 in. fixture, 12 V DC ballast, cigarette lighter adaptor and clip-on car battery cables. (Photo courtesy of Kino Flo, Inc. Sun Valley, CA.)

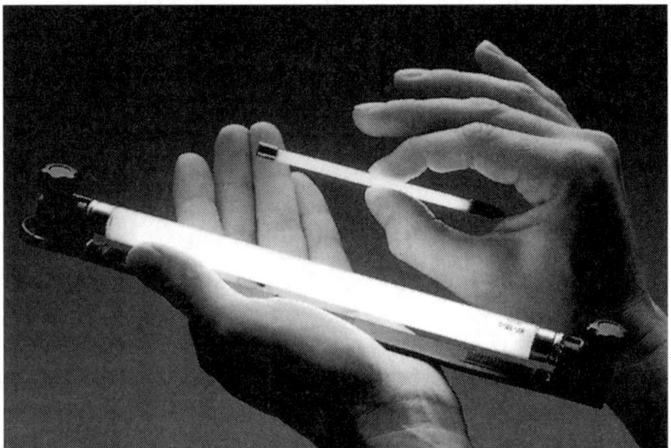

Figure 3.47 Kino 9 in. Mini-flo (reflector and doors removed) and 4 in. micro flo tube Kino Flo lights. (Photo courtesy of Kino Flo, Inc. Sun Valley, CA.)

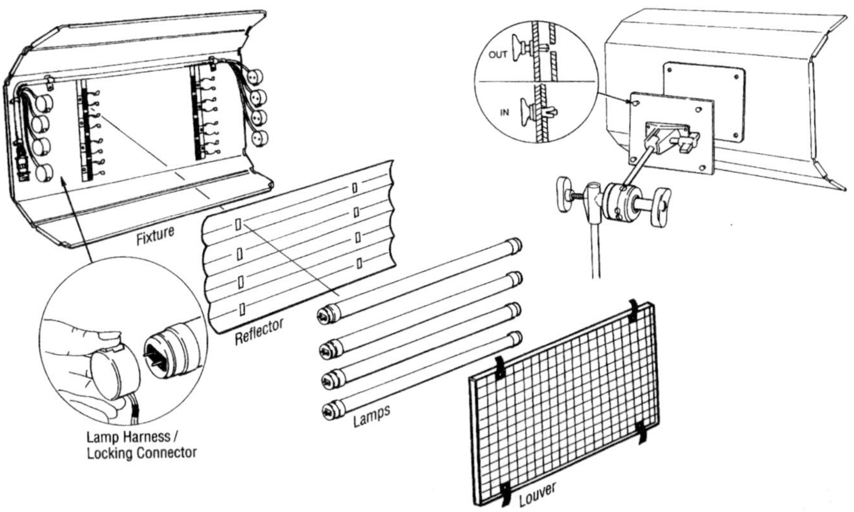

Figure 3.48 Component parts of the portable Kino Flo luminaires and how they fit together. (Courtesy of Kino Flo, Inc. Sun Valley, CA.)

Bare tubes can be neatly mounted to a surface using plastic cable ties and adhesive cable tie mounts or by applying double-stick tape to the tube.

You can order a special Y-splitter, which splits a four-bank cable (or two-bank cable) into single harnesses, so you can mount tubes end to end, for example. Be sure to order additional single harnesses and cables with the splitter.

Ballast features

- **Standard ballasts** Kino Flo standard ballasts (four-bank, double-bank and single) provide a three-position toggle selection switch (all lamps/off/half the lamps).
- **Select ballasts** Kino Flo Select ballasts (four-bank, double-bank and single) feature an additional high-output/standard-output toggle switch. Use the high-output setting for 4 ft lamps and the standard setting for 2 ft and 15 in. lamps. Operating 2 ft and 15 in. lamps in the HO setting will cause the colour temperature and green output to be higher. The Select ballast also features more advanced electronics than the standard ballast, which gives it more reliable and consistent performance.
- **Dimming ballasts** Kino Flo Dimming ballasts (four-bank, double-bank and single) feature a slider to adjust light output in a full range with no change in colour temperature. A trim adjustment allows you to set and return to a particular setting easily, and to turn the lamp on at a preset level. Dimming ballasts provide a jack for attachment of a remote cable. Multiple dimming ballasts can be wired to and controlled by a standard dimmer board.
- **Slimline Select and Mega-ballast** The Kino Flo Slimline Select powers single-pin 6 ft and 8 ft tubes. The Kino Flo Mega-ballast powers 6 ft and 8 ft luminaires only (four-bank, double-bank and single).

Troubleshooting

From time to time one or more tubes in a luminaire will not light. The problem could be in the ballast, the lamp harness, or the lamps. The best way to proceed is as follows:

1. Double-check that the ballast is hot, plugged into a live AC service.
2. Check that the extension is properly connected at the ballast and harness.
3. Check that the harnesses are properly secured to the tubes and that the head cables are fully connected at both ends. Harness connectors are colour-coded; the same colour must be on both ends of the lamp.
4. Switch the ballast to full ON position. Note which lamps do not work, and try another ballast. If the same lamps still do not fire, change out those lamps. If the lamps still do not fire, change out the harness.

When renting Kino Flos in large numbers, it is prudent to include a few extra back-up four-bank ballasts (one for every twelve systems). Newer Kino Flo ballasts have a latch-up feature to protect the solid-state circuitry from abuse during operation. However, many older style ballasts are still in circulation. Single and double systems generally do not require back-up ballasts.

Kino Flo portable luminaires are made with wire barn-door 'hinges' (the flexible metal rods at the corners of the doors), which are made to be disposable. If one breaks, it can be easily replaced by removing the end screw, pulling out the broken wire, and replacing it with a length of good wire.

Some additional notes about fluorescent lights

Effect of temperature

Fluorescent lamps are sensitive to extremes of temperature. Standard fluorescents are designed for maximum output between 20°C and 25°C. Fluorescents operating on high-frequency ballasts will operate in temperatures below freezing. With all fluorescents, even those operating on high-output ballasts, the operating temperature affects both the colour and the intensity of the light. In freezing conditions, the high-intensity ballast can get the tube started, but it takes a few minutes for the tube to reach the proper colour and output. In hot temperatures or if the tubes are enclosed in an unventilated space, the colour may wander toward the blue-green end of the spectrum and additional colour correction may be needed.

Effect of voltage shifts

Voltage shifts do not appreciably affect the colour temperature of fluorescents. If the voltage is too low, however, the light will go out completely or will not start. A 10 per cent decrease in power will yield a 10 per cent decrease in light output.

Calculating power needs

Fluorescent lights are generally of nominal wattage and therefore pose no special power demand concerns. However, when a large number (hundreds) of fluorescent lights are to be powered, one must keep in mind some additional factors. The wattage rating on a fluorescent tube is the power consumed by the tube alone. The ballast typically consumes an additional 10 per cent to 20 per cent. Thus, a 40 W tube actually consumes as much as 48 W of power (20 per cent of 40 = 8, 40 + 8 = 48). In addition, power factor must be taken into account (reactive current and power factor are explained in Chapter 8).

4

Stands and rigging

We constantly need to hang lights in awkward places, so naturally, over the years, a myriad of stands, clamps, arms and suspension rigs have been devised to secure a lantern or flag almost anywhere.

Stands

Stands come in two basic types. Baby stands have a 16 mm (⅝ in.) spigot that fits into the baby receiver found on most lights of baby 2 kW or smaller (Figure 4.1).

Junior stands (combo stands) have a 28 mm (1⅛ in.) receiver that takes the junior spigot found on larger lights (see Figure 4.3). Stands of both types come in short, 'low boy' versions as well as the standard height with two-sections or three-sections. Stands may be made of aluminium, which is lightweight, or of steel, which can bare more weight.

Baby stands

The most versatile baby stand for location work is a steel three-section stand with a lazy leg (also called mountain leg) (see Figure 4.1). The legs can be quickly retracted by loosening the T-handle on the top collar and pulling up. The lazy leg makes it easy to level the stand when it is placed on uneven ground, on a stair, over the edge of a kerb, or leaning against a set wall (Figure 4.2).

Rolling stand

Baby rolling stands are convenient when working in the studio on a level surface. Many rolling stands have brakes that snap into a locked position.

Lightweight kit stands and blade stand

Blade stands are extremely lightweight, which is their one advantage. They are also somewhat flimsy and unstable. They are best used with small lights. It is

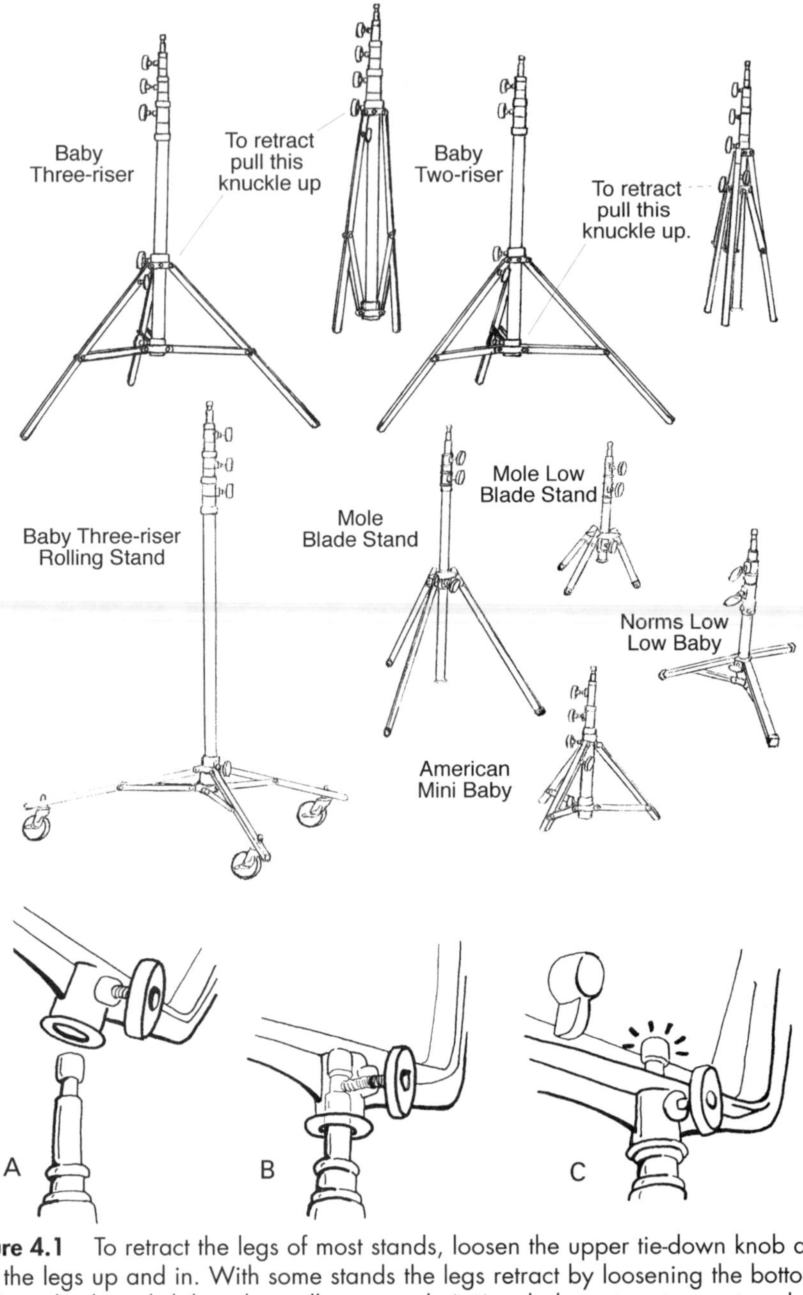

Figure 4.1 To retract the legs of most stands, loosen the upper tie-down knob and pull the legs up and in. With some stands the legs retract by loosening the bottom tie-down knob and sliding that collar upward. A ⅝ in. baby spigot inserts into the receiver on a fixture (A). When mounting the light, the spigot should be flush with the receiver and not stick through. This ensures that the T-handle is engaging the indent of the spigot (B). Also some lights (notably the baby junior) will not tilt properly if the spigot sticks through (C)

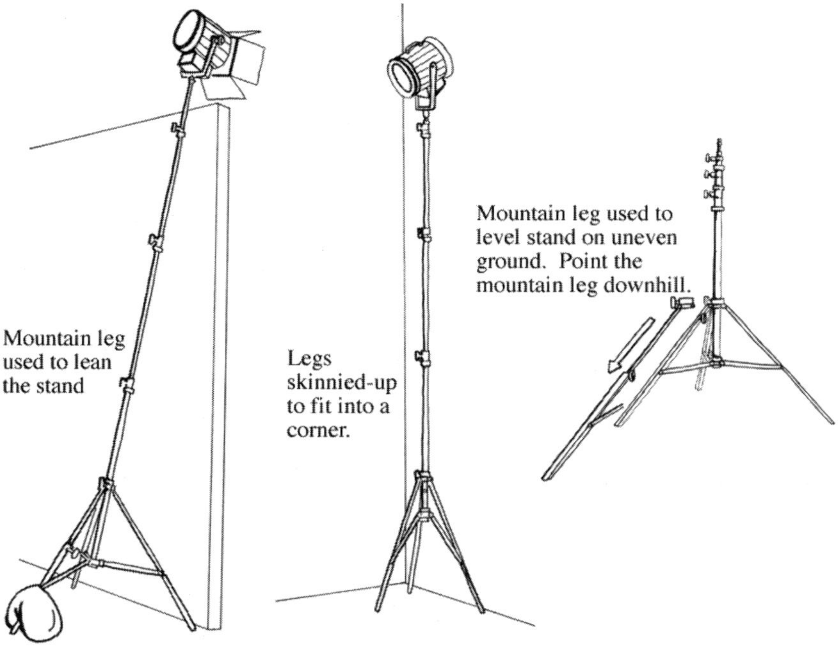

Figure 4.2 Alternative stand configurations

wise to stabilize a lightweight stand by hanging a small sandbag on the bottom T-handle.

Low stands

When you need a light placed low, a mini-baby (22 to 50 in.) or preemie (31 to 70 in.) stand comes in handy. Table 4.1 lists the basement and top floor for many common stands.

Junior stands

Combo

The junior combo stand is so named because it was designed to handle both luminaires and reflector boards. Larger luminaires, Studio 2 kW Fresnel and larger, have a 28 mm (1⅛ in.) spigot. A typical two-section combo has a maximum height of about 11 ft (335 cm). A three-section combo has a maximum height of 14 ft (426 cm). Figure 4.3 illustrates the junior stand and some common stand accessories: the *Universal head* with 28 mm receiver and baby pop-up spigot, the angled drop-down offset, and the spigot adapter (spud adaptor).

Low boy

The minimum height of a typical combo stand is 48 in. (121 cm). If the light must be lower than that, you need a low boy junior stand, which has a minimum height of

Table 4.1 Stands

Name	*Type*	*Risers*	*Min*	*Max*	*RM Leg*	*Brand*
			Height			
Low Baby Stands						
Runway Base Only		0	11″	11″		Matthews
Mini Preemie	St	2	20″	39″		Matthews
Preemie Baby	Al	2	31″	5′10″		Matthews
Mini Baby	St/Al	2	22″	50″	X	American
Low Low Baby	Al	2	20″	3′3″		Norms
Low Hefty Baby	Al	2	33″	5′7″		Norms
Baby Stands						
Steel Maxi	St	3	34″	10′		Matthews
Beefy baby standard	Al	2	37″	8′3″		Matthews
Beefy baby 3-riser	Al	3	45″	12′	X	Matthews
Baby 2-riser	St/Al	2	40″	9′4″	X	American
Baby 3-riser	St/Al	3	44″	12′5″	X	American
Baby Light 2-riser	Al	2	44″	9′4″		Norms
Baby Light 2-riser	St	2	52″	10′6″		Norms
Hefty Baby 2-riser	Al	2	47″	9′10″	X	Norms
Hefty Baby 3-riser	Al	3	50″	12′10″	X	Norms
Low Jr. Stands						
Low Boy	St	2	33″	6′9″	X	Matthews
Low Boy	Al	2	37″	6′9″	X	Matthews
Low Combo 1-riser	St	1	29″	4′0″	X	American
Low Combo 2-riser	St	2	32″	5′6″	X	American
Low Combo 2-riser	St	2	33″	5′7″	X	American
Low Boy		2	36″	5′8″	X	Norms
Junior Stands						
Combo	St	2	48″	11′	X	Matthews
Sky High	St	3	52″	14′	X	Matthews
Mombo Combo	St	4	76″	27′	X	Matthews
Light Duty Combo	St	2	48″	10′5″	X	American
Heavy Duty 2-riser	S	2	50″	11′3″	X	American
Heavy Duty 3-riser	St	3	51″	14′3″	X	American
Alum Combo 2-riser	St/Al	2	48″	10′3″	X	American
Alum Combo 3-riser	St/Al	3	51″	13′9″	X	American
Mombo Combo	St	4	5′8″	23′5″	X	American
Standard		2	54″	11′2″	X	Norms
Sky High		3	58″	13′	X	Norms
Sky High	Al	3	61″	13′	X	Norms

Note: RM leg stands for Rocky Mountain leg. St/Al means the stand has steel legs and aluminium risers.

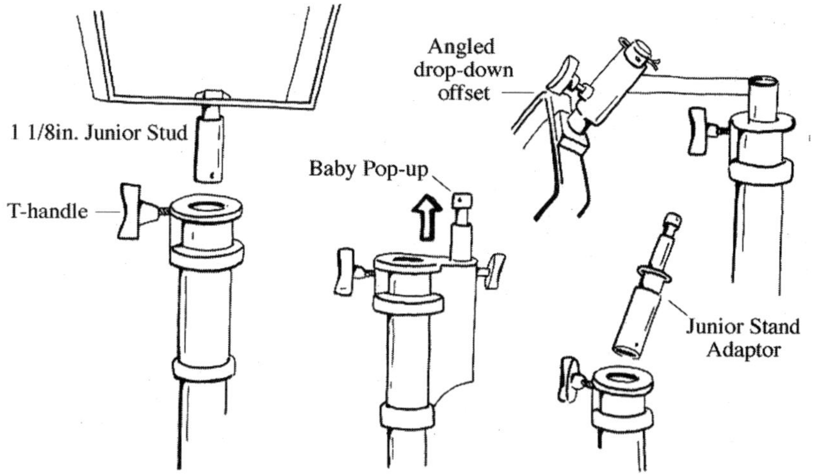

Figure 4.3 The 28 mm (1⅛ in.) spigot fits into the receiver on the stand. The T-handle should engage the indented part of the spigot. A Universal head provides 16 mm pop-up spigot and 28 mm receiver, which allows the stand to support either a baby or a junior fixture. An angled drop-down offset allows a light or reflector to hang lower than the lowest height of the stand. The 45° angle holds the light away from the stand. In the absence of a baby pop-up, a stand adaptor can be used

around 33 in. (86 cm). If you need to mount a light lower than 33 in., you'll have to use a turtle stand or T-bone.

T-bones and turtle stands

A T-bone is simply a metal T fitted with a junior receiver (Figure 4.4). A T-bone can be nailed or screwed into place in green beds (decks or bridges) or on a scaffold tower.

A turtle stand is nothing more than three legs joined in the centre to a junior receiver. It sits flat on the floor, providing a low position for larger lights. Arri and Matthews make a C-stand with removable legs, which serve as a turtle stand. They also make low wheeled stands with Universal or junior receiver. Matthews calls theirs a runway stand.

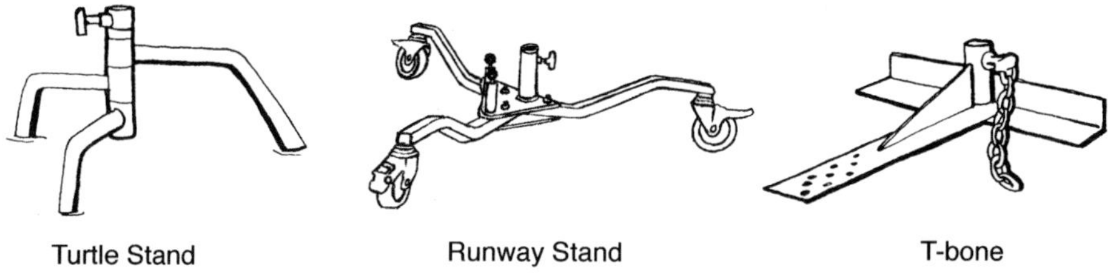

Figure 4.4

Mombo combo

A mombo combo is a very substantial, four-section, steel stand with a very wide base (no wheels), which allows a maximum height of more than 26 ft (792 cm).

Offsets, side arms, extensions and right angles

Offsets

Figure 4.5 shows various types of baby offsets that can be used to put the position of the head out away from the stand. They are useful when some obstruction, such as furniture or a set piece, prevent the stand from being placed under the light. Note that an offset or side-arm puts the stand off its centre of balance. Use sandbags on the legs to counterweight.

Risers/extensions

Risers come in many sizes, typical sizes would be 6, 12, 18 and 24 in. A riser is a handy piece of hardware when a light mounted to a plate or clamp is not quite high

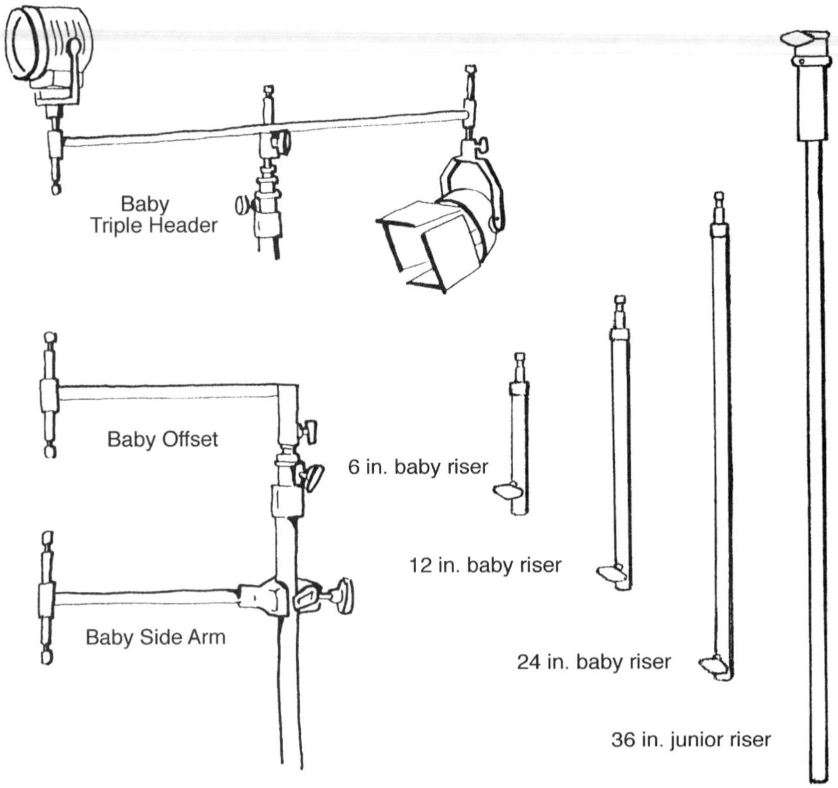

Figure 4.5 Offsets, side arms, double-headers and triple-headers are available in baby and junior sizes (babies are shown here)

enough. A 36 in. junior stand extension essentially adds an additional section to a stand. It can also be inserted into the receiver on the dolly or the crane when a light is to ride with the camera.

Booms

Boom poles allow a lantern to be suspended over or behind the actors in places where it could not be mounted by other means. Booms vary in size and strength. The small ones mount on a baby stand and provide about a 4-ft arm with almost as much counterweight length. The larger ones mount on a combo stand, have more length and more counterweight, and provide either a junior or a baby mount for the light. Sandbags can be added for additional counterweight.

A *C-boom clamp* allows you to use a C-stand as the boom by clamping around the C-stand's main tube (1¼ in.). The 'fork' slides into a 4½ in. grip head.

Using stands

- See Chapter 2, Table 2.3, for check-out procedure.
- 'Righty tighty, lefty loosey.' Lock-off knobs (T-handles) tighten when turned to the right (clockwise) and loosen when turned to the left.
- Extend the top section first. If you extend the second section first, you will raise the first section out of your reach, and you'll look like an idiot. One exception, if the light is heavy for the stand, you can add strength to the stand by not using the first section, or by using only part of it.
- Bag any raised stand. A good rule of thumb is one sandbag per section. If the light is extended all the way up on a three-section stand, you would use three bags. Place the sandbags on the legs so that the weight rests on the stand, not on the floor.
- Get help when needed. As a rule, use two people to lift any light of 5 kW or larger. Depending on the height of the stand and the awkwardness of its position, mounting a 12 kW or Dino can require three or even four people. Don't hesitate to round up the other electricians when you need them. It is poor judgement to bite off more than you can chew. A heavy light can get away from you and cause injury and damage. Moreover, handling large lights alone will tire you out before the day is over and, in a short time, is likely to lead to back and knee problems. I know too many people in their mid and late thirties who have done permanent damage by abusing themselves when they were younger. Lifting equipment is not a contest; the lighting crew works as a team.

Crank-up and motorized stands

Crank-up stands provide a mechanical advantage needed for raising heavy lights. Table 4.2 gives the weights and weight capacities of crank-up and motorized stands. They have a chain-, cable- or screw-driven telescoping extension system with a crank and clutch, so that the crank will not reverse and spin out of control under weight. Do not crank up a stand without some kind of weight on it, as this can cause problems in the inner mechanisms.

Table 4.2 Weight capacities of crank-up and motorized stands

	Floor	*Ceiling*	*Capacity*	*Type*
American				
Roadrunner 220	4′2″	11′3″	220 lb (100 kg)	Crank
Big Fresnel Lamp Stand (BFL)	4′2″	12′6″	300 lb (136 kg)	Motor
Arri				
Baby 2-section Supercrank	3′2″ (97 cm)	5′5″ (165 cm)	220 lb (100 kg)	Crank
Short Base 3-section Supercrank	4′8″ (153 cm)	11′3″ (345 cm)	154 lb (70 kg)	Crank
2-section Supercrank	4′10″ (147 cm)	7′7″ (232 cm)	198 lb (90 kg)	Crank
3-section Supercrank	5′5″ (165 cm)	11′5″ (348 cm)	176 lb (80 kg)	Crank
4-section Supercrank	5′11″ (182 cm)	15′7″ (477 cm)	154 lb (70 kg)	Crank
5-section Supercrank	7′9″ (237 cm)	20′4″ (620 cm)	154 lb (70 kg)	Crank
Matthews				
Lite Lift	4′1″	8′6″	85 lb (38 kg)	Crank
Crank-O-Vator	4′11″	12′	150 lb (68 kg)	Crank
Low Boy Crank-O-Vator	3′2″	5′5″	150 lb (68 kg)	Crank
Super Crank	5′9″	12′6″	200 lb (90 kg)	Crank
Cine-Vator	4′6″	12′	300 lb (136 kg)	Motor
Mole-Richardson				
Folding Crank-up Litewate Stand	4′5″	10′	–	Crank
Molevator	5′1″	11′1″	250 lb (113 kg)	Motor

The Arrivator, Cine-Vator, Molevator and similar motorized stands power the telescoping mechanism with an electrical motor that is operated by a single up/down toggle switch (Figure 4.6).

These stands can handle the heaviest lights made (up to 136 kg [300 lb]).

- When rolling a large light on a crank stand or motorized stand, push the stand from the back with the swivel locks on the two rear tyres unlocked and the front tyre locked. Steer by pushing the back wheels left or right. If you put two tyres in front, they can catch in a rut and the whole stand will tip over.
- When the stand is in place, prevent the stand from rolling by swivelling each wheel straight out from the stand and locking each swivel. Additionally, wedges in the tyres and cup blocks under the tyres will prevent them from turning.
- Before raising the stand, make sure it is totally levelled with cup blocks, wedges and apple boxes if necessary.
- Use your strong arm to turn the crank to raise and lower the light. Never release the clutch without having a good grip on the crank. If the crank gets away from

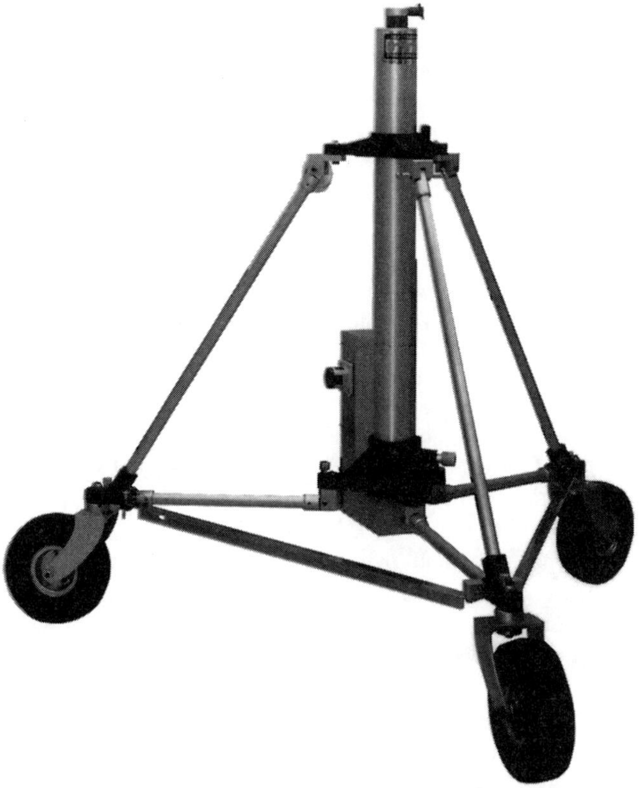

Figure 4.6 A Cine-Vator stand. (Photo courtesy Matthews Studio Equipment, Burbank, CA.)

you, there is a good chance you will not be able to get hold of it again before the light hits you on the head. There is also a good chance you'll hurt yourself trying to grab hold of the spinning crank. If you lose control, let go of the clutch and get out of the way of the light.

Flag stands and overhead stands

Stands with *grip heads* are used to support overhead sets and flags, scrims (nets), diffusion frames and so on.

C-stands

Q: How do you drive an electrician crazy?
A: Lock him in a small room with a C-stand.

Given enough C-stands and enough time, one could build a scale model of the Eiffel Tower. They are like an erector set. A Century Stand (*C-stand* or *flag stand*) uses a

2½ in. *grip head* to hold an *arm*. The stand comes in various sizes 20 in., 30 in., 40 in. and 60 in. as do the arms (20 in. or 40 in.). The legs of the stand may be either fixed or removable, or they may have a sliding leg which allows the stand to be levelled on uneven surfaces. Various manufacturers also make attachments such as the Arri Flexation Attachment or Arri Magic Arm (a jointed lightweight arm used to support small flags, postage stamps, fingers and dots) which both provide the ability to set flags in ways that would otherwise be difficult.

C-stand associated equipment

An equipment trolley (called a taco cart in the USA) is dedicated to holding C-stands, apple boxes, wedges, cup blocks and cribbing, as well as providing drawers for hardware and consumables and space for milk crates (which hold mounting hardware). A flag box attaches to the front and holds 2 × 3 ft and 18 × 24 in. flags, scrims (nets) and silks. Another trolley typically holds 4 × 4 ft flags, scrims (nets), silks and bounce boards.

- **Flags** Black duvetyn fabric stretched over a metal frame and used to cut a selected portion of a light beam. Common sizes include: 12 × 18 in., 18 × 24 in., 24 × 36 in., 30 × 36 in. and 4 × 4 ft.
- **Scrims** (net) Bobbinet stretched over a metal frame and used to reduce the strength of a selected portion of a beam of light. Single scrim has green edges. Double has red edges. Common sizes include: 12 × 18 in., 18 × 24 in., 24 × 36 in., 30 × 36 in. and 4 × 4 ft.
- **Silks** White silk stretched over a metal frame and used to reduce and soften a beam or light. Common sizes : 12 × 18 in., 18 × 24 in., 24 × 36 in., 30 × 36 in. and 4 × 4 ft. Thinner silks, called half silk and quarter silk, are also available.
- **Frames** Empty metal frame on to which diffusion and gel is mounted (using snot tape) in order to diffuse or colour a beam of light. Common sizes include 18 × 24 in., 24 × 36 in., 2 × 2 ft, 3 × 3 ft and 4 × 4 ft.
- **Cukes and celo cukes** A cuke is a piece of ¼ in. plywood with holes cut in it in random shapes. It is used to break up a beam of light into a pattern. A celo cuke uses a painted wire mesh instead of plywood to give a more subtle effect. Common sizes include 18 × 24 in., 24 × 36 in. and 4 × 4 ft.
- **Cutters** Long narrow flags used to create shadows or to cut the light. Common sizes include 10 × 42 in., 18 × 48 in. and 24 × 72 in.
- **Dots and fingers** Very small flags and scrims (nets) used to make very small cuts.

Setting a C-stand

- Place the longest leg under the extended arm. This helps stabilize the stand. Always sandbag the legs when putting weight on an extended arm (A C-stand may also be used as a lighting stand as shown in Figures 4.7 and 4.8.)
- Work with gravity, not against it. When you are standing behind the stand with the arm pointing away from you, the knuckles should be on your right. In this way, when weight is put on the arm, gravity pulls the grip head clockwise, which tightens it. If the knuckle is on the left, the weight will eventually loosen the knuckle, and the whole rig will collapse (very bad form).

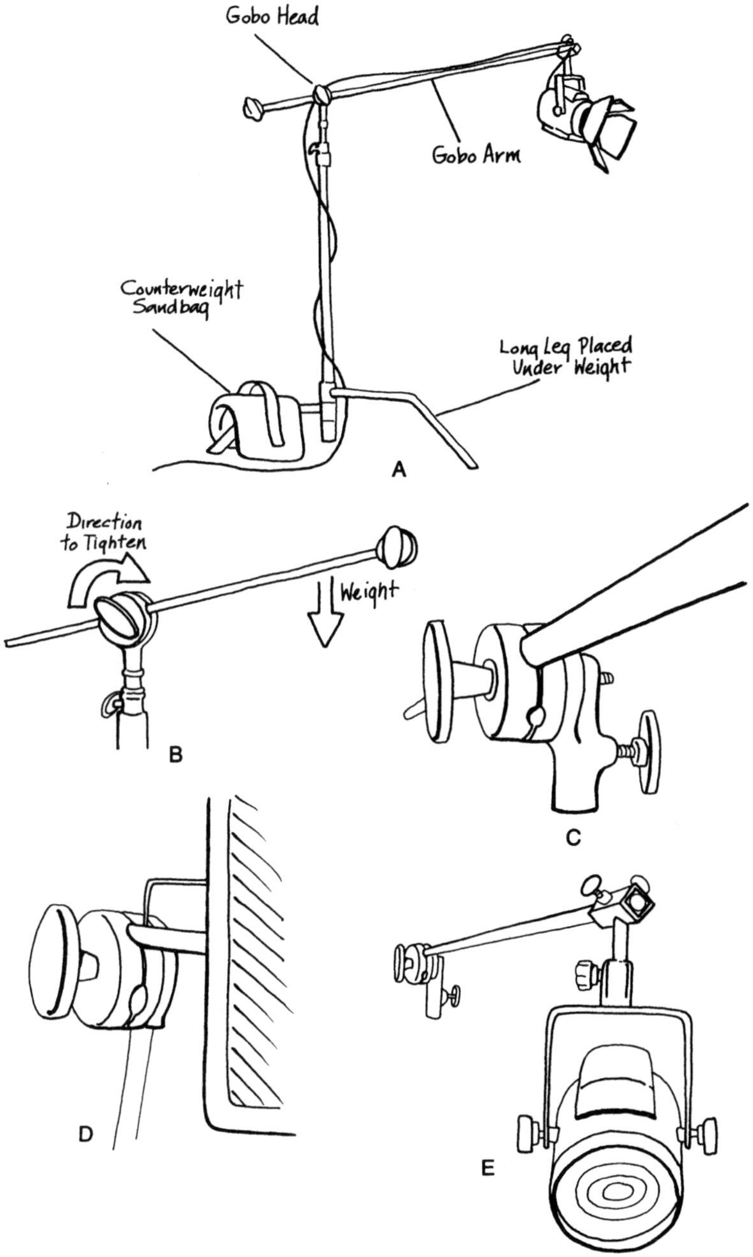

Figure 4.7 (A) A C-stand supporting a light fixture. (B) Orient the knuckle so that gravity tightens it (righty tighty). (C, D) The grip head accepts various sizes: a ⅝ in. hole for the gobo arm or a baby spigot; a ⅜, ½ or ¼ in. hole for nets and flags. (E) The light fixture shown uses a bar clamp adaptor (used on furniture clamps) to attach to the gobo arm. (Equipment courtesy of Concept Lighting, Sun Valley, CA.)

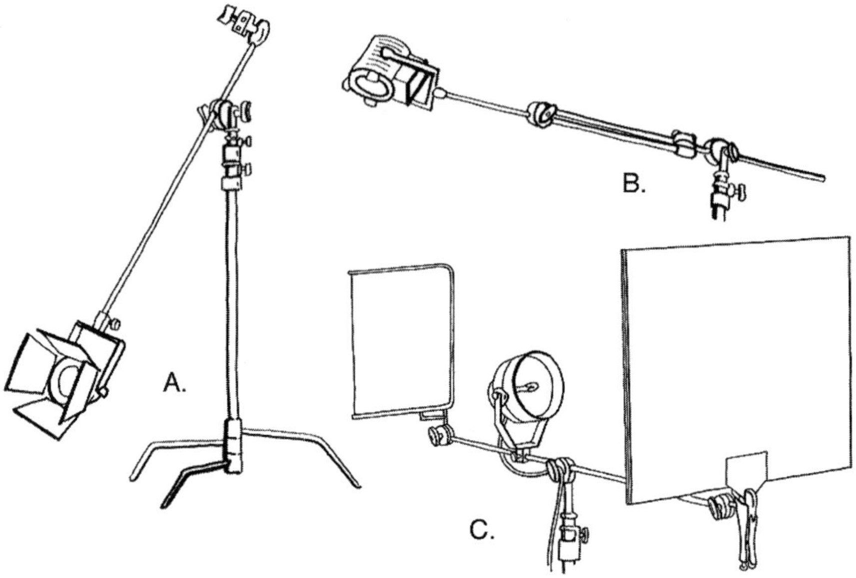

Figure 4.8 Some special uses for C-stands: (A) to place the light in a low position. (B) To arm the light out over the action. Here, two gobo arms are coupled together. (C) A bounce card rig like this uses a single stand to support the light, bounce card and a net

- Avoid configurations in which the back end of the arm sticks out, especially at eye level; it could hurt someone. There is almost always an alternative configuration that eliminates the hazard. If it's unavoidable, place a tennis ball or Styrofoam cup on the end of the arm so people will see it.
- Place the sandbag on the top leg so that the weight is on the leg and not resting on the ground.
- Always place the C-stand on the 'off-stage side' of the light , the outside, as viewed from the camera. This helps keep grip equipment out of the movie.
- When a lot of torque is placed in the gobo head, configure the stand so that the flag rests on the T-handle. Do not rely on the strength of the grip head alone.
- Take wind into account. When setting 4-by frames or flags in a wind, use a larger stand with a wide base, such as a combo stand. A C-stand does not handle big flags or frames well in any kind of wind.

Overheads/butterflies and associated stands

An *overhead set* or *butterfly set* is large frame with one of several types of material stretched across it. Overhead sets are used on exteriors to shade the action (see Figure 4.9). Standard sizes are 20 × 20 ft, 12 × 12 ft and 6 × 6 ft. An overhead set includes a single black net (which cuts light by a half stop), a double black net (cuts a full stop), a silk (diffuses light, softens shadows) and a black-out made of black

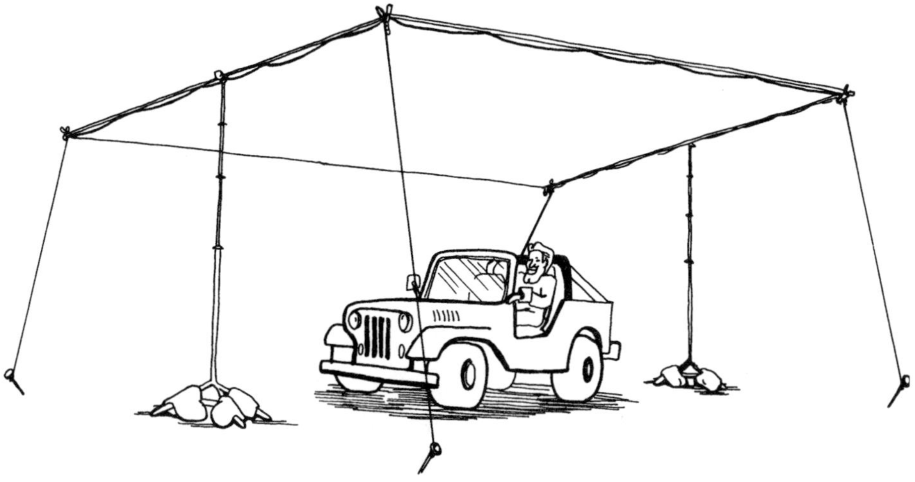

Figure 4.9 A 20 ft × 20 ft overhead silk reduces and softens direct sunlight

duvetyn shades action completely. A set may also include: ½ Silk, ¼ Silk, Rosco Soft, Grid Cloth, ½ Grid, ¼ Grid, griffolyn (black/white), a silver reflector (lamé), a gold reflector (lamé), silver/black scrim, single and double white net, and a windbag (muslin).

- **Griffolyn (griff)** A nylon/plastic sheet that is white on one side and black on the other. When stretched in an overhead frame, the white side provides a big bounce source for exterior fill; the black side absorbs light for negative fill (Figure 4.10).
- **Silver and gold reflectors** A silver is a reflective silver fabric used as a large, strong exterior bounce source. A gold has a reflective gold side to create a golden bounce light. A 12 × 12 or 20 × 20 reflector can fill a tremendously large space with relatively soft light.

Medium, hi, and hi-hi walkers and rollers

A medium roller stand is slightly taller than a junior combo, about 14 ft maximum, and has wheels, which makes it easy to move around. The wheels have brakes that should be locked once the stand is placed. In addition to a junior receiver, roller stands provide a 4½ in. grip head for mounting overhead frames, large flags, and other grip gear. A hi-hi roller is especially useful when height is required; it has a maximum height of 20 ft. A hi or hi-hi walker stand has no wheels.

Stand maintenance

Modern stands are made of chrome-plated steel, stainless steel and aluminium. Stainless steel stands are extremely weather resistant. A well-made stand will not rust or corrode. When stands get muddy, they should be cleaned so that dirt does not get

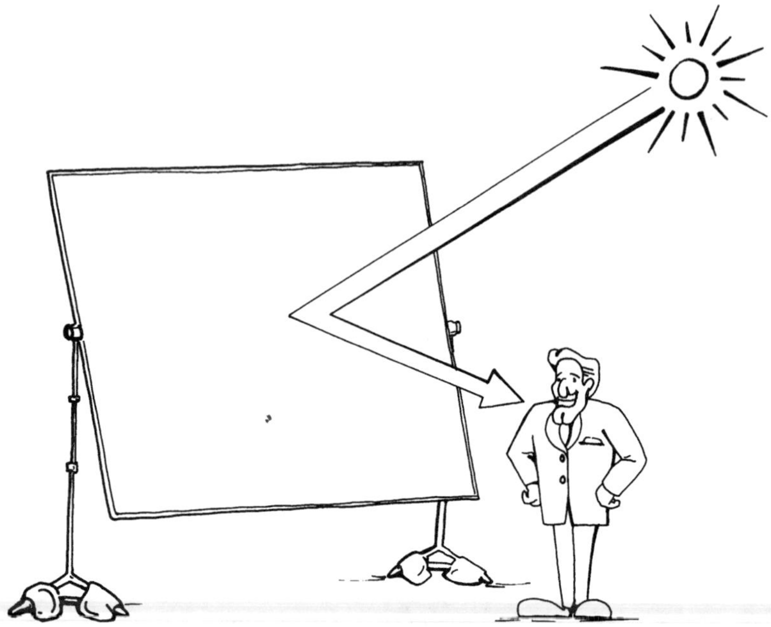

Figure 4.10 A white griffolyn can be used as a giant soft bounce source. Gold and silver lamé give even stronger light

inside between the sections. Wipe each section down with a rag or towel. If a section starts to bind, lubricate with silicone spray.

Occasionally the Allen screws that secure the bonnet castings and the section castings to the tube parts of a stand get loose and the castings come off. It is a simple matter to push the castings back into place and tighten down the Allen screws. Be sure to keep the castings tight. If the casting comes off while you are raising a light, the section will separate from the stand and you'll wind up balancing the lighthead on a pole like an acrobat does with teacups.

Rigging hardware

Baby and junior nail-on plates

A nail-on plate, also called a baby plate, wall plate or pigeon plate (Figure 4.11), mounts to a surface with screws.

Use a cordless electric drill with a Phillips bit and wood screws or drywall screws. The plate can be mounted on a horizontal surface, a wall or a ceiling, but be sure you are screwing into something solid. If you are screwing into a set wall (usually ¼ in. plywood), you will need to place a piece of cribbing on the other side of the wall to give the screws something to hold to.

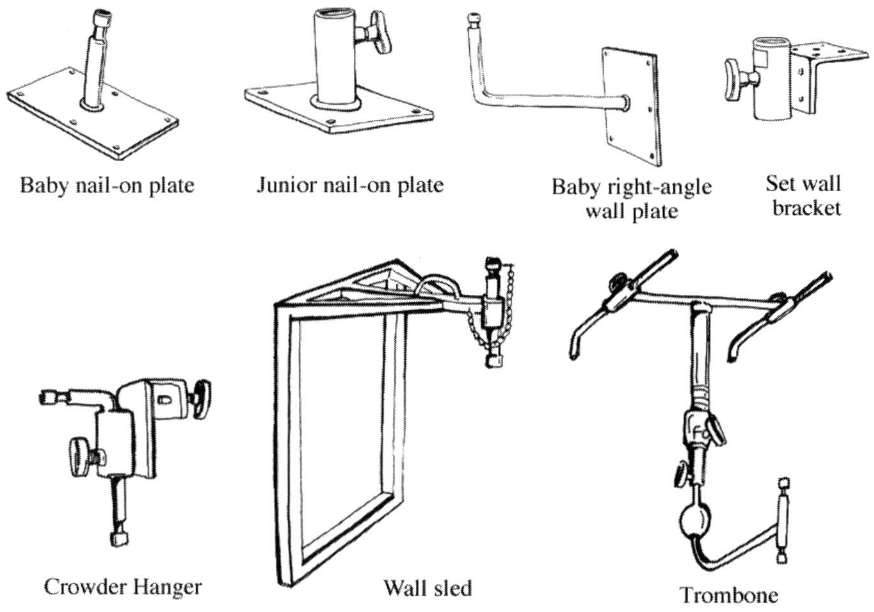

Figure 4.11 Plates and hangers for set walls

Typically you would prepare several apple boxes with nail-on plates. This is handy for mounting a light on the floor or on a counter top.

Set wall mounts

See Figure 4.11.

Set wall bracket

A set wall bracket is a right-angle plate that mounts to any right-angle corner, such as the top of a flat.

Crowder hanger

A crowder hanger fits over the top of a door or on a 2 × 4 in. beam. It can be used with a baby adaptor that provides two mounting positions, one above and one below the hanger.

Edge plate bracket

An edge plate bracket is similar to a crowder hanger. It is used to mount lights to the side edge of a green bed.

Wall sled

A wall sled is suspended on rope from the top of a set wall. The weight of the light holds the sled in position against the wall without screws or tape. Wall sleds are made with either a junior or a baby mount.

Trombone

Like the crowder hanger, a trombone also fits over the top of the set, but it is adjustable to any width of wall. It provides an adjustable drop-down position for the light. Use a rubber ball on the telescoping arm to prevent it from scraping the wall. A trombone can have either a junior or a baby mount.

Clamps

C-clamp

C-clamps (Figure 4.12) come in various sizes: 4, 6, 8 and 12 in. Each one has two baby spigots or a 1⅛ in. junior receiver welded to it. The feet are either round and flat, or squared off. The squared metal clamps are designed for mounting to bar/barrels.

With any of the clamps shown, to prevent puncturing or marring the beam and to increase the surface area of the clamp, insert two pieces of 1 by 3 in. cribbing between the clamp and the surface. Wrap the cribbing in duvetyn when it is important not to scratch the finish.

A common problem when mounting lights to a C-clamp on top of the set wall is that the light cannot be tilted down far enough. Use the angled spigot on a C-clamp to get around this problem.

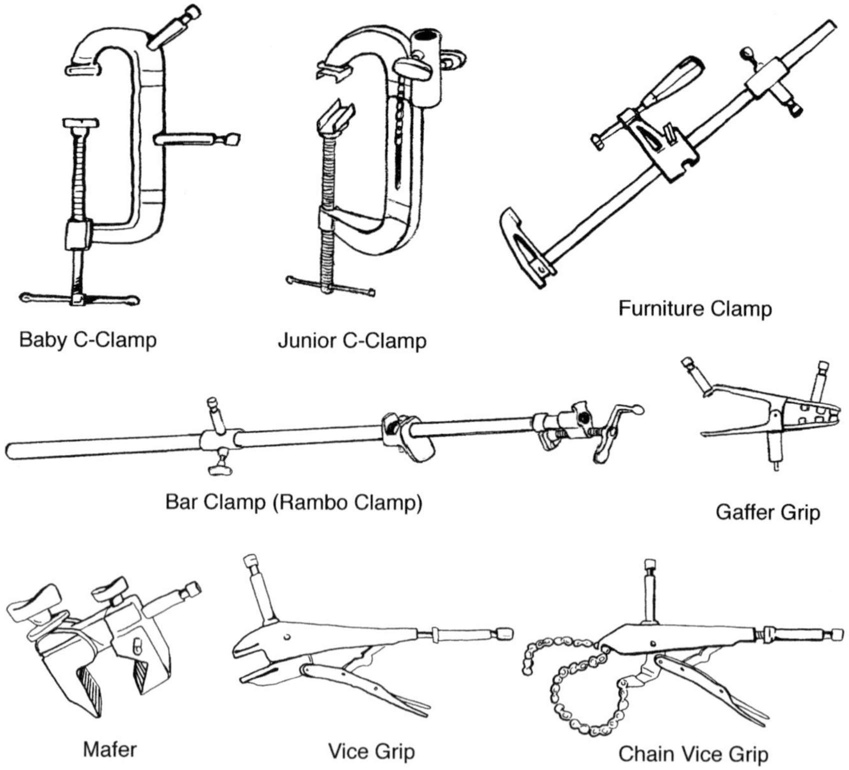

Figure 4.12 Clamps

Furniture clamp and bar clamp

A furniture clamp, or bar clamp, holds itself in place by applying pressure on either side of the beam to which it is attached. Furniture clamps come in various sizes (6, 12, 18, 24 and 36 in.); standard bar clamps are 48 in., all of which are adjustable. Furniture clamps can be used to put lights on top of set walls, suspend them from ceiling beams, or mount them to furniture. As with C-clamps, use cribbing to increase the surface area of the clamp and to protect the surface to which you attach the clamp.

Gaffer grip

A gaffer, or gator, grip is a spring clamp with rubber teeth. It is used to mount smaller lights to doors, bar/barrels and furniture.

Mafer/Arri super clamp

A mafer (pronounced mayfer) (Arri calls theirs a super clamp) is a very strong and versatile mount, a favourite clamp-type mount. A cam-operated screw mechanism closes and opens the rubber-lined jaws. It can attach to any round surface from ⅝ in. (16 mm) to a 2 in. (51 mm) diameter and any flat surface from 1⁄16 in. to 1 in. thick. The baby spigot snaps into place with a spring-loaded lock. The removable spigot can be exchanged for accessories, such as a flex arm, a double-header offset arm, or a right-angle baby spigot. Arri also makes a heavy duty version.

Vice grip

The adjustable width of a vice grip provides a strong grip. As with any vice grips, the clamp is released by pressing the unlocking handle.

Chain vice grip

A chain vice grip provides a very solid mount to any pipe up to 6 in. in diameter. It is used to mount a light to a pipe or small pillar. It is also often used to secure a stand to a standing post to hold the stand when there is no room to spread the legs. To make sure that the vice grip does not open, wrap tape around the handle after the chain vice grip is in place.

Bars, barrels, grids and green beds

Pipe clamp and hook clamp

Pipe clamps (Figure 4.13) are used when hanging lights from an overhead bar, barrel or grid. Pipe clamps come with a safety pin attached to the clamp with a safety bond. The cotter pin prevents the receiver from slipping off the spigot. Always use the safety pins when hanging lights. A hook clamp is a less heavy duty version of the same idea.

Barrel clamp, grid clamp, Big Ben

A *barrel clamp* hinges completely around the barrel or bar and tightens with a threaded bolt (like a 'cheeseboro'). The Arri version offers a Universal head (both 28

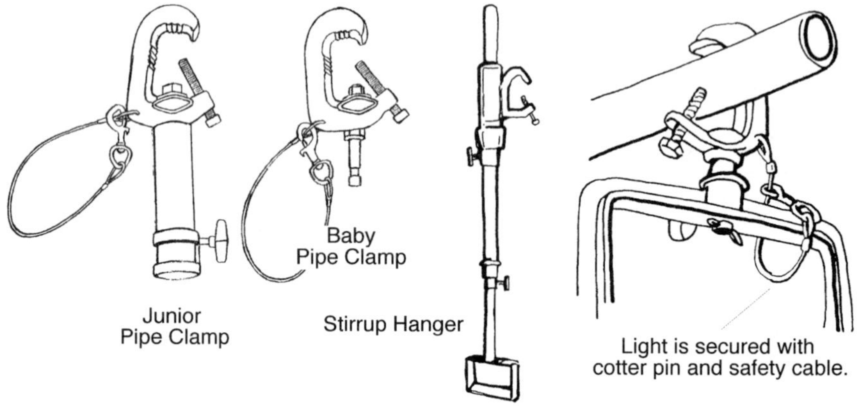

Figure 4.13 Barrel clamps

mm receiver and 16 mm spigot). A baby or junior *grid clamp* is the same thing, but offers only one or the other.

A *Big Ben clamp* is a similar type of 'cheeseboro' clamp which offers a male 28 mm spigot. It is handy for such things as supporting a small grid, or creating a *goal post*.

Telescoping stirrup hanger

To get a light lower than the height of the grid, use a telescoping hanger to lower it to the desired height. Hangers have a baby spigot, junior receiver or Universal head. Some end in a stirrup to which you attach a pipe clamp.

Greens and bazookas

In most studio sound stages, wooden catwalks called greens, decks or bridges are suspended above the set to provide lighting positions. Along the edge of the greens, at 18 in. interval, are holes on to which a junior spigot fits. A light may be inserted directly into this receiver, or a bazooka can be inserted into the hole. A bazooka is like a one-section stand with no legs. An L-shaped bracket fits over the catwalk's handrail to support it.

Location rigging hardware

Wall spreader and tube stretcher

Wall spreaders (Figure 4.14) support lights by exerting pressure against two opposite walls or the floor and ceiling. A 2 × 4 in. or 2 × 6 in. piece of timber creates the span. The hardware mounts to either end of the timber and uses a threaded post to apply pressure against the walls. Timber must be cut to fit the particular span needed.

A wall spreader can create a secure overhead beam of up to about 16 ft (4.8 m) from which lanterns can be hung. With a long span be sure the hardware is aligned with wall studs, and screw the wall spreaders to the wall. A tube stretcher essentially adapts a wall spreader for use with scaffold tube instead of timber.

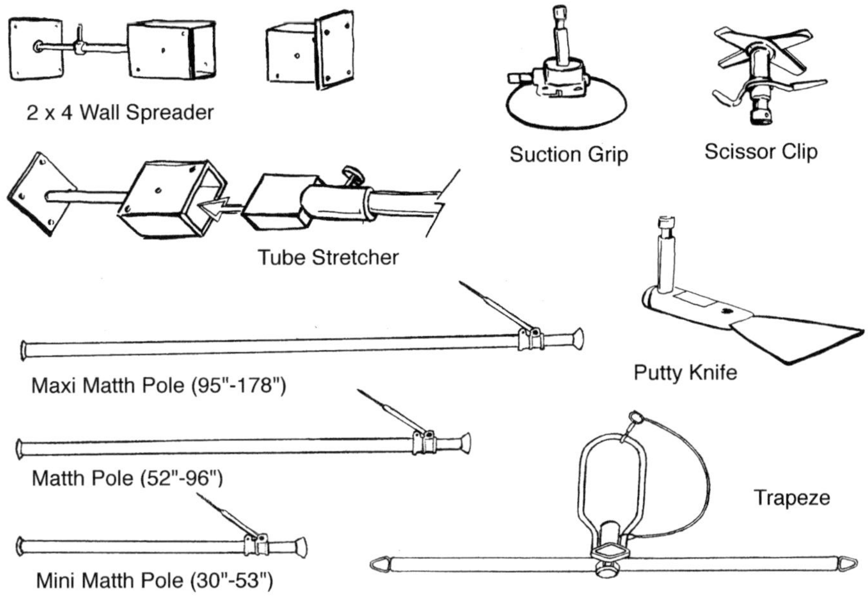

Figure 4.14 Location rigging equipment

Polecat/autopole/barracuda/Matth pole

All names for essentially the same thing: A smaller, lighter duty version of a wall spreader, especially useful in doorways or narrow halls. An autopole can support lightweight lanterns and grip equipment.

Suction grip/limpet mount/ pump cup

Suction grips of 4 or 6 in. can be used to affix small lighting units to non-porous surfaces, such as a window or a car bonnet. These grips generally use a cam to create the suction; they are not as strong as the larger pump-type grips. Suction grips come with baby spigot only and should be limited to use with smaller lights.

Scissor clip

A scissor clip is used to mount a light to the metal supports of a dropped ceiling. The scissor closes over the metal strips that support the ceiling tile. It is tightened in place by turning the 16 mm (⅝ in.) spigot. Cables can be dressed above the ceiling or clipped to the metal strips with small grip clips.

Putty knife/sparrow plate

A putty knife can be wedged in a windowsill or door frame. It provides a baby spigot for a small lantern.

Trapeze

A trapeze is used to dead hang a light of any size from a rope. It provides a junior receiver. Eyelets at each end of the trapeze are provided for guy wires, which prevent the light from turning once placed in position.

Shiny boards

This is a 42 × 42 in. silver-covered board that mounts on a combo stand. Reflectors are used to bounce light, usually sunlight. They can be panned, tilted, and locked into position. They normally have a hard side that reflects a hard square-shaped patch of light, and a soft side that reflects a slightly broader, less intense, area with soft edges.

- **2 × 2 ft shiny board** Similar to the larger ones, but this uses a baby stand.
- **Mirror boards** A mirror board is a shiny board with a mirror surface. Quite a bit heavier than shiny boards, it gives off a very bright, sharply delineated square of light.

5

Lighting objectives and methods

We've talked a great deal about equipment. Let's put hardware aside for the moment and discuss the bigger question of what we want to accomplish with lighting and how we go about it. What are the considerations the DP and gaffer keep in mind when they make lighting decisions? To begin we'll look at some technical considerations: how to take and interpret light-meter readings, how to use and control contrast, how to use the zone system to understand the placement of light and dark values, and what factors affect our working lighting levels for a given scene.

With these technical questions out of the way, we'll examine the conceptual basis the DP and gaffer use to generate ideas and devise schemes for lighting each scene. Each lighting decision begins with the consideration of four basic objectives: mood, visibility, naturalism and composition. We arrive at the placement of each light, its direction, colour, softness and strength by considering how we wish to fulfil these objectives for a given lighting set-up. Finally, we will look at lighting method: lighting the actor and lighting the scene.

A brief overview of cinematography

An incident light reading can be expressed one of two ways, in terms of light level (foot-candles or lux) or in f-stops. Thinking in terms of the light level has advantages when working with the lights, but ultimately it is the f-stop that is set on the camera, and most DPs think of their exposure range in terms of stops.

Light level: foot-candles or lux

A light reading expressed in foot-candles or lux is an absolute measurement of light level (one foot-candle equals 1 lumen per square foot; one lux equals 1 lumen per square metre. One foot-candle is 10.764 lux). A light reading expressed in f-stops depends on additional variables. A light meter, such as the digital Spectra Professional IV (Figure 5.1), tells you the intensity of light in foot-candles (or lux)

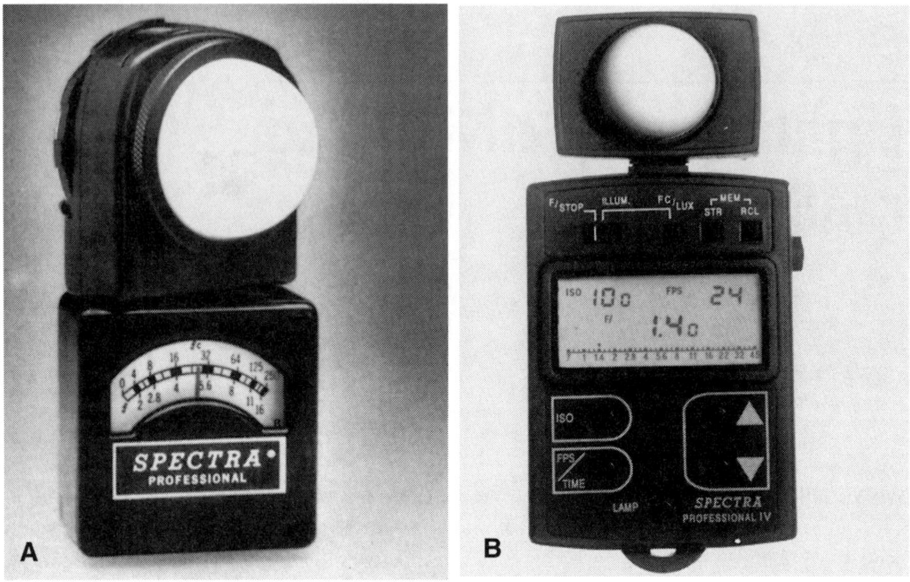

Figure 5.1 Light meters: (A) Spectra Professional incident light meter; (B) Spectra Professional IV digital/analogue light meter. The latter reads incident or reflected light directly in f-stops and photographic illuminance in foot-candles or lux, with a range from 0.1 to 70,000 FC. (Photos courtesy of Spectra Cine, Inc., Burbank, CA.)

(Figure 5.2 shows the foot-candle scale).This meter also gives the reading as a working f-stop, taking into account the film ISO and shutter speed.

The advantage of working in foot-candles or lux rather than f-stops is that a gaffer very quickly learns how many foot-candles he or she will get from a given light at a given distance (Table 5.1 lists some approximate data. Table A.14 in Appendix A is a more comprehensive list.) If the gaffer is lighting to a given FC level, he or she will always call for the right light for the job. F-stops, on the other hand, do not correspond directly with light level. F-stop depends on a number of other variables, how the film stock is rated, what filters are being used, the frame-rate, and so on. It is, therefore, not so straightforward to calculate which light will give a particular f-stop.

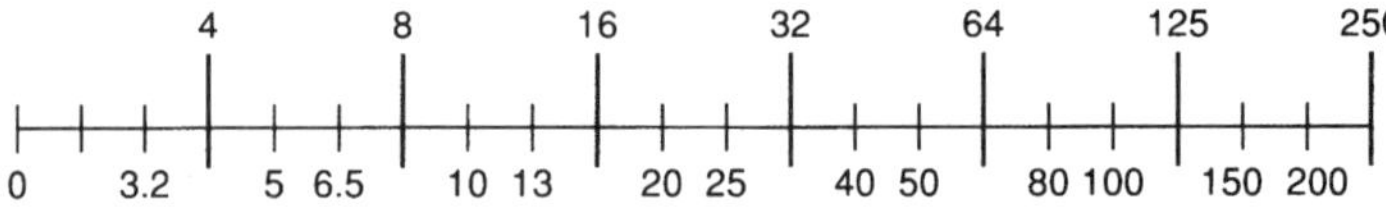

Figure 5.2 Actual numerical increments between standard foot-candle readings

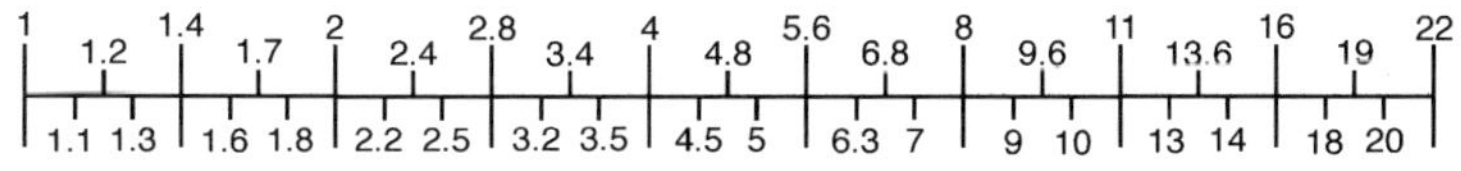

Figure 5.3 The actual numerical increments between f-stops

F-stops

F-stop settings are inscribed on the aperture ring of the lens of the camera by the manufacturer in standard increments: 1, 1.4, 2, 2.8, 4, 5.6, 8, 11, 16 and 22, as shown in Figure 5.3. The lower the f-stop, the larger the aperture, and the more light passes through the lens.

A light meter gives the f-stop by taking into account the film speed and exposure time. (For normal filming at a crystal sync speed of 24 or 25 fps, and with a standard 180° shutter, the exposure time is 1/48th or 1/50th of a second.) Many meters (e.g., Minolta) only read out in f-stops.

The f-stop scale in Figure 5.4 shows how foot-candles compare with f-stops for 320 ISO film. As you can see, the foot-candles double with each f-stop.

Table 5.1 Relative strengths of various light sources

Source	*fc spot*	*fc flood*
Direct Sunlight		6400–8600
Skylight on an overcast day		450–1800
Brute Arc at 30′	9000	1190
12 kW HMI at 30′	8250	500
9-lite PAR 64 at 30′	NS lens 3600	WF lens 450
2500 HMI PAR at 30′	NS lens 2880	WF lens 247
4000 HMI Fresnel at 30′	2305	247
10 kW at 30′	2465	460
5 kW baby senior at 30′	655	110
PAR 64 at 30′	VNS lens 560	MF lens 150
2 kW Junior at 20″	1000	130
1 kW baby at 20′	440	45
2 kW zip soft light at 10′		100
650 pepper at 10′	528	110
750 soft at 10′		30
200 Mini at 10′	195	25
100 pepper at 10′	55	23

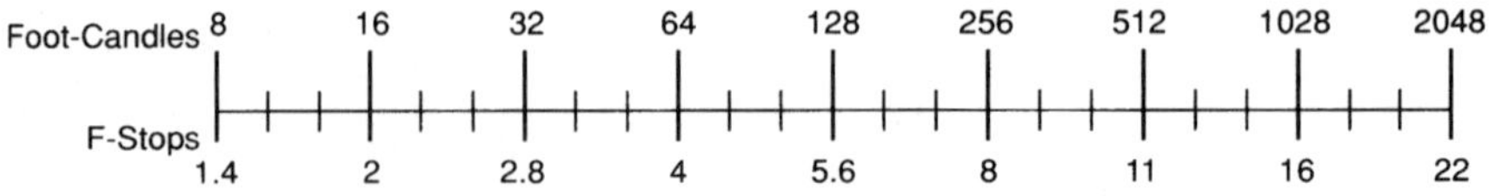

Figure 5.4 Comparison of foot-candles to f-stops with 320 ASA film

Each incremental f-stop cuts the light by a half. f/4 lets half as much light through as f/2.8, so it takes twice as many foot-candles at f/4 (64 FC) to get the same exposure as at f/2.8 (32 FC). Table 5.2 correlates f-stop to foot-candle level for all film speeds.

Taking readings with an incident light meter

Incident light meters measure the amount of light falling on the face of the light meter. A hemispherical light collector, or photosphere (commonly known as 'the ball'), collects light from the sides, top and bottom as well as from the front. The reading is taken by holding the meter up in the position of the subject. When the ball faces the camera, the meter gives an average reading of the total amount of light falling on the subject as viewed from the camera.

Alternatively, by pointing the ball at the light source, you can read the amount of light from that source. However, keep in mind that when light hits the subject from

Table 5.2 F-stop versus foot candles for various film speeds

Incident light in foot-candles

Frame rate: 24 fps

Exposure time: 1/50 sec (180 degree shutter opening)

ASA	f/1.4	f/2	f/2.8	f/4	f/5.6	f/8	f/11
25	100	200	400	800	1,600	3,200	6,400
50	50	100	200	400	800	1,600	3,200
64	40	80	160	320	640	1,250	2,500
100	25	50	100	200	400	800	1,600
125	20	40	80	160	320	640	1,250
160	16	32	64	125	250	500	1,000
200	13	25	50	100	200	400	800
320	8	16	32	64	125	250	500
400	6.4	13	25	50	100	200	400
500	5	10	20	40	80	160	320

the side or back, relative to the camera, less light is reflected towards the camera than when that light hits the subject from the front. Making allowance for this, the reading of a side-light can be accurately taken by turning the meter, splitting the angle towards camera.

When reading the output of individual lights, some cinematographers replace the hemispherical collector with a flat disk collector. The flat disk reads only light coming from the front. The disk is also used when photographing flat art work, such as a painting or front-lit titles.

When taking a reading, use your free hand to shade unwanted light off the photosphere. If you were reading the intensity of frontal lights, you would shade off any light coming from high backlights. The facial tones are not affected by the light hitting the back of the hair and shoulders, and if you do not shade the meter from the backlights, the reading will be incorrect. Backlight would be measured separately.

You can get an impression of the relative strengths of various lights, key and fill, for example, by shading the photosphere from one source, usually the key, and noting the change in the reading. You would use this technique to determine the contrast ratio.

When the reading is halfway between two numbers, it is called a split. For example, a 2.8/4 split would be halfway between f/2.8 and f/4. Increments between stops are also commonly expressed in thirds of a stop, so you might say 'one-third stop closed from a 4' to indicate that the aperture is one-third of the way towards f/5.6.

The use of terms such as warm and cool can cause confusion. To the gaffer, warm 4 means that there is slightly more light than a 4, the aperture is a high-side 4. To the camera assistant, a warm 4 could mean to open the aperture from a 4, which would increase the light, a low-side 4. Establish common terminology with the people you are working with, and use clear language. Double-check if you are not sure what someone means.

F-stops for the electrician

When setting a light, an increase of one stop means doubling the light output. The gaffer might tell the electrician to 'remove a double', 'spot it in a double's worth' or 'move the light in one stop closer'. An experienced electrician can approximate by eye.

Contrast ratio

Contrast ratio is used when the key light is angled so that the actor's face takes on a light side, *the key side*, and a shadow side, *the fill side*. The contrast ratio is the ratio of brightness of one to the other. The exposure is set for the key side. The darkness of the fill side greatly influences emotional tone of the image.

The fill light typically comes from the direction of the camera and fills in the whole face. The key light hits selected parts of the face, favouring one side. Therefore, to determine the contrast ratio you compare the light on the key side, which is key plus fill, to the shadow side, which is fill alone (key + fill:fill alone).

If key plus fill reads 120 FC and fill alone reads 60 FC, the contrast ratio is 120:60, or 2:1. A 2:1 ratio has a one-stop difference between key plus fill and fill alone. A 2:1 ratio is relatively flat, a typical ratio for ordinary television productions. It provides modelling while remaining bright and void of noticeably strong shadows. With a two-stop difference, or 4:1 ratio, the fill side is distinctly darker and paints a more dramatic, chiaroscuro style. For most normal situations, the contrast ratio is kept somewhere between 2:1 and 4:1. A three-stop difference, or 8:1 ratio, puts the fill side in near darkness, just barely leaving detail in the shadow areas. A bright, sunny day typically has between a 6:1 and 8:1 ratio, requiring the addition of fill light to lower the contrast ratio.

Contrast viewing glasses

A contrast viewing glass is a dark-tinted glass that typically hangs around the gaffer's neck like a monocle. By viewing the scene through the glass, the gaffer can evaluate the relative values, highlights and shadow areas. The glass darkens the scene so that the highlights stand out clearly, and shadow areas sink into exaggerated darkness. The glass helps evaluate if a particular highlight is too bright or a shadow too dark. On the other hand, if nothing stands out when viewed through the contrast glass, the scene lighting has become too flat and the tonal range has been compressed; you might want to reduce the fill level, flag or net light off the backgrounds and find places to add highlights.

Contrast glasses are available in various strengths which are meant to approximate the contrast characteristics of different film stocks. The glass becomes ineffective when it is held to the eye long enough for the eye to adjust to it. Encircle the glass with your hand so that your hand forms a light-tight seal around your eye. Use the rest of your hand to shade the contrast glass from flare. You can also evaluate contrast without the aid of a contrast glass by doing it the old-fashioned way, by squinting.

Gaffers also frequently use a contrast glass to check the aim of the lights. By positioning oneself on the actors' marks, a gaffer can centre the aim of the lanterns, without getting blinded, by viewing each light through the dark glass. Similarly, a contrast glass is used to view the movement of clouds in front of the sun on days with intermittent cloud cover.

Film latitude and the zone system

The human eye can see detail in a much wider range of contrast than film emulsion. Although a person looking at a scene may see detail in every shadow and every highlight, on film anything too dark or too bright relative to the chosen exposure starts to lose definition as it approaches the extremes of the film's latitude. Details disappear into obscurity, and objects become either more and more bleached out or increasingly lost in blackness.

It is helpful to think of the tones in a black-and-white picture. Between pure black and pure white there is a range of values, shades of grey that define the picture. The goal in choosing the exposure and in illuminating the scene is to place those values so that they will be rendered on film as the cinematographer has envisioned them.

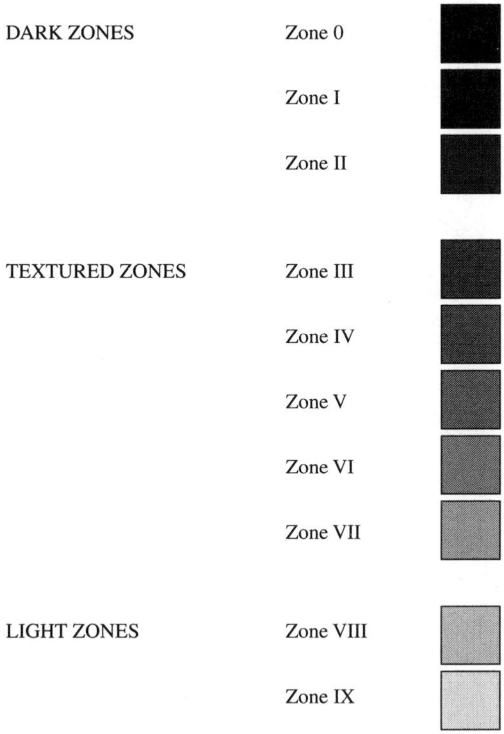

Figure 5.5 The eleven values of the zone system. Zone X is pure white. It is not shown here. (From Chris Johnson, *The Practical Zone System: A Simple Guide to Photographic Control*, [Boston: Focal Press, 1986.] p. 31. Reproduced with permission of Focal Press.)

Ansel Adams, the American still photographer, invented the zone system as a tool for understanding how the values in a scene will be rendered on film. There are eleven zones, as shown in Figure 5.5. Zone 0 is pure black and zone X is pure white. Each zone is one stop lighter than the last.

The range of brightness and darkness in which film emulsion can capture an image is known as its latitude. Each film emulsion has its own latitude characteristics within this ten-stop range. Cinematographers must therefore be familiar with the response of different film stocks.

Zone V, middle grey, is a very important value for determining exposure. Middle grey is 18 per cent reflective and is commonly called 18 per cent grey. An incident light meter works by defining this midpoint in the latitude of the film. It gives an exposure reading that will make a middle-grey object appear middle grey on screen. When you define the exposure of middle grey, all the other values fall into place (to the extent of the film's latitude). On the outer edges of the exposure latitude, the image begins to lose detail and textured areas become less defined until, at the extremes of the scale (zones I and IX), no detail is visible and (zones 0 and X) only pure black and pure white.

Zone appearance on film

- 0 Total black. With a film stock that holds blacks well, the blacks on the edge of the frame merge with the black curtains surrounding the screen.
- I. Threshold of tonality, but with no texture.
- II. First suggestion of texture. Deep shadows represent the darkest part of the frame that still shows some slight detail.
- III. Average dark materials and low values, showing adequate texture.
- IV. Average dark foliage, dark stone, or sun shadow. Normal shadow value for white skin in sunlight.
- V. Middle grey (18 per cent reflectance). Clear northern sky near sea level, dark skin, grey stone, average weathered wood.
- VI. Average white skin value in sunlight or artificial light. Light stone, shadows on snow, and sunlit landscapes.
- VII. Very light skin, light grey objects, average snow with acute side lighting.
- VIII. Whites with texture and delicate values. Textured snow, highlights on white skin.
- IX. White without texture, approaching pure white. Snow in flat sunlight.
- X. Pure white. Spectral reflections, such as sun glints or a bare light bulb.

The way the cinematographer lights the set and sets the exposure determines the various values of the scene. Normally the actor's face is lit for the correct exposure (though there are lots of situations where underexposure or overexposure is appropriate and more expressive). The intensity of backlights, kicker lights, backgrounds, practical lights, windows and so on must be manipulated to place their relative intensity in the zone desired. A spot meter can be used to measure and compare reflective values, but with practice one mostly balances levels by eye.

To give a practical example, suppose that the exposure outside a room with windows is five stops brighter than inside the room. If the aperture is set for the interior exposure, all details in the exterior portion of the image will fall into zone X and will be completely bleached out; the edges of the windows will likely get 'blown-out,' with soft fringes around them. A compromise somewhere between the exterior and the interior exposures is not much better; the interior will still be very dark and muddy (zone III) and the exterior will be hot (zone VIII). The lighting must bring the outside and the inside exposures closer together.

To look natural during daylight, the exterior should be brighter than the interior, but by two or three stops, not by five. To close the gap you could either reduce the exterior exposure two stops by gelling the windows with 0.6 neutral-density gel; or you could light the inside, bringing it up to a level that is two stops less than the outside exposure; or you could combine these techniques.

Negative film stocks tend to have greater latitude in overexposure than they do in underexposure. As a general rule, a neutral-grey object can be overexposed by as much as four stops and underexposed by up to about three stops before it becomes totally lost, either washed out or in dark shadow.

Reversal film stocks have the opposite response; they have greater latitude in underexposure, and they lose definition faster in overexposure. Reversal stocks tend to be more contrasty and have less latitude in general than negative stocks. Similarly, video cameras have narrow latitude; typically detail is well rendered only within a range of four to five stops.

Spot meters

A spot meter (Figure 5.6) is a reflected light meter with a very narrow field of acceptance (usually less than 2°). An incident meter reads the amount of light hitting the light meter, and a reflected meter reads the amount of light reflected back from the subject.

The reading depends on the reflectance of the object as well as the amount of light. From behind the camera, the DP or gaffer can sight through the meter and pick out any spot in the scene he or she wants to measure. By taking readings of various areas of the scene, he or she can compare the exact reflectances of face tones, highlights and shadows.

Digital spot meters typically display readings in either f-stops or EV (exposure value) units. Some meters display readings only in EV units; the corresponding f-stop is found using the conversion dial on the meter. Table 5.3 shows how spot-meter readings correspond to reflectance. The f-stops listed down the left side of the table represent the aperture setting on the camera lens. The zones across the top of the table indicate the actual reflectance, which corresponds to spot meter readings taken off various areas of the composition.

Exposure value units are handy because they put reflectance value on a linear scale in one-stop increments. Each EV number represents a one-stop difference in value from the last. It eliminates the mental gymnastics involved in counting on the

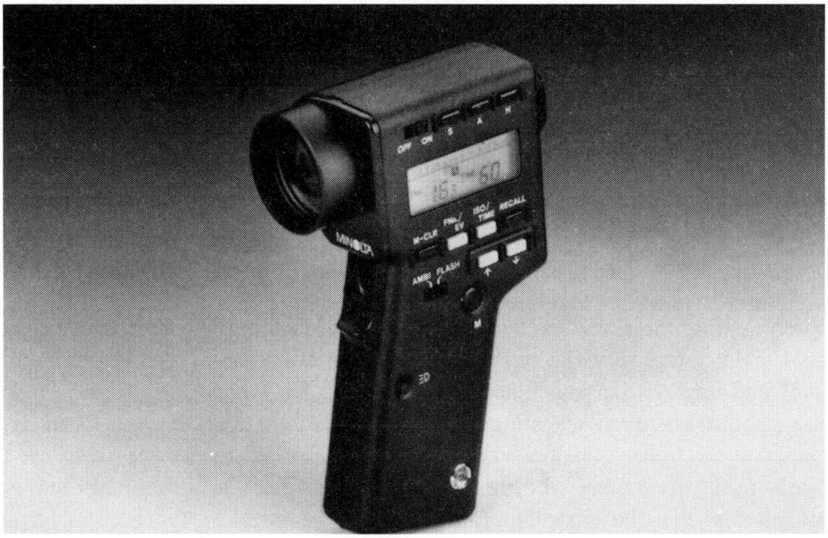

Figure 5.6 Minolta spot meter F. (Photo courtesy of Minolta Corp., Cypress, CA.)

Table 5.3 Spot-meter readings, reflectance and f-stop

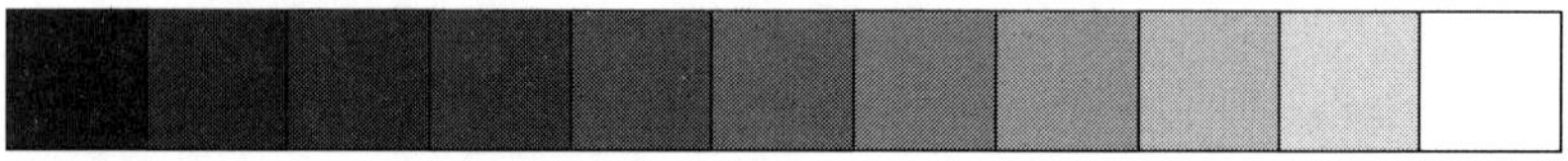

	O	I	II	III	IV	V	VI	VII	VIII	IX	X
Aperture Setting	*f-stop*										
1.0	–	–	–	.5	.7	1.0	1.4	2.0	2.8	4	>5.6
1.4	–	–	.5	.7	1.0	1.4	2.0	2.8	4	5.6	>8
2.0	–	.5	.7	1.0	1.4	2.0	2.8	4	5.6	8	>11
2.8	.5	.7	1.0	1.4	2.0	2.8	4	5.6	8	11	>16
4	.7	1.0	1.4	2.0	2.8	4	5.6	8	11	16	>22
5.6	<1.0	1.4	2.0	2.8	4	5.6	8	11	16	22	>32
8	<1.4	2.0	2.8	4	5.6	8	11	16	22	32	>44
11	<2.0	2.8	4	5.6	8	11	16	22	32	44	>64
16	<2.8	4	5.6	8	11	16	22	32	44	64	>88
22	<4	5.6	8	11	16	22	32	44	64	88	>128

f-stop scale. For example, if a skin tone reads f/8, and a highlight reads f/45, how many stops brighter is the highlight? Before you start counting on your fingers, let's ask the same question in EV: The skin tone reads EV 10, the highlight EV 15; it's easy, the difference is five stops. You can even set the ASA on the spot meter so that EV 5 represents the f-stop on the lens. By so doing you calibrate the meter to read out in zones; EV 0–10 equal zones 0–X. EV readings are not affected by the shutter speed setting of the meter, only the ASA.

A great many DPs rely almost exclusively on their spot meter for light readings. Knowing that the reflectance of average Caucasian skin is about zone VI and one stop lighter than 18 per cent grey (zone V), the DP can base his or her f-stop on a spot reading taken off an actor's face or alternatively take a reading off his hand which can be placed in the path of the light. The DP makes the necessary one-stop compensation mentally.

When reading the reflectance of white skin, the reading will be a half to one and a half stops brighter than the setting on the lens. Brown and olive skin falls around zone V, and dark brown and black skin values fall between zone II and IV. When lighting and exposing black skin, the shinyness of the skin plays a larger role in determining the light value than it does with lighter skin. Reflective glints off black skin may range up to zone VI or higher. There is a tremendous range of tonal values in human skin that the cinematographer observes and takes into account. You can find out the exact reflectance of a particular actor by comparing the reading of the face to that of a grey card or one's own hand.

A spot meter is also particularly handy for measuring naturally luminescent sources, such as television screens, table lamps, illuminated signs, stained glass windows, neon lights, or the sky during sunrise and sunset. It is also handy for getting readings on objects that are inaccessible or far away.

Light level

A single parameter that greatly affects all of a gaffer's major decisions is the amount of light the DP will want to film a scene. One DP I have worked with likes to shoot ASA 50 film at a f/4 or f/5.6, requiring a light level of 400 to 600 foot-candles. To do this requires many large HMI units, heavy 4/0 cable, many large power plants, and lots of hard-working hands. Another DP shoots ASA 500 film with a very low f-stop, requiring only about 32 foot-candles of illumination. For this the biggest light needed is a 2 kW or baby, and the biggest cable is banded 2 AWG cable. The choice of light level affects everything: what lights will be ordered, the power requirements, and the time and manpower needed.

Film speed

A DP's choice of film stock depends on many factors, including the subject matter of the film, the director's ideas about how it should look, the types of locations, the need for matching with other stocks (matte work and opticals), and his or her own style of lighting and personal preferences about grain and colour.

As illustrated in the examples above, the speed of the film, or ISO (also termed ASA or EI) is the primary determinant of light level. A high-speed film emulsion is very light sensitive and requires little light to gain an exposure. Slower film stocks require more light but have less apparent grain, finer resolution, and more deeply saturated colours.

The choice of film stock also affects the look of the lighting. If a slow film stock is used in an interior scene, a fairly drastic increase in light level is required, virtually replacing all natural light with brighter artificial sources. The large lights must very often be hung above the set, giving limited realistic lighting angles. Faster film stocks and lenses enable a more subdued lighting approach with fewer and smaller artificial lights brought to bear. The small lights are easier to hide, allowing more realistic angles for the light. The cinematographer can use existing light to a greater extent.

Optimizing lens characteristics

Lenses tend to have the greatest clarity and definition in the middle of the f-stop scale, between f/4 and f/8. Some loss of quality occurs at the ends of the scale. For this reason, many cinematographers ask for sufficient foot-candles to work in the centre of the scale. Also, because lens characteristics change very slightly at different f-stops and for simplicity of lighting, DPs often prefer to shoot all the shots for a particular sequence at the same f-stop.

Depth of field

Depth of field is the amount of foreground and/or background either side of the point of focus that will appear sharp. As the iris is opened up to lower f-stops, the depth of field decreases. (Depth of field also decreases with an increase in the focal length and with a decrease in the subject's distance to the lens.)

Depth of field is directly proportional to the f-stop. If the DP wants shallow focus with a given lens, he or she needs to use a low f-stop (f/2 or f/2.8), and therefore low light levels. If the DP wants to have lots of depth, he or she needs a higher f-stop, necessitating higher light levels. Thus the depth of field also affects the size and type of lanterns used to light the scene.

Varying exposure time

When the camera is operated at high speed for slow-motion photography, the exposure time is decreased and the aperture must be opened up to compensate. For example, when filming a car stunt at night with multiple cameras, the working light level must be high enough to accommodate a lower f-stop setting on high-speed cameras. An f/2.8 (uncompensated) would force a camera running at 120 fps to expose at under an f/1.4. This could be accomplished with the use of super-speed lenses, which open up to about f/1.4, but could not be accomplished with many standard lenses (which typically open up to between f/2 and f/2.8), or zoom and telephoto lenses, which are slower still. Similarly, if the shutter angle is reduced, the exposure time is reduced.

When shutter speed or shutter angle is not standard, everyone must be very clear when giving f-stops as to whether the f-stop compensation has been taken into account. When giving the f-stop, you would say it is an 'f/4 on the lens', meaning that the compensation has been taken into account. If not, you should say you are giving an uncompensated reading.

Genesis of lighting ideas

If ten world-class DPs each planned the lighting for a particular room, each of the ten lighting schemes would be different from the rest, as different as the mind and imagination of its creator. There can be no set prescription for 'good lighting'; it is not the object here to present formulas. In fact, a gaffer or DP who always lights by formula or habit undervalues the potential impact of the lighting. The psychological effect of the script is played out not only through the dialogue and acting, but also in the lighting and camera work. Good lighting comes from the ability to visualize how light can underscore the drama and mood of a written scene. Mood is perhaps the most powerful contribution of lighting to a motion picture. It starts in the DP's imagination. He or she looks at the room to be lit, and returns in his or her mind to the script: the events, the emotions, the personalities that inhabit the space in the story. In collaboration with the director and production designer, the DP arrives at a sense of what each scene should feel like. The lighting may be gritty and hyper-realistic, slick and clean, high-tech and stylish or lush and glamorous. It may be naturalistic, or it may be stylized and theatrical. He or she is seeking conceptual ideas that will inspire his or her approach to the lighting.

- What are the conditions, the weather, the time of day? Are they dictated by the script? If not, does the tone of the scene suggest an approach to take?
- How should the audience experience this character, radiant with charisma, frazzled and imperfect, strong and determined, or what?
- How is light treated by the character in the story? Would she invite sunlight to pour into the room like butterscotch, or would she close it out, leaving us in a musty dark room, the sunlight seeping around the edges of thick curtains?
- Does light connect the central character to his surroundings or does it isolate him? Is he surrounded with glowing human faces with whom he might interact, or anonymous figures who leave him alone and alienated?
- What colour and quality of light support the character's inner emotional state, and what light sources could be introduced in the scene to motivate that light on the actor or in the room?
- Where does the arc of the story take us? How does the space change in appearance and feel from one part of the film to the next? Is it a long day's journey into night, an emergence from darkness into light, or what? How will each scene in this progression be augmented?

The lighting does not necessarily follow a literal interpretation of the script's mood. It can be ironic, a miserable lonely person faced with a beautiful sunny day. This might be more compelling than giving the character a dull rainy afternoon to mope about, especially if the writer uses irony as a device elsewhere.

There are infinite creative possibilities that wed the lighting to the story. New ideas constantly suggest themselves from the dialogue, the setting, the actual location. Even the props, the set dressing and the characteristics of the actors themselves can contribute to lighting ideas. Very often on location scouts the natural fall of the light lends itself to a particular scene, stimulating ideas for how that feeling can be recreated. A set painter's work light might be doing something interesting quite by accident.

Imaginative previsualization of each scene, based on story-driven concepts, stimulates an inexhaustible supply of lighting ideas. It brings variety to the cinematography and avoids a monotonous, formulaic approach. It offers the DP and gaffer a cohesive vision, which will result in creative, effective, and appropriate lighting design.

Lighting objectives

What else are we thinking about as we face an unlit set, before we can name and place the particular lights we will use? Take a moment to consider the overall objectives of lighting.

Visibility (or selective visibility)

A film without sound is called a silent movie. A film without light is called radio. Obviously, you must have light to expose the film. Exposure and contrast are two essential elements of selective visibility in cinematography. Much of the artistry of cinematography is in the control of lightness and darkness throughout the film's latitude, selectively exposing objects and characters to appear bright and glowing, slightly shaded, darkly shaded, barely visible or completely lost in darkness, as desired.

Equally important is the direction of light. One of our first concerns is how we will light the actor's face. What angle of light shall we use to reveal the face? How much of the face do we wish to reveal? Where does the actor stand? Which way will he face?

Naturalism

Lighting helps set the scene; it locates the scene in time and space. The quality and direction of the light and the sources it implies are part of what makes a scene convincing. Often unconsciously, we recognize lighting that portrays time, season, place and weather conditions. The lighting is evocative of the way the air feels and smells, whether it is musty or clear, cool or hot, humid or dry.

In lighting a scene, the DP strives to evoke as much about the place and time as he or she can imagine. The crew won't necessarily shoot a given scene at the time specified in the script. In fact, day scenes are often shot at night, and night scenes during the day. To create natural-looking lighting and to keep things consistent, one must control the existing sources and utilize or invent techniques to recreate realistic, natural lighting using artificial sources.

The opposite of natural lighting is lighting that gives away the artificial setting to the audience: when multiple shadows are cast on the walls and floor by an actor, when a lamp or wall sconce casts its own shadow, when you can trace the diverging rays of light back to a lamp outside a window, when 'direct sunlight' comes into a room at different angles at each window.

Composition

Lighting is used as a means of emphasis and delineation. It helps separate the layers of the three-dimensional world on the flat two-dimensional screen. It can also create purely graphic effects that contribute to the design of the composition.

Emphasis

In some situations the DP will need to selectively emphasize characters or elements, letting the lighting direct the eye within the frame. For example, imagine a wide shot looking down over the congregation in a large church. The shot immediately conveys the grandeur of the ceremony, but without further help our eye wanders without a focus. An increased light level surrounding the figures at the front of the church draws the eye to our hero and heroine making their vows at the altar. The light falls off a little on peripheral figures.

Separation

When the three-dimensional world is telescoped on to a piece of celluloid and projected on to a flat screen, our natural stereoscopic ability to detect depth is lost. The cinematographer can re-emphasize depth in the image by accentuating the outlines of characters and objects, contrasting the brightness and colour of the different layers, and by moving the camera, which reveals depth with the relative motion of different planes.

A common problem is that when foreground and background share the same value they blend together. Suppose we are shooting a courtroom drama. The district attorney (DA) has brunette hair and is wearing a dark blue suit. The courtroom is panelled in dark wood, and the reporters and onlookers in the audience are wearing dark grey and black suits. The DA's dark hair will blend into her dark surroundings, making it hard to say just where her head stops and everything else starts.

The cinematographer may choose to remedy this with a strong backlight that creates a rim around her hair and shoulders to separate her from the background. The amount of backlight needed depends on the reflectance of the subject and how pronounced an effect is desired. Suppose the public defender is a dapper, blond-haired man sporting a cream-coloured jacket. He will require little or no backlight to separate him from the dark background, but a small amount of backlight might be used if the DP wants to glamorize the character with highlights in his hair. If we were to measure the intensity of the backlight, the light might be one stop under the key light. The dark hair of the DA will absorb light like a sponge, so her backlight would be set one or two stops over the key light.

There was a time in movie history when a bright glamorous backlight was an accepted convention. Today audiences tend to recognize it as artificial. Strong backlight can still look natural if it is well motivated; otherwise, it has to be subtle. Perhaps the DA's kicker could be motivated by a shaft of sunlight. A bright window in the background of the shot often helps in this type of situation; it provides a sense of source.

Backlight is not the only way to create separation. The cinematographer might choose to separate the foreground, middle ground, and background simply by lighting them to contrasting levels of brightness. The dark-haired DA could be separated by lightening the background behind her. Because the DP does not want to lose the sense of solemn darkness in the audience, he might choose to throw a shaft of sunlight across just one or two rows of the dark suits. The gaffer places the shaft so that it will line up behind the DA in a pleasing composition. A light dose of smoke in the air gives substance to the translucent shaft of light, leaving the audience in atmospheric dimness behind it. The DA's dark head of hair stands against lighter values, nicely separated and defined.

Depth

Another important compositional element is depth. A composition that includes surfaces at various distances receding into the distance increases the shot's sense of perspective and scale. If the shot includes some sense of space beyond the plane of the facing wall, outside a window or through an open doorway into other rooms, the gaffer can create planes of light and dark that recede deep into the picture. Depth offers opportunities for interesting lighting and composition.

Graphic effect

A DP often wants light that simply creates graphic shapes or lines that enhance or distort shapes in the scenery. He or she might throw a diagonal slash across the background, a pattern of moving foliage, a window frame, a venetian blind, or use objects in the set dressing to create irregular shadows.

Lighting a textured surface at an oblique angle emphasizes the texture of the surface. The wall of a corrugated metal building appears as a pattern of vertical lines, a brick wall becomes a pattern of regular rectangles. Breaking up the background with textured light goes a long way towards creating an exciting image from one that would otherwise be dull.

Time constraints

One final objective that has been conveniently ignored up until now is to work within the time frame permitted by the production schedule. In an ideal world, the DP can devote planning and attention to all the objectives previously discussed. In real life, however, speed often becomes the top priority, and the lighting has to be designed accordingly. There is little time to contemplate stylistic concerns; it is simply a matter of getting the scene lit fast and making it look as good as possible. The lighting crew spends all its energy trying to get out of the fire and back into the frying pan.

The speed of the lighting depends a great deal on the complexity of the DP's approach. One cinematographer might light a scene beautifully with a single soft source. Another might have a very detailed, painstaking approach, using dozens of lanterns and lighting practically every person and every object on the set individually, which takes much more preparation time.

Speed also depends on the gaffer's and best boy's planning and the flexibility of the rigging. With thoughtful planning and some prerigging time, the time spent on lighting during shooting can be quite minimal, and yet the lighting can still be complex. Without proper planning and a flexible rigging design, much time is wasted (rerouting cable, rigging and hanging new lights, and so on), stress is higher, more effort is expended, and the lighting can become rushed and sloppy.

The process of creating natural lighting

Many DPs have said that the best lighting is usually the simplest; with each additional light, you add at least one new problem. Two carefully placed lights usually give far better results than lighting a subject with five or six lights. DPs strive to find lighting that is deliberate, clean and simple. This is not to say that a DP will never use dozens, or even hundreds, of lights to illuminate a scene. A scene may call for many small pools of light. Each light is controlled and serves a distinct purpose. As an actor walks through the room, he may pass through twenty lights, but at any one moment no more than two or three sources are illuminating him.

Motivating light sources

It is sometimes helpful for the DP and gaffer to designate what the motivating sources of light are for a scene. These sources may be real or imagined; identifying them gives the DP and gaffer a starting point, a quality of light to emulate. Ostensibly, a scene could be lit by direct sunlight pouring through the windows, by soft light filtering through a skylight, by candles on a dining-room table, by a table lamp and wall sconces, by moonlight, by torch-light, by the light of an instrument panel (in an aeroplane, a car, a spaceship, a submarine, etc.), by a flashing neon sign outside the window of an urban apartment, by the flashing lights of an ambulance, by the headlights of a passing car, or by the flickering glow of a bonfire on a beach. If the DP has previsualized the scene, he will already know what type of light source is appropriate. Now, taking into account the specific blocking, architecture of the set, and placement of practical lights in the set he will determine which source will act as key light on the actors face, which source might motivate lighting on the background, which source he might use to motivate backlights and so on.

Reinforcing the motivating source

A source may be shown on screen, a table lamp for example, or may simply be suggested, a flashing neon sign for example. In either case, the actors are illuminated either by the source itself or by lanterns that strengthen the effect of the motivating source.

In most cases if the source is bright enough to provide illumination for the actors, it will appear too bright itself. For example, suppose an actor is sitting on a couch beside a table lamp. If we rely solely on the lamp to provide the exposure on the actor's face, the lamp will be greatly overexposed. Conversely, if we dim down the lamp to look natural (zone VII), the actor's face will be too dark. The actor's face therefore needs to be illuminated separately by a source that mimics the soft, golden quality of the table lamp. This also affords us the opportunity to 'cheat' the key light where it will look best on the actor's face. What matters is that the quality of the light, of the key source in particular, be that of a realistic and plausible lighting source and that the general direction of the light have continuity and not shift between camera angles. A diffused Fresnel aimed around the front of the lamp would serve this purpose. Care must be taken not to let light spill on to the lamp itself or to let the lamp cast a shadow from the Fresnel, as this would destroy the illusion of light originating from the lamp.

It is nice if the director, production designer and DP consider the movement of the actors in relation to the placement of lighting sources. Light naturally influences behaviour. For instance, a patch of sun moves across my living room floor during the afternoon, and my cat moves every 15 minutes to keep up with it. People also gravitate to light to read, work, and talk to one another. The lighting will therefore directly affect the blocking, and vice versa.

When no plausible sources exist to light the actors, as in a dark bedroom at night, a little dramatic licence must be taken. The idea is to create a look that is psychologically palatable to the audience, if not wholly realistic. One approach to lighting a supposedly non-illuminated night scene is to create a low base level of non-directional blue light and underexpose it. Then, very selectively, add chips and slivers of light, and perhaps use subtle backlight to define the contour of the actor where he disappears into dark shadow. The success of such an effect is a delicate matter requiring an experienced eye and good judgement.

Establishing the key light

The first light to establish is the key light. The key light typically establishes the exposure for the scene. All the other lights, fill light, backlight, practicals, scenery lighting and so on, are set relative to the key light. The key is the strongest light on an actor's face. It may cover a large area, the sun, for example, is one of the larger key lights, or it may cover only the immediate area around the motivating source. If the set is large, a number of different sources will be key lights in different areas of the set. For example, as an actress moves from a window to a sofa that is in front of a fireplace, she walks out of the soft, blue, window light and into the warm, flickering firelight.

The shape of a face is revealed to the eye by the way light falls on the curves and planes of features. Tonal variations, the shading and shadows, are what tell our brain the shape of an object. Certain features can be emphasized or de-emphasized by the placement of the lights. Often a DP's efforts are focused on de-emphasizing trouble spots, such as a double chin or sunken eyes. We may hide a double chin by keeping the light high and the chin in shadow.

The placement of the key light and the angles at which light strikes the subject greatly affect the associations evoked in the audience. Yet no particular meaning is necessarily associated with a given angle of light. Do not be limited by pedantic assumptions, a low light always denotes something sinister, or that the classic key position bestows glamour. Lighting is a subjective matter. The art of the gaffer and DP is to respond to the context of the moment being photographed.

Rembrandt cheek-patch lighting

The conventional key light position is at 45° above and 45° to one side of the actor (Figure 5.7). This position throws the shadow of the nose across the opposite side of the face, leaving a patch of light on the cheek. This patch is known as the Rembrandt cheek patch, after portraits by the seventeenth-century Dutch painter. This lighting angle puts light in both eyes and models the nose, lips, chin and cheeks nicely. It is considered the most natural key light position. It is very important to notice the differences in each actors face: one has a large nose; another has a broad face or a chin that sticks out or droops. Some have deeply set eyes that are difficult to get light into, or hair that interferes with the light or wrinkles they wish their public not to see. The DP responds to these differences in the treatment given to each face and quite often the 45° rule quickly becomes academic.

Most often the key is somewhere between 0 and 90° from a frontal position to the subject and between 0 and 45° above the subject's head; however, it can come from

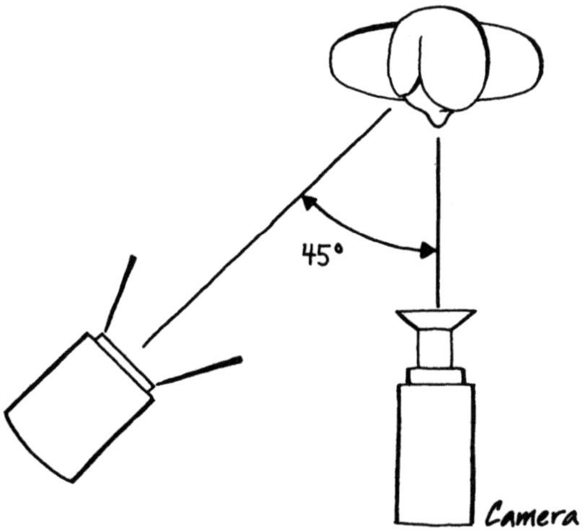

Figure 5.7 Conventional key position, 45° above and 45° to one side of the actor

any direction that will reveal at least some of the features of the face: from below, from high overhead or high to the side, and even from a three-quarter back/side position.

Side light

A direct side light at eye level puts one whole side of the face in shadow. When this half-light effect is desired, the best position for the key light is not at 90° to the face, but slightly less than 90°. At 90°, the cheek on the key side of the face tends to make an unattractive shadow. By bringing the light slightly forward of 90°, the shadow disappears, and the result is a pleasing half-light effect. It models the face nicely and gives a pronounced sense of contrast and direction. Light does not fall on the far eye. If desired, fill light or eye light may be added to put a glint in both eyes.

A nice addition to a side light key is to wrap the light around on to the far cheek with a very subtle soft source in a three-quarters frontal position on the same side as the key with little or no additional fill. The result, a very soft, high-contrast side light, gives an appealing gradation of tones across the face. This look came into vogue in the 1980s in testimonial commercials: a yuppie talking candidly, and presumably impromptu, about his stockbroker or the merits of his long-distance service. The technique is useful in all sorts of situations.

One of the pitfalls of a side light position is that if the actor turns her head away from the source, the face goes completely into shadow. The addition of a back/side kicker on the non-key side can help define the features in such a case (Figure 5.8). Alternatively, you could let the face go dark, and define the profile by silhouetting it against a lighter background.

An eye-level side light also tends to cast the shadow of one actor on to another. This problem can be remedied by raising the light higher, throwing the shadow downward.

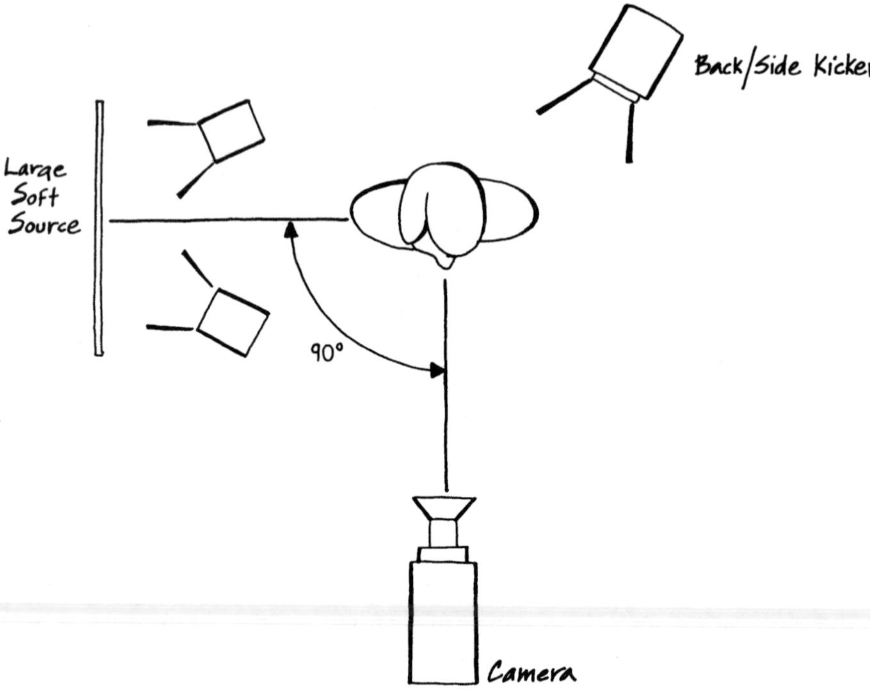

Figure 5.8 Soft side key light with opposite side kicker

In dance performances, floor-level side lights are used because they accentuate the form and muscle shapes of the dancers. The low position allows the light to be cut off the stage surface, which increases the apparent height and duration of dancers' leaps and enhances the illusion of effortless flight.

Far-side key

The previous discussion concerns lighting an actor who is more or less facing the camera. Consider now what happens when an actor is facing three-quarters to the camera (Figure 5.9).

From the camera's perspective, the key light, which is lighting one whole side of the actor's face, is a deeply set side light. The effect is to give the far side of the actor's face an illuminated edge and to place a patch of light on the near-side cheek, while leaving the rest of the near-side portion of the face in shadow. By adding a very limited amount of fill light, the far-side key conveys darkness in the room.

Front light

When a key light is brought to the front, the scene becomes flatter. Using a direct frontal soft light as the key light is a technique of glamour still photography, where the goal is less to reveal the form as to hide the blemishes. Actors who have undesirable wrinkles are often given stronger doses of super-soft front light.

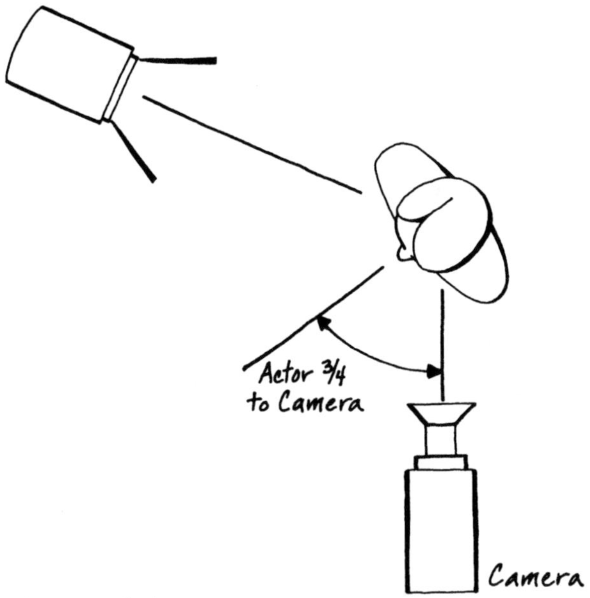

Figure 5.9 Far-side key

Hard front light was a convention of glamour cinematography of the black-and-white era. By placing the light so that it shoots directly on to the face, the nose and chin shadows are minimized to a small underline. The eyes appear very bright, and the sides of the face, the temples, and jaw fall off in brightness.

To prevent the front light from flattening out the entire scene, it is often desirable to angle the light down such that it can be cut off from the background with toppers and siders (Figure 5.10). It is also helpful to have some distance between the actor and the background; otherwise, a hard shadow becomes unavoidable.

Bottom light

When you think of bottom light, you automatically imagine an eerie, unnatural visage with lighting under the eyebrows, nose and chin casting shadows upward from the eyebrows. However, a low light source does not necessarily have that effect. Light that is bounced up from a light-coloured floor or table surface can lend the face a soft radiance. Again, lighting angles do not necessarily have any particular meaning.

Naturally, a low position may be used when a light source is at ground level, a camp fire, for example, or when the actor is elevated. Any time you place a light in a low position, you have to be prepared to deal with, or learn to love, the shadows cast upward on the background and ceiling.

High in front or high to the side

A high position can give a dramatic effect by putting the eye sockets in deep shadow and underlining the nose, lips, and chin in shadow. In *The Godfather*,

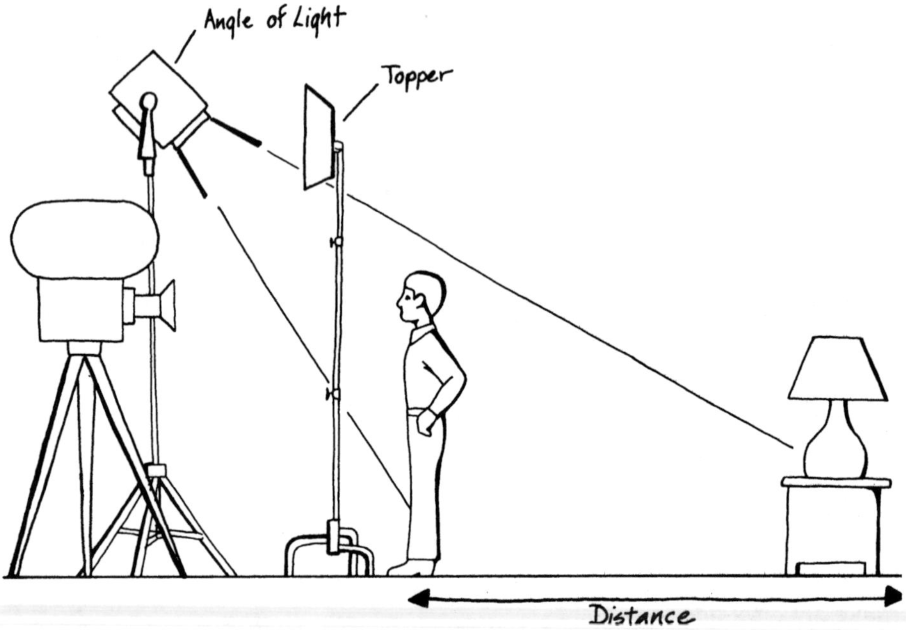

Figure 5.10 On the nose key. Usually requires a topper to prevent the front light from flattening out the background

Gordon Willis used soft, high frontal sources to give Marlon Brando a low-key, intimidating presence.

Eye light

An eye light is usually placed as close to the camera lens as possible. Eye light makes the eyes twinkle or brings them out of darkness by creating a reflection in the eyeball. The bigger the dimensions of the source, the bigger the reflected dots. Eye light does not have to be very intense, however, because the eyeball is very reflective. An eye light need not flatten out the overall composition.

An obie light is a light positioned directly over the camera lens, mounted close to the matte box (lens hood). It has the advantage of panning, tilting, and dollying with the camera. The obie light maintains a minimal level of frontal fill on actors as they pass in and out of other lights while the camera moves with them through a set. Obie lights have dimming shutters, so brightness can be adjusted without affecting colour temperature.

Backlights, kickers and hair lights

Backlight highlights the edges of the face, hair, and shoulders of an actor. It strengthens the lines that delineate the figure from the background. The various backlight positions can also emphasize features of the face and hair. Scenes that occur in relative darkness are often back lit in order to give delineation to the figures and set dressing without lighting them. Backlight is also the best angle to make rain, snow and smoke visible to the camera.

Three-quarter backlight kicker

A kicker is normally relatively low, from a three-quarter backlight position. A light glancing off the side of the face and hair gives form to the jaw, cheek, and hair, and separates that side of the figure from the background. Because of its low, back position, it does not cause problems by spilling on to walls and can easily be kept off the ground. As with all backlights, the problem is always keeping it out of frame and preventing flare on the lens. It is nice to be able to hide the light behind a set piece or furniture.

High side backlight

High side backlights, one on either side of the subject, soak the performer in backlight; the effect is powerful and dramatic. You see this technique used in rock concerts and dance performances. It works equally well for an effect in motion pictures. When blended with the frontal lights and applied with more subtlety, a pair of high side backlights rims the head and shoulders evenly and highlights the hair. News reporters and talk show hosts seem to have one or two backlights with them wherever they go. Keep in mind high backlights tend to light up the ground, table tops and other horizontals.

Rim light

A high direct backlight rims the head and shoulders, pulling the actor out from the background. A rim light is a thin highlight. Again, the light will spill on to the floor and must be shaded off the lens.

Hair light

Positioned somewhere between a rim and a top light, a hair light creates a flattering halo effect. Applied with subtlety, it brings out the colour and texture of the hair.

Top light

A top light (directly overhead) primarily lights the actor's hair and shoulders. It does not light the face at all, other than the forehead and the bridge of the nose. Although it can be used for dramatic effect, this is not a great position from which to light a person, unless the person is reclining. It can be effective to create a sense of faceless anonymous figures in a room, lighting table tops and horizontal surfaces without illuminating faces. Sometimes a DP will bounce a top light off of a table to illuminate an actor's face.

Fill

The next important consideration is fill. The object of fill light is to bring up the light level in the dark shadow areas of the face created by the key light. To do this soft light must come from a more frontal position than the key light, usually from near the camera. When low light levels are being used, the ambient light level may be sufficient to fill the shadows, or often the fill can be accomplished with a white board placed to bounce light into the shadow areas of the face. When a lantern is used, it must be a large, soft source that will not create additional shadows, a light bounced into a 4 × 4 piece of foam core, or put through heavy diffusion such as 216, or a large source such as a soft light, chimera or home-made soft box.

The amount of fill light determines the contrast ratio and has a great deal to do with the apparent lightness or darkness and, to some extent, the mood of the scene. If the fill light is strong, bringing the contrast ratio up to 2:1, the scene appears very bright and flat, a look that is termed *high key*. Reducing the amount of fill light brings out the directionality of the key lights, separates the elements of the frame, and makes the colours appear more saturated. Reducing the fill even more allows deep shadows to appear. A high key:fill ratio gives the sense of night or darkness in the room, especially if the scene is lit with edge and side light. This kind of look is termed *low key*.

Most DPs fill by eye, rather than by using a meter. Judging fill light takes some experience and familiarity with the characteristics of the film stock. It may be helpful to turn the fill light off and on to judge its effect.

Set light

It is sometimes the case that the key lights illuminate the set, and there is need for very little further treatment of it. It may be lit with practicals, which give it pools of light and dark, or the gaffer may place bulbs behind items of set dressing to add interest. When light needs to be added to bring out the background, it is best to be selective with it. Light tends to build up on backgrounds and can start to flatten everything out. Look for ways to break it up or create variation, gradation, or specific highlights.

Backdrops

On a sound stage, the exterior scene outside the windows of the set is very often created using a translight or scenic backing. A translight is a gigantic photograph which is back-lit (usually with sky pans). Day and night translights are created depicting a back yard, the view from a high-rise office building, and so forth.

Specials

If some object in the set requires a separate treatment, for example, a crystal ball, that object is given a special. In the case of the crystal ball, a special might shoot up into the ball through a hole in the table.

Lighting the scene

The discussion thus far has dealt with lighting a single, stationary actor. Very few films, however, are about a single individual who never moves. The following light plots show how two different sets might be lit for a scene.

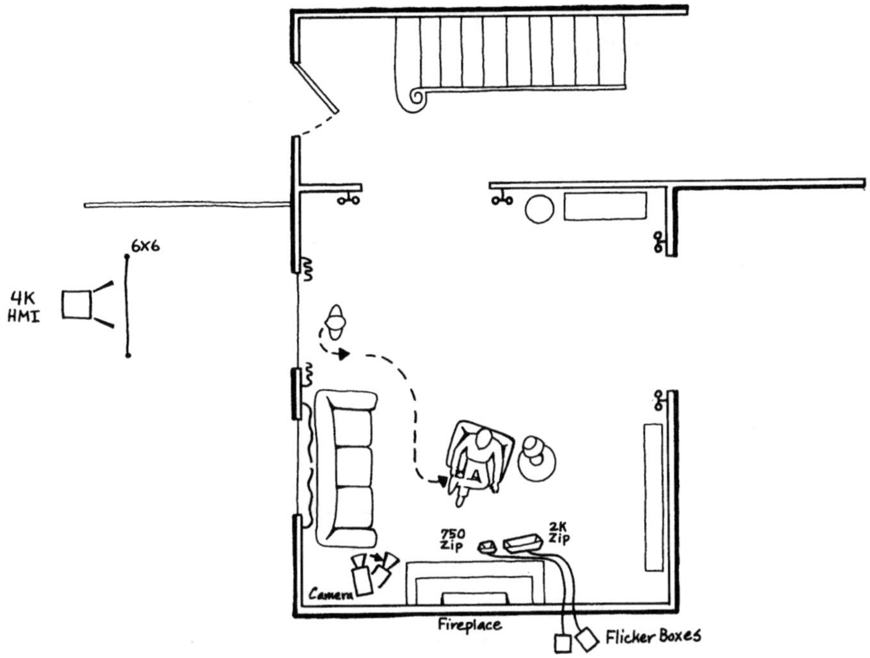

Figure 5.11 Living-room scene and key light positions. The 4 kW HMI through silk gives a soft cool light through the window while the two small soft lights on the flicker boxes create the illusion of firelight

Living-room scene

Figure 5.11 shows a living-room set built on a sound stage. The scene at hand is set on a cold, overcast winter day. A fire is burning in the fireplace. The actor starts the scene at the window, looking out at the falling snow, then he moves to the armchair and sits down in front of the fire.

The motivating sources for the scene are the lights from the window, the table lamp next to the armchair, the fire, and the chandelier in the front hall. Before we can plan how these sources will function, we first need to know where the camera will be placed. For the shot at hand, the camera will be placed on the right side of the fireplace, taking a profile angle of the actor at the window, panning with him as he moves to the chair, and taking a three-quarter frontal angle of him as he sits down.

The key light at the window naturally comes from outside. The light should be soft, diffuse, and slightly blue in contrast to the warm interior. We use a 4 kW HMI Fresnel shining into a 6 × 6 ft frame of light grid cloth. A half CTO orange gel is applied to the light to correct the blue HMI source halfway to tungsten. We adjust the light's intensity so that we read the target f-stop on the subject's face when he stands by the window. The intensity falls off as he moves away from the window. The window frame cuts the light, reducing the spill on the back wall and preventing it from spilling on to the armchair.

As the actor approaches the chair, the key shifts from the window to the fireplace. A firelight rig is placed on the floor just out of the frame. The firelight is exposed a half-stop under the target f-stop, coloured slightly orange, and made to flicker randomly. (Some techniques for creating this effect are explained in Chapter 6.) The shadows in the room should shift slightly with the dancing movement of the make-believe flames. Because the light from the fire is close to the subject, intensity rapidly falls off behind him. Shadows are cast on the chair but do not reach the back wall.

Backlights and kickers

Now that the two key lights are set, we can consider what other lights we would like (Figure 5.12).

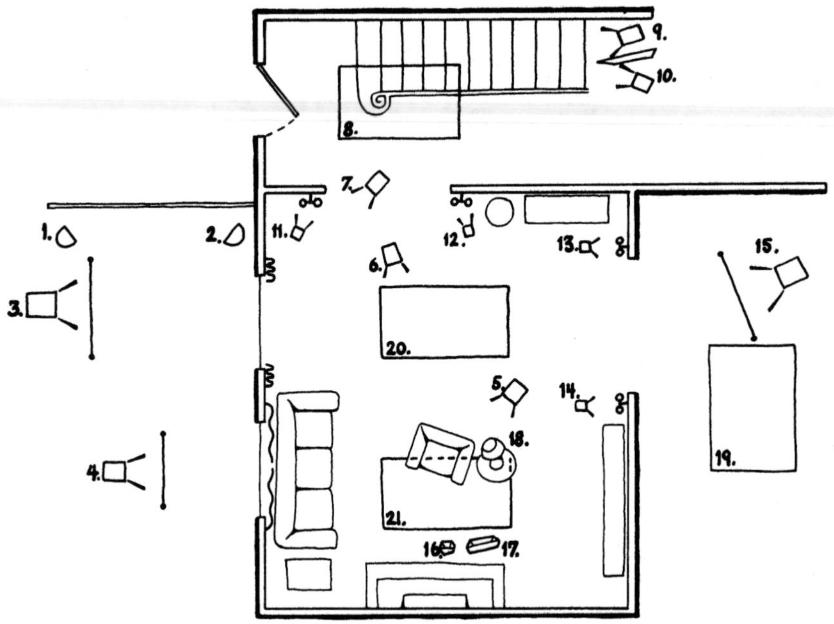

Figure 5.12 Living-room scene with back and fill lights added: (1, 2) scoops lighting the painted flat, (3) key at the window, (4) light giving glow around edges of closed curtains, (5) rim light motivated by table lamp, (6) backlight at chair motivated by hallway light, (7) backlight at window, (8) soft box to fill hallway with top light, (9) light on stairs and banister poles, (10) slash on the back wall, (11 to 14) small Fresnels producing light around wall sconces, (15) light spilling into living room from dining room, (16) 750 W soft firelight, (17) 2 kW zip firelight, (18) table lamp, (19) dining-room soft box to light visible walls of next room, (20, 21) soft top fill, put low on dimmers for ambient warm fill

The position of the table lamp motivates a nice kicker for the seated position. A 650 W Fresnel is placed on a stand just out of the frame to the right, aimed around the back of the table lamp. The combined light reading of the practical and the kicker is to be one stop over the target f-stop.

We could also introduce two backlights coming in from the hallway: one to rim the actor's back at the window and one for his shoulders when in the chair. The backlight at the window should be cut so that it does not throw light on the wall and curtains next to him.

Fill

Finally, we will need some fill light. We want to keep contrast in the scene, so we will only need enough fill to give a little detail on the shadowy part of his clothes at the window and as he moves to the chair. A soft source next to the camera would have to be carefully positioned so as not to light up the camera-left wall and to avoid causing a glare in the panelling on the far wall. The scene might also be filled by hanging soft boxes overhead.

Background

Additionally, we must consider treatment of the back walls, hallway, stairs, dining room, and scenery outside the windows, which will all be in the background of the various shots filmed in this room. As the scene continues, we are likely to have actors coming into the hallway, the dining room, the stairway and so on. We must consider each area that may be used or seen.

In the firelight scene described earlier, it may be enough to bring out the back walls with the glow from the sconces on either side of the hallway entrance. We may want to reinforce the sconces with small Fresnels positioned overhead, throwing soft blobs of light on the walls around the sconces. A light shining down from the top of the stairway would provide an edge light to an actor standing in the hall or on the stairs, and would create a diagonal slash on the far back wall. The hallway might also be lit with a skirted overhead soft box. The scenery flat outside is lit with several blue-gelled scoops or sky pans.

Exterior night scene

Typically, when shooting moody, dark scenes or night scenes, the key lights move around to side and back positions. The back cross is a common technique used to light two or more people from the back.

Figure 5.13 shows a set-up for a face-to-face conversation at night. The camera position for the master shot has both actors in profile. Actor A is keyed from the back right, actor B from the back left. From the camera's point of view, these two lights are far-side keys; they put very little light on the visible side of either actor's face, giving a sense of overall darkness. Note that actor B's key light acts as a kicker, or backlight, for actor A, and actor A's key light does the same for actor B. A small amount of fill light is required to keep the side of the faces visible to the camera from going totally black; however, the fill light's

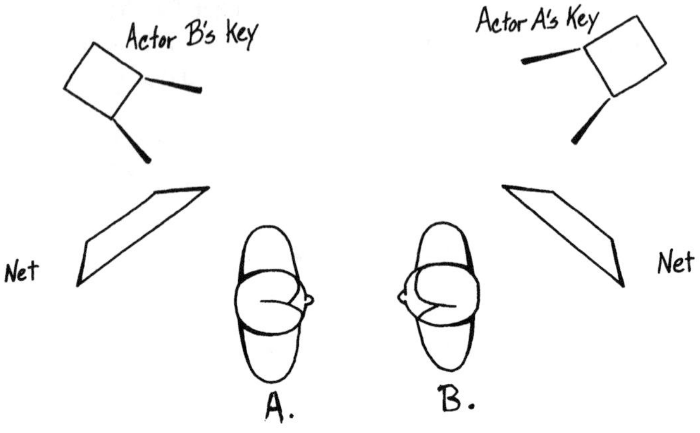

Figure 5.13 Back cross master shot

intensity must be very carefully controlled to get detail in the faces without overfilling.

Once the master shot is completed, individual, over-the-shoulder (OTS) close-ups will be shot. Figure 5.14 shows the camera placements.

Notice that our key lights are already in good positions to light the faces. We will now bring in backlights to keep a rim on the non-key sides of the faces. The fill light moves with the camera, placed on the non-key side, and is cheated back and forth for each close-up.

Moving into position for the first close-up, we will want to check the intensity at which actor B's key hits actor A's back. Because A is closer to the light, it may be too hot or bright. Placing a net to bring down the level of B's key will solve this problem. Similarly, when we move the camera for the second close-up, we reduce the level of A's key hitting B.

When shooting the first close-up, we turn off actor A's backlight because it draws attention away from actor B. Likewise, when shooting the second close-up, we turn off actor B's backlight so as not to detract from actor A.

The background consists of shopfronts across the street. The DP wants the background shadowy and underexposed two to three stops. Starting with total darkness, we need to bring the light level on the street and shopfronts up to a low base level. Our aim is to create an ambient light: moonlight or streetlight. The whole background must be covered completely. If the camera sees the edge of a light's field, where true darkness begins, the ambient effect will be destroyed. To accomplish a widespread and even field, we need to put a fairly big lantern high up and a long way off, typically a 12 kW discharge source on a condor crane 50 to 80 ft in the air and perhaps 150 ft away. The size of the light, its height, and its distance depend on the size of the area to be lit. Notice in Figure 5.14 that for each shot a new background will be seen, and quite a bit of real estate may have to be covered.

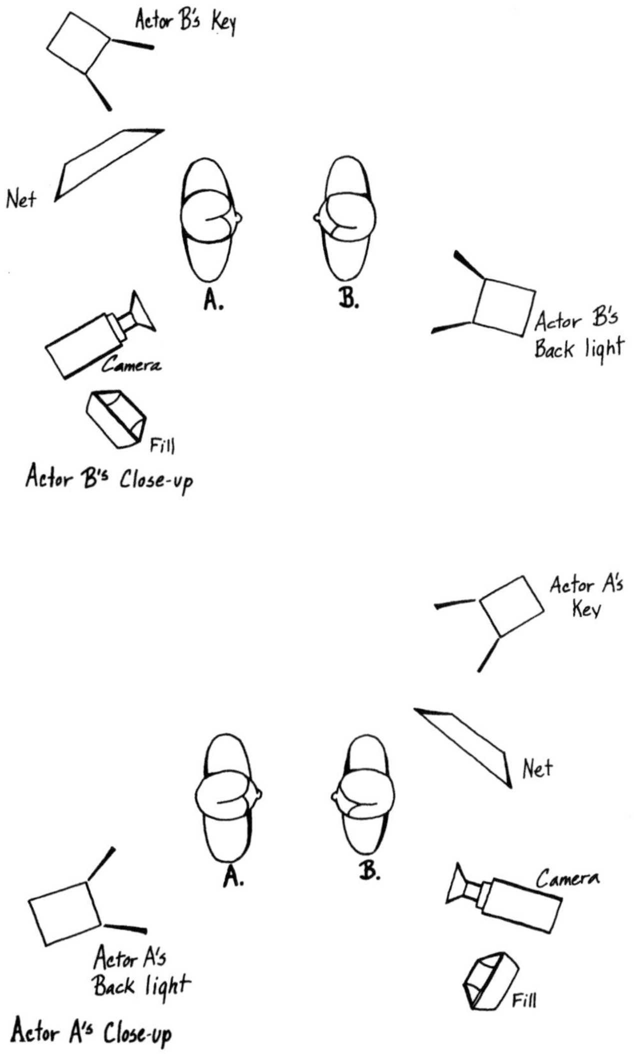

Figure 5.14 Back cross setup for OTS reverse close-ups

To accentuate the darkness of the background, it would be nice in this situation to have a few self-luminous sources in the picture: neon signs, car headlights, or perhaps some steam (back lit) rising out of a manhole. Cinematographers often like to wet down the pavement during night scenes so they can pick up reflections from the shiny surface.

6

Manipulating light:

tools, techniques and the behaviour of light

I can't stand a naked light bulb any more than I can a rude remark or vulgar action.

(Tennessee Williams, *A Streetcar Named Desire*)

Light has five properties: colour, brightness, form, shape/pattern, and movement. The set electrician uses the techniques discussed in this chapter to manipulate and control these five properties.

Colour

The lighting crew has two goals when it comes to colour. The first is the technical process of matching the colour temperature of the light sources to each other and to the rated colour balance of the film stock. The second is aesthetic: introducing colour into the light to simulate realistic sources, such as firelight, neon light or blue moonlight. The DP may use tints to enhance the colours of the actors' faces, their clothes and their surroundings, and give the scene mood, such as warmth, eeriness, bleakness.

Colour correction

Light is a narrow band of the electromagnetic spectrum as shown in Figure 6.1. Wavelengths from 380 to 760 nanometers (nm) are detectable to the human eye as visible light.

The colour of a light source is determined by the intensity of the various wavelengths that make up the light. When the full range of wavelengths is combined, the result is said to be white light. None the less, all light has colour; every light source has its own balance of wavelengths. Because the human eye adapts to its surroundings, shifts in balance are not always apparent to the human eye unless one light source is next to another in direct contrast.

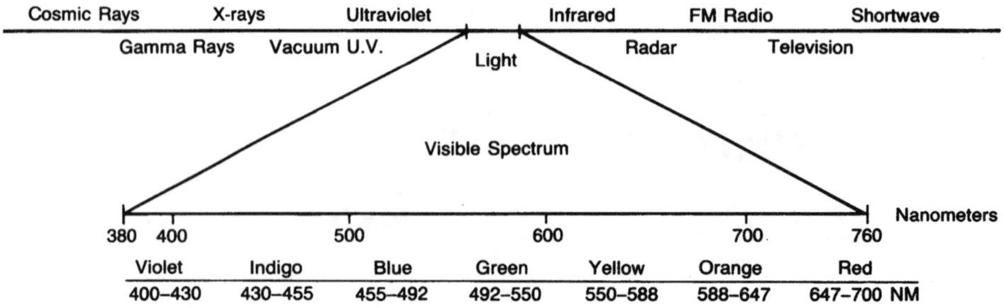

Figure 6.1 The colour spectrum is a narrow band within the electromagnetic spectrum. Individual colours of light within the visible spectrum combine to make 'white light'

An incandescent lamp produces light that is orange compared to an HMI, which is stronger on the blue end. Standard fluorescent tubes produce light that has strong spikes at several places in the spectrum, which give it a strong green hue.

Unlike the human eye, film stock cannot adjust to these variations. Colour rendition is always relative to the colour balance of the film stock: either tungsten (3,200 K) or daylight (5,600 K). To appear white on film, the colour balance of the light must match that of the film. This is accomplished by applying colour correction gels to unmatched sources. The gels redistribute the spectrum by reducing the intensity of selected wavelengths in a given source. CTO (colour temperature orange) must be applied to daylight sources to match with tungsten film. CTB (colour temperature blue) must be applied to incandescent sources to match to daylight film. A magenta gel must be applied to fluorescent lights to remove the green appearance.

A gel having a secondary colour diminishes the amount of the opposite primary colour in the light (see Figure 6.4 later in this chapter). Conversely, a gel having a primary colour diminishes the strength of the opposite secondary colour in the light. For example, amber gel diminishes blue light, and blue gel diminishes amber light. Magenta gel diminishes green light, and green gel diminishes magenta light.

Kelvin colour-temperature scale

The colour makeup of any source that has a continuous spectrum, such as an incandescent light, can be measured and quantified in degrees Kelvin. (Kelvin measurements are based on a scale starting at absolute zero (–273°C) using the same degrees as Centigrade.)

Figure 6.2 shows how the distributions of wavelengths differ for sources of different colour temperatures.

The *colour temperature* scale is based on raising the temperature of a blackbody until it glows. How much it is heated determines the colour make-up of the light. When heated a little, it glows red. Heated more, it becomes yellow, then white, then pale blue and finally brilliant blue. The higher the Kelvin reading, the bluer the light.

Table 6.1 shows the colour temperature of various sources. You can see that household lamps are in fact quite yellow (2,800 K to 2,900 K). Tungsten lamps are much less so (3,200 K), but still look orange compared to daylight (5,600 K).

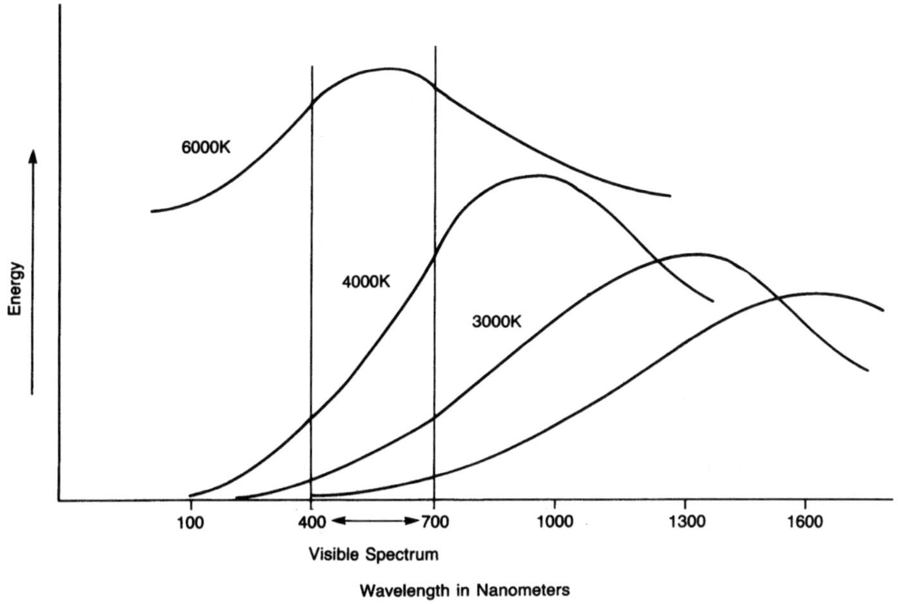

Figure 6.2 Distribution of energy for various colour temperatures across the visible spectrum

The colour make-up of sources that do not have a continuous spectrum, HMIs and fluorescents, can also be given an equivalent Kelvin rating termed the correlated colour temperature (CCT).

Using MIRED units to calculate colour shifts

Tables F.1, F.2 and F.3 inclusive (Appendix F) advise you which gel to use to get from any colour temperature to any other colour temperature. Although the Kelvin scale is useful for defining the colour temperature of a source, it is an awkward scale to use when quantifying the effect of a colour correction gel or filter. You cannot simply state that a particular gel creates a 200 K shift. The Kelvin shift of a given correction filter depends on the colour temperature of the light source. A blue gel that alters a tungsten source 200 K (from 3,200 K to 3,400 K) alters a daylight source 650 K (from 5,600 K to 6,250 K).

When gel manufacturers quantify the effect of colour correction gel, they use micro reciprocal degrees (MIRED units), rather than degrees Kelvin. Micro reciprocal degrees provide a linear scale on which to calculate the shift of a given gel on any source.

The MIRED value is equal to 1 million divided by the Kelvin colour temperature:

$$\frac{1{,}000{,}000}{K} = \text{MIRED value}$$

Table 6.1 Colour temperature of various sources

Source	*Kelvin*	*MIREDs*
Match or candle flame	1,900	526
Dawn or dusk	2,000–2,500	500
Household lamp	2,800–2,900	357–345
Tungsten halogen lamps	3,200	312
Photo flood lamps	3,400	294
1 hour after sunrise	3,500	286
Late afternoon sunlight	4,500	233
Blue glass photoflood lamp	4,800	208
3,200 K lamps with dichroic filter	4,800–5,000	208–200
FAY lamps	5,000	200
Summer sunlight	5,500–5,700	182–175
White flame carbon arc light with Y–1 filter	5,700	175
HMI light	5,600 or 6,000	179 or 167
Sunlight with blue/white sky	6,500	154
Summer shade	7,000	141
Overcast sky	7,000	141
Colour television	9,300	108
Skylight	10,000–20,000	100–50

Table F.4 (Appendix F) lists the MIRED value for any Kelvin number from 2,000 K to 9,900 K. Tables F.5, F.6 and F.7 list the colour shift in MIREDs of colour correction gels of various manufacturers.

The MIRED shift of a particular gel needed to get from any Kelvin temperature (K1) to any other Kelvin temperature (K2) is as follows:

$$\text{MIRED shift} = \frac{1{,}000{,}000}{\text{K1}} - \frac{1{,}000{,}000}{\text{K2}}$$

Note that tungsten colour temperature is 312 MIREDs, and daylight is about 179 MIREDs. To correct a daylight source to tungsten, a shift of +133 MIREDs is required. To correct a tungsten source to daylight, a shift of -133 MIREDs is required.

Colour-temperature meter

A colour-temperature meter gives a Kelvin reading of the light hitting the cell of the meter. It is important to realize that although a cinematographer's colour meter, such

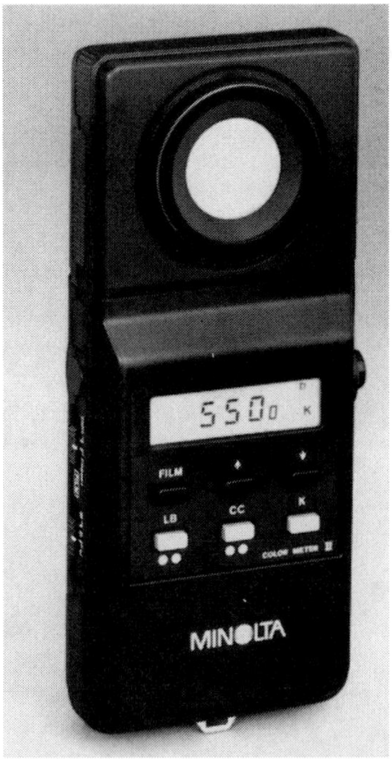

Figure 6.3 Minolta Colour Meter II. (Photo courtesy of Minolta Corp., Cypress, CA.)

as the Minolta Colour Meter II (Figure 6.3), is calibrated at the factory, the readings of two identical meters will often differ, albeit by a relatively small amount.

This type of colour meter is accurate for comparing the colour temperatures of several light sources, but no Kelvin reading should be taken as an absolute value. When more than one meter is being used to take readings on the set, the meters should be checked side by side under the same light to determine the variation between them.

- **Light-balancing scale, orange/blue shift** The Minolta colour meter automatically calculates the MIRED shift from the Kelvin reading. Minolta calls this shift the light-balancing (LB) index number. This number indicates the amount of amber or blue correction gel needed to match the source to the colour temperature of the film stock (refer to Tables F.1 to F.4 in Appendix F to determine the closest correction gel to use). The colour balance of the film stock must be preset on the meter. A three-position selection switch offers the standard film colour temperatures: film type B 3,200 K, film type A 3,400 K (which is used for some still film stocks), or film type D (daylight) 5,500 K. The meter also has a manual mode that allows you to input any target Kelvin temperature. Manual mode comes in handy when the cinematographer needs to have all the lights balanced to a non-standard Kelvin rating. A chart on the back of the colour meter also gives the Kodak filter number and the amount of exposure change corresponding to the LB reading (Table F.8 in Appendix F). Kodak filters are used in the camera in situations where an overall colour correction is needed. For example, when filming a scene in which the practical lamps are unavoidably yellow, the DP can add 1/4 CTO to his lights to match them to the practicals, then cancel out the yellow cast with a blue filter on the lens.

- **Colour-compensation scale, green/magenta shift** The colour temperature meter also gives a colour-compensation (CC) reading that indicates the amount of green or magenta gel needed to correct a source to appear white on film. Such a correction is typically required by fluorescent lights. A CC reading of 30 M (+13 on Colour Meter II) is typical for a cool white lamp, for example. This excess green can be filtered out with a full minus-green (magenta) gel. Table F.9 (Appendix F) lists green/magenta correction gels and the corresponding colour meter readings.

Colour-correction gels

All correction gels come in densities of full, half, quarter and eighth correction. Correction gel typically comes in rolls 48 or 54 in. wide and 22 or 25 ft in length. When gel is cut from the roll, the cut pieces should be labelled (F, H, Q or E) and organized by size and colour.

Converting daylight sources to tungsten

CTO gels are orange, and they warm up daylight-balanced sources. Sunlight and HMI sources are corrected to 3,200 K by 85 gel. Full CTO or extra CTO corrects skylight to tungsten, or 5,500 K sources to a warm yellow 2,800 K.

- **Gelling window** When the outside of the window is accessible, gel can be stapled or taped over the outside window frame, which hides the gel more easily. When stapling gel, apply a square of gaffer's tape to the gel and staple through the tape to prevent the gel from ripping. The key to gelling windows is to keep the gel tight and free of wrinkles.

  CTO correction is also available in 4 × 8 ft acrylic sheets. Using acrylic sheets avoids the problems of wrinkles, movement, and noise that gel makes.

  With a very light dusting of spray adhesive (Spray 77) you can stick gel directly on to a window or acrylic sheet. Press bubbles and wrinkles out to the edges with a duvetyne-covered block of wood. If gelling windows promises to become an everyday process on a particular location, an elegant system is to cut acrylic inserts to fit the windows, then add ND and CTO gel (using the spray adhesive technique) as needed to suit the light conditions and time of day. If necessary you can move the inserts around from shot to shot depending on the camera angle.

  You can also use snot tape (3M transfer tape) or secure it by carefully taping around the edge of the gel with tape that matches the colour of the window frame. Another fast method is to spray water on the windows and apply the gel with a squeegee. This method will not last all day, but it saves so much time that it doesn't matter if it must be redone.

- **Neutral-density and combination neutral-density/CTO correction gels** Neutral-density (ND) gel is grey; it decreases the intensity of a light source without altering colour. Neutral-density gel 0.3 reduces the intensity one stop, ND 0.6 two stops, ND 0.9 three stops and ND 1.2 four stops. Combination CTO/ND gel and acrylic sheets are commonly used to reduce the brightness of windows.

Converting tungsten to daylight

CTB correction gels change the colour temperature of a tungsten source towards that of daylight. Typically quarter or half CTB is used when the DP desires a cool blue look to a particular light source.

When the DP is using a daylight-balanced film, tungsten sources are typically avoided. HMI lanterns provide daylight-balanced light that is cleaner, brighter, cooler and a more efficient use of power. Tungsten lights are very weak on the blue end of the spectrum. Full CTB reduces light transmission by 85 per cent, or about two stops. (The gel is having to absorb 85 per cent of the energy from the light and consequently the hot-burning lights also burn out blue gel very quickly.)

Dichroic filter

The most common type of dichroic filter is a glass filter that fits on to the front of some open-face lights to make a tungsten to daylight conversion (3,200 K to 5,600 K). The filter reduces light output by two stops. The filter is easily identified by its strange red/blue reflective appearance, like petrol in a water puddle.

A dichroic filter works by optically cancelling out certain wavelengths of light. It does not involve dyes or pigment, but rather reflects selected wavelengths of light by the thickness of a chemical coating on the glass. The thickness of the coating is a quarter of the wavelength of the selected colour's chromatic opposite. Manufacturers can custom make dichroic glass filters in practically any colour. Their advantage over gel is that they never fade. They are ideal for long-term installations, where the cost and trouble of replacing faded gel every week outweighs the initial expense of buying glass filters. The one trick to them is that light has to pass through the filter exactly perpendicular to the plane of the glass or the colour will start to vary. For some lights a curved glass filter is necessary. Manufacturers include Rosco (Permacolour Glass Filters) and Automated Entertainment Manufacturing (HD Dichroic).

Before the dichroic filter came along, the *MacBeth* filter was used. It is simply a blue glass filter.

Green/magenta colour correction

Green and magenta colour correction gels were developed primarily to allow colour matching between fluorescent lights and other sources. A comprehensive list of fluorescent lamp types and the correction they require is given in the *American Cinematographer Manual*, in the table entitled 'Colour balancing for existing fluorescent lighting'. This table represents the result of comprehensive testing and is by far the best reference. For copyright reasons it cannot be reproduced here.

However, there are still many variables that no table can account for, so testing with a colour meter remains the best approach. Table F.9 (Appendix F) lists green

Table 6.2 Strategies for matching mixed colour sources

Strategy	*Ceiling fluorescents*	*Tungsten fixtures*	*HMI fixtures*	*Windows*	*Fluorescent floor fixtures*	*Film stock and camera filters*
Match to Tungsten Used when the daylight sources are small and manageable (e.g. sound stage, a night scene, or a location with windows).	Replace with Phillips Col/93 or equivalent. Add 1/4 or 1/8 Minus Green as necessary Gel Warm Whites with Full minus green Gel Cool Whites with Fluoro Filter	**Use Tungsten lights to light the scene** As is.	Apply Full CTO gel	Apply Sun 85 or Full CTO gel	Kino Flo. (with KF-32 tubes)	Tungsten balanced film, no filter
Match to Daylight Good approach in room with many large windows.	Replace with Phillips Col/95 or GE Northlite (5,600 K). Add 1/4 or 1/8 Minus Green as necessary. Gel Cool Whites with Full Minus Green.	Apply Full CTB gel (very inefficient)	**Use HMIs to light the scene** As is.	As is, or with ND as needed	Kino Flo (with KF 55 tubes)	Tungsten blanced film with 85 filter. Daylight balanced film, no filter.
Match to Fluorescent Daylight Resort to this if the ceiling lights must remain on and (1) there are too many fluorescent lights to gel or replace them all, (2) the lights are not accessible, or (3) there is absolutely no other alternative.	Cool whites as is.	Apply Plus Green 50 or Full CTB and Full Plus Green gel.	Apply Full Plus green gel	Gel with Window Green	Kino Flo with K55 tubes and Full Plus Green Other types use same type of bulb as in ceiling fixtures.	Tungsten balanced film with 85 and FLB filter, or correct green in lab printing. Daylight balanced film with FLB or take out green in lab printing.

and magenta correction gels and Kodak filter numbers and corresponding colour meter readings that may be useful in this process.

There are three general approaches to matching the colour temperatures of fluorescent lights, tungsten lights, HMIs and daylight:

1. Match all the sources to daylight (5,600 K).
2. Match all the sources to tungsten (3,200K).
3. Match all the sources to fluorescent daylight (5,600 K plus green).

Table 6.2 details each approach.

When gelling overhead fluorescent fixtures that have frosted plastic panels, you can cut sheets to lay inside each fixture. If you have to gel tubes individually, place tabs of snot tape along the tube and roll the tube up in gel. Carefully cut away excess gel.

Rosco makes tubular sleeves of colour correction gel that can make gelling tubes easier. You can also get clear plastic sleeves that are meant for protection in case of lamp breakage; cut and roll the gel inside them.

Fluorescent tubes, colour rendering

Manufacturers provide two ratings to indicate the type and quality of the colour rendered by their fluorescent tubes: the correlated colour temperature (CCT) and the colour rendering index (CRI). The CCT and CRI are printed on the packaging of the tubes and sometimes also on the tubes themselves. While CCT and CRI ratings give the gaffer valuable information about the general performance characteristics of a given tube, they can be misleading in terms of the colour rendering of fluorescent light on film. CCT and CRI are based on the colour perception of the human eye, not the peculiarities of film emulsions. Specific colour information must be gathered with a tri-stimulus meter, such as those manufactured by Minolta.

Correlated colour temperature

The CCT gives the effective colour temperature of the tube to the human eye when the spikes in the colour curve are combined together. Fluorescent lights come in various colour temperatures. Daylight tubes are designed to light spaces that have supplementary daylight, such as offices with large windows. The light is colour balanced towards the blue end of the spectrum (5,000 K to 6,500 K) to blend with the window light. Warm lights, which have a colour temperature closer to that of household lamps (3,000 K) are generally used in enclosed spaces where supplementary light comes from table lamps and wall sconces.

Colour Rendering Index (Ra)

The CRI is a rating, from 1 to 100, of the accuracy of a light's colour rendering properties when compared with a perfect reference source. Light sources with different relative spectral power outputs have different colour rendering properties. Sodium lamps, as everyone knows, emit a yellow light, almost from one single monochromatic spike and its colour rendering is extremely poor. Daylight and tungsten lamps have a broad spectrum and correspond to the blackbody curve, thus producing an Ra of 100. The Colour Rendering Index is derived from measuring the reproduction from eight test colours when lit by the light source in question.

Table 6.3 Applications of Colour Rendering Index (Ra)

CIE colour rendering index (Ra)	*Typical application*
Greater than 90	Where accurate colour matching is required, e.g. colour print inspection.
80 to 90	Where accurate colour judgements are necessary and/or good colour rendering is required for reasons of appearance, e.g. shops and other commercial premises.
60 to 80	Where moderate colour rendering is required.
40 to 60	Where colour rendering is of little significance but market distortion of colour is unacceptable.
20 to 40	Where colour rendering is of no importance and market distortion of colour is acceptable.

Note: For film or TV use we would need an Ra index of at least 80.

On location you will come across standard fluorescents, which are often used for general lighting and fluorescent fittings designed to give more accurate colour reproduction, such as those used in shops, museums, art galleries and in the graphical industry. Because fluorescent lamps are low pressure mercury discharge, with special phosphors in the fluorescent coating, they always have a tendency to have the typical mercury spikes of blue and green. A high CRI tells you that the tube has a nearly complete spectrum of light frequencies and is therefore capable of rendering colours well; however, they may still have a green spike and require colour correction, which typically involves a combination of magenta and CTO gels. The amount of magenta filtering varies and does not necessarily correspond to the colour rendering of the tube. Generally tubes with a high CRI are less efficient in light output than tubes with lower colour rendition properties.

A low CRI rating indicates the tube emits a limited spectrum of light and is incapable of rendering all colours accurately. Fluorescents are designed to maximize lumen output and utilize energy efficiently. They produce two to four times the light output per watt of an incandescent lamp, and they last five to fifteen times longer. Thus, for economic reasons standard fluorescent tubes, with their greater efficiency, are widely used in office buildings, warehouses, factories and commercial buildings. However, they generally have low CRI ratings, 50 to 70, and should be replaced with tubes with a high colour rendition value which, hopefully, will avoid the need for filtering.

Table E.2 (Appendix E) lists specifications for various types of American fluorescent tubes.

Colouring light

Colour chips and grey scale

When the film laboratory makes a print or video transfer from a developed negative, the timer or colourist adjusts the exposure and colours of the print to make them look natural. When a DP introduces colours into the lighting, she must take steps to prevent the timer from removing the colour in the lab. To give the lab a reference at the beginning of each film roll, the AC films about ten seconds of colour chips or grey scale under white, properly colour-balanced light. The chip chart, or colour chart, has a set of standard colours or a scale of grey tones from white to black from which the timer can work. The chip chart must be filmed under light that is exactly the proper colour temperature. A light that has been checked beforehand with a colour-temperature meter should be standing by for chip chart shots. When filming the chip chart, no other light should fall on the chart. You may need to turn off or block lights momentarily to prevent extraneous light from discolouring the chip chart. It is also helpful to the colourist to see skin tone with the chip chart, and even to see the scene in the background with all its 'non-standard' colour.

When working with television cameras, the engineer puts a line-up chart in front of the cameras before beginning shooting and electronically adjusts the signal from each camera for proper colour rendition. Note: Only one chart and one light should be used, thus guaranteeing consistency between cameras.

Colour correction gels for tints

Colour correction gels are used for tints largely because they are readily available and because they warm or cool the light in a way that occurs naturally in real life and is familiar, in the Kelvin scale. They shift the colour along a single dimension between orange and blue.

Eighth, quarter and half CTO and CTB gels are often used to warm up or cool down a source or even an entire scene. A fire light might use half, full or, even, double CTO. A sunset or dawn scene might be filmed with a full CTO on the lights to simulate the golden light of the low sun. An exterior winter scene shot on a sound stage might use soft overhead lights gelled with a half CTB to cool the scene to 4,100 K. 'Clean' non-gelled directional sources would be added to make sunlight.

When using HMI lights in a tungsten-balanced scene, the amount of blue tint in the light is controlled by the amount of CTO correction applied to the light. When a slightly cool light is desired, a half-CTO is applied, bringing the 5,600 K source down to about 3,800 K. This accomplishes the same thing as applying a half CTB to a tungsten source.

Theatrical gels for tints

For a more complete palette of tints, theatrical gels offer a vast array of alternative possibilities (Table F.10 in Appendix F). Theatrical gels, also called effects gels or party gels, come in more than 400 shades (in sheets 21 × 24 in. or 20 × 24 in. or in 4 × 25 ft rolls). Instead of using a quarter CTO, the DP can choose from dozens of warming shades, such as gold, amber, straw, fire, salmon, pink, rose, apricot and so on. For bringing colour to face tones, there are various cosmetic gels: cosmetic peach, burgundy, rose, rouge, etc. (also listed in Table F.10). Colours such as salmon, pink and, even, chocolate are also used to enhance skin tones. Straw and bastard amber often simulate a low afternoon sun or a flame.

Film emulsions vary in their sensitivity to different colours. A tint may not look quite the same on film as it does to the eye. It must also be remembered that tints must be compatible with the pigments of the wardrobe and set. The colour of the light mixes by a subtractive process with these colours. The cinematographer may even conduct screen tests to see on film exactly what effect a given tint will have on a particular face or costume. A test is also the best way to compare the effects of several possible tints side by side.

Saturated colours

A deeply coloured gel effectively narrows the range of wavelengths to those of a specific colour. For example, a red gel transmits only the wavelengths around 650 nm. All other wavelengths are absorbed by the gel. The more deeply saturated the gel, the more heat it retains and the more susceptible it is to losing its colour and melting. Pairing tungsten lights with red, orange and yellow gels, and HMI or arc lights with blue and purple gels uses the light spectrum more efficiently and puts less stress on the gels. Protect saturated gels by affixing them away from the heat of the lens, on the barn doors or on a frame. Narrow-beam punchy sources such as PARs will play havoc on saturated gels. Heat-shield is a clear heat-resistance film used to protect coloured gels from fading or melting under heat stress. Leave a couple inches of space between the heat-shield and the gel. Rosco's Therma-shield is a sturdier (and more expensive) version that will hold up better than standard heat shield films. Par lights and 2 kW open-face units often require heat-shield, especially with dense colours.

Heat-shield will retard the fading of a gel but is ineffective when a light is simply burning through a gel. In that case, the gel must be placed further from the source, spreading the light over a greater area of gel. Sheets of gel may have to be seamed together with clear J-lar tape to cover the larger beam.

Additive mixing of colours

When differently coloured lights overlap, they mix to make new colours. This is sometimes desirable, sometimes undesirable. Either way, it is important to know how coloured lights mix.

The primary colours of light are red, blue, and green. By mixing these three colours of light, all other colours can be made. Theoretically, if three lights that are gelled primary red, blue and green are aimed at a white surface with their beams overlapping, as in Figure 6.4, the area of intersection of all three lights is white. The intersection of two primaries makes the secondary colours (cyan, magenta and amber).

Subtractive mixing of colours

When two gels are combined in one light or when coloured light is directed at a coloured surface, the colours combine using a subtractive process. Only the colours

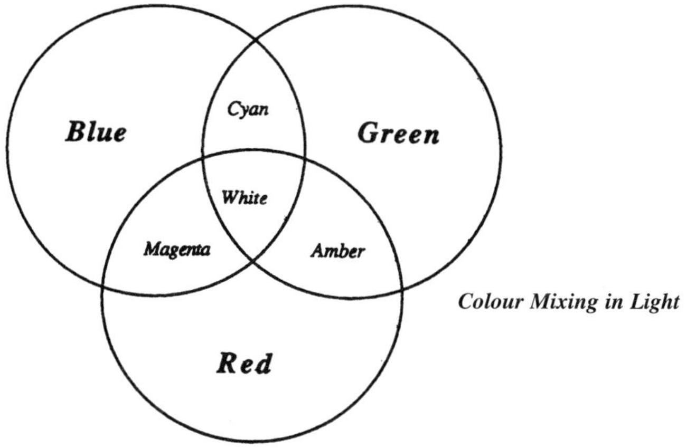

Figure 6.4 Additive mixing of coloured light. The overlapping of all three primary colours creates white light. The combination of two primary colours creates the secondary colours (amber, cyan and magenta). (Reprinted with permission from Paul Carter's *Backstage Handbook* [New York: Broadway Press, 1988].)

common to both are seen. Having a feeling for subtractive mixing is important for anticipating how the set, wardrobe and actor's skin tone will appear in tinted or coloured light. A red light directed at a blue-green dress, for example, will turn the dress black.

Brightness

Methods of control

There are many ways to adjust a lamp's intensity. On the set you quickly learn to consider not only which method is the quickest and easiest, but also which method best accomplishes the effect needed.

- **Scrim** Dropping a scrim in the light is the fastest and easiest way to reduce intensity without affecting anything else.
- **Distance** It is often surprising how little you need to move a light to make a big difference in the brightness. This is because the intensity of a light decreases in proportion to the square of its distance from the subject. This is known as the *law of squares*. By examining Figure 6.5 you'll observe that if a luminaire produces 120 FC at 10 ft, at twice the distance (20 ft) the intensity will be one-quarter, or 30 FC. At three times the distance (30 ft), the intensity will be one-ninth, or about 13 FC.
- **Flood or spot** Flooding dims the light and increases its coverage; spotting brightens the light and narrows its coverage. With PAR lights, you can change to a wider or narrower lens.

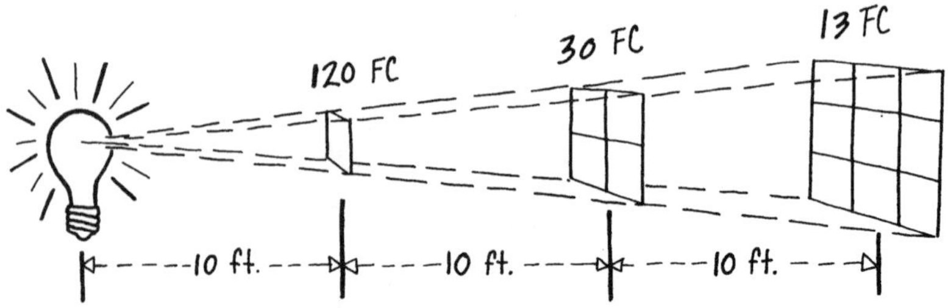

Figure 6.5 Law of Squares: If a square surface of 1 ft × 1 ft is illuminated to 120 FC 10 ft from the light source, at 20 ft the same amount of light is now spread over a 4 ft × 4 ft area. The amount of light on a 1 ft × 1 ft area is a quarter of what it was at 10 ft (120/4 = 30 FC). At 30 ft, the intensity is one-ninth of what it was at 10 ft (13 FC)

- **Dimmer** Dimmers provide a variable control of intensity but also affect colour temperature. See 'Dimmers' section below.
- **Nets** Nets are especially useful to control a selected portion of the beam. They are framed on three sides and open on one side. The open side makes it possible to hide the shadow line of the net.
- **Fingers and dots** Fingers are used to reduce the intensity of a sliver of the beam. Dots are used to reduce the intensity of a very small circular area and can be used to even out hot spots in the centre of beam field. Both come as single nets, double nets, silks and solids.
- **Bobinette** Black net fabric that comes in bolts. It is handy because it can be cut to any shape and size, and draped or taped in place. It would be a quick way to dim down a too-bright neon or fluorescent practical, for example.
- **Neutral-density gel** Neutral-density gel is useful for controlling the brightness of a source that cannot be dimmed, and is fixed in place, such as a xenon follow spot.
- **Diffusion** Diffusion media dim and soften the light. The many kinds of diffusion media affect brightness and softness to varying degrees.
- **Wattage** You can replace the lantern with a bigger or smaller unit, or in some instances you can replace the lamp with a higher or lower wattage (lamp substitutions are listed in Table E.3 of Appendix E).
- **Shutters** Shutters can smoothly reduce the amount of light getting to the subject. They are handy when the light level needs to change during a shot.

Dimmers

A dimmer reduces light intensity by reducing the current to the light source. In the case of tungsten sources, this reduces the colour temperature of the light, turning it gradually more yellow and orange as it is dimmed, as shown in Table 6.4. The light changes 5 K per volt on a 240-volt system. Dimmers are useful, therefore, only to the extent that the colour change is not noticeable or when it is acceptable to the DP.

Table 6.4 Square law dimming figures

The square of the fader setting gives the percentage light output e.g.: Fader at '6' equals light output of 36 per cent.

Fader setting	*Light output %*	*CT (K)*	*%*	*Output volts 240*	*120*	*Current %*	*Power %*
10	100	3,200	100	240	120	100	100
9	81	3,120	93	224	112	96	89
8	64	3,040	88	211	106	93	82
7	49	2,960	81	194	97	88	72
6	36	2,860	74	178	89	85	63
5	25	2,750	66	158	79	78	52
4	16	2,600	59	142	71	73	43
3	9	2,400	51	122	61	67	34
2	4	2,200	39	94	47	59	23
1	1	–	23	55	27	46	11
0	0	–	0	0	0	0	0

Several kinds of dimmers are used in film production: household, Variac, plate dimmers, and electronic dimmers.

Discharge and fluorescent sources can be dimmed without noticeable colour changes over certain ranges, but these require special types of dimming ballasts.

Household dimmers (American)

Small 600 W and 1,000 W household AC resistance dimmers, are often used to control practical lamps and small luminaires.

A 150 W *socket dimmer* screws into the lamp socket. They are handy for controlling low-wattage practical lamps.

Variac dimmers

The Variac dimmer, an AC dimmer, is a type of variable transformer called an auto-transformer. It can boost the power up to 285 V (on a 230 V system) or decrease it to zero. They come in 1 kW, 2 kW and 5 kW sizes (Figure 6.6). Typically they are fitted with an on/off switch as well as a large rotary knob. Some have a three-way switch: normal/OFF/boosted.

There is an important difference between a household resistance dimmer and a Variac dimmer. A variable resistor, or rheostat, works by interposing a resistance on one wire of the circuit, in series with the light. The resistance opposes the flow of

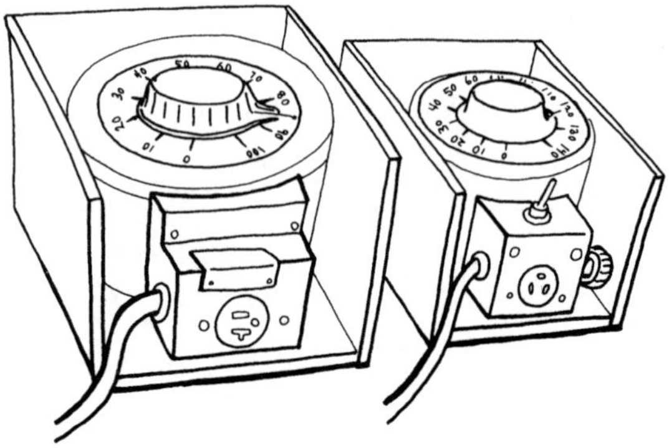

Figure 6.6 Variac dimmers in 2 kW and 1 kW sizes. (Equipment courtesy of Hollywood Rental, Sun Valley, CA.)

current to the light, which causes the light to dim. A Variac does not use resistance; instead, it uses coils to induce a current (like a transformer), the voltage of which can be varied. For dimming filament lamps, the effect of either dimmer is the same; however, for controlling fluorescent ballasts or fan motors (inductive loads), a rheostat will not work. A Variac must be used.

Plate dimmers

Plate dimmers are large variable-resistance dimmers that can be used with either AC or DC circuits running incandescent lights (Figure 6.7).

Because better dimmers are available for AC circuits, plate dimmers see most of their action dimming DC in the older studio sound stages. Unlike other types of dimmers, a plate dimmer can provide blackout dimming only when a minimum wattage is pulled through it; if the lamp connected to it is too small, the dimmer will not dim all the way down to blackness. To provide sufficient wattage, it may be necessary to run a ghost load, an additional light that does not light the set but provides the added wattage to make the dimmer operate.

Plate dimmers come in various sizes: 1 kW (775 W minimum), 2 kW (1,655 W minimum), 3 kW (2,705W minimum) and 5 kW (500 W minimum, a huge 88 lb. unit). Each is equipped with an ON/OFF switch. DC sound stages use large consoles housing twelve or so plate dimmers. The console typically has a number of 1 kW circuits, some 2 kW circuits and a couple of 5 kW circuits.

Electronic dimmers

Dimmers used in the UK come in various shapes and sizes, the most popular being 2.5 kW (10.42 A), 3 kW (12.5 A), 5 kW (20.84 A), 6 kW (25 A) and 10 kW (41.67 A). These may be stand-alone (*in-line*) units which usually have a slider fader on the unit as well as a DMX port to control the dimmer from a console or, when a large number of incandescent lights are to be controlled, *dimmer packs*, or *modular dimmer racks*, are commonly used. A portable

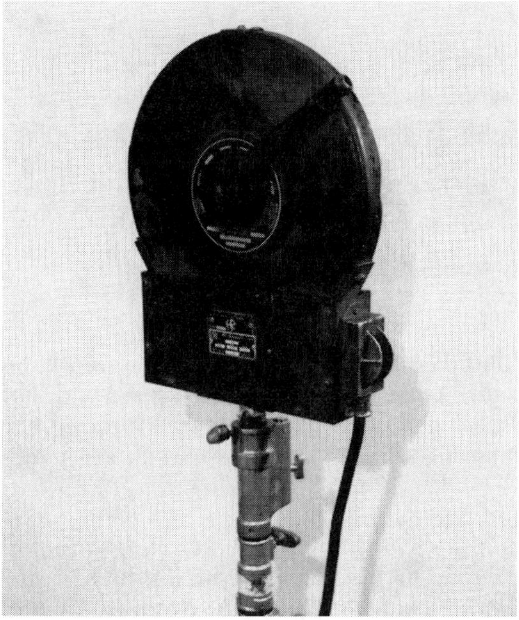

Figure 6.7 Mole-Richardson 2 kW plate dimmer. (Equipment courtesy of Hollywood Rental, Sun Valley, CA.)

unit like the twelve-channel pack shown in Figure 6.8 is compact and relatively lightweight, ideal for location work. Electronic dimmers are covered in more detail in Chapter 9.

Separate dimmer circuits are controlled remotely from a *control console*, commonly called a *desk*. A simple console provides sliding faders to set output levels for each channel. Two or more packs may be daisy-chained together and controlled by a single control console when larger numbers of channels are needed. Multiple packs are typically mounted on a rack. To eliminate dimmer hum from the sound stage, dimmer racks must be placed in a separate dimmer room or housed in a soundproof, air-conditioned cabinet.

Shape, pattern and form

In the following sections we look at how light can be manipulated as it travels from the light source to the subject. We begin by discussing the manipulation of hard light, and then move on to ways of creating and manipulating soft light. This discussion encompasses the properties of form, shape and pattern.

Once a light is placed and turned on the gaffer will want to cut it off areas where it is not wanted (be it with barn doors or flags). He will often want a key light cut off a background wall, or net off an actor who stands closer to the light source. The

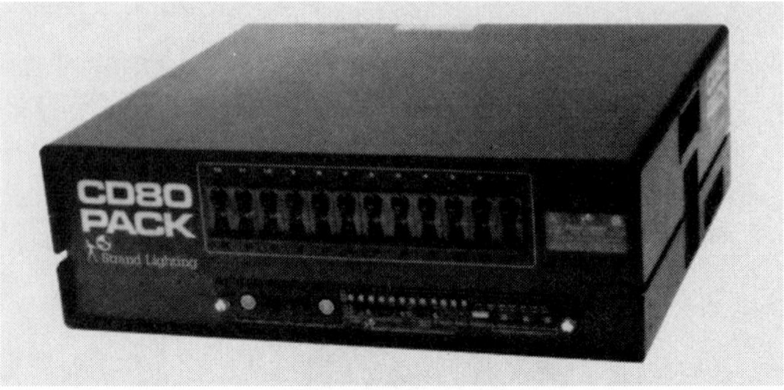

Figure 6.8 Strand CD80 dimmer pack. The twelve-channel pack shown here has twelve dimmer circuits each protected by a circuit breaker. The dimmer pack's brains (the controller card) is attached to the face plate (below the breakers) which contains the control cable inputs/outputs, diagnostic indicators and set-up switches. (Photo courtesy of Strand Lighting, Inc., Rancho Dominguez, CA.)

gaffer will want to break up the background with a pattern, a streak, or a line of shadow. Side-spill leaks should automatically be cleaned up with a flag or blackwrap. To accomplish any of these important goals, there are a few basic laws of physics to be aware of, as well as a number tricks you can use.

Making cuts and patterns

A *topper* is a flag or net used to cut off the top of a light. Toppers are often used to keep light off background scenery, which also helps the boom operator avoid casting shadows on the walls. Similarly, *siders* and *bottomers* trim light from the side or bottom. A lenser cuts light off the camera lens to prevent flair in the filters and lens. A *courtesy flag* is one set up to shade glaring light off the director, DP or others.

Flags and nets come in various standard sizes shown in Figure 6.9.

A few simple, but very important, rules apply when using any flag, net, pattern or set piece (such as a window) in front of a light:

- To make a soft cutoff (fuzzy shadow line), place the flag closer to the light. To make a hard cutoff (cleanly defined shadow line) place the flag closer to the surface on to which the shadow falls. For example, if you put a slash of light on a background wall, and want to light gradually taper off towards the top, you would use a soft-cut topper (a barn door works fine). If you want a hard, defined shadow line, on the other hand, you would want to place the flag well out in front of the light. For the sharpest definition, back the light up and place the flag as close to the wall as possible (without it encroaching into the frame). A larger flag may be necessary to cover the whole beam.
- When setting a lenser, a hard cutoff is preferable. If the camera is on a long lens, the flag can be placed close to the camera. However, when a wide lens is being

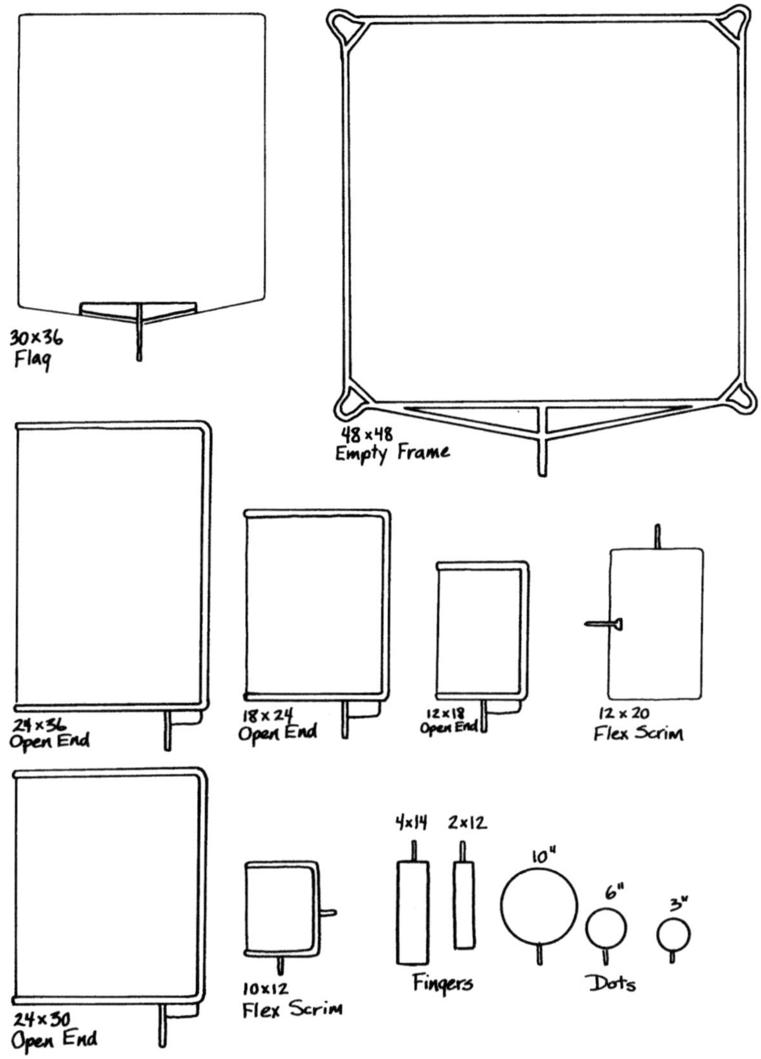

Figure 6.9 Common sizes of flags, nets, frames and silks including finger dots and postage stamps

used, you will run into trouble with the flag encroaching into the frame and it must be worked closer to the light. Halfway between the camera and the light is usually a good, effective placement when practicable.

- In order to avoid the encroachment problem, always place the stand on the off-stage side of the flag. First prepare the flag on the stand, then slide it in from the off-stage side until the shadow covers the lens and filters. A lenser must block light from the entire inner face of the matte box. If light hits the filters in the matte box,

the image may flare. Try to overhear or observe what lens is being used, and learn to guesstimate the frame line accurately.
- With Fresnel lights in flood position, the beam width is roughly equal to the distance from the light. If the flag is placed 3 ft in front of the light, a 2 × 3 ft flag will be sufficient. If a harder shadow is needed, you'll have to use a longer cutter (24 × 72 in.) placed further from the light.

Use of the net

A net can reduce the intensity in a specific area with much greater accuracy than a half-scrim in the light. You can help hide the shadow line of a net by making a soft cutoff. If a double net is making an obvious shadow line, you can use two single nets clipped together and staggered, so the thickness builds up gradually. You can fine-tune intensity with a net by angling the net slightly. The more oblique the angle, the thicker it gets.

Break-up patterns

A break-up pattern is very often used to give texture to the background of a shot. Breaking up the light with a tree branch, gobo pattern, venetian blind, window pattern or just random streaks of shadow gives the image greater contrast and tonal variation, and helps set off the foreground subject. The gaffer may want to exploit whatever shadow-projection possibilities are offered by the set and set dressing: foliage moving in the wind, a slow-turning fan, water running down glass, lace curtains, a banister.

Again, in order for the pattern to be cleanly defined, the pattern-maker must be as close to the surface as possible.

You will get a cleaner shadow:

- from a point source than from a larger one
- from a stronger light placed further away
- from a Fresnel luminaire than from an open-face reflector luminaire
- at full flood than when spotted in
- from the edge of the beam than from the centre
- by removing the lens from the luminaire altogether (though you also lose intensity and flood/spot control)
- by using a doughnut to remove the edges of the beam with ellipsoidal and xenon lights.

The distance also affects the size of the projected shadows. When the pattern is close to the subject and far from the light, the pattern will be of only slightly larger dimensions than the pattern-maker itself. When the pattern-maker is very close to the light, however, the pattern will be projected over a large area, extremely enlarged and distorted in shape, more expressionistic. Thus the size of lamp used, the size of the pattern-maker needed to cover the beam, and the distance of the light and the pattern from the subject must all be taken into account before placing the light. In fact, these considerations may have to be taken into account when designing and placing the sets. For example, if a light is to shine through a window and needs to be placed a considerable distance from the window, ample space must be provided for lights around the set.

Cucaloris

A *cucaloris*, also called a cookie or cuke, is a plywood flag with odd-shaped holes cut in it. It is used to break up the light into random foliage-like splotches. A celo cuke is made with painted wire mesh and creates a more subtle effect because the mesh reduces the light rather than blocking it completely. A cookie does not look convincing if it moves during a take. For realistic moving foliage, use a branchaloris.

Branchaloris

A *branchaloris* is nothing more than a leafy branch found on the ground or broken off a bush and placed in front of a light on a C-stand. It breaks up the light, projects the shadows of branch and leaves on to the scene, and can be made to move naturally as if in the wind.

Tape on an empty frame

To make lines through the light, to simulate the frame of a window, for example, take an empty frame (18 × 24 in., 2 × 3 ft, or 4 × 4 ft, depending on the size of the source and the frame's distance from it) and run strips of black tape across it. It is easier to build the pattern with the lantern in place and turned on, so you can see the effect it is creating.

Soft light

Soft light results when light is bounced or diffused over a relatively large surface by one of several means: light shining through a large frame of diffusion, light bouncing off of a large white surface such as a foamcore bounce board, a white griffolyn or a piece of show card; light bouncing from the large face of a softlight; or using a soft box.

With soft light we are no longer dealing with parallel (slightly diverging) rays of light from a single point source, but with rays that are bounced or diffused so they are diffracted at all angles, moving in all directions. Light from a soft source comes to the subject from all points of a diffuse luminous surface, resulting in three qualities that are often very desirable:

1. It creates soft shadows. No clean, sharply discernible line is projected. The shadow lines are broad and fuzzy. Shadows appear as gradations of tone so that the entire image is imbued with a softness that is natural and also very beautiful. The fuzzy quality of soft shadows also makes them easier to hide in situations where multiple shadows would be distracting.
2. Soft light wraps around the features of the subject. Whereas a face lit from one side by hard light is like a half moon, bright on one side and black on the other, lit by a large soft source it shows a gradual drop off of light from one side to the other. Soft light tends to fill in blemishes in the skin. The overall picture has a full

tonal range, light to dark, with no harsh shadow lines and with lower overall contrast than when lit with harder light.
3. When lighting shiny or glossy subjects such as an automobile, the reflection of a soft light source in the contours of the metal forms interesting patterns that emphasize shape and curves. Hard light, on the other hand, is reflected as a bright, glaring hot spot.

A soft source can be used to create a soft highlight in dark wood, bringing out dark furniture or panelling by catching a reflection of the light source. The gaffer places the light where it is reflected directly into the camera. Especially in cases where you don't want to throw a lot of light on to the walls, this approach yields a subtle and more natural effect.

Along the same lines, a soft source makes a nice eye light. It reflects in the shiny part of the eye, giving the eyes a special brightness. A large, soft source reflected in this way need not actually shine a lot of light on to the subject; it need only be bright enough to create a visible highlight by reflection.

Softness of light

Three factors affect the softness of light: the size of the face of the source, its distance from the subject and how much the light has been diffused. The larger the source, the softer the shadows and the greater the wrapping effect, because the larger source yields more light rays that can come from angles that encircle the features of the subject. This is why it is important when focusing a light on to a diffusion frame or bounce board to completely fill it with light. The surface of the diffusion frame or bounce board becomes the source of light for the scene; the larger the source, the softer the effect.

The smaller the subject, in relation to the face of the source, the more the light engulfs the subject. If the subject is too small it becomes overwhelmed and the image starts to appear flat.

Obviously, the size of the source in relation to the subject also depends on the distance between them. The further away the source, the smaller its effective size. (The sun, for example, is a very large source but as it is 93 million miles away, its rays are completely parallel, so direct sunlight is about as sharp a light as you will find.)

Bringing a soft light in as close to a subject as possible maximizes its softening effect. This also has the effect of localizing the light, creating a soft pool around the actor, which then falls off very quickly into darkness. This happens because light level falls off with distance at a geometric rate, so the closer the source is to the actor, the more dramatic the fall off. Conversely, move the source out if you want the light to carry across more space; the further the source is from the actor, the less the fall off around him (relative to the light level at his position).

Controlling soft light

Soft light is more difficult than hard light to cut and control, and the softer the light (the heavier the diffusion), the more difficult it becomes. The larger the source, the larger the flags required to block the light. Boxing-in a 4 × 4 frame of heavy diffusion typically requires 4 × 4 or 4 × 8 flags. Flags and nets used close to a large source are ineffectual; the light engulfs the flag. To be useful, the flag must be far enough from the source that it blocks a direction the light is travelling, rather than merely blocking a portion of the face of the source. Large cutters, 2 × 6 ft, are necessary as toppers, placed well out in front of the source. An even larger teaser may need to be fashioned from a length of duvetyne attached to a length of 1 × 3 batten.

With soft light you might use a small flag where normally you would use a net. Because the shadow is so nebulous, the flag serves to create an area of lesser brightness, rather than a well-defined cutoff. The flag can be angled to increase or decrease its effective size.

Diffusion

Diffusion materials

There are five basic types of diffusion, each with its own character: spun, frost, white diffusion, silks (and other fabrics), and silent diffusion. Each type is manufactured in several densities (Table F.11 in Appendix F). Spun, or spun glass, gives the beam a mild soft edge, but with minimal beam spread, so that the shape of the beam and the effectiveness of barn doors are maintained. Frost, such as Opal or Hampshire Frost, yields slightly more beam spread and softening, but still maintains a discernible beam centre. The original direction of the beam is still dominant.

A medium weight diffusion such as 250 diffracts much more of the light. As a result, the beam spreads as it passes through the diffusion. As the diffusion surface itself becomes the source of rays of light equally with the lantern, the effective size of the source is enlarged to the size of the diffusion frame. Shadows are softened. The light starts to wrap around the edges of objects.

A dense diffusion, such as a heavy frost, 216, or grid cloth, causes wide beam spread. The original direction of the beam becomes secondary to the diffuse multidirectional rays emitted from the diffusion. The light rays are deflected in all directions over the entire area of the diffusion frame. This creates the ideal source for shadow-less, wrapping light because the greatest number of light rays are diverted at angles that can accomplish these ends, and because the dominant direction of the light from the lantern is completely removed. It creates a shadow-less, even field of light, with no discernible beam centre or edge.

Fabrics such as silk, muslin and grid cloth are dense diffusions often used on large frames. Many gaffers like the diffusing effect of muslin. You can bounce light off it or use it as a diffuser, directing light through it. The fabric is inexpensive and durable, and can be made in any size up to huge 40-ft squares and larger. Unbleached muslin has a yellow tint, which warms the light without the need for gels. Bleached muslin has less of a tint but retains the warming effect.

Silk is commonly used on a 12-in. or 20-in. overhead frame. Silk has a relatively low transmission; it reduces light intensity by about 2⅔ stops, but despite its density, silk has only a moderate diffusing effect. A light passing through silk still casts a hard shadow, but the silk helps to fill. China silk or ¼ silk is much lighter, reducing transmission by only ½ stop.

Silent diffusions, such as Soft Frost and Hilite, are made of a rubbery material that does not rattle and crinkle when caught by wind, as other diffusions do. These materials are not as heat resistant as normal diffusion, however, and should not be used directly on a luminaire.

As with coloured gel, label each piece of diffusion when it is cut from the roll. Mark the type on the corner of the piece with an indelible marker.

Diffusion on the lantern

Attaching diffusion material to the barn doors of a Fresnel or open-face light takes the hard edge off the beam. It diffuses the light, evens out the intensity across the field, and reduces or removes the central hot spot.

To create as large a source as possible, open the barn doors wide and attach the diffusion to the outside. When using dense diffusion medium, the flood/spot mechanism works in reverse. To maximize the light output, flood the light to fill the diffusion with light. Maximum output is found just shy of full flood.

Diffusion attached inside the barn doors does allow the barn doors still to have some effect and creates fewer problems with spill and reflections off the back of the diffusion; however, it does not increase the size of the source and therefore does little more than take the curse off the hard light.

Other ways of making soft light

Croney cone

The Croney cone, which is named for its inventor, Jorden Crownenweth, ASC (Blade Runner), is a cone that fits in place of the barn doors on the front of the light. A frame fitted with grid cloth or some other diffusion slides into slots on the front of the cone, turning the Fresnel into a soft source with a larger face

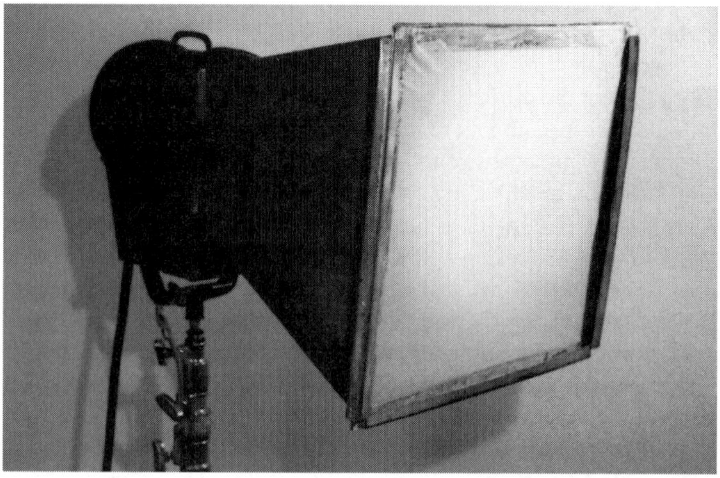

Figure 6.10 A Croney cone. (Equipment courtesy of Hollywood Rental, Sun Valley, CA.)

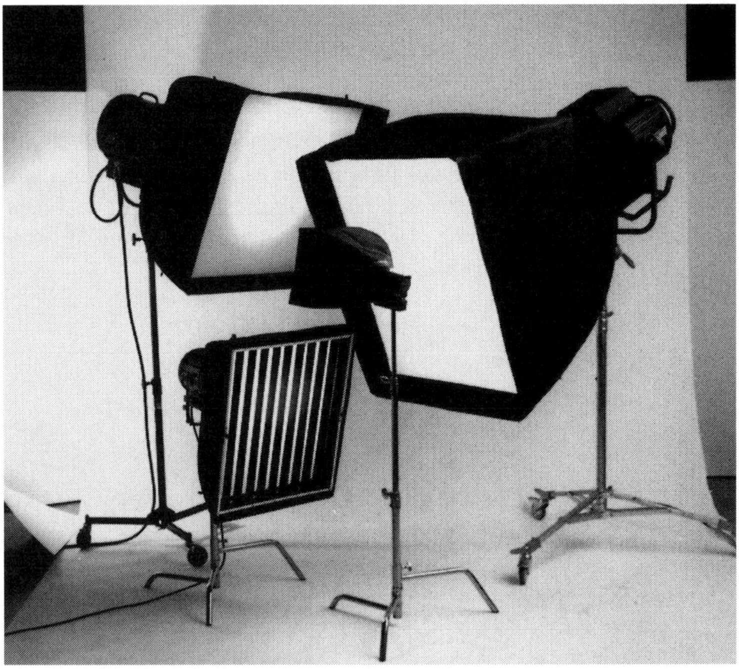

Figure 6.11 Chimera soft boxes. (Photo courtesy of Chimera Photographic Lighting, Boulder, CO.)

(Figure 6.10). The diffusion frame can be exchanged easily when a different type of diffusion is desired.

Chimera

Chimera Photographic Lighting makes a variety of collapsible, heat-resistant, fabric soft boxes (Figure 6.11) that incorporate a great many refinements on the basic Croney cone design.

Chimeras are made of heat-resistant fabric stretched and held in shape by flexible, interior, stainless-steel poles. The interior fabric is soft silver reflective material, which increases light output and further diffuses the light. Their design includes two effective ways to reduce side spill, 60- and 90-honeycomb grids, and louvres. A second interior diffusion baffle can be added to double-diffuse the light. This ensures that even an intense and punchy light source will be fully diffused.

Chimeras can be fitted to almost any Fresnel, PAR, and open-face lantern in place of barn doors. A 'speed ring' is needed to adapt the Chimera to each light. The Chimera light banks are available in four models. Video Pro and Quartz banks are standard depth and are best used with open-face lanterns. Daylite and Daylite Junior banks are deeper; they are useful for narrower beam lanterns such as Fresnels.

The flaps that close the chimera around the face of the light will get burned by most lights. The flaps are fitted with Velcro, so they can be folded back away from the face of the light. Always fold the flaps and open the ventilation holes.

Home-made diffusion box

You can build an inexpensive soft box, with many of the same advantages as the chimera. This type of soft box diffuses light from a lantern while also containing the light (Figure 6.12A). It has two separated layers of diffusion. Light becomes diffused as it passes through the layers and also bounces between the layers, further scatter-

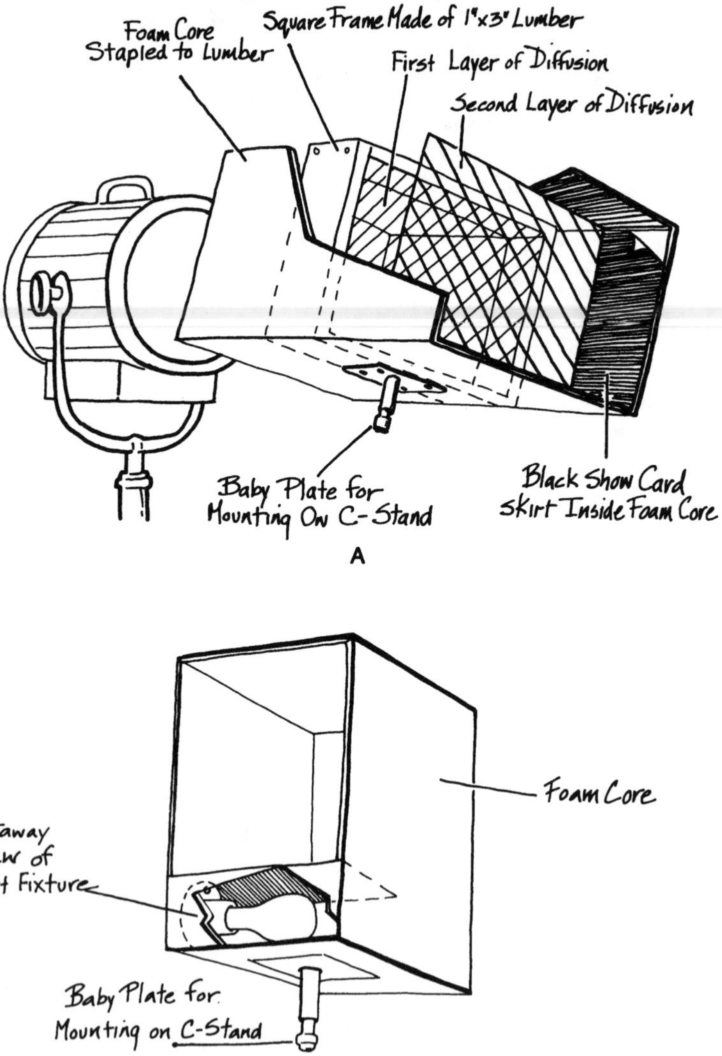

Figure 6.12 (A) A portable diffusion box. (B) The 'garbage box' improvised by DP, Greg Gardener

ing the rays and softening the light. The hood, made of black show card, adjusts the spread of light. A nail-on plate is screwed on for mounting the unit on a C-stand.

A box like this can be made any size or shape, but if you make it just slightly larger than the size of standard frames (24 × 36 in or 18 × 24 in), you can make a slot in the side of the box so that diffusion and colour can be easily changed by sliding in a new frame.

Home-made soft box

Another approach to take is to construct a soft box with light bulbs installed inside the soft box itself. The advantage is that it is self-contained and very lightweight. You can position such a box without having to contend with a heavy lantern (a short C-stand easily supports it).

Soft boxes can be made quite simply out of light lumber, foamcore, staples, screws and diffusion. Remember that these materials are flammable, and light bulbs get very hot. Be sure to cut ventilation flaps or holes in the bottom and the top of the box to create a ventilation flow. Leave plenty of space on all sides around the lamps. Do not put power cords or tape on the inside of the box, where they could come loose, fall near a lamp, and catch on fire. Build these home-made devices with large doses of common sense and caution.

Construct the box with black foamcore on the outside, white inside. Use porcelain sockets for regular lamps, photofloods and mushroom floods, or bayonet mount FEV sockets for small tungsten lamps. Use several lamps, and wire each socket separately so that you can vary the brightness by switching lamps on or off. Cut flaps so that you can reach inside to change lamps when needed. Place the mounting plate at the centre of gravity so that the box balances on the plate and does not create excessive torque on the C-stand. (If you build a snoot for the box, you may need to determine a second centre of gravity with the snoot in place and add a second nail-on plate.)

Garbage box

This type of soft box got its name when an inventive gaffer (now DP, Greg Gardener) hurriedly pulled a cardboard box from the garbage and transformed it into a soft light (Figure 6.12B). The box is lined with foamcore. A ledge shields direct light from the lamp. A white wrap foil lining around the lamp should be used to protect the foamcore from heat. This type of light is used close in to a subject.

Chicken coop

A chicken coop hangs overhead on rope. This kind of light might be used, for example, over a large dinner table. It is usually rigged so that it can be raised and lowered to increase or decrease the intensity of the light. The one shown in Figure 6.13A is fitted with six photoflood lamps. A small, single-lamp version is shown in Figure 6.13B. The coop has a duvetyne skirt that can be lowered or raised independently on all four sides to control the amount of light falling on the walls of the room.

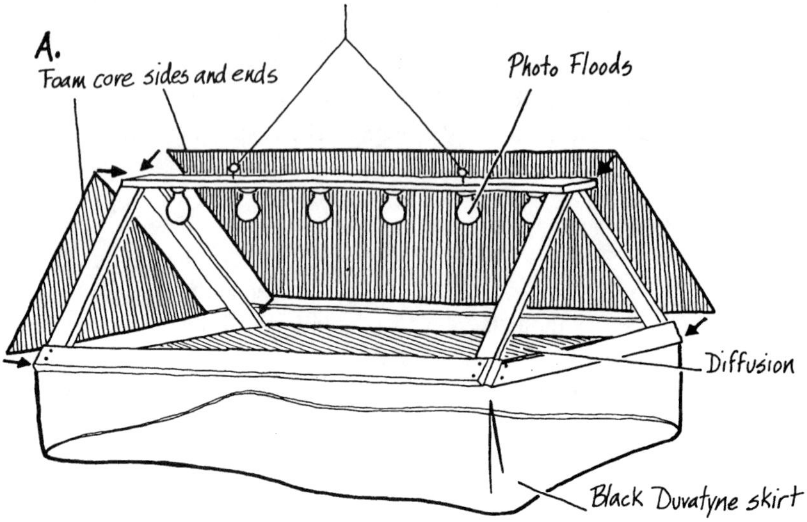

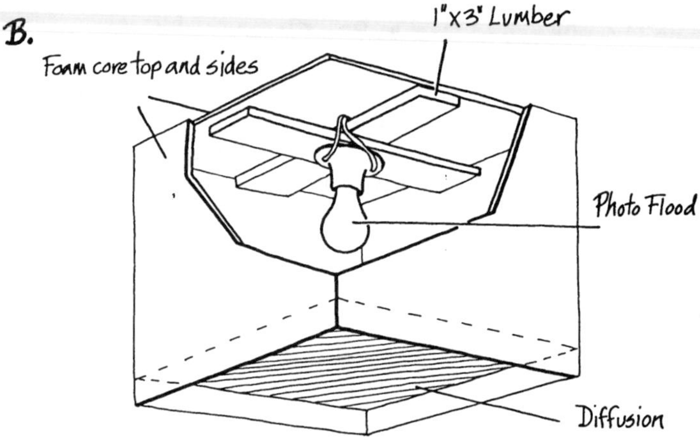

Figure 6.13 (A) A home-made skirted six-light chicken coop. (B) A single photoflood soft box

Nook light coop

Figure 6.14 shows nook lights mounted in a chicken coop frame and pointing upward into the foamcore to create an even, less direct soft light.

China lanterns

Paper Chinese lanterns are an inexpensive, lightweight soft light or ambient light source. They come in various sizes, 12, 24 and 30 in. spheres, as well as rectangular boxes. Rig the lantern to a C-stand, with a photoflood lamp in a porcelain socket (do not use the 60 W plastic sockets that are sometimes sold with the lanterns; the

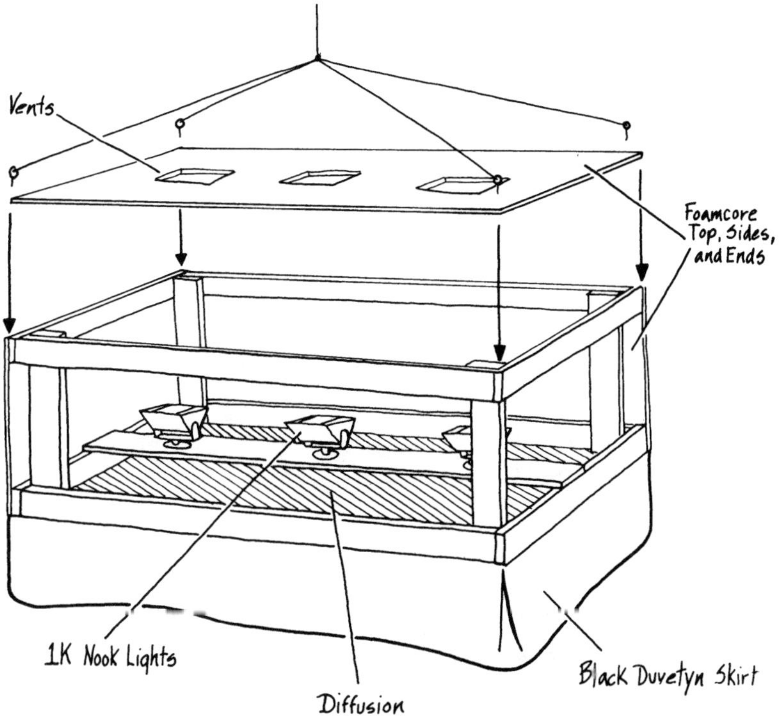

Figure 6.14 A home-made skirted nook light bounce box

photoflood lamps will melt them). I always use them on a dimmer. Hidden in the set, or positioned just off screen and used in close, the lanterns are nice soft 'glow lights' and give a localized warm glow. A large ball hung above the set achieves a nice low ambient light level. The ball can be skirted, if desired, to keep spill off walls. The popularity of lanterns inspired manufacturers to come up with more durable luminaires of this type. K 5600 Lighting makes a 200 W HMI lantern in 20 in. or 30 in. diameter. Chimera has 22 in. and 30 in. lanterns which fit video pro ring sizes, or can be fitted with a tungsten halogen socket.

Bounce light

Soft light can be created by simply bouncing a specular source off a white surface. The following list provides some examples:

- **Poly and foamcore** In many situations, a piece of white board can be used to bounce existing light on to the shadow areas of the face to reduce contrast. This is especially common when shooting outside in direct sunlight, where the contrast is very high. A 2-ft or 4-ft square of foamcore, taped to and reinforced by a piece of 1-in. polystyrene, is standard equipment for fill light. Similarly, a piece of show card placed in the lap of the driver of a car helps fill in shadows. To fill a fairly

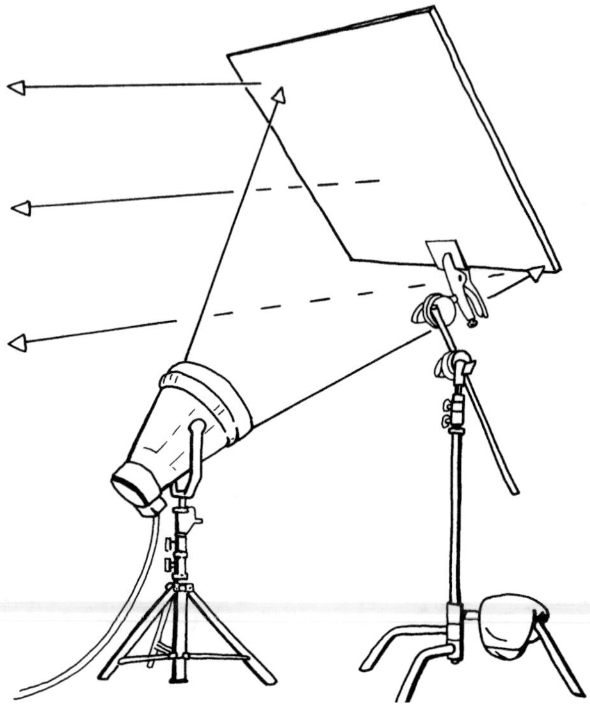

Figure 6.15 A strong large soft source produced by bouncing a 2,500 W HMI PAR off of a 4 × 4 poly

large room with soft light, a strong light, such as a 2,500 HMI PAR, can be aimed at a 4 × 4 ft or 4 × 8 ft piece of poly or foamcore (Figure 6.15). Remember that the angle of incidence equals the angle of reflection. If you put the bounce board up high and angle it downward, you can place the lights below and in front of the board, pointing up into it.

- **Show card, cove light** In a small room where it is difficult to hide lamps, you can tape a piece of white show card into an off-screen corner (Figure 6.16). The reflected light can be better controlled if the show card is curved into a parabola. The lantern is hidden under or above, pointing at the show card, creating a soft light from that direction. You can also use a silver or gold show card.
- **Ceiling** A fast and easy way to fill a room with soft, even illumination is simply to bounce a strong light off a white ceiling. If the ceiling is not white, you can rig a sheet of foamcore to the ceiling.
- **Griff** To create a very big, soft source that might simulate skylight when shooting inside a studio or when a large area needs to be covered with soft light, the gaffer may bounce light into a 12- or 20-ft square of griffolyn. A couple of large HMIs, one on each side, will do the trick. For exterior scenes, a griff works the same way, bouncing sunlight.

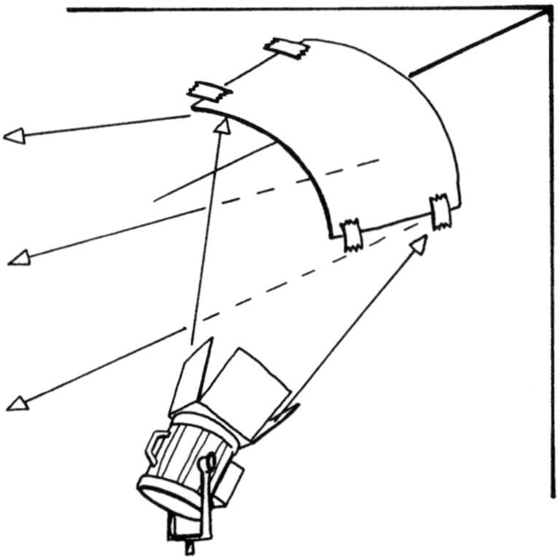

Figure 6.16 Show card taped into a corner creates a soft source without rigging a fixture into the corner

- **Negative fill** To some extent the shine in a person's face reflects the colour and lightness of surfaces around them. Placing a 4 × 4 ft flag near an actor removes these reflections, as well as shading off any wayward light.

Movement

The final property of light that can be manipulated is motion: the jumping glow of a television screen, the dancing flames of a fire, the passing of car headlights at night, disco and concert lights, the movement of a hand-held lantern or flashlight, a swinging lamp hanging from the ceiling, the projection of rain running down a windscreen, the slow, smooth motion of sunlight through an aeroplane's windows as it banks and turns. Movement contributes to a scene's naturalism, mood and visual interest.

Flicker effects: television screen, flame and fire

Sit in a dark room with only the television on but don't look at it. Watch the way the light shifts on the walls and faces in the room. You will notice that the blue television light quickly changes in intensity and colour when there is a cut on screen and gradually shifts in intensity as the camera pans or as characters move around.

The pace of the shifts depends on what you are watching. MTV creates a constantly changing image. Old movies, on the other hand, tend to play scenes in wide master shots or to intercut reverse close-ups, leaving at least several seconds and even 20 or 30 seconds between cuts. When you are creating an off-screen television effect, you must find a way to mimic the pace of the shifts with the intensity of the light. There are many different ways to do this, and any method that works is as good as another. A common way is to make a soft box out of foamcore and light wood, and place several small lights inside it. Use blue gel and diffusion on the front of some or all the lights, as desired. To make the lights flicker, some sort of controller must be used.

Flicker boxes

Television screen and flame effects are often created using a flicker box such as that shown in Figure 6.17. There are a variety of such boxes on the market. A flicker box typically creates increase and decrease in intensity at random intervals. The rate of flicker, as well as the brightness of the light at its peak and lowest intensities, can be set with controls. Some flicker boxes also make blinking light effects and even lightning flashes. Flicker boxes having three circuits can produce co-ordinated flicker effects and chase effects.

Some gaffers use a circular disc of mercury switches to flicker the lights. The switches contain liquid mercury, which completes the circuit when tilted such that the mercury spills over the contacts. By artfully tipping and rotating the disc, different lights turn on and off in a controllable yet unregimented way that is very convincing. Operating this type of controller requires a practised hand. Another gaffer uses two short fluorescent tubes and has an electrician move his arms in front of the light – simple, but effective.

Fire effect

Flicker boxes are also commonly used to create a fire effect. When a flame moves, the shadows from the firelight move up and down and from side to side. To get a convincing effect, it is necessary to use at least two lights to simulate a flame.

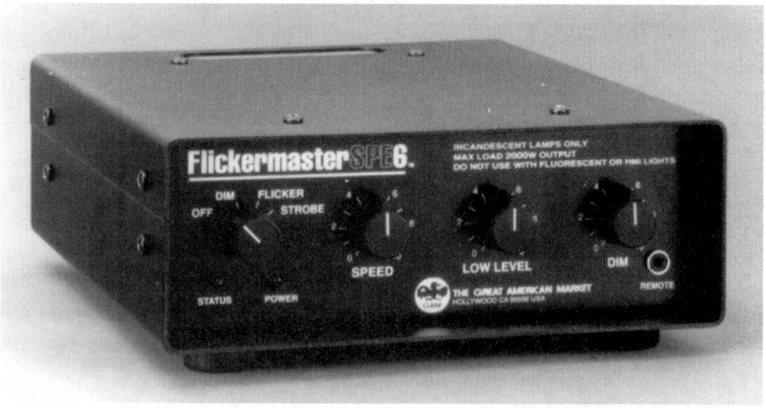

Figure 6.17 The Flickermaster SPE-6 supplies a 2,000 W circuit which can be set to flicker up to a set peak, and down to a set base level. It can function as a random flicker, or strobe (with adjustable speed) or as a dimmer. (Courtesy of The Great American Market, Hollywood, CA.)

The best way to get a fire effect is to use fire. If practical considerations (such as the location, the need for fire marshals, and so on) allow it, a fire bar (a gas-fuelled pipe with holes along it) can be supplied by the effects department and used as a portable lighting source. If the intensity of the flame is insufficient, supplemental light can be imbued with the look of flame by shining a luminaire through the flame of the fire bar.

Moving lights

Lights are often mounted on a crane or dolly, or hand held by an electrician to make the light move. Reflecting a PAR 64 into a shiny silver tray of water creates lively water striations. Sequences of dimmer cues can be set up to create breathtaking shifts in angle and colour. Various special effects lights can be used to create moving projections (scene machine), or dynamic concert lighting effects (automated luminaires). There are many exciting ways to move light. The possibilities are limited only by your imagination.

7

Electrician's set protocol

Staging area

Upon arrival at each new shooting location, one of the first jobs is to establish a staging area where electrical equipment is kept, ready to go on to the set when needed. The best boy will have picked out a spot that is convenient to the set, but not so close as to block access. Stake out the spot early before all the good ones are taken. The entrance to the staging area must be clear of obstructions. You don't want a line of producers and stars sitting in chairs in front of the area. You need to be able to carry equipment in and out fast.

While the director and DP are deciding on their shots, the electricians can 'head-up' a selection of lights on stands in the staging area, ready to be brought into the set when called for. Line up the lights on stands. Organize them in rows – row of midgets, row of tweenies, row of babies, row of juniors, and so on – so that each type of light is readily accessible. Skinny up the legs of the stands so they can be packed together closely. To be totally proper about it, the lights should be arranged with the stand fully lowered, T-handles lined up in a straight line down the back of the stand, power cord hanging on hanger, gels and scrims hanging on the stand (not in the light) and doors closed.

The staging area should be arranged in an orderly fashion for easy access to all the equipment to include: crates of 25-ft and 50-ft stingers, gel crate, gel rolls, boxes of practical lamps and associated electrical parts, dimmers, black wrap, tape rolls, clothespegs/croc-clips and similar electrical expendables. It is often convenient to keep a selection of essentials (tape, black wrap, clothespegs and gel) even closer at hand, in a set box – a crate that is kept on or immediately outside the set.

When a light, stinger, or cable is no longer needed on the set, it goes back to the staging area where it will not create clutter. The light should be 'head wrapped', the stand is fully lowered, the cord coiled, the barn doors closed, and the scrims removed and hung on the stand. If a particular gel or diffusion is being used on all the lights, store it in the scrim box.

Lighting the set

Electricians have to be alert and always have one eye on the gaffer. You tune into the sound of his or her voice, and learn to pick it out from the general rumble of noise. An experienced electrician has a sense of the ebb and flow of activity on the set, and knows when he or she needs to work fast and when there is time to spare. When lighting begins on each new set-up all the electricians should automatically come to the set. There is a great deal of activity as the broad strokes of the lighting are put in.

The director's monitor and the camera dolly should be given power immediately. The director often needs the monitor to set up the new shot.

A period of tweaking and adjusting follows the broad strokes; a few small lights may be added. Finally the DP declares that the lighting is ready, and the AD calls the actors into the set. Each time the first AD announces a new shot, the electricians working the set should quietly get close to the lights that may need to be moved and watch the gaffer and DP for orders. Even when lighting activity is at a minimum, there should always be one electrician on the set (unless the AD clears the set for a particular performance). Before you leave the set to grab a drink, conduct business or go to the toilet, be sure that another electrician is on the set and knows that you are stepping out. If the gaffer needs to step out, he will assign the best boy or a set electrician to cover him, and that person must remain next to the DP until the gaffer returns.

Setting lights

What's needed

The gaffer gives an instruction: 'Put a baby over in that corner to key these two actors. Give it opal and quarter CTO.' You will need a baby stand, a baby with scrim set and barn doors, gels and diffusion. You will probably also need a 25-ft stinger to run power to the light. You may want to bring a couple of additional gels and diffusion along so that if the gaffer changes his or her mind, you don't have to go back for them later.

A complete set of appropriate-size scrims and a set of barn doors should be brought to the set with every light. Hang the scrim box on the stand. When the gaffer wants a little less from a light, you should be able to drop in the scrim in seconds. It is very bad form to have to search for scrims. They should always be with the light.

It is also worth repeating that each raised stand should be bagged. The more time you spend on sets, the more you see just how easily stands are toppled. It becomes second nature to check that stands are properly bagged. Similarly, when working in a wind, around Ritter fans, or around helicopters, the grips may need to tie guy lines (not less than three) to the top of the light stand and secure them to bull stakes driven well into the ground. Propeller-wash from a helicopter will blow over a Dino on a supercrank as if it was a piece of paper, even with 130 lb of sand on it.

Teamwork

It is important for each electrician to watch for a chance to back up another electrician and jump into the game. When a light is called for, one electrician sets the light while another runs the power. When an HMI is called for, one person connects the head, the other connects the ballast. If a light is called for at the last minute, all the electricians work in a team: one person carries the head, another grabs a stand, and two more carry the ballast together throwing the head cables over their shoulders. By the time the head is on the stand, the ballast cable is attached to the ballast, and someone has run power to the ballast. The whole drill takes only a minute.

The trick to teamwork is communication and jumping in to help without getting in another person's way. Communicate. If you're running someone's power for them, or fetching gel for their light, be sure to tell them so. There are some things that are better accomplished by one person alone. If three or four people all jump to set one light, the set becomes like a primary-school football match, with everybody playing out of position, chasing after the ball in one roving mass. The DP is continually in a race against time. The grip/electric crew can win or lose that race for him or her. When things gel between crew members, set-ups come together like a well-practised play on the sports field, allowing the DP time for finesse. In this way a sharp crew can vastly improve the look of the photography, not to mention keeping the days to a reasonable length.

Warnings

When carrying large, heavy or hot equipment through the set, call out warnings such as, 'Coming through, watch your back' or 'Hot points, coming through'. You don't want to singe the director's arm with a hot light. I once heard a grip carrying dolly track use the warning, 'Duck or bleed!' This cleared the way quite effectively.

When turning a light on, call out, 'Light coming on' before you hit the switch. This is a courtesy to the actors, stand-ins and crew who are in front of your light. It is meant to warn them not to look at the light. Unfortunately, when novices hear the warning, they often do just the opposite and momentarily blind themselves, but after that they quickly learn. It is a good idea to tilt the light up away from the set or to put a gloved hand in front of the light as you turn it on. That way the light doesn't come on suddenly, and you give the actors or stand-ins a second to adjust to it before you pull your hand away. This kind of courtesy is not just a matter of politeness, but also one of professionalism. Saying 'Light coming on' also alerts the gaffer and DP that your light is in place, powered and ready to be focused. Similarly, avoid blinding people in general. If a working light needs to be moved, don't let it swing around and blast into people's faces.

If you are about to plug in a light and you can't tell if the switch is on or off, you can give the warning, 'Possible hot stab'. This is especially important if the light is aimed at someone or if the light coming on is likely to be an annoyance to the DP or gaffer. An accidental hot stab can be forgiven if you give a warning. It is important to make a habit of turning lights off at the switch before unplugging them to avoid hot stabs.

Whenever a flash camera is used on the set, the photographer should call out, 'Flashing' before snapping the shot. This is mainly a courtesy to people in front of the camera, but it also alerts the electricians that a camera is about to flash. This way, the flash is not mistaken for an electrical arc or a lamp exploding or burning out.

Safety bonds

When a lantern is hung above the set (i.e. suspended from the ceiling, set walls or overhead grid), a safety bond should be attached to the yoke and around a permanent structural support capable of holding the weight of the lantern if it should become detached from its suspension point. The best type of safety bond is aircraft wire cable, with a loop in one end and a karabiner at the other. In the absence of aircraft cable, sash cord or safety chain can be used. Be sure to leave enough slack in the safety line for the light to be panned and tilted. Under European regulations the lantern must not be able to fall more than 300 mm.

Barn doors should also come with safety bond connecting them to the light, to prevent them from falling. If a light does not have a barn door safety bond, use bailing wire or safety chain to attach the doors before hanging the light.

Focusing lights

Once the light is in place, notify the gaffer that you are ready to focus it. When you turn the light on the real craft begins, manipulating the light so that it accomplishes the desired effect. While the electrician handles the light, the gaffer either stands on the set with the light meter or views the scene from the appropriate camera angle. Very often the gaffer will start with the light at full spot to aim the beam. A gaffer will hold out a fist where he or she wants the beam spotted. The electrician spots the light on to his or her hand, then returns the light to full flood. Another way gaffers sometimes focus the light is to view the light fixture through a contrast glass. The gaffer then directs the lamp operator with hand signals. The following are common instructions:

- **Pan lamp-left or lamp-right** Lamp-left is your left when you are facing in the same direction that the light is pointing. Lamp-right is your right.
- **Camera-left or camera-right** Camera-left is your left when you are facing in the same direction that the camera is pointing. Camera-right is your right.
- **Tilt up** Tilt the light up.
- **Tilt down** Tilt the light down.
- **Flood it out** Turn the flood/spot knob slowly towards flood until told to stop. Say 'Flooding.'
- **Full flood** Go directly to full flood.
- **Spot it in** Turn the flood/spot knob slowly towards spot until told to stop. Say 'Spotting'.
- **Full spot** Go directly to full spot.
- **Stem up** Raise the stand.
- **Stem down** Lower the stand.
- **Walk it back** Move the stand and light back.
- **Walk it in** Move the stand and light closer to the action.
- **Lock it down** The light is aimed correctly; tighten the T-handles to lock that position.
- **Walk away** It's perfect. Make sure that everything is secure, and you're done with that one. 'That's a purchase' is a similar phrase to 'Walk away'.

- **A scosh** Technical term for an increment slightly less than a smidgen or a tad, as in 'Flood it out a scosh'.
- **Door it off the back wall** Lower the top barn door.
- **Drop in a double** Put in a double scrim. Say 'Double in' when finished. You also hear expressions like 'Slow it down' or 'Bring it down to a dull roar'.
- **Home run** Two doubles in a light.
- **Grand slam** Two doubles and a single in a light.
- **Pull the wire** Pull out all scrims. Say 'Wire out' or 'It's clean' when no scrims are in.
- **Bottom half-double** Put in a half-double scrim oriented to cut the bottom. Say 'Bottom half-double in'.
- **Waste some of that** Pan or tilt the light so the hot spot isn't directly on the action.
- **Do off/on or A-B** Switch the light off and on so that the gaffer can observe what the light is accomplishing. Announce 'On' as you turn it on and 'Off' as you turn it off.
- **Shake up that shiny board** As the sun moves, shiny boards have to be readjusted. Move the board to check that it is properly aimed. The phrase can refer to lights in the same way.
- **Flag the light** Pass your hand back and forth in front of the lens to show where the beam is hitting.
- **Give me a slash here** Bring the barn doors together to create a line where indicated.
- **Rotate the beam** PAR lights have an elliptical beam, rather than a round one. You can turn the lamp housing to orient the beam horizontal, vertical, or at any angle.
- **Dress the cable** Tidy up the cable or run it out of sight or out of the way.
- **Dress the light** Something is hanging off the light (that is, a safety chain or diffusion is hanging into the shot). Clean it up.
- **Change that out for a deuce** Replace the light with a 2 kW fixture.
- **Count to ten** Hold off on what you are doing; things are changing and it may not be needed after all.
- **Cancel the baby** Yes, sure enough we don't need that light.
- **Fire it up** Turn it on.
- **Cool the light** Turn it off. You also often hear 'Save the lights'.
- **Strike the light** When referring to an HMI, strike means turn it on, as in 'Strike it up'.
- **Strike the set** Take down all the lights and return them to the staging area.

It is customary for the electrician to respond to the gaffer's directions by repeating each direction back as he performs it. This assures the gaffer that they have been heard and someone is following their instructions. When they say, 'Flood it out', the electrician responds, 'Flooding' as he does so. When delay is involved, he or she lets the gaffer know he or she has heard before proceeding; if they ask for a light, the electrician responds, 'Flying in' as he goes to fetch it.

Walkie-talkies and radio headsets

The clamour of the crew calling out these sorts of instructions to one another can be a distraction for the director, actors and DP when they are trying to communicate on set. Walkie-talkies or radio headsets are an invaluable tool for the electric crew. They cut down on the noise on the set and save the electricians a lot of running around. If you need something from the staging area, for example, and someone has just gone over there, you can quietly ask that person to bring you what you need on the way back without yelling or running.

When using headsets or walkie-talkies, be sure to use proper mike technique: Press the button fully, allow a second for the transmitter to engage before you start speaking and don't release it until after you have finished your last word, otherwise your first and last words will be cut short. When speaking, keep the mike about an inch from your mouth for a clear, strong signal.

Typically a walkie-talkie has many channels, which may be assigned to various departments. Usually the assistant directors are on channel one, while the electric, grip and transportation departments claim their own channels.

The gaffer initiates a conversation by asking for someone by name: 'David, come back', or simply a general call for aid: 'Electric'. Respond with your name: 'Go for David'. Always acknowledge a transmission by saying 'copy' or some similar response. If the gaffer's transmission is interrupted by another transmission, say 'You were stepped on, say again'. If the signal breaks up during transmission, say 'You broke up, come again', or repeat back what you think he said and ask for confirmation. A broken signal is often an indication that the battery on the transmitting unit is low and should be exchanged for a fresh one. Common usage has evolved to include various CB radio codes, such as:

Q: 'What's your 20?' = Where are you?
A: 'I'm ten one-hundred' = I'm in the toilet.

Use concise phrases. Brevity is the soul of wit, as Shakespeare said; try not to clutter up the frequency with rambling. If a lengthy explanation is unavoidable, you may want to change to an unused channel so as not to monopolize the frequency. Say 'Go to three'. Then change to channel three and wait for a response. When the conversation is finished, say 'Back to five' or whatever the original channel was.

Last but not least, if you are not wearing a headset, turn down the volume on your walkie-talkie to zero during takes, and remember to turn it back up again when the take is finished. There are few blunders more embarrassing and less forgivable than ruining a take by allowing your radio to blurt out, 'Hey Hank, when's lunch?' in the middle of a tense performance.

Hand signals

Even when working on a show with radios, you will still find times when hand signals are needed. These are shown in Figure 7.1.

Applying gel to the fixture

The most common way of attaching gel or diffusion to a Fresnel or open-face light is to clip it on with croc-clips or clothes-pegs (Figure 7.2B). Look out for light reflecting off the back of the gel and bouncing on to the walls of the set. Encircle the gaps in the barn doors with black wrap to block gel-reflection spill.

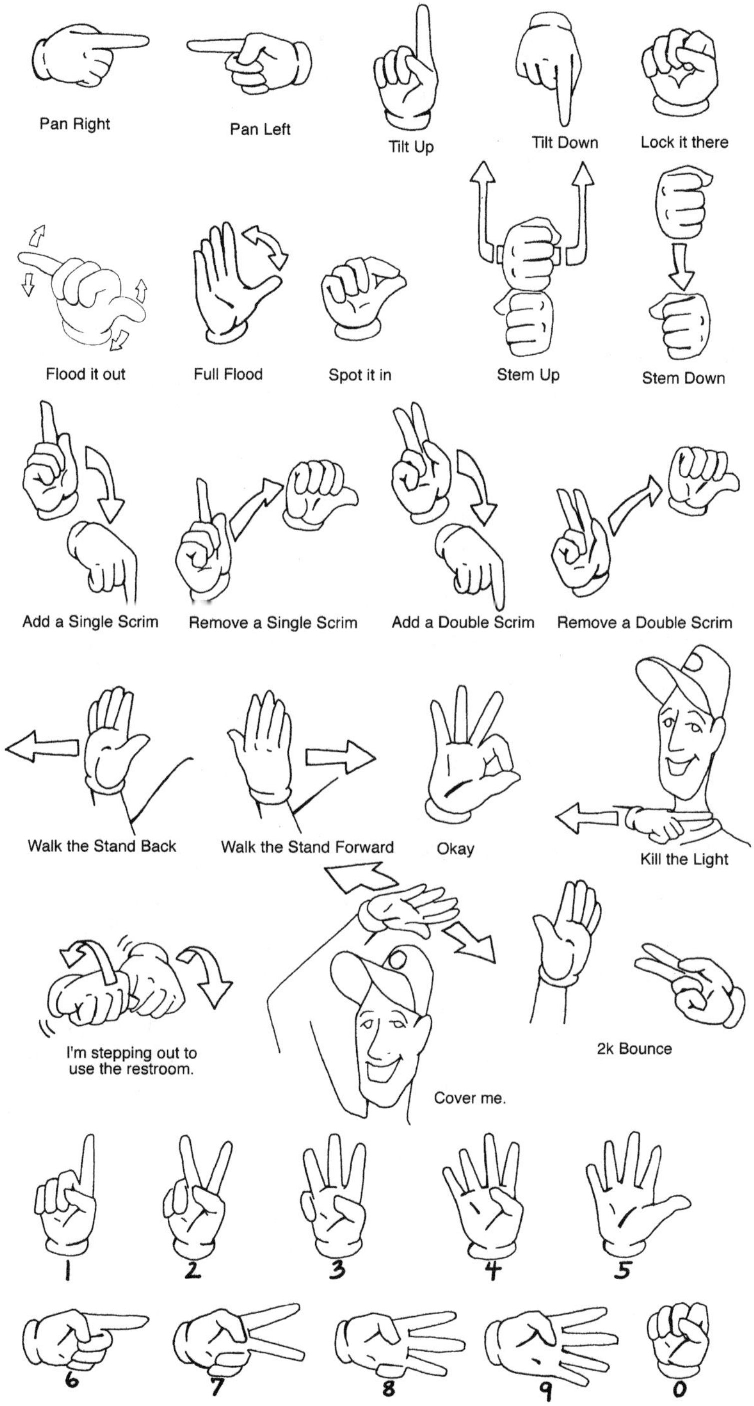

Figure 7.1 Hand signals

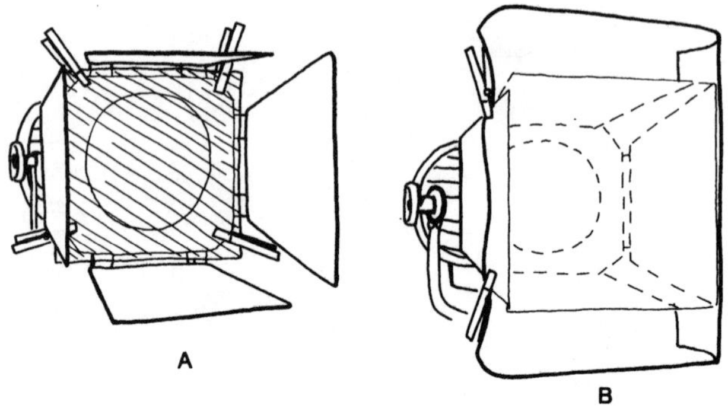

Figure 7.2 Gel and diffusion can be attached either inside the barn doors (A), or outside the doors (B)

Don't be stingy with gel; cut a square of gel big enough so that light does not leak around the side of the gel causing white spill. Placing the gel on the inside of the barn doors (Figure 7.2A) also prevents spill but will put more heat stress on the gel. Generally this works well with Fresnel fixtures when they are flooded out. When using a dense gel, a particularly hot fixture (PAR or open face), or when the lamp is spotted, the gel will lose colour.

Gel frames can be used in some circumstances with some types of fixtures but generally the scrim slot is too hot a place for gel. Never put a scrim next to a gel frame. The hot scrim will melt the gel.

Stingers (extension cables) and cabling

A set can quickly become a rat's nest of tangled cables if care is not taken when running cables and stingers. Here are some guidelines.

Circuit balance and capacity

The best boy electric is responsible for distributing the loads on the cables and the power source so that circuit loads are balanced and cables are operating within their capacities. Each electrician must know the cable layout, know where you can find outlets and keep tabs on the amperage on circuits that are operating near capacity. When balance (between phases) or circuit capacity are critical, keep the best boy abreast of new lights being added. With large lights (5 kW or larger), consult with him as to which circuit should be used before plugging in.

Exceeding the amperage capacity of a wire or plug causes it to heat up and eventually to melt the insulation. A bad connection inside a socket or plug also overheats the insulation. When lights are left on for more than 20 minutes, it is good practice to touch the cables and plugs from time to time to check for overheating. It is normal for cables to run warm, but if they become hot to the touch replace cables as necessary and notify the best boy electric.

If a fuse blows repeatedly, there is something wrong: The circuit is overloaded or there is a short in the light, the plug or the outlet. Redistribute the plugs, add more circuits, repair the short. Do not replace the fuse with an oversized fuse, it will eventually cause a meltdown. It is helpful to tag the plug of 2 kW lights so that you can identify them among the many cords at the outlet box, and keep them on separate circuits.

Cables crossing the set

Keep cables out of the shot and out from underfoot. An electrician rarely runs a cable in a direct line from the power source to the light. Before running the cable, consider the best way to run it. Avoid crossing doorways, especially if there is a chance that the door will work in the scene. Run stingers around the edge of the set. Gaffers often say you can tell a good electrician by the cable you can't see. The most convenient set-up is to have the distribution cables run above the set with power drops in strategic locations. This eliminates a lot of cable running around the set.

Cables crossing work areas

When cable has to cross an area where there is foot traffic, a hallway or doorway, use cable crossovers (Figure 7.3) or put a rubber mat over the cable and tape it securely to the floor with wide gaffer's tape.

If there is a danger of people tripping on the bulge of the mat, put diagonal stripes of yellow tape across it so that it will be noticed. When cables cross an area where vehicles or carts will be moving, the cables should be protected with cable crossovers. Cables for any discharge sources should never be left in vulnerable positions.

Appropriate length

Use appropriate length stinger to reach the light. A '*clothes line cable*', one that is taut and off the floor, is an accident waiting to happen, someone is sure to trip on it. Stingers normally come in lengths of 25 and 50 ft. Use the appropriate length. A rule of thumb for fast identification is as follows: A 25-ft stinger has about seven coils, and a 50-ft stinger has 14. When a light is on a stand, the power cord should fall

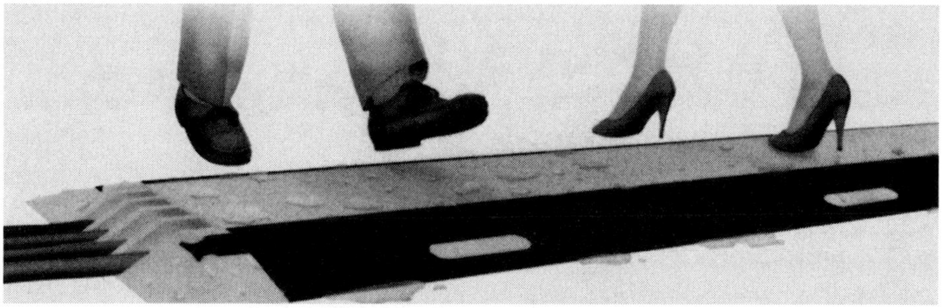

Figure 7.3 Cable crossover. (Photo courtesy of Peterson Systems International, Duarte, CA.)

straight to the ground at the base and have some slack coiled or in a figure eight at the base. Keep excess cable coiled neatly. Place the coil such that if the stand is moved, the cable will pay out from the top of the coil, not from the bottom.

When lights are hung from barrels, be sure to leave two loops of slack cable hanging at the light. If the light later needs to move its position or pan around 180°, you'll need slack to play with. Run the power cable down the barrel to the service, or to the end of the barrel. Tie it to the barrel at intervals with tape or sash cord.

Preventing 'kick-outs'

When connecting two cables, use a stress knot or the cables' tie-rope to hold the connection together (Figure 7.4). This helps prevent a 'kick-out' (accidental unplugging). In the event of a kick-out or 'gap in the line', the electrician must quickly track down the culprit connection. As with everything else on the set, remaining aware of what is happening around you will help you spot kick-outs immediately.

Repatching

You will sometimes need to unplug a light that is in use in order to replace a cable, run power from a different direction or readjust the loads of various circuits. Before you unplug the light, inform the gaffer of the need for a repatch, and as you disconnect it, call out 'Repatch'. This assures everyone that the light has not gone out accidentally. Frequent repatches can be irritating for the gaffer and DP. In many situations it may be best to find another way to solve the problem.

Standby stingers at outlet boxes

To streamline the process of powering lights as they are added, have at least two stingers standing by at each power drop or gang box, coiled and ready to be used.

Labelling stingers and power cords

Labelling cables helps immensely in identifying problems and recabling lights when needed. When a cable runs out of the set through a rat hole, over the top of the set or

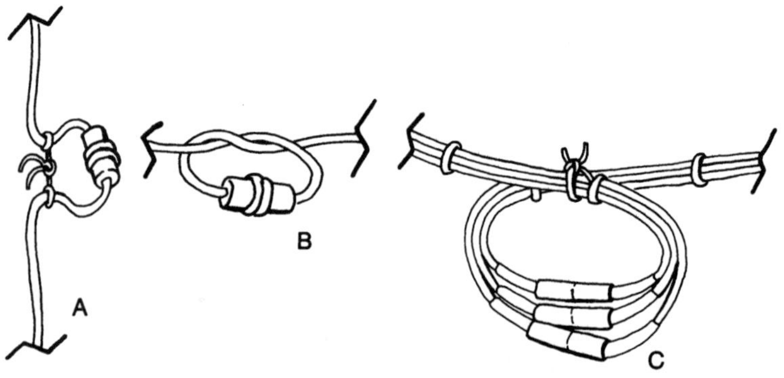

Figure 7.4 When there is danger of an accidental kick-out, use a strain relief. (A) A dangling connection held with the tie-ropes. (B) A simple strain relief for a stinger running along the ground. (C) Banded cable connection point

up into the grid or catwalks above the set, both ends of the cable or stinger should be labelled with tape. Indicate the lights it is powering, for example, '2 kW window light' or 'stair sconces'. Similarly, when using a dimmer board the gang box or female receptacle of the power cord is marked with the channel number. See 'Rules for cabling' in Chapter 9 for notes on labelling and laying out distribution equipment.

When lights are hung from a grid it is helpful to be able to identify each light by number. Label each light so the number is visible to the gaffer on the ground below. Write the numbers large and legible on 2-in. tape on the underside of each unit. Mark the tails (the plugs) with the same numbers. With the lamps numbered, it is easy for the gaffer to communicate what he wants: 'Plug lamps 10, 14 and 18 into the same dimmer and work them on a cue.'

Labelling dimmer settings

When setting a dimmer level, start with the dimmer at line voltage. Say 'line voltage'. The gaffer may then specify a setting to try, 'set it at 90 per cent', or he or she may just say 'lower, lower, lower, good'. Keep telling him or her the level, 'that's 80 per cent, 70 per cent, 60 per cent'. Once it is set, make a mark on tape to indicate the setting. If several settings are used, number them. After the shot is completed, leave these markings on the dimmer, they may be needed again.

Dimmers hum. At close range they will create problems for the sound recordist. The electrician can anticipate this and position dimmers accordingly.

Coiling stingers and cable

All cables and stingers are coiled clockwise. Each loop puts a twist in the cable. When uncoiled it must be allowed to untwist, or it will start to twist on to itself.

The stranded copper wire inside a cable has a natural twist; coiling counterclockwise works against the grain. When a cable is consistently coiled in the same manner each time it is used, the cable becomes 'trained' to coil that way. A trained cable will coil easily. If a cable is coiled different ways with each use, it becomes confused and unmanageable.

The over and under method shown in Figure 7.5 is used for coaxial cable, dimmer control cables and audio cable. Every other loop counteracts the twist so the cable can be unravelled without twists. Using the occasional underhand loop sometimes makes a cord more co-operative.

Small lamps, practicals

Types of lamps

Photoflood lamps and PH lamps

Photoflood lamps are colour-balanced for use in photography (3,200 K, 3,400 K and 4,800 K) and come in various wattages. They are often used in table lamps and suspended China-hat practicals. Higher wattage photofloods are often used in soft boxes, Chinese lanterns, and scoop lights such as Smith Victor lights. Most

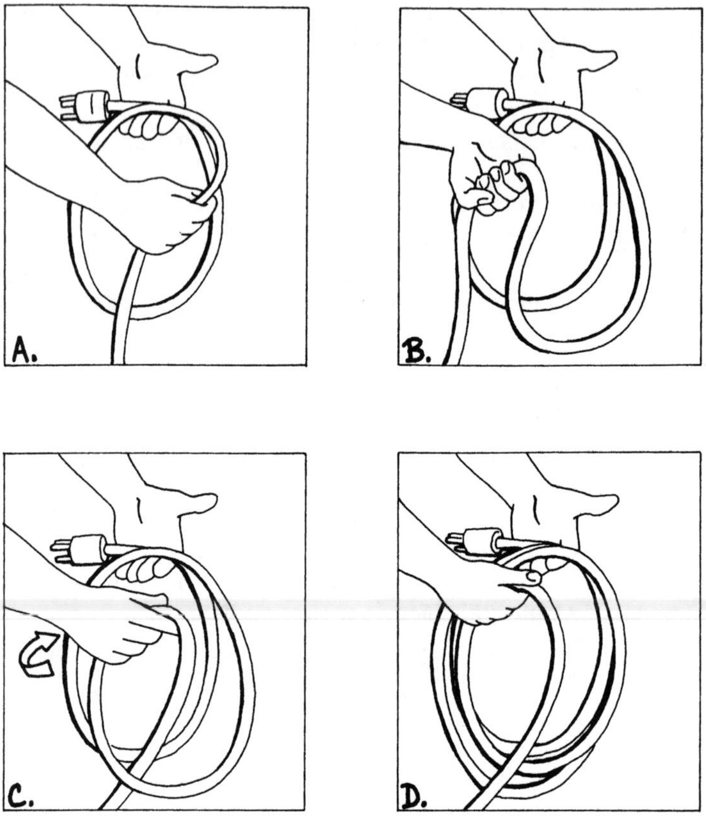

Figure 7.5 The over-under method of coiling control cables: (A) Start with a normal loop. (B, C) Give the second loop a twist to the inside. (D) Make the next loop normal. Alternate back and forth between a normal loop and a twisted loop

photoflood lamps burn very hot and have a short life, in order to provide the high colour temperature.

Household lamps

A selection of low-wattage household lamps, 15 W, 25 W, 40 W, 60 W, is handy for making practicals glow without being overly bright. A household lamp's colour temperature falls between 2,600 K and 2,900 K, which appears yellow on film. If the colour shift is objectionable, it can be removed with CTB gel. Alternatively, the DP may add ¼ CTO to the artificial lights to match the warmth of the practicals. The colour shift can be removed in the lab or with the use of a blue filter on the lens (Kodak 82 series, see Table G.8 in Appendix G). In many instances a warm colour shift is appropriate for the scene; for example, lamps naturally appear slightly warm, and the DP leaves it.

Candela-base lamps

Some candelabra wall sconces and chandeliers take candela-base lamps; this is something to check during location scouts. The lamps, usually low wattage, and are around 2,600 K. Round make-up table lamps (40 W and 60 W) are small, soft, very warm (2,600 to 2,700 K) lamps that can be grouped to make an inexpensive, soft glow-light.

Mushroom floods, R-40 and others

Flood and spot lights of the mushroom-shaped variety incorporate a silver reflector inside the lamp for better output and throw. Common wattages are 75 W, 150 W, 300 W and 500 W (EAL). Tungsten 3,200 K lamps are available in 200 W, 300 W, 375W and 500 W wattage (see Table E.1 in Appendix E). The rest fall between 2,800 K and 2,900 K. The R-40 size is the most commonly used. A Lowel K-5 kit includes sockets, mounting bracket and barn doors that snug on to the front of an R-40 lamp. There are a wide variety of other reflector lamps. The size is indicated by the number; for example, in R-40/FL, R stands for reflector and 40 is the size in eighths of an inch (40/8 = 5 in.). FL indicates flood. Smaller R-30 and R-20 lamps are great for track lighting, lighting wall art at close range.

MR-16

MR-16 lamps are tungsten halogen projector lamps with a 2-in. parabolic reflector. They are 3,200 K and very bright. They are now commonly used in track-lighting fixtures. They come in a variety of wattages, voltages, and reflector types. The track-lighting type is 12 V, uses a transformer, and has a GX-5.3 base, shown in Figure E.1 (Appendix E). The tiny size, brightness, and colour temperature of MR-16s make them a very useful lamp for making small pools of light.

Linestra tubes

These are incandescent tube-shaped lamps 12, 20 or 40 in. long and 3/4 in. diameter. Their colour temperature is 2,800 K. They are very lightweight, and can be attached with tape or bailing wire. They are used in sets, lighting shelving, for example.

Fluorescent lamps

The most common types of practical fluorescent lamps you will encounter are T-8 (bi-pin) in the UK and Europe and T-12 (bi-pin) or Slim-line (single pin) in the USA. Tubes commonly come in 8-ft, 6-ft, 5-ft, 4-ft, 3-ft and 2-ft sizes. These lamps can be easily replaced with High CRI tubes. Older desk lamps sometimes take small T-5 tubes.

Controlling practicals

It is standard practice to put practical lamps on dimmers so that their intensity can be easily adjusted. However, there are other ways to dim a lamp that do not alter the colour temperature. Spraying the lamp with a light speckle of black streaks and tips is a fast way to reduce the lamp's intensity. (Don't spray a hot lamp, it will burst.) Sometimes you will only want to reduce brightness in one direction. This can be done by spraying one side and not the other. Holding a lighter close to the lamp and letting the carbon build up on the lamp is another way to dim it. The carbon wipes off more easily than streaks and tips. Placing diffusion on the inside of the lamp shade and installing ND gel around the lamp are also ways to dim a practical.

Light cues

Hand cue

If an actor turns a wall switch on or off during a scene, the wall switch can be wired to a relay which activates a remote contactor (such as in a deuce board) that controls the set lights. On location it is often necessary for an electrician to perform the lighting cue with a dimmer or switch when the actor reaches for the light switch. The electrician must position him or herself somewhere out of the way and out of the shot, but where he or she can see the action to hit the cue. Experienced actors help sell the cue by covering the switch with their hand so that the camera does not see the exact moment that the switch flips.

Switch-over

In a night scene, when an actor turns off a bedroom light and the room goes dark, the lighting must switch from practical sources to moonlight or exterior sources. Darkness is commonly simulated by underexposed, blue, directionless lighting. The transition may require a switch-over in which some lights are turned off and others are turned on in the instant that the actor turns off the lights. The problem is that the time required for one group of filaments to dim and the other group to heat up prevents the switch-over from being instantaneous, and the audience can see the new lights coming on. Some special techniques can be helpful to sell the switch-over.

One solution is to have the night group on the whole time. Unfortunately, this can look false because the moonlight appears to be as bright as the light in the room, and the blue colour of the night group discolours the lamplight. However, if the change happens before any of this becomes too noticeable, this can be a workable solution. If the scene ends with the lights turning off, the blue group can be kept very low so as not to distract for the bulk of the scene.

If the scene carries on in darkness after the lights go off and the actors must be visible in the dark, then a special transition is needed. Here is a clever way to handle this transition: Keep the night group on throughout the scene, but at levels that are one and a half to two stops below the lamplight. This will look natural. When the interior light is turned off, begin to open the camera aperture on a slow 5-second change. The effect is similar to that of the human eye adjusting to the dark. Additionally, the audience's eyes will be adjusting to the new light level, which hides the aperture change.

Wiring small fixtures

Practical lamps

On any interior set, the art department will provide practical sources: table lamps, wall sconces, floor lamps, desk lamps, china hats or a chandelier, for example. Each time you begin shooting on a new set, one of the first things to take care of is the wiring and testing of practicals, and changing the lamps as desired by the gaffer.

Practical outlets

A well-made set will have practical wall outlets. These are very convenient for plugging in practical, set dressing appliances (a toaster, for example) and small lights. These wall outlets will be supplied by short lengths of cable fitted with an appropriate plug and connected to a dedicated circuit (13 A).

Lamp repair

When a lamp fails, be sure to label the light so that it doesn't get brought back on to the set by mistake. Put an X across the lens with 1-in. tape, and write 'NG' (no good) or 'BO' (burned out) on it. If you know what is wrong with the light, write that on it also (for example, blown lamp, bad switch, bad plug).

Common repairs include changing the lamp, replacing the power switch or plug, reconnecting the power cord to the head, repairing the flood-spot mechanism and cleaning corroded contacts with contact cleaner. Most lights are not too complicated and can easily be repaired if replacement parts can be obtained. Before starting any type of repair, double-check that the fixture is disconnected from the power. If time allows, the best boy simply has new equipment delivered in exchange for the broken equipment.

Safety

You don't have to work on sets long before you see that in a rush people can forget their common sense. This is how people get hurt and equipment gets broken. Make safe work practices habitual, and you will avoid needless injuries, especially when working under pressure. Work swiftly but never run.

Ladders

When working with suspended lights, you must often work from a ladder. If the ladder seems at all shaky, have someone hold it and spot you at the bottom of the ladder. Use the appropriate size of ladder. Don't use the top step. Don't stretch to reach a light that is too far from the ladder; instead, get a taller ladder or climb down and move the ladder you have.

Two people often need to work from two sides of the same ladder when rigging two lights very close together. When you step on to someone's ladder, say 'On your ladder', and when you step off again, say 'Off your ladder'.

Parallels (scaffold platforms)

Parallels are quite frequently used as a lighting platform. They are quick and easy to assemble and, if used with proper caution, can be safe. However, caution is the watchword. Almost any veteran electrician can tell you a story about an accident involving parallels.

Parallels must be set on level ground or be levelled with levelling jacks. On uneven ground it can be hard to tell what is level; a plumb line or bubble level should be used. A leaning parallel is an accident waiting to happen. Be sure that weight is distributed evenly on the platform, especially when people are climbing or lifting equipment up to the platform. Use bodies as counterweight when necessary. Never mount lights outside the perimeter of the railing.

Large light stands should be strapped down to the platform. Ratchet straps and nylon webbing are ideal, although chain or rope can do the trick if properly used. Remember to take account of the force of the wind blowing on 4-by frames. Tie guy lines to the yoke or stand when needed. Tie the power cable to a vertical post on the platform, leaving plenty of slack to manoeuvre the light.

Working at heights

Anytime you work at a height, on a ladder, greens, catwalk, parallels or truss, remove your tool belt. Tie any tools you need to your belt. If you do drop something, yell a warning, such as 'Heads up', 'Headache', or just 'Look out below!' Dropping a tool from the catwalks can get you kicked off a studio lot.

Remember to bring a tag-line so you can hoist equipment up as you need it. The tag-line should be tied off at the top end so that it cannot fall. Call 'Line out' before you toss down the line. When you toss an item up to a worker, call 'Airmail' to alert the people around you; then if the catcher misses, no one gets cracked on the head.

Protecting floors

Protecting the floor becomes a concern when shooting in a private home or in a set where the floors might be scratched by metal stands. A number of precautions can be taken. One is to put crutch tips on the feet of each stand. Tape the rubber tips in place with gaffer's tape. A stock of crutch tips should be ordered in advance after the location is initially scouted.

Layout board (1/4 in. hard cardboard that comes in 4×8 ft sheets) can provide a protective covering over the floor. It is usually laid out over the entire area and taken up wherever it will be seen in the camera's frame. A more temporary substitute is a furniture pad placed under the stand.

Sprinkler systems

With the fire marshal's permission, make a practice of putting Styrofoam cups over sprinkler heads to insulate them from the heat of the lights. In the category of big blunders, few are more conspicuous than activating the emergency sprinkler system and dousing the actors and sets in water. Placing a hot light too close to a sprinkler head can easily melt the soft alloy valve that normally holds back the flood. There is no way to stop an activated head from flowing once it has started, and the water in the pipes will continue to drain through for hours even if the sprinkler system is immediately turned off at the source.

Smoke, fire and other bad smells

Lights get very hot and can easily start a fire. Common sense and proper care are essential to the prevention of accidents. In the event of a small fire, a quick electrician may be able to smother the flames with gloved hands or with a furniture pad. Know where the fire extinguishers are situated.

An electrician with a good nose and good eyes can detect a potential fire before it becomes serious. If you smell smoke, don't cause a panic, but let the other electricians and grips know so they can help look for the source. The smell of burning wood may be caused by a toasting clothespeg or a light placed too close to a wooden set piece. The smell of burning plastic or rubber may be traced to smouldering insulation on a cable connection or in-line switch. An overheated stinger is a common offender. Check the lights for burning gel or diffusion, or smoking flags or nets. Check the set walls and ceiling for bubbling or smouldering paint. On DC stages, keep your nose open for the sharp, metallic-burning smell of an arcing paddle connector. When a paddle comes partially unplugged it will arc, which eventually burns up the contacts on the plugging box. Keep looking until you find the source of the smell. The problem may be something obscure, such as burning Bakelite plastic in a defective deuce board.

A smoking light is usually the result of some foreign matter getting into the light and burning up. Dusty lights will often smoke for a short time when they are first turned on. Moths are relentless kamikazes. They will keep an open-face fixture smoking all night as they bake themselves one after another. Outside in a ventilated area this does not pose a danger to anyone but the moths. Inside, though, it may be necessary to turn off a smoking light and clean it out. Sometimes the only way to clean the light is just to let the substance burn off. For example, after a light is repainted, it should be taken outside and turned on for 10 or 15 minutes until it stops smoking.

The wrap

When filming is completed at a given location, all the equipment has to be packed back into the van. It may take two or three hours when a lot of equipment is in use. Especially after a long day, it is everyone's dearest wish to get the van packed as quickly as possible and get home. It is one of the best boy's responsibilities to begin the wrap early and have as much of it done as possible before the actual wrap is called. Early in the day, the best boy organizes the removal of superfluous equipment

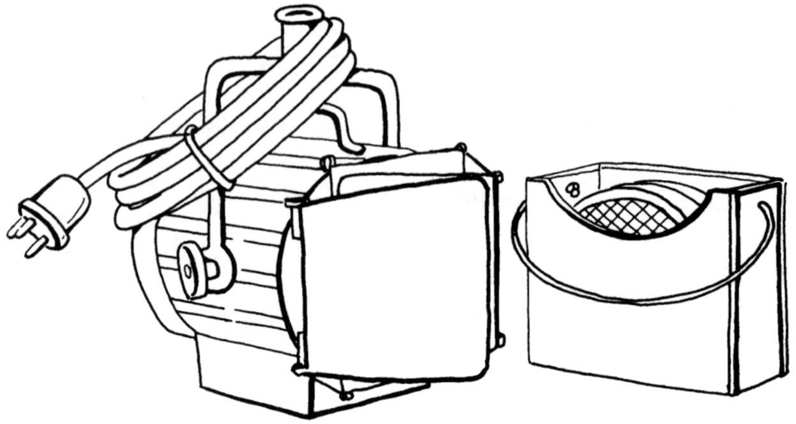

Figure 7.6 A properly wrapped light. Some electricians prefer to tuck the cable inside the yoke to prevent it from getting caught on other equipment

from the set, and the coiling of cable that will no longer be needed. Once the last set-up is lit, any equipment not in use should be stowed and ready to drive away.

When wrap is called, lights are switched off and the equipment starts coming back to the van. I find it works best if the best boy remains at the van and packs the equipment as it is brought to the lift gate by the electricians. This avoids equipment getting piled up at the gate.

Wrapped lights should look like the one shown in Figure 7.6. The yoke is swivelled up over the top of the light. The power cord is coiled, tied, and hung over the yoke. The barn doors are shut. Scrims, diffusion and gel have been removed and returned to the scrim and gel boxes. Spreader lenses are removed from PAR lights. The lamps should be removed from larger lights (12 kW and 18 kW HMIs) before travel.

Coiling feeder cable

The fastest way to coil feeder cable is to stand with your legs apart and coil in a clockwise circle on the ground. With a little practice you can get into a rhythm, pulling the cable towards you with one hand, then the other, guiding it into a coil. If you are fighting the natural twist of the cable, the coil will not want to lie flat, and the unnatural twist will age the cable. The ideal size for a coil is tight enough not to be floppy and unmanageable, but not so tight and tall that it becomes impossible to stack. Use the tie strings to secure both ends firmly. Loose ends tend to swing around and hit people and generally get in the way. Lift with your knees, not with your back. Never jump down (off the lift gate for example) with heavy cable on your shoulder. You will know as soon as you do it that it was a mistake. Your knees and ankles may never forgive you.

Inventory

The best boy conducts an equipment inventory as he loads. If each shelf has been labelled with the type and quantity of lights it holds, this process is quite straightforward. Bungy off each shelf as soon as it is complete; this helps you keep track of what is still missing, and once all the shelves are filled the van is ready to go without further delay. Putting each light in its proper place is not just a matter of organization, it can be crucial to fitting everything on the van. Before leaving any location, someone should make an idiot check of the set, looking in each area where lights were placed during filming.

8
Electricity

Units of measurement and their fundamental relationships

The four basic units of electrical measurement are:

- amperes (current)
- volts (electromotive force)
- watts (power)
- ohms (resistance).

To understand these units and how they relate, it is helpful to use the analogy of the flow of water from a water tank through a hose. Before we begin to explore this analogy, we must first introduce one more unit of electricity, the coulomb. The coulomb can be thought of as a specific quantity of electrical power, in the same way that a gallon is a specific quantity of liquid. Don't try to imagine how much a coulomb is; just remember that it is a quantity of electricity.

Rate of flow: current

When water flows through a hose running from a tank of water, the size of the hose determines how much water will flow in a given amount of time (Figure 8.1). We measure this rate of flow in gallons per minute. In an electrical circuit, the rate of flow of electricity from a battery or generator is measured in coulombs per second, commonly known as amperes, or amps (A) for short. One coulomb per second equals one ampere. The volume of electricity per second is called the current (also known as amperage).

Pressure of flow: voltage

When water flows out of a drinking fountain, it is under a small amount of pressure and rises in a small arc. If the same amount of water is delivered under high pressure, because of a clogged fountain spigot for example, it shoots high into the air,

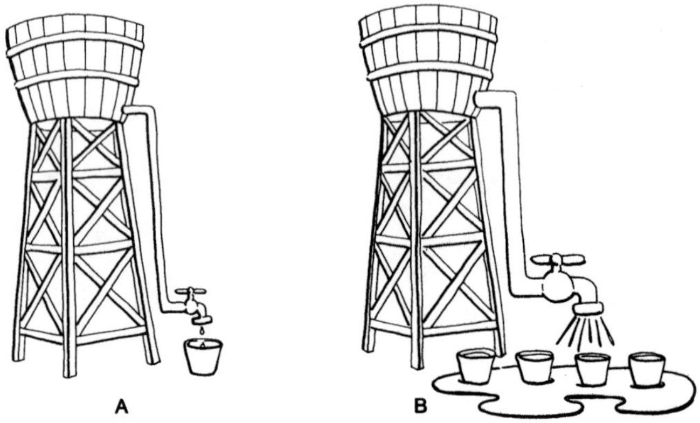

Figure 8.1 Amperage is analogous to the rate of flow

goes up your nose or hits you in the eye. In the water tank example, the height of the tank above the ground determines the water pressure in the hose (Figure 8.2).

A water tank raised 100 ft in the air provides ten times the pressure (in pounds per square inch) as that same tank when it is 10 ft off the ground.

The pressure under which electricity is delivered is called the voltage (V). A torch operates on 1.5 V, a car battery at 12 V, and a wall socket at 120 V in America and 240 volts in the UK. Voltage is the force with which current is pushed through a resistance.

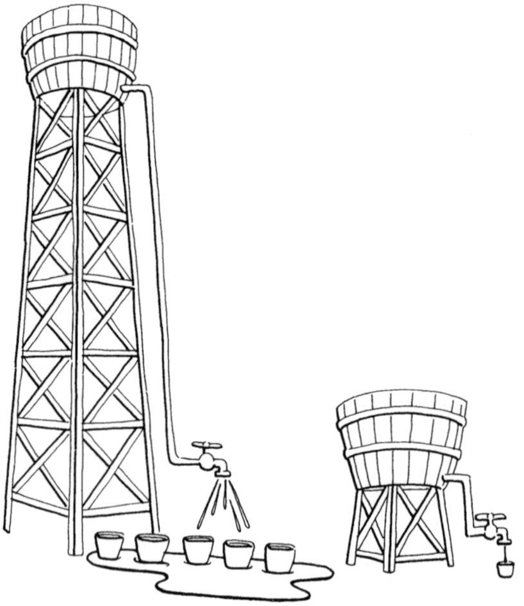

Figure 8.2 Voltage is analogous to the pressure of flow

Another way to think of voltage is as the difference in potential energy between two points in a circuit. The potential energy of the water in the tank is proportional to its height above the tap at the end of the hose, the difference in their heights. When we measure voltage with a voltmeter, we read the difference in voltage potential between the live wire and the neutral wire, or between two phases.

Work: wattage

Returning to the water tank analogy, the amount of water flowing from the tank at any one moment is the product of flow rate and pressure. The size of the pipe and the height of the tank together determine the total amount of water that will flow from the tank.

The total amount of useful electrical power being delivered at any one moment is measured in watts. The wattage is the product of the amperage (flow rate) and the voltage (pressure). Wattage is the measure of the amount of work being done in any one instant. It is the same idea as horsepower; in fact, 746 W = 1 horsepower. Wattage can be thought of as total power output; in the case of lighting fixtures, wattage directly corresponds to the light output.

For the purpose of billing, the power company's meter counts the electricity consumed in kilowatt-hours (abbreviated kWh). (As we have already established, one kilowatt is 1,000 W, abbreviated 1 kW or simply 1 k.) The wattage being used at any given time is reflected in the speed at which the disc in the meter is turning. Kilowatt-hours measure the total amount of electrical power consumed over a given amount of time, and is calculated from the rate at which power is consumed in kilowatts, multiplied by the hours that power is consumed at that rate.

The power equation

Watts are mathematically related to volts and amps as follows:

$$\text{watts} = \text{volts} \times \text{amps}$$

Electricians use this important equation frequently when making load calculations. An easy way to remember it is to think of West Virginia (W = VA).

There are other ways to state the same relationship:

$$\text{volts} = \frac{\text{watts}}{\text{amps}}$$

$$\text{amps} = \frac{\text{watts}}{\text{volts}}$$

To give an example of how both amperage and voltage contribute to the wattage, consider two 60 W bulbs: a household bulb and a car headlight. The household bulb runs on 240 V (in the UK) and pulls a current of 0.25 A . The car headlight uses a 12 V battery but pulls electricity at a rate of 5 A. The total power consumed is the same for the 60 W household bulb and the 60 W car headlight:

Household bulb (UK): 240 V × 0.25 A = 60 W

Household bulb (USA): 120 V × 0.5 A = 60 W

Car headlight: 12 V × 5 A = 60 W

In formulas, voltage, wattage, amperage and resistance are represented by the symbols E, W, I and R, respectively.[1] The relationship between these four forces can be stated numerous ways. All the possible permutations are shown in the formulas wheel (Figure 8.3).

The magic circles illustrated in Figure 8.4 provide an easy way to use these two equations.

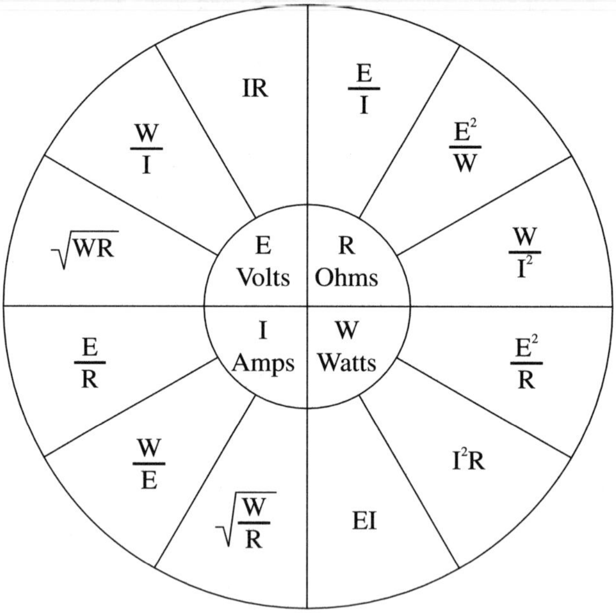

Figure 8.3 The formulas wheel gives every permutation of the relationships between voltage, amperage, wattage, and resistance. (Reprinted with permission from Paul Carter, *Backstage Handbook* [New York: Broadway Press, 1988].)

1. P is also commonly used as an abbreviation for power. W (watts) will be used in this book.

Calculating the current of luminaires

To calculate the current drawn by a given luminaire, divide the lamp's wattage by the line voltage. For example, for a 1 kW light operating at 230V, we make the following calculation:

$$\frac{\text{watts}}{\text{volts}} = \text{amps}$$

$$\frac{1000\text{ W}}{230\text{ V}} = 4.3\text{ A}$$

Table 8.1 gives the amperage of a variety of luminaires for various voltage systems.

Table 8.1 Amperage of luminaires of various wattages

Wattage of lamp	*Voltage system* 240 V	230 V	220 V	120 V	30 V	12 V
100	0.42 A	0.43 A	0.45 A	0.83 A	3.33 A	8.33 A
200	0.83 A	0.87 A	0.91 A	1.67 A	6.67 A	16.67 A
300	1.25 A	1.30 A	1.36 A	2.50 A	10.00 A	25.00 A
400	1.67 A	1.74 A	1.82 A	3.33 A	13.33 A	33.33 A
500	2.08 A	2.17 A	2.27 A	4.17 A	16.67 A	41.67 A
650	2.71 A	2.83 A	2.95 A	5.42 A	21.67 A	54.17 A
750	3.13 A	3.26 A	3.41 A	6.25 A	25.00 A	62.50 A
1,000	4.17 A	4.35 A	4.55 A	8.33 A	33.33 A	83.33 A
1,500	6.25 A	6.52 A	6.82 A	12.50 A		
2,000	8.33 A	8.70 A	9.09 A	16.67 A		
3,000	12.50 A	13.04 A	13.64 A	25.00 A		
4,000	16.67 A	17.39 A	18.18 A	33.33 A		
5,000	20.83 A	21.74 A	22.73 A	41.67 A		
6,000	25.00 A	26.09 A	27.27 A	50.00 A		
8,000	33.33 A	34.78 A	36.36 A	66.67 A		
9,000	37.50 A	39.13 A	40.91 A	75.00 A		
10,000	41.67 A	43.48 A	45.45 A	83.33 A		
12,000	50.00 A	52.17 A	54.55 A	100.00 A		
20,000	83.33 A	86.96 A	90.91 A			

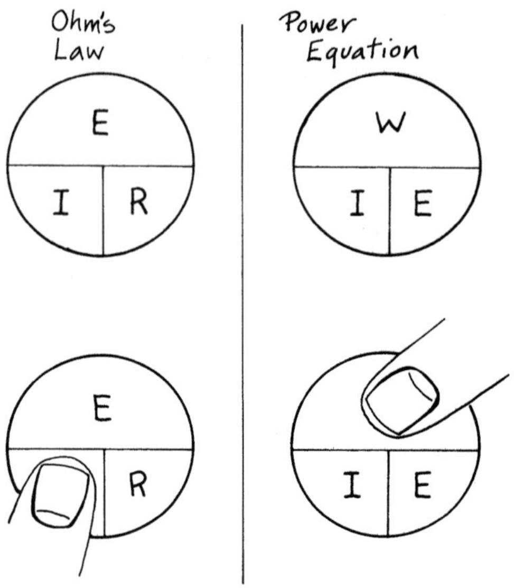

Figure 8.4 A simple way to remember the most common of the formulas in Figure 8.3 is to use 'magic circles'. On either of the circles shown, cover the symbol you want to find with your finger. The relationship that remains is the formula. For example, to determine amperage (I) from a known resistance (R) and voltage (E), put your finger on the I, and read E divided by R. To determine wattage (W) from amperage and voltage, put your finger over the W, and read I times E

Resistance and Ohm's Law

So far we have a mental picture of a lamp operating at the UK standard 240 volts and drawing current (amps) in order to generate a particular wattage output. However, this is an incomplete picture of the forces acting on a circuit. What prevents an ambitious 60 W light bulb from drawing more current and becoming a 600 W light bulb? The force we are missing is resistance. Understanding resistance and how it relates to power and current gives a much clearer picture of the forces at work in a circuit.

Resistance is the opposition to the flow of current created by the load put on the circuit by the fixtures plugged into it, and by the resistance of the wires themselves. Resistance is measured in ohms, which is abbreviated as the Greek letter omega (Ω).

The resistance of a particular conductor or lamp filament can be considered constant[2] determined by its physical properties and construction. The resistance of the

2. The resistance of a piece of wire is constant at a given temperature. Any metal has less resistance at a lower temperature; as temperature increases, so does resistance. With tungsten this effect is very pronounced – when cold it has very little resistance but when heated it has very high resistance. As a result, tungsten lights have high inrush current with a cold start. Once at operating temperature, however, resistance is constant. In contrast, the resistance of copper changes little with temperature.

filament limits the amperage that can be pushed through it by a particular voltage, and therefore determines its ultimate output in watts.

Ohm's Law

Ohm's Law can be stated three ways:

$$I = \frac{E}{R} \qquad \text{amps} = \frac{\text{volts}}{\text{resistance}}$$

$$R = \frac{E}{I} \qquad \text{resistance} = \frac{\text{volts}}{\text{amps}}$$

or

$$E = I \times R \qquad \text{volts} = \text{amps} \times \text{resistance}$$

I = E/R calculates the amperage drawn by a particular load, knowing the line voltage and the load's resistance. To see how this equation works, we'll use it to illustrate the dramatic effect of line loss. All conductors, such as cable, have resistance. In a long length of cable, the resistance causes a perceptible drop in voltage from source to load because resistance turns some power into heat in the cables. This is known as *line loss*. Looking at I = E/R, we can see that if voltage decreases (due to line loss), the amperage will also decrease. We can calculate that if the voltage is reduced to 216 V (on a 240 V system), a 2,000 W load (normally 8.3 A, 28.8 Ω), will only draw 7.5 A:

$$I = \frac{E}{R} \quad \frac{216\ \text{V}}{28.8\ \Omega} = 7.5\ \text{A}$$

The total power output of the load is down to 1,620 W:

$$W = E \times I \qquad 216\ \text{V} \times 7.5\ \text{A} = 1620\ \text{W}$$

A 2 kW light only operates at full efficiency at its rated voltage. Operating at 216 V (90 per cent of its rated voltage) the 2 kW will in fact only produce about 72 per cent of its normal light output. That's one weak 2 kW, a 28 per cent loss of output caused by a 10 per cent loss of voltage. Light output decreases dramatically with line loss.

Resistance of a luminare

Ohm's Law, stated as R = E/I, can be used to calculate the resistance of a load (a lamp). The resistance of a particular load can be calculated by dividing its rated voltage (at full) by the amperage. For example, a 5 kW bulb (rated 5,000 W at 240 V) pulls 20.83 A. The resistance of the lamp can be calculated as

$$\frac{240\ \text{V}}{20.83\ \text{A}} = 11.52\ \Omega$$

Resistance of cable

The resistance of a particular length of cable is equal to the voltage drop in the cable divided by the amperage running through it. If there is a 4 V drop in a length of cable carrying a 40 A load, the resistance of that length of cable is

$$\text{ohms} = \frac{\text{volts}}{\text{amps}} \qquad R = \frac{E}{I} \qquad \frac{4\ \text{V}}{40\ \text{A}} = 0.1\Omega$$

Line loss

The (UK) IEE Regulations state that the voltage drop should not exceed 4 per cent of the nominal voltage i.e. 9.2 V in a 230 V system, or 9.6 V in a 240 V system.

You can anticipate there will be significant line loss any time there is a fairly long run of cable and the cable is being loaded near its maximum rating. Table C.1 (in Appendix C) gives voltage drop per 100 ft for various cables.

The three variables that affect the amount of line loss are length, wire thickness and amperage load. Remember these three principles:

1. The resistance of a conductor increases directly with its length. The longer the run, the greater the line loss.
2. The resistance of a conductor decreases in proportion to its cross-sectional area. The larger the conductor, the less the line loss.
3. Voltage drop varies directly with the load. The larger the amperage load, the larger the line loss.

To overcome the line loss, the generator operator will often simply increase the voltage at the generator so that the voltage on the set is correct. However, if you increase the voltage at the generator to overcome line loss, keep two things in mind. First, if equipment is being powered at the upstream end of the cable run (such as the producer's trailer at base camp), the upstream equipment will be over voltage (the producer's computer is toast). Secondly, voltage drop is proportional to amperage load. When the amperage load is reduced significantly, voltage must be turned down at the generator to prevent any remaining lights from being over voltage. If a lot of big lights are suddenly turned off, the voltage will jump up and the remaining load is over voltage (the sound desk is toast). To avoid these problems, it is necessary to minimize line loss by increasing the conductor size.

Effects of line loss and low voltage

If line loss results in low voltage at the set, it causes a number of serious problems for the operation of lights. As we have already discussed, light output falls off dramatically as the voltage decreases. The dramatic loss of output was shown in our earlier example.

Additionally, as the light intensity decreases, so does the colour temperature of the emitted light. As the intensity decreases, the colour goes from white to yellow to orange. However, colour temperature falls much less sharply than the light output which is one of the reasons we can dim lights over a reasonable range without too many problems. It should be borne in mind that in our example the line loss to the 2 kW lamp was 24 volts which is 115 K, about 12 MIREDs.

One final reason why it is important to keep line loss within reasonable tolerances is that a loss of voltage also translates into a loss of power. From the equation $W = I^2R$, we see that the power loss in a given cable increases as the square of the amperage. If you double the ampere load on the cable, the voltage drop will also double, but the power loss will increase fourfold. The power source has to work harder, burning more fuel, or more kilovolt-amperes, because it is using power overcoming the resistance of the cables in addition to running the lights. The performance of the generator, its maximum effective load, is reduced.

Other causes of line loss

Line loss also occurs when a connection is weak or loose, when a cable is frayed, when a connector is only partially inserted and when a connector or conductor is loaded beyond its capacity. Each of these situations creates a hot spot in the cable and connector, which further degrades the insulation. Circular coils in a single-conductor, current-carrying cable create impedance, resulting in line loss and increased heating. Good set practices, such as checking for good contact between connectors, taping connectors, avoiding circular coils of cable and replacing overheating parts, help rid you of the annoyance of inexplicable line loss and melted connectors.

Line loss calculations

The figures in Table C.1 (Appendix C) were calculated using Ohm's Law: $E = IR$. Using Ohm's Law, we can calculate the thickness of cable needed to limit the voltage drop to a selected percentage, the distance a particular cable can carry a known amperage, or the exact voltage drop for a particular cable.

We can calculate the theoretical line loss in any cable by inserting the resistance of the cable into Ohm's Law: voltage drop = amperes × ohms.

Table 8.2 Cable voltage drops

Typical current rating	*Conductor size*	*Type*	*Millivolt drop per meter per amp*	*Number of current-carrying wires in insulation*
16 A	2.5 mm^2	Copper	19	2
45 A	6.0 mm^2	Copper	7.7	2
125 A	25 mm^2	Copper	1.7	2
180 A	120 mm^2	Copper	0.46	2
400 A	185 mm^2	Copper	0.27	1 (short runs)
400 A	240 mm^2	Aluminium	0.45	1 (long runs)

The resistance of copper cable in ohms per 100 ft is given in Table C.2 (Appendix C).

In the UK the method of determining volt drop is as follows. The IEE and the cable manufacturers produce tables which give the volt drop in millivolts per ampere per metre. Different figures are given to take account of single- and three-phase systems together with allowances for 'impedance' losses. The tables give the total volt drop in all the circuit conductors for each metre of cable route. The values given assume the maximum operating temperature of the cables. In most practical cases the volt drop will be less because the cables will probably not be at full capacity and the conductor temperatures will not be at maximum rating, therefore, the resistance will be lower than that given in Table 8.2.

For example: two 120 mm^2 feeder cables, rated for 85°C, used as a phase and neutral are taken 200 metres from a generator to a distribution point. The volt drop for this cable is given as 0.46 mV/A/m. If we assume the cables are loaded to 180 amps the volt drop will be

$$0.46 \times 180 \times 200 = 16{,}560 \text{ millivolts} = 16.56 \text{ volts}$$

British regulations require that the volt drop should be no greater than 4 per cent, in most cases, which amounts to 9.6 volts on a 240 volt system. As can be seen the above value will not be acceptable, therefore either a larger conductor size, or parallel feeders would have to be used.

Overcurrent protection

From Ohm's Law (R = E/I), you can see that the higher the amperage flowing through a fixture, the lower the resistance in the circuit, and conversely, the lower the resistance of a fixture, the more amperage is allowed to flow. But what happens if there is no resistance? If you create a dead short by touching the two wires together, the uninhibited current flow rapidly increases to the maximum available from the power source, which may be thousands of amps. The amperage in the circuit becomes extremely high, far beyond the amperage capacity of the cables. The wires heat up, burn and melt (quite possibly setting the building on fire) or, if the amperage is high enough, will vaporize the cables in a matter of seconds. Overcurrent protection is needed for this reason.

An overcurrent device (a fuse or circuit breaker) cuts off power to the circuit if the current exceeds a specified limit. The amperage capacity of cables used downstream of the overcurrent device should be greater than the amperage capacity of the overcurrent device. Thus, circuit protection is designed to prevent the possibility of thermal meltdown from an overloaded or shorted circuit.

Fuses and circuit breakers

There are two functions required from the protective devices we use, one of which they will protect for normal overload conditions, such as lamps failing or incorrectly plugged luminaires creating too much current on a circuit. In addition, the devices have to be adequately rated so that they safely stand fault currents caused by short circuits.

The wiring going from the switchgear to the distribution units and dimmer racks has to be protected by either fuses or some form of circuit breaker. Before we go any further it would perhaps be wise to look at the magnitude of currents that flow from the main switchgear to the dimmer racks. In a fairly straightforward simple installation using packs of 6 × 2.5 kW dimmers, each pack connected to 240 V single phase, would consume 62.5 A on full load. At the other end of the scale, if we were using 192 5 kW dimmers, spread over three phases (240 V), we would have 1,333 A per phase on full load.

If we placed a piece of wire across a 240 V supply and switch on, the wire disappears rather quickly. By using a simple bit of Ohm's Law it will soon be realized that the current is governed by the resistance of the piece of wire and if the piece of wire does not have much resistance the current can become quite large. For example, if a piece of wire with a resistance of 0.01 Ω is placed across a 240 V supply, the current flowing through the piece of wire would be 24,000 A and this is called the fault current. It is obvious that with a current flow of this magnitude, unless we are using an enormously thick piece of wire, the wire would actually vaporize and thus fuse. In practice we wouldn't just be concerned with a piece of wire across the 240 V supply, because in addition to the resistance of the wire is the resistance of all the cables feeding the point where the wire is inserted in the circuit. Thus, the nearer we are to the point of supply the greater will be the fault current. On the input to the main we can get very high fault currents indeed. If, however, the fault occurs at the end of a 100 metres of cable run the fault current will be relatively low.

Why should we be worried about a short circuit in the wiring system? We are concerned with avoiding short circuits in our lighting feeders because of the danger due to the magnetic and thermal effects it can produce in the conductors and on busbar systems. We must therefore place protective devices in the conductors which must operate sufficiently quickly and in absolute safety to prevent this kind of danger. If we are going to use a fuse, we can meet the fault current requirement by selecting fuses with a high rupturing capacity, for example BS 88 in the UK allows for a rupturing capacity of 80 kA. Another method of protecting circuits is by using an air circuit breaker (acb) or a moulded case circuit breaker (mccb). These will also have to be rated to meet the prospective fault current.

Thus the switchgear feeding the dimmer racks will be provided with, say, fuses to handle 400 A running current and if a normal overload occurs will rupture relatively quickly. In addition, they will have to fuse immediately with a fault current of around 20,000 amps. Acbs and mccbs are often specified for high current applications of about 400 A and greater on switchgear. Fuses are generally used below this point.

Most of the devices to protect the installation will have to be carefully selected. We have to bear in mind that there will be more than one device protecting the circuits so the protection devices have to be carefully integrated with each other so that discrimination is achieved. For example, it's no good having the mccb feeding a dimmer rack failing when only one outgoing dimmer circuit has a fault.

Residual current devices

A residual current device (RCD) is an additional protective device (either incorporated into a specially designed circuit breaker or into a wall outlet) that detects fault currents much smaller than that which would trip a normal circuit breaker or fuse. It is designed to protect people against shock current in the event of a fault. In household wiring RCDs are required to be installed in bathroom outlets, outlets near sinks, outdoor circuits and on any electrical equipment operated in proximity to a swimming pool or the like. Similarly, when filming in a bathroom or near a pool, an RCD should be incorporated into the circuits powering the lights near the water. The danger of wet environments is that water underfoot greatly increases the conductivity of one's body to earth. Should leakage current occur, the RCD will trip so fast that the shock current is less than that required to cause any serious injury.

An RCD works by continuously comparing the current of the phase wire to that of the neutral wire. Normally the current flowing to a load on the phase is identical to the current returning on the neutral. However, if there is a defect in the wiring or the fixture, some current will leak to earth, causing a differential between the two wires. If there is a differential of 30 mA the RCD will disconnect the circuit in less than 40 ms.

However, it must be realized that if an operator gets hold of the phase and neutral at the same time, the same current will flow in each conductor *and the device will not trip*!

Some rental houses can provide special distribution boxes with RCD circuit breakers or outlets for use near water. It is simple to build an RCD-protected outlet box. You can buy all the parts at an electrical supply store, or even a hardware store. *Note*: Unlike normal circuit breakers, an RCD breaker has a neutral terminal as well as a phase, to which the load wires are connected. An RCD breaker has a wire, which connects to the neutral. All RCD circuits are equipped with a test button (which, when pressed, should cause the circuit to shut off) and a reset switch. RCDs are called ground-fault circuit interrupter (GFCIs) or ground fault interrupters (GFIs) in the USA, and earth leakage detectors (ELDs) in Australia. Finally it must be pointed out that many of these devices are not guaranteed to work with distorted waveforms such as dimmer outputs unless a specially designed trip is being used.

Cable and current-carrying capacity

The amperage capacity, or *ampacity*, of cable is assigned to each type of cable based on the wire gauge, the maximum operating temperature of the insulation, and the conditions under which it will be used. Let's look at these factors individually.

Cable (UK and Europe)

Conductor size in the UK and Europe is given in square millimetres. The conductor size, type of insulation, operating temperature and number of conductors (cores) is marked on the cable. The cable reference codes are usually marked 'CENELEC'. A typical code would be HO7RN-F1, which would indicate the cable rated for 750 V (7), heat and oil resistant (HO), rubber insulated on the conductors (R), with neoprene outer insulation (N) and the (F) indicates flame retardant. The number following the (F) indicates the number of cores.

In the UK cables are often marked with their British Standard Code number which does not immediately give information, but references look-up tables.

It is incumbent upon hire companies to provide equipment rated for the purpose intended, and failure to do so is punishable under the law in the UK. You can generally count on materials being held to a high standard.

American Wire Gauge

Wire sizes in the USA are numbered using the American Wire Gauge (AWG) sizes shown in Figure 8.5.

For wire sizes from 18 AWG to 1 AWG, the smaller the number, the bigger the wire. Cables larger than 1 AWG are numbered 0, 00, 000, and 0000 (pronounced 'one ought,' 'two ought,' 'three ought,' and 'four-ought'). These sizes are usually written 1/0, 2/0, 3/0, and 4/0.

Cables bigger than 4/0 are referred to by their cross-sectional area, measured in circular mils (cmils), and are rarely used as portable power cable in film production.

Multiconductor cable is labelled with the gauge and the number of conductors denoted as follows: 12/3, where 12 is the AWG gauge of the cable, and 3 is the number of conductors.

Type W cable

Type W cable is a portable, extra-hard-usage power cable manufactured to meet the requirements of NEC Article 400 (portable cords and cables) and is acceptable for

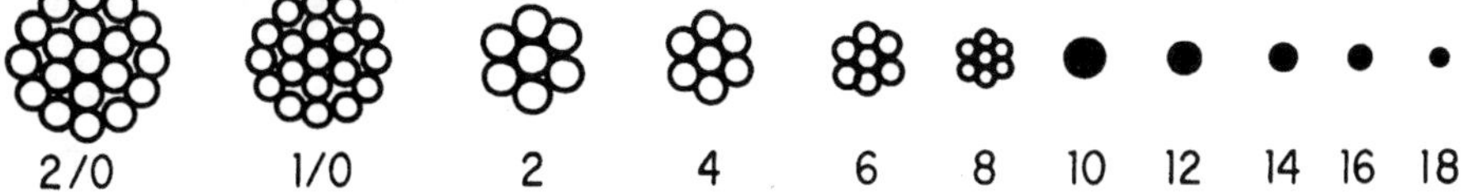

Figure 8.5 Actual diameters of common US sizes of copper wires without insulation. (From H. Richter and W. Schwan, *Practical Electrical Wiring*, 15th edn. [New York: McGraw-Hill, 1990]. Reproduced with permission of McGraw-Hill.)

temporary wiring according to Articles 520 (Theatres and Similar Locations) and 530 (Motion Picture and Television Studios and Similar Locations). It is flexible and abrasion resistant. It may be oil, solvent and sunlight resistant, and flame tested. Carol Super Vu-tron cable is also flexible down to –50°C.

Entertainment industry and stage-lighting cable EISL (types SC, SCE, and SCT)

Entertainment cable is a portable, extra-hard-usage cable with the same insulation characteristics as type W cable, but is 20 per cent smaller and lighter than type W due to the improved materials used in the insulating jacket. You will often see 105°C cable used, but it is not listed in the ampacity tables because the temperature rating must also match the temperature rating of the circuit protection, which is usually not more than 90°C. Use the 90°C column of the table for 105°C cable.

Welding cable

For many years welding cable was commonly used for feeder because it was more flexible and lighter than other types of cable available at the time. However, welding cable has never been approved for this purpose. The misapplication of welding cable became an issue during the 1984 Olympic Games in Los Angeles, after which there was a general conversion to type W and entertainment cable on the West Coast. Although some small rental houses may still rent it, the National Electric Code (NEC) prohibits the use of welding cable in motion picture distribution systems, except as an earth (grounding) wire.

Decoding feeder cable labels

Electricians learn to identify wire gauge by appearance. Occasionally, however, you have to check the gauge by reading it off the insulation. For example, 2/0 type W cable is almost as large as type SC 4/0 cable.

Single-conductor feeder cables are imprinted something like this:

> Royal Entertainment Industry & Stage-Lighting Cable 2/0 AWG 90°C 600V (UL) NEC 520 & 530 Outdoor

- Royal' is the manufacturer.
- Entertainment …Cable' is the type of cable.
- 2/0 AWG' is the size of the cable according to the American Wire Gauge standard.
- 90°C' is the maximum operating temperature of the insulation.
- 600V' is the maximum voltage of the cable.
- UL' indicates that the cable is listed with Underwriters Laboratories.
- NEC 520 & 530' indicate that the cable meets the requirements of National Electrical Code Articles 520 and 530, which apply to the entertainment industry.
- Outdoor' indicates that the cable is approved for outdoor use.

Decoding multiconductor cable labels

Multiconductor cable, used for stingers and power cords, is marked as follows:

12/3 Type SJOW-A 90°C P-123-MSHA,Type SJO 90°C

- '12/3' indicates the gauge (12) and the number of conductors in the cable (3).
- 'Type SJOW-A' is a code for the type of insulation (S cord with a light oil- and water-resistant jacket).
- 90°C' is the maximum operating temperature of the insulation.
- 'P-123-MSHA' indicates that the cable is approved by the Mine Safety and Health Administration (MSHA).
- Type SJO 90°C' is an alternative designation given to this particular cable.

Maximum operating temperature

Testing laboratories test each type of cable insulation and assign it a maximum temperature rating. The more current run through the cable, the warmer it becomes. The rating reflects the temperature that the wire can safely reach without damaging the insulation. When insulation becomes overheated, it may become brittle, crack apart or melt. The temperature rating provides a margin of safety between the maximum operating temperature of the cable and its breakdown point.

Tables B.1 and B.2 (Appendix B) list the current-carrying capacity (ampacity) of various sizes and temperature ratings of cable. Note that the current-carrying capacity of a cable rated at 60 or 75°C is substantially lower than that of cable rated at 90°C. Be sure you assign the proper amperage to the cable you are using. In the UK and Europe almost all cable is rated at 85°C.

If a cable rated at 90°C is connected to a fuse rated at only 75°C, the cable may transfer heat and may overheat the fuse. In this case, a larger jumper cable must be used to prevent heat transfer. The jumper cable must be sized to carry the needed amperage at the lower temperature rating.

Other factors that affect current-carrying capacity (ampacity)

Current-carrying capacity (ampacity) is not printed on cable because outside factors influence the operating temperature of the cable, which may lower its effective maximum amperage. The ambient temperature around a cable, the number of cables and the distance between them, whether the cables are in a raceway or conduit or standing in free air, and whether the circuit is run continuously or intermittently (periodically allowed to cool) all affect the operating temperature of the cable and, therefore, the allowed current-carrying capacity. Electrical regulations specify how much a cable must be derated in each of these circumstances. Keep this in mind when cabling. When cable runs are in well-ventilated areas and the room temperature is normal or cool, no derating is necessary. When cables are tightly bundled or stacked one on another, placed in narrow raceways, or subject to hotter than normal ambient temperatures, the insulation may be overheated if the cable is loaded to full current-carrying capacity. Keep this in mind when selecting cable gauge under such circumstances.

Current-carrying capacity (ampacity) of connectors

Like cable, connectors have a maximum amperage rating. Obviously, you must not run more power through a cable than the connector is rated for, regardless of the rating of the cable. Connectors tend to be the weakest part of the system. Connectors will overheat and melt if they are overloaded or (most commonly) if there is poor electrical contact between connectors. If left too long the connector melts and is destroyed. More on this in Chapter 9.

Parallel and series circuits

Several lamps can be connected in a single circuit in one of two ways: in *parallel* or in *series* (Figure 8.6). Lighting equipment is almost always connected in parallel.

In a parallel circuit, the voltage is the same at every point of the circuit. The current of the whole circuit is equal to the sum of the current drawn by the individual units. In a parallel circuit the loss of one branch circuit only affects that branch. In a series circuit, current is constant throughout the circuit. The sum of the voltages of the lights is equal to the voltage of the circuit. For example, to use 28 V ACL PAR lights (aircraft landing lights) with a 120 V source, four 28 V lights are connected in series (28 + 28 + 28 + 28 = 112 V). The total resistance in the circuit is equal to the sum of the resistance's of the fixtures. In a series circuit, if there is a break in the circuit at any point (if a filament blows, for example), the entire circuit is interrupted and none of the lights receive power.

Types of distribution circuits

There are various voltage configurations which are used in various parts of the world. The UK and Australia generally uses a three-phase star-connected 415/240 V

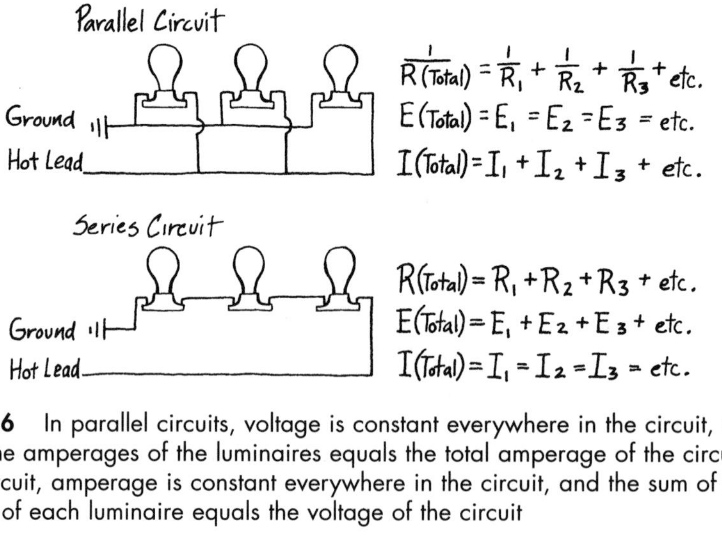

Figure 8.6 In parallel circuits, voltage is constant everywhere in the circuit, and the sum of the amperages of the luminaires equals the total amperage of the circuit. In a series circuit, amperage is constant everywhere in the circuit, and the sum of the voltages of each luminaire equals the voltage of the circuit

AC system. The European 'harmonized standard' is star-connected 400/230 V AC. Many West European countries still use 220 V service (three-phase delta-connected 127/220). In the USA and Canada three-phase systems are either star-connected 208/120 V AC, or delta-connected 240/120 V AC. Single-phase AC is 240/120 V. On top of that, many sound stages in Hollywood still use 240/120 DC. Appendix H gives a complete listing for nations around the world.

Before we start to look at how each of these circuits work, lets look at the difference between AC and DC current.

Direct current and alternating current

A direct current power source, a battery or DC generator, has a positive terminal and a negative terminal. Electrons flow from the negative terminal through the circuit to the positive terminal. The polarity (direction of flow) never changes, and the voltage remains (relatively) constant.

Alternating current, which is supplied by the power company or by an AC generator, consists of a phase wire and a neutral wire.[3] The polarity of the circuit alternates from positive to negative and back to positive again. It does this 50 times every second – 50 cycles per second is 50 hertz (Hz) (Figure 8.7). (In the USA, alternating current operates at 60 Hz.)

During each cycle, the voltage of a 50 Hz 240 V system goes from 0 to +340 V, back to 0, reverses polarity, goes down to –340 V, and back to 0 again. It does this 50 times every second. Because the cycles occur rapidly, there is no time for the filament of a bulb to dim during the short time when the voltage passes 0, which is the reason the bulb provides a constant glow. The *effective*, or *RMS* (root mean square), voltage of a circuit is 240 V:

$$\frac{\sqrt{2}}{2} \times \text{peak voltage}$$

or

$$0.707 \times 340 = 240 \text{ V}$$

A voltmeter reading will give you the effective voltage. A lamp connected to the circuit will operate at the effective voltage of 240 V.

Alternating current and direct current on the set

Both AC and DC power are used on sound stages and on location. Many of the large

3. The neutral lead is also sometimes called the common lead, and in America the technically correct name for it is the grounded wire. As the term neutral is the most familiar term to most electricians I have adopted it for this edition of this book. Technically, however, this is considered incorrect use of the term – in the US. Anyway the common wire is not actually 'neutral' (in the sense that it carries no current) unless the phase leads are equally loaded. Also, do not confuse the term grounded wire with grounding wire. They serve two completely different functions in a circuit. See Earthing later in this chapter.

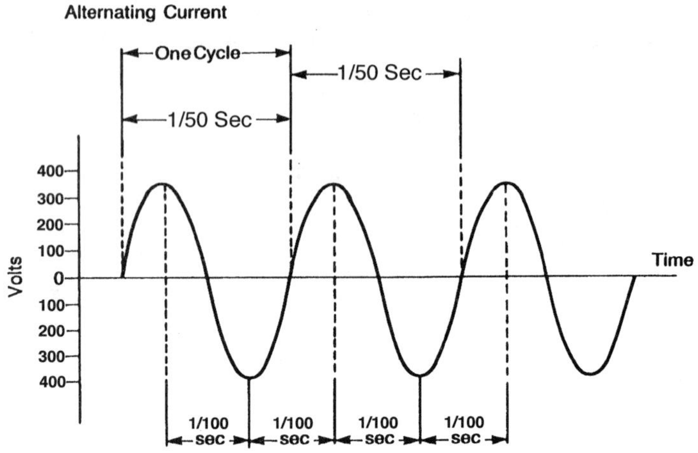

Figure 8.7 Fifty-hertz alternating current makes one full cycle in 1/50 second and hits peak voltage every 1/100 second. Notice that the effective, or RMS, voltage is 240 V

Hollywood studios still use DC power in some or all of their stages, including Warner Brothers, Paramount, Universal, Sony, Twentieth Century Fox, Walt Disney Studios, CBS Studio Centre and Culver Studios. Most new studio facilities use AC, and AC is used for most location filming as well.

Either AC or DC can be used to power tungsten lights. A 120 V DC circuit will light the bulb to the same brilliancy as a 120 V AC circuit. DC current cannot be used with AC discharge sources, Variac dimmers, or other equipment that uses an AC transformer. Plate dimmers or electronic DC dimmers must be used to dim DC circuits. Carbon arc lights run on DC. To convert AC power to DC a *rectifier* must be used. To convert DC to AC an *inverter* must be used.

Safety considerations

Direct current is often used when filming near water because it is considered to be safer. You are less likely to get a shock from a DC system. With an AC system, you can complete a circuit by touching a hot wire (phase) and standing on the ground, but with a DC circuit, you can only complete the circuit by touching the positive and the negative wire simultaneously. The earth beneath your feet does not complete the circuit unless the DC system is earthed, and few are. Also, the shock from a DC circuit and the shock from an AC circuit are different. (See 'Electrical shocks' later in this chapter.)

Switches and breakers

There are some important differences between AC and DC switches and circuit breakers. It is a property of DC current that when there is a narrow gap between contacts, the current will arc and begin to burn the contacts (a carbon arc light operates on this principle). Every time a switch is opened or closed, a short gap exists for an instant. If the current is allowed to arc each time the switch is opened or closed, it will burn away the contacts of the switch very quickly. To prevent the arc, DC switches and circuit breakers are spring-loaded so that the contacts snap together or break quickly.

The most common household switches, AC-only switches, do not require this feature and operate quietly, without a snap. Do not use AC-only switches or breakers with DC circuits. The letters AC appear after the rating on the switch.

AC-DC switches can be used with either AC or DC power. If AC does not appear on the rating of the switch, it is an AC-DC type. If an AC-DC switch is to be used to control an incandescent light, it must have a 'T' (tungsten) rating (a slightly stronger switch is needed to handle the high initial inrush current drawn by a cold tungsten filament).

DC three-wire system

Most DC stages are actually powered by two generators connected in series to provide a three-wire system with two hot legs (red and blue) and one common leg (white) (Figure 8.8) – this is a US colour-coding.

Connecting the load between either one of the hot legs and the common leg gives 120 V. Connecting the load between the negative blue leg and the positive red leg gives 240 V. Location generators usually provide only two-wire DC.

The common neutral

You might wonder whether using the neutral wire to serve two circuits doubles the load on the neutral wire. Would the neutral wire have to be twice as thick as in a single circuit to carry twice the current? The answer is no. The current flowing through one leg always flows in the direction opposite that of the current in the second leg. When the loads are the same on both legs, the current in the common (neutral) wire is effectively zero. When the load on one leg is greater than that on the second, the neutral wire carries the *difference* in amperage of the two legs.

For example, assume that leg A and leg B are carrying 50 A each. The loads are even, so the two loads travelling through the neutral wire cancel each other out. If we remove 10 A from the leg A and put it on leg B, making leg A 40 A and leg B 60 A, the neutral wire will carry the difference (20 A).

Polarity

Polarity is the direction of flow of electricity in a circuit. In DC circuits, electricity flows from the negative terminal of the power source, through the circuit, to the positive terminal. DC polarity is important when powering carbon arc lights. This equipment will not operate properly if the polarity is reversed. In a three-wire DC circuit, the blue leg is always negative and the red leg is always positive (see Figure 8.8). If you were connecting a carbon arc light to the blue leg, you would connect the positive lead to the white wire. If you were connecting it to the red leg, you would connect the negative lead to the white wire. The white wire is negative with respect to the red leg and positive with respect to the blue leg.

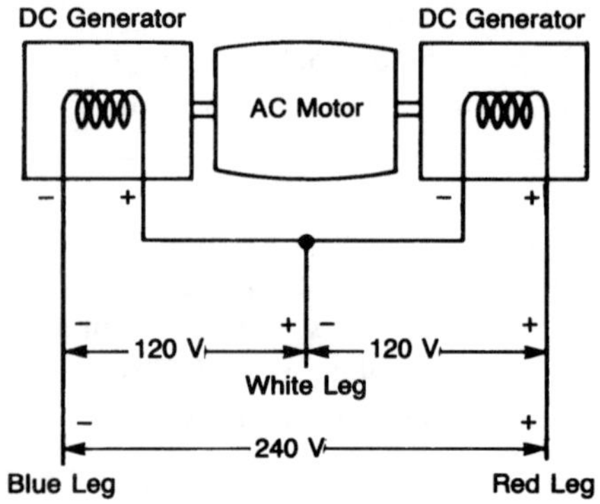

Figure 8.8 A three-wire 120/240 V DC generator configuration for DC sound stages. An AC motor drives two DC generators connected in series. The blue leg is usually the negative leg, and the red leg is the positive. The voltage potential between them is 240 V. The white leg gives a voltage potential of 120 V when connected to a circuit with either hot leg

You can check the polarity of a DC circuit by using a DC voltmeter or a magnetic compass, which will point in the direction of flow when held next to a current-carrying wire.

Three-phase, four-wire systems

Most commercial buildings, including sound stages, have three-phase power. Location generators also provide three-phase power. You will sometimes see the word phase abbreviated with the Greek letter phi (Ø).

A three-phase, four-wire system consists of three 240 V phase wires (we'll call them phases A, B and C) a neutral wire and an earthing wire. The three phases each operate at 50 cycles per second. Each phase, however, operates a third of a cycle out of sync with the next (Figure 8.9). If you think of one cycle as a 360° circle, each phase begins the cycle 120° after the last.

The circuit shown in Figure 8.10 is a wye-connected three-phase system. It is called a *wye* or *star* because of its shape. When a load is connected to any one of the phases and the neutral wire, the voltage is 240 V. When a load is placed between any two phases, because the two phases are 120° apart the voltage is 415 V.

Circuits derived from wye-connected systems

Five types of circuits can be derived from a wye-connected, four-wire, three-phase system. For the purpose of this discussion we'll refer to the UK 415/240 V system (Figure 8.11), but the same derivations are possible with the 400/230 V system, 208Y/120 system or any other wye-connected system. (*Note*: All AC systems also include an earth wire which is not counted in the discussion below. A 'four-wire' three-phase system actually has five wires including the earth.)

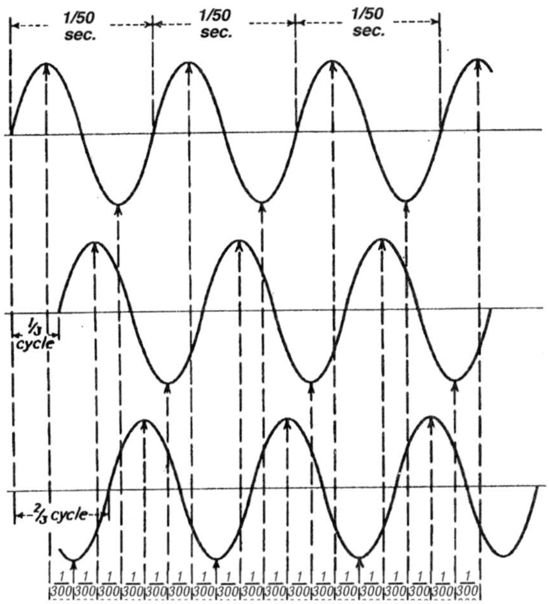

Figure 8.9 Three-phase cycles. (Modified from H. Richter and W. Schwan, *Practical Electrical Wiring*, 15th edn [New York: McGraw-Hill, 1990]. Reproduced with permission of McGraw-Hill.)

- **240 V, two-wire circuit, single-phase** Three separate branch circuits can be made by connecting to any one of the phase wires and the neutral wire. When loading the three phases, it is important to keep them balanced. (Branch circuits on a 400/230 V system would be 230 V, and 120 V on a 208/120 V system.)
- **415 V, two-wire circuit, single-phase** This circuit is made by connecting to any two of the three phases. Some older larger discharge source ballasts run on 415 V. Again, as much as possible, keep the load balanced between the phases by connecting to A and B, B and C, and C and A evenly. (These branch circuits would be 400 V on a 400/230 V system, and 208 V on a 208/120 V system. In the USA the larger lights (12 kW, 20 kW etc.) use 208 V service.]
- **415/240 V, three-wire circuit, single-phase** By connecting two of the three phases and the neutral leg, you can derive a single-phase three-wire branch circuit. This gives you the option of providing 240 V or 415 V power and you can use a three-wire single phase distribution system. Be sure to label each distribution box (so you remember which distribution box is plugged into which phases. Keep the load balanced by connecting evenly: A and B, B and C, and C and A. (These branch circuits would be single-phase 400/230 V on a 400/230 V system, and 208/120 V on a 208/120 V system. In the USA this provides for both 208 V and 120 V luminaires.)
- **415 V, three-wire circuit, three-phase** This type of circuit uses all three phase wires and has no neutral. It is a balanced system, generally used for machinery,

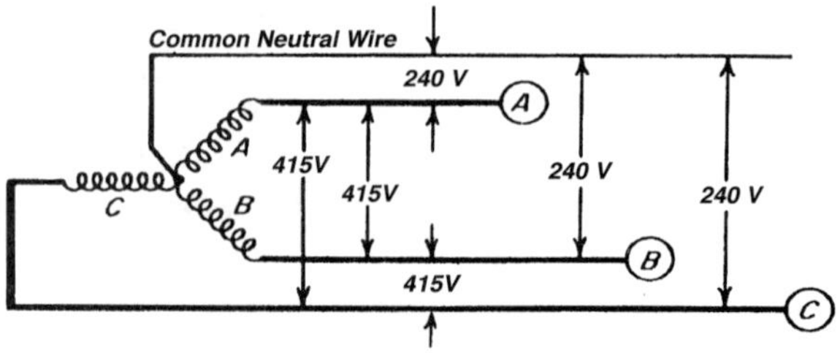

Figure 8.10 415Y/240. The three coils shown represent the secondary coils of the transformers that step down the voltage from the power line. A 415Y/240 system can supply 240V single-phase circuits and 415-V three-phase circuits at the same time. (From H. Richter and W. Schwan, *Practical Electrical Wiring*, 15th edn [New York: McGraw-Hill, 1990]. Reproduced with permission of McGraw-Hill.)

such as a large air-conditioning units and three-phase motors. Such circuits are not suitable for providing temporary supplies. It is unsafe and forbidden to use a neutral from another circuit to make single-phase circuits from the wires of a three-wire, three-phase system. (This circuit would be three-phase, three-wire 400 V on a 400/230 V system, and 208 V on a 208/120 V system.)

- **415/240 V, four-wire circuit, three-phase** Branch circuits which use all four wires provide all the possibilities mentioned above.

Colour-coding

The UK system of colour-coding for fixed wiring (permanent building wires) is as follows:

Earth (protective conductor)	Green/Yellow
Single phase (live)	Red (or Yellow or Blue)
Neutral	Black
Phase R	Red
Phase Y	Yellow
Phase B	Blue

The UK system of colour-coding for flexible cables is:

Earth (protective conductor)	Green/Yellow stripe
Neutral	Blue
Phase wires	Brown or Black

Four and five core cable: If conductors of the same colour are used for the three phases or for different functions, then coded sleeves are added to the cores (e.g. L1, L2, L3).

Other systems used in the USA

As we have already mentioned, the predominant system in the USA is 208Y/120V

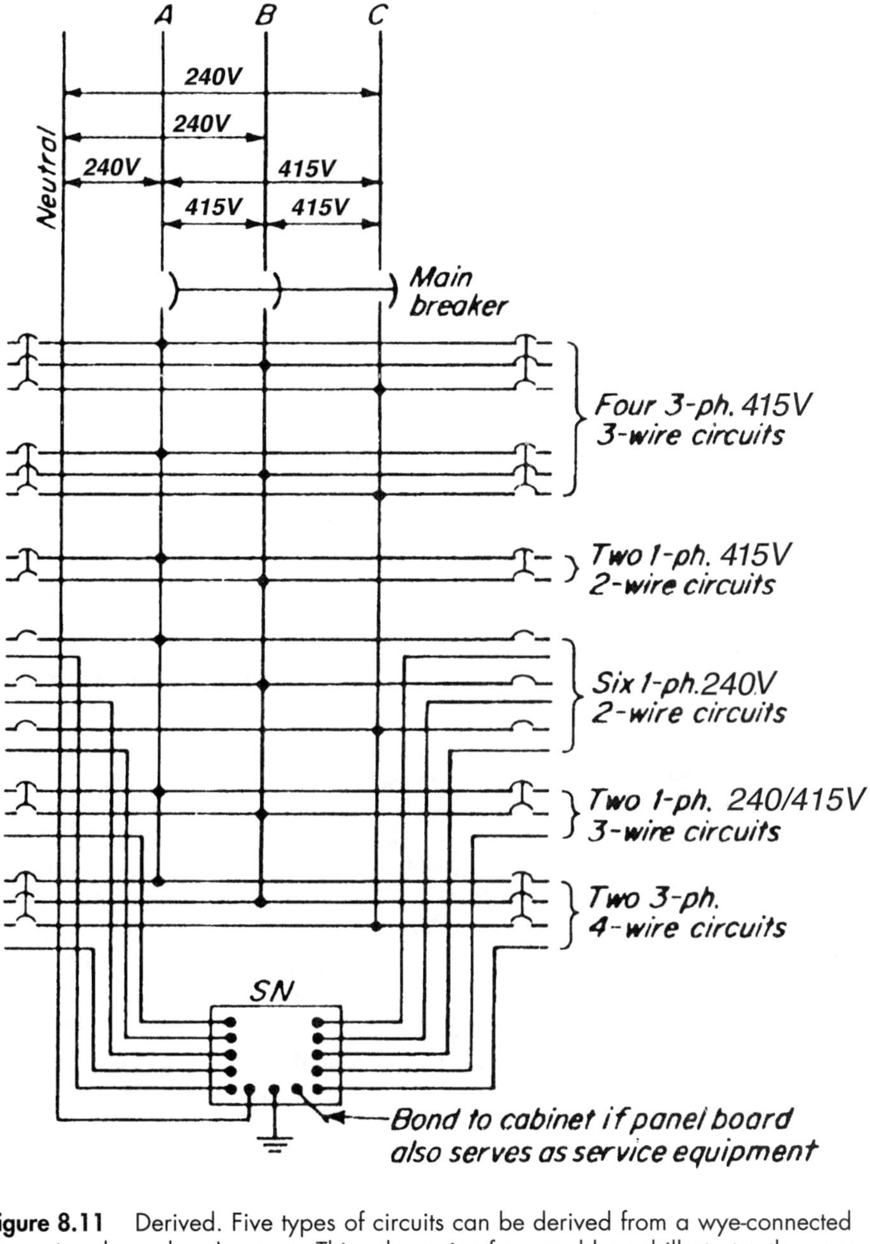

Figure 8.11 Derived. Five types of circuits can be derived from a wye-connected (four-wire, three-phase) system. This schematic of a panel board illustrates the way the circuits are connected. (Modified from H. Richter and W. Schwan, *Practical Electrical Wiring*, 15th edn [New York: McGraw-Hill, 1990]. Reproduced with permission of McGraw-Hill.)

AC, and the circuits derived from it. However there are other systems which are commonly used as well.

240/120 AC single-phase, three-wire circuits

Like the three-wire DC system, this system consists of two hot 120 V wires and a neutral wire. By connecting the load between one hot and the neutral, you get 120 V. By connecting the load between the two hot legs, you get 240 V.

In North America most incandescent lights run on 120 V, and larger discharge sources and 20 kWs run on anything between 208 V and 240 V. A single-phase, AC system, which provides both 120 V and 240 V power from three wires, meets this dual voltage requirement and is commonly used in film distribution systems as well as in homes and commercial buildings (Figure 8.12). In America the neutral wire is always white. The two hot legs will be two other colours (blue, red or black), but never white or green. The earth (ground) wire is always green.

Note that although this type of circuit is known as a three-wire circuit, it actually uses four wires. The fourth wire is a green-coded earthing wire used for earthing metallic parts of the lights and electrical hardware (see 'Equipment earthing' later in this chapter).

Delta-connected systems

In factories and large industrial buildings, you will sometimes come across a four-wire, three-phase delta-connected system. Its name comes from the circuit's resemblance to the Greek letter delta (Δ). The voltage across each of the secondary coils of the transformer is 240 V (Figure 8.13).

To supply 120 and 240 volts, one coil is tapped in the centre. The tap is earthed and becomes the neutral lead for a three-wire, single-phase 120/240 V circuit. Single-phase 120 V power can be gained by connecting to A and N, or B and N. The tapped coil is usually larger than the other two, so it can handle the extra load.

Connecting to C and N produces 208 V, single-phase power (Figure 8.14). This is called the *high leg*, and it has caught many an electrician by surprise. If you are used to a wye configuration, you would expect any of the three phases to give 120 V when connected with the neutral. In wye connected three phase there is only one coil between the neutral and phase connections. The high leg on a delta-connected system gives an unexpected output because it is across more than one coil, and the product of the out of phase components is 208 volts. Obviously, the high leg would burn out any 120 V light connected to it.

There are a couple of variations on the delta-connected system. Three-wire systems may be either 240 V or 480 V across each coil. A centre-tapped 480 V coil could be used to provide 480/240 power. In an alternative delta configuration, one corner of the delta is sometimes earthed.

Fluorescent installations

Large American fluorescent lighting installations operate more efficiently on 277 V power, so some industrial buildings use a wye-connected 480 Y/277 V system. The cables are usually coded Brown, Orange and Yellow. This system has no direct appli-

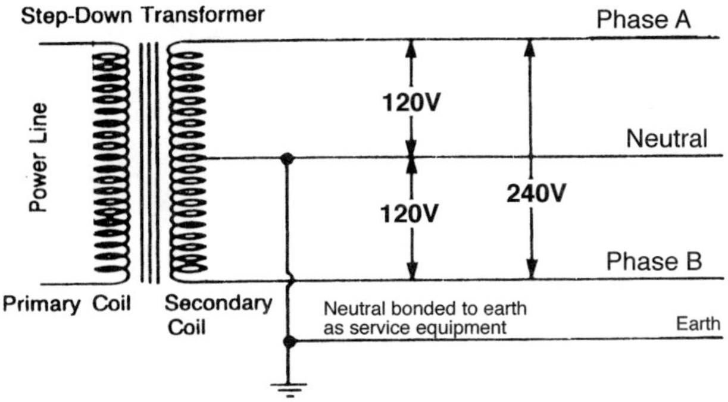

Figure 8.12 A 240/120 single phase. The coils represent the primary and secondary coils of the transformer that steps down the voltage from the power lines. The neutral wire taps into the midpoint of the secondary coil and is an earthed wire. The voltage potential is 240 V between phases and 120 V between neutral and either of the phases

cations for film lighting and would require a step-down transformer to be a useful as a power source. (Mole-Richardson is one manufacturer offering step-down transformers of this type.)

What happens when a circuit is incorrectly connected?

When laying out new distribution on location or on stage it is important to check the voltage at the distribution boxes before plugging in any equipment. With many systems it is possible to accidentally connect the main feeders incorrectly. If a phase wire and neutral wire get crossed, one leg of the distribution will deliver 415 V to the outlets – which would burn out any lantern plugged into it.

Secondly, be sure that the neutral is never inadvertently disconnected once the lights are on. The following example uses the American 120/240 single-phase system to illustrate what happens if the neutral is taken out of the circuit. An over-voltage situation would result if this happened with any system.

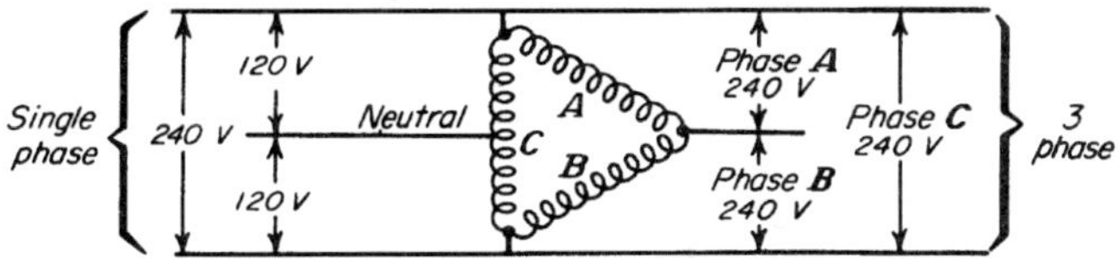

Figure 8.13 Delta. A 240 V three-phase delta-connected system delivers single-phase 240/120 V current and three-phase 240 V current. (From H. Richter and W. Schwan, *Practical Electrical Wiring*, 15th edn [New York: McGraw-Hill, 1990]. Reproduced with permission of McGraw-Hill.)

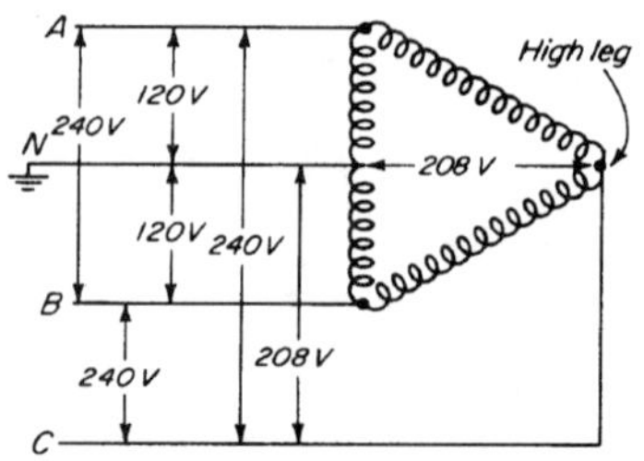

Figure 8.14 Delta with high leg. In a delta-connected system the voltage from the neutral to the high leg is 208 V power, not 120 V power as you would expect from a wye-connected system. (From H. Richter and W. Schwan, *Practical Electrical Wiring*, 15th edn [New York: McGraw-Hill, 1990]. Reproduced with permission of McGraw-Hill.)

When the neutral is removed (Figure 8.15) the voltage applied to the circuit becomes 240 V, and the two sides of the circuit become connected in series. Keep in mind these are 120 V lamps. Theoretically, if the amperage load on both legs were exactly the same, the voltage on each side would still be 120 V (240 divided by 2). However, chances are that one leg is pulling more amperage than the other. The difference in resistance creates an imbalance in the voltage. The voltage on one side of the series circuit drops, while the other side shoots up, and will start to blow out bulbs on that side of the circuit in a matter of seconds.

Consider a simple example of a three-wire system with a 5 kW luminaire on the red leg and a 2 kW luminaire on the blue leg (Figure 8.16).

With the neutral connected, each light receives 120 V. The 5 kW pulls 41.67 A and has a resistance of 2.88 W. The 2 kW pulls 16.67 A and has a resistance of 7.2 Ω. If the neutral wire were disconnected, the two lights become connected in series, in a 240 V circuit. Unlike a parallel circuit, the amperage in a series circuit is the same in every part of the circuit, and the total resistance of the circuit equals the sum of the resistances of all the lights.

We can calculate the amperage for the circuit as follows:

$$\text{I (amperage)} = \frac{\text{E (voltage of circuit)}}{\text{R (sum of the resistances)}} = \frac{240}{(2.88 + 7.2)} = 23.81 \text{ A}$$

Knowing the amperage of the whole circuit, we can now calculate the voltage (E = I × R) being applied to each light:

Voltage of the 5 kW: 23.81 A × 2.88 Ω = 68.6 V

Voltage of the 2 kW: 23.81 A × 7.2 Ω = 171.4 V

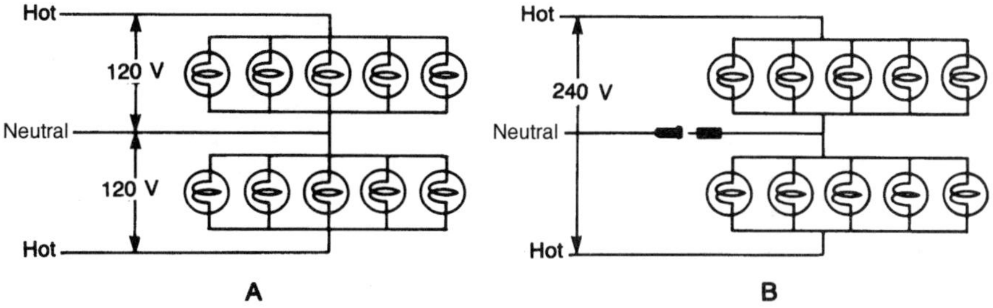

Figure 8.15 Removing neutral. (A) A typical three-wire 120/240 V system with five lamps connected to each leg. The red and blue legs are separate circuits sharing the neutral lead. (B) When the neutral wire is pulled, the hot legs become connected in series with 240 V total voltage. If both sets of lamps have exactly the same resistance, the voltage is divided evenly in two, at 120 V each. However, if one leg has more resistance, it receives more voltage and the other leg receives less. (They always add up to 240 V.)

From this we can see that the fixture with the greater resistance, the 2 kW, will receive a higher voltage, which will blow the lamp. Notice that the sum of the voltages of the lights is equal to the voltage of the whole circuit (68.6 + 171.4 = 240).

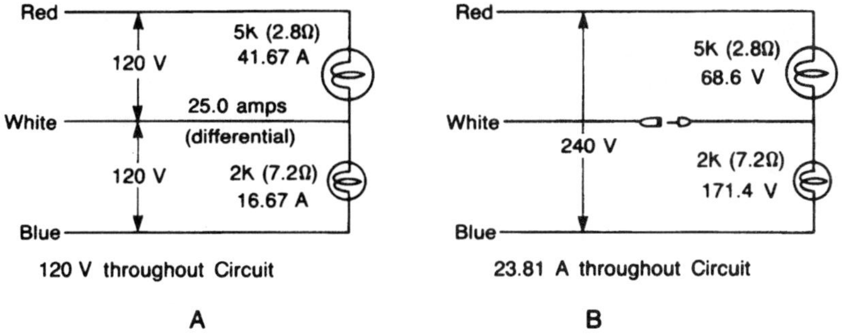

Figure 8.16 5 kW and 2 kW without neutral. (A) A three-wire system with 5 kW on one leg and 2 kW on the other. (B) With the white wire pulled, two legs are connected in series with 240 V applied to the circuit. The 2 kW will be blown by the 171 V power

Equipment earthing

Earth wires are not meant to carry current under normal circumstances. They carry current only when there is a fault inside a piece of equipment and the housing becomes live. If no earth wire were connected (Figure 8.17A), anyone who touched the fixture would complete the circuit to earth through his or her body and would receive a shock. With an earth wire connected to the housing (Figure 8.17B), electricity seeks the path of least resistance, and the bulk of the electricity completes the path to earth through the earthing wire instead of through a human body. The faulty

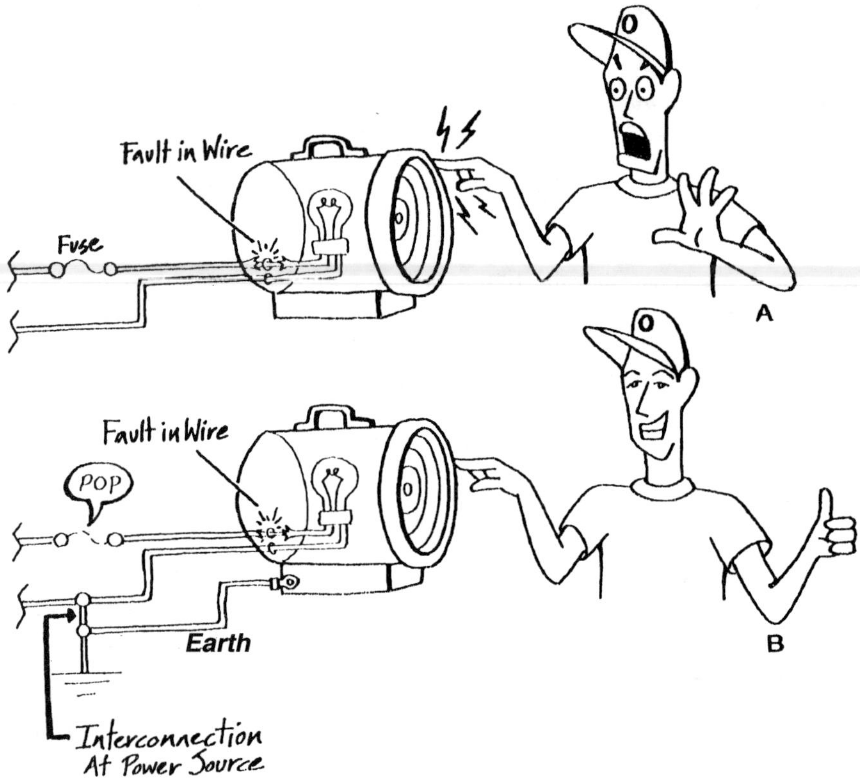

Figure 8.17 (A) A fault in a metal fixture energizes the entire housing. Anyone who touches the fixture may complete a circuit to earth and get a shock. (B) An earthing wire carries the fault current safely to earth. Because the earthing wire and the neutral wire are bonded at the service entrance, this creates a dead short between the hot wire and neutral. If enough current flows through the earthing wire, the fuse or circuit breaker will pop in response. However, if the fault only makes loose contact (high resistance), it will create a lot of heat but may not pop the fuse

fixture remains safe to touch. If enough current flows through the earth wire, it will blow the fuse or trip the circuit breaker protecting the circuit.

Proper equipment earthing is essential to safety. It is one of the things that the fire marshal and electrical inspector will look for on the set.

The earthing wire can be smaller than the current-carrying wires; however, it must not be so small that the resistance in the wire prevents it from tripping the breaker in case of a fault. The various national electrical codes provide tables indicating the minimum sizes for earthing wires (Table B.3 in Appendix B is taken from the US National Electrical Code).

Power factor

When we calculate cable loads and generator loads we use the equation: watts/volts = amps. However, with some AC equipment this statement is not true: It underestimates the actual current. When a piece of equipment has inductive properties (magnetic ballasts) or capacitive properties (electronic ballasts and electronic dimmers), power factor must be considered in order to make proper load calculations. Power factor is sometimes denoted as pf.

A load such as an incandescent light or heating element has no inductive or capacitive properties. It merely creates resistance in a circuit. A purely resistive circuit is said to have *unity power factor* – a power factor of 1.0 or 100 per cent, and the equation watts/volts = amps is correct. When the load involves coils such as those in a transformer, motor, or magnetic ballast, inductive reactance comes into play, and the power factor is less than 100 per cent. Inductance opposes the flow of current, causing current to lag behind voltage. The increase and decrease of current (which normally corresponds with the increase and decrease of voltage, 50 times a second) lags behind the voltage. With voltage and current out of phase, more current is required to accomplish the same amount of work. If you measure the amperage and the voltage, then multiply the two together, you get what's called the apparent wattage (expressed in *volt-amperes*). When power factor is low, apparent wattage will be higher than the true power (the watts of power actually used by the equipment). As one electrician put it, if apparent wattage is a pint of Guinness, power factor is the head of foam that prevents you from filling the glass to the brim. The size of the feeder cables, and the rating of the power source, must be sufficient to supply the apparent wattage (beer plus foam), even though only the beer counts as far as how much actual drinking is being accomplished. Load calculations must therefore include power factor. Similarly, if the circuit has a capacitive component, such as with some electronic ballast's, capacitive reactance produces a power factor of less than 100 per cent. Capacitive reactance causes current to lead voltage, which once again results in reduced efficiency. Modern discharge source ballasts have power factor correction circuits, which restore the efficiency of a ballast. This factor is very important when using limited power sources or domestic sockets to supply power to lights on location.

Power factor calculations

Power factor is the percentage ratio of watts to volt-amperes:

$$\text{pf} = \frac{\text{rated wattage}}{\text{volt-amperes}}$$

$$\text{watts} = \text{volt-amperes} \times \text{pf}$$

For single-phase circuits, volt-amperes = volts × amps. For three-phase circuits, volt-amperes = 1.732 × volts × amps (1.732 is the square root of 3).

The power factor of a ballast or motor is sometimes, but not always, written on the equipment. To calculate the actual amperage needed to power equipment when the power factor is known, use the following equation:

$$\frac{\text{rated wattage}}{\text{volts} \times \text{pf}} = \text{required amperage}$$

To illustrate, suppose you are powering four 6 kW HMIs. If we made the mistake of discounting the power factor, we would incorrectly calculate the amperage as follows:

$$\frac{4 \times 6{,}000}{240} = 100 \text{ A}$$

If the units have a power factor of 80 per cent, the actual amperage required will be

$$\frac{4 \times 6{,}000}{240 \times 0.8} = 125 \text{ A}$$

From this we see the importance of taking power factor into account. The amperage is significantly higher than thought – 25 A higher.

Harmonic currents on the neutral wire

With incandescent lights, if we draw equal current from two phases (assume a single-phase, three-wire, 120/240 V system), there will be no return current on the neutral; the current cancels out between legs. In theory this would allow the neutral wire of the feeder cables to be smaller than the phase wires (although this practice is no longer permitted by current electrical codes).

When using magnetic ballasts, it is normal to have as much as 20 to 25 per cent of the total current return on the neutral when the phases are evenly loaded. The current returning does not completely cancel between legs because inductance causes current to lag behind voltage. For this reason, when using many magnetic ballasts, it is wise to provide a neutral that is at least as large as the phase wires.

With electronic ballasts that do not have power factor correction, current leads voltage, and with this equipment about 80 per cent of the current does not cancel out between legs. When operating many electronic ballasts, the neutral wire of the feeder *cable must be substantial enough to carry the sum of the currents* of the phases, times 80 per cent.

It is common practice to *double or triple the neutral wire* when powering large numbers of electronic dimmers or electronic ballasts. By the same token, you can overload the neutral wire of the transformer or generator if it is not sized to handle return current, especially with 208 Y/120 circuits.

Meters for measuring electricity

Set electricians should carry some kind of voltage tester with them at all times (Figure 8.18). An inexpensive voltmeter (Figure 8.18C) is quite adequate because with constant use meters run the risk of being damaged. Meters and testers come in many shapes and sizes. A simple voltage tester (Figure 8.18H), when connected across a circuit, indicates with a LED display whether a circuit is 120 V, 220 V, 230 V or 240 V. An inexpensive, needle-type AC/DC voltmeter reads voltage from 0 to 500V with adequate accuracy. This type of meter can usually also measure resistance in ohms.

Most electricians invest in a small digital multi-meter (8.18I), such as the Beckman DM73 or equivalent, which measures AC and DC voltage, detects continuity, and measures resistance. More expensive digital multipurpose meters, such as those manufactured by Fluke (8.18E), incorporate frequency and current measuring ranges in addition to voltage, resistance, and continuity. The best boy electric must be able to make measurements of this kind. Voltmeters, ammeters, frequency meters and continuity testers are also manufactured as separate meters.

Measuring voltage

A voltmeter has two probes. Touch the probes to the terminals of the circuit to be measured. When probing exposed terminals, be careful as you position the probes not to put your fingers on or close to the terminals. When measuring a DC circuit, if the needle deflects to the left, off the bottom of the scale, the polarity is reversed. Check that your probes are properly connected; reverse them to get a measurement. A digital meter reading will show a negative sign to indicate reversed polarity.

Measuring frequency (hertz rate)

A frequency meter is used to measure the frequency of an AC circuit in cycles per second (Hz). There are several types of frequency meters. The most popular frequency meters simply plug into an outlet (Figure 8.18D). In addition, some clamp-on ammeters have a frequency function.

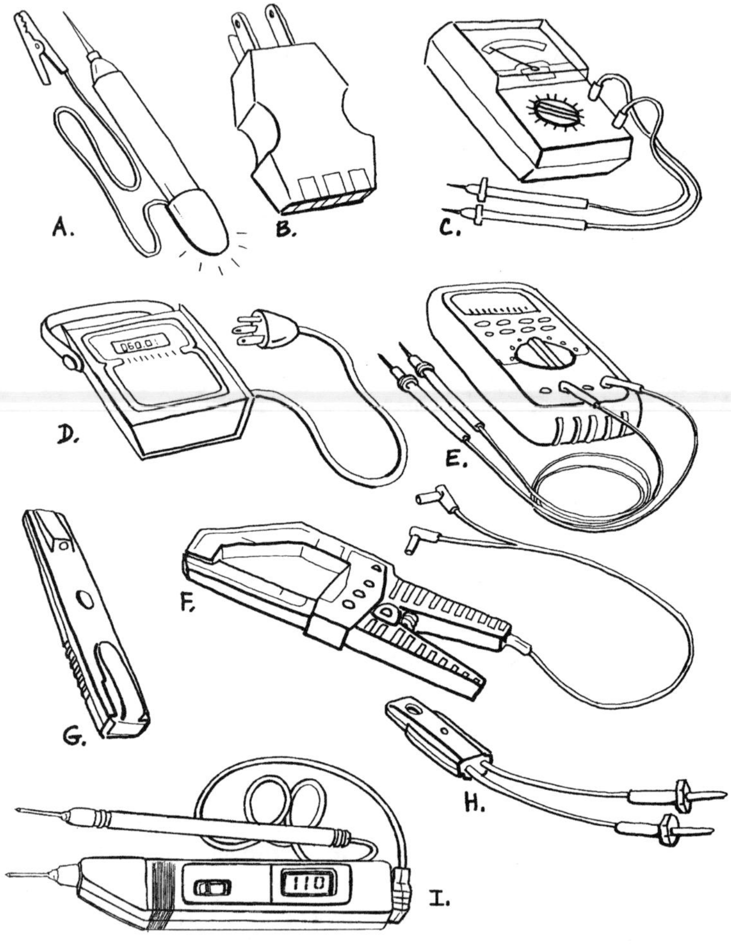

Figure 8.18 Meters for measuring electricity: (A) continuity tester, (B) circuit tester, (C) voltmeter, (D) line frequency tester, (E) digital multimeter, (F) amp clamp attachment for multimeter, (G) voltage sensor, (H) voltage tester, and (I) a common digital multimeter

Another type of frequency meter, the 'Cinecheck', does not take the reading from the power lines at all, but instead from the light emitted by an discharge source (magnetic ballast only). Simply hold the meter up to the light and read the frequency.

Measuring amperage

A current clamp (Figure 8.18F) is used to determine the current through a single conductor. Current clamps are generally AC only; however, some more sophisticated clamp meters can measure DC current as well. The clamp has two curved fingers that close around an insulated single conductor cable. The clamp measures the strength of the magnetic field created around the cable by the current running through it. The strength of the field is proportional to the current running through the wire. The clamp gives a reading in amperes.

Testing continuity

Unlike all the other testing equipment discussed in this section, a continuity tester (Figure 8.18A and I) is only used when power is not connected to the circuit. The tester is used to check for a break in the line. If the line is continuous, the tester will beep or light up.

A continuity tester is handy to check if a bulb or fuse has blown. If the filament of the bulb is intact, the tester will show continuity across the terminals of the bulb.

Testing circuits

A circuit tester (Figure 8.18B) is used to test 13 amp sockets. It tells if the circuit is live, if the polarity is correct and if the earthing wire is present.

A voltage sensor (Figure 8.18G) is a handy device that senses the magnetic field of electricity. Although it gives no quantitative reading of amperage, the sensor is extremely useful for checking if a wire is live. Put the sensor near the wire, and press the button. If it beeps or lights up, then the wire is live.

Electrical shocks and muscle freeze

In the event that an electrician comes into contact with a live wire and completes a circuit, the biggest danger is that his or her muscles will be frozen by the current and he or she will not be able to pull away from it. If this happens, the most important thing is to get the electrician away from the current as quickly as possible. The length of time a person is connected to the mains supply will determine the severity of injury and the likelihood of cardiac arrest and death. Do not touch someone who is being electrocuted. Unless you can move faster than 186,000 miles per second (the speed of light), you will become part of the circuit. Pushing the victim with a wooden plank or an apple box is a safe way to disengage him from the circuit. A running, jumping body block can work as long as you are in the air when you hit the victim

Table 8.3 Effect of resistance on amperage of shock

Condition	*Resistance*	*Amps*
Dry skin @ 100 V	100,000	1 mA
Wet skin @ 100 V	1,000	100 mA
Open cut @ 100 V	500	200 mA
Dry skin @ 10,000 V	100,000	100 mA

and do not complete a circuit to earth.

Once the victim is away from the circuit, check for pulse and breathing. Begin resuscitation immediately if there is no pulse. Call for professional medical assistance.

In addition to the duration of contact, the severity of damage from a shock is proportional to the number of vital organs that the current passes through, especially the heart. The most lethal path electricity can take is into one arm and out of the other. As electricity travels across the chest and through the heart, it can very easily cause ventricular fibrillation or stop the heart entirely. For this reason, when dealing with live exposed wires, many electricians handle the wire with one hand and put the other hand in their pocket or behind their back if possible.

The severity of a shock is a combination of the voltage in the circuit, the frequency of the supply and the resistance present (Table 8.3). Shocks are very time dependent and if the time of contact with the mains is very brief (around 40 ms or less) little or no harm will be done. It is this fact that ensures that GFCIs (RCDs) do their work safely and efficiently.

However, in many of the situations cited in this book earth leakage trips will not be protecting the circuits so the maximum caution should be exercised. The resistance of dry skin, for example, is about 100,000 Ω. This resistance is enough that contact with a 100 V circuit will allow about 1 milli-ampere (mA), or 0.001 A, to flow through the body, which will not be felt (Table 8.4). In contrast, the resistance of wet skin is about 1,000 Ω which allows about 100 mA to flow through the body. This is enough to cause ventricular fibrillation, impede breathing and cause unconsciousness and possibly death. Wearing thick rubber electricians gloves is recommended any time you are exposed to live lugs and cables.

AC current can be more deadly than DC current for several reasons. Although both types of current have the effects listed in Table 8.4, AC can freeze a body to a conductor with one fifth as much current as DC. Alternating current can more easily cause fibrillation and cardiac arrest because the 50 Hz polarity cycle is a harmonic of the rhythm of the heart and because AC has a peak voltage of 340 V, while DC is a constant 120 V. In Europe the problem is greater because of the higher AC voltages used. However, this is not to say that DC power cannot hurt and kill a person.

Every electrician must have a healthy respect for electricity if he or she aims to

Table 8.4 Effect of amperage on shock victim

Current	*Effect on body*
1 mA or less	No sensation (not felt)
More than 5 mA	Painful shock
More than 10 mA	Muscle contractions; could cause a 'freezing' to the electrical circuit for some people
More than 15 mA	Muscle contractions; can cause most people to become frozen to the electrical circuit
More than 30 mA	Breathing difficult; could cause unconsciousness
50–100 mA	Ventricular fibrillation of the heart possible
100–200 mA	Ventricular fibrillation of the heart certain; death is possible
Over 200 mA	Severe burns and muscular contractions; the heart is more apt to stop beating than to fibrillate; death is likely
1 A or more	Permanent damage to body tissues; cardiac arrest, severe burns, and probable death

have a long and successful career. People are killed every year by electrocution, the majority of accidents are caused by faulty equipment that has been poorly maintained, but some people are injured or killed by their own ignorance or foolishness. Pressure from the powers that be, long hours and physical exhaustion can cloud good judgement and clear thinking. Be aware of your physical and mental state. As a professional, your judgement of a situation has weight; don't discount it. No matter how frantic things get, when it comes to dealing with exposed live conductors, remember to slow down, think about what you are doing and don't let anyone distract you. No situation in film-making is worth the risk to your life and health.

9

Electrical distribution

The component parts of a distribution system are as follows:

- **Power supply** The power may come from one or more of a number of sources: a mobile generator; designated studio circuits, which are powered by a municipal transformer or turbine generators; a tie-in to the service panel on location; a location power drop; a battery or battery pack; or available wall circuits. Power sources are covered in Chapter 10.
- **Intake switch (main disconnect)** The main disconnect, an isolator switch with current-limiting fuses or breaker or circuit breakers, provides a main switch to shut down all power at the end of the day or in an emergency. It also provides main circuit protection for the power supply. In the case of a generator, the main breaker switch or fuse is part of the generator.
- **Main feeder cable** This cable, usually 400 A or 150 A single core cable, carries power from the power supply to the set.
- **Main distribution junction box or control centre** The main feeder terminates into distribution boxes which function as a junction, dividing the power into multiple outlets for smaller intermediate feeder cable.
- **Distribution boxes or portable remote switchboards** Distribution boxes provide circuit protection and subdivide power further, providing outlets of different sizes to supply lights of various sizes, and subsequent smaller outlet boxes.
- **Dimmers** Dimmer packs are powered from the main feeder, and may control some or all of the lights.
- **Extensions** Extension cables, run from the distribution boxes to the larger lights and outlet boxes.
- **Final outlet boxes** Provide outlets for plugging the smaller lights.

European distribution systems

There are many similarities between the UK and American systems of distribution, although the amperage requirements are much less in Europe, due to the higher volt-

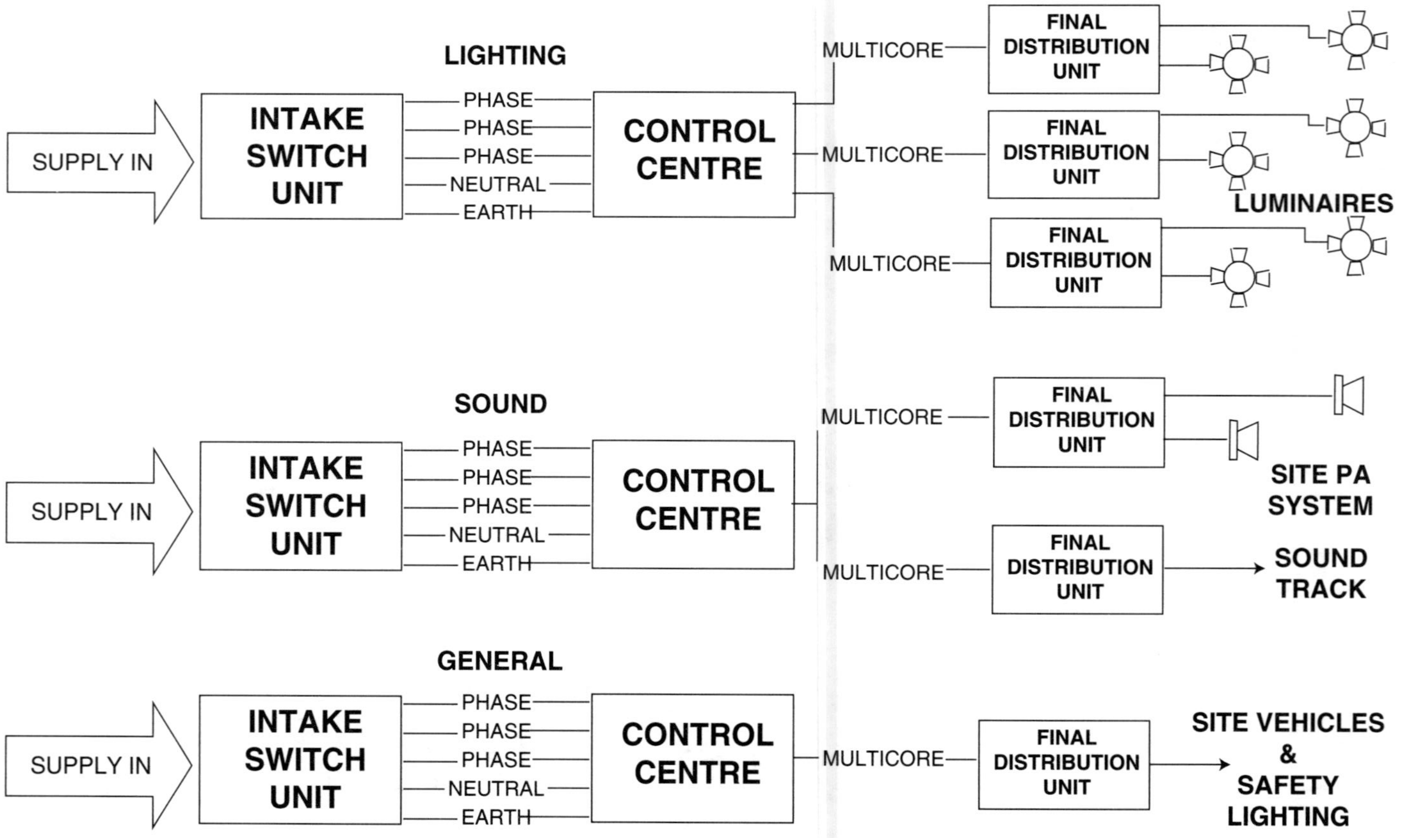

Figure 9.1 Distribution systems overview

ages used. The UK system of distribution is based upon BS 5550, which was introduced in 1981 and is periodically revised. It has been very successful in streamlining the number of connectors and cable systems in use, together with the types of switchgear and distribution units. The primary distribution units consist of the following (see Figure 9.1):

1 Intake switch unit (ISU) – power intake from the mains or generator – 400 A
2. Control centre (CC) – Intermediate distribution – 400 A/125 A/63 A
3. Final distribution unit (FDU) – 125 A/32 A/16 A.

The main power distribution cables are single core, typically 400 A, 250 A or 150 A and commonly use BAC connectors. BAC, Spade, Tec connectors or bare wires are used to connect to the power supply. It is essential to identify each of these cables clearly to show whether it is a phase, neutral or earth conductor. Obviously, any mis-plugging can cause a huge fault, or a very dangerous situation. Several modern distribution systems do have sensing circuits to prevent any mis-plugging. The system (shown in Figures 9.2, 9.3 and 9.4) is used by Michael Samuelson Lighting Ltd of Pinewood Studios. It incorporates four system status lights on the top of each distribution unit. A green light indicates the box is properly grounded. Red light warns of reversed polarity, and a blue light and buzzer indicate ground leakage. The buzzer lets an electrician know that there is a ground leak as soon as a lantern is plugged in, even when the flashing blue light is out of sight. The buzzer can be turned off with a key (held by the gaffer) in which case a yellow light comes on to indicate when the buzzer is disabled.

The main feeder cables terminate into a control centre (CC) distribution box. In a three-phase system this box feeds multiple three-phase 125 A subfeeders which run to either a splitter unit (which separates the phases into three 125 A single phase runs), or into a distribution unit which offers a variety of single-phase outlets.

Generally, multi-core connectors and cables are used for circuits 125 A and less. BS 4343 connectors are commonly used. Figure 9.2 shows the four single-phase connector sizes. Typically these would be colour-coded blue for single-phase. There are three families of connectors which are colour-coded: red for 3-phase connectors, blue for single-phase ones and yellow for low voltage connectors.

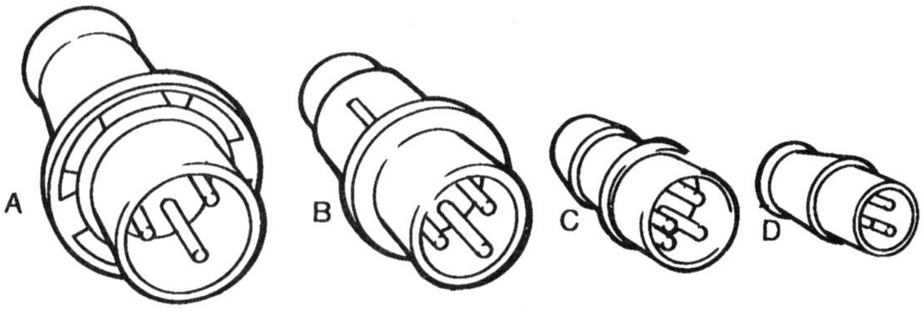

Figure 9.2 BS 4343 1-phase plugs: (A) 125 A; (B) 63 A; (C) 32 A; (D) 16 A. (From David Samuelson's *'Hands-on' Manual for Cinematographers*, [Oxford: Focal Press, 1994]. Reproduced with permission of Focal Press.)

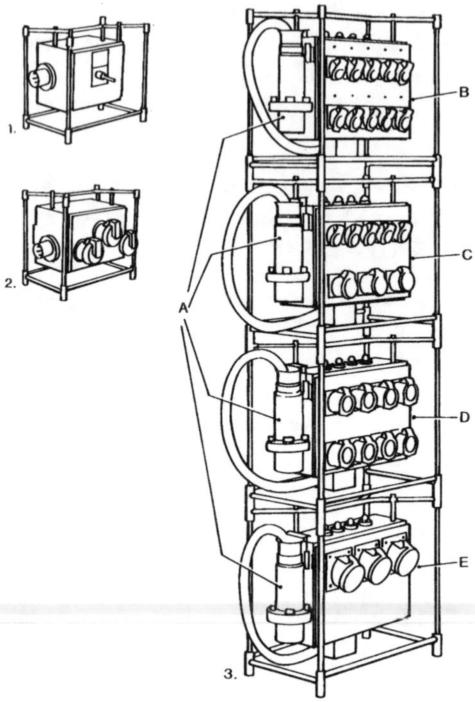

Figure 9.3 MSL electric distribution system: (1) '125' isolation switch unit, (2)'125' 3-phase splitter unit, (3) stacked '125' distribution units: (A) 125 amp 1-phase (with inlet plugs on short cables); (B) 10 × 16 amp outlets; (C) 5 × 16 amp + 3 × 32 amp outlets; (D) 8 × 32 amp outlets. (From David Samuelson's *'Hands-on' Manual for Cinematographers*, [Oxford: Focal Press, 1994]. Reproduced with permission of Focal Press.)

There are several different input and output power arrangements of the units to cater for the variety of connectors used and for three-phase and single-phase operation. Figure 9.3 shows some examples. Figure 9.4 shows the step-down structure generally used with DC circuits, single-phase AC circuits and three-phase AC circuits.

The six boxes shown here form a system: 125 A Intake Switch Unit (1), 125 A three-phase to three 125 A single-phase splitter unit (2), and junction boxes that distribute power to all the various outlet sizes (3). The system also incorporates splitter units to divide 125 A to 63 A outlets, and 63 A to 32 A outlets. There are outlet boxes with 63 or 32 A inputs and multiple 16 A outputs, and Y-splitters and jumper leads to adapt to domestic type plugs. 16 A connectors are typically used on luminaires up to about 3,500 W. 32 A connectors can be used on luminaires up to about 7,000 W. 63 A connectors are typical for luminaires up to 12 kW.

Distribution units are fitted with the necessary power intake switchgear and subdistribution fuses or MCBs contained within one unit, which makes rigging so much safer by reducing the amount of interconnections on site. Each outlet has its own

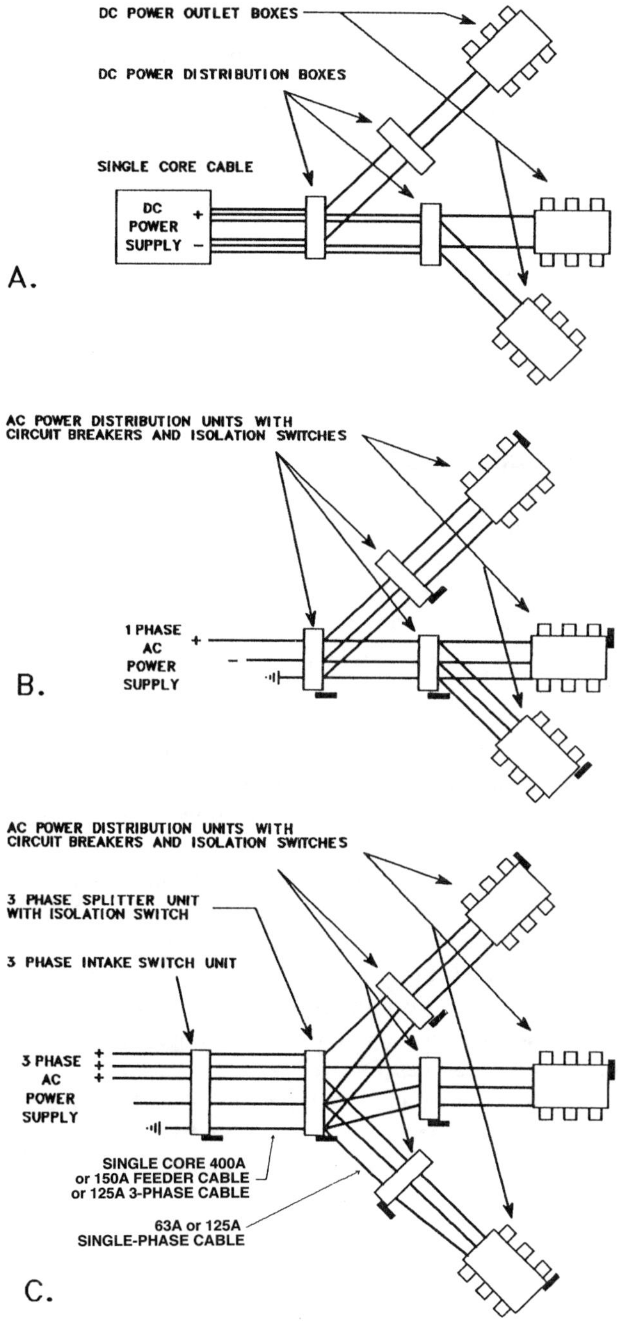

Figure 9.4 Power distribution schematics. (A) DC System, (B) Single-phase AC System, (C) Three-Phase System. (From David Samuelson's *'Hands-on' Manual for Cinematographers*, [Oxford: Focal Press, 1994]. Reproduced with permission of Focal Press.)

mechanical circuit breaker and neon indicator. Most modern distribution units are fitted with RCDs and to prevent nuisance tripping; they are also fitted with a bypass system accessed by the use of a key.

There are many other types of connectors used for various purposes and by various vendors. Electrical regulations specify that all connectors must be approved to either a British Standard or an International Standard, and should only be used with the correct pin connections and relevant colour codes. Under the British Health and Safety regulations all items used on the temporary installation must be tested for electrical safety prior to being delivered to site and they have to be marked that the test was satisfactory. It is essential that when any temporary installation is complete, wherever it is, that it is fully checked to ensure that all connections and equipment have been installed correctly prior to the application of power to the system.

American distribution systems

Many systems of cable, connectors, junction boxes and distribution boxes are in use in the American motion picture industry today (Figure 9.5). You can often find two or more different systems working on a set servicing different pieces of equipment. The basic structure of distribution is the same.

Feeder cable

The first thing to determine in planning a cable run is the size of the main feeder by estimating what the maximum total amperage requirement will be (including headroom for discharge sources starting currents and allowing for line losses based on the length of the main run).

A small set-up, 380 A or less, can run on three-wire, single-phase *banded cable*. A medium-size set-up, using more than two large lights (12 kWs, 10kWs, maxi-brutes), will typically require 2/0 cable (300 A per leg max., 600 A single-phase, 900 A three-phase max.). A large set-up (or especially long run) will require 4/0 cable (400 A per leg, 800 A single-phase, 1,200 A three-phase max.). On a large studio sound stage, or for a night scene that takes in a lot of acreage, multiple cable runs may be required involving multiple power sources.

Starting at the power source and moving towards the load, the first type of connector encountered attaches the distribution system to the power supply. Generators are commonly fitted with bus bars for lug cable, and/or Cam-Lok receptacles and/or mole-pin receptacles.

Sister lugs

Lugs are heavy-duty copper or bronze-cast clamps that screw on to the copper bus bars of the power supply and spider boxes.

Lug cable, heavy, single-conductor, usually 4/0 or 2/0 cable with lugs at both ends, is used for primary feeders, running from the bus bar to the spider box and from spider box to spider box.

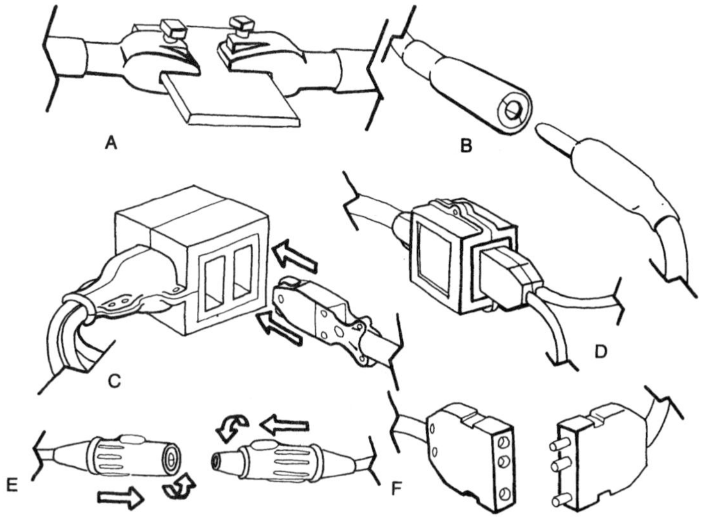

Figure 9.5 US connectors: (A) lugs attached to bus bar or spider;, (B) ½ in. mole-pins; (C) four-hole stage box and paddle; (D) one-hole stage box with two half paddles plugged into it; (E) Cam-Lok connectors; (F) Bates three-pin connectors

Spider boxes

A spider box is an intermediate cable splicing point used to join lengths of lug cable, or to divide power in several directions. A spider box houses several ¼ in. thick copper bars held in a transparent Plexiglas insulated frame. Spider boxes provide a bar for each wire of the distribution cable; each bar can accommodate between four and eight lugs. Spider boxes may have two, three, four, or five bars, depending on the number of wires in the circuit. Holes in the Plexiglas frame provide access to the lug bolts, which are tightened to the bars using a T-handle 3⁄16 in. Allen wrench (Figure 9.6).

Warning: Never use a green bus bar as a current-carrying bus; it is an earthing bar only. The green bus bar is connected directly to the external metal straps, which will create a serious short and shock hazard if the bus bar is connected to a hot lead. The ampacity per cable and per bar of a spider box is determined by the number of lugs per bar.

Mole-pin feeder cable

Mole-pin connectors are single-conductor, ½ in. diameter, slip-pin connectors. Mole-pins are used on feeder cables and on the head cables of some larger lights. A lug-to-mole-pin adaptor, or jumper (Figure 9.7A), connects mole-pin feeders to the spider box or deuce board.

Mole-pin feeder cables are widely used for 2/0 cable and on banded 2 AWG cable. On banded cable, the legs are colour-coded with rubber sheaths at the base of the

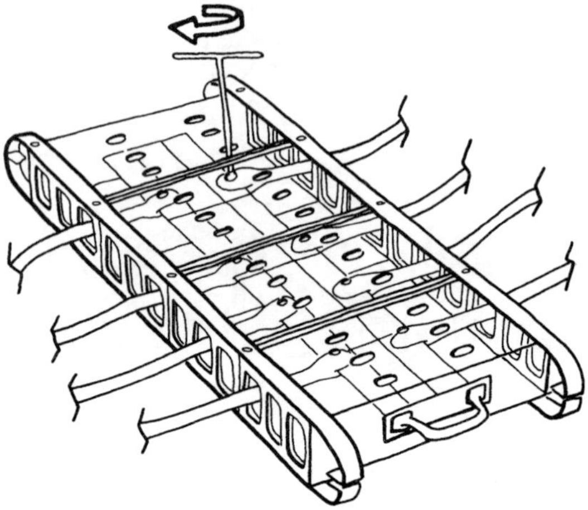

Figure 9.6 Spider boxes allow up to six lugs per bar. Lug nuts are tightened with a T-handle Allen wrench through the holes in the Plexiglas frame

connectors. Mole-pins are made that can fit cable sizes from 4/0 to as small as 10 AWG.

The 1996 NEC (where adopted) requires that feeder cable connectors on AC circuits have a mechanical locking mechanism to hold them together. Since then Mole and other manufacturers have come up with different types of locking sheaths.

Reversed ground system

With all types of pin connectors, the male and female are oriented with 'pins to power,' meaning that the male pins point towards the power plant and the female end goes towards the lights. This ensures that only female connectors are live parts and if correctly designed, 'finger proof'. This is true of all cable, except when a reverse earthing is used; the pin on the grounding wire is pointed downstream.

Table 9.1 Amperage capacity of stage boxes

Stage box	*Circuit type*	*Amps per hole*	*Amps per side*	*Amps total*
One-hole	Two-wire	50	–	50
Two-hole	Two-wire	45	–	90
Four-hole	Two-wire	85	–	170
Four-hole	Three-wire	85	110	220
Six-hole	Two-wire	85	170	265
Six-hole	Three-wire	85	170	340

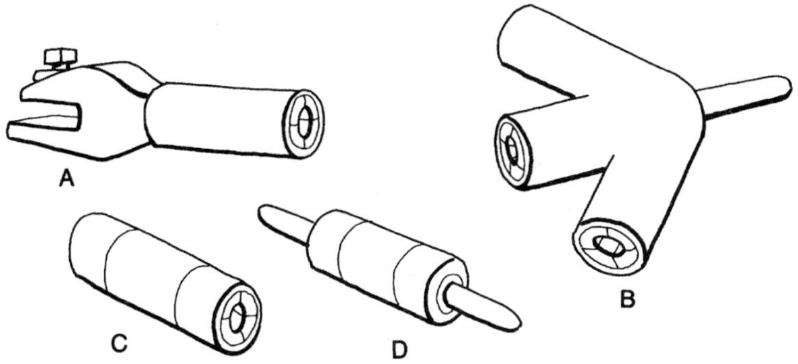

Figure 9.7 Mole-pins: (A) lug-to-mole-pin adaptor; (B) mole-pin three-fer; (C) female-to-female mole-pin adaptor; (D) suicide pin male-to-male mole-pin adaptor

Some rental houses and studios make their banded cable with the earthing pin reversed; the female end points towards the power source. Many best boys also run their single conductor cable with the earthing wire connectors in reverse. The idea is to make it impossible to plug a hot wire into the earthing wire by mistake.

Three-fers

Three-fers are used to branch three feeder cables off of one (Figure 9.7B). A standard three-fer interconnects one male pin with three female receptacles. One three-fer is used on each leg. They are colour-coded.

Earthing stars and earthing clusters

An earthing three-fer, or grounding star used with a reverse earth system, interconnects three male pins with one female receptacle. An earthing cluster or 'squid' is a soft-wired set of connectors that serves the same purpose.

Suicide pins

A suicide pin is a male-to-male mole-pin adaptor (Figure 9.7D). It gets its name from the fact that when the adaptor is plugged in, it exposes a hot pin. Obviously, you should never leave a bare suicide pin plugged into a live wire. Suicide pins are used to reverse the direction of the connectors on the earthing wire or to make a feeder loop (see 'Rigging' later in this chapter).

Cam-Lok cable

Cam-Lok connectors are single-conductor connectors used on 4/0 and 2/0 feeder cable, an alternative system to lugs and spider boxes. Cam-Lok is also the most common input connector for dimmer packs.

The male and female connectors twist-lock together with a cam mechanism which ensures full contact yet is easy to connect and disconnect. However, to ensure a good connection, the connectors must be twisted until tight, not simply inserted. The connectors are shielded with rubber so that bare metal cannot be left exposed, and the

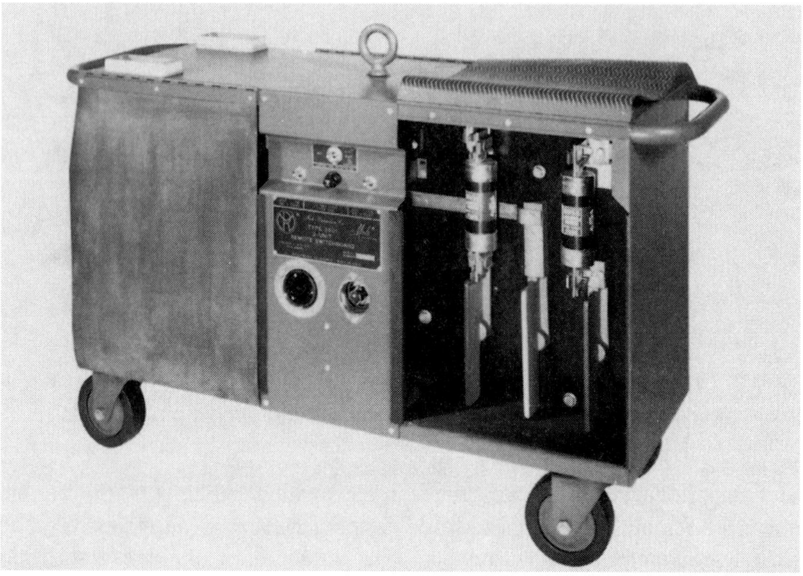

Figure 9.8 Deuce boards with two high-amperage, remote-control, fused switches in a stackable casing. The deuce board shown is designed for a three-wire 800 A AC or DC input and two three-wire 400 A outputs (200 A per leg). (Photo courtesy of Mole-Richardson Co., Hollywood, CA.)

connection is protected from water. The rubber is colour-coded red, blue, black, white, or green appropriately.

Remote switchboards

Switchboards (commonly called location boards or deuce boards) work with any three-wire system: AC or DC. On DC sound stages switchboards are commonly used to provide circuit protection at a workable amperage, 200 A per leg. (In most cases, the circuit protection for DC cans is located in the powerhouse, not in the sound stage, and is set at 1,200 A per leg.) Once the feeder cables have reached the vicinity of the set, they are usually connected to a switchboard. These switches control power to various areas of a large set or to several separate sets within one stage. An ace board has a single switch (400 A total). A deuce board divides power between two switches (800 A input total) (Figure 9.8).

A four-way board divides power between four switches (1,600 A input total). The input feeder lugs connect to bus bars on the switchboard. Sets of output bus bars are provided on the front of the unit. Each output circuit has individual circuit protection and separate toggle switches that control internal high-amperage contactors. The contactors can be controlled by toggle switches on the switchboard or from a remote toggle switch box or a practical switch wired into the set. A main switch is provided in both locations to switch all contactors at once. Control cables run down to stage level, from which all the switches throughout the stage can be controlled. Switchboards are designed to be stacked. An eyelet is provided on the top of each unit for hoisting it into catwalks.

On DC sound stages, stage boxes (paddle connectors) and stage extensions run from the deuce boards to the lights and floor drops. (More about the DC paddle system will be discussed later.) On AC systems banded cable runs from the deuce boards to 400A distro boxes around the set. AC deuce boards are also available with 100A Bates outlets and circuit breakers.

AC power distribution boxes

Whatever the feeder cable, lug, mole-pin, Cam-Lok, or what have you, the feeder cable terminates into a *distribution box.* The distribution (distro) box provides a fused step-down point for the subsequent smaller circuits that service the lights. Circuit protection (breakers or fuses) are required within 25 ft of any reduction in

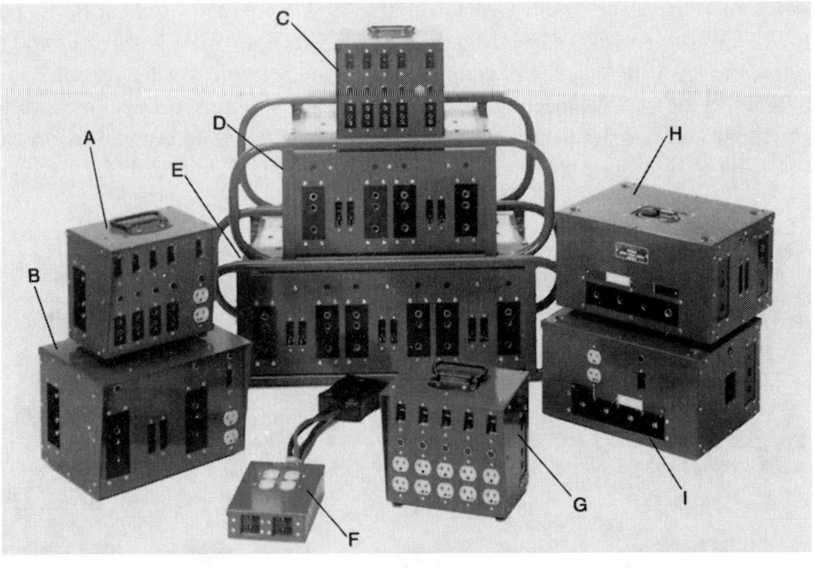

Figure 9.9 Mole distro boxes: (A) Bates/Edison outlet box: 100 A Bates in, four 20 A Bates out, one 20 A duplex Edison out, 100 A Bates feed-through; (B) Bates step-down box: 100-A Bates in, two 60 A Bates out, 100 A Bates feed-through; (C) Bates outlet box: 100 A Bates in, five 20 A Bates out, 100 A Bates feed-through; (D) single-phase spider/distribution box: lugs in (red, blue, white, and green), four 100 A Bates out; (E) three-phase spider/distribution box: lugs in (red, blue, black, white, and green), six 100 A Bates out, two 208 V 100 A Bates out; (F) gang box: 100 A Bates in, four 20 A Edison out; (G) Edison 'lunch box': 100 A Bates in, five 20 A Edison out; (H) banded pin box: mole-pins in, single phase; four 100 A Bates out; pin feed-through; courtesy duplex Edison receptacle; (I) 240 V banded pin box: mole-pins in, single phase; two 240 V 100-A Bates out; pin feed-through, courtesy duplex Edison receptacle. (Photo courtesy of Mole-Richardson Co., Hollywood, CA.)

cable size (NEC 240-21). 100 A Bates outputs are widely used on distro boxes. Some boxes also offer 240 V 100 A Bates, 60 A Bates or Edison outlets. Figure 9.9 shows the line of Mole-Richardson distribution boxes.

Some questions to consider when ordering boxes: Single-phase or three-phase? Input connector type? AC/DC or AC only? Do you need 240 V 100 A outlets for 12 kW and 20 kWs? Do you want some boxes that feed through? Most boxes have indicator lights (help with trouble shooting) and courtesy outlets (in a dark stage it's good to have a small work light at each box).

Bates three-pin connectors

Bates connectors come in several sizes: 20 A, 60 A, 100 A, and 240 V 100 A (Figure 9.10). They are three-pin connectors: hot wire, neutral and ground (except the 240 V 100 A connector, which is a ground and two hot wires, no neutral). 100 A and 60 A extensions (100 ft, 50 ft or 25 ft) run from the distro boxes to the lights and gang boxes. 100 A Bates connectors are used on lights of more than 7.2 kW such as 10 kW Fresnels, 9 kW maxi-brutes, 8 kW softlights. 60 A Bates are used on lights from 2 kW to 7.2 kW such as 5k W Fresnels, 9-lite FAYS (5,850 W), 4 kW softlights, 5 kW sky pans, etc. A 100 A-to-60 A adaptor/splitter must typically be used to connect these lights to the 100 A outlet on the distro box. Twenty amp Bates plugs are found only on theatrical lamps (ellipsoidal spotlights and parcans) and in television studios in which all the lighting equipment is used in-house only. Such facilities are installed

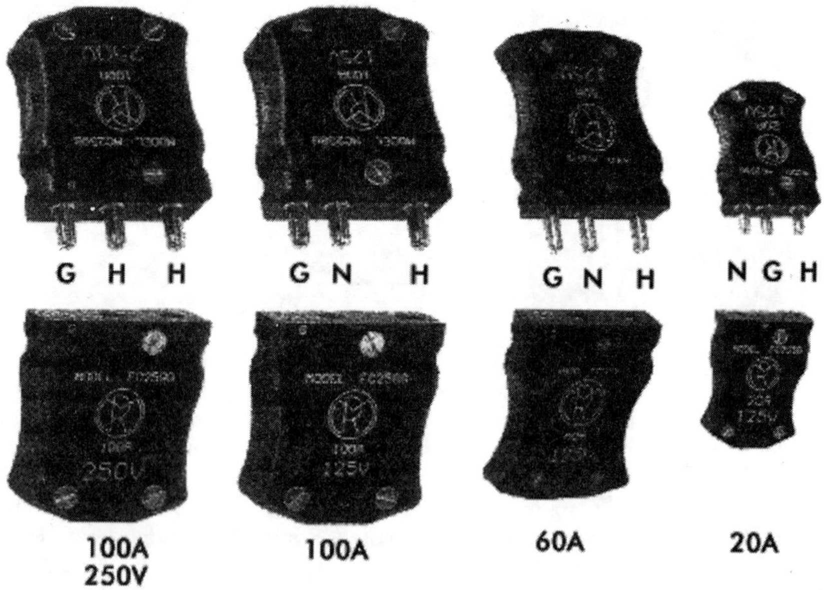

Figure 9.10 Bates connectors. The 100 A, 240 V connector is similar to the 100 A connector but the neutral pin is instead a hot pin and is positioned closer to the centre of the plug

with permanent numbered circuits around the walls of the stage, in the floor and mounted to overhead pipes. This permanent feeder system is hard-wired to a patch panel and dimmer board. Twenty amp Bates extensions are used instead of Edison stingers. Distro boxes with 20 A Bates outlets can be ordered if a large number of Bates-fitted lamps will be used, but ordinarily in location work Edison outlets are used for lamps 2 kW or less. Lamps with 20 Bates plugs require an adaptor pigtail (Edison male/Bates female).

Bates connector pins are sized and positioned asymmetrically so they make ground first, break ground last, and they are polarized, they cannot be plugged in incorrectly. Bates connectors will melt if they become overheated; keep them strictly within their designed amperage limits. Where one Bates cable plugs into another, tape the connection so they don't pull apart.

Edison boxes

Edison *gang boxes* are fitted with either a 100 A or a 60 A male Bates. A 'lunch box' (Figure 9.9G) provides five 20 A duplex circuits (ten Edison outlets) with 20 A circuit breakers and indicator lights on each circuit. Some also provide a 100 A female outlet, so you can feed through to subsequent boxes.

Adaptors

There are as many kinds of adaptors as there are different combinations of connectors: lugs to mole-pin, lugs to Cam-Lok, full stage to 60 A Bates, 20 A Bates to Edison, 20 A twist-lock to 20 A Bates, and so on. Adaptors often come in the form of a *pig tail*: a soft-wired adaptor, which is nothing more than a foot or so of cable with a different connector on each end. When ordering equipment, the best boy must take care to order the adaptor needed to connect each piece of equipment. When referring to an adaptor, designate the male end first.

- **100A to 2 100 A splitters** The idea of this splitter is to give you more outlets for 60 A splitters, 100 A gangs, and lights. *Note*: Under no circumstances should this splitter be used to pull more than 100 A total.
- **100 A to 2 60 A splitters** Order as many of these as you have lights and gangs with 60 A tails. *Note*: some adaptors are fitted with in-line 60 A fuses. Be sure to stock spares and be on the lookout for burn-outs.
- **240 V 100 A Bates snake bites** (mole-pin to Bates adaptors) If you get caught without a 240 V Bates outlet for a 20 kW, this solves the problem. *Note*: Although very handy, there is no circuit protection here either.
- **3-wire 100 A Bates snake bites** (3-wire mole-pin to 2 100 A Bates) In the absence of a distro box, a snake-bite patches directly into three-fers. *Note*: Although very handy, there is no circuit protection here either.
- **Edison to 20A Bates pigtails** You will need adaptors with any theatrical lights you order.
- **100 A Bates to mole-pin adaptors** Be sure to ask for the type of connector for

any large lights you order. If the light has mole-pins, you may need to adapt to 100A Bates.

- **Cam-Lok jumpers** (lug to Cam-Lok) Jumpers are typically used to lug dimmer packs into a spider box.
- **Lug jumpers** 10 ft lug jumpers are handy to connect deuce-boards to a near-by spider box.
- **Banded jumpers** Handy to wire a 400 A distro box into a spider box.

DC paddle/stage box system

The paddle/stage box system is a two-pole, non-polarized, ungrounded system of plugs and receptacles that has been in use longer than any other system. It is still used today for DC rigging on sound stages. It was originally designed as a DC system and, strictly speaking, was never approved for use with AC power. However, as AC power became more common on sets, the system came to be used for both AC and DC. Many rental houses retrofitted their stage boxes with grounding leads to meet NEC grounding requirements for AC power. In 1992 authorities began to enforce the 1987 NEC ban on the use of stage boxes and paddle plugs with AC current.

Stage boxes

Stage boxes are referred to by the number of holes they have: one-hole, two-hole, four-hole or six-hole box. Lights with stage, or paddle, connectors plug directly into the stage box. A gang box plugs into the stage box with a paddle connector (Figure 9.11).

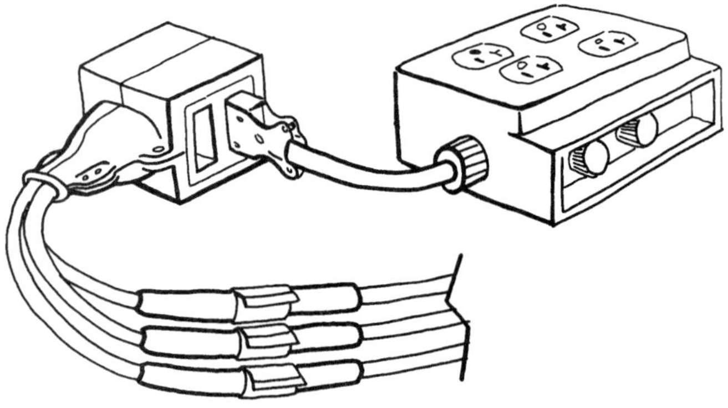

Figure 9.11 A fused gang box plugged into a stage box

A normal full stage plug (1 in. thick) can carry a maximum of 85 A. A half stage plug (½ in. thick) can carry 20 A and can fit two to a hole in a stage box (Table 9.1).

Stage boxes come in both two-wire (single-circuit) and three-wire (120/240) versions. The colour-coded sheath at the base of the mole-pins or lugs identifies the legs. When you connect the box normally, blue to blue, red to red, and white to white, you get two 120 V circuits (Figure 9.12A).

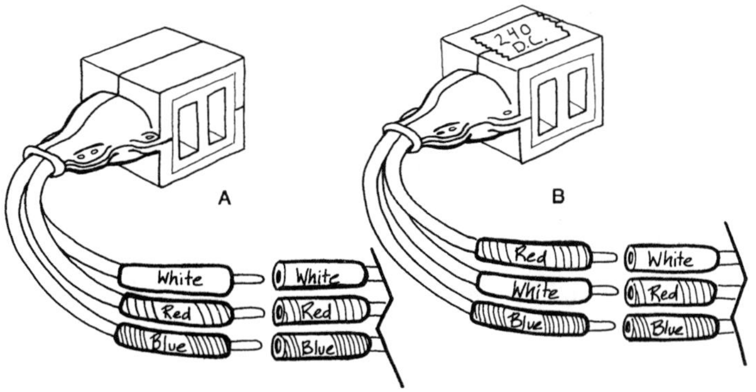

Figure 9.12 (A) A four-hole stage box connected normally provides four 120 V outlets: two on the red leg and two on the blue leg. (B) A four-hole box connected red to white and white to red provides 240 V power on the blue side and 120 V power on the red side

Three-wire boxes are painted red on one side and blue on the other to show the leg into which the paddle is plugged.

Connecting a stage box for 240/120 V power

To get 240 V current from a stage box, connect the feeder to the box as follows: red to white, white to red, and blue to blue (Figure 9.12B). This connects the two hot legs to the blue side of the stage box, making it 240 V. The red side still runs 120 V on the red leg. Whenever you '240' a stage box, be sure to mark it boldly with a big piece of tape.

Stage extensions

A stage extension has a stage plug on one end and a one-hole or two-hole box on the other. It is used as an extension for the bigger lights that have paddle connectors, or for Edison gang boxes.

Precautions with the stage box system

1. The holes of stage boxes are large enough to put your fingers into, which presents a hazard. Tape over holes that are not in use, especially when children or animals will be present.
2. Be very careful not to incorrectly connect a three-wire system to the stage box and run 240 V accidentally. Always label 240 V circuits.
3. There is little to prevent moisture from getting into the connections when water is present. When shooting around moisture (e.g., on dewy grass, near a sprinkler system, in the rain, in a bathroom, near a pool), raise pin and stage box connections up on apple boxes. Wrap the connections in visqueen or plastic garbage bags.
4. When plugging in cables and lights using DC current, make sure that the fixtures are turned off. Making a hot stab, plugging in a light when it is turned on, with

DC is a dangerous business because the contacts will arc and start to weld before they can become fully connected. Gases can build up and cause an explosion. If you have to make a hot stab, insert the connector with one well-aimed, straight, firm motion, so it goes in all the way at once. Avoid hot stabs whenever possible.

Meltric/Abbott system

The Meltric/Abbott system (Figure 9.13) is used on a limited number of stages around Hollywood.

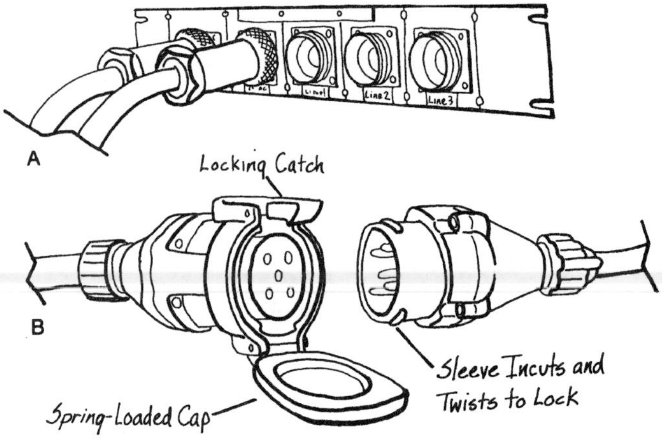

Figure 9.13 (A) An Abbott sequentially locking panel, (B) Meltric connectors

The system uses 400 A or 200 A Abbott connectors on the feeder cable and Meltric 225 A, 100 A, and 60A connectors for the sub-feeders. The entire system is equipped with five wires for three-phase AC power, but it can be used for single-phase AC if not all of the wires are used. Wheeled distribution boxes provide step-down points with circuit protection. There are several kinds of distribution boxes: the main disconnect, the feeder splicing block, the feed-through feeder distribution box, and the subfeeder distribution boxes. Meltric 100 A banded cable extensions are used for subfeeder. Meltric 100 A to 100 A 'octopus' three-fers and Meltric 100 A to 60 A 'squid' three-fers divide the three-phase power into single-phase 120 V circuits. Fused 90 A and 50 A gang boxes provide Edison or twist-lock outlets for the smaller luminaires.

Meltric connectors

Meltric connectors feature a positive mechanical lock, spring-loaded connector caps, and a five-wire polarized 'make first, break last' pin configuration that prevents wires from being plugged incorrectly. The connectors are spring-loaded so they spring apart when released and must be pushed together with force to connect them. Because of their rugged design and many features, the connectors are larger and heavier than other distribution connectors.

Abbott connectors and sequentially locking panels

The sequential safety-lock panel is designed to make it impossible to connect and disconnect the feeder cables in the wrong order. A locking mechanism prevents any connectors from being connected before the earth. Once the earth is connected, the neutral must be connected next, and only then can the hot wires be connected.

Other brands of connectors have similar sequentially locking panels. Posi-loc is a system for Cam-Lok connectors, and VEAM B-lok is a similar panel for VEAM single-conductor connectors. Sequentially locking panels are not required by code, and while some feel that they make the distribution system idiot-proof, the use of panels on every female connection is generally an unnecessary encumbrance.

Rigging

On large sets, a rigging crew prerigs the cabling and hangs whatever lights are to be used prior to shooting. The rigging crew is supervised by the rigging gaffer, who plans the cabling for the sets. She/he sees to it that the lights on the floor and above the set are supplied with adequate power. She/he strategically places power drops so that distro boxes are readily available at any place on or above the set to allow additional lights. The rigging gaffer plans the placement and cabling of switchboards and dimmer racks as required by the situation or as requested by the DP and the gaffer. She/he oversees the rigging and testing of the power system from beginning to end. On smaller productions, the best boy may serve as the rigging gaffer and go out with a couple of extra electricians to prerig locations.

Distribution strategy

Planning the cabling and distribution for a set or location requires planning, forethought, and calculation. During filming, an electrician working the set should only need to glance around the immediate area to find power for the light, and yet the cable must remain neat and invisible to the camera at all times. An electrician should rarely require a 50 ft stinger on a set that is properly cabled, nor should a stinger have to cross a room if the distribution is effectively laid out. You should never find yourself having to run four or five stingers out a door and around a corner; one properly placed distro box can eliminate a lot of work, mess, and task-time. No matter how far away the gaffer wants a light, getting power should not create a crisis; cable should be standing by, ready to be run out to it.

Set power, the 'ring of fire'

Here are some rules of thumb for laying out set power on location and on sound stage alike. Provide a 'ring of fire', surround the set with power on all sides. Rigging is not only a matter of having sufficient amperage available, but of having outlets placed so that one is always close at hand. No matter where the camera is placed, you should have an outlet box ready to pull in behind camera. In each room where action is to take place, have cable and outlet box coiled outside each door ready to come in when needed. In a room with only one door, provide power on the opposite side of the room (through a window, through a rat hole in the set, over the top of the set wall, or dropped from the grid), ready to come in should the door have to close. Provide at least 63 A to each side of a room. In a large room provide power boxes every 50 ft (hidden outside windows, in side rooms, through rat holes, or ready to drop from the grid). In a house with a staircase, you will need power at the top of the stairs. Hide cables that cross doorways by routing the cable up and over the top of the door.

Substantial amounts of power are often required outside windows to power large units pointing into the room, as well as units lighting up an exterior (at night). When shooting on a stage, a translight or scenic painting will often be hung outside windows to provide an exterior backdrop (a cityscape, suburban street, mountain woodland, or what have you). Translights are typically back lit with a row of skypans. When shooting in a room with a lot of windows, you can expect that the gaffer will want to put some large units outside. Have the necessary distribution box positioned accordingly.

The DP may want to place lights inside buildings across the street, or create a streetlight effect on background buildings. To provide for this eventuality, you may need to have several hundred feet of cable ready to run out, hidden from the camera.

Planning the rig

The process of planning a rig:

1. Walk the set, and decide where you will need service: floor drops and high boxes. Add up the amperage demand.
2. Add to that the amperage demand of the prerigged lights.
3. The total will be the amperage carried by the main feeder run. On a large studio stage, several separate circuits supply cans are installed throughout the stage; for each area, power is drawn from the nearest can. In this case, add up the amperage demand for each circuit, which gives the amperage of the cable run from each can.
4. Calculate the number of switchboard circuits and dimmer circuits that will be needed. Decide where this equipment can be most strategically placed so as to minimize the length of cable needed.
5. Estimate the amount of cable and distribution equipment needed to run from the switchboards or dimmer circuits to the lights and plugging boxes.

You now know all the equipment that will be needed for the rig: feeder cable, switchboards, dimmers, distro boxes, subfeeder cable, extensions, and plugging boxes. The best boy can place the equipment order with the rental house or studio lighting department.

Direct current cable runs

This section describes the somewhat antiquated system still used in Hollywood for rigging DC. 4/0 cable has a maximum amperage rating of approximately 400 A. A normal three-wire circuit using 4/0 cable delivers 400 A per leg and 800 A total. If more amperage is required, the cable can be doubled (back in the heyday of DC rigging this was known as a half-million run), tripled (a 750 run), or quadrupled (a million run). Table 9.2 shows the maximum amperage that can be drawn by various configurations, and Figure 9.14 shows the configuration of wires for each run.

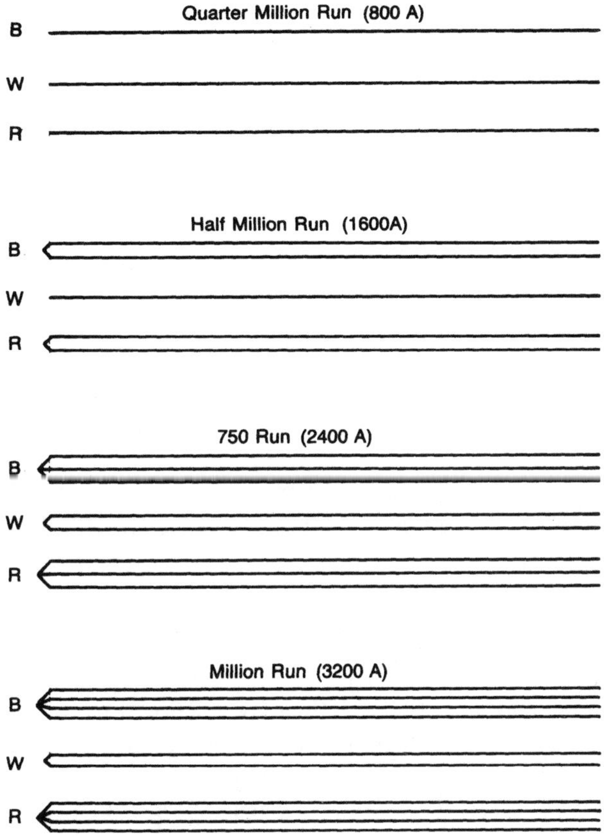

Figure 9.14 Wire configurations

Table 9.2 DC cable runs

Type of run	*Number of 40/0 Pcs*	*Amps per leg*	*Amps total*	*Configuration* Hot	Ntrl	Hot
4-2-4 (Million Run)	10	1,600	3,200	4	2	4
3-2-3 (750 Run)	8	1,200	2,400	3	2	3
2-1-2 (1/2 Million Run)	5	800	1,600	2	1	2
1-1-1 (1/4 Million Run)	3	400	800	1	1	1
2-wire	2	400	400	1	1	0

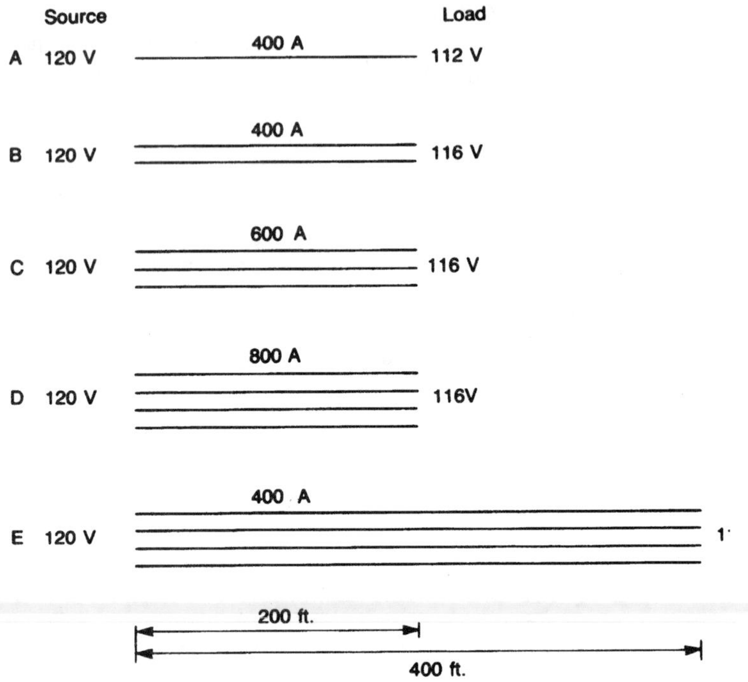

Figure 9.15 Double, triple, and quadruple cable and the effect on line loss

When running fewer neutral wires than hot leg wires, it is crucial that you maintain a balanced load. The neutral wires will not be overloaded as long as the two hot legs remain evenly balanced. Remember that the neutral only carries the difference in amperage between the two hot legs. During operation, the best boy must never let the two legs become unevenly loaded by more than the amperage capacity of the neutral wires.

Line loss

Figure 9.15 shows the effect on line loss by increasing the number of cables used. Doubling the cable (see Figure 9.15B and E) allows you to have a longer run for the same line loss, but you cannot then add amperage without the problem of line loss returning. Appendix C gives the line loss per 100 ft for various types of cable and load circuits.

Making a cable loop (ring circuit)

A trick used to either *double the effective amperage of the cable or to cut line loss by half for the same current* is to form a complete circle of cable around a set, by joining the legs at the back of the set at a spider box or with suicide pins (American system). Effectively the cables are now in parallel, and if we only require a total of 152 amps from the circuit we will have reduced the line loss to half. Joining the cables does not change the total maximum amperage, but it doubles the maximum amperage you can have at any point. For example, if the cable were 2 AWG (rated at 152 A), the maximum amperage you could have without joining the cables would be 152 A on each cable run. With the cables joined, you can run up to 304 A anywhere in the circle (Figure 9.16).

Rigging the set

During rigging, the distribution system remains disconnected from the power source and from the lights and electrical appliances. Only after the whole distribution system has been laid out and the system has been tested for shorts and discontinuity is the system connected to the power source and the main switch turned on. The best boy checks the line voltage before any lights are plugged in to make sure that the power plant has been adjusted and is running properly and that cabling is properly connected.

Rules for cabling

When laying cable, the crew typically starts at the power source and works towards

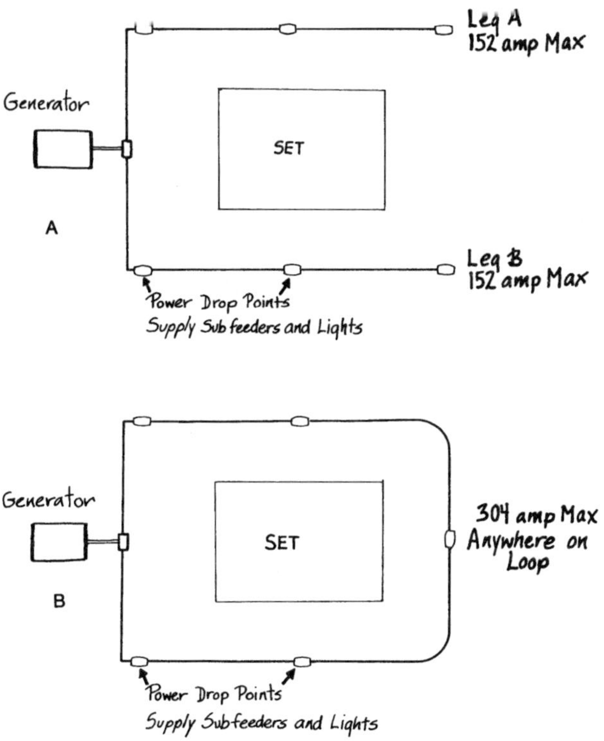

Figure 9.16 (A) Two runs of 2 AWG banded cable allow 152 A per leg on each run. (B) By connecting the cables at the ends, up to 304 A can be run anywhere in the loop

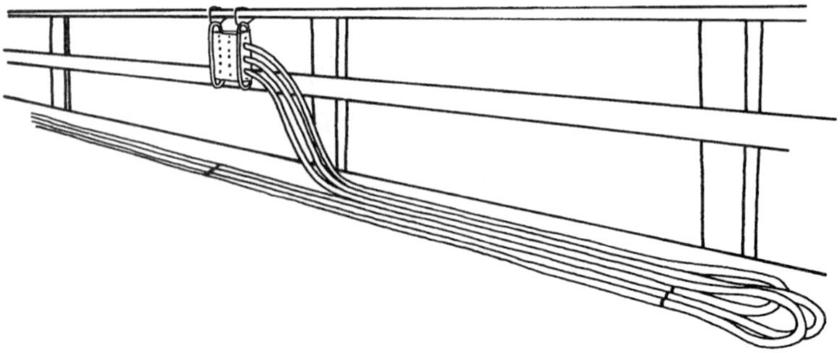

Figure 9.17 Cable laced back on itself

the set, first laying out the feeder cable, then placing and connecting the switchboards, then running power to the catwalks and stage floor and, finally, hanging the lights.

Keep the cables neat, as out of the way as possible, and well organized. Keep the cables on the sides of the catwalks to provide room to walk. In catwalks, cables may also be strung along overhead hooks called deer antlers.

Excess cable

Any excess cable should be left at the load end of the cable, where it will be available if it is needed later. Excess cable should be run out in a straight line and then turned back on itself and run to its end point (Figure 9.17).

Avoid sharp bends in cable. They will cause hot points in the cable. Never leave a live cable in a circular coil because (a) the induction associated with AC circuits can cause serious line losses and can heat up and ruin the cable, and (b) the heat from adjacent coils can cause severe overheating and possibly a fire.

Root out bad contacts

Each time you attach two pieces of cable, check the pins and be sure each connector is making solid contact. Use a pin-splitter tool to straighten bent pins. Nightmarish flicker problems are caused by bad, bent contacts in cable. Having to track down a bad cable because lights start flickering during filming is a horrible experience. The expression on the DP's face as he watches banks of lights go dark one after another while his crew scrambles around behind the sets yelling 'repatch' is enough to ruin a gaffer's whole day. Any questionable cable should be put aside, tagged boldly with tape.

Identifying cable, switchboards and spider boxes

When laying out single conductor cable, it is extremely important to identify each cable properly. Each end of each cable can be identified with knots in the tie ropes (Figure 9.18A shows a system of knots used in the USA) or with coloured tape. Mark the cable at both ends before uncoiling it.

Many different runs of cable are often placed in a single catwalk. It is useful to be able to identify quickly the cables of a single run. To do this, lace the wires of each

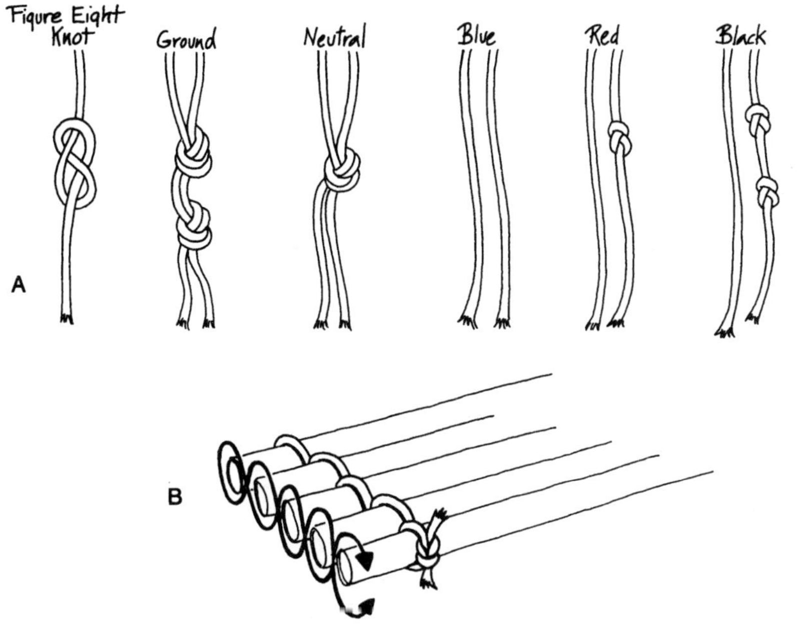

Figure 9.18 (A) On single conductor cable, use knots in the tie ropes to identify the wires. Figure eight knots are easy to untie after use. Knots have the advantage of being readable in the dark. (B) By lacing a five-wire cable run with sash, you can separate the cables of one run from those of other runs

run together, as shown in Figure 9.18B. Lacing the cables also helps keep the runs neat.

At each junction point between cables, the switch number, circuit number, or dimmer number should be labelled with 2 in. white tape on the spider box, deuce board or distribution box. Switchboards should be labelled with the switch number and circuit number. It is also helpful to identify the intended function of the circuit, such as drop-in, high box, top lights and so forth. A set lighting technician who is unfamiliar with the layout must be able to understand the circuitry by reading the labels on the cables and equipment.

When AC and DC are being used on the same set, be sure to mark all outlet boxes either AC or DC. Write DC labels in black pen and AC labels in red pen so that the type of power is immediately obvious.

On single-phase circuits and single-phase branch circuits derived from three-phase it is useful to identify from which phase the circuit is drawing power. This information is important for balancing the load. You can colour-code the distro boxes with coloured electrical tape or simply label them with tape. During filming an electrician can immediately see what leg he is plugging into and tell the best boy if need be.

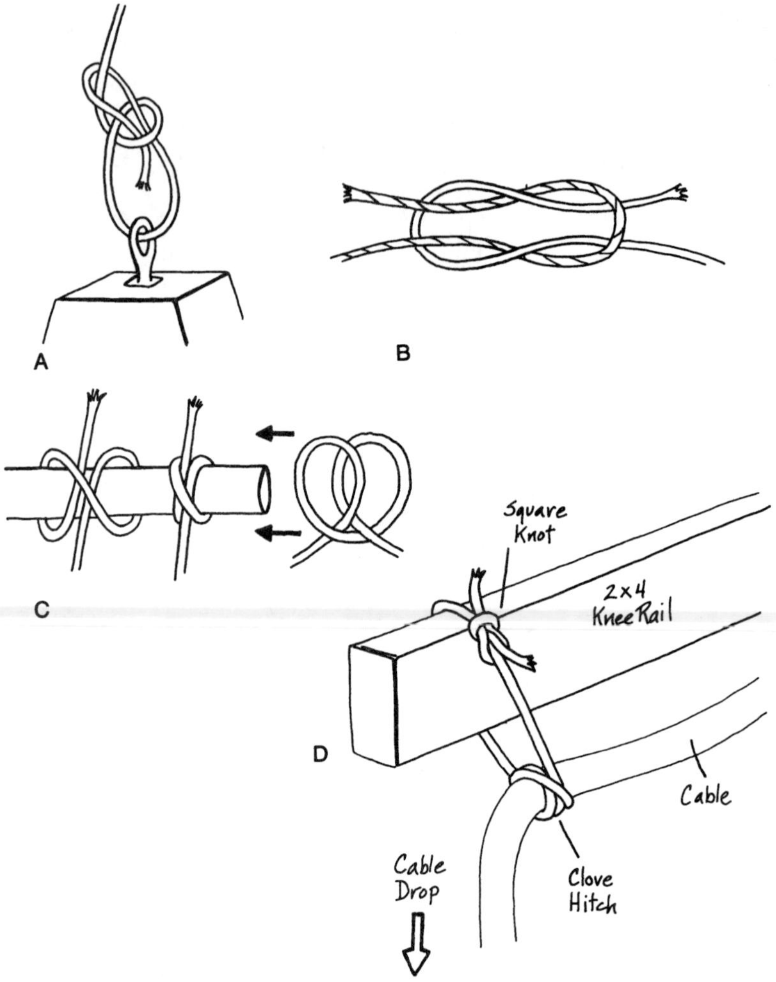

Figure 9.19 Useful knots: (A) The bowline is a very reliable knot that will not come loose when stressed. It is often used for tying ropes to equipment for lifting aloft. A real ace can tie this knot with one hand (a useful trick); (B) the square knot is used to tie one rope to another; (C) the clove hitch is used to hold tight to a dead weight such as a vertical cable drop; (D) the clove hitch and square knot are used as tension relief on a cable drop

Dimmer circuits

Each dimmer circuit serves a single light or a group of lights that always acts as a single unit. Each circuit has a number that corresponds to a fader number on the control console. Every cable between the dimmers and the lights is labelled with the circuit number. When rigging lots of dimmer circuits, affix white tape to both ends of all the cable before you run it. That way it is an easy matter to mark the cable as you run it and you don't have to carry tape around with you. Tab spare cable also so that it can be easily labelled when it is added.

Knots

Every electrician should know the following knots.

Bowline

When lifting equipment on to a catwalk, use a bowline (Figure 9.19A) to tie the rope to the equipment.

Clove hitch

A cable tension relief is made using a clove hitch on the cable (Figure 9.19C). A clove hitch uses the weight of the cable to grip the cable tightly. The two loose ends of rope are looped around a support and tied with a square knot (Figure 9.19B). When tying off a cable drop from a catwalk or green bed, tie the cable to the knee rail or standing post (Figure 9.19D). Do not tie off to wood smaller than a 2 × 4.

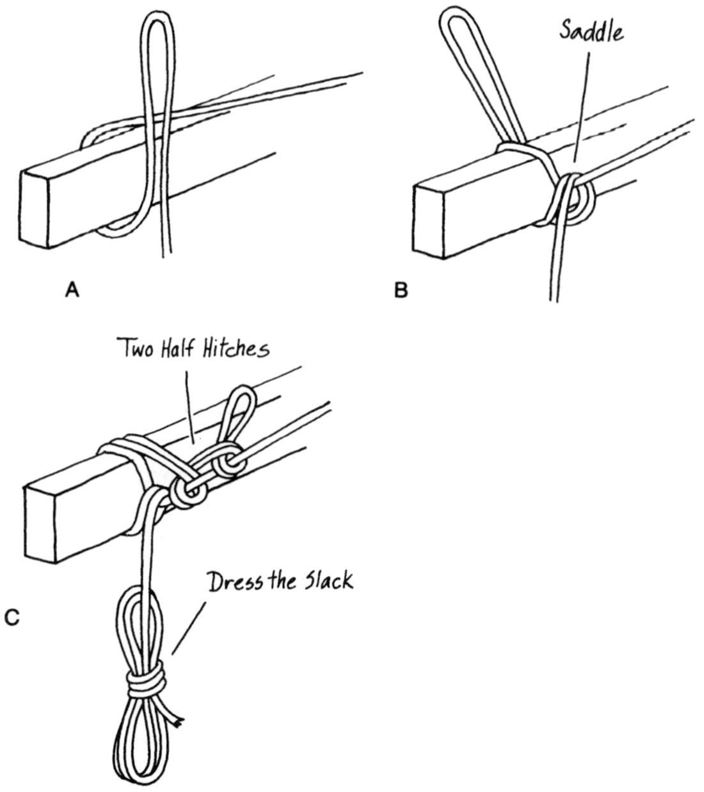

Figure 9.20 The high safety knot is used to tie off a taut line

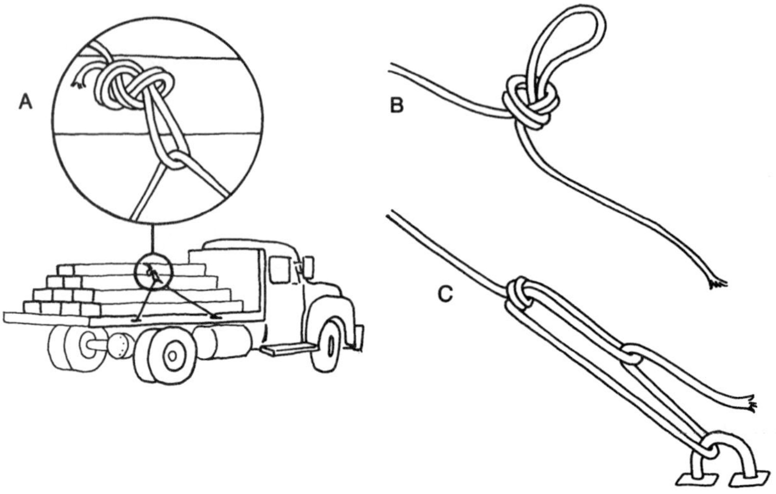

Figure 9.21 The trucker's hitch is used to tighten a rope around equipment to secure it in place. (A) A trucker's hitch using two ropes. (B and C) A trucker's hitch using a single rope

High safety knot

A high safety knot (Figure 9.20) is used to tie off a line that has tension on it, such as that from a dead weight or block and tackle. The saddle cinches the line so that it will not slip while you tie the two half-hitches to secure it.

Trucker's hitch

The trucker's hitch (Figure 9.21) is used to tighten a rope, as when tying something down or securing a rope around equipment to hold it during travel. A fancy trucker's hitch is shown in Figure 9.22.

Rigging lights

When lights are mounted to pipe, all cable should run to one end of the pipe and from there up to a tie-off point. The bundle of cable is lashed to the pipe at regular intervals. Leave two loops of slack at each head so it can be panned and tilted.

In some situations lights must be suspended (Figure 9.23) by rope using a block and tackle to hoist them into position. A one-to-one block and tackle can be used for smaller lights. For larger and heavier lights, a two-to-one or three-to-one block and tackle is necessary (Figure 9.24).

Testing

Once the entire distribution system is in place, it must be thoroughly checked, that is, each circuit from beginning to end must be tested for short circuits, continuity, correct voltage and line loss. In the process of testing you may find blown fuses, tripped circuit breakers, blown bulbs, bad connections, burned-out

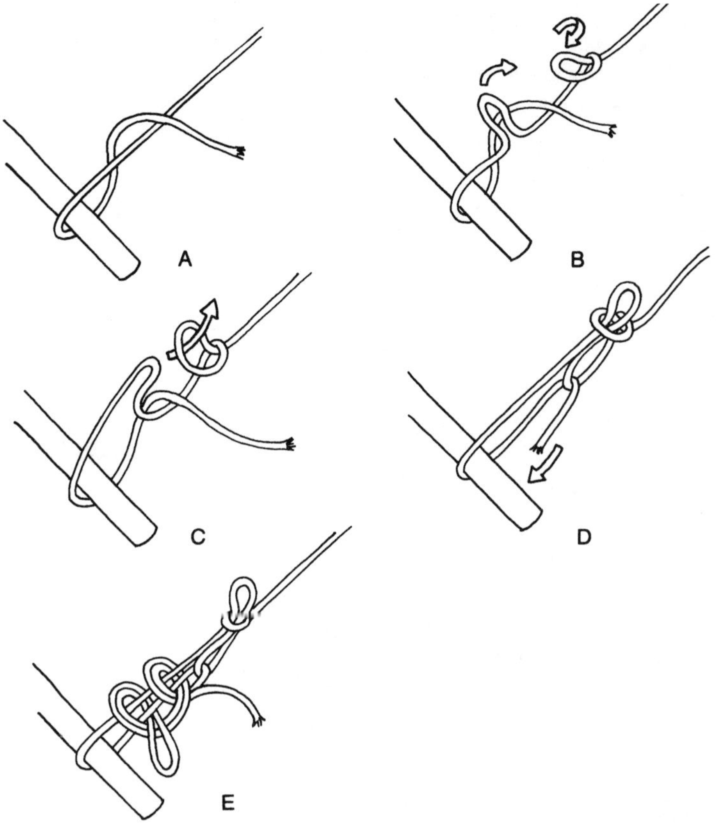

Figure 9.22 This hitch allows you to tighten the rope as you would a trucker's hitch; however, it is more easily adjustable, and the knot can be removed quickly by simply removing the half hitches and tugging on the loose end. Unlike the standard trucker's hitch, no knots are left in the rope

cable and so on. By the time you are finished, you have a pristine rig ready for the shooting crew.

Check for shorts

Before connecting the feeders to the power source, check all lines for short circuits. You can do this quite simply by using a continuity tester which bleeps when a circuit is made. Normally, all neutral to live and/or live to live combinations should not activate the bleeper. Obviously there should be no short circuits to earth from any of the phase connections. Check each wire in combination with each of the other wires. Make certain that all isolators are open and that all the luminaires are either unplugged or switched off.

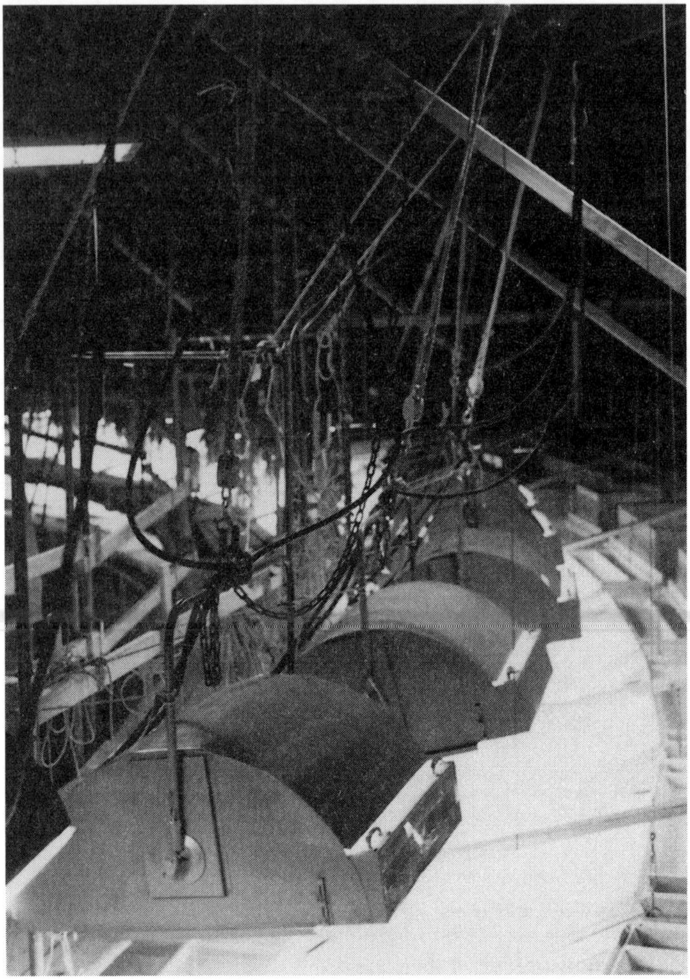

Figure 9.23 A row of eight-banger soft lights shining down through the ceiling of the set, rigged to the rafters with blocks and tackle. This rig creates soft top light for a three-level set built for *Star Trek: Deep Space Nine* on Stage 17 at Paramount Studios. Note that the blocks and tackle are tied off to the hand rail with high safety knots. In addition, each light is tied off with guy wires and secured with chain. (Rig by Frank Valdez. Photo by author.)

Check the voltage

Next, turn the power on, and check the voltage at each outlet box. Be sure that none of the boxes accidentally has the wrong voltage (120 or 240).

Check the lights

At this point, you can plug in all the lights and begin to turn them on. Check that each light is working.

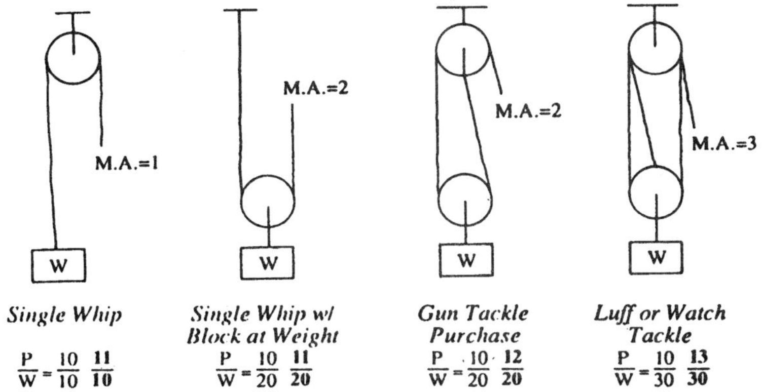

Figure 9.24 Block and tackle mechanical advantage configurations. The moving part of the block and pulley is called the 'sheave'. Heavy lights, like the eight-bangers shown in Figure 9.23, are rigged with the luff tackle, which gives a three-to-one mechanical advantage. Smaller lights could have a single whip with no mechanical advantage. (Reprinted with permission from Paul Carter's *Backstage Handbook* [New York: Broadway Press, 1988]).

Check for line loss

With all the lights on, use a precise voltmeter to check for line loss. First check the voltage at the power supply; then check it at the end of each run. Be sure that you are checking at the furthest point from the power source on each run. If the line voltage is abnormally low, check for bad connections and bad cable on that run.

Check the hertz rate

If magnetic HMI ballasts are to be used, check the line frequency. It should be constant at 50 Hz (UK) or 60 Hz (US).

Electronic dimmer systems

An electronic dimmer system consists of a control console (desk), which controls and displays the status of the dimmers and the dimmer packs (See Figure 6.8).

How an SCR dimmer works

An electronic dimmer is a silicon-controlled rectifier (SCR). Rather than increasing or decreasing voltage (the amplitude of the AC sine wave), as with a variable transformer, an SCR dimmer increases and decreases power by chopping up the sine wave (Figure 9.25).

At 100 per cent power the sine wave looks normal. At 50 per cent power the dimmer delays switching on the circuit during the first 90°, then switches on at the

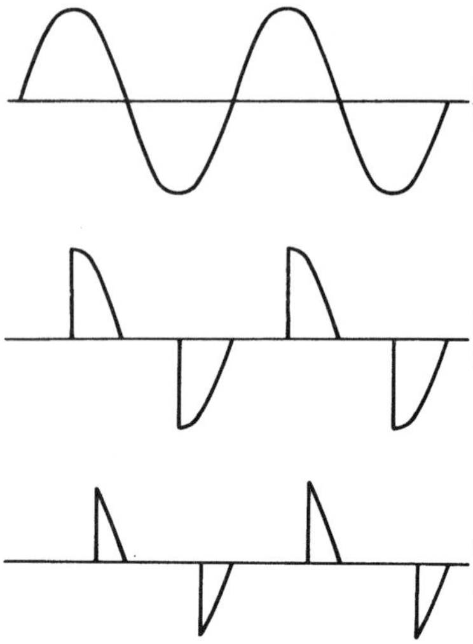

Figure 9.25 The AC wave form of a SCR dimmer circuit. At half power the sine wave is actually clipped off half way through its cycle

peak of the wave. The level to which the dimmer is set determines the point in the sine wave at which the dimmer activates. The dimmer deactivates each time the wave passes through zero. *Note*: Because the sine wave is chopped up, SCR dimmers cannot be used on line with fluorescents, HMI fixtures, or electric motors (such as motorized stands and fans). Using electronic dimmers with such loads can cause damage to both the dimmer and the load.

Control signals

The console communicates with the dimmers using a small signal cable. Older consoles use an analogue system with individual 10 V DC control signal circuits running to each dimmer requiring a multi-core cable (one wire per dimmer plus a common). The dimmer matches its power output proportionally to the voltage of the control signal from 0 to 10 V. Modern systems communicate using a multiplexed analogue signal (AMX192) or digital protocol (DMX512). Dimmer levels are encoded by the control console and connected using an AMX four-wire or DMX five-wire control cable. A control card in the dimmer pack decodes the multiplexed or digital signal. An AMX192 signal can control as many as 192 channels with a single control cable. DMX 512 protocol can control up to 512 channels. The control cable from the console is daisy-chained from one dimmer pack to the next, looping the signal through as many packs as needed.

Control consoles

There are three levels of sophistication to control consoles: manual boards, memory boards and fully automated computer boards. The manual board has a set of sliding faders that directly correspond to the channel numbers. A typical 2-preset board has a duplicate row of faders used to preset the fader positions for the next lighting cue. The two sets of faders are typically referred to as scenes X and Y. A crossfade fader is provided to make a smooth transition from dimmer settings for scene X to those of scene Y. Most modern boards provide a single-handle or split-handle proportional dip-less crossfade, which crossfades smoothly between presets without an intensity dip during the fade. Each set of fader levels is called a *scene preset*. In the days when manual boards were in common use, the board operator had to write down all the fader settings as the lighting designer created them during the prelight or tech rehearsals. During the performance, the board operator was constantly busy setting faders for the next lighting cue on the inactive scene preset. When prompted, they executed the crossfade to the new scene, and then began to reset all the faders for the next cue. Because cues sometimes needed to follow each other in rapid succession, boards with three, four, or more scene presets (hundreds of faders) were common.

Fortunately, the memory board was invented. A memory board is an enhanced manual board that memorizes and replays channel settings, freeing some or all of the faders to be reset to a new state. In this way, a number of presets can be set up, memorized and replayed without having to reset fader levels.

Other common features are separate non-dim (switch) circuits, timed cross-fades, a grand master blackout switch, and usually chase effects circuits. Momentary switches, which allow the board operator to flash the lights with a touch of his fingers, are a common feature on rock-and-roll boards.

Most dimmer boards provide sub-master faders, which allow you to group faders and control each group with a separate sub-master fader. When a sub-master is created, the board records the levels of all the dimmers and assigns those levels a given sub-master fader. When the board operator brings the sub-master fader up to full, all the dimmers come up to their assigned levels. A board may have anywhere from four to several dozen sub-masters, and each sub-master can be 'piled on' to the others. In other words, if the board operator creates a sub-master for the key lights, and another sub-master for the gobo pattern lights, and a third sub-master for back-lights, each group of lights can be added to the others. When a dimmer is assigned different levels in two or more active sub-masters, the dimmer takes the level of the higher sub-master setting.

Sophisticated computer boards provide automatic, timed, crossfade memory so that the cues crossfade automatically at the pre-programmed speed. All the board operator has to do during the performance is hit the cue button when prompted; the board automatically executes the crossfade. A crossfade may be programmed to happen instantaneously, to dim smoothly over a couple of seconds, or even to fade almost imperceptibly over a matter of minutes. Computer boards can handle hundreds of complex timed level manipulations and even overlap multiple cues with ease.

Definitions

As you can already tell, when you start talking in detail about dimmer systems, you quickly run into a whole new language. It is important to understand the standardized meanings of terms like patch, circuit, channel, preset, cue, etc. These terms are very often misused or used interchangeably. Understanding the following list of definitions also helps clarify the way this equipment works in general. Most of what follows is taken almost directly out of the Strand CD80 operator's manual.

- **Circuit** Everything downstream of the dimmer, from the dimmer's output connector to the luminaires themselves.
- **Dimmer** The device controlling power to a circuit and luminaires. Two lights on one dimmer circuit cannot be separately controlled.
- **Channel** Device controlling a dimmer or group of dimmers. In a simple system there is a slider for each channel. On most current control systems, channels are numbers, accessed by numeric keypads. Multiple dimmers may be controlled by a single channel to which they are patched.
- **Patch** Historically, the process of physically connecting circuits to dimmers. Now usually refers to electronic assignment of dimmers to channels. 'Patch' does not refer to the assignment of channels to cues or sub-masters.
- **Preset** A predefined set of intensities for a set of channels, stored in memory for later replay.
- **Memory** Storage location for channel, grouping and timing information.
- **Cue** Process of recalling information from its memory location and putting the result on stage.
- **Sub-master** A controller (usually a linear slider) that allows manual control of groups, effects, cues or channels.
- **Fade** A gradual change in stage levels from one set of intensities ('look') to another.
- **Up-fade** The portion of a fade that involves only channels that are increasing in level.
- **Down-fade** The portion of a fade that involves only channels that are decreasing in level.
- **Crossfade** A fade that contains both an up-fade and down-fade. Also may refer to any fade where the levels of one cue are replaced by the levels of another cue.
- **Bump** An instantaneous change in stage levels from one set of intensities ('look') to another.

Strand CD80 Digital Pack

The Strand CD80 Digital Pack is among the most commonly used portable dimmer packs in motion picture work. What follows are some crib notes on operation and troubleshooting.

CD80 packs are configured in various ways; groups of six 2.5 kW, 5 kW or 10 kW dimmers are common.

For larger dimming jobs, a rolling rack combines multiple packs into a single compact rolling welded aluminium cabinet:

- Forty-eight 2.5 kW dimmers, 10 A circuits
- Twenty-four 5 kW dimmers, 20 A circuits
- Twenty-four 10 kW dimmers, 40 A circuits.

Some dimmer packs are fitted with Socapex outputs. A single Socapex cable carries six separate circuits. When lights are being individually controlled, Socapex cable makes cabling much less cumbersome. It comes in long lengths: 200, 150, 100, 50 and 25 ft. At the lamp end of the cable, a fan-out adaptor connects to the Socapex cable, providing six numbered receptacles. A fan-in adaptor connects the cable to the power source. ('Break-out' and 'break-in' are the American terms.)

Installation and setup

CD80 packs must receive adequate ventilation and be kept within reasonable temperature and humidity levels with no condensation. The packs are not designed to be used outdoors. As many as eight packs may be stacked vertically. Do not place more than two units side by side unless there is at least 24 in. between packs, otherwise the exhaust heat from one pack is blown directly into the intake vent of the next pack. Keep vents clear from obstruction, dirt, fibres, paint particles and so forth.
Ideally, the rack is mounted in a special air-conditioned, soundproof cabinet, which eliminates both the problems of cooling and noise.

Digital Pack Controller 'card'

The brains of the CD80 pack is the *Digital Pack Controller*, commonly known as the *card*. The digital controller is made of a face plate mounted on a control card. The control card slides into slots in the front panel of the dimmer pack. Two thumbscrews secure it in place. In case of failure, the entire card can be replaced in the field. The Digital Pack Controller can be removed and installed without disconnecting any wiring. With the input power turned OFF, loosen the thumbscrews and pull on the thumbscrews to slide the controller out of the pack.

To install the controller (again power OFF at supply), line the controller up with guides on each side of slot and slide the module in carefully until it touches the connector in the pack. Firmly set the controller by pressing on both ends of the module. Tighten in place with thumbscrews.

The face plate contains the connectors, buttons and indicator lights that affect everything the dimmer pack does (Figure 9.26).

- Input and output connectors for AMX control cable (4-pin XLR).
- Input and output connectors for DMX/SMX control cables (5-pin XLR).
- Input connectors for twelve or twenty-four discrete analogue control signals.
- Input connectors for fibre optic cable (not used).
- RS232 connector for connection with computer (not used).
- Three power indicator lights (green) that show each input power phase present (øA, øB, øC). Use these to check the input power lines.

- Three protocol indicator lights (yellow), which show the protocol currently being decoded (AMX, DMX, or analogue).
- Six MODE select DIP switches used to set various important parameters of operation. Table 9.3 outlines the function of each of these six DIP switches. Be especially sure switches 2 and 6 are set properly or the dimmer pack may not work properly. If you change dip switch settings during operation, press the RESET button to enter changes.
- Over-temperature indicator light (red), the dimmer pack will shut down automatically and this light will come on if the heat sink temperature exceeds 85°C. This would happen if the vents were blocked, if ventilation were inadequate, or if the fan motor failed.
- Three numbered thumbwheels used to assign the first dimmer number for the pack. For example, when several twelve-channel packs are daisy-chained together, the first pack would be assigned channels 1 to 12 by setting its thumbwheel to 1. The second pack's thumbwheel would be set to 13 (assigned channels 13 to 24).
- Recessed 'panic' button. When pressed this button turns all dimmers ON. Push it again to return dimmers to normal operation. Use a bent paper clip or other small probe to get to the recessed button.
- Recessed RESET button. When pressed this button tells the card's processor to restart.
- Twelve or twenty-four two-position push-buttons. When set to the IN position, each button turns ON the associated dimmer to full and overrides the control signal, or operates the dimmer in the absence of a control signal. When the button is in the OUT position, the dimmer operates normally and the back-lit button shows the approximate level of the associated dimmer.

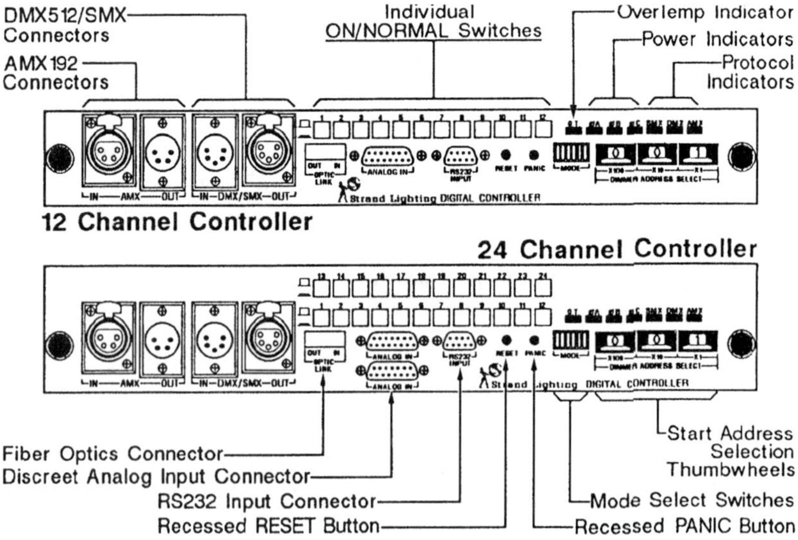

Figure 9.26 CD80 dimmer pack controller card face plate

Table 9.3 CD80 pack MODE select dip switch settings

Position 1	OFF	no effect
	ON	no effect
Position 2	OFF	Three-phase operation
	ON	Single-phase operation
Position 3	When using analog and multiplexed protocol simultaneously, this switch determines if the output signal to the dimmer is the *sum* of the two signals (up to 100%) or the *highest* of the two signals (pile-on)	
	OFF	Highest takes precedence (pile-on)
	ON	Dimmer level is analogue + protocol
Position 4	OFF	0–15 VDC input level for analogue input
	ON	0–10 VDC input level for analogue input
Position 5	OFF	In the event of loss of control signal, the dimmers will retain current levels for 30 minutes
	ON	In the event of loss of control signal, the dimmers will black out
Position 6	OFF	Uses every *other* control signal starting with the thumbwheel number (use with 6 kW and 12 kW dimmers when using Strand lighting systems AMX192 where 6 kW/12 kW dimmer assignment is being made in the control console
	ON	Uses sequential control signals starting with the thumbwheel number

Phase fuses

Three small (250 mA fast blow) phase fuses are located on the controller card. If phase B or C fuse blows, the controller will not work the dimmers connected to that phase. If the phase A fuse blows, the controller will be completely disabled. Replacing the fuses requires no special tools or procedures. With input power turned OFF, remove the controller card from the pack, replace the faulty fuse, and carefully reinsert the controller module.

Dimmer law selection

Dimmer law refers to the response of the dimmer to the control signal over the range of fader settings. A direct one to one relationship between control signal and dimmer output (*linear law*) gives a fairly abrupt rise in light level as the fader is increased, whereas a *modified square law* gives smoother control over the lower end of the dimming curve. Dimmer law selection is made using the jumper on the control board as shown in Figure 9.27.

To match the law with an analogue control signal, disable the jumper. To use the modified square law, install the jumper as shown.

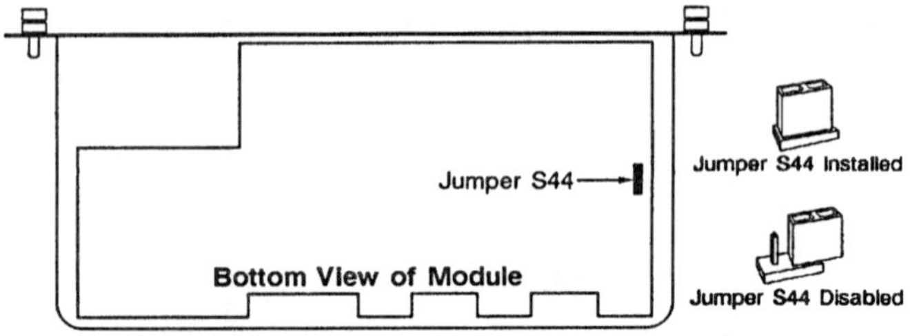

Figure 9.27 Dimmer law curve jumper location on controller card

Single/three-phase selection

In addition to MODE switch 2 (setting for single- or three-phase), smaller packs have an interior single-/three-phase selection plug on the power terminal block. The factory default setting is three-phase. To check the setting, remove the top cover of the pack and check the position of the phase selection plug shown in Figure 9.28.

Close up the pack and connect the input leads. Check the green power indicator lights to confirm that proper phases are powered.

Thumbwheel setting

Set the thumbwheels to the first dimmer number to which this dimmer pack is to respond. The digital controller will start looking at dimmer signals starting at the signal number set on the thumbwheel.

For example, if you had three twelve-channel packs that are to be controlled by a thirty-six channel console, you would set pack one thumbwheel to 1, pack two thumbwheel to 13 and pack three thumbwheel to 25. This assigns channels 1 to 12 to the first pack, channels 13 to 24 to the second pack, and channels 25 to 36 to the third pack.

Each pack is independent of the others. You can set two packs to the same set of signal numbers if you require more than one physical dimmer for each dimmer number.

The start numbers do not have to be a multiple of 6 or 12. You can start one dimmer pack at 1 (dimmers 1 to 12) and the second pack at 9 (dimmers 9 to 20). This will give you two dimmers each on dimmers 9 to 12.

Troubleshooting

Neutral current and line noise

Although a tungsten lamp presents a resistive load to a dimmer, the dimmer output consists of a chopped waveform at any point below maximum output. The chopped wave form has a high third harmonic content which produces neutral current, even with balanced loads. The harmonics are greatest when the dimmer is at 90° conduction (half power). In all situations the neutral conductor needs to be at least the size of the phase conductors and on some occasions doubled or trebled when powering large numbers of dimmers. If suitable precautions are not taken these harmonics will also cause *electromagnetic interference*, commonly called *line noise*. All live and neutral conductors should be run as pairs so that the interference is mutually self cancelling. With a large 'out of balance' load it is possible to get spurious triggering effects due to the neutral wandering away from its 'zero' point. Symptoms of this

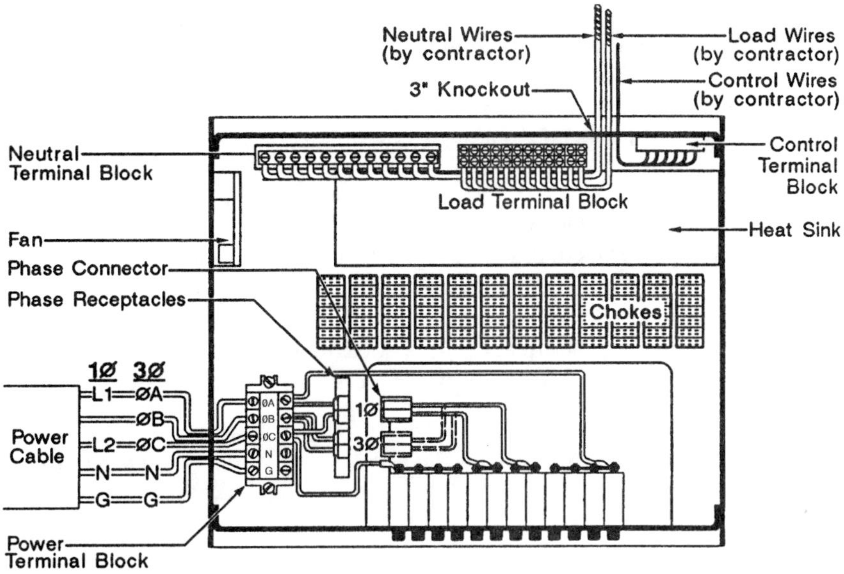

Figure 9.28 The CD80 internal phase selection plug (smaller models only) factory default setting is three-phase

problem are random triggering of dimmers on other phases causing the lights to come 'on' when in theory they are 'off'.

Problems which affect the entire pack

No phase LED lit

- No power to the dimmer pack. Check distribution and cable connectors.
- Controller may not be seated correctly. Remove and reinstall the controller.
- Fuse F1 (phase A) may be open (blown). Replace with a 250 mA fast blow fuse if required (see 'Phase fuses').
- If the fuses are okay and you can turn the dimmers ON with their individual push-buttons, the controller module is defective. Replace it with a spare and return it to owner or Stand Lighting for repair.

Phase B or C LED not lit

- Fuse F2 or F3 is probably open. Replace the fuse. (See 'Phase fuses'.)

All phase LED lit but no protocol indication

- Control console is unplugged or control cable is disconnected.

Incoming control wiring may be incorrectly wired, or one or more conductors broken. Replace control cable or check its continuity and wiring.

No control of dimmers (dimmers are always OFF)]

- If the OverTemp light is ON, the pack has shut down from overheating. Make sure that the air intake and exhaust are not blocked and wait for the thermostat to reset.
- The thumbwheel settings may be set to an incorrect address. Double-check your settings.

No control of dimmers (dimmers are always ON)

- The 'panic' button may be ON, or the individual dimmer push-buttons may be ON.

Problems confined to one phase

Problems that are confined to one phase are usually related to controller problems or to the dimmer pack being incorrectly set up for the type of power in use.

Consecutively numbered dimmers will not go ON

- One phase of the power feeding the pack is off or not connected.
- The controller module may be incorrectly inserted. Remove it and carefully reinsert it into the dimmer pack.
- One or more output control circuits (in the controller) have failed. Swap the controller card with a known good spare. If the problem goes away, return the defective controller for repair.

One or more dimmers on the same phase do not come up to full or do not track correctly

- MODE switch 2 may be incorrectly set. Make sure the pack is set up for the type of power being used.
- The phase fuse may be open.

One or more output control circuits (or the controller) may be defective

- Replace the controller with a spare, and return the defective card for repair.[blr]

Problem with individual dimmers

- Check dimmer circuit breaker ON.
- Check load wiring and lamp are operating properly (not burned out).
- Check load wiring and lamp by turning ON the push-button switch for that dimmer circuit. If nothing comes on, the problem is in the wiring or the lamp itself.
- If you still have a problem it is either a defective controller, defective discrete analogue control wiring, or a defective SSR, circuit breaker or choke. Each of these parts is designed to be easily replaced in the field.
- Check the controller module by replacing it with a known good spare. Make sure the MODE switches are set the same way on the replacement controller. If the problem goes away with the new controller, return the defective controller for repair.
- Check for defective SSR, choke, or circuit breaker by checking the voltage at the circuit breaker output, choke output, and SSR output with the dimmer ON (see Figure 9.28). The component with an input but no output is defective (most commonly the SSR). Replace the defective component.
- If the dimmer works from the console (protocol input), but not from the discrete analogue input, there is a problem in the discrete analogue circuitry, external to the pack.
- Dimmers flicker when at 50 per cent. Control card is defective. Replace.

10

Power sources

Putt-putts (portable Honda generators)

For small amounts of remote power, a portable Honda-style 'putt-putt' generator is a very handy unit to carry on any show. In rough terrain it enables lighting in places a heavy diesel plant cannot reach. At night a putt-putt can save running hundreds of feet of cable to power one 2,500 PAR to light the deep background. A Honda can power work lights during wrap, allowing the main plant to be shut down and the cable wrapped. One Hollywood insert company (which shoots mostly MOS establishing shots and pick-ups for films and television shows) lights all their night exteriors quite nicely with little more than three putt-putts and a dozen Par 64s.

A typical 5,500 watt Honda generator that you get from a film equipment supplier will have been retrofitted with precision speed control and appropriate output connectors. (There is also a 6,500 watt model, which is significantly noisier.) Fuel capacity is generally 4.5 to 5 gallons, which will last six to eight hours. The arrangement of the electrical circuits is also commonly modified for our use. In UK/Europe output is a single 240 V circuit. (In the USA, the alternator has two windings, wired in series, which provide two 20 A 120 V circuits and one 45 A 240 V circuit. In this configuration you cannot pull more than 20 A per side, and it works best if you keep the two circuits evenly loaded. When Crawford or Young retrofit a generator, they split the windings so that you can switch between parallel windings [one 45 A 120 V circuit] or series [two 20 A 120 V, one 45 A 240 V circuit].)

Troubleshooting

With such a small engine, the governor can be touchy and is easily upset by variations in the load or in the fuel flow. The resulting variations in the frequency can cause discharge sources to produce flicker as they are not in synchronization with the camera shutter. It is a wise precaution to monitor the frequency with an in-line meter, and many gaffers use flicker-free ballasts when powering discharge sources from a putt-putt to allow greater tolerance for variations in the generator frequency. The governor tends to be less stable with light loads. You will get more consistent performance if you load the unit to near full capacity and do not change the load during the shot (with flicker devices or sudden light cues).

Hiccups in the power line are commonly caused by inconstant fuel flow. The generator must be on level ground. The fuel tank is mounted only slightly above the carburettor; on a slope, with the fuel tank on the low side, fuel can get too low to flow properly, which disrupts the power. When powering lights on a moving vehicle or vessel, rocking or jerking can interrupt fuel flow, which causes hiccups in the power line. This can be helped by keeping the tank topped up, but the best solution is to use a unit which has been retrofitted with a fuel pump.

A common breakdown on the Honda is the circuits that recharge the battery. If they fail, the battery will go flat; as it does, the governor will have difficulty maintaining consistent RPM. First the hertz rate becomes unstable, starts oscillating, and then slowly drifts lower and lower. If this happens you can fix the problem temporarily (and get the shot) by jumping the battery with a car battery.

Another common trouble with these units is difficulty in starting due to flooding. In order to avoid flooding the carburettor during transport the fuel valve must be shut off. The carburettor has a very low head and will flood and dribble fuel all over the place if the valve is left open.

The performance of a small engine is greatly affected by air density. At high elevations (above 3,000 feet) power output decreases 3 per cent per 1000 feet. In the mountains the mixture will need to be weakened or the fuel/air mixture will be too rich, causing the engine to run rough and possibly foul the spark plugs.

Young Generators, Inc. extensively retrofit their Hondas to remedy the weaknesses mentioned. A fuel pump reduces fuel flow problems. The circuitry is completely reworked, with a split solenoid (50 A 120 V, or 120/240 V AC), stronger regulator, better battery charging system, and numerous other refinements. A fuel solenoid automatically shuts off fuel upon shutdown to eliminate dribbling and flooding. The generator is mounted on four large pneumatic tyres and encased in a protective metal roll-cage. It weighs about 440 pounds.

Full-size generators

Film generators are baffled to minimize noise for sound recording. They are very precisely electronically governed at 50 ± 0.2 Hz to be reliable when used with discharge lights, and are equipped with a frequency readout, and frequency adjustment on the main control panel. Similarly, voltage is precisely maintained electronically and can be adjusted. Dual plants of 100 kW to as much as 200 kW are commonly mounted on a carrier (see Figure 2.2). Trailer-mounted 'mobile' or 'tow plants' are also common, ranging from small 15 kW up to 140 kW. The smaller sizes up to 60 kW commonly use petrol engines. Larger plants require diesel engines. Generators are rated in kilowatts. A 60 kW generator is said to have a 250 A capacity at 240 V; a 140 kW generator has a 583 A capacity, and so on. A 120 kW AC/DC generator, like the one shown in Figure 10.1, is the typical workhorse for motion picture work.

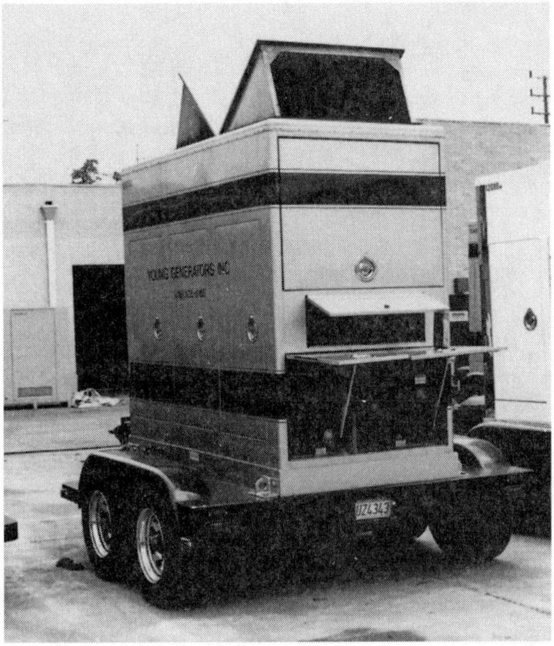

Figure 10.1 Trailer-mounted 120 kW (1,000 A) generator. The vents on the top open automatically when the engine is turned on. The side doors provide access to the engine. On the back of the unit, the bottom doors cover the bus bars and power distribution outlets and above that the digital control panel

Most generators used today are relatively simple to operate, fully automated, and self-diagnostic. The Young generator (American) shown in Figure 10.1 is typical. It has a selection switch (either on the control panel or inside one of the rear doors) that allows you to choose between single-phase, three-phase, or two-wire DC with up to 200 A single-phase AC delivered concurrently. Circuit breakers or electronic overcurrent protection protect the generator from short circuits. Most generators on the West Coast provide copper bus bars for the connection of lug feeder cable. Generators are fitted with receptacles appropriate to the main distribution cable (Figure 10.2 shows the American, lug bus bars, Cam-Lok and mole-pin). The Young generator shown has dual voltage regulators, dual electronic governor controllers, and dual fuel pumps to provide redundancy in case a part fails. Young generators will automatically shut down when they are about to run out of fuel. (This is not true of all generators. You can have significant downtime when a diesel motor has run out of fuel because you have to bleed the fuel lines to get the air out.)

Smaller trailer-mounted generators typically have a fuel capacity of 80 to 150 gallons. A 60 kW diesel generator under full load burns fuel at a rate of about 3.8 gallons per hour. The larger plants typically hold 200 gallons. A 90 kW plant burns between 3 and 8 gallons per hour depending on the load. A 140 kW plant burns 15

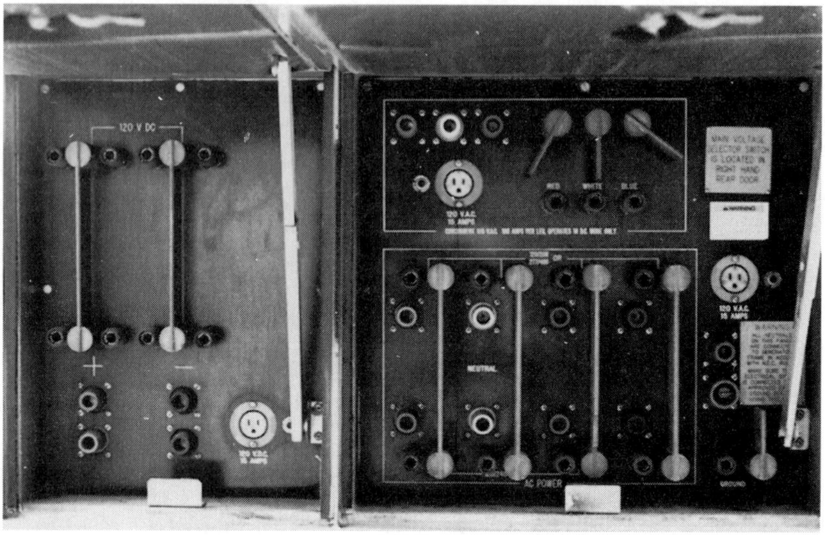

Figure 10.2 The distribution panel provides bus bars and mole-pin and Cam-Lok connectors for each wire. On the left are the DC bus bars. On the bottom right are the AC bus bars, which can service three-phase 120/208 V power or single-phase 120/240 V power using the three left bus bars. Above right are 120/240 V bus bars for AC when run concurrently with DC. There is also a 15 A courtesy Edison outlet. At the far right bottom is the earthing bus

gallons per hour at full load, 8 at half load. A 60 kW petrol generator consumes about 6 gallons per hour at any load.

Generator placement

The sound department has a vested interest in where the generator is placed. Despite baffles that deaden engine noise, generators can still be a nuisance for the sound department. Place the generator around the corner of a building or behind a big vehicle, far from the set. Point the noisiest parts (the exhaust ports) away from the set. Electricians must sometimes run very long lengths of feeder cable to get the generator far enough from the set; once placed it can be a lot of trouble to move it, so it is worth getting it well placed initially.

The quieter the location, the harder it is to hide the generator. For example, one crew was shooting in the desert where it is very quiet and very hard to find large structures to hide things. The crew had already run every piece of cable they had, and the generator was sitting miles away but was still ruining the sound takes. Finally, out of desperation, the best boy had a hole dug 14 ft deep and backed the generator into the hole. There is a theory among best boys that if the sound mixer can't see it, he won't hear it. Unfortunately, in this case the sound mixer could still hear the interred generator. This just goes to show that you can't always please the sound mixer, no matter how hard you try, but you have to exhaust every possibility before you can give up. (Another tactic I've tried on a remote western shoot was to build a thick haystack around the plant on three sides (allowing plenty of clearance so as not to create a fire hazard.)

The generator operator or transportation personnel must make sure the plant is secured and stationary. The emergency brake must be engaged, if equipped, or chocks placed under the wheels to prevent movement (fire code regulations). It is a common misconception that the generator must be perfectly level to operate. Although a good policy when possible, this is not generally true. The main consideration is for the fuel in the fuel tank, but if the fuel intake is properly installed (in the centre, kerb-side at the bottom of the tank), being out of level will not adversely affect fuel intake. If conditions dictate that you must run the generator out of level, make sure the fuel filler and vents are high and the fuel pick-up point is low.

Finally, the fire marshal will have several concerns related to generators. The generator must not be parked under anything that is likely to catch fire, such as dry foliage. (Remember exhaust ports point up.) It must not block fire hydrants or exits. A multipurpose fire extinguisher (20-BC) or equivalent must be available. If the generator requires refuelling, it must be shut down before refuelling begins, and a 'static line' attached between the fuel truck and the generator. There must be no smoking near the generator.

Generator operation

Walk-around inspection

Before starting the generator each day, the operator makes a walk-around inspection of the plant to include the following:

1. Open manual air vents if necessary. Most large generators' vents open automatically when the engine is started (they use oil pressure to hold them open). This is a great convenience, but it also serves to help you forget to open them when they must be opened manually. The engine will overheat very quickly without proper cooling. In rain or snow, the top air intake must be closed to prevent water getting in the air supply. The secondary air intake door must be opened instead. A valve, usually found near the back doors, may have to be closed to cut off oil pressure from the top door.
2. Check the oil at the beginning of every day. Add oil when needed. Inspect the engine compartment for leaky hoses or oil-soaked insulation.
3. Check the water level once or twice a week, and add water if necessary.
4. Remove the fuel cap and check the fuel level. The tank should be topped off each night to prevent water condensation inside the fuel tank overnight. (With petrol engines, do not switch a flashlight on at the mouth of an open fuel tank. The spark in the switch can ignite the gas fumes.)
5. Check the Racor fuel filter for water and crud, which may have collected on the bottom of the clear bowl. Drain if necessary (see 'Draining the Racor filter').
6. Check fan and alternator belts.

Starting the generator

1. Run the distribution cables. Be sure no lights or other loads are connected to the distribution system. Connect the feeder cables to the generator. Place the generator's master power switch in the OFF position.
2. Check that the generator is set for single-phase AC, three-phase AC, or DC operation as desired. Some generators use a large selection switch (located inside, back, right) to switch large contactors from one configuration to another. Be aggressive when turning this switch. A solid connection is needed. Make sure the switch is fully locked in position. If the switch fails to make full contact or is left between settings, the results can be catastrophic.
3. Flip the STOP/RUN switch to RUN (Figure 10.3), press the ignition switch or turn the ignition key. Leave the IDLE/RUN switch in IDLE while the generator is not feeding the distribution system. Most generators have automatic starters and start easily. Allow the generator to warm up in IDLE for a few minutes before switching it to RUN. Look up as soon as the engine starts; watch that the cooling doors are open and watch the exhaust colour (more on exhaust shortly).
4. When the best boy is ready to turn on the power, alert the gaffer and electricians that 'the lines are going HOT'. You do not want to shock someone down the line who may still be connecting the lugs to a spider box.
5. When you are ready for power, flip the IDLE/RUN switch to RUN, and turn the main power switch ON.

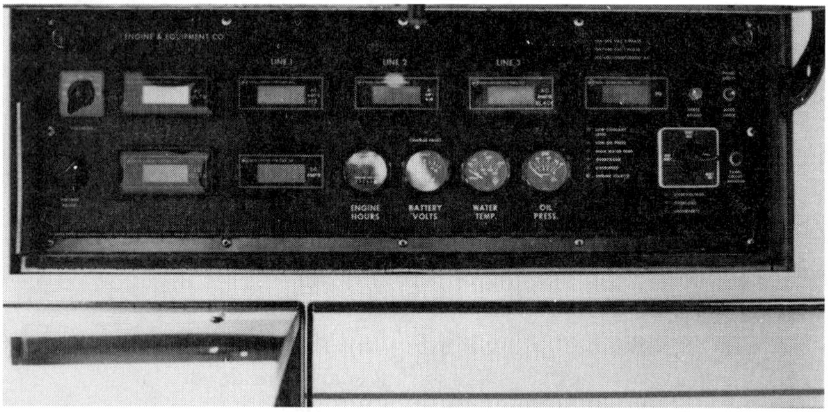

Figure 10.3 The digital control panel. Top row, from left to right: voltmeter selector switch, which selects which leg the voltmeter reads; AC voltmeter; three ammeters, one for each leg; and frequency meter. The lights below the frequency meter show engine diagnostics; the lights above the frequency meter indicate which type of power is being used. To the right of the frequency meter are the hertz adjustment bolt and the panel-lights switch. Bottom row, from left to right: voltage adjustment knob, DC voltage meter, DC ammeter, four engine instruments, and ignition switch/power switch. (Courtesy Young Generators, Inc Arroyo Grande, CA.)

6. Check the voltage output meter and set the voltage using the adjustment knob. Be sure to recheck voltage after changing from single-phase to three-phase or vice versa. Voltage will need adjustment. You can use this knob to offset voltage drop in the cables. The voltage reading should be taken from the farthest outlet from the generator.
7. Check the hertz reading. It should be hovering right around 50 ± 0.2 Hz, and it should be stable, never jumping more than 0.1 Hz at a time. If a small adjustment is necessary, adjust the frequency with the adjustment knob or screw.
8. If you are in a public area, cover the live panel with rubber matting and mark it 'Danger Live Wires'.

During operation periodically monitor the ammeters. It is best to keep the load evenly distributed between legs, no more than 50 A between legs as a rule of thumb.

Periodically check the engine instruments: oil pressure, battery charge, water temperature, and fuel pressure (if installed). These gauges can warn you of impending problems such as a fuel filter clogging or a battery losing its charge, problems that could very soon shut down the generator (and the production). More on this in 'Basic troubleshooting'.

Shutting down the generator

1. Turn off all the lights and other loads.
2. Turn off the generator's main breaker or power switch.
3. Switch the generator to IDLE and allow several minutes for cool down.
4. After 3 to 5 minutes turn the ignition switch OFF.
5. Close manual air vents if necessary.

Earthing generators

At this writing, according to the latest Los Angeles City regulations, a generator that is fully insulated from the ground by rubber tyres or other means need not be earthed with an earth spike. However, if the generator cannot be insulated from the ground, then the earth bus must be connected to a grounding electrode. The grounding electrode may be either an 8-ft copper or steel stake driven fully into the ground (NEC Section 250-6[c]) or a building's grounding electrode. The connection to the electrode must be made with an approved bolted clamp; spring clamps are not allowed. Do not use a water pipe or lawn sprinkler system pipe for ground. The pipe may not be metal underground, and it is not an approved ground in any case.

When a generator is being used in addition to a tie-in to the mains supply in a building, the generator should be grounded with a stake, and the ground must also be bonded to the ground of the building. This puts both systems at the same voltage potential. By neutralizing any difference in potential, you eliminate the chance of getting a shock from touching a light powered by the generator while touching the building ground, for example, through a metal handrail, radiator, or plumbing pipe. However, if the generator is only powering equipment on the outside of the building and equipment powered by the two sources are never used in proximity to each other, the generator need not be bonded to the building ground.

When a generator is fully insulated from the ground, it operates as a closed system. All the lighting fixtures are grounded to the generator. If there is a ground short, the generator's circuit breakers will trip to protect the circuit.

Selecting a generator

The size of generator selected for a job should be based on the power requirements for that job. While one naturally might want a larger generator 'just in case,' overkill can be bad for the plant. A generator should not be run continuously at less than 20 per cent of its maximum load. Over time, running under very light loads causes all sorts of problems, including glazing the cylinders, which can destroy the engine. Nothing is better for a rough-running engine than to be run at full capacity for a couple of hours. You'll see a lot of soot and smoke in the exhaust at first until the engine has cleaned itself out. Generator rental companies use load banks (big resistance banks) for this very purpose as part of regular maintenance schedule.

Carrier-mounted plants

Flexibility in load capacity is one reason it is advantageous to have two carrier-mounted plants. In addition to having backup in case one plant fails, you have the ability to run a lot of power or very little as necessary. Carriers provide increased fuel capacity, up to 300 gallons, enough to keep a plant running for as long as three or four days.

Mobile tow plants

The advantage of a tow plant is that it is generally quieter than a carrier-mounted plant, the large flat fuel tank effectively blocks sound so it does not reverberate out from under the plant as it does with a carrier-mounted plant. When filming a period western in a peaceful, remote stretch of New Mexico, you can hear a car three miles away, let alone a 200 hp diesel engine 500 ft up the mesa. You need a quiet plant or you'll be running cable up hill and down dale.

Generator vans

Young Generator Inc. has also built custom cargo vans with 30 kW, 60 kW and, even, 90 kW capacity generators installed inconspicuously inside. The van makes relocating the generator fast and easy, and allows it to be hidden in the shot if necessary.

Petrol versus diesel

Either a petrol engine or a diesel engine drives the alternator. There are pros and cons to each. The advantages of a petrol engine are that it runs very quietly, has low emission (nitrogen oxide), and is not as heavy as a diesel engine. A basic carburettor can digest inferior fuels without serious effects on the engine's operation better than a fuel injection system used by diesel engines can. The disadvantages of petrol engines are that gas engines have limited power output, up to 60 kW (250 A at 240 V), they have higher fuel consumption (gas engines have static fuel consumption under any load, even under no load), and they use flammable petrol, which is not permitted in harbours and other fire critical areas.

The primary advantages of a diesel engine are high reliability, low maintenance, and high fuel efficiency. It has more power and can turn larger alternators. Also, diesel fuel is 'combustible' rather than 'flammable,' so it is safer. On the down side, diesel engines are hard cold-starters; diesel engines are more sensitive to fuel contamination and more critical of lubricants and coolants. As a result of the higher combustion pressures, diesel engines must be made of heavy materials. A 140 kW tow plant can weigh upwards of 10,000 lb. High combustion pressure also means more noise (you can always tell the distinctive diesel knock), higher emissions and soot, but much lower hydrocarbon and ROG emissions.

Electrical configurations

Generators use three-phase alternators. The alternator has three sets of coils, each 120° offset from the last, creating three-phase AC current. In order to have the ability to select between several possible output voltages, many motion picture generators are designed using a twelve-lead 'reconnectable' alternator. Alternator coils are tapped at twelve strategic places (Figures 10.4 and 10.5). Depending how the coils

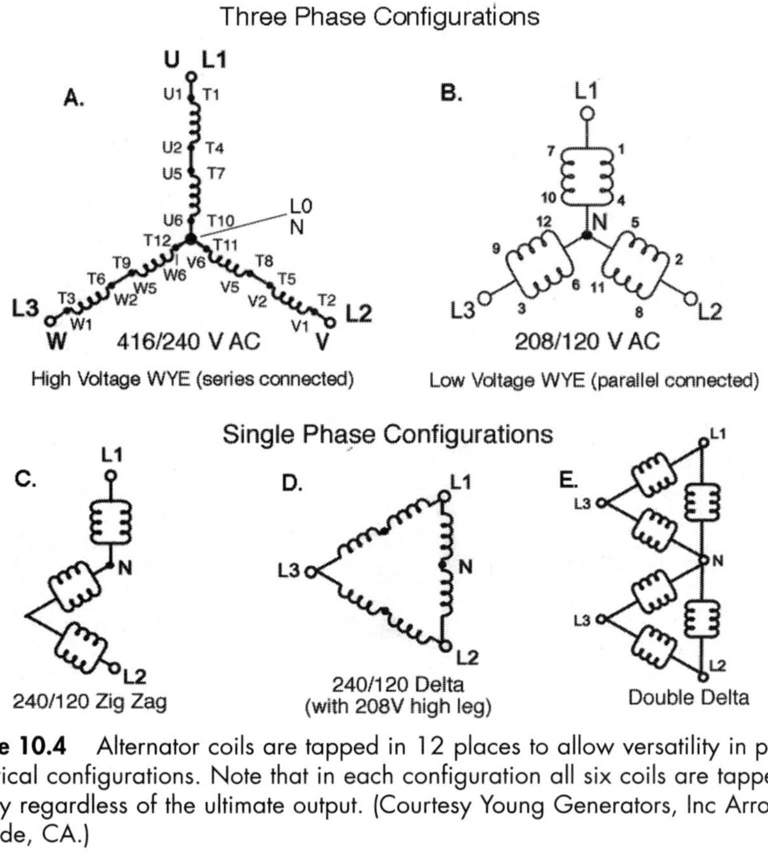

Figure 10.4 Alternator coils are tapped in 12 places to allow versatility in possible electrical configurations. Note that in each configuration all six coils are tapped evenly regardless of the ultimate output. (Courtesy Young Generators, Inc Arroyo Grande, CA.)

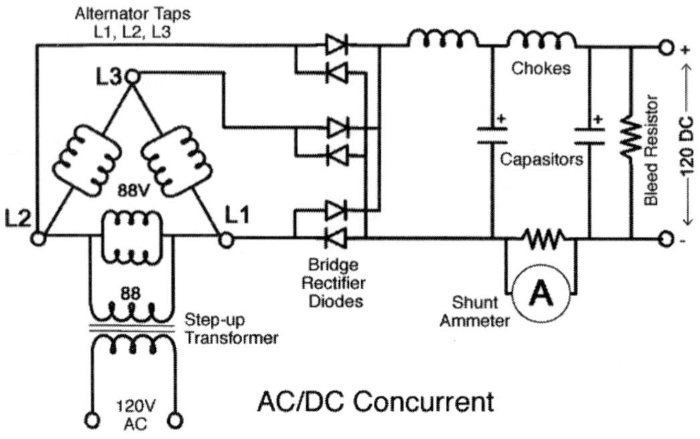

Figure 10.5 AC and DC derived concurrently from an 88 V Delta three-phase AC configuration. A step-up transformer creates 120 V AC by tapping between L1 and L2 (a second transformer between L2 and L3 would be used to create 120/240 AC). The three 88 V AC legs are converted to 120 V DC using rectifier diodes, chokes and capacitors. (Courtesy Young Generators, Inc Arroyo Grande, CA.)

are connected the output may be three-phase 416/240 AC (high wye), 208/120 AC (low wye), single-phase (480/240 AC), or even 240/120 AC with 120 V DC concurrently (with the addition of a rectifier and other circuitry) (Figure 10.5).

Each phase (marked U, V and W) is tapped in four places (e.g. U1, U2, U5, U6 etc.). World-wide there are actually two standard systems used for identifying the load leads from an alternator: the International Electrotechnical Commission (IEC) identifies the phases as U, V and W, and numbers the twelve taps U1, U2 etc. In the USA the National Electrical Manufacturers Association (NEMA) identifies the phases L1, L2 and L3, and numbers the taps T1 to T12. Both systems are shown in Figure 10.4A. The rest of the schematics are shown here using the NEMA nomenclature.

High and low voltage configurations are possible because each of the phase coils is essentially split in half, and can be connected in series (Figure 10.4A, high wye) or in parallel (Figure 10.4B, low wye).

Basic troubleshooting

A fully equipped, modern generator will automatically shut down if it senses a mechanical problem, such as low oil pressure, low coolant pressure, high water temperature, over-speeding or over-cranking. Any of these problems is easily diagnosed by inspecting the engine warning lights and instruments followed by poking around inside the generator housing, and looking for the problem. If a generator shuts down, check the indicator lights before turning the start switch off.

If you have a knowledge of engines, you may be able to make a reasonable guess at the cause of the shutdown. Overheating could be caused be a rupture in the cooling system (low coolant pressure and high temperature) or a blocked or burnt-out thermostat (high water temperature). Most likely is a plugged radiator (pollen, insulation fluff, etc.) or broken fan belt.

Low oil pressure indicates a ruptured oil line, leaking oil, or low oil.

A 'charge' light indicates the battery has not been charging, pointing to a problem with the alternator, a broken belt, a break in the wiring between the alternator and the battery (some generators have a fuse or circuit breaker in this line), or a bad battery. An important note here is that the electronic governor that controls the engine speed relies on battery power to operate. Unlike a car motor, which requires little battery power to run, the electronic governor requires a much larger amount of battery power. A failed charging system typically shows itself in a slow loss of AC hertz rate and an inability to pick up a load.

Troubleshooting: mechanical

Fuel system

The fuel system is vital to the proper running of a diesel engine and the biggest area of potential problems. Bubbles of air in the fuel lines can make it impossible to maintain consistent hertz rate. Contaminants in the fuel can clog fuel lines over time.

Fuel is drawn into the pickup at the bottom of the fuel tank. If you have problems after the plant has been moved and there is a lot of crud coming into the fuel filter, it may be because the fuel intake is raised off the bottom of the tank and crud on the bottom of the tank has become stirred up. Or the tank may now be on a slight incline, causing water at the bottom of the tank to reach the intake. The water and crud on the bottom of the tank will gradually build up until it reaches the (raised) fuel intake, at which time the engine will not run because it is drinking pure water and crud.

Fuel is pumped through the Racor filter, which separates out any water and contaminants. The clear bowl on the bottom of the filter shows any water or crud that has accumulated. It can be drained out using the valve on the bottom of the bowl. In wet, humid climates the Racor will fill up much faster than in dry climates.

To drain water, hold a container under the drain, open the valve at the bottom of the filter bowl, and then activate the electric fuel pump to force the water from the bottom of the filter assembly. If your generator does not have a fuel pump upstream of the Racor, you may have to loosen the T-handle and remove the top cover before draining fuel from the valve. Refill the filter with clean fuel before closing the cover.

Fuel is pumped to the primary and secondary fuel filter canisters, which are usually close to the main fuel pump. This pump raises fuel pressure to 20 to 50 psi and pumps fuel to the fuel injector. A fuel pressure gauge is sometimes installed at this point in the system. The fuel pressure gauge is helpful to forewarn the operator if a clog is developing somewhere in the fuel system. Make note of the normal fuel pressure. A downward trend in fuel pressure usually indicates a clogging fuel filter. If pressure is unstable and the gauge is all over the map, it indicates that the system is sucking air.

Bleeding the lines

If a diesel engine is allowed to run out of fuel, the fuel lines get air in them, and must be bled before the generator will restart. Use the following procedure:

1. Fill the fuel tank.
2. Activate the electric fuel pump. On some plants this is accomplished by pressing the engine ON/OFF button. Others have a switch installed next to the pump inside the engine housing. If the fuel pump stops clicking, repeat this step.
3. Bleed the Racor filter. Unscrew the top of the filter and let the fuel pump fill the filter to the top. Then screw the top back down.
4. Operate the small hand pump on the side of the injector pump for 60 seconds.
5. Start the generator.
6. If it doesn't start, open the injector #1 with a 19 mm or 11⁄16 in. wrench until fuel spurts out.
7. Repeat steps 5 and 6 with injectors 2, 3 and 4.

Bad fuel

If you get bad fuel in the system, you must clean out the entire system. Start by adding a de-watering additive and/or biocide to the fuel (see 'Fuel care and additives' below). Switch to the backup fuel system (if equipped). Next clean the fuel filters and fill them with clean fuel. There are four of them: one in the electric fuel pump, the Racor filter, and two canister filters near the injectors.

Fuel care and additives

Condensation on the insides of the fuel tank will cause water in the fuel. Avoid this by filling the tank before leaving it overnight. Daily use of a de-watering additive is a great insurance policy, as they remove their weight in water, eliminating the most common cause of generator failure, dirty fuel. Additives such as Fuel Power combine a water dispersant and anti-gumming agent; they clean the injectors and reduce smoke.

Cold weather

There are two types of diesel fuel. In warm states such as California, you only ever see one type, diesel 2; however, diesel 2 turns to a gel and becomes gooey and waxy at 9° to 0°C. In cold climates diesel 1, which is thinner, becomes necessary. Diesel 2 is normally preferable because it contains more BTUs (more energy). Use local fuel when in cold climates. 'Pour point depressants', such as Polar Power, prevent diesel fuel from waxing up at freezing temperatures. Use it before the fuel has a chance to gel. If you get caught in the sudden freeze with diesel 2 in the tank, use Melt Down additive to unclog gooey fuel lines. (Kerosene is sometimes used but is illegal because of EPA requirements.) Warming the fuel tank with a heater also helps.

Troubleshooting: electrical problems

The two control systems of the electrical component of a generator are the voltage regulator and the electronic governor. The voltage regulator increases or decreases the magnetic field strength inside the alternator to control output voltage. It then compares output voltage to a preset (adjustable) target value and automatically adjusts field strength to match to it.

The electronic governor controls the engine revs, which is directly proportional to the frequency, so delicate control of the throttle (petrol engine) or fuel injector (diesel) is required. The governor receives a signal from a sensor, which tells it how fast the engine is turning. (The sensor is a magnetic pickup that actually counts teeth on the flywheel as it turns.) The governor compares this speed to the desired speed (which results in 50 Hz) and increases or decreases the gas accordingly.

Snags in either the voltage regulator system or the governor system can cause electrical problems; however, more often than not, problems that show up in fluctuations in voltage or hertz rate are caused by other factors.

Visible flicker in the lights

Visible flicker is rarely caused by faulty frequency regulation, as is often erroneously assumed. Do not confuse the flickering caused by discharge sources (a pulsing visible only on film) with visible flicker. Most often visible flicker is caused by poor connections in the distribution cables. I have tracked down many a flicker and found a bad connector or pin connector was at fault. Especially if flicker is limited to particular lights, or a single leg of power, the problem is unlikely to be with the generator.

Lights flicker on all phases

Voltage periodically jumps and dips. Peaks and dips in voltage are sometimes caused by build-up of corrosion on the voltage adjustment knob on the control panel. Several swift twists back and forth (load disconnected) will usually clean it out and should get rid of the problem. This knob is one of the weakest links in the system. Subjected to the elements, the rheostat can get a build-up of dirt and corrosion. Faulty contact in the rheostat can make it very hard for the voltage regulator to work effectively.

A second possibility is that flicker and voltage fluctuations occurring on all three phases are often caused by a bad neutral connection. Feel the cable connections for hot spots. This will lead you to the problem cable or connector.

A third possibility is fluctuations coming from the voltage regulator itself. This usually occurs as a 'bouncing' instability, about two pulses per second. Very occasionally you'll have to switch to the backup voltage regulator, which can be selected with a switch inside the generator housing. Be sure to shut down the generator before changing from one to the other. Never switch between regulators with the engine running.

Generator does not produce any power

The voltage regulator power input or field output has become disconnected, or the regulator may have failed.

Voltage goes through the roof

High voltage indicates that the voltage regulator's sensing input is disconnected. If the sensing input is disconnected, the voltage regulator will sense that the voltage is too low (it senses zero voltage). It will increase voltage in the field output more and more to try to compensate, and the generator output voltage will go through the roof.

Unpredictable, irregular changes in frequency
Look for air bubbles rising up through the Racor fuel filter. Air bubbles may be caused by low fuel in the tank or by a pinhole leak in a fuel line. A restriction in the fuel line has a similar effect.

Unstable frequency, governor lever is 'hunting', overshooting, then undershooting
Check that there is no play in the throttle/governor linkage, and that the linkage moves freely without stickiness. Clean it and spray it with lubricant if necessary. In the case of an engine with a carburettor, the problem may be caused by a sticky throttle due to: high venturi pressure hampering the throttle valve (wiping some oil on the bearings will often free up a stiff butterfly and allow the governor to control the hertz rate properly); or carburettor ice – placing a load on the generator will lower the vacuum and usually eliminate the problem; otherwise, shut down and allow the ice to melt.

Unstable frequency, governor lever oscillates and does not stabilize
Governor control may need calibration. An adjustment is made with the 'I', 'A' and gain controls on the little electronic governor box.

Engine over-speeds
The 'I' pot on the governor controller adjusts overshoot. The engine will over-speed briefly when load level changes if it is set too high. Alternatively, the frequency may be set too high or be faulty, or the governor is faulty.

Slow frequency drift (typically downwards)
Battery going flat (failed engine alternator), moisture in electronic governor controller (dry it with a hair dryer or work light), or a bad electronic governor controller.

Wet cell battery packs

In situations in which no other power source is practical, such as when shooting in a moving car, a boat, a remote cave or some equally inaccessible place, battery packs can provide the needed power. By connecting ten 12 V wet cell (lead-acid) batteries in series, a DC voltage of 120 V can be obtained. Commercially available battery packs are specially made with non-spill caps on the cells, typically housing five 12 V cells to a case. Each case weighs about 130 lb. Batteries are made in various capacities, ranging up to 100 ampere-hour (AH) and more; however, a 45-AH rating is typical. As an example, when fully charged and operated continuously at 26°C, the Molepower battery pack, manufactured by Mole-Richardson, provides power as follows:

- 4,000 W for 20 minutes
- 3,000 W for 40 minutes
- 2,000 W for 1 hour
- 1,000 W for 2 hours and 40 minutes.

As you can see, a battery's capacity is affected by its rate of discharge: the lower the rate, the greater the total power output. At lower temperatures, wet cell batteries have reduced capacity; the times noted should be reduced by 7 per cent for each 6°C below 26°C. Additionally, if the battery is not run continuously, its total running time will be greater than the times noted. Finally, the performance of wet cells decreases with age. In a given battery pack, there will likely be a mix of newer and older cells, making it hard to predict the battery's performance precisely.

The voltage of a lead-acid battery decreases as it discharges, very slowly at first, and more rapidly as it nears the end of its charge. The state of charge can be found by checking the specific gravity of the electrolyte with a hydrometer. The water level should be checked and topped off with distilled water when necessary.

It takes six to eight hours to charge a wet cell battery pack properly. A trickle charger is often used (input: 120 V AC, 15 A; output: 120 V DC, 12 A). A battery pack can be shock-charged in about fifteen minutes, but this is very dangerous, it can cause permanent damage to the batteries, does not fully charge the electrolyte and is not recommended.

Great care must be taken not to tip a lead-acid battery. Spilled sulphuric acid will cause serious damage to the equipment and people with whom it comes into contact. If a battery spills, the area must be thoroughly doused in water to dilute the sulphuric acid.

There is also a more expensive, lightweight, maintenance-free, lead-acid battery that is fully sealed, in which the electrolyte is in the form of jelly or absorbent felt. The battery can be operated in any orientation except completely upside down without any danger of spill. Fully sealed lead-acid batteries typically have a lower AH capacity than other types: 20 to 30 AH is typical.

Power on location

When shooting in a location where a generator is impractical, you can use one of the following alternatives to provide power: have the power company make a line drop and install a kilowatt-hour meter at the location; or tie into the building's service at a switchboard.

Line drops

A line drop is sometimes less expensive than renting a generator. If shooting will take place in one location over several weeks and the building cannot supply sufficient power, you can have the power company make a line drop from the power lines and install a kilowatt-hour meter at the location. An electrician can then install a switchboard with main breakers for the system from which the film's distribution system can draw power. The line drop has advantages over a tie-in because it is a designated circuit with sufficient power available; it has advantages over a generator because it is silent and does not burn fuel.

Tie-ins

A tie-in taps power directly from a building's service box, drawing power from the building's permanent feeder cables. In many locations, such as homes, hotels and warehouses, a tie-in to house power may save a tremendous amount of cabling and expense.

Tying-in is potentially very dangerous. You can be killed by inadvertently contacting live wires. Furthermore, a mistake can cause serious damage to the facility and to the film equipment. Tie-ins should only be undertaken by experienced personnel or qualified electricians.

Power demand

Depending on the demands of the situation, a tie-in can work in one of two ways: by adding to the load of an existing service or by replacing the load of an existing service. If the power demand is not very large, for example, when running a few supplemental lights that are hard to reach with generator power, a tie-in may be made that relies on the surplus amperage available on house circuits. A current clamp should be used to measure the existing current flow to determine the surplus that may be used and to monitor the loads once the tie-in is made.

On the other hand, if the power demand is large or if there is not enough surplus power available from the existing service, then the only way to use house circuits is to shut off or disconnect the circuits to supply the needed amperage to the film's distribution system. In a factory warehouse, for example, there might be some large machinery that won't be operating during filming and that has 100 A or 200 A breakers in the switchboard. An electrician can remove these breakers, disconnect the wires to the machinery, and install breakers with wires running to the film's distribution system.

Types of service

The amperage rating of the service will vary with the size of the installation. A small older house, for example, might be equipped with two 30 A fuses (three-wire, single-phase). A commercial building is likely to have three-phase service panels of 72 kW or more. In addition, this type of installation often has three-wire, single-phase subfeeders of sufficient amperage to be of use.

Commercial buildings may also have high amperage, three-wire, three-phase circuits designated for large air-conditioning units or other big machinery. These circuits are inappropriate for tie-ins because they are designated specifically for the machinery they feed, and they do not provide a grounded neutral lead.

Every switchboard has a small metal placard that gives the amperage, voltage and number of phases of the panel. This information should be confirmed by

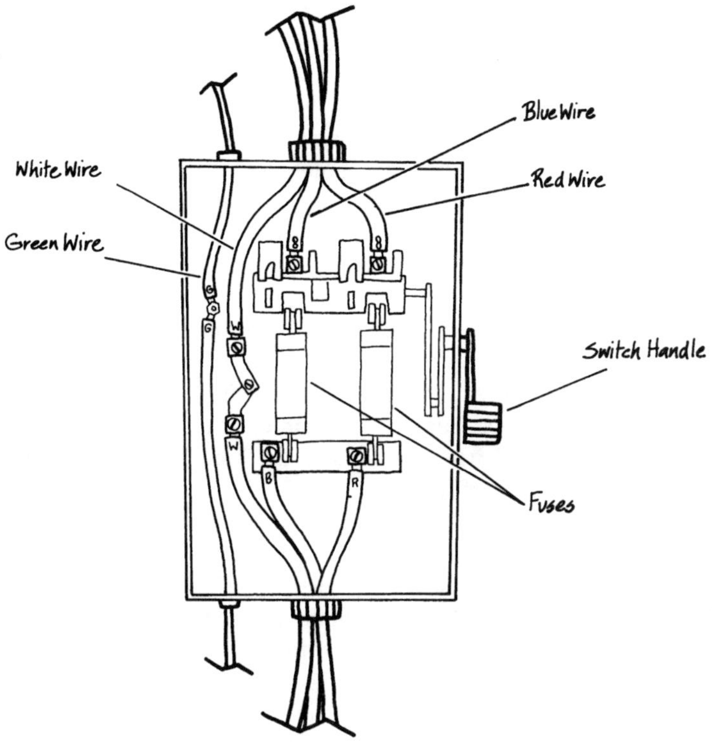

Figure 10.6 A single phase three-wire bull switch

inspecting the panel carefully and measuring the voltage across the phases with a voltmeter.

Before tying-in

Ideally, the power should be turned off at a main switch (Figure 10.6) while the tie-in is performed. If there is a main switch that can be shut off, shut it off. More often than not, power cannot be cut off, and the tie-in must be made to a live circuit.

An assistant should always be present while the electrician makes the tie-in. The assistant is there to help the electrician should he get into trouble. If there is a main switch for turning off the power in an emergency, the assistant should stand with their hand on the switch. (Should an accident occur, the priority becomes saving the electrician from electrocution, and the switch should be used and the consequences dealt with later.) If there is no switch, the assistant should hold a piece of 2 × 4 or an apple box to use to knock the electrician away from the switchboard should he make contact and become frozen to the terminals. The assistant should have a flashlight handy in case the lights go out. They can also help guard against distractions. Make it a policy not to let anyone talk unnecessarily while the electrician is making a tie-in.

The electrician performing the tie-in must be insulated from the ground. He or she should stand on an apple box or a piece of rubber matting.

Making the connections

The electrician first suspends the tie-in cables from a structural support above the box with sash cord so that the ends of the cable dangle. This takes the weight off the connections. The tie-in cables are not connected to the rest of the distribution system when making the tie-in. An isolator should be connected immediately downstream of the tie-in, and it should be switched off.

If it is possible to make the tie-in with one hand, it is good practice for the electrician to put the other hand in his pocket or behind his or her back to prevent the possibility of completing a circuit through the heart.

The tie-in is made downstream of the main breaker or fuses. It should never be made upstream (on the service side) of the main breakers. If a short circuit is accidentally created upstream of the main breaker, the breaker at the local transformer will trip and could shut off electricity for a whole city block.

Connecting to circuit breakers

If there are identifiable circuits that are not needed during filming, the easiest way to tie in is to remove one or more of the installation's circuit breakers and replace them with two larger breakers of equivalent total amperage (Figure 10.7).

If the switchboard has 100 A or 200 A breakers in it already, they can be disconnected from the house load and connected instead to jumper cables that lead to suitable connectors. This approach guarantees that the distribution system will not overload the switchboard.

After tying-in

To comply with the NEC regulations, once the tie-in is complete the open switchboard must be guarded from accidental contact. Rubber matting attached to the face of the switchboard provides proper protection. You can secure the matting with the screws and screw holes of the switchboard cover. The switchboard can be further guarded by locking the door to the room. Place a sign that says 'Danger Live Cables' or 'Danger High Voltage' across the face of the switchboard. Place additional signs across the doorway to the room to prevent people from getting near the open switchboard.

When the system is ready to be energized, notify the gaffer and electricians. Everyone must be warned before current starts running through the cables. Once the connection is made and the isolator is on, make a point of telling the gaffer and other electricians, 'We're hot'.

Using available power

Sometimes you simply don't have the option of using your own distribution system. You are forced to use the existing circuitry at the location. When you use available power, the best boy electric should first find the breaker box and check the current

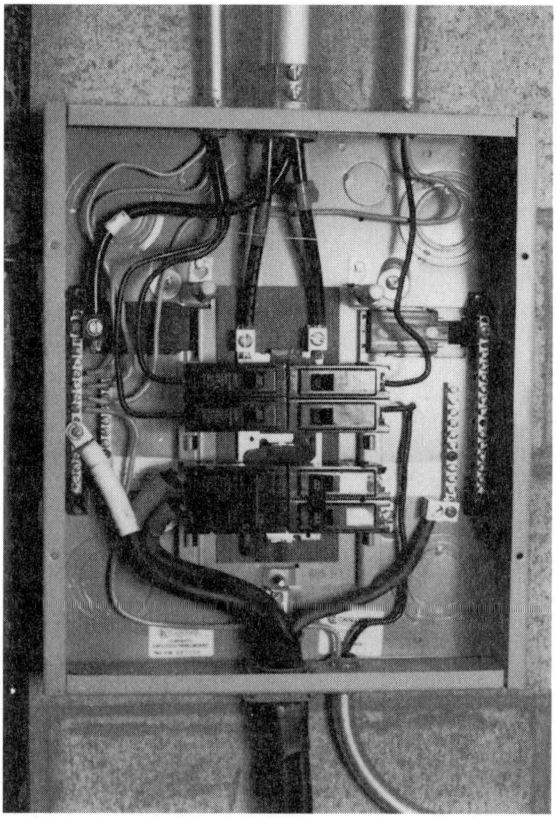

Figure 10.7 A tie-in to 100 A breakers. The tie-in cables are the black cables that are run out the bottom of the panel box. The bus on the left is the neutral wire. The smaller bus on the right is the earthing wire

capacity of the circuits. Count the number of separate circuits. Number the circuits and label the outlets with the circuit numbers. If hair-curling irons or blow dryers are going to be plugged in, determine which circuit they are on. Run extension cables from different sections of the house so that as many circuits as possible are available to you.

The American electrical code specifies that in new houses there must be two designated 20 A circuits around the counter of the kitchen. These circuits are handy because they are not wired to any other outlets. Other designated circuits are those for the laundry and the water heater. Wall outlets usually share circuit breakers with other outlets and overhead fixtures. Small houses may have only one circuit per floor. Larger houses may have two or three circuits per floor.

Small apartments often have as few as one or two circuit breakers per apartment. Each apartment has separate circuits, however, so if it is possible to run power from other apartments, you can power more lights.

11

Special circumstances and equipment

Theatre and concert lighting luminaires

Each lighting venue has its own set of demands. The luminaires designed and developed for lighting the stage have been perfected for that task. The ellipsoidal reflector spotlight (ERS) gives the stage lighting designer the strong throw, versatility, and control needed to light a stage from some distance. The PAR can give the concert designer a highly durable, reliable luminaire that has the raw strength to pump light through saturated gels on to the concert stage. Each type of luminaire is an answer to a particular lighting need.

Naturally, these luminaires are employed when filming stage performances, but their special qualities are also very handy in other situations. A Leko can provide a hard cutoff where there is no room to make a sharp cutoff with a flag. For example, a woman answers her front door; she is lit by light bounced off a piece of show card taped to the inside wall beside the door. An ellipsoidal can make the hard cutoff necessary to prevent direct light from hitting anything but the card.

Ellipsoidal reflector spotlights

The ellipsoidal reflector spotlight (ERS – known as an ellipsoidal or Leko[1] in the USA and as a profile spotlight in Europe) is the workhorse of theatre lighting (Figure 11.1). Ellipsoidal spotlights are listed in Table A.12 (Appendix A).

The luminaire is designed to give a long controllable throw in order to light a stage from fairly distant positions. The luminaire is able to project a beam that can be shaped by shutters or by an iris, or to project a gobo pattern. The shape of the beam is determined by the shape or pattern in the gate aperture. Light collected from a highly efficient ellipsoidal reflector passes through the gate; the shape or pattern in the gate is then brought into focus by a lens assembly in the barrel. The gate can be brought into sharp or soft focus by sliding the barrel forward or back-

1. Leko is a trademark of Strand Lighting, but it is widely used to refer generally to ellipsoidal spotlights.

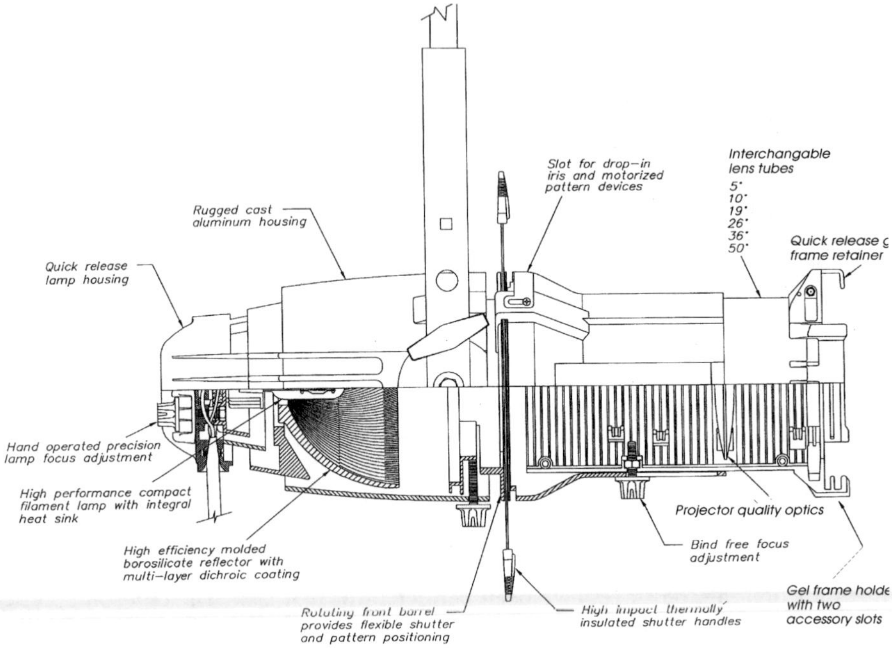

Figure 11.1 The Source Four. Innovative advances in the design of the lamp, reflector and lens assembly allow this 575 W light to out-perform standard 1 kW ellipsoidals while providing exceptionally sharp shutter cuts without halation, even distribution of light through the field, extended pattern life, and eliminating shutter jams due to heat-warping. You can put two Source Fours on a 1.2 kW dimmer circuit, doubling the dimmer capacity. (Courtesy of ETC – Electronic Theatre Controls, Inc., Middleton, WI.)

ward. The narrower the beam angle of the lens, the greater the throw and intensity.

Four shaping shutters (top, bottom, left and right) can be pushed into the path of the beam to shape it into a square, rectangle, triangle, or whatever is needed. Immediately in front of the shutters is the gobo slot, into which a metal cut-out pattern can be inserted. Hundreds of gobo patterns are available – a wide variety of window and venetian blind patterns, foliage patterns, clouds, cityscapes, stars, flames, practically anything you can name. Motorized rotating gobo devices are available that create theatrical moving flame and water patterns by projecting two counter-rotating gobo patterns. Many luminaires also have a rotatable front barrel, which provides flexibility in the positioning of shutter cuts and gobo patterns. An iris can be placed in the gobo slot to adjust the aperture of the circular beam, or to use the lamp as a follow spot. Coloured gel is placed in a gel frame holder at the front of the light.

A donut is a metal mask accessory that slides into the gel frame slot. It is used to sharpen gobo patterns and clean up colour fringes at the beam edge (at the expense of some light output).

The field of an ellipsoidal is normally very even. If the lamp gets out of alignment in relation to the reflector, the lamp shows a noticeable hot spot. A screw or hand-operated knob in the back of the luminaire adjusts the alignment. To change a burned-out lamp, the back section of the luminaire is removed.

Ellipsoidal luminaires are designed with either a fixed beam width or a 'zoom' barrel. Some manufacturers refer to individual luminaires by lens diameter and focal length (6 × 9 in. has a 6-in. lens and a 9-in. focal length). Others refer to lamps by field angle (such as 40°, 26°, 20°, 10° and 5°).

Gaffers often have to scratch their heads when they see these figures, not knowing which type will work for which application. You can easily calculate the beam diameter and light intensity of any luminaire using data given in Table A.12 (Appendix A). Generally speaking, wide-beam Lekos of 250 W and 500 W are used above stage in small theatres, 750 W and 1,000 W 6 × 9 and 6 × 12 luminaires are used above stage and in the front of the house in medium-sized theatres, and 6 × 16 or 8 × 16 1 kW and 2 kW luminaires are used for long throws from the front of house.

Note: It is generally accepted that luminaire output figures usually refer to the beam angle, however in the case of profile spotlights you may see field angle quoted. Due to the sharp cutoff at the edge of the beam, the field angle and beam angle are virtually the same thing.

PAR cans

PAR cans are the workhorse of rock-and-roll lighting (Figure 11.2). They are popular because they put out a lot of light per watt, more than any other incandescent luminaire, and can drive light through even the most saturated gel colours. They are simple, lightweight, maintenance-free and made for the heavy-duty life of the concert tour. Their design is as simple as they come, a PAR lamp mounted inside a can that provides a gel frame slot at the front of the barrel. PAR cans don't generally

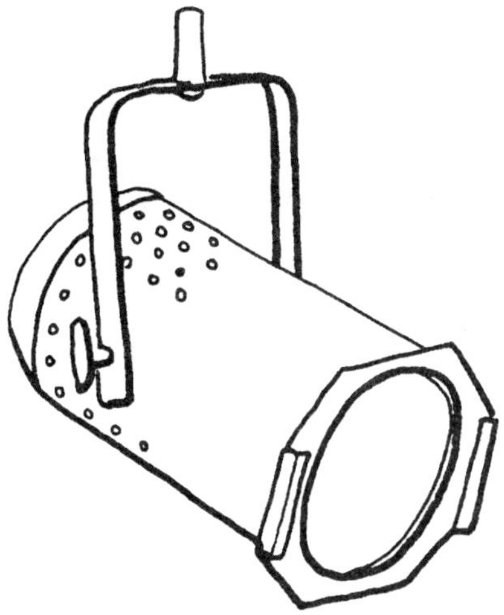

Figure 11.2 PAR can

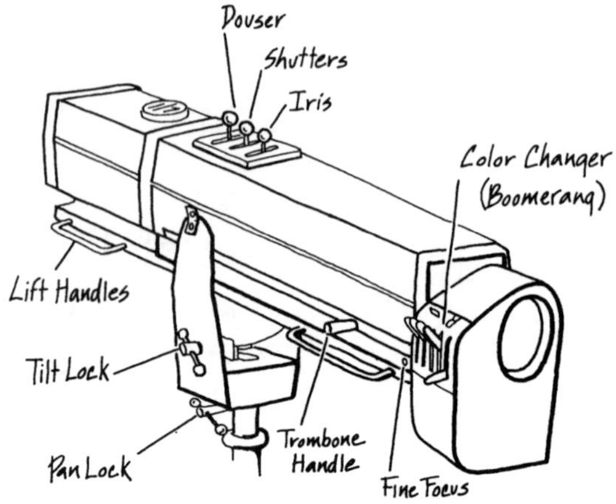

Figure 11.3 The Strong Super Trouper follow spot. (Equipment courtesy of Strong International, Inc., Omaha, NE.)

come with scrims. The gel frame is typically 10 in. in diameter and any 10 in. scrims (Mighty-Mole) will fit the slot.

PAR cans use 1 kW PAR-64 lamps (the same lamps used in maxi-brutes and Mole-PARs, see Tables E.4, E.5 and E.6 in Appendix E). Smaller PAR cans using PAR-56 and PAR-36 lamps are also available. The beam pattern is oblong, not round, but the lamp can be turned in the housing to make the best use of its orientation. PAR lamps come with various spreads: wide flood (WFL), medium flood (MFL), narrow spot (NSP) and very narrow spot (VNSP). For an even narrower, very intense beam, an aircraft landing light (ACL) can be fitted into a standard PAR-64 housing. ACL lamps operate on 28 V but can be run with a step-down transformer or in series in gangs of four (USA 110 V) or eight (Europe 220 V).

Follow spots

Follow spots (or front of house lights), with their powerful long throw, are a staple of music concerts, skating events, circus events and theatrical performances (Figure 11.3).

Follow spots are designed to follow a performer on a distant stage, necessitating the following controls: an iris lever, which controls the size of the circular pool of light; a douser lever for 'blacking-out'; shutters, which 'strip out' the top and bottom of a circular pool, creating more of a rectangle; and a colour changer, which introduces any of several coloured gels. The trombone handle is used to set the size and intensity of the beam. A fine focus knob is used to sharpen or soften the edges of the beam. The setting of this knob varies with the distance of the subject and the trombone setting used. Follow spots are mounted on gimbals, which allow the operator to pan and tilt the light smoothly to follow action on the stage.

The size and light source type vary with application. Small 1 kW quartz-lamp follow spots, such as the Strong Trouperette, are common for short throws of 30 to 60 ft (100 FC), such as in a night club or school auditorium. Slightly larger 575 W HMI and 700 W xenon units have throws of 50 to 160 ft (100 FC). Large follow spots, such as the Strong Super Trouper with a 1 kW or 2 kW xenon lamp, are used for lighting performers from the back of very large auditoriums and arenas. The Super Trouper has a throw of 130 to 340 ft (100 FC). The Gladiator and other similar follow spots using 2,500 W and 3,000 W xenon lamps have throws of up to 460 ft (100 FC).

Operating the follow spot

Operating a follow spot smoothly and properly is something of a speciality. There are a few important points to remember. Unless otherwise specified, the trombone and iris should be arranged to light the performer from head to foot. Always keep the performer's face lit, if necessary losing other parts of the body. Panning and tilting must be smooth and in perfect harmony with the movements of the performer, neither leading them nor getting left behind, and keeping small movements fluid and subtle so as not to be distracting. When you receive direction to iris out from head-and-shoulders to full-body, tilt the light down as you iris out so that the light stays centred on the body. If you are to come out of black on a performer, get the light aimed before opening the douser. If necessary, you can surreptitiously get accurate aim by closing the iris down to a pinpoint, then quickly open the douser, aim the light, douse it and open the iris up again. Very often follow spots are used to ballyhoo, the classic sweeping of light over the stage and the audience in big random figure of eight's. You can expect to be asked to 'ballyhoo' at some point. When a group of performers are to be covered with a single light, the beam has to be widened out so much that the top and bottom of the beam start to create unwanted spill problems. In this case, you may be asked to strip it out using the shutter to cut the top and bottom of the beam, again making the beam cover the performers from head to foot.

In film work it is convenient to be able to adjust the intensity of the beam. This can be accomplished in a couple of different ways. The simplest way is to use the trombone. Trombone forward to intensify the light, and trombone back to dim it. The gaffer will meter the light on stage and give you one or more working intensity settings, mark the settings on the barrel and make sure the trombone does not slide out of adjustment. Once the trombone is set for intensity, the iris is used to size the beam. A second way to dim a spot is to put neutral density gel in one or two gel slots.

The boomerang (colour changer) typically has six gel frames, which can be introduced into the beam using one of six levers on the end of the barrel. By common convention, the changer levers are numbered from 1 to 6 from front to back. Most changers are designed so that you can roll through the colours; as each new lever is applied, the previous lever automatically releases. You can release all the levers and go to white light by pressing a button underneath the changer levers.

When the spot is not in use on stage, it may be panned off into the ceiling of the arena or into the sky, or it may be doused. Xenon lights should not be turned off unnecessarily, as this drastically decreases the life of the very expensive xenon lamps. The douser can be closed for several minutes without causing damage to the light. Do not use the iris or shutter to do this, however, as they will be damaged. Like any xenon light, xenon follow spots use a power supply that converts the current to DC. Xenon lamps are flicker-free at any frame rate and have a daylight colour temperature. The lamps are extremely sensitive to temperature and must be cooled with fans when running. After shutdown the lamp must be allowed to cool with fans running for at least five minutes. Never shut down the power before the light has been allowed to cool.

Follow spots are designed to be used with coloured gels. Despite their candlepower, they should not burn through gel; the optics are arranged so that the beam is least hot as it passes through the gel stage of the barrel. In addition, large follow spots use cooling fans to cool the gel in use. If the gel burns through quickly in one place, it is a sign that the lamp or reflector may be out of alignment. There are adjustment knobs on the back of the larger lights that are used to align the lamp. If the gel fades quickly, you may want to check that the gel fan is working (on the underside of the boomerang) and that the air intake is not clogged.

Effects lights

Xenon lights

On a sunny day in Los Angeles my light meter will typically give a reading somewhere between 6,000 and 8,000 foot-candles (depending on the smog). A 12 kW HMI 50 feet away, full spot, gives me around 3,000 foot-candles. The new 24,000 W HMIs will bring that figure up to around 6,000 foot-candles (at 50 feet). So what could be brighter than that? A 7 kW xenon 'searchlight' at 50 feet puts out almost that much when fully flooded. At full spot it ratchets up to a screaming 30,000 foot-candles. A 10 kW xenon can deliver more than 8,000 foot-candles at a distance of 150 feet!

Xenotech, Phoebus, Tek Lighting and other manufacturers, have developed lines of high-output, flicker-free xenon lights designed primarily for concert, event, theatrical and film use. They are made in various sizes from a powerful 75 W flashlight torch (Xenotech) with clip-on battery, through a full range of units – 150 W, 500 W, 750 W, 1,000 W, 2,000 W, 4,000 W, 7,000 W – up to a 10,000 W unit, the brightest lighting unit in existence to my knowledge.

A xenon 'searchlight' creates an intense, sharply defined shaft of daylight-balanced (5,600 K) light with a beam unlike that of any other luminaire. Light emanates from the luminaire in a narrow column of almost perfectly parallel rays with very little scatter and a powerful throw. At 50 feet, full spot, the beam of a 7 kW is still only 30 inches across (Figure 11.4). Xenon searchlights are used aboard police and rescue helicopters, on armoured tanks and in prison towers. Film xenons are commonly used to re-create these types of searchlight effects. Everyone immediately thinks of Jorden Crownenweth's masterful work in *Blade Runner*. The moving searchlights seem both ominous and poetic in the thick atmosphere of that movie. Nowadays xenons are practically standard procedure for futuristic shows.

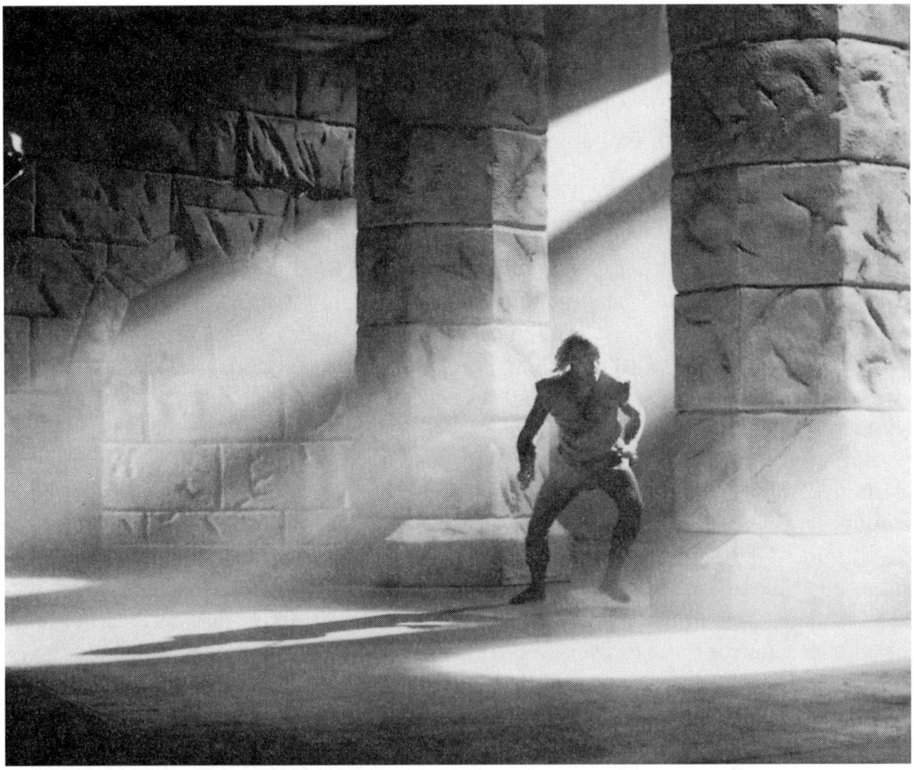

Figure 11.4 Xenon lights have a very small arc gap, allowing the beam to be focused into an intense, very narrow shaft. (Photo courtesy of Xenotech, Inc., Sun Valley, CA.)

A xenon's unique beam characteristics makes it useful as more than a mere effect unit. Say you wish to simulate hard parallel shafts of sunlight piercing a row of skylights in a musty (lightly fogged) attic. In this case you might opt for xenons over HMIs because the spread of the beam from a PAR or fresnel gives away the artificial source. This is especially true if you have space restrictions above the set and can't get the luminaires backed away enough to get nice parallel rays. The highly focused beam of a xenon also has the strength to give you nice hot highlights even when the shaft has to travel through a large set before splashing on to the floor or walls. The clean beam edges look great with a little atmosphere in the air. (I've found you can sharpen up the beam edge even more if necessary by masking out the beam edges with a donut. I found this necessary when shooting miniatures.)

The magic of a xenon lies in the special characteristics of the lamp. To be able to focus light into a collimated shaft of parallel rays, you have to start with practically a point source – a point source that is also very bright. The problem is, with most types of lamps, the brighter the light, the larger the source has to be (the filament size in tungsten lamps, or arc length in HMIs). Xenon lamps have a very short arc length and an extremely bright arc, which makes them easy to collimate into a highly focused beam. The short arc length also means generally they are easy to hot-restrike. The lamp is mounted axially, with the arc positioned at the focal point of a highly polished parabolic reflector. The terminal cap at the front-end of the luminaire blocks direct light from the lamp, so all light is reflected by the parabolic reflector and directed into parallel rays.

The one major drawback to the design of any xenon searchlight is the shadow in the beam. Because the lamp is double-ended and must be axially mounted, the luminaire requires a structure at the front of the lamp to hold the terminal at that end of the lamp. The shadow of the structural parts is projected within the beam and creates a distinctive Mercedes-Benz emblem-like shadow, and a small donut hole in the centre of the beam. In most cases I've found that disguising this shadow, and hiding the round beam-edge is not difficult, but the shadow can sometimes be a problem so you have to allow for it.

Coloured gel (CTO) is typically snot taped right to the front of the luminaire. Saturated party colours can sometimes be a challenge; they tend to burn right through.

The other restriction to keep in mind when planning to use xenons is that they sometimes don't like to be tilted down. Beyond about 15 degrees below horizontal they will very often become troublesome – the arc wanders, they shut off or won't start up. It is best to use a mirror if the beam is to be directed downward. Xenotech offers 45 degree mirrors which mount to the ears of their luminaires from 2 kW up to 7 kW.

The Xenotech 75 W flashlight runs on a clip-on battery or off the mains. (The flashlight is reported to deliver 600 FC, at full spot, at a distance of 100 ft!) The power supplies for larger units (2,000 W – 10,000 W) may take either 208-230 V single-phase or three-phase depending on the type. With some three-phase power supplies you can get them to work on two legs of single-phase but you have to use the right two legs (the last time I used one I dropped the blue, and used red and black (US phase colours)).

Xenon lamps run on very high current, low voltage DC necessitating a transformer/rectifier power supply which usually tends to be quite large and heavy. A 2 kW xenon lamp characteristics are 2,000 W at 25 V DC, drawing 80 A and producing 80,000 lumens. The lamp also requires a very high voltage of approximately 40,000 V to restrike it when it is hot. Tek Lighting has a unique design for their 2 kW, 4 kW, 7 kW and 10 kW units which incorporates the power supply right into the heads. They are reportedly brighter, quieter and have a smaller black hole in the beam than other xenon heads. On all xenon lights ON/OFF and flood/spot functions can be controlled from the ballast and the head. Xenon lights operate on a pulse DC (equivalent to square-wave current), which allows flicker-free filming at any frame rate up to 10,000 fps.

Xenotech lights can be ordered with a normal yoke or with a remote-control articulating base and colour changer and douser accessories. When operated by computer-controlled remote, a line of xenon lights can be preprogrammed to perform moving beam effects in unison, or each unit can be controlled separately for different purposes.

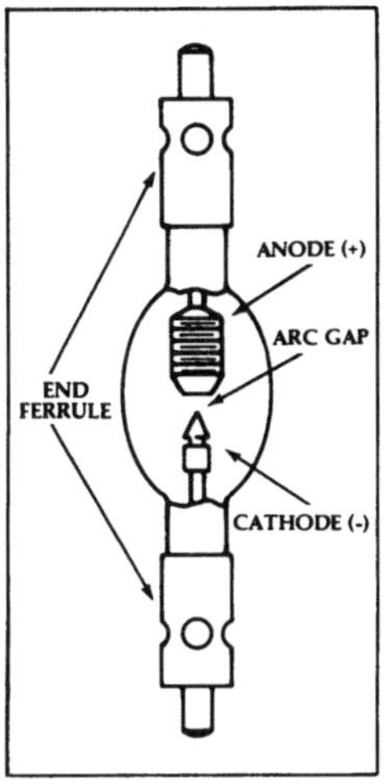

Figure 11.5 A xenon lamp

Xenon lamps have long lives: greater than 2,000 hours. There is no colour shift over the life of the lamp, and the colour temperature is independent of voltage and current fluctuations. Xenon lamps require very careful temperature regulation, and they must use forced air cooling, which makes them somewhat noisy. Forced air cooling should continue for at least five minutes after the light has been turned off. Never turn off the power supply before the lamp has been allowed to cool.

Like HMIs, xenon lamps put out large amounts of ultraviolet radiation which is filtered out of the beam by the front glass. During the life of the lamp, evaporated tungsten is deposited on the upper inner wall of the envelope and slowly reduces light output. The lamp should be turned over after half its rated life. These unavoidable deposits are what define the end of a lamp's usefulness. Frequent ignition charges accelerate the wear of the electrodes and hasten the darkening of the envelope. Xenon light operators should therefore try to avoid unnecessary shutdowns and start-ups. If the light is temporarily not needed, pan it into the sky rather than shutting it off.

A xenon lamp (Figure 11.5) is always under substantial internal pressure, and the pressure increases when hot. A xenon lamp does not break; it explodes! According to one xenon technician I talked to, if a lamp explodes and you are not protected, shards of quartz can become lodged under your skin. They are invisible to x-rays, so the only way a doctor can remove them is to poke around in your open cuts – very painful. Clearly it is necessary to wear serious protection when handling the lamp. The 'bomb suit', a kevlar vest and gloves, and full-face shield should be worn (xenon vendors will provide the suit on request). Handle the lamp with the utmost care and never handle one until completely cooled. For safety reasons, lamps should not be operated more than 25 per cent past their rated lifetime. Xenon lamps must be installed with proper polarity. If operated with improper polarity, the lamp can be rendered useless in a short amount of time.

Automated lights

Impressive lighting showmanship has always been a tradition in rock-and-roll lighting. State-of-the-art automated luminaires are capable of creating breathtaking effects in the hands of a creative designer and a skilled console operator. Dozens of lights can be programmed, choreographed to make sweeping pans and flourishes, weaving beams of light into patterns in the air. The lights have dozens of features. The operation of lighting systems such as Vari-lite, Intellabeam, Cyberlight, Roboscan and others is complex, typically requiring the skills of a specialist. However, without getting into too much detail, we can get a general idea of what is possible by looking at one luminaire as an example.

The Cyberlight, designed by Lightwave Research, employs a 1,200 SE HMI source (5,600 K). Light travels through a complex tunnel of mechanisms, including: motorized zoom, variable iris, variable frost (hard or soft edge), optical dimming and blackout, a three-tier colour system (infinitely variable dichroic colour mixing system, eight-position colour wheel, colour correction), bi-directional variable speed rotating gobo wheel (four gobos), fixed gobo wheel (eight gobos) and variable-speed strobe shutter. The light can also produce a number of optical effects, such as a multi-image prism, split colour, near photo-quality image projection, wave glass and a mosaic colour effect. The light comes out of the end of the luminaire and is aimed by use of mirror, which is panned and tilted by a high-resolution, micro-stepping motor capable of panning the beam smoothly 170° and tilting 110°. All features are remotely controlled using a special LCD lighting controller or a USITT DMX-512 console. The control cable is standard XLR. The luminaire is 44 in. long and weighs 91 lb.

Blacklights

Ultraviolet (UV) light, blacklight, occupies a place in the electromagnetic spectrum just below violet, the shortest visible wavelength of light. It is invisible radiant energy. The UV spectrum is subdivided as follows:

- UV-A 350+380 nm black light
- UV-B 300+340 nm used for sun tanning
- UV-C 200+280 nm very dangerous.

Right around 365 nm, in the middle of the UV-A spectrum, you get maximum transmission for exciting luminescent pigments and materials. When acted upon by UV rays, fluorescent and phosphorescent materials are excited and emit visible light and vibrant colour. Because blacklight works on some materials and not others, you can create interesting images, such as a disembodied pair of white gloves juggling three glowing orange balls.

Blacklight Blue fluorescent lamps (BLB, 4 ft, 40 W typically) don't have a lot of punch; however, when used in close they can be quite effective. With a bright reflector and high-output ballast (e.g., Kino Flo), fluorescents offer an even, soft light from a large source.

In order to create radiant energy at about 365 nm, one needs a light with high UV output (Mercury Vapour or Metal Halide) and a carefully designed UV filter that blocks the visible light (400 to 700 nm) and the UV-B and UV-C wavelengths. Theatrical rental houses typically stock Mercury Vapour or Metal Halide floodlights ranging from 250 W to 400 W. These lamps use a deep-dyed, pot-poured, rolled, or blown glass filter.

For lamps larger than 400 W, a UV dichroic coating is necessary to take the extreme heat. Such filters can be used on luminaires up to 18 kW HMI and on xenon lights. Xenotech and Phoebus both carry dichroic UV lenses for their xenon lights. Automated Entertainment in Burbank has developed UV filters for 12 kW and 18 kW HMIs, and 200 W, 1,200 W, 2,500 W and 4 kW SE Pars. Automated Entertainment also have their own UV and 'glow in the dark' pigments and dyes.

Wildfire Inc. is another innovator in this area. They have developed a line of UV lights, including a 400 W Fresnel, 400 W floodlight, 400 W ellipsoidal spotlight and 250 W wide profile spotlight in a 20°, 50° or 90° beam diameter. The units operate with ballasts and head feeders like HMIs. Wildfire also offers a wide variety of luminescent materials and paints, including non-toxic dyes, hair spray, lipstick, fabrics, plastics, adhesive tapes, confetti, PVC flexible tubing and more.

DN Labs is also active in this market, with a line of small lights and specially formulated, highly efficient luminescent rods and sheets that can be machined and won't break.

Photographing with blacklight

To determine the exposure with blacklight, take spot meter readings of the luminescent materials to be filmed under the UV lights. In order to glow vibrantly on film, they should be overexposed by one stop. The effect is less vibrant at exposure and slightly dull one stop under exposure. A UV filter must be used on the camera lens because the lens cannot focus UV light the same way it can focus the visible spectrum. Without the UV filter, UV produces a hazy softening in the image.

Ultraviolet light can be combined with conventional light and still create a luminescent effect. The balance depends on how much the effect is to be featured. One could light the scene normally and add UV lights on luminescent materials to give them an extra vibrancy, or a scene could be lit to a lower level with conventional lights so that the luminescent materials stand out. With nothing but blacklight lighting a scene, a woman wearing a luminescent wig and dress, for example, will appear to have no hands or face, only the clothes and hair will show up.

Lighting automobiles

Directors of photography sometimes specialize in one type of work; photographing automobiles for commercials is one such niche, sometimes referred to as sheet-metal photography. Lighting a car requires special consideration because the metal is glossy and highly reflective. When lighting any shiny object, you are not so much projecting light on to the subject as creating an environment around it that, when reflected, defines its shape, separates it, and creates highlights and shadow. By manipulating the shape of the reflected highlights and shadows, you can actually alter the apparent shape of the subject. Car lighting specialists use this technique to de-emphasize less appealing contours of their subject with the same delicate care that feature DPs often take in lighting the face of a star.

Fisher lights are large rear-lit soft banks specifically designed for this type of work (Fisher Productions, Inc.). They are made in 10 × 40 ft and 17 × 52 ft sizes. The bank is suspended from overhead crane or rigged to building structures and can be panned, tilted, and angled remotely. The banks are lit with rows of 1 kW tungsten lamps, which are individually controlled by a dimmer, 40 kW (10 × 40) or 96 kW (17 × 52). Dimmers are standard 208Y/120 three-phase AC with Cam-Lok tails (adaptors when necessary). When flicker-free daylight-balanced light is needed, the 10 × 40 bank can also be fitted with a 50 kW DCI system (twenty 2,500 W DCI lamps, powered by dimmable electronic ballasts). By manipulating brightness and colour across the whole area of the bank, effects such as twilight sky can be created. Fisher supplies their own technicians with the special rig.

Chimera Photographic Equipment also makes large soft banks called F-2 Banks (5 × 10, 10 × 20, 10 × 30, 15 × 30 or 15 × 40 ft). Lights can be rigged to the centre suspension bar or to a grid above.

Fibre optics

A fibre optic cable is a flexible or semi-flexible glass cable that conducts light energy produced by an illuminator light box. There are a number of fibre optic systems available, with different features and applications.

LTM makes a flicker-free 250 V HTI (5,600 K) illuminator and a system of fibre optic cables that is commonly used for filming model sets, to light car interiors, and for table-top product shots where a conventional lamp would melt the product or cause an electrical hazard, lighting up inside soaps or fluids, or underwater. The light emitted from the end of the fibre optic cable comes out as a beam and can be fitted with a 2½ in. Fresnel lens and barn doors, a miniature light-bar, or used bare. The system gives a choice of two cable configurations: either the CML-4 (four 8 ft long, ⅜ in. cables) or CML-100 (100, 2½ ft long, 3/16 in. diameter fibre bundles). Various lens attachments, extensions, and accessories are available. The cables are extremely small and flexible, can be easily hidden, and can get into some tight little spots. Because of the make-up of the cable, the light can become green in lengths longer than 8 ft, and a magenta correction gel may need to be used.

DN Labs makes a 1,200 W HMI illuminator (either electronic or magnetic) that illuminates eleven 1½ in. diameter fibre optic cables very brightly. DN Labs also makes a 250 W (3,000 K) illuminator, and a 75 W 12/24 V AC/DC illuminator, which is ideal for moving car work. These illuminate a single fibre optic cable. Clearflux™ fibre optic cable comes in various sizes and types: OD ¼ in., ⅜ in., ½ in.

and ¾ in. core, either side lit (entire length glows) or end lit (which transmits light to the end).

Innovision Optics makes a fibre optic system that uses either 150 W or 250 W tungsten, or a 150 W metal halide illuminator that has a choice of dichroic coloured glass filters built into it. Flexible and semi-flexible optic cables come in various types and sizes. One type glows along its entire length like a flexible neon rope. It can be heated and bent into semi-permanent shapes and letters. Core sizes are 3/16 in., ¼ in., ⅜ in. and ½ in., in up to 70 ft unspliced lengths. To increase intensity, you can attach an illuminator at both ends.

Neon

When the art department provides neon lights, it is often necessary to dim the neon to make it look good on film. Bobinette or black hose stockings work if the neon is out of focus in the background, but when the neon is seen clearly, it is useful to dim them electronically. Variac or triac dimmers can generally be used for short periods, but when the neon is to be left on, the art department should order special neon dimmers. Other dimmers can overheat and burn out the neon transformer. The way to know if a dimmer is overheating a transformer is to use an ammeter on the power line either going into or coming out of the dimmer. If the dimmer setting is a bad match for the transformer, the amperage flow will jump way above the rated amperage of the transformer. A transformer rated at 2 or 3 amps can start drawing 15 or 20 amps and burn up.

Neon transformers are sized to the particular tube they are lighting. The voltage and current output of the transformer will depend on a number of factors, including the type of gas used and the length of the tube. If you run into trouble with the neon going out when dimmed, using a larger transformer will help. The current output of the transformer drives the neon tubes. A transformer with a higher current output will keep the tube lit when dimmed.

Camera-synchronous strobe lighting

Clairmont Camera and Unilux, Inc. have designed high-speed strobe lighting systems that synchronize the flash of the lighting units with the shutter of the camera. Each frame of film is given a very bright, very short flash of light. When a camera operates at 24 fps, the exposure time is normally 1/48 second. With the Unilux strobe unit, the flash is 1/100,000 second. The effect is to remove all motion blur from an image. Strobe units are often used for shooting slow-motion close-ups of pouring liquids, such as in beer and soft drink commercials. Each drop of beer is sharp because in each frame the moving drops are frozen by the very brief flash. The lights can be synchronized with the camera shutter at frame rates from 1 fps up to 650 fps.

Unilux strobes have been used in music videos to capture dance in an ultra-sharp, jerky style. By using a special-effects generator box, the lights can create a strobe effect by not exposing every frame. This appears on film as a series of flashes with performers jumping suddenly from one position to another. Using a sequencer circuit, the lights can also be made to chase so that in each frame light comes from a different head.

Unilux H3000 system

Unilux has been designing and improving strobe systems since the late 1960s. The first such system was so large that it required a special studio. With each model, the lights have become smaller, lighter and simpler to operate. Today's strobes are as portable and as easy to operate as 1,200 W HMIs.

The H3000 system consists of three heads and a control console to which the three lights are connected. Figure 11.6 shows a system using two control units and five heads.

Control consoles can be daisy-chained together to control as many lights as needed. The H3000 system takes single-phase, 50 or 60 Hz, 220 V power at about

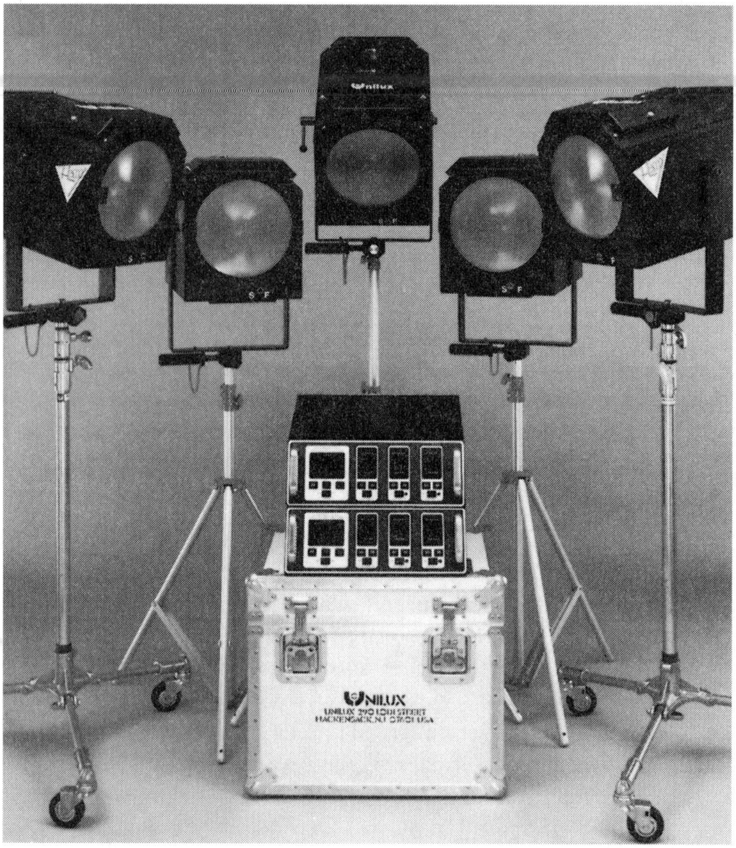

Figure 11.6 The Unilux H3000 system. Pictured here: five heads, two control units and the shipping case. (Photo courtesy of Unilux, Inc., Hackensack, NJ.)

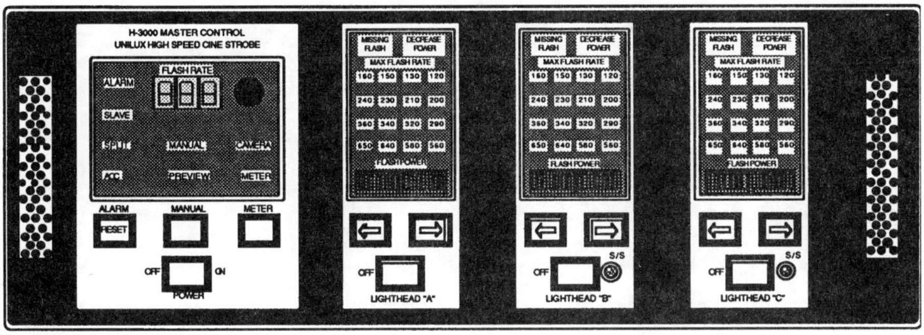

Figure 11.7 The front of the Unilux H3000 control unit. (Illustration courtesy of Unilux, Inc., Hackensack, NJ.)

10 A per head. An older Unilux system uses three-phase 220 V power and draws about 5 A per head.

Unilux heads use a special spiral-shaped quartz xenon lamp (which resembles something out of Dr Frankenstein's laboratory). They have a daylight colour temperature of 6,000 K, and they operate relatively coolly. The heads can be oriented in any position.

The strobe system synchronizes to the speed of the camera using a sync cable connected to the camera's speed control accessory receptacle. The strobe speed follows the camera shutter speed to give one flash each time the shutter is open and one flash each time it is closed, which is when the camera operator can see through the lens.

Operation

Figure 11.7 shows the front panel of the control console.

When you turn the power switch on, the lights go into preview mode. They flicker at 60 flashes per second at a relatively low light level. This speed is just fast enough that the strobing is not annoying while setting the lights. Once the lights are roughly positioned, you are ready to take some light readings. Before you can take readings, however, you must select the maximum flash rate for each light. The maximum flash rate settings are, in frames per second, as follows: 120, 130, 150, 160, 200, 210, 230, 240, 290, 320, 340, 360, 560, 580, 640 and 650 fps. The maximum flash rate should be set at or above the fastest film frame rate that will be used in the shot. If filming at less than 120 fps, set the flash rate to 120 fps. The brightness that the lights can attain is inversely proportional to the speed of the flashes that you set. When you set the flash rate you are also setting the intensity of the flash. When the camera rolls, the flashes will be uniform in intensity at any speed up to the maximum speed you've set. Electronics within the control console monitor the operation of the equipment and signal errors such as camera speeds above the maximum flash rate setting or missing flashes.

Note that high-speed cameras sometimes give off a spike pulse when they are coming up to speed. This will trigger an alarm on the console. Press the alarm reset button. If the alarm is not triggered again, you can safely assume that there is no problem once the camera is at speed.

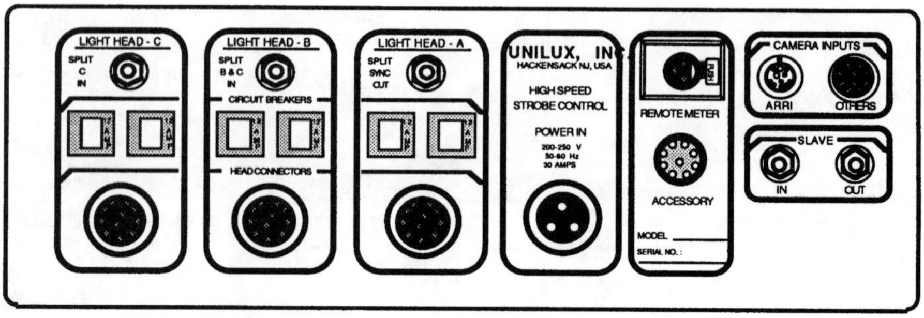

Figure 11.8 The back of the Unilux H3000 control unit. (Illustration courtesy of Unilux, Inc., Hackensack, NJ.)

Let us say that we will be filming at 200 fps. We set the maximum flash rate to 200 for each of the light heads. Now we are ready to take light readings. A word of warning: If the main power switch is turned off, the settings will be lost, so it is helpful to circle the setting numbers on the console with a white grease pencil.

Strobe light must be measured with a flash meter. A flash meter is able to sense and capture an exposure measurement from a quick flash of light. Unilux provides Minolta flash meters with their lights. To take a reading, press the meter button on the control console (Figure 11.7). The lights will come up to the intensities you've set. Note that the lights continue to flash at 60 flashes per second in meter mode. When you're done taking readings, press the meter button again to return to preview mode. The control console will automatically return the lights to preview mode after three minutes.

When you are ready to start filming, the lights will automatically come up to the preset intensity when you turn the camera on. The flash rate is slaved to the camera speed and will increase and decrease speed in tandem with the camera motor. The frame rate at any given moment is shown on the control console. The control console also displays the source of the flash rate signal: camera, meter mode, preview, accessory port (such as the special effects generator) or slave input (used when the console is slaved to another console).

Controlling the light

A focusing snoot can be used to concentrate the beam into a spot of adjustable size. Unilux lights don't generally come with barn doors, but Mole Studio Junior barn doors and 10⅛ in. scrims fit the ears.

Mixing sources

In many instances, cinematographers find that the Unilux image is overly sharp. To make the image look more natural you can mix Unilux with tungsten or flicker-free discharge sources. A good mix is to set Unilux two stops brighter than the supplemental sources.

To calculate the exposure when mixing Unilux with supplemental sources, measure the two sources separately and then add the two readings. Remember that twice as much light equals one stop more, so if the Unilux reading and the supplemental readings are the same, effectively doubling the light, the exposure is one stop more than the individual readings. If Unilux is one stop brighter, the supplemental lighting is half as bright, and you would add a half-stop to the Unilux reading. If Unilux is two stops brighter, the supplemental light is one quarter as bright. You would add a quarter stop to the Unilux reading.

When Unilux lights are used alone, changing the frame rate does not change the exposure. Because the heads flash the same amount of light on each frame, the exposure time does not change with the frame rate as it does with normal lights. When mixing Unilux with supplemental light, if you double the frame rate, the exposure time of the supplemental light is cut in half. You would need to double the intensity of the supplemental light to keep the same proportion of light from the two sources. In other words, the f-stop you read from the tungsten sources must take the frame rate (shutter speed) into account before it is compared with the Unilux reading for the purpose of setting light levels.

Sync delay box

The sync delay box is a separate circuit box that comes with every system. With all cameras except Arriflex, the camera sync cable is connected to the sync delay box, and the box is then connected to the 'others' camera input on the back of the control console. The sync delay box serves three potentially helpful functions: shutter sync, cut-off speed and polarity.

Shutter sync

With each camera used, the shutter sync should be checked by removing the lens and observing the shutter opening with the Unilux lights running. If the shutter is not completely open each time the light flashes, the sync delay circuit should be used. Turn the circuit on, and set the angle of shutter delay from 1° to 359°.

Cut-off speed

When set to automatic, the cut-off speed circuit does not let the flash rate go below 60 fps. This is to avoid annoying strobe speeds as the camera slows down at the end of each take (used when filming at frame rates above 60 fps). The switch can also be set to cut off at 10 fps or at 1 fps.

Polarity

With some Panavision cameras, the polarity of the sync pulse is inverted. The polarity switch flips the polarity so that the control console gets a usable signal. If the shutter won't sync up, try changing the polarity.

Split sync

The split sync configuration allows you to get two stops more light when operating at frame rates above 60 fps with any camera that has a rotating shutter. As noted earlier, each head normally flashes twice for each shutter rotation: once for an exposure (shutter open) and once for the camera operator (shutter closed). The split-sync configuration eliminates the second flash, which cuts the flash rate in half, provides extra power to the heads, and quadruples their light output.

To provide light for the viewfinder, the viewfinder flash is diverted to one or two separate heads. The viewfinder lights do not affect the exposure because they are off when the shutter is open. When the system is in meter mode, the viewfinder light is off so that it will not affect the exposure readings.

Special effects generator

The special effects generator makes strobe and chase effects possible. These are used quite often for music videos. Strobe effects have also been used on such features as Throw Momma from the Train and Jacob's Ladder to create the flashing light of a train passing in a tunnel.

The special effects generator has eight channels. Each channel can control an individual light or an entire console of three lights. Each channel can be set to skip between one and nine frames between flashes.

A sequencer circuit makes the channels chase, firing each head separately in sequence. Simply select the number of channels, from one to eight.

Caution

Be aware that the strobe lighting can trigger a seizure in people who have photosensitive epilepsy. Make sure that everyone on the set is aware that strobes will be used. People with this very rare reaction generally know to stay away from strobes and will avoid them. Strobe lighting can also synchronize with moving machinery and make it appear to be still, which can easily cause an accident.

High platforms for lighting

There are various hydraulic and motorized lifts and arms that are commonly used as platforms for lights and for rigging lights aloft. Telescoping boom platforms, scissor lifts and man lifts are invaluable tools, both on the sound stage and on location.

Telescoping boom platforms (Condors)

The standard moonlight rig consists of one or two 12 kW HMIs mounted to the basket of a telescoping boom platform, raised high above the scene. Condor, Snorkelift, JLG and Simon are the dominant makes, but 'Condor' is the common name for boom platforms. An electrician is designated to operate the platform and the lights mounted on it. In the USA the operator remains with the lights throughout their use. In Europe this is not allowed by safety code; the heads are therefore equipped with remote control units.

Operation

This type of platform is self-propelled at speeds of 0.7 to 3 miles per hour (mph). Some are designed with an electric motor for indoor use; larger platforms use petrol or diesel motors. The boom and turret can be controlled from either the basket or a side panel on the chassis. The drive train can only be controlled from the basket. Platforms come in various sizes and have maximum heights of 30, 40, 60, 80 and 120 ft.

The operation of different makes varies little. The Snorkelift TB-A80, which has an 80 ft boom is shown in Figure 11.9.

The controls are similar for most other types and sizes. The better rental companies include an operator's manual in a weatherproof canister on the equipment, so if you are not familiar with a particular model, you can consult the manual. Most operations are self-evident, however, once you understand the basics.

Safety precautions

Electronics provide ramping in all the controls, including boom operations, which helps smooth out the natural jerkiness of the machinery. You will run into older or less sophisticated models for which the controls act very abruptly. All models, especially these, require considerable care in operation, especially when lights are rigged in the basket.

When driving the platform any significant distance, it is good practice to drive with the boom fully retracted and parallel to the ground. This position gives the operator the best field of view over the top of the chassis. The most natural (and therefore the simplest and safest) configuration for driving is with the steering tyres towards the front and the boom slung off the back (see Figure 11.9D). When the boom is raised and extended, the platform automatically drives at a slower speed.

The use of a safety body harness attached to a short rope (not more than 4 ft free fall) and a large snap hook that hooks on to the basket rail is required by OSHA when operating a boom platform. Boom platforms are normally very stable, even when the arm is fully extended. However, physics being what it is, stability is severely compromised if the chassis is not level. Do not operate the machinery on more than a 5° gradient (6 in. rise in 10 ft). Some lifts have an automatic safety device that precludes operation on uneven ground. The transportation or grip department can help level the vehicle. When a slight gradient is unavoidable, it is best to orient the chassis pointing up and down the hill, and to rotate the boom with the weight on the uphill side or, if necessary, the downhill side, but not out to one side. Chock the wheels. The vehicles can creep if left on an incline.

A chassis can be driven when the boom is extended; however, this is not recommended when the chassis is not on perfectly level ground or when the weight is off-centre. At full extension, this can be a dicey business. It is best to avoid making the boom sway with jerky starts and stops, as this will throw the operator around in the basket and can even catapult him/her out of the basket entirely.

Do not use the boom arm as a crane. Don't sling objects below the basket. When working over pedestrian or automobile traffic, use cones, signs, or flags to mark the

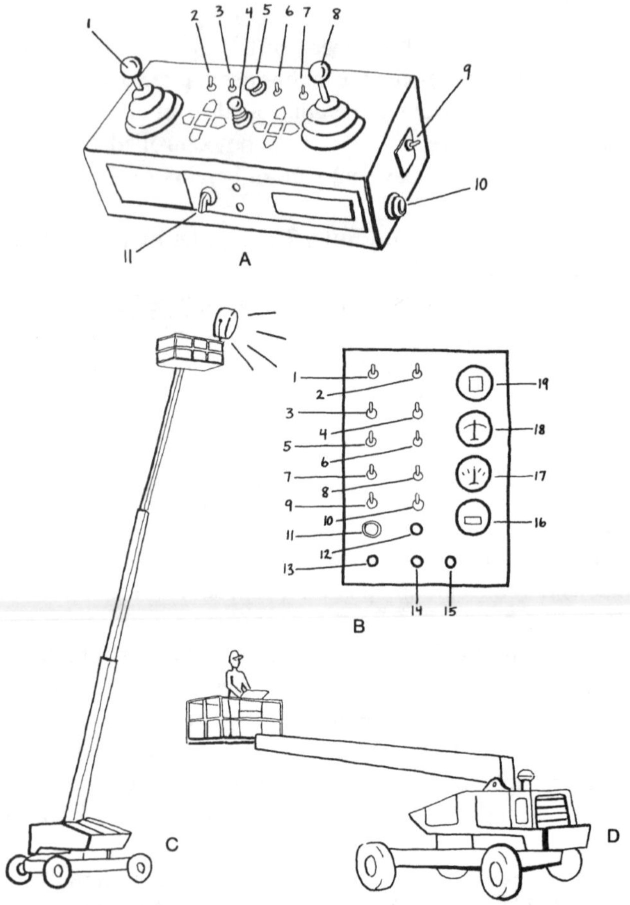

Figure 11.9 Snorkelift operation: (A) Platform basket control panel: (1) boom control lever (up/down, rotate left/right), (2) engine throttle (low/high), (3) drive range (low gear or high gear), (4) boom arm (retract/extend), (5) panic button for emergency stop, (6) platform level (tilts the basket), (7) emergency power on/off switch (battery power), (8) drive lever (forward/reverse, steering left/right), (9) platform rotate, (10) horn, (11) ignition switch and circuit breaker; (B) Ground control panel on side of chassis: (1) platform/ground control selector switch, (2) boom/axles selector switch, (3) engine throttle (high/low), (4) emergency power on/off switch, (5) boom arm (extend/retract), (6) boom control lever (up/down), (7) boom control lever (rotate left/right), (8) platform level, (9) platform rotate, (10) ground controls (on/off), works like dead-man pedal: must be held on to operate boom functions, (11) start button, (12) choke, (13) system circuit breaker, (14) throttle circuit breaker, (15) choke run circuit breaker, (16) Hobbs meter, (17) Amp meter, (18) oil pressure, (19) engine temperature; (C) Boom arm extended; (D) Boom arm retracted in position to drive chassis. Note that the boom is raised so that the driver can see over the top of the chassis. The steering wheels are at the front. (Equipment courtesy of ADCO Equipment Rental, City of Industry, CA, and Snorkelift, St Joseph, MO.)

area and control traffic around the base of the boom. Do not use reverse or forward as a brake when moving in the opposite direction.

Never operate a boom within 10 ft of power lines. Ten feet is the absolute minimum clearance recommended, but most experienced operators double that figure.

Rigging lights to the basket

When two lights are to be rigged to the basket, weight becomes a concern. Most platforms have a 500 lb weight limit. The maximum weight limit is printed next to the panel door on the chassis. The make of the luminaires and weight of the cables, grip rigging, and the weight of the electrician must be considered. With two 12 kW luminaires in the basket and a small electrician, you will be operating right at the weight limit. Ballasts should not be put in the basket. See weight data in Table A.5 (Appendix A).

Condor mount

Various manufacturers make hardware for securely mounting large lights to the basket of a boom platform. The grips who rig the mount will need to be given an idea of which way the light will need to face in order to position the mount conveniently. To mount the lights, tilt the basket forward so that it is easy to reach from the ground. Lift the light on to the mount. Then, with someone holding the light, tilt the basket back to level.

Grip equipment, such as a 4-by gel frame, can be secured out in front of the light using ear extensions (Figure 11.10A) or a grip helper (Figure 11.10B).

A meat axe is commonly secured to the rail of the basket to provide a means of manipulating nets and flags out in front of the light. A flag is often needed.

Always tie a safety around the yoke to the basket. The safety should be ½ in. hemp, nylon rope or, best of all, 1-in. tubular webbing. A 10-ft length is sufficient to run a loop through the knee rail and over the yoke with plenty of slack for manoeuvring the light. Loop the safety around the knee rail so that if the light falls, it will swing under the basket and not smash into it.

Once the lights are rigged on the basket, the operator must use a light touch on the controls and operate the chassis and boom as smoothly as possible. Jerking the lights around with abrupt movements puts a great deal of stress on the mount.

Rigging without a platform mount

A luminaire can be mounted by securing a steel junior stand to the inside corner of the basket with chain vice grips. This is not a recommended method, however, because the stress can bend or break the stand. If you are going to mount lights in this manner, use only steel hardware (aluminium stands should never be used for 12 kWs) and do not drive with lights rigged. If the chassis must be moved, remove the heads first.

Cabling

The cable from the luminaire must be long enough to reach the ballast unit on the ground when the boom is at its full height. A cable extension is usually required to

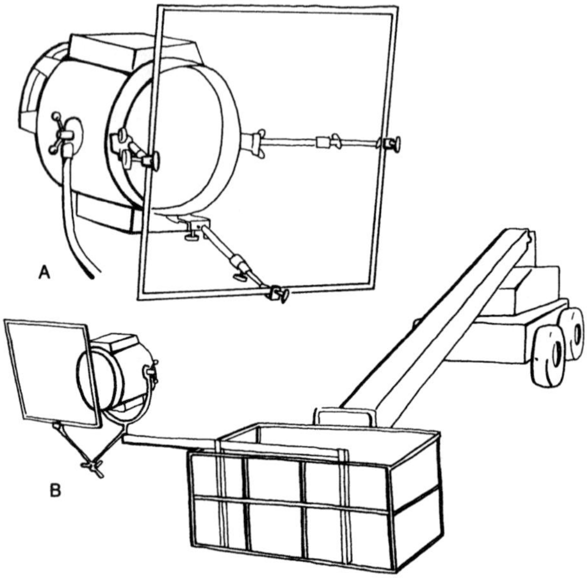

Figure 11.10 Mounting 4-by frames. (A) Ear extensions made by American Studio Equipment. (Equipment courtesy of American Studio Equipment, Sun Valley, CA, and Concept Lighting, Sun Valley, CA.) (B) Grip helper and Condor bracket manufactured by Matthews Studio Equipment, Inc., Burbank, CA

make the run. As always, the head cable should have a strain relief at the lamphead. A second strain relief should be attached to the basket. Leave plenty of slack head cable in the basket so that the luminaire can be manoeuvred.

When there is more than one cable, run all cables together in a single bundle. It is best to position the cables so they leave from the centre of the basket next to the control console, where the boom joins the basket. This minimizes strain on the platform hydraulics (four 12 kW feeder cables may weigh 120 lb or more).

It is easiest if the cable can hang straight down to the ground from the basket. In some situations, this is not possible: It may block traffic, get into the shot, or cause other problems. When the cable cannot be hung straight down, it must be tied to the boom arm. The best way to do this is to extend the arm out fully at ground level and tie the cable to the arm at the top of each boom section. Some boom arms have eyelet rings on the arm. Thread motorcycle straps or ¼ in. hemp through the eyelets and loop them around the cable.

Never place the ballast behind or in front of the chassis. If you need to move the chassis, this causes delay. In the worst case, you could run it over.

Be aware that you can sometimes receive a shock by touching two heads at the same time. This is also true when touching two ballasts or when touching two platforms. This is not normal, but it has been known to happen. You can check for current between units with a voltmeter.

Man lifts and scissor lifts

A man lift is a small portable lift, usually having a capacity of around 300 lb and a maximum platform height of 20 to 36 ft (Figure 11.11A).

It is commonly used on sound stages as a platform from which to work on hanging lights and cables. A man lift has wheels and casters to roll the unit from place to place. Outriggers stabilize the unit for extension. An electric motor powers a cable system that raises and lowers the platform.

A scissor lift is a battery-powered, electrically self-propelled hydraulic lift (Figure 11.11B). A typical scissor lift has a 700- to 1,500-lb capacity and a maximum height of 20 to 40 ft (depending on the model). Scissor lifts can be used as lighting and camera platforms. Again, only use this equipment on level ground, and always extend the outriggers before elevating the platform.

When fully charged, the batteries should last for many hours of intermittent operation; however, scissor lifts should always be plugged in and charged overnight. If the lift will not operate, check the DC voltage across the batteries (usually 24 V powered from four 6 V batteries arranged in series). If the batteries are drained, the lift will need to be charged for several hours before it can be operated, and it should remain on charge until fully charged.

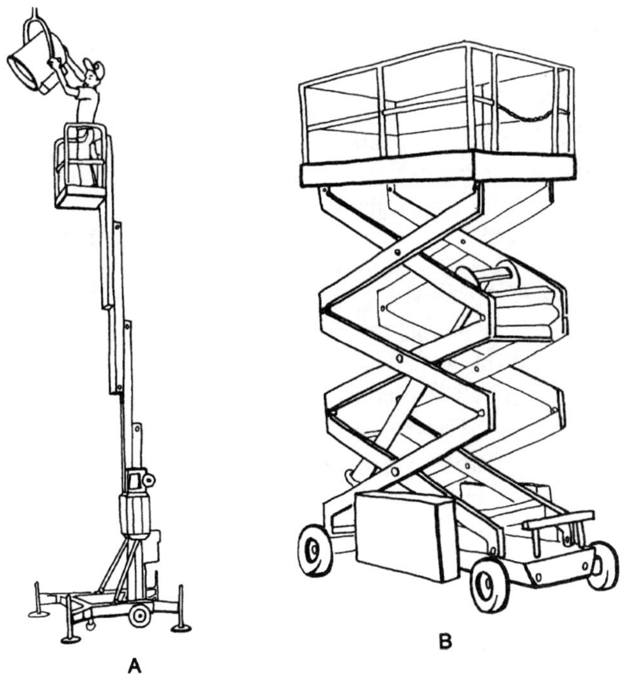

Figure 11.11 (A) Man lift. (B) Scissor lift

Musco lights

The Musco Light Company began as a mobile sports lighting service but has found a place in the motion picture industry for lighting very large expanses. A Musco consists of a truck-mounted boom arm with a bank of 6 to 15 high-efficiency 6 kW open-face discharge luminaires. Because of its high-efficiency reflector, each 6 kW unit puts out as much light as a standard 12 kW HMI Fresnel. The smallest Musco truck has a maximum boom height of 80 ft, and the largest goes to 100 ft (120 ft with a jib arm). The trucks are completely self-contained and self-sufficient, with their own sound-baffled generators and operators (Figure 11.12).

The lights can be controlled by the gaffer or DP with a hand-held remote-control unit or by the Musco operator with levers at the base of the boom. Each light can be panned 360°, tilted 220°, flooded and spotted remotely. The entire boom arm rotates 180° on its base.

The luminaires have a daylight colour temperature of 5,600 K. Some are available with flicker-free electronic ballasts. A 15-head array can flood a 300 sq. ft area up to half a mile away from the truck at a level of 20 FC. At maximum spot, a 50 sq. ft area that is 100 ft from the light can be illuminated to 13,000 FC.

When gel or diffusion is needed, it is placed on a large frame that surrounds the entire bank of lights on three sides. The frames can be gelled ahead of time by Musco's field operators, or they can be gelled by set grips on the day before use. It takes exactly three rolls of 48-in. gel to cover the whole frame of the fifteen-light array.

Other moonlight rigs

When more height is required than a boom platform can provide, a crane truck can be used. The larger crane trucks have boom heights of 225 ft with caged platforms. These types of cranes usually come with their own driver.

Some gaffers prefer to use a large, soft source for night moonlight ambience. This has prompted the design of rigs such as a suspended 12 × 12 ft soft box lit with an array of 2,500 PARs or 12 kWs.

Fisher Productions, Inc. (who make specialized suspended soft banks for car photography) makes a special rig, named appropriately, the 'Moonlight'. It is a 8 × 17 ft soft bank lit with ten 2,500 W DCI lamps (an 18 kW tungsten version is also available). Because a large source can only create soft shadows if it is relatively close to the subject, rigs of this type are best positioned fairly close overhead. Distant backgrounds can be more easily lit with standard hard sources.

Helium balloons

Another ingenious contribution to our lighting arsenal is the helium balloon. By placing HMI or tungsten lamps inside a sealed diffusion ball and filling it with helium, you can create soft 360° light without the need for a high platform. The balloon is attached to a tether and winch to set the height of the balloon. Balloons are

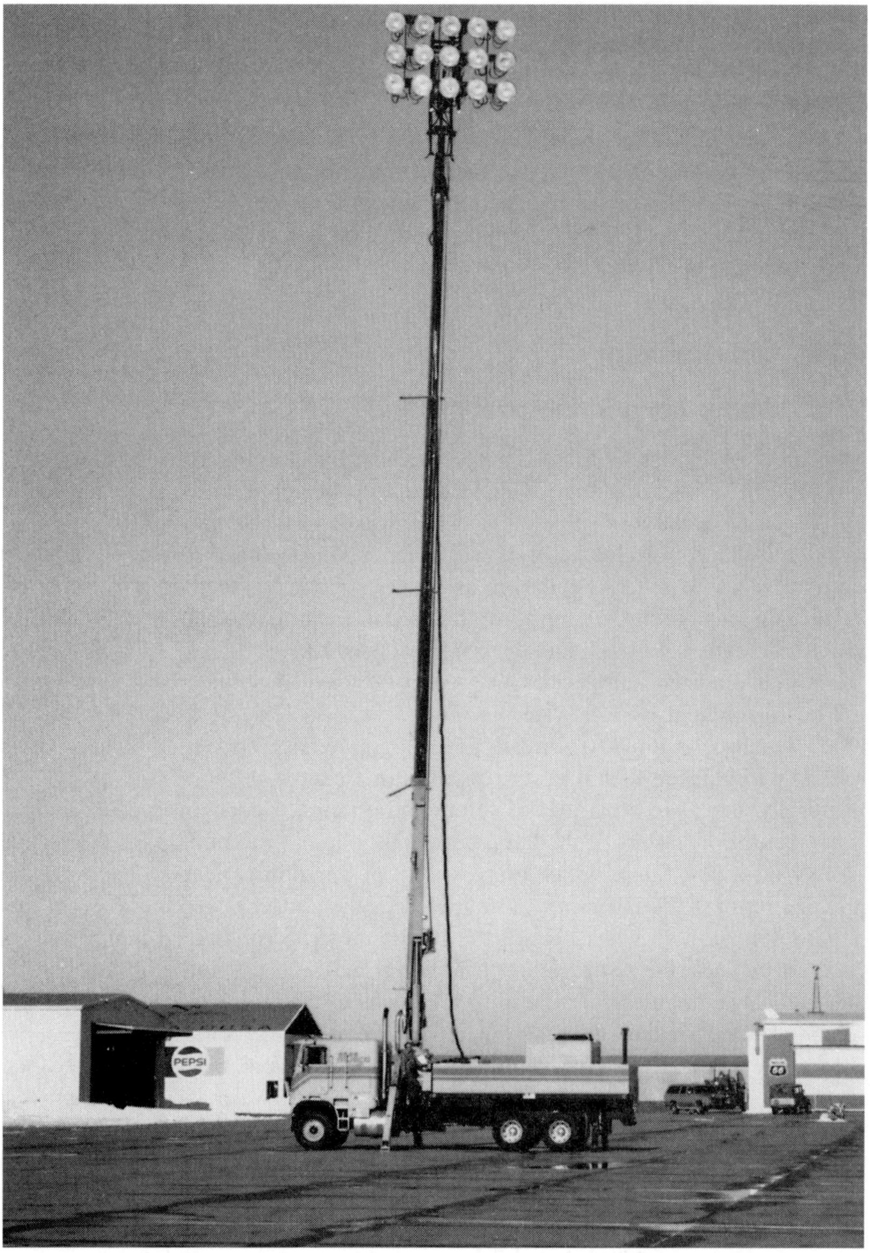

Figure 11.12 A Musco truck. (Photo courtesy of Musco Mobile Lighting, Ltd, Oskaloosa, IA.)

particularly useful in delicate interior locations, such as an old cathedral, where rigging lights could do damage to the location.

Balloons are available in sizes from a 5.25 ft diameter, 2,000 W tungsten unit with an operating height of 10 to 30 ft (Lunix 160 by Airstar) up to an 18.4 ft diameter, 12,000 W unit with a maximum height of 164 ft (Solarc 500, Airstar). Helium is an inert gas and is not combustible; in fact, it is a cool gas, which helps ventilate the enclosed lamps. When stabilized with guy lines the largest balloon is safe in winds up to about 22 mph. For manufacturers and distributors, see Appendix G, under Airstar, Leelium or LTM.

Underwater lighting

The old drop-a-lamp-in-the-pool method

In the days of Esther Williams, it was standard procedure to light water ballet sequences by submerging bare 10 kW incandescent lamps in the pool. Power was DC. The feeder cable was soldered to the terminals of the lamp, and the connection was potted with a big glob of epoxy or latex rubber to make it watertight. (In the early days, they used tar.) As daring as it may sound, this technique and a similar scheme using a small PAR lamp were the predominant methods of underwater lighting until the early seventies, and they are still used today.

Note that tungsten halogen lamps cannot be used underwater in this way; they must be surrounded by air. Water cooling would prevent the lamp from reaching 250°C, which is required to activate the halogen cycle. Without the halogen cycle, the lamp will blacken with tungsten deposits in a matter of hours.

Naturally, there are a number of safety and efficiency concerns with this type of arrangement. For starters, if the lamp burns out, you have to pull up the whole cable to solder on a new lamp, which creates a lot of downtime. Second, having a large amperage running though every cable increases the danger posed in the event that a hot wire contacts the water. Third, the lamps must be submerged before they are turned on because the temperature differential between the hot lamp and the cool water can cause the glass of a lamp or PAR lens to crack or explode. Finally, if the lamp breaks under water, the result is a live wire in contact with water.

In the late 1960s, Birns Oceanographic lights, which were underwater lights manufactured for the oil industry, began to be used in underwater cinematography. The Snooper, Snooperette and 2 kW Columbia consisted of standard double-ended tungsten lamps mounted in front of a reflector in a casing with a heavy cover glass. They can be used to depths of 3,000 ft. The lights have to be submerged before they are turned on to prevent the cold water from shock-cooling the glass and cracking it. The lights were an improvement over what was available before, but they are heavy and very inefficient.

Modern underwater luminaires

For an underwater lighting system to be safe, it must be a completely sealed system, watertight from cable to lamp; provide a sensing device and shutdown mechanism in case an electrical fault occurs; and overcome the problem of thermal stress on the glass that is in contact with water.

James Cameron's epic adventure film, The Abyss, revolutionized underwater lighting technology. Forty per cent of the live action footage was filmed underwater in a huge tank, 209 ft in diameter and 55 ft deep. The project offered two young inventors the opportunity to realize a project they had had in mind for some time. Pete Romano, an underwater cameraman, and Richard Mula, a gaffer and engineer, developed the 1,200 W HMI SeaPar, an efficient underwater PAR light, to meet the needs of this extremely demanding project. The SeaPar and other underwater luminaires are now supplied by HydroFlex. Additionally, they offer the 1,200 W HMI HydroPar (an update of the SeaPar), the 1,000 W Incandescent HydroPar, and a small, handy incandescent 650 W SeaPar (Figure 11.13A and 11.13B). SeaPars work equally well out of water, in the rain or submerged to depths of more than 250 ft. Birns and other manufacturers now also offer similar systems.

The lights find use not only in underwater scenes but in any scene in which water is present. For example, a scene in Batman II has the actors wading knee-deep in floods. If a SeaPar head accidentally falls into the water, there is no danger and no harm done; and power cords can be run underwater.

Safety features

The system is watertight. Ballasts and main distribution cables remain above the surface. The head cables run down into the water. SeaPars use watertight plugs that can be plugged and unplugged underwater with the power off. The connectors have locking sleeves to prevent kick-outs. A hot female lead can be left unplugged in water because the female plug naturally holds air within the deep contact pockets so that electricity does not come into contact with water. All cables and connectors are watertight. Regular type W and entertainment cable are approved for use in water. The connection point on the head is made so that, even if the head cable gets cut, water cannot enter the head.

To provide a fault-sensitive shutdown mechanism, the system operates on AC current with a grounding lead. All metal parts are grounded. The HMI ballasts are fitted with two ground fault interrupter (GFI) circuits that sense the presence of leakage current. If there is more than a 5 mA differential between the hot leg (outgoing current) and the neutral leg (incoming current), indicating that fault current is leaking through to ground, a relay cuts power to the ballast in less than $\frac{1}{60}$ second. This is less current than is required to harm an individual, even if the person is in contact with the fault source.

The second GFI serves as a redundant backup. In addition, a fourth lead is used: A ground-return lead connected to a relay circuit constantly monitors the integrity of the grounding lead and will shut down the power if ground is removed or lost. Finally, the outside glass covers on SeaPar luminaires are made of special thermoshock-resistant glass that can withstand sudden extreme temperature changes.

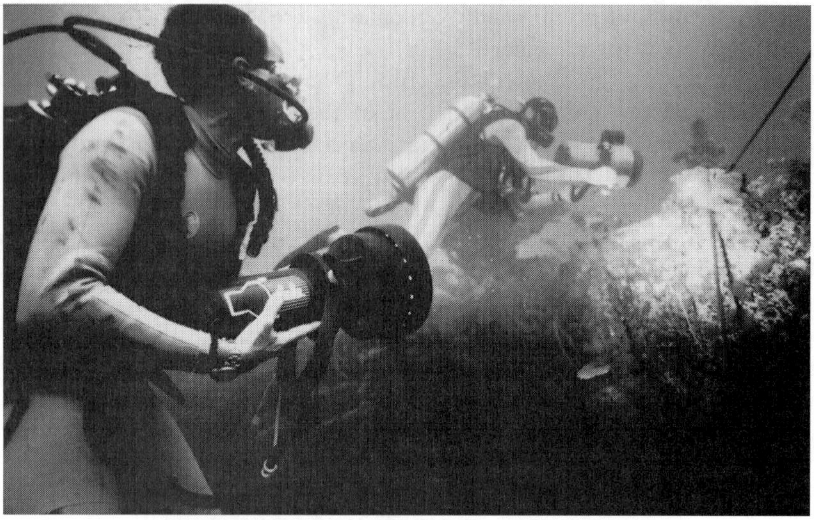

A

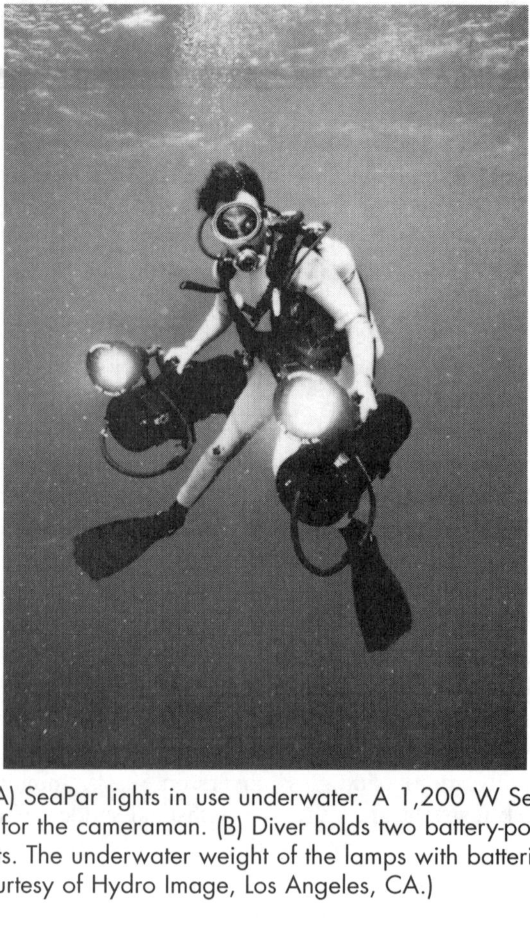

B

Figure 11.13 (A) SeaPar lights in use underwater. A 1,200 W SeaPar HMI lights a rusted wreckage for the cameraman. (B) Diver holds two battery-powered incandescent PAR 46 lights. The underwater weight of the lamps with batteries is about 2 lb each. (Photos courtesy of Hydro Image, Los Angeles, CA.)

Operational features

Spreader lenses are held inside the watertight cover glass. On some lights, the spreader lens is factory mounted to the PAR lamp. On the newer ones, the spreader lenses can be exchanged (out of water) by simply unbuckling the cover on the front of the luminaire. Spreader lenses have very little effect underwater if they are on the outside of the luminaire.

A retaining ring buckles to the front of the luminaire. The retaining ring holds scrims, gels, and diffusion, and simultaneously prevents any light leakage to the sides. The retaining ring allows water to circulate around the gel for heat dissipation. Barn doors and snoots can be mounted to the front of the retaining ring.

There are two lock knobs on the yoke on either side of the light. One is the tilt lock. The other, the rotation lock, is used to orient the elliptical beam. The luminaires can be used in any orientation.

Lighting underwater

During the filming of The Abyss, director of photography Mikael Salomon used the lights in all the ways you normally do in a dry sound stage. He bounced light off griffolyn, used griffolyn flags to control the light (duvetyne turns brown in water), used colour and diffusion on the lights, and so on.

Water acts as a colour filter. Within 10 ft of the surface, 70 to 80 per cent of the red end of the spectrum is absorbed, leaving only blue light. The brilliant colours of sea life appear dull in the blue light that filters down from the surface. Only when you shine a light on them do the magnificent colours come to life. Fill light is therefore used to help bring back good colour to subjects at depths greater than about 16 ft, even when existing exposure is sufficient. Fill light may also be called for when shooting a subject from below. Light can be bounced off the bottom of a white pool, off a white board or shone directly at the subject. At depths greater than 130 ft, supplemental light is necessary to get an adequate exposure and, of course, underwater lights come into play whenever you are shooting at night.

Water is usually somewhat cloudy and acts as a diffusion, much like fog. It reduces light transmission and softens the light as it bounces off the particles in the water. However, the beam angle of the light in clear water is the same as in air. It is important to keep the cloudiness consistent. In a pool, a filtering system must be used, and the floor of the pool must be vacuumed to start with a clean pool. Once all the divers are in the water, you can add substances to make it murkier if necessary. When filming The Abyss, fuller's earth, diatomite (a swimming pool filter agent), small amounts of milk and blue detergent were added to the water to make it very blue and hazy. To avoid stirring up particles resting on the bottom, underwater crews often do not use fins. Instead, they wear weights and walk around on the bottom of the pool.

Exposure readings are taken using an underwater reflected light meter. The Sekonic Marine II, for example, has a 10° angle of acceptance. You aim the meter in the direction you wish to shoot and set the aperture accordingly. The water is brighter above the diver and falls off into darkness below the diver, so meter readings should be taken in the appropriate direction. Underwater cinematographers generally have underwater housings for other light meters as well.

An underwater scene lit only from underwater looks dead and flat. Except for the bubbles, you can't even tell that you are underwater. To bring the water to life, you need light coming through the surface, creating dancing striations of light. For a night scene, you might use a heavy backlight from above the surface and a small amount of soft underwater bounce (a 1,200 W HMI into a 4-by-4 white griffolyn, for example).

Underwater lights are often used to light up swimming pools or fountains, even when the camera will not be submerged. A light placed at the bottom makes the entire pool glow and throws moving highlights on surrounding people, buildings, trees and so on.

Electricity and water

The danger of water is that it is a conductor. Salt water (which is essentially what the body is made of) is a better conductor than fresh water. Neither is a very good conductor, but enough of one to pose a threat to life under certain circumstances.

Remember that to get a shock, a diver must become part of a closed circuit. Water is ground, and in water a diver becomes part of the ground. The greatest danger is to reach out of the water and touch a hot wire or a metal housing with a fault in it, directing electricity exclusively straight through the body: in through the arm, through the lungs and heart, and out through the lower half of the body. This scenario could very easily kill a person. That is why it is so critical that the casing of a light and all accessible metal parts be at ground potential and, if there is a ground fault, that the circuit is automatically interrupted by the ground fault interrupter (GFI) before an accident can occur.

As a matter of safety, all electrical equipment, including submersibles, submarines, pumps, cables and lights, should be routinely checked for leakage current before being put in the water.

A bare wire underwater sets up an electrical field around it as current flows out of the fault point, and returns to the power system via all parallel paths. Generally this would mean flowing from a single point to all grounded objects, mainly via the path of least resistance. If the neutral or grounding wire is close by, as in the case of a sheared cable, the field will be very strong between the two wires and will spread around the fault, weakening with distance. The size of the field is determined by the magnitude of the fault current. If a power cord gets cut in a boat propeller, for example, a fault current of 10 A in fresh water will set up a field with a diameter of about 5.6 ft (minimum safe distance). A fault current of 100 A, on the other hand, sets up a field 49 ft in diameter.

The magnitude of the fault current is dependent on only two factors; it is proportional to system voltage and inversely proportional to the impedance imposed by the size and length of cable. A smaller cable imposes more resistance and will therefore limit the fault current to a greater extent than a larger cable. This fact has been used to argue that using a number of small cables (a 'maxi brute' made of ten individual

1 kW PARs, for example) is safer than using one large cable (to power a 10 kW, for example [This is an academic argument because there is no such thing as a waterproof AC 10 kW unit at this time. I mention this phenomenon here in order to present the reader with as comprehensive an understanding of all factors possible.]). It turns out, however, that due to a complicated phenomenon – involving the increased capacitance due to increased total cable length – the impedance in the ten 1 kW cables is no greater than that of the 10 kW, and therefore no safer in a fault situation.

In the past, gaffers preferred using many small amperage cables to a few high amperage ones because GFIs on 20 A circuits are very dependable. The higher the amperage, the greater the noise in the system and the less dependable the GFIs become. In the 1990s, however, more sophisticated GFIs have become available. The Shock-Block (manufactured by K-Tec Corporation) is a 100 A GFI housed in a waterproof enclosure that can operate on very noisy power supplies with variable voltages such as those of dimmer systems. The Shock-Block allows GFI protected loads of up to 12 kW on 20–120 V model and 25 kW on the 208–250 V model. The Shock-Block GFI also features a 5-LED display which indicates the amount of ground leakage at any moment. Lighting technicians can use this feature to easily identify and isolate faulty circuits where multiple loads are connected to the 100 A circuit.

A diver can feel when he is coming close to an electrical field. If you have ever put your tongue on a 9 V battery, you know the taste that comes into your mouth, and you can feel a tingle in the fillings in your teeth. Closer to the field, you begin to feel the tingle of electricity in your body. A diver who is inside a strong field may experience the effects of electrical shock: trouble breathing, muscle freeze, cardiac fibrillation and cardiac arrest.

In an earlier chapter, the effects of AC and DC on the body were discussed. DC current poses a less lethal threat because it requires more amperage to cause muscle freeze and to interfere with other important muscles, such as the heart and lungs. Although HMIs are always AC (even AC/DC ballasts run AC to the head), their increased light output means that they replace an incandescent light of much higher amperage, so they pose no greater threat than the alternative. However, because AC circuits are grounded, the safety features previously discussed diminish any potential threat to a safe level.

Shooting in the rain

The primary concerns when shooting in the rain, real or artificial, are that all the electrical circuits are safe and that the lights are covered and stay dry.

Cabling and distribution

The preceding section discussed the electrical safety hazards posed by water. Similar hazards exist any time the ground is thoroughly wet. In fact, water is a better conductor when it is mixed with the minerals of soil. A muddy field is more conductive than a freshwater pool. Guard against bare contacts coming into contact with water and ground by elevating all connection points on apple boxes. Use watertight connectors or wrap electrical connections in visqueen or heavy-duty plastic garbage bags to prevent water falling on to connection points. When cable is to be run in wet areas, it should be inspected prior to use. Look for deep nicks in the outer sheath.

Rain poses an additional hazard: Everything and everyone tends to get wet, and wet hands and feet will pose little resistance should you come into contact with a fault. Luminaires must be grounded. It is a wise precaution to test luminaires for ground fault leaks prior to use in a wet environment.

Rain tents

Lights must be protected from falling and blowing moisture. If water falls or blows on to the hot lens, the thermal shock can crack or shatter the lens, especially when the lamp is in flood position and the lens is hottest. If water leaks into the housing and touches the lamp, the lamp will burn out or explode. With HMIs water causes serious problems with the electronics. Water can also cause corrosion to the metal parts of the luminaires.

Protect the lens with a gel frame of heat-shield gel or a thin colour (1/8 CTO or 1/8 CTB). Place rain hats over the lights. Celo screen, a tough, plastic-covered wire screen, works well to cover luminaires. Bend it over the light and grip clip it to the yoke on either side. Alternately, a flag covered with a garbage bag works for small lights. Larger lights require a 4-by flag wrapped in visqueen or a griffolyn. (Check for holes in the griff first.) A 12-by or 20-by griff is handy to cover a number of units at once. Rain hats should be positioned so that rain runs off away from the luminaire; don't let rain collect and form a pool in the flag.

Lighting rain

Falling water is most visible to the camera when lit from the back. Rain shots are typically done by placing rain between the lens and the actors, and the general area before the camera, and supplementing it with rain falling in puddles, on the tops of cars, and in places where it would be noticeably lacking were it not there. A gentle trickle of rain might also be used over the actors to keep them dripping. Back light makes the rain visible to camera.

Whenever the ground is wet, the camera will pick up reflections and highlights of sources within the frame. The DPs often deliberately place self-luminous dressing in the frame to pick up these highlights.

Lightning effects

Creating a convincing lightning effect can be difficult. It requires a very bright, very brief flash, several stops brighter than the exposure used for the set lighting. To be convincing, it should flicker slightly and vary from flash to flash. For a small area, shutters are sometimes used in front of a fairly large luminaire; however, this is a marginally effective technique when used in a large area.

For many years, the brightest and most convincing lightning effect was accomplished with a scissor arc. A scissor arc consists of a bundle of carbon rods wrapped in wire and attached to a scissor device that brings the carbons into contact with the opposite electrode. When the two are brought together, all hell breaks loose, and an extremely bright sputtering flash lights up everything within a street. The scissor arc is positioned a distance from the action and is placed up high on a scaffold. Should you ever be on a set where a scissor arc is used, stand clear of the contraption, and watch out for fragments of hot carbon falling from the luminaire. A hot piece of carbon can melt right through asphalt.

Lightning strikes

More recently, Optec Inc. has developed Lightning Strikes, a programmable lightning machine that can drench the set in light for up to three seconds. The light comes in two sizes, 70,000 W and 250,000 W, and several heads can be connected to a central control unit and fired simultaneously or separately. The colour temperature is 5,600 K, and the unit is dimmable to about 20 per cent output with no change in colour temperature. The units can be very precisely controlled and flash sequences can be programmed, so identical flashes can be repeated in take after take. The 70 kW head's peak output yields 350 FC at 100 ft with a 45° beam spread. The units can be ordered with fully sealed waterproof housings for use with rain towers.

There are a variety of different control units. The Undulating Controller comes as standard with each light and is used for manual or automatic random lightning flashes. The Precision Fader is a programmable controller with which one can create, repeat and loop up and down fades. It is great for creating an explosion effect, for example, with a big initial flash and slow decay, spiked with lesser secondary explosions. Each sequence can be up to four seconds, and the unit can hold up to four sequences. The unit comes with four preprogrammed sequences, but you can create custom sequences using a simple joystick to edit the sequence. Each sequence can change level up to twenty-four times a second. Machine-gun fire flashes can also be created with an on, off, on, off pattern.

The Quad Controller controls up to four lights separately or in unison with eight memory banks that record firing sequences for playback. The control unit can also be hooked up to a MIDI music system plus video or audio playback unit to cue the flashes using time-code as a timing base.

The lights can also be run using a DMX controller. Brightness level and 'mode' are controlled on two adjacent channels: constant, slow undulation, medium undulation or fast undulation are controlled by the 'mode' pot. Multiple lights can be synchronized or operated separately.

Each head operates on 208 and 250 V service (single-phase or two legs of a three-phase service; 220 V or more is preferred).

Luminaire	70,000 W	250,000 W
Weight	35 lb	55 lb
Dimensions	33 × 14 × 10 in.	42 × 17 × 11 in.
Mount	1-⅛ in. Jr. Pin	1-⅛ in. Jr. Pin
Voltage	208–250 V AC 50/60 Hz	208–250 V AC 50/60 Hz
Current	300 A momentary	1,000 A momentary
Power requirements		
Mains or house	63 A minimum	200 A minimum
	100 A optimum	300 A optimum
Generator	45 kW or 52 kVA	145 kW or 185 kVA

Generator companies recommend that when two 70,000 W heads are used, the plant should have at least a 90 kVA capacity; when three 70,000 W heads are used, the plant should have at least a 140 kVA capacity. The 70 kW unit draws about 300 A when fired. Because the time is so short, it can safely be run on 100 A house current. (It is treated like an electric motor starting load.) Although this is a fairly substantial intermittent load, the peak power is within 5 per cent of nominal RMS power, meaning that there is no momentary drain much greater than the nominal power, as there is when striking HMI units, for example. A sudden heavy load like this will affect all the lights on a generator. They may blink each time the strike hits. To guard against surge current affecting the set lighting, most gaffers order an additional generator to handle the Lightning Strikes units. If you have to run both on the same generator, use the smaller 70 kW unit, keep the bursts short, and do not have more than half the amperage capacity of the generator devoted to lightning units.

Shooting on moving vehicles

The standard method of shooting a scene in a moving car is to tow the car and mount the camera to the side door or the bonnet of the car. The tow vehicle is equipped with a sound-baffled generator and various rails and platforms to which lights can be mounted. Specialized vehicles support the camera on a crane arm, which makes placing the camera a relatively easy task and provides an opportunity to approach a driving scene with some dynamic camera moves (Figure 11.14A).

Another approach is to put the car on a low-riding flatbed trailer, a *process trailer*, and to tow the trailer (Figure 11.14B). The trailer rides low to the ground so that the height of the car above the pavement looks normal to the camera. Taking the air out of the car's tyres once it is on the trailer also helps. The largest trailer for this purpose is two lanes wide, allowing room for the camera, lights, and crew.

It usually works out well to tie HMI ballasts to the rigging on the roof of the cab. Run cables along the speed-rail, keeping them neatly tied and out of the way. Be sure nothing is going to slip loose, rattle, drag or get under the tyres when the car gets on the road.

There are many techniques for lighting the interior of a car. The basic problem with daytime car interiors is the contrast between interior and exterior. The light level

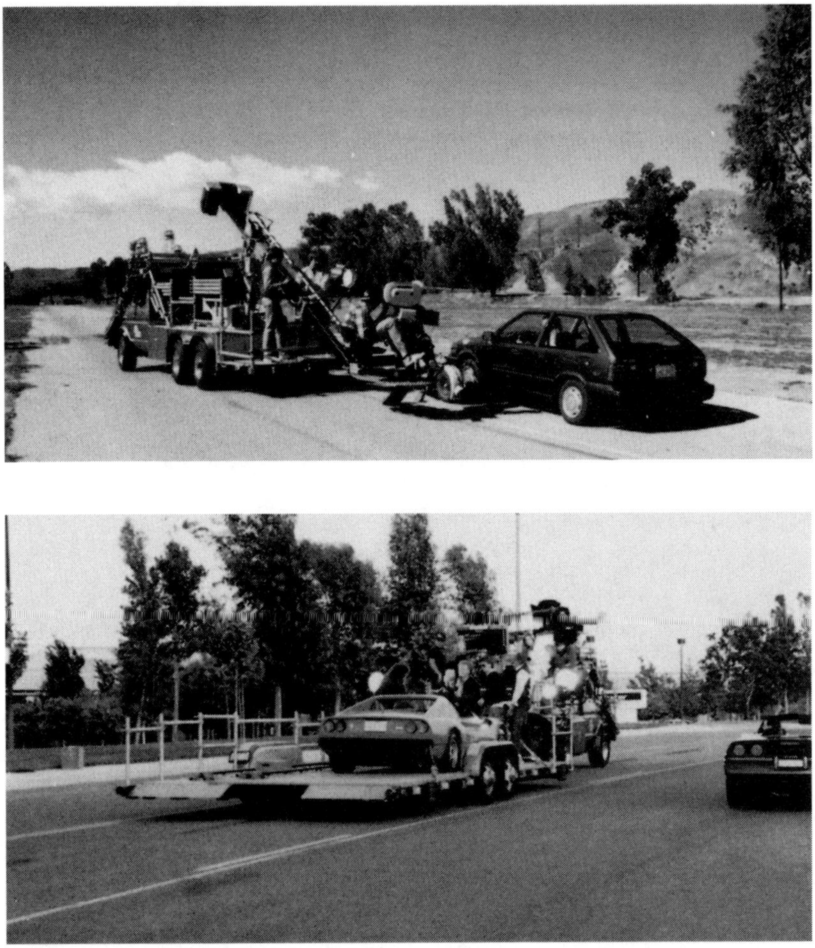

A

B

Figure 11.14 Rigging lights to moving vehicles: (A) Shotmaker truck towing a car. (B) A car on a process trailer. (Photos courtesy of Shotmaker Co., Valencia, CA.)

on the faces has to be brought up so that the exterior scenery is not overexposed. When lighting a car on a sunny day, one approach is to use large HMI sources on the tow vehicle to simulate sunshine on the actors' faces. On an overcast day, the supplemental lights may be shone through diffusion material attached on the windscreen (assuming that the camera does not see the windscreen).

Shooting at night poses a different set of problems. For a city street scene, an open aperture is needed to make naturally lit shopfronts visible. You would therefore shoot at relatively low light levels with small luminaires taped to the dashboard, for example. Some DPs like to have several small lights mounted at various angles to achieve the appearance of passing traffic and streetlights by bringing the lights up and down on dimmers or panning them across the actors.

With fast film, the lighting need not consume a lot of power. A night scene could be very minimally lit using a couple of 12 V luminaires (Kino Flos, stick-ups, Dedolights or other 12 V luminaires) running off the car battery or a deep-cycle marine battery. I once liberated a headlight from the grip truck; bounced, diffused and wrapped in blackwrap, it looked fantastic.

Appendix A

Luminaire specification tables

The tables in this section offer lots of potentially helpful information about all types of luminaires. Beam angle and candle-power data allow you to calculate the beam diameter of any light at any distance. This is particularly helpful when choosing ellipsoidal spotlights. Knowing candle-power allows you to calculate intensity in foot-candles at any distance you choose. Here's how it works.

Calculating field diameter

Table A.12 lists specifications for various commonly used ellipsoidal spotlights. Included in this table (and in any manufacturer's catalogue) is the multiplier used to calculate field diameter at a given throw. For example, the Source Four 36° fixture has a multiplier of 0.65. If the throw is 20 ft, we can calculate the field diameter as follows:

$$\text{Distance} \times \text{multiplier} = \text{field diameter}$$

$$20\ \text{ft} \times 0.65 = 13\ \text{ft}$$

For most other luminaires you can use the beam angle to look up the beam diameter at any distance using Table A.13.

Calculating intensity

We can use Table A.14 to ascertain the light level of most luminaires at any distance. We can also calculate the intensity of a light at any distance using the inverse square law. To find the amount of light, divide the source candle-power given in candela (cd) by the distance squared:

$$\frac{\text{Source cd}}{D^2\ (\text{feet})} = \text{FC} \quad \text{or} \quad \frac{\text{Source cd}}{D^2\ (\text{metres})} = \text{lux}$$

European measurements are based upon the standard unit of length which is the metre. As there are 3.28 ft per metre, there are 3.28 × 3.28 (10.76) sq. ft to the sq. metre. Thus if we multiply the light level reading in foot-candles by 10.76 we obtain the reading in lux. For example, a Source Four 36° fixture has a source intensity of 84,929 cd. The intensity at 20 ft (6.1 metres) is therefore:

$$\frac{84{,}929}{20^2} = 212\ \text{FC or}\ 212 \times 10.76 = 2{,}281\ \text{lux}$$

You can use this equation to calculate the source intensity (cd) of a given fixture by measuring the FC level at a given distance, or to calculate the distance necessary to achieve a particular FC level from a given fixture.

$$\text{cd} = \text{FC} \times D^2$$

$$D = \sqrt{\frac{\text{fixture intensity (cd)}}{\text{light level (FC)}}}$$

Table A.1 Tungsten Fresnels

	Watts	*Lamp ANSI code*	*Lens*	*Scrim (in.)*	*Chimera ring size (in.)*
Altman					
300L	300	FKW	3″	5″	5″
650L	650	FRK	4.5″	6 5/8″	6 1/2″
1000L	1 kW	EGT	5″	7 3/4″	7 5/8″
Studio 1 kW	1 kW	EGT	7″	9″	9 5/8″
2000L	2 kW	CYX	7″	9″	9 5/8″
Studio 2 kW	2 kW	CYX	10″	13″	13 1/2″
5000L	5 kW	DPY	10″	13″	13 1/2″
Studio 5 kW	5 kW	DPY	12″	15 1/2″	16 1/8″
Arri					
300W	300	FKW	3.2″	5″	5″
650W	650	FRK	4.3″	6 5/8″	6 1/2″
1000W	1 kW	EGT	5.1″	7 3/4″	7 5/8″
Studio 1 kW	1 kW	EGT	6.9″	9″	9 5/8″
2000W	2 kW	CYX	6.9″	9″	9 5/8″
Studio 2 kW	2 kW	CYX	10″	13″	13 1/2″
5000W	5 kW	DPY	10″	13″	13 1/2″
Studio 5 kW	5 kW	DPY	11.8″	15 1/2″	16 1/8″
Studio 10 kW	10 kW/12 kW	DTY[a]	16.7″	19 1/2″	20″
Cinemills					
20 kW	20 kW	20 kW	24″	29″	29″
DedoTech[b]					
DLH	100	FCR		3″	3″
	50	BRL			
	20	–			
DLHM	100	FCR		3″	3″
DLH-150	150	FCS		3″	3″
COOLH	250	ELC		3″	3″
DeSisti					
Leonardo 1 kW	1 kW	EGT	6″	7.25″	7 3/8″
Piccolo 2 kW	2 kW	CYX	6″	7.25″	7 3/8″
Leonardo 2 kW	2 kW	CYX	10″	12″	12 3/8″
Piccolo 5 kW	5 kW	DPY	10″	12″	12 3/8″
Leonardo 5 kW	5 kW	DPY	12″	15.5″	15 3/4″
Leonardo 5 kW	5 kW	DPY	14″	15.5″	15 3/4″
Piccolo 10 kW	10 kW	DTY	14″	15.5″	15 3/4″
Leonardo 10 kW	10 kW	DTY	24″	29.75″	—
Super Leo 20 kW	20 kW	20 kW	24″	29.75″	—
Leonetti (Sunray)					
20 kW	20 kW	20 kW	24″	29″	29″
Mole-Richardson					
Tiny Mole	200	FEV	2″	5″	3″
Mini Mole	200	FEV	3″	4 7/16″	4 1/2″
Midget	200	FEV	4 15/36″	5 1/8	5 1/8″
Betweenie	300	FKW	3″	5 1/8″	5 1/8″
Tweenie	650	DYS	4 1/2″	5 1/8″	5 1/8″
Tweenie II	650	FRK	4 1/2″	5 1/8″	5 1/8″
Baby Baby	1 kW	EGT	5″	7 3/16″	7 1/4″
Baby	1 kW	EGT	6″	6 5/8″	6 5/8″
Baby Junior	2 kW	EGT	6″	9″	9″
Junior Solarspot	2 kW	CYX	9 7/8″	10 1/8″	10 1/8″

Table A.1 Tungsten Fresnels (*continued*)

	Watts	*Lamp ANSI code*	*Lens*	*Scrim (in.)*	*Chimera ring size (in.)*
8″ Junior	2 kW	CYX	8″	9″	9″
Baby Senior	5 kW	DPY	9 7/8″	13 1/2″	13 1/2″
Senior Solarspot	5 kW	DPY	14″	15 1/2″	15 1/2″
Baby Tenner	10 kW	DTY	14″	18 1/2″	18 1/2″
Tenner Solarspot	10 kW	DTY	20″	21″	21″
Big Eye	10 kW	DTY	24 3/4″	29″	29″
20 kW 'Big Mo'	20 kW	20 kW	24 3/4″	29″	29″
LTM Peppers					
Pepper 100/200	100	ESR	2″	3″	3″
	200	FEV	—	—	—
Pepper 200	200	FEV	3 1/8″	4 1/4″	4 1/4″
Pepper 300	300	FKW	3 1/8″	4 1/4″	4 1/4″
Pepper 420	420	EKB	3 1/8″	4 1/4″	4 1/4″
Pepper 650	650	FRK	4 3/8″	5″	5″
Pepper 500/l kW	500	EGN	5″	6 5/8″	7 1/4″
	1 kW	EGT	—	—	—
20 kW Pepper	20 kW	20 kW	24″	29″	29″
Sachtler					
Director H	300	FKW	3″	5 1/4″	5 1/4″
Director C	500	FRG	3″	5 1/4″	5 1/4″
Director H	650	FRK	5″	7 3/4″	7 3/4″
Director C	1 kW	[c]	5″	7 3/4″	7 3/4″
Director H	1 kW	EGT	6″	9″	9″
Director C	2 kW	[d]	6″	9″	9″
Director H	2 kW	CYX	8″	12″	12″
Director H	2 kW	CYX	10″	13.5″	13.5″
Director H	5 kW	DPY	10″	13.5″	13.5″
Director H	5 kW	DPY	12″	13.5″	13.5″
Director 10 kW	10 kW	DTY	—	—	—
Strand Quartz Color					
3″ Mizar	200	FEV	3″	4 3/8″	4 1/4″
3″ Mizar 300/500	300	FKW	3″	4 3/8″	4 1/4″
	500	FRK	—	—	—
5″ Bambino 1 kW	1 kW	EGT	5″	7 1/4″	7 1/4″
6″ Polaris 1 kW	1 kW	EGT	6″	9″ or 7 7/8″	7 5/8″
6″ Bambino 2 kW	2 kW	CYX	6″	9″	7 5/8″
10″ Castor 2 kW	2 kW	CYX	10″	12 5/8″ 13 1/2″	12 3/4″
10″ Bambino 5 kW	5 kW	DPY	10″	12 5/8″ 13 1/2″	13 1/2″
12″ Pollux 5 kW	5 kW	DPY	12″	16″	15 3/4″
14″ Vega 10 kW	10 kWk	DTY	14″	16″	15 3/4″
20″ Draco 20 kW	20 kW	20 kW	20″	29″	29″

[a] Uses Koto 12 kW tungsten lamp and maximized reflector/lens system for output rivaling a 20 kW.

[b] All power supplies have selectable input voltage: 110, 120, 220, 230, or 240 V AC and three-position switch selects output level.

[c] Uses special Philips blue pinch 1 kW bulb with GY 9.5 base.

[d] Uses special Philips blue pinch 2 kW bulb with G22 base.

Table A.2 Soft lights

	Watts	*Lamp*	*ANSI code*	*Face dimensions*	*Candle-power*
Arri					
Arrisoft 1000	1000	1	FCM	9.5″ × 7.7″	9200
Arrisoft 2000	2000	2	FCM	8.2″ × 17.1″	16,700
DeSisti					
Botticelli 2 kW	2000	2	FCM	21″ × 1″	—
Botticelli 4 kW	4000	4	FCM	32″ × 21″	—
DN Labs					
Spectra-flux 200T	100	1	GCC	6″ × 6″	—
	200	1	GCB	—	—
Lowel					
Softlight 2	2000	2	FCM	28″ × 24″	—
LTM					
400 Soft	400	1	FDA	4 3/4″ × 6 7/8″	1000
1000 Soft	1000	1	FCM	11.5″ × 17″	5000
2000 Soft	2000	2	FCM	20.5″ × 17″	10,080
4000 Soft	4000	4	FCM	42″ × 42″	18,000
Mole-Richardson					
Mini-Softlite	650	1	FAD	6 1/4″ × 6 1/4″	2400
750 Baby Soft	750	1	EJG	8″ × 8″	3000
1 kW Super Soft	1000	1	FCM	18″ × 18″	5000
2 kW Zip Baby Soft	2000	2	FCM	8″ × 17 1/2″	10,080
2 kW Super Soft	2000	2	FCM	24″ × 24″	10,080
4 kW Baby Soft	4000	4	FCM	18″ × 18″	18,000
4 kW Super Soft	4000	4	FCM	36″ × 30″	24,320
8 kW Super Soft	8000	8	FCM	36″ × 30″	48,000
Strand					
Arturo 1000/1500	1000	1	FFT	—	—
	1500	1	FDB	—	—
Arturo 2000	2000	2	FFT	—	—
Arturo 4000/6000	4000	4	FFT	—	—
	6000	4	FDB	—	—

Table A.3 Open-face fixtures

	Watts	*Lamp*	*Scrim*	*Chimera ring size*
Arri				
Arrilite 600	600	DYS	5″	5 1/8″
	250	DYG	—	—
Arrilite 650	650	FAD	7 1/4″	7 1//4″ *
Arrilite 1000	1000	DXW	7 1/4″	7 1/4″ *
Arrilite 2000	2000	FEY	10″	10″
DeSisti				
Minilite 1000	1000	FHM	—	—
Lee Colortran				
Mino Pro Broad	650	FAD	—	—
Mini-Broad	650	FAD	—	—
Broad	1000	FHM	—	—
Mini-lite Nook	1000	FHM	—	—
Set Light Nook	1000	FHM	—	—
Lowel				
Pro-light	125	FSH	Special	Special*
	250	GCA		
	200	GCB		
	100	GCC		
V-light	500	GDA	Special	Special*
Toto-light	300	EHZ	Special	Special*
	500	FCZ		
	750	EMD		
Omni-light	420	EKB	Special	Special*
	600	DYS		
DP Light	500	EHC	Special	Special*
	1000	FEL		
LTM				
Pepper 650 Flood	650	FRK	6″	6″
Mole-Richardson				
Teenie Weenie	600	EKD	5 1/8″	5 1/8″
Teenie Mole	650	FAD	6 1/4″	6″ *
Mickey-Mole	1000	DXW	7 3/16″	7 1/4″
Mighty	2000	FEY	10″	10″
1 kW Broad	1000	FHM	8 1/2″ × 12″	—
2k Super Broad	2000	FFW	10 1/4″ × 12″	—
650 Nooklite	650	FAD	—	—
1 kW Nooklite	1000	FCM	—	—
2 kW Nooklite	2000	FEY	—	—
1 kW Molette	1000	FCV	—	—
2 kW Molette	2000	BWG	—	—
Sachtler				
Reporter 20	20, 70	—	—	—
Reporter 50	30, 50	—	—	—
Reporter 100	100	—	—	—
Reporter 250	250	—	—	—
Reporter 300	150, 300	—	—	—
Reporter 650	650	—	—	—
Reporter 1000	1000	—	—	—

Table A.3 Open-face fixtures (*continued*)

	Watts	*Lamp*	*Scrim*	*Chimera ring size*
Strand Quartz Color				
Pulsar 600	600	DYS	—	Special*
Ianabeam 650 'Redhead'	650	FAD	7 1/4	Special*
Ianabeam 1000 'Redhead'	1000	DXW	7 1/4	Special*
Ianabeam 2000 'Blonde'	2000	FEY	10″	10 5/8″

* Fixture takes a dedicated nonstandard Chimera ring.

Table A.4 Tungsten PAR lights

	Watts	*Lamp*	*Weight*	*Scrim*
ETC				
Source Four Par	575	HPL575	7.5 lb	7.5″
Mole-Richardson				
Molepar	1000	PAR 64	4 3/4 lb	10 1/8″
PAR CAN	1000	PAR 64	4 1/2 lb	10″
Lee Colortran				
Cine-Queen	1000	PAR 64	—	9″

	Heads	*Watts*	*Bulb*	*Weight*
Mole-Richardson				
Molefay	1 × 650	650	PAR 36	2 1/4 lb
2-light	2 × 650	1300	PAR 36	9 lb
4-light	4 × 650	2600	PAR 36	10 1/2 lb
6-light	6 × 650	3600	PAR 36	17 lb
9-light	9 × 650	5400	PAR 36	29 1/2 lb
12-light	12 × 650	7800	PAR 36	26 1/2 lb
5-light	5 × 650	3250	PAR 36	10 lb
3-light obie	3 × 650	1950	PAR 36	4 1/2 lb
6-light	6 × 1000	6000	PAR 64	45 1/2 lb
9-light	9 × 1000	9000	PAR 64	63 1/2 lb
24-light	24 × 1000	24000	PAR 64	131 lb
Molecool	1 × 600	600	DYS	3 1/4 lb
		250	DYG	—
2-light	2 × 600	1200	DYS	9 lb
9-light	9 × 600	5400	DYS	29 1/4 lb
Ultra Light Mfg.				
24-lt. Dino	24 × 1000	24 kW	PAR 64	—
30-lt. Dino	30 × 1000	30 kW	PAR 64	—
Ultra Dino	36 × 1000	36 kW	PAR 64	190 lb

Colour temperature, beam angle, and intensity depend on the globe used. See bulb data in Appendix E. Source Four Par uses interchangeable, rotatable lenses (Clear, VNSP, NSP, MFL, and WFL). Lumen output is equivalent to 1 kW PARs with smoother, rounder beam. Optional MCM reflector removes 90 per cent of heat from beam. Molepar accessories include intensifier and dichroic daylight conversion filter.

Table A.5 Discharge Fresnels

	Lamp	*Lens*	*Scrim*	*Chimera ring size*	*Head weight*
Altman					
575 SE	575 SE	5″	7 3/4″	7 5/8″	16 lb
1200 SE	1200 SE	7″	9″	9 5/8″	17 lb
2500 SE	2500 SE	10″	13″	13 1/2″	38 lb
4000 SE	4000 SE	12″	15 1/2″	16 1/8″	65 lb
Arri					
200W	200	4.3″	5 1/4″	—	5.5 lb
200 SE	200 SE	4.3″	6 5/8″	6 1/2″	8 lb
575W	575	6.9″	8.5″	8 1/2″	18 lb
Compact 575W	575 SE	5.1″	7 3/4	7 5/8″	12 lb
1200W	1200	11.8″	13″	12 3/4″	35 lb
Compact 1200W	1200 SE	6.9″	9″	9 5/8″	20 lb
2500W	2500	13.8″	16″	15 1/2″	66 lb
Compact 2500W	2500 SE	10″	13″	13 1/2″	31 lb
4000W	4000	19.7″	21″	21″	95 lb
Compact 4000W	4000 SE	11.8″	15.5″	16 1/8″	49 lb
6000W	6000	19.7″	21″	21″	96 lb
Daylight 6000	6000	19.7″	21″	21″	85 lb
Daylight 12000	12000	19.7″	21″	21″	137 lb
Cinimills					
12 kW Silver Bullet	12 kW	24″	29″	29″	135 lb
18 kW Silver Bullet	18 kW	24″	29″	29″	150 lb
DeSisti					
Rembandt 200	200 SE	4.8″	6″	6″	5.29 lb
Piccolo 575	575 SE	6″	7 1/4″	7 3/8″	15.21 lb
Rembrandt 575	575	6″	7 1/4″	7 3/8″	—
Piccolo 1200	1200/SE	6″	7 1/4″	7 3/8″	18.74 lb
Rembrandt 1200 SE	1200/SE	10″	12″	12 3/8″	27.78 lb
Rembrandt 1200	1200	10″	12″	12 3/8″	—
Piccolo 2500	2500/SE	10″	12″	12 3/8″	33 lb
Rembrandt 2500	2500	12″	15 1/2″	15 3/4″	—
Rembrandt 4000	4000	14″	15 1/2″	15 3/4″	—
Piccolo 6000	6000 SE	14″	15 1/2″	15 1/2″	—
Rembrandt 6000	6000	14″	15 1/2″	15 3/4″	—
Rembrandt 12 kW	12 kW	20″	24 1/4″	24 1/2″	117 lb
Rembrandt 18 kW	18 kW	24″	—	26 1/2″	148 lb
Mole-Richardson					
575W Solarspot	575 SE	6″	6 5/8″	6 5/8″	11.25 lb
1,200W Solarspot	1200W SE	8″	9″	9″	20.25 lb
2,500W Solarspot	2500W SE	9 7/8″	13 1/2″	12″	28 lb
6,000W Solarspot	6000W SE	14″	18 1/2″	18 1/2″	31 lb
12 kW Solar-arc Solarspot	12 kW	24 3/4″	29″	29″	150 lb
18 kW Solar-arc Solarspot	18 kW	24 3/4″	29″	29″	125 lb
LTM					
Bonxia 200 SE*	200 SE	3 1/8″	4 1/4″	4 1/4″	3.3 lb
Luxarc 200	200	5″	6 5/8″	6 5/8″	6 lb
Luxarc 575	575	7″	9″	9″	12 lb
Luxarc 1200	1200	10″	12″	12″	22 lb
Luxarc 2500	2500	12″	15 1/2″	15 3/4″	50 lb

Table A.5 Discharge Fresnels (*continued*)

	Lamp	*Lens*	*Scrim*	*Chimera ring size*	*Head weight*
Luxarc 4000	4000	14″	18 3/8″	18 1/2″	58 lb
Luxarc 6000	6000	20″	21 1/2″	21″	105 lb
Super Lite 12 kW	12 kW	24″	29″	29″	125 lb
Luxarc 18 kW	18 kW	24″	29″	29″	130 lb
Super 1218 kW	12 kW or 18 kW	24″	29″	29″	143 lb
Sachler					
Director 125D	123 W/SE	3″	5 1/4″	5 1/4″	4.4 lb
Director 270D	250 W/SE	5″	7 5/8″	7 5/8″	10 3/4 lb
Director 575D	575 SE	6″	8 1/2″	8 1/2″	14 lb
Director 1200D	1200 SE	8″	12″	12″	—
Director 2500D	2500 SE	10″	13.5″	13.5″	—
Director 4000C	4000 SE	10″	13.5″	13.5″	—
Director 4000D	4000 SE	12″	13.5″	13.5″	—
Strand Color Quartz					
575 Sirio	575	6″	9″	9″	24 lb
1200 Sirio	1200	10″	12 3/4″	12 3/4″	44 lb
2500 Sirio	2500	12″	16″	15 3/4″	58.5 lb
Supernova 25/12	2.5 kW/1200 SE	10″	13 1/2″	13 1/2″	36 lb
Supernova 40/25	4 kW or 2.5 kW SE	12″	16″	15 3/4″	43 lb
4000 Sirio	4000	14″	16″	15 3/4″	72 lb
6000 Sirio	6000	14″	16″	15 3/4″	68 lb
12 kW Sirio	12 kW	20″	29″	29″	187 lb
Sunray					
Sunray 12/18 kW Combo	12 kW or 18 kW	24″	29″	29″	138 lb

Can operate on 30 V battery with special DC electronic ballast.

Table A.6 Discharge PAR and SE PAR fixtures

		Lamp	*Scrim*	*Chimera ring size*	*Head weight*	*Lens*	*Beam angle*	*Candela*
Arri	Arrisun 5 PAR	575 PAR	—		11 lb	Very narrow spot	14° × 8°	450,000
						Narrow spot	14° × 10°	400,000
						Medium flood	26° × 12°	150,000
						Wide flood	50° × 45°	25,000
	Arrisun 1200W PAR	1200 PAR	—	10″	19 lb	Very narrow spot	14° × 7°	1,800,000
						Narrow spot	11° × 8°	1,300,800
						Medium flood	22° × 10°	600,000
						Wide flood	54° × 19°	169,600
	Arrisun 12 plus	1200 SE	13″	13 1/2″	25 lb	Super spot	3.5°	5,625,000
						Spot	6.5°	2,500,000
						Medium	12° × 20.5°	192,000
						Super wide	21° × 47°	110,000
						Frosted Fresnel	39°	53,250
	Arrisun 40/25 2500W Bulb	2500 SE	15.5″	16 1/8″	43 lb	Super spot	5°	8,750,000
						Spot	8.5	3,375,000
						Medium	11° × 20°	1,800,000
						Wide	11° × 44°	450,000
						Super wide	48°	200,000
						Frosted Fresnel	18°	202,500
	Arrisun 40/25 4000W Bulb	4000 SE	15.5″	16 1/8″	43 lb	Super spot	4.5°	10,500,000
						Spot	10°	4,500,000
						Medium wide	12° × 21°	2,150,000
						Wide	19° × 45°	600,000
						Super wide	50°	250,000
						Frosted Fresnel	22°	270,000
	Arrisun 60	6000 SE	19.5″	—	59 lb	Super spot	7°	14,900,000
						Spot	10°	7,175,000
						Medium	11° × 20°	3,375,000

Table A.6 Discharge PAR and SE PAR fixtures (*continued*)

		Lamp	*Scrim*	*Chimera ring size*	*Head weight*	*Lens*	*Beam angle*	*Candela*
						Wide	20° × 38°	1,225,000
						Super wide	42°	675,000
						Frosted Fresnel	37°	337,500
LTM	Cinepar 200S/E	200 SE	6 5/8″	6″	2.4 lb	VNSP, NSP, MF, WF	—	—
	Cinepar 200	200W PAR	6 5/8″	6″	4 lb	NSP, M, WF, WF	—	—
	Cinepar 575 S/E	575 S/E	6 5/8″	6 5/8″	7 lb	NSP, MF, SWF, FF	—	—
	Cinepar 575	575 PAR	7 1/4″	7 1/4″	8 lb	VNSP, M, WF, SWF	—	—
	Cinepar 1200 S/E	1200 SE	9″	9″	16 lb	VNSP	4°	4,601,600
						MF	25° × 12°	490,800
						WF	54° × 21°	131,300
						SWF	53°	72,100
	Cinepar 1200	1200 PAR	9″	9″	13 lb	VNSP	12° × 6°	2,000,000
						NSP	12° × 8°	1,375,000
						MF	23° × 9°	805,100
						WF	54° × 22°	198,800
						SWF	64°	89,400
	Cinepar 2500 S/E	2500/SE	13″	12 3/4″	32 lb	VNSP	6°	5,832,000
						NSP	8°	2,592,000
						MF	27° × 11°	856,000
						WF	60° × 25°	222,400
						SWF	54°	124,800
	Cinepar 4000 S/E	4000/SE	15 1/2″	15 3/4″	40 lb	VNSP	5°	10,530,000
						M	23° × 10°	1,260,000
						WF	38° × 15°	540,000
						SWF	20°	261,000
						FF	33°	180,000
	Cinepar 6000 S/E	6000S/E	19 1/2″	—	48.5 lb	M, WF, SWF, FF	—	—

VNSP: very narrow spot; MF: medium flood; WF: wide flood; SWF: super wide flood; FF: frosted fresnel.

Table A.6 Discharge PAR and SE PAR fixtures (*continued*)

	Lamp	*Scrim*	*Chimera ring size*	*Head weight*
Cinemills				
200W Wallylight	200 PAR	7.25″	7 1/8″	11.5 lb
200W SE	200 SE	7.25″	7 1/8″	6 lb
575W SE	575 SE	7.25″	7 1/8″	12.5lb
1200W PAR	1200 PAR	10″	9″	16 lb
1200W SE	1200 SE	10″	10 1/8″	16 lb
2500W SE	2500 SE	13.5″	13 1/2″	24.5 lb
4000W SE	4000 SE	13.5″	13 1/2″	24.5 lb
6000W SE	6000 SE	13.5″	16 1/8″	—
DeSisti				
Remington 200	200 SE	—	—	—
Caravaggio 575	575 PAR	—	7 3/8″	
Caravaggio 1200	1200 PAR	—	—	19 lb
Remington 2.5/4 kW	2500 SE	—	—	—
	4000 SE	—	—	—
Remington Piccolo 6 kW	6000 SE	—	—	—
DN Labs				
575 Durapar PAR	575 PAR	7.5″	7 7/8″	10 lb
575 Durapar SE	575 SE	10″	—	15 lb
1200 Durapar PAR	1200 PAR	10″	10 1/8″	13 lb
1200 Durapar SE	1200 SE	12″	12″	21 lb
2500 Durapar SE	2500 SE	12″	12″	21 lb
10 kW Durapar (4-light cluster)	4 × 2500 SE	—	—	82 lb
40 kW Durapar (16-light cluster)	16 × 2500 SE	—	—	338 lb
4000W Durapar	4000 SE	16″	15 3/4″	33 lb
6000 SE Durapar	6000 SE	16″	15 3/4″	48 lb
6000 DE Durapar	6000W DE	22″ × 25″	—	65 lb
12kW Durapar	12 kW DE	22″ × 25″	—	80 lb
K 5600				
Joker 200*	200W SE	5″	5″	4.4 lb
Joker 400	400W SE	6 5/8″	6 5/8″	5.2 lb
Joker 1200	1200W SE	9″	9″	12 lb
Mole-Richardson				
200 Molepar	200 PAR	6 1/4″	6″	7.5 lb
575 Molepar	575 PAR	7 3/16″	7 1/4″	10 lb
1200 Molepar	1200 PAR	10 1/8″	10″	13 lb
1200 Molepar	1200 SE	10 1/8″	10″	15 lb
2500 Molepar	2500 SE	12″	12″	27 lb
4000W Molepar	4000W SE	13 1/2″	13 1/2″	28.5 lb
6000W Molepar	6000W SE	15 1/2″	—	39 lb
Sachtler				
Production 575D	575 SE	6″	9″	14 lb
Production 1200D	1200 SE	8″	9.5″	—
Sunray				
575 PAR	575 PAR	7 1/4″ 12″**	7 3/8″	3 lb
575 SE Par	575/SE	7 1/4″	7 3/8″	11 lb

Table A.6 Discharge PAR and SE PAR fixtures (*continued*)

	Bulb	*Scrim*	*Chimera ring size*	*Head weight*
		12″**		
1200 PAR	1200 PAR	10″	10 1/8″	10 lb
		15 1/2″**		
1200 SE Par	1200/SE	10″	10 1/8″	15 lb
		15 1/2″**		
2500W SE	2500/SE	10″	10 1/8″	20 lb
		15 1/2″**		
4000W SE	4000 SE	15 1/2″	15 1/2″	30 lb
		21″**		
Strand Quartz Color				
Quasar 12	1200 PAR	10 3/16″	10 5/8″	19.8 lb
Super Quasar 25/12	2500 SE or			
	1200 SE	10 3/16″	10 5/8″	34 lb
Super Quasar 40/25	4000 SE or			
	2500 SE	12 5/8″	12 3/4″	44 lb

* Can operate on 30V batteries with 200W Slimverter inverter.
** With intensifier.

Table A.7 Discharge sunguns

	Globe	*Scrim*	*Chimera ring size*	*Power supply*
DeSisti				
Tiziano		—	6″	24-30 V DC Electronic Ballast 120 V AC Mains Adaptor
Remington 200	200W SE	—	—	24-30 V DC Electronic Ballast 120 V AC Mains Adaptor
DN Labs				
200 PAR	200 PAR	—	5 1/4″	—
LTM				
Sungun 200S/E	200W SE	5 7/8″	6″	DC Ballast: 30 V electronic AC Ballast: 100-260 V auto
Blue Torch 270	250W SE	5 7/8″	6″	DC Ballast: 24-30 V AC Ballast: 110 V
Bonzai 200 S/E	200W SE	4 1/2″	4 1/4″	DC Ballast: 20-30 V AC Ballast: 120-250 V
Sachtler				
Reporter 125D	123W SE	5 1/4″	5 1/4″	—
Reporter 270D	250W SE	7 5/8″	7 5/8″	—
Production 575D	575W SE	8 1/2″	8 1/2″	—
Production 1200D	1200W SE	12″	12″	—

Table A.8 Other discharge fixtures

Description	*Manufacturer*	*Name*	*Globe*	*Dimensions*	*Weight*
Chickencoop	Cinemills	4000W/2500W	2500W DE 4000W DE	49″ × 39″	55 lb
Softlights	DeSisti	Raffaello 575	575W DE	12 5/8″ × 15″	20.5 lb
	DeSisti	Raffaello 1200	1200W DE	12 5/8″ × 19″	24.5 lb
	DeSisti	Raffaello 2500	2500W DE	17″ × 24 3/4″	50.2 lb
	LTM	Softarc 575	575W DE	14″ × 20 1/4″	18 lb
	LTM	Softarc 1200	1200W DE	19″ × 30″	31 lb
	DN Labs	Durapar 200T	—	—	—
Scoop	DN Labs	Spectra-Flux 1200	1200 SE	21″ round	21 lb
Bare bulb in Pyrex tube used for Chinese Lantern	K 5600	Bug Light	200W SE	Pyrex Tube	3.5 lb
Open Face. 130° spread. Can be used in any orientation	DeSisti	Goya 1200 Shadowlight	1200W SE	—	—
	DeSisti	Goya 2500/4000 Shadowlight	2500 SE 4000 SE	20″ × 22″	37 lb

Table A.9 Mole-Richardson studio arc fixtures

	Grid input Watts	*Amps*	*Volts*	*Carbon dimensions (in.)*	*In/hr*	*Head lens*	*Scrim*	*Weight*
150	18 kW	150	120 DC	Pos .63 × 25 Neg 11/16 × 9	9″ 4 1/2″	—	—	181 lb
Baby Brute	27 kW	225	120 DC	Pos .63 × 22 Neg 17/32 × 6 3/4	20″ 10	14″	18 1/2″	126 lb
Litweight Brute	27 kW	225	120 DC	Pos .63 × 22 Neg 17/32 × 6 1/4	20 10	24 3/4″	29″	152 lb
Brute	27 kW	225	120 DC	Pos .63 × 22 Neg 17/32 × 920	20 10	—	—	225 lb
Titan	42 kW	350	120 DC	Pos .63 × 25 Neg 11/16 × 920	20 10	—	—	250 lb

Table A.10 Fluorescent fixtures

Fixture	*Lamps*	*Lamp length*	*Bulb type*	*Dimensions of face (in.)*	*Weight (lb)*	*Ballast*
Lowel						
Light Array	6	4 ft.	T-12	30 × 54	18	Detatchable, flicker-free
Mole-Richardson						
Eight-tube, 18 in.	8	18 in.	T-12	16.4 × 19	25.25	Built-in, conventional
Four-tube, 4 ft.	4	4 ft.	T-12	21.75 × 55.25	42.74	Built-in, conventional
Leonetti Sunray						
Four-tube, 4 ft.	4	4 ft.	T-12	8 × 48	23	Flicker-free
Eight-tube, 4 ft.	8	4 ft.	T-12	16 × 48	36	Flicker-free
LTM						
Mini Moonlight	2	18 in.	Osram FT 36 DL/835 (3200K) Philips PL-L 36W/95 (5100K)	2 × 18	—	Built-in, flicker-free
Moonlight Single	6	18 in.	Osram FT 36 DL/835 (3200K) Philips PL-L 36W/95 (5100K)	18 × 18	25	Built-in, flicker-free
Moonlight Double	12	18 in.	Osram FT 36 DL/835 (3200K) Philips PL-L 36W/95 (5100K)	36 × 18	50	Built-in, flicker-free
Moonlight Triple	18	18 in.	Osram FT 36 DL/835 (3200K) Philips PL-L 36W/95 (5100K)	54 × 18	75	Built-in, flicker-free
Moonlight Quadruple	24	18 in.	Osram FT 36 DL/835 (3200K) Philips PL-L 36W/95 (5100K)	36 × 36	100	Built-in, flicker-free
Moonlight Sextuple	36	18 in.	Osram FT 36 DL/835 (3200K) Philips PL-L 36W/95 (5100K)	36 × 54	150	Built-in, flicker-free

Table A.11 Kino Flo fixtures

Name	*Length*	*Tubes*	*Ballast*	*Mount*	*Weight (lb)*	*Amps*	*Volts*	*Lamp*	*Output at 6ft. (fc)*
Portable Fixture Systems									
Four Bank	4-ft.	4	Stnd, Slct, Dim	3/8 stud	10.5	5	117 V AC	F40/T12	80
	2-ft	4	Stnd, Slct, Dim	3/8 stud	6.5	3.5	117 V AC	F20/T12	45
	15-in.	4	Stnd, Slct, Dim	3/8 stud	5	2.5	117 V AC	F14/T12	25
Two Bank	4-ft.	2	Stnd, Slct, Dim	3/8 stud	7	2.6	117 V AC	F40/T12	53
	2-ft.	2	Stnd, Slct, Dim	3/8 stud	4	1.8	117 V AC	F20/T12	23
	15-in.	2	Stnd, Slct, Dim	3/8 stud	3	1.4	117 V AC	P14/T12	14
Single	4-ft.	1	Stnd, Slct, Dim	3/8 stud	4	1.3	117 V AC	F40/T12	25
	2-ft.	1	Stnd, Slct, Dim	3/8 stud	2	0.9	117 V AC	F20/T12	10
	15-in.	1	Stnd, Slct, Dim	3/8 stud	1.5	0.7	117 V AC	F14/T12	6
Wall-O-Lite	4-ft.	10	Built-in	Jr. stud	47	12	117 V AC	F40/T12	180
Four Bank	8-ft.	4	Mega	—	—	—	117 V AC	—	—
	6-ft.	4	Mega	—	—	—	117 V AC	—	—
Two Bank	8-ft.	4	Mega	—	—	—	117 V AC	—	—
	6-ft.	4	Mega	—	—	—	117 V AC	—	—
Single	8-ft.	4	Mega, Slimline	—	—	—	117 V AC	—	—
	6-ft.	4	Mega, Slimline	—	—	—	117 V AC	—	—
12V DC Systems									
12V Single	4-ft.	1	12VDC Single	3/8 stud	—	4.5	12 V DC	F40/T12	—
	2-ft.	1	12VDC Single	3/8 stud	—	2.6	12 V DC	F20/T12	—
	15-in.	1	12VDC Single	3/8 stud	15 oz.	2.3	12 V DC	F14/T12	—
Mini-flo	9-in.	1	Mini-flo 12VDC	—	8 oz.	.8	12 V DC	F6/T5	—
Micro-flo	6-in.	—	Micro-flo 12VDC	—	—	—	12 V DC	—	—
Micro-flo	4-in.	—	Micro-flo 12VDC	—	—	—	12 V DC	—	—
Studio Fixtures									
Image 80	4-ft.	8	Built-in	Jr. stud	29	10	117 VAC	F40/T12	155
Image 40	4-ft.	4	Built-in	Jr. stud	14	5	117 VAC	F40/T12	78
Image 20	2-ft.	4	Built-in	Jr. stud	6	1.8	117 VAC	F20/T12	45
Trans-Panel Modules									
Trans-panel	4-ft.	12	Built-in	Hooks	50	2.1	117 VAC	F40/T12	—

Ballast types: Standard (Stnd), Select (Slct), Dimmable (Dim), Mega-ballasts and Slimline (8-ft. and 6-ft. lamps). 12VDC ballasts come with transformer for use with 120VAC or 220VAC service.

Table A.12 Ellipsoidal spotlights

Fixture	*Field angle*	*Multiplier*	*Candle power (cd)*	*Lamp*	*K*	*Watts*	*Weight (lb)*	*Gel frame (in.)*
Altman			***Flat Field Data***					
Shakespeare 50	50°	0.93	27,500	FLK (HX600)	3200	575	18	6 1/4″
Shakespeare 40	40°	0.73	43,500	″	″	″	18	6 1/4″
Shakespeare 30	30°	0.54	104,000	″	″	″	18	6 1/4″
Shakespeare 20	20°	0.35	119,000	″	″	″	18	6 1/4″
Shakespeare 10	10°	0.17	265,000	″	″	″	30	6 1/4″
Shakespeare 1535Z	15°–35°	0.26–0.63	233 kW–58 kW	″	″	″	30	7 1/2″
Shakespeare 3055Z	30°–55°	0.54–1.04	74 kW–23.5 kW	″	″	″	30	7 1/2″
ETC			***Flat Field Data***					
Source Four 450	50°	0.93	34,866	HPL 575	3250	575	16	6 1/4″
Source Four 436	36°	0.65	84,929	″	″	″	16.3	6 1/4″
Source Four 426	26°	0.46	138,079	″	″	″	16	6 1/4″
Source Four 419	19°	0.31	167,435	″	″	″	16	6 1/4″
Source Four 410	10.3°	0.178	800,300	″	″	″	16.3	12″
Source Four 405	6.8°	0.119	996,000	″	″	″	17.5	14″
Altman			***Peak Field Data***					
Micro-Elipse	—			MR-16 EYC/EYJ	3050	75	5	3 3/8″
3.5Q 3.5 × 5	48°	0.89	12,000	EHD	3000	500	9	4 1/8″
3.5 × 6	38°	0.69	15,200	″	″	″	9	4 1/8″
3.5 × 8	28°	0.50	16,000	″	″	″	9	4 1/8″
3.5 × 10	23°	0.41	17,200	″	″	″	9	4 1/8″
3.5 × 12	18°	0.32	20,000	″	″	″	9	4 1/8″
4.5-1530 Baby zoom	15°–30°	0.26–0.54	88 kW–55 kW	EHF	3200	750	15	6 1/4″
4.5-2550 Baby zoom	25°–50°	0.44–0.93	80 kW–40 kW	″	″	″	15	6 1/4″
4.5-3060 Baby zoom	30°–60°	0.55–1.15	50 kW–26 kW	″	″	″	15	6 1/4″

Table A.12 Ellipsoidal spotlights (*continued*)

Fixture	*Field angle*	*Multiplier*	*Candle power (cd)*	*Lamp*	*K*	*Watts*	*Weight (lb)*	*Gel frame (in.)*
360Q 4.5 × 6.5	56°	1.06	51,200	EHF	3200	750	13.5	7 1/2″
6 × 9	35°	0.63	88,000	″	″	″	14	7 1/2″
6 × 12	25°	0.44	152,000	″	″	″	15	7 1/2″
6 × 16	21°	0.37	184,000	″	″	″	15	7 1/2″
6 × 22	11°	0.19	216,000	″	″	″	15	
Altman			***Peak Field Data***					
1KL6-12	12°	0.21	342,400	FEL	3200	1 kW	24	7 1/2″
1KL6-20	20°	0.35	257,600	″	″	″	25	7 1/2″
1KL6-30	30°	0.54	195,200	″	″	″	24	7 1/2″
1KL6-40	40°	0.73	148,800	″	″	″	25	7 1/2″
1KL6-50	50°	0.93	97,600	″	″	″	24	7 1/2″
1KL8-10	10°	0.17	490,000	″	″	″	26	10″
1KJL 10-5	5°	0.09	1,008,000	″	″	″	32	12″
1KL6-2040Z	20°–40°	0.35–0.73	275 kW–85 kW	″	″	″	28	7 1/2″
1KL8-1424Z	14°°–24°	0.25–0.43	489 kW–262 kW		″	″	″ 34	10″
Colortran			***Peak Field Data***					
5/50 Series 650-012	50°	0.93	28,700	FEL	3200	1 kW		
5/50 Series 650-022	40°	0.73	48,000	″	″	″		
5/50 Series 650-032	30°	0.54	118,000	″	″	″		
5/50 Series 650-042	20°	0.35	171,000	″	″	″		
5/50 Series 650-052	15°	0.26	298,000	″	″	″		
5/50 Series 650-072	10°	0.17	563,000	″	″	″		
5/50 Series 650-082	5°	0.09	938,000	″	″	″		

Table A.12 Ellipsoidal spotlights (*continued*)

Fixture	*Field angle*	*Multiplier*	*Candle power (cd)*	*Lamp*	*K*	*Watts*	*Weight (lb)*	*Gel frame (in.)*
Colortran		***Peak Field Data***						
Mini-zoom 213-302	40°– 65°	1.27–0.73	32 kW–8.9 kW	FMR	3000	600		
Mini-zoom 213-312	25°–50°	0.44–0.93	49 kW–18.3 kW	″	″	″		
Mini-zoom 213-322	15°–30°	0.26–0.54	61 kW–44.5 kW	″	″	″		
Mini Ellipse 213-152	50°	0.93	9,000	EVR	3000	500		
Mini Ellipse 213-152	40°	0.73	16,500					
Mini Ellipse 213-152	30°	0.54	24,000					
Ellipsoid 213-052	40°	0.73	48,000	FEL	3200	lk		
Ellipsoid 213-062	30°	0.54	118,000	″	″	″		
Ellipsoid 213-072	20°	0.35	171,000	″	″	″		
Ellipsoid 213-092	12°	0.21	298,000	″	″	″		
Ellipsoid 213-102	10°	0.17	563,000	″	″	″		
Ellipsoid 213-112	5°	0.09	938,000	″	″	″		
Ellipse Zoom 213-162	15°–35°	0.26–0.63	206 kW-82 kW	″	″	″		
Strand			***Peak Field Data***					
Quartet PC	7.5°–55.5°	0.13–1.05	64,000	FRK	3200	650	7.3	6″
Quartet 25	25°	0.44	36,000	″	″	″	10.5	6″
Quartet 22/44	22°–44°	0.39–0.81	408,000	″	″	″	10.6	6″
Leko 15	15°	0.26	190,800	FEL	3200	1 kW	17	7.5″
Leko 20	20°	0.35	185,000	″	″	1 kW	13.2	7.5″
Leko 30	30°	0.54	449,850	″	″	1 kW	13.2	7.5″
Leko 40	40°	0.73	118,825	″	″	1 kW	13.2	7.5″
Leko 50	50°	0.93	63,000	″	″	1 kW	13.2	7.5″
8″ Leko	12°	0.21	582,400	″	″	1 kW	22	10″
10″ Leko	9°	0.15	880,000	″	″	1 kW	26	11 3/4″
4 1/2″ Variable Focus	25°–50°	0.44–0.93	24,698	EVR	″	500	15	6 1/4″

Table A.12 Ellipsoidal spotlights (*continued*)

Fixture	*Field angle*	*Multiplier*	*Candle power (cd)*	*Lamp*	*K*	*Watts*	*Weight (lb)*	*Gel frame (in.)*
6″ Variable Focus	15°–40°	0.26–0.73	92,800	FEL	″	1 kW	27	7 1/2″
Cantata 11/26	11°–26°	0.19–0.46	265,000	″	″	″	28	7 1/2″
Cantata 18/32	18°–32°	0.32–0.57	165,000	″	″	″	26.5	7 1/2″
Cantata 26/44	26°–44°	0.46–0.81	108,800	″	″	″	24	7 1/2 ″
Optique 8/17	8°–17°	0.17–0.30	395,000	T-29	″	1200	28	7 1/2 ″
Optique 15/42	15°–42°	0.26–0.77	119,790	″	″	″	28	7 1/2″
Alto 8/16 (2 kW)	8°–16°	0.14–0.28	595,200	CP92	″	2 kW	37.5	9.6″
Alto 14/32 (2 kW)	14°–32°	0.25–0.57	357,192	″	″	″	37.5	9.6″
Alto 20/38 (2 kW)	20°–38°	0.35–0.69	207,500	″	″	″	35	9.6″
Toccata 10/26	10°–26°	0.17–0.46	605,756	″	″	″	45.2	9.6″
Toccata 15/38	15°–38°	0.26–0.69	348,480	″	″	″	43.56	9.6″

Lamp intensities for ETC Source Four and Altman Shakespeare fixtures are *cosine flat field* candle power. All others are *peak* candle power. Comparing the two is misleading because peak readings tend to exaggerate performance.

Altman 360Q lamps are manufactured with either a bi-pin base, or a mini-can base. The bi-pin bulb type is listed here.

Each fixture can take a variety of bulbs. The highest wattage bulb is shown here. See Table E.3 for bulb substitutions.

To determine beam width, multiply *multiplier* by distance.

To determine footcandle level, divide candle-power by distance squared, or use Table A.14.

Table A.13 Beam diameter at various distances

Beam angle degree	*Multiplier*	*Distance in feet* 5	10	15	20	25	30	40	50	75	100	150	200	250
2	0.03	0.2	0.3	0.5	0.7	0.9	1.0	1.4	1.7	2.6	3.5	5.2	7.0	8.7
4	0.07	0.3	0.7	1.0	1.4	1.7	2.1	2.8	3.5	5.2	7.0	10.5	14.0	17.5
6	0.10	0.5	1.0	1.6	2.1	2.6	3.1	4.2	5.2	7.9	10.5	15.7	21.0	26.2
8	0.14	0.7	1.4	2.1	2.8	3.5	4.2	5.6	7.0	10.5	14.0	21.0	28.0	35.0
10	0.17	0.9	1.7	2.6	3.5	4.4	5.2	7.0	8.7	13.1	17.5	26.2	35.0	43.7
12	0.21	1.1	2.1	3.2	4.2	5.3	6.3	8.4	10.5	15.8	21.0	31.5	42.0	52.6
14	0.25	1.2	2.5	3.7	4.9	6.1	7.4	9.8	12.3	18.4	24.6	36.8	49.1	61.4
16	0.28	1.4	2.8	4.2	5.6	7.0	8.4	11.2	14.1	21.1	28.1	42.2	56.2	70.3
18	0.32	1.6	3.2	4.8	6.3	7.9	9.5	12.7	15.8	23.8	31.7	47.5	63.4	79.2
20	0.35	1.8	3.5	5.3	7.1	8.8	10.6	14.1	17.6	26.4	35.3	52.9	70.5	88.2
22	0.39	1.9	3.9	5.8	7.8	9.7	11.7	15.6	19.4	29.2	38.9	58.3	77.8	97.2
24	0.43	2.1	4.3	6.4	8.5	10.6	12.8	17.0	21.3	31.9	42.5	63.8	85.0	106.3
26	0.46	2.3	4.6	6.9	9.2	11.5	13.9	18.5	23.1	34.6	46.2	69.3	92.3	115.4
28	0.50	2.5	5.0	7.5	10.0	12.5	15.0	19.9	24.9	37.4	49.9	74.8	99.7	124.7
30	0.54	2.7	5.4	8.0	10.7	13.4	16.1	21.4	26.8	40.2	53.6	80.4	107.2	134.0
32	0.57	2.9	5.7	8.6	11.5	14.3	17.2	22.9	28.7	43.0	57.3	86.0	114.7	143.4
34	0.61	3.1	6.1	9.2	12.2	15.3	18.3	24.5	30.6	45.9	61.1	91.7	122.3	152.9
36	0.65	3.2	6.5	9.7	13.0	16.2	19.5	26.0	32.5	48.7	65.0	97.5	130.0	162.5
38	0.69	3.4	6.9	10.3	13.8	17.2	20.7	27.5	34.4	51.6	68.9	103.3	137.7	172.2
40	0.73	3.6	7.3	10.9	14.6	18.2	21.8	29.1	36.4	54.6	72.8	109.2	145.6	182.0
42	0.77	3.8	7.7	11.5	15.4	19.2	23.0	30.7	38.4	57.6	76.8	115.2	153.5	191.9
44	0.81	4.0	8.1	12.1	16.2	20.2	24.2	32.3	40.4	60.6	80.8	121.2	161.6	202.0
46	0.85	4.2	8.5	12.7	17.0	21.2	25.5	34.0	42.4	63.7	84.9	127.3	169.8	212.2
48	0.89	4.5	8.9	13.4	17.8	22.3	26.7	35.6	44.5	66.8	89.0	133.6	178.1	222.6
50	0.93	4.7	9.3	14.0	18.7	23.3	28.0	37.3	46.6	69.9	93.3	139.9	186.5	233.2
52	0.98	4.9	9.8	14.6	19.5	24.4	29.3	39.0	48.8	73.2	97.5	146.3	195.1	243.9

Table A.13 Beam diameter at various distances (*continued*)

Beam angle degree	*Multiplier*	*Distance in feet* 5	10	15	20	25	30	40	50	75	100	150	200	250
54	1.02	5.1	10.2	15.3	20.4	25.5	30.6	40.8	51.0	76.4	101.9	152.9	203.8	254.8
56	1.06	5.3	10.6	16.0	21.3	26.6	31.9	42.5	53.2	79.8	106.3	159.5	212.7	265.9
58	1.11	5.5	11.1	16.6	22.2	27.7	33.3	44.3	55.4	83.1	110.9	166.3	221.7	277.2
60	1.15	5.8	11.5	17.3	23.1	28.9	34.6	46.2	57.7	86.6	115.5	173.2	230.9	288.7
62	1.20	6.0	12.0	18.0	24.0	30.0	36.1	48.1	60.1	90.1	120.2	180.3	240.3	300.4
64	1.25	6.2	12.5	18.7	25.0	31.2	37.5	50.0	62.5	93.7	125.0	187.5	249.9	312.4
66	1.30	6.5	13.0	19.5	26.0	32.5	39.0	52.0	64.9	97.4	129.9	194.8	259.8	324.7
68	1.35	6.7	13.5	20.2	27.0	33.7	40.5	54.0	67.5	101.2	134.9	202.4	269.8	337.3
70	1.40	7.0	14.0	21.0	28.0	35.0	42.0	56.0	70.0	105.0	140.0	210.1	280.1	350.1
72	1.45	7.3	14.5	21.8	29.1	36.3	43.6	58.1	72.7	109.0	145.3	218.0	290.6	363.3
74	1.51	7.5	15.1	22.6	30.1	37.7	45.2	60.3	75.4	113.0	150.7	226.1	301.4	376.8
76	1.56	7.8	15.6	23.4	31.3	39.1	46.9	62.5	78.1	117.2	156.3	234.4	312.5	390.6
78	1.62	8.1	16.2	24.3	32.4	40.5	48.6	64.8	81.0	121.5	162.0	242.9	323.9	404.9
80	1.68	8.4	16.8	25.2	33.6	42.0	50.3	67.1	83.9	125.9	167.8	251.7	335.6	419.5
82	1.74	8.7	17.4	26.1	34.8	43.5	52.2	69.5	86.9	130.4	173.9	260.8	347.7	434.6
84	1.80	9.0	18.0	27.0	36.0	45.0	54.0	72.0	90.0	135.1	180.1	270.1	360.2	450.2

Simply multiply distance times multiplier to get diameter at any distance.

Table A.14 Brightness of luminaires at various distances

		Footcandles at various distances														
		Distance in feet														
Fixture	*Approximate candella range*	5	10	15	20	25	30	40	50	60	70	80	90	100	150	200
100W Pepper: Flood	1,875–2,500	75	19	8	5	3	2	1								
	2,500–3,200	100	25	11	6	4	3	2	1							
750 Zip Soft	3,200–3,750	128	32	14	8	5	4	2	1							
200W Pepper: Flood	3,750–5,000	150	38	17	9	6	4	2	2	1						
1 kW Soft	5,000–6,400	200	50	22	13	8	6	3	2	1						
300W Pepper: Flood	same as above															
200W HMI Fresnel: Flood	6,400–7,500	256	64	28	16	10	7	4	3	2	1					
650W Fresnel: Flood	7,500–10,000	300	75	33	19	12	8	5	3	2	2	1				
2 kWSoft	10,000–12,500	400	100	44	25	16	11	6	4	3	2	2	1			
	12,500–15,000	500	125	56	31	20	14	8	5	3	3	2	2	1		
4 kW Soft	15,000–20,000	600	150	67	38	24	17	9	6	4	3	2	2	2	1	
1 kW Baby Fresnel: Flood	same as above															
1 kW Mickey Mole: Flood	same as above															
575W HMI Fresnel: Flood	20,000–25,000	800	200	89	50	32	22	13	8	6	4	3	2	2	1	
	25,000–30,000	1,000	250	111	63	40	28	16	10	7	5	4	3	3	1	
2 kW Mighty Mole: Flood	30,000–40,000	1,200	300	133	75	48	33	19	12	8	6	5	4	3	1	
8 kW Soft	40,000–50,000	1,600	400	178	100	64	44	25	16	11	8	6	5	4	2	1
2 kW Arrilite/Blonde: Flood	same as above															
1 kW PAR 64: WF	same as above															
2 kW 8" Jr. Fresnel: Flood	50,000–60,000	2,000	500	222	125	80	56	31	20	14	10	8	6	5	2	1
1200W HMI Fresnel: Flood	60,000–80,000	2,400	600	267	150	96	67	38	24	17	12	9	7	6	3	2
5 kW Baby Senior Fresnel: Flood	80,000–100,000	3,200	800	356	200	128	89	50	32	22	16	13	10	8	4	2
1200 W HMI PAR: SWF	100,000–120,000	4,000	1,000	444	250	160	111	63	40	28	20	16	12	10	4	3
10 kW BabyTenner Fresnel: Flood	120,000–160,000	4,800	1,200	533	300	192	133	75	48	33	24	19	15	12	5	3
1 kW Mickey Mole: Spot	same as above															
2500W HMI Fresnel: Flood	same as above															
2500W HMI SE PAR: SWF	same as above															
1 kW PAR 64: MF	same as above															
4000W HMI Fresnel: Flood	160,000–200,000	6,400	1,600	711	400	256	178	100	64	44	33	25	20	16	7	4
1200W HMI PAR: WF	same as above															
4000W HMI SE PAR: FF	same as above															
2 kW Mighty Mole: Spot	same as above															
2500W HMI SE PAR: WF	200,000–240,000	8,000	2,000	889	500	320	222	125	80	56	41	31	25	20	9	5

Table A.14 Brightness of luminaires at various distances (*continued*)

Fixture	*Approximate candella range*	*Footcandles at various distances* *Distance in feet* 5	10	15	20	25	30	40	50	60	70	80	90	100	150	200
4000W HMI SE PAR: SWF	240,000–320,000	9,600	2,400	1,067	600	384	267	150	96	67	49	38	30	24	11	6
6000W HMI Fresnel: Flood	320,000–400,000	12,800	3,200	1,422	800	512	356	200	128	89	65	50	40	32	14	8
6000W HMI SE PAR: FF	same as above															
1 kW PAR 64: NSP	same as above															
20 kW Fresnel: Flood	400,000–480,000	16,000	4,000	1,778	1,000	640	444	250	160	111	82	63	49	40	18	10
12 kW HMI Fresnel: Flood	480,000–640,000	19,200	4,800	2,133	1,200	768	533	300	192	133	98	75	59	48	21	12
4000W HMI SE PAR: WF	same as above															
1 kW PAR 64: VNSP	same as above															
18 kW HMI Fresnel: Flood	640,000–800,000	25,600	6,400	2,844	1,600	1,024	711	400	256	178	131	100	79	64	28	16
1200W HMI PAR: MF	800,000–960,000	32,000	8,000	3,556	2,000	1,280	889	500	320	222	163	125	99	80	36	20
2500W HMI SE PAR: MF	same as above															
4000W HMI SE APR: MF	960,000–1,280,000	38,400	9,600	4,267	2,400	1,536	1,067	600	384	267	196	150	119	96	43	24
1200W HMI PAR: NSP	1,280,000–1,600,000	51,200	12,800	5,689	3,200	2,048	1,422	800	512	356	261	200	158	128	57	32
	1,600,000–1,920,000	64,000	16,000	7,111	4,000	2,560	1,778	1,000	640	444	327	250	198	160	71	40
1200W HMI PAR: VNSP	1,920,000–2,560,000	76,800	19,200	8,533	4,800	3,072	2,133	1,200	768	533	392	300	237	192	85	48
2500W HMI SE PAR: NSP	2,560,000–3,200,000		25,600	11,378	6,400	4,096	2,844	1,600	1,024	711	522	400	316	256	114	64
	3,200,000–3,840,000		32,000	14,222	8,000	5,120	3,556	2,000	1,280	889	653	500	395	320	142	80
	3,840,000–5,120,000		38,400	17,067	9,600	6,144	4,267	2,400	1,536	1,067	784	600	474	384	171	96
2500 W HMI SE PAR: VNSP	5,120,000–6,400,000		51,200	22,756	12,800	8,192	5,689	3,200	2,048	1,422	1,045	800	632	512	228	128
	6,400,000–7,680,000		64,000	28,444	16,000	10,240	7,111	4,000	2,560	1,778	1,306	1,000	790	640	284	160
12 kW HMI Fresnel: Spot	7,680,000–10,240,000		76,800	34,133	19,200	12,288	8,533	4,800	3,072	2,133	1,567	1,200	948	768	341	192
4000W HMI SE PAR: VNSP	>10,240,000			45,511	25,600	16,384	1,378	6,400	4,096	2,844	2.090	1,600	1,264	1,024	455	256
6000W HMI SE PAR: VNSP	>12,800,000			56,889	32,000	20,480	4,222	8,000	5,120	3,556	2,612	2,000	1,580	1,280	569	320
Overcast Day (ballpark)		1,800	1,800	1,800	1,800	1,800	1,800	1,800	1,800	1,800	1,800	1,800	1,800	1,800	1,800	1,800
Sunlight: Direct		6,400	6,400	6,400	6,400	6,400	6,400	6,400	6,400	6,400	6,400	6,400	6,400	6,400	6,400	6,400
Sunlight: Direct		8,000	8,000	8,000	8,000	8,000	8,000	8,000	8,000	8,000	8,000	8,000	8,000	8,000	8,000	8,000

Footcandle figures are based on the lower number in the candella range.
Candella ranges are in 1/3 stop increments.
Footcandle data represents the peak beam intensity. A reading at the beam edge is one-stop less than the peak beam reading.
Data is based on manufacturers marketing data and represents performance under ideal conditions (new bulb, clean new lens and reflector, no atmospheric interference). Performance data varies with fixture design and manufacturer. These figures are meant to represent an average fixture of each type.

Appendix B

Ampacity of cords and cables

Note: There are no direct metric equivalents to American cable sizes, and in all the cable tables given it has been necessary to use metric cable sizes with the nearest current carrying capacity.

Table B.1 Ampacity of type W and entertainment cable types SC, SCE and SCT

Size of cable		*No. of current-carrying wires in cable* *1*[a]	*2*[b]	*3*[c]
Cable rated at 90° C and 105° C				
4/0	(120 mm^2)	405	361	316
3/0	(95 mm^2)	350	313	274
2/0	(70 mm^2)	300	271	237
1/0	(50 mm^2)	260	234	205
2AWG	(35 mm^2)	190	174	152
4AWG	(25 mm^2)	140	130	114
6AWG	(16 mm^2)	105	99	87
8AWG	(10 mm^2)	80	74	65
Cable rated at 75°C				
4/0	(120 mm^2)	360	317	277
3/0	(95 mm^2)	310	275	241
2/0	(70 mm^2)	265	238	208
1/0	(50 mm^2)	230	207	181
2AWG	(35 mm^2)	170	152	133
4AWG	(25 mm^2)	125	115	101
6AWG	(16 mm^2)	95	88	77
8AWG	(10 mm^2)	70	65	57
Cable rated at 60°C				
4/0	(120 mm2)	300	265	232
3/0	(95 mm2)	260	230	201
2/0	(70 mm2)	225	199	174
1/0	(50 mm2)	195	173	151
2AWG	(35 mm2)	140	128	112
4AWG	(25 mm2)	105	96	84
6AWG	(16 mm2)	80	72	63
8AWG	(10 mm2)	60	55	48

Source: Reprinted with permission from NFPA 70-1993, The National Electrical Code ®, Copyright © 1992, National Fire Protection Association, MA 02269. This reprinted material is not the complete and official position of the National Fire Protection Association on the referenced subject, which is represented only by the standard in its entirety.

Note: The metric sizes quoted are the nearest equivalent current rating given in the British IEE Regulations.

[a] These amperage capacities are based on an ambient temperature of 30°C (86°F). They are allowable only where the individual conductors are not installed in rackways *enclosed* and are not in physical contact with one another, except in lengths not to exceed 24 in. where passing through the wall of an enclosure.

[b] See footnote b in Table B.2. [c] See footnote c in Table B.2.

Table B.2 Amperage capacities for flexible cords, stingers, and zip cord[a]

AWG Size		*No. of current-carrying wires* 2[b]	3[c]	Asbestos[d]
18	(1.0 mm²)	10	7	6
16	(1.25 mm²)	13	10	8
14	(1.5 mm²)	18	15	17
12	(2.5 mm²)	25	20	23
10	(4 mm²)	30	25	28
8	(4 mm²)	40	35	—
6	(6 mm²)	55	45	—
4	(10 mm²)	70	60	—
2	(16 mm²)	95	80	—

Source: Reprinted with permission from NFPA 70-1993, The National Electrical Code ®, Copyright © 1992, National Fire Protection Association, MA 02269. This reprinted material is not the complete and official position of the National Fire Protection Association on the referenced subject, which is represented only by the standard in its entirety.

Notes:

[a] These amperage capacities apply to the following types of cord: thermoset types C, E, EO, PD, S, SJ, SJO, SJOO, SO, SOO, SP-1, SP-2, SP-3, SRD, SV, SVO, and SVOO and thermoplastic types ET, ETT, ETLB, SE, SEO, SJE, SJEO, SJT, SJTO, SJTOO, SPE-1, SPE-2, SPE-3, SPT-1, SPT-2, SPT-3, ST, STO, STOO, SRDE, SRDT, SVE, SVEO, SVT, SVTO, and SVTOO.

[b] The amperage capacities in this column apply to multi-core cable in which two of the wires are current-carrying (such as a phase and neutral wire, or the two legs of a 240 V single-phase circuit). The neutral wire of a balanced 240/120 V single-phase circuit is not considered a current-carrying wire for the purpose of this table, with one exception: If the major portion of the load consists of electronic ballasts, electronic dimmers, or similar equipment, there are harmonic currents present in the neutral conductor and it shall be considered to be a current-carrying conductor. The green grounding (earth) wire is never considered to be a current-carrying wire.

[c] The amperage capacities in this column apply to multi-core cable in which three of the wires are current-carrying (such as a three-wire three-phase circuit, a balanced four-wire three-phase circuit, or a single-phase three-wire circuit derived from the neutral and two of the phase legs of a wye-connected three-phase system). The neutral wire of a balanced four-wire three-phase circuit is only considered a current-carrying wire when there are harmonic currents present. A cord or cable with four or more current-carrying wires must be derated in accordance with NEC Section 400-5. Cords and cables in which four to six of the conductors are carrying current must be derated to 80 per cent of the current-carrying capacity given in this table.

[d] This column gives the amperage capacities of asbestos cords (types AFC, AFPD, and AFPO), which are often used inside luminaires. In Europe the use of asbestos as an insulating material for the wiring inside luminaires has been abandoned due to Health and Safety legislation.

Table B.3 Minimum size of grounding (earth) wires

Rating of circuit protection device (A)	*Gauge of grounding conductor* *Copper Wire No.*		*Aluminium and Copper-Clad Aluminium Wire No.*	
15	14AWG	(2.5 mm^2)	12AWG	(4.0 mm^2)
20	12AWG	(4.0 mm^2)	10AWG	(6.0 mm^2)
30	10AWG	(6.0 mm^2)	8AWG	(10 mm^2)
40	10AWG	(6.0 mm^2)	8AWG	(10 mm^2)
60	10AWG	(6.0 mm^2)	8AWG	(10 mm^2)
100	8AWG	(10 mm^2)	6AWG	(16 mm^2)
200	6AWG	(16 mm^2)	4AWG	(25 mm^2)
300	4AWG	(25 mm^2)	2AWG	(35 mm^2)
400	3AWG	(35 mm^2)	1AWG	(50 mm^2)
500	2AWG	(35 mm^2)	1/0	(50 mm^2)
600	1AWG	(50 mm^2)	2/0	(70 mm^2)
800	1/0	(50 mm^2)	3/0	(95 mm^2)
1000	2/0	(70 mm^2)	4/0	(120 mm^2)
1200	3/0	(95 mm^2)	250kcmil	(150 mm^2)
1600	4/0	(120 mm^2)	350kcmil	(185 mm^2)

Source: Reprinted with permission from NFPA 70-1993, The National Electrical Code ®, Copyright © 1992, National Fire Protection Association, Quincy, MA 02269. This reprinted material is not the complete and official position of the National Fire Protection Association on the referenced subject, which is represented only by the standard in its entirety.

Note: The metric sizes quoted are the nearest equivalent current rating given in the British IEE Regulations.

Appendix C

Line loss and resistance tables

Table C.1 Voltage drop per 100 ft

	Three-phase			*Single-phase circuits from 3-phase feeders*		*Single-phase and DC circuits*			
Amps per leg	*4/0 feeder*	*2/0 feeder*	*#2 banded*	*#2 banded and '100A'*	*#6 '60A'*	*4/0 feeder*	*2/0 feeder*	*#2 banded and '100A'*	*#6 '60A'*
25	0.2	0.4	0.7	1.1	2.7	0.3	0.4	0.8	2.1
50	0.4	0.7	1.4	2.1	5.3	0.5	0.8	1.6	4.1
75	0.7	1.1	2.1	3.2	8.0	0.8	1.2	2.4	6.2
100	0.9	1.4	2.8	4.2	10.7	1.0	1.6	3.2	8.2
125	1.1	1.8	3.5	5.3		1.3	2.0	4.1	
150	1.3	2.1	4.2	6.3		1.5	2.4	4.9	
175	1.5	2.5	4.9	7.4		1.8	2.8	5.7	
200	1.8	2.8	5.6	8.4		2.0	3.2	6.5	
225	2.0	3.2				2.3	3.6		
250	2.2	3.5				2.5	4.1		
275	2.4	3.9				2.8	4.5		
300	2.6	4.2				3.1	4.9		
325	2.9					3.3			
350	3.1					3.6			
375	3.3					3.8			
400	3.5					4.1			

Note: For a distance of 100 ft (30.48 metres) along the route taken by the cables, and represents the total of the voltage drops in all the circuit conductors.

Table C.2 Resistance of copper wire at 25°C

Size	*Cross-sectional area (cmils *)*	*Cross-sectional area (mm²)*	*Lb (kg) per 100 ft (30.48 m)*	*Ohms per 100 ft (30.48 m)*	*Length in feet (metres) for one ohm*
4/0	211,600	107.30	65.3 (30 kg)	0.00509	19,646 (5,988 m)
2/0	167,800	85.10	51.8 (24 kg)	0.00642	15,576 (4,747 m)
2 AWG	66,360	33.60	20.5 (9.3 kg)	0.0162	6,173 (1,881 m)
4 AWG	41,740	21.20	12.9 (5.9 kg)	0.0259	3,861 (1,177 m)
6 AWG	26,240	13.30	8.0 (3.6 kg)	0.0410	2,439 (743 m)
8 AWG	16,510	8.37	5.1 (2.3 kg)	0.0640	1,529 (466 m)
10 AWG	10,380	5.26	3.1 (1.4 kg)	0.1018	982 (300 m)
12 AWG	6,530	3.31	2.0 (0.9 kg)	0.1619	617 (188 m)
14 AWG	4,110	2.08	1.2 (0.6 kg)	0.2575	389 (119 m)
16 AWG	2,580	1.31	0.8 (0.4 kg)	0.4094	244 (74 m)
18 AWG	1,620	0.82	0.5 (0.3 kg)	0.6510	154 (47 m)

Notes:
Weights listed are of the copper itself, not the total weight or an insulated cable. Resistance at 25°C.
* Cmils is the measure of wire area in thousands of an inch thus: 1 square inch = 1,000 × 1,000 = 1,000,000 cmils.
To calculate mm² of American cables, take the cmils figure and multiply by 0.000507.
There are no direct metric equivalents to American cable sizes, and in all the cable tables given it has been necessary to use metric cable sizes with the nearest current carrying capacity.

Appendix D

Flicker-free frame rates

Table D.1 Flicker-free frame rates with 60 Hz current

Frames/Second	*Optimal Shutter Angle*
120.000	180
60.000	180
40.000	120
30.000	180
24.000	144
20.000	180
17.143	
15.000	
13.333	
12.000	180
10.909	
10.000	
9.231	
8.000	198
7.058	
6.000	
5.000	
4.000	
3.000	
2.000	
1.000	

Table D.2 Additional flicker-free frame rates at specific shutter angles with 60 Hz current

Frames/Second	*Shutter Angle*
57.6	172.8
50	144
48	144
45	135
36	108
35	105
32	92 or 96
28	168
26	156
25	150
22	198 or 132
18	162
16	192 or 144

Table D.3 Flicker-free frame rates with 50 Hz current

Frames/Second	*Optimal Shutter Angle*
100.000	180
50.000	180
33.333	
25.000	180
20.000	144
16.666	
14.285	
12.500	
11.111	
10.000	
9.090	
8.333	
7.692	
7.142	
6.666	
5.000	
4.000	
3.125	
2.500	
2.000	
1.000	

Table D.4 Additional flicker-free frame rates at specific shutter angles with 50 Hz current

Frames/Second	*Shutter Angle*
48	172.8
40	144
36	129.6
32	115.2
30	108
28	108.8
26	187.2 or 93.6
24	172.8
22	158.4
18	194.4 or 129.6
16	172.8 or 115.2
12	172.8 or 129.6
8	172.8 or 144

Appendix E

Lamp tables

Table E.1 Photoflood and practical lamps

Type	*Lamp and base type*	*Volts*	*Watts*	*K Colour*	*Life (hr)*
Standard and Pear-shaped (PS) Photofloods					
PH-211	A-21 Medium	120	75	3200	100 hr
PH-212	A-21 Medium	120	150	3050	100 hr
PH-213	A-21 Medium	120	250	3400	3 hr
BBA (No 1)	A-21 Medium	120	250	3400	3 hr
BCA (B-1)	A-21 Medium	120	250	4800	3 hr
ECA	A-23 Medium	120	250	3200	20 hr
BAH	A-21 Medium	120	300	3200	20 hr
EBV (No 2)	PS-25 Medium	120	500	3400	6 hr
EBW (B-2)	PS-25 Medium	120	500	4800	6 hr
ECT	PS25/5 Medium	120	500	3200	60 hr
Mushroom Bulbs					
DAN (R-20)	R-20 Medium	118	200	3400	4
BEP (R-30)	R-30 Medium	118	300	3400	4
EBR (R-30)	R-30 Medium	118	375	3400	4
DXH (PH/RFL-2)	R-40 Medium	118	375	3200	15
BFA (R-34)	R-40 Medium	118	375	3400	4
DXC (PH/RFL-2)	R-40 Medium	118	500	3400	6
EAL	R-40 Medium	120	500	3300	15
FAE	R-40 Medium	118	550	3400	10
MR-16 Bulbs Medium Screw Base					
FSA (NSP) or JDR120V75W NSP	MR-16, Medium	120	75	3000	—
BSB (MFL) or JDR120V75W MFL	MR-16, Medium	120	75	3000	—
FSD (WFL) or JDR120V75W WFL	MR-16, Medium	120	75	3000	—
FSC (NSP) or JDR120V100W NSP	MR-16, Medium	120	100	3000	—
FSE (MFL) or JDR120V75W MFL	MR-16, Medium	120	100	3000	—
FSF (WFL) or JDR120V75W WFL	MR-16, Medium	120	100	3000	—

Notes:

The lamp type designation indicates type and size (in eighths of inches). For example, R-40 indicates it is a reflector lamp with a 5-in. diameter (40/8 = 5). An R-30 bulb is 3 6/8 in. diameter, an MR-16 is 2 in. diameter, and so on.

The mushroom floods listed here are all 3,000 K or more. Mushroom floods also come in a wide variety of wattages that have lower colour temperature, flood, and spot. R-40s, for example, come in 75 W, 150 W, and 300 W.

The MR-16s listed are 120 V medium screw base. MR-16 and MR-11 lamps also come in a wide variety of other configurations. The 6 V and 12 V versions with a small 2-pin base are the most common type.

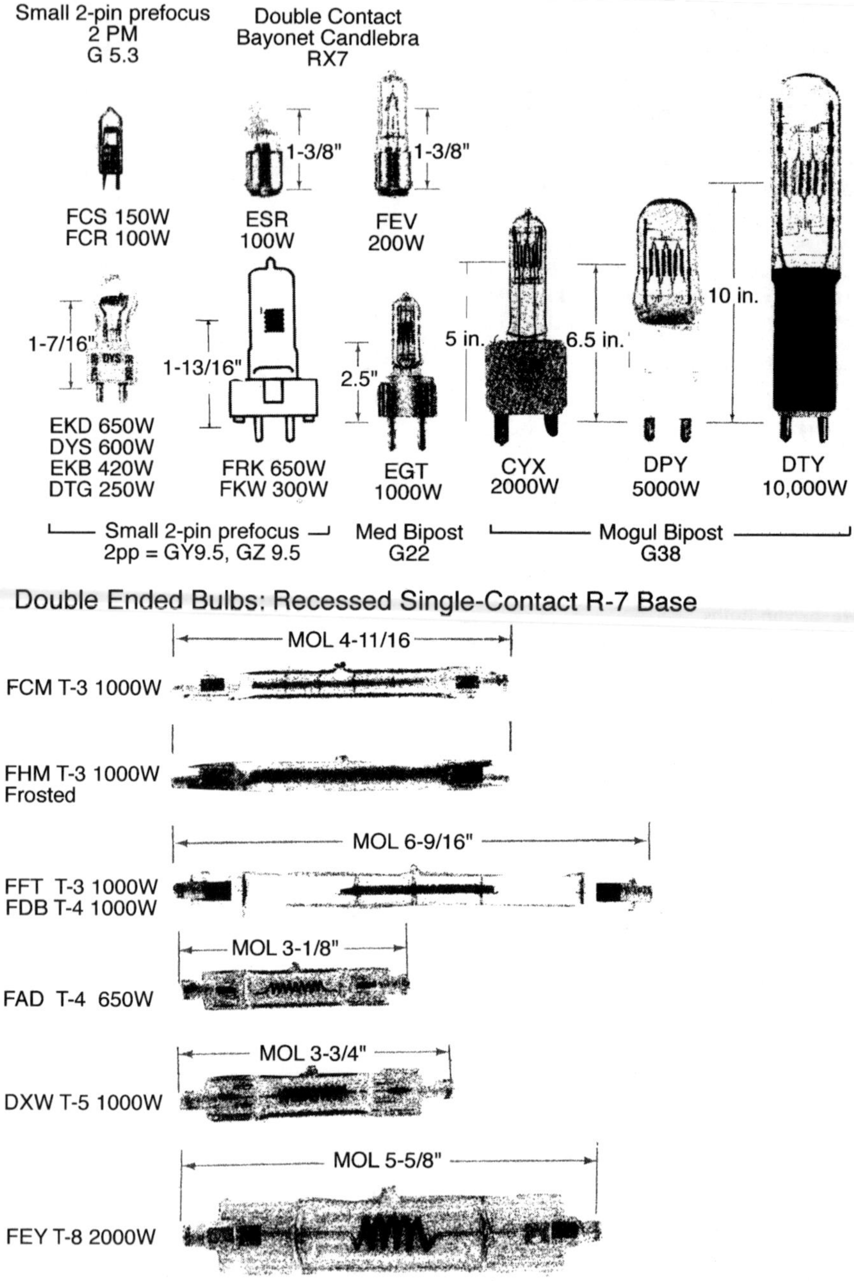

Figure E1 US lamps and bases

Table E.2 Fluorescent lamps

Watts	*Lamp*	*Diameter*	*Length*	*Description*	*Kelvin*	*Base*
KF55 (Daylight) Lamps						
6	T5	5/8″	9″	F6T5/KF55	5500K	Mini Bipin
14	T12	1 1/2″	15″	F14T12/KF55 SFC	″	Med. Bipin
20	T12	1 1/2″	24″	F20T12/KF55 SFC	″	″
30	T12	1 1/2″	36″	F30T12/KF55SFC	″	″
40	T12	1 1/2″	48″	F40T12/KF5S SFC	″	″
55	T12	1 1/2″	72″	F72T12/KF55/SL SFC	″	Single Pin
85	T12	1 1/2″	72″	F72T12/KF55/HO SFC	″	Med. Bipin
75	T12	1 1/2″	96″	F96T12/KF55/SL SFC	″	Single Pin
110	T12	1 1/2″	96″	F96T12/KF55/HO SFC	″	Med. Bipin
KF32 (Tungsten) Lamps						
6	T5	5/8″	9″	F6T5/KF32	3200K	Mini Bipin
14	T12	1 1/2″	15″	F14T12/KF32 SFC	″	Med. Bipin
20	T12	1 1/2″	24″	F20T12/KF32SFC	″	″
30	T12	1 1/2″	36″	F30T12/KF32 SFC	″	″
40	T12	1 1/2″	48″	F40T12/KF32SFC	″	″
55	T12	1 1/2″	72″	F72T121KF32/SL SFC	″	Single Pin
85	T12	1 1/2″	72″	F72T12/KF32/HO SFC	″	Med. Bipin
75	T12	1 1/2″	96″	F96T12/KF32/SL SFC	″	Single Pin
110	T12	1 1/2″	96″	F96T12/KF32/HO SFC	″	Med. Bipin

Other US Fluorescent Lamps

Make and name	*Colour temp (°K)*	*Colour rendering Index*	*Minus-green (/k) index correction required*
Duro Test Optima 32	3200	82	0–1/4
Duro Test Vita-Lite	5500	91	1/8–1/4
GE Chroma 50	5000	90	1/2
GE IF 27	3000	—	—
GTE Sylvania Design 50	5000	91	1/2
Warm White (WW)	3000	52	Full
Deluxe Warm White (WWX)	3000	77	Full
Cool White (CW)	4500	62	Full

Coloured Fluorescent Lamps

Lamp	*Description*
Super Blue	420 nm blue spike for blue screen opticals
Green	560 nm green spike for green screen opticals
Black Light	UV A stimulates luminescent materials
Red	Party colours
Pink	Party colours
Yellow	Party colours

Table E.3 Tungsten halogen lamp specifications

Conversion figures for bulb dimensions

1.181″	= 30 mm	1 3/8″	= 35 mm	1 7/16″	= 36mm
1 13/16″	= 46.5 mm	2 3/8″	= 60.5mm	2 1/2″	= 63.5 mm
3 1/8″	= 78 mm	3 1/2″	= 88.9 mm	3 3/4″	= 93 mm
4 11/16″	= 118 mm	5″	= 127 mm	5 1/4″	= 133 mm
5 5/8″	= 143 mm	6 1/2″	= 165 mm	6 9/16″	= 167 mm
10″	= 254 mm	13.937″	= 354 mm		

Bi-pin single-ended tungsten halogen bulbs

Watts	*ANSI code*	*Colour temp (°K)*	*LCL*	*Finish*	*Volts*	*Bulb life (hr)*	*Amps*
100W and 200W Fresnels: Peppers, Midget, Tiny Mole, Mini Mole, etc. Base: Double-contact bayonet candelabra RX7. Bulbs: B-12, G-16 1/2, T-4 and T-8. Burn within 30° of vertical, base-down.							
250	ESS	2950	1 3/8″	C	120	2000	2.1
200	**FEV**	**3200**	**1 3/8″**	**C**	**120**	**50**	**1.7**
200	BDJ	3200	1 3/8″	C	120	20	1.7
200	CCM	3075	1 3/8″	C	115-125	25	1.7
150	CGP	3075	1 3/8″	C	115-120	25	1.3
150	ETF	3000	1 3/8″	F	120	2000	1.3
150	ESP	2900	1 3/8″	C	120	1000	1.3
150	ETC	3000	1 3/8″	C	120	2000	1.3
100	**ESR**	**2850**	**1 3/8″**	**C**	**120**	**750**	**.5**
100	100Q/CL/DC	3000	1 3/8″	C	120	1000	.8
100	CEB	2975	1 3/8″	C	115-125	50	.8
75	CBX	2925	1 3/8″	C	115-125	50	.6
50	CAX	2875	1 3/8″	C	115-125	50	.4
100W and 150W Dedo. Base: Small 2-pin: 2 PM = G 5.3 Bulb: T-3 1/2, T-4. Burn base down to horizontal							
150	**FCS**	**3400**	**1.181″**	**C**	**24**	**100**	**6.25**
100	**FCR**	**3300**	**1.181″**	**C**	**12**	**50**	**8.3**
50	BRL	3300	1.181″	C	12	50	4.2
300W, 650W Fresnels: Tweenie II, Betweenie, 300W Pepper, etc. Base: Small 2-pin prefocus: 2 PP = GY 9.5. GZ 9.5. Bulb: T-6. Burn with coil horizontal.							
650	**FRK**	**3200**	**1 13/16″**	**C**	**120**	**200**	**5 4**
500	FRB	3200	1 13/16″	C	120	200	4.2
300	**FKW**	**3200**	**1 13/16″**	**C**	**120**	**200**	**2.5**
Small 1 kW Fresnels (special high seal temp bulb made for specially designed high-temp heads – Sachtler, DeSisti). Base: Small 2-pin prefocus GY9.5. Bulb: Philips							
1000	Blue Pinch	3200	1 13/16″	C	120	250	8.3
Old Style Tweenie, 420 Pepper, Teenie Weenie Open Face. Base: 2-pin prefocus: 2 PP = GY 9.5. GZ 9.5. T-6 or T-7 bulb. Burn with coil horizontal.							
650	**EKD-Q650/3CL2PP**	**3400**	**1 7/16″**	**C**	**120**	**25**	**5.4**
600	**DYS/DYV/BHC**	**3200**	**1 7/16**	**C**	**120**	**75**	**50**
420	**EKB-Q420/4CL/2PP**	**3200**	**1 7/16″**	**C**	**120**	**75**	**2.5**
250	**DYG-Q250/4CL/2PP**	**3400**	**1 7/16″**	**C**	**30**	**15**	**5.3**
100	EYL	3300	1 7/16″	C	12	50	63

Table E.3 Tungsten halogen lamp specifications (*continued*)

Watts	*ANSI code*	*Colour temp (°K)*	*LCL*	*Finish*	*Volts*	*Bulb life (hr)*	*Amps*
1 kW Fresnels Base: Medium bipost., G22. Bulb: T-6, T-7, T-20 or T-24. Burn within 45° of vertical base-down.							
1000	**EGT-Q1000T7/4CL**	**3200**	**2 1/2″**	**C**	**120**	**250**	**8.3**
1000	EGT	3200	2 1/2″	C	120	250	8.3
1000	EBB-1M24/13	3350	2 1/2″	C	120	12	8.3
750	EGR-Q750T7/4CL	3200	2 1/2″	C	120	200	6.3
750	EGR	3200	2 1/2″	C	120	200	6.3
750	DVH-750T24/16	3200	2 1/2″	C	120	50	6.3
500	EGN	3200	2 1/2″	C	120	100	4.2
500	DVG-500T20/63	3200	2 1/2″	C	120	50	4.2
Small 2 kW Fresnels (special high seal temp bulb made for specially designed high-temp heads – Sachtler, DeSisti). Base: Medium bipost., G22. Bulb: T-8 Philips							
2000	Blue Pinch	3200	2 1/2″	C	120	500	16.7
2 kW Fresnels Base: Mogul bipost., G38. Bulb: T-7, T-8, T-9 1/2, and T-48. Burn within 45° of vertical base down.							
2000	**CYX-Q2000T10/4**	**3200**	**5″**	**C**	**120**	**250**	**16.7**
1500	CXZ-Q1500T10/4CL	3200	5″	C	120	300	12.5
1000	CYV-Q1000T7/4CL/BP	3200	5″	C	120	200	5.3
5 kW Fresnel Base: Mogul bipost., G38. Bulb: T-17 and T-20. Burn base-down to horizontal.							
5000	**DPY-Q5000T20/4CL**	**3200**	**6 1/2″**	**C**	**120**	**500**	**41.6**
5000	DPY	3200	6 1/2″	C	120	500	41.6
10 kW and 12 kW Tungsten Fresnel Base: Mogul bipost., G38. Bulb: T-24. Burn within 45° of vertical base-down.							
10,000	**DTY**	**3200**	**10″**	**C**	**120**	**300**	**83.3**
12,000	**Koto 12 kW**	**3200**	**10″**	**C**	**120**	**—**	**100**
20 kW Fresnel Base: Mogul bipost., G38. Bulb: T32. Burn within 45° of vertical, base-down.							
20,000	KP200 208V	3200	13.937″	C	208	300	83.3
20,000	KP200 220V	3200	13.937″	C	220	300	83.3
20,000	**KP200 240V**	**3200**	**13.937″**	**C**	**240**	**300**	**83.3**
1 kW Molipso Base: Medium prefocus, P28. Bulb: T-5 or T-6. Burn any position.							
1000	**EGJ-Q1000/4CL/P**	**3200**	**3 1/2″**	**C**	**120**	**500**	**8.3**
1000	EGM-Q1000/CL/P	3000	3 1/2″	C	120	2000	8.3
1000	EGJ	3200	3 1/2″	C	120	400	8.3
750	EGF-Q750/4CL/P	3200	3 1/2″	C	120	500	8.3
750	EGG-Q750/CL/P	3000	3 1/2″	C	120	2000	6.3
750	EGF	3200	3 1/2″	C	120	250	6.3
750	EGG	3000	3 1/2″	C	120	2000	6.3

Table E.3 Tungsten halogen lamp specifications (*continued*)

Watts	*ANSI code*	*Colour temp (°K)*	*LCL*	*Finish*	*Volts*	*Bulb life (hr)*	*Amps*
2 kW Molipso							
Base: Mogul bipost., G38. T-8 bulb. Burn any position.							
2000	**BWA-Q2000/4CL/**	**3200**	**5″**	**C**	**120**	**750**	**16.7**
2000	BWA	3200	5″	C	120	500	16.7
1 kW Molette, Ellipsoidal Spotlights							
Base: Medium 2-pin. G9.5. T-4 or T-6 bulbs. Burn any position.							
1000	**FFL-Q1000/4CL**	**3200**	**2 3/8″**	**C**	**120**	**500**	**8.3**
1000	**FCV-Q1000/4**	**3200**	**2 3/8″**	**F**	**120**	**500**	**8.3**
1000	FEL	3200	2 3/8″	C	120	300	8.3
1000	FCV	3200	2 3/8″	F	120	300	8.3
750	EHF-Q750/4CL	3200	2 3/8″	C	122	300	6.3
750	EHF	3200	2 3/8″	C	120	300	6.3
750	EHG	3000	2 3/8″	C	120	2000	6.3
500	FHC/EHB	3200	2 3/8″	C	120	200	4.2
500	EHC/EHB-Q500/5CL	3150	2 3/8″	C	120	300	4.2
500	**EHD-Q500CL/TP**	**3000**	**2 3/8″**	**C**	**120**	**2000**	**4.2**
500	EHD	3000	2 3/8″	C	120	2000	4.2
2 kW Molette							
Base: Mogul screw. T-8 bulb. Burn any position.							
2000	BWF-Q2000/4CL	3200	5 1/4″	C	120	750	16.7
2000	BWF	3200	5 1/4″	C	120	400	16.7
2000	**BWG**	**3200**	**5 1/4″**	**F**	**120**	**400**	**16.7**

Double-Ended Tungsten Bulbs

Watts	*ANSI code*	*Colour temp (°K)*	*MOL*	*Finish*	*Volts*	*Bulb life (hr)*	*Amps*
400W and 650W Soft Lights and Open Face Lights							
Base: Recessed Single-Contact R7S. 3 1/8″ double-ended T-4 bulb. Burn any position.							
650	**FAD**	**3200**	**3 1/8″**	**C**	**120**	**100**	**5.4**
650	FBX	3200	3 1/8″	F	120	100	5.4
650	DWY	3400	3 1/8″	C	120	25	5.4
420	FFM	3200	3 1/8″	C	120	75	3.5
400	**FDA (400T4Q/4CL)**	**3200**	**3 1/8″**	**C**	**120**	**250**	**3.3**
400	EHR (400T4Q/CL)	2900	3 1/8″	C	120	2000	3.3
300	EHP (300T4Q/CL)	2900	3 1/8″	C	120	2000	2.5
1 kW Open Face, Mickey, 1 kW Arrilite							
Base: Recessed Single-Contact R7s. 3 3/4″ double-ended T-3 bulb. Burn any position.							
1000	**DXW**	**3200**	**3 3/4″**	**C**	**120**	**150**	**8.3**
1000	FBY	3200	3 3/4″	F	120	150	8.3
1000	BRH	3350	3 3/4″	C	120	75	8.3
1000	DXN	3400	3 3/4″	C	120	75	5.0
600	FCB	3250	3 3/4″	C	120	75	5.0
500	FGD	3200	3 3/4″	C	120	100	4.2

Table E.3 Tungsten halogen lamp specifications (*continued*)

Watts	*ANSI code*	*Colour temp (°K)*	*MOL*	*Finish*	*Volts*	*Bulb life (hr)*	*Amps*
1 kW Nook, 1 kW, 2 kW, 4 kW and 8 kW Soft lights							
Base: Recessed Single-Contact R7s. 4 11/16″ double-ended T-3 bulb. Burn horizontal ± 4°.							
1000	**FCM-Q1000T3/4CL**	**3200**	**4 11/16″**	**C**	**120**	**500**	**8.3**
1000	FCM-Q1000T3/4	3200	4 11/16″	F	120	500	8.3
1000	FCM	3200	4 11/16″	C	120	300	8.3
1000	**FHM**	**3200**	**4 11/16″**	**F**	**120**	**300**	**8.3**
750	EJG-Q750T3/4CL	3200	4 11/16″	C	120	400	8.3
750	EMD-Q750T3/4	3200	4 11/16″	F	120	400	6.3
750	**EJG**	**3200**	**4 11/16″**	**C**	**120**	**400**	**6.3**
500	FDF-Q500T3/4CL	3200	4 11/16″	C	120	400	4.2
500	FDN-Q500T3/4	3200	4 11/16″	F	120	400	4.2
500	EDF	3200	4 11/16″	C	120	400	4.2
500	EDN	3200	4 11/16″	F	120	400	4.2
500	Q500T3/CL	3000	4 11/16″	C	120	2000	4.2
500	Q500T3	3000	4 11/16″	F	120	2000	4.2
500	FCL	3000	4 11/16″	C	120	2600	4.2
500	FCZ	3000	4 11/16″	F	120	2600	4.2
300	EHM-Q300T2 1/2CL	2980	4 11/16″	C	120	2000	2.5
300	EHZ-Q300T2 1/2	2950	4 11/16″	F	120	2000	2.5
2 kW Nook							
Base: Recessed Single-Contact R7s. 5 5/8″ double-ended T-6 or T-8 bulb. Burn any position.							
2000	**FEY-Q2000T8/4CL**	**3200**	**5 5/8″**	**C**	**120**	**500**	**16.7**
2000	FEY (2MT8Q/4CL)	3200	5 5/8″	C	120	400	16.7
1000	FER/EHS-Q1000T4/6CL	3200	5 5/8″	C	120	500	8.3
1000	FER (1000T6Q/4CL)	3200	5 5/8″	C	120	500	8.3
1000	DWT-Q1000T6/CL	3000	5 5/8″	C	120	2550	8.3
1000	DWT (1000T6Q/CL)	3000	5 5/8″	C	120	2000	8.3
Cyc Strips							
Base: Recessed Single-Contact R7s. 6 9/16″ double-ended T-3 or T-4 bulb. Burn horizontal ± 4°.							
1500	**FDB-Q1500T4/4CL**	**3200**	**6 9/16″**	**C**	**120**	**400**	**12.5**
1500	FGT-Q1500T4/4	3200	6 9/16″	F	120	400	12.5
1000	**FFT-Q1000T3/1CL**	**3200**	**6 9/16″**	**C**	**120**	**400**	**8.3**
1000	FGV-Q1000T3/1	3200	6 9/16″	C	120	400	8.3

LCL = Light Centre Length, the distance from the centre of the bulb's filament to the bottom of its base. If the wrong LCL is used, the filament will not be centred on the reflector and fixture performance will be greatly reduced.
MOL = Maximum Overall Length, the distance from the top of the lamp to the tip of the pins on the base, or from end to end for double-ended lamps. For double-ended lamps, MOL is necessary to match lamp to fixture size.
Interchangeability = Bulbs within each grouping in this table are interchangeable – they have the same base (type and dimensions) and the same LCL (or MOL in the case of double-ended lamps).
The most commonly used lamps for motion picture work are highlighted in bold print.
C = Clear finish
F = Frosted finish

Table E.4 PAR 64 lamp types (120 V)

	500W	*1000W*			*1200W*
Beam	*2800K (2000 hrs)*	*3000K (4000 hrs)*	*3200K (800 hrs)*	*5200K (200 hrs)*	*3200K*
Very narrow spot	—	—	FFN (VNSP) Q1000PAR64/1	—	GFC (VNSP)
Narrow spot	500PAR64NSP	1000PAR64QNSP	FFP (NSP) Q1000PAR64/2	FGM (NSP) Q1000PAR64/3D	GFB (NSP)
Medium flood	500PAR64MFL	1000PAR64QMFL	FFR (MFL) Q1000PAR64/5	FGN (MFL) Q1000PAR64/7D	GFA (MFL)
Wide flood	500PAR64WFL	1000PAR64QWFL	FFS (WFL) Q1000PAR64/6	—	GFE (WFL)
Extra wide flood	—	—	GFF (XWFL)	—	GFD (XWFL)

Table E.5 PAR 64s: performance data for theatrical PARs and aircraft landing lights

ANSI code	*Volts*	*Watts*	*Base*	*Colour temp*	*Ave. life (hr)*	*Beam*	*Beam angle (degrees)*	*Candle power*
FFN	120	1000	EMEP	3200	800	VNSP	12 × 6	400,000
FFP	120	1000	EMEP	3200	800	NSP	14 × 7	330,000
FFR	120	1000	EMEP	3200	800	MFL	28 × 12	125,000
FFS	120	1000	EMEP	3200	800	WFL	48 × 24	40,000
GFF	120	1000	EMEP	3200	800	XWFL	—	—
GFC	120	1200	EMEP	3200	400	VNSP	10 × 8	540,000
GFB	120	1200	EMEP	3200	400	NSP	10 × 8	450,000
GPA	120	1200	EMEP	3200	400	MFL	24 × 13	160,000
GFE	120	1200	EMEP	3200	400	WFL	58 × 25	45,000
GFD	120	1200	EMEP	3200	400	XWFL	—	—
ACL (Aircraft Landing Light) Bulbs in PAR 64 size								
4559	28	600	Screw Terminal	—	25	VNSP	12 × 11	600,000
Q4559	28	600	Screw Terminal	—	100	VNSP	12 × 8	600,000
Q4559X	28	600	Screw Terminal	—	100	VNSP	11 × 7 1/2	600,000

Table E.6 PAR 36 lamp types (120 V)

Beam	*5000K (35 hr)*	*3400K (30 hr)*	*3200K (100 hr)*
Spot	—	FBJ Q650PAR36/3	—
Medium	FAY Q650PAR36/3D	DXK Q650PAR36/2	FCX Q650PAR36/7
Wide	—	—	FCW Q650PAR36/6

Appendix E.7: European lamps

CP stands for colour photography because the lamps were originally imported from the USA by the British film industry. All CP lamps have a colour temperature of 3,200 K, are single-ended and range in power from 300 W to 20 kW.
P class are double ended linear lamps also rated at 3,200 K and range in power from 250 W to 2 kW.

Note: The European voltage is being harmonized at 230 V but lamps are being produced as 220 V, 230 V and 240 V versions to allow for various countries deviations from the standard voltage.

The American National Standards Institute (ANSI) adopted a different coding system, generally using three letters arranged in alphabetical order. The following table gives some of the equivalent types and can be used to find alternative lamps.

Table E.7 European lamps

Single-ended tungsten halogen incandescent lamps

	European code (LIF)	*USA code (ANSI)*	*Volts*	*Colour temp.*	*Life*	*LCL (mm)*	*Base*
250 W	—	DYG	30	3400	15	36.0	GY9.5
300 W	CP-81	FKW	120	3200	150	46.5	GY9.5
	CP-81	FSL	220/230	3200	150	46.5	GY9.5
	CP-81	FSK	240/250	3200	150	46.5	GY9.5
500 W	CP-82	FRG	120	3200	150	46.5	GY9.5
	CP-82	FRH	230	3200	150	46.5	GY9.5
	CP-82	FRJ	240	3200	150	46.5	GY9.5
	M-40	—	220/240	2900	2000	46.5	GY9.5
	—	BTM	120	3200	150	55.5	P28s
	—	EHC	120	3200	300	60.5	G9.5
	—	EHD	120	2900	2000	60.5	G9.5
	—	EGN	120	3200	150	63.5	G22
	—	EGE	120	2900	2000	88.9	P28s
575 W	HX600	FLK	115	3200	300	60.5	G9.5
	HX601	—	115	3000	1500	60.5	G9.5
600 W	—	DYS	120	3200	75	36.0	GY9.5
	—	FMB	120	3050	2000	51.0	GY9.5
	HX602	—	220/240	3100	300	60.5	GY9.5
650 W	—	DYR	220/240	3200	50	36.0	GY9.5
	—	DYS	120	3200	75	36.0	GY9.5
		EKD	120	3400	25	36.0	GY9.5
	CP-89	FRK	120	3200	200	46.5	GY9.5
	CP-89	FRL	220	3200	150	46.5	GY9.5
	CP-89	FRM	240	3200	150	46.5	GY9.5
	CP-23/CP-67	—	120	3200	100	55.0	GX9.5
	CP-23/CP-67	FVD	220/240	3200	100	55.0	GX9.5
	CP-51/CP-69	FKL	120	3200	100	55.5	P28s
	CP-51/CP-69	FKM	220/240	3200	100	55.5	P28s
	CP-49	—	220/240	3200	50	55.5	P28s
	—	FKR	220/240	3100	300	60.5	G9.5

Table E.7 European lamps (*continued*)

Single-ended tungsten halogen incandescent lamps

	European code (LIF)	*USA code (ANSI)*	*Volts*	*Colour temp.*	*Life*	*LCL (mm)*	*Base*
	—	FKV	120	3150	300	60.5	G9.5
	CP-39/CP-68	FKG	120	3200	100	63.5	G22
	CP-39/CP-68	FKH	220/240	3200	100	63.5	G22
	—	DTA	120	3200	300	87.0	P40s
750 W	—	BTN	120	3000	750	55.5	P28s
	—	BTP	120	3200	200	55.5	P28s
	—	EHF	120	3200	300	60.5	G9.5
	—	EHG	120	3000	2000	60.5	G9.5
	—	EGR	120	3200	200	63.5	G22
	—	EGG	120	2900	2000	88.9	P28s
900 W	—	BVA	120	3200	75	44.5	GY9.5
	—	DZJ	220/240	3200	75	44.5	GY9.5
1000 W	CP-98	—	220/240	3200	125	46.0	GY9.5
	CP-24	—	120	3200	200	55.0	GX9.5
	CP-24		220/240	3200	200	55.0	GX9.5
	CP-70	FVA	220	3200	200	55.0	GX9.5
	CP-70	FVB	240	3200	200	55.0	GX9.5
	CP-52	FKN	220/240	3200	200	55.5	P28s
	—	BTR	120	3200	250	55.5	P28s
	CP-77	FEL	120	3200	300	60.5	G9.5
	CP-77	FEP	220/240	3200	300	60.5	G9.5
	—	FCV	120	3200	300	60.5	G9.5
	CP-40/CP-71	FKJ	220/240	3200	200	63.5	G22
	—	EGT	120	3200	250	63.5	G22
	—	EGJ	120	3200	500	88.9	P28s
	—	EWE	220/240	3200	250	88.9	P28s
	—	BVT	120	3050	500	100.0	P40s
	—	BVV	120	3200	250	100.0	P40s
	—	CYV	120	3200	250	127.0	G38
	CP-106	—	220/240	3200	400	127.0	G38
	—	DSE	120	3200	500	N/A	E40s
1200 W	CP-93	—	120	3200	200	63.5	G22
	CP-93	—	220/240	3200	200	63.5	G22
	CP-90	—	120	3200	200	67.0	GX9.5
	CP-90	—	220/240	3200	200	67.0	GX9.5
1500 W	—	DTA	120	3200	300	87.0	P40s
	—	CWZ	120	3200	300	100.0	P40s
	—	CXZ	120	3200	300	127.0	G38
	—	DSF	120	3200	750	241.0	E40s
1900 W (2 filaments: 1250 W + 650 W)							
	CP-105	—	220/240	3050	250	143.0	GX38q
2000 W	CP-43/CP-72	—	120	3200	400	70.0	GY16
	CP-43/CP-72	FTM	220	3200	400	70.0	GY16
	CP-43/CP-72	FTL	240	3200	400	70.0	GY16
	CP-79	—	220/240	3200	350	70.0	GY16
	CP-75	—	220/240	3200	400	75.0	G22
	CP-53/CP-74	—	120	3200	400	87.0	P40s

Table E.7 European lamps (*continued*)

Single-ended tungsten halogen incandescent lamps

	European code (LIF)	*USA code (ANSI)*	*Volts*	*Colour temp.*	*Life*	*LCL (mm)*	*Base*
	CP-53/CP-74	—	220/240	3200	400	87.0	P40s
	CP-28	—	220/240	3200	300	87.0	P40s
	CP-92	—	120	3200	400	90.0	G22
	CP-92	—	220/240	3200	400	90.0	G22
	—	BVW	120	3200	400	100.0	P40s
	CP-41/CP-73	FKK	220/240	3200	400	127.0	G38
	—	CYX	120	3200	400	127.0	G38
	CP-34	—	220/240	3200	300	127.0	G38
	—	BWA	120	3200	500	127.0	G38
	—	FWG	120	3200	500	128.0	E40s
	CP-59/CP-76	—	220/240	3200	300	133.0	E40s
	—	BWF	120	3200	400	133.0	E40s
	—	FWH	120	3200	500	171.0	E40s
2500 W	CP-91	—	120	3200	400	90.0	G22
	CP-91	—	220/240	3200	400	90.0	G22
	CP-94	—	220/240	3200	400	127.0	G38
2500 W (2 filaments, each 1250 W)							
	CP-30	—	220/240	3200	300	143.0	GX38q
3000 W	HX-48	—	120	3200	400	127.0	G38
	HX-48	—	220/240	3200	400	127.0	G38
3500 W	CP-107	—	220/240	3200	400	165.0	G38
3750 W (2 filaments: 2500 W + 1250 W)							
	CP-58	—	220/240	3200	300	143.0	GX38q
5000 W (2 filaments, each 2500 W)							
	CP-32	—	220/240	3200	300	143.0	GX38q
5000 W	CP-29/CP-85	—	220/240	3200	500	165.0	G38
	CP-29/CP-85	DPY	120	3200	500	165.0	G38
	CP-46	—	220/240	3200	400	165.0	G38
	CP-46	ECN	120	3200	400	165.0	G38
10000 W	CP-80	—	220/240	3200	400	254.0	G38
	CP-80	EBA	120	3200	400	254.0	G38
	CP-83	—	220/240	3200	500	254.0	G38
	CP-83	DTY	120	3200	500	254.0	G38
20000 W	CP-27	—	220/240	3200	500	420	G38
	CP-99	BCM	220/240	3200	350	354	G38

Special 'pinch protected' tungsten halogen lamps

The lamp manufacturers state that 'pinch protected' lamps should only be used in specially designed luminaires and under *no* circumstances should they be used in existing standard luminaires. This is because 'pinch protected' lamps have either a shorter 'light centre length' than normal or a higher wattage for the same 'light centre length' to enable manufacturers to design smaller luminaires. The pinch temperature of a standard tungsten halogen lamp is typically 400°C, whereas 'pinch protected' lamps can work at temperatures up to 500°C.

Table E.7 European lamps (*continued*)

Special 'pinch protected' tungsten halogen lamps

Wattage	*Ref. No.*	*Volts*	*Col. temp.*	*Life*	*LCL (mm)*	*Base*
75	VL75BP	30	3200	75	36.5	GZ9.5
150	VL175BP	30	3200	75	36.5	GZ9.5
250	VL250	30	3200	75	36.5	GZ9.5
400	VL400BP	120/230/240	3200	75	36.5	GZ9.5
800	VL800BP	120/230/240	3200	75	36.5	GZ9.5
1000	6995IBP	120/230/240	3200	250	46.5	GY9.5
2000	6994MBP	120/230/240	3200	500	63.5	G22
2500	86863HBP	120/230/240	3200	500	179.0	Fa4
5000	6963MBP	120/230/240	3200	525	127.0	G22
5000	6963NBP	120/230/240	3200	525	127.0	G38

Double-ended tungsten halogen incandescent linear lamps

	European code (LIF)	*USA code (ANSI)*	*Volts*	*Colour temp.*	*Life*	*Length (mm)*	*End caps*
250 W	P1/8	—	30	3400	12	78.0	R7s
300 W	—	EHM	120	2950	2000	78.0	R7s
400 W	—	EHR	120	2900	2000	78.0	R7s
420 W	—	FFM	120	3200	100	78.0	R7s
500 W	P2/30	FDF	120	3200	400	118.0	R7s
	K1	—	220/240	2900	2000	118.0	R7s
	—	FCL	120	3000	2000	118.0	R7s
625 W	P2/10	—	220/240	3200	200	189.0	R7s
	P2/10	—	120	3200	200	189.0	R7s
	P2/15	—	220/240	3400	75	189.0	R7s
650 W	P2/6	FAD	120	3200	100	78.0	R7s
	—	DWY	120	3400	25	78.0	R7s
750 W	—	EJG	120	3200	400	78.0	R7s
800 W	P2/13	DXX	220/240	3200	75	78.0	R7s
	P2/11	EME	220/240	3200	150	118.0	R7s
1000 W	—	DXW	120	3200	150	93.0	R7s
	P2/35	—	220/240	3200	150	93.0	R7s
	P2/28	FCM	120	3200	300	118.0	R7s
	P2/28	—	220/240	3200	300	118.0	R7s
	P2/29	FHM	120	3200	300	118.0	R7s
	P2/20	—	220/240	3200	300	118.0	R7s
	—	FFT	120	3200	500	167.0	R7s
	P2/7	EKM	220/240	3200	200	189.0	R7s
1250 W	P2/12	—	220/240	3200	200	189.0	R7s
1500 W	—	FDB	120	3200	400	167.0	R7s
2000 W	P2/27	FEX	220/240	3200	300	143.0	R7s
	–	FEY	120	3200	300	143.0	R7s

Table E.7 European lamps (*continued*)

Par sealed beam incandescent tungsten halogen lamps

	Wattage	*LIF*	*ANSI*	*Volts*	*Col. temp.*	*Life*	*Beam angle°*	*Base*
Par 36	650	—	FCX	120	3200	100	40×30	Ferrule cap
	650	—	DWE	120	3200	100	40×30	Screw terminal
	650	—	FBO	120	3400	30	25×15	Screw terminal
	650	—	FBE	120	5000	35	25×15	Screw terminal
Par 64	500	CP-86	—	220/240	3200	300	10×7	GX16d
	500	CP-87	—	220/240	3200	300	11×9	GX16d
	500	CP-88	—	220/240	3200	300	21×10	GX16d
	1000	—	FFN	120	3200	800	10×7	GX16d
	1000	CP-60	EXC	220/240	3200	300	12×6	GX16d
	1000	—	FFP	120	3200	800	13×10	GX16d
	1000	CP-61	EXD	220/240	3200	300	13×10	GX16d
	1000	—	FFR	120	3200	800	25×14	GX16d
	1000	CP-62	EXE	220/240	3200	300	25×14	GX16d
	1000	—	FFS	120	3200	800	70×70	GX16d
	1000	CP-95	EXG	220/240	3200	300	70×70	GX16d

Discharge lamps

When selecting an alternative discharge lamp consult the luminaire and/or the ballast manufacturer or their representative for a suitable replacement. Lamps of the same rating may have different operating characteristics or may be 'hot restrike' which require higher ignition voltages.

Double-ended linear discharge lamps

Wattage	*Code*	*Lamp volts*	*Correlated colour K*	*Life hrs*	*Maximum length (mm)*	*End caps*
HMI (OSRAM) *Hot Restrike*						
200	HMI200W	80	6000	300	75	X515
575	HMI575W/GS	95	6000	750	135	SFc10
1200	HMI1200W/GS	100	6000	750	220	SFc15.5
2500	HMI2500W/GS	115	6000	500	355	SFa21
2500	HMI2500W/S	115	6000	500	210	SFa21
4000	HMI4000W	200	6000	500	405	SFa21
6000	HMI6000W	123	6000	500	450	S25.5
12000	HMI12000W	224	6000	500	470	S25.5
12000	HMI12000W/GS	160	6000	500	470	S30
18000	HMI18000W	225	6000	250	500	S30
HTI (OSRAM) *Hot Restrike*						
270	HTI250W/D	45	4600	250	93	MO-PIN-1 mm
300	HTI300W/DE	100	6500	600	92	SFc10.4
400	HTI400W/D	55	4600	250	100	MO-PIN-1 mm
600	HTI600W/D	95	5300	250	100	MO-PIN-1 mm
MSI (PHILIPS) *Hot Restrike*						
200	MSI200W	80	5600	300	75	X515
575	MSI575W	95	5600	750	145	SFc10.4

Table E.7 European lamps (*continued*)

Double-ended linear discharge lamps

Wattage	*Code*	*Lamp volts*	*Correlated colour K*	*Life hrs*	*Maximum length (mm)*	*End caps*
1200	MSI1200W	100	5600	750	220	SFc15.5.6
2500	MSI2500W	115	5600	500	355	SFa21.12
4000	MSI4000W	200	6000	500	405	SFa21.12
6000	MSI6000W	123	6000	350	450	S25 5×60
12000	MSI12000W	225	6000	250	470	S25 5×60

Single-ended linear discharge lamps

Wattage	*Code*	*Lamp volts*	*Correlated colour K*	*Life hrs*	*Light centre length (mm)*	*Base*
HMI (OSRAM) ***Hot Restrike***						
125	HMI123W	80	6000	150	26.7	Special
200	HMI200W/SE	70	6000	200	39.0	GZY9.5
270	HMI250W/SE	50	6000	250	35.0	FaX1.5
400	HMI400W/SE	67	6000	650	60.0	GZZ9.5
575	HMI575W/SE	95	6000	750	70.0	G22
1200	HMI1200W/SE	100	6000	750	107.0	G38
2500	HMI2500W/SE	115	6000	500	127.0	G38
4000	HMI4000W/SE	200	6000	500	142.0	G38
HTI (OSRAM)						
150	HTI150W	90	6500	750	30	GY9.5
HTI (OSRAM) ***Hot Restrike***						
270	HTI250W/SE	45	4600	250	35	FaX1.5
400	HTI400W/SE	55	4800	250	35	FaX1.5
600	HTI600W/SE	95	5300	300	35	FaX1.5
1200	HTI1200W/SE	100	6000	600	59	GY22
2500	HTI2500W/SE	115	6000	600	85	G22
HSR (OSRAM)						
400	HSR400W	67	5600	650	62	GX9.5
700	HSR700W	72	6000	1000	75	G22
MSR (PHILIPS)						
200	MSR200	70	5600	200	39	GY9.5
400	MSR400	70	5600	650	62	GX9.5
575	MSR575	95	5600	750	125	GX9.5
700	MSR700	72	5600	1000	75	G22X42
1200	MSR1200	100	5600	800	85	G22/30X53
MSR/SA (PHILIPS) ***Hot Restrike***						
220	MSR200SA	34	5400	500	36.5	GY9.5
400	MSR400SA	54	5400	400	36.5	GY9.5

Table E.7 European lamps (*continued*)

Single-ended linear discharge lamps

Wattage	*Code*	*Lamp volts*	*Correlated colour K*	*Life hrs*	*Light centre length (mm)*	*Base*
MSR/HR (PHILIPS) ***Hot Restrike***						
125	MSR125HR	80	5600	200	39	GZX9.5
200	MSR200HR	70	5600	200	39	GZX9.5
400	MSR400HR	70	5600	650	60	GZZ9.5
575	MSR575GR	95	5600	750	70	G22
1200	MSR1200HR	100	5600	800	107	G38
2500	MSR2500HR	115	5600	500	127	G38
4000	MSR4000HR	200	5600	500	142	G38
SB (PHILIPS)						
220	SN250	75	5600	2000	55	GY9.5
440	SN500	75	5600	2000	70	GX9.5
660	SN660	65	5600	500	80	GY16
880	SN1000	75	5600	750	95	GY16
MSD (PHILIPS)						
200	MSD200	68	5600	750	55	GY9.5
700	MSD700	72	5900	2000	85	G22
CSR (GE)						
400	CSR400/CS	67	5600	650	62	GX9.5
700	CSR700/CS	72	5600	1000	75	G22
1200	CSR1200/CS	100	5600	750	85	G22
CSR (GE) ***Hot Restrike***						
575	CSR575/HR	95	6000	750	70	G22
1200	CSR1200/HR	100	6000	750	107	G38
2500	CSR2500/HR	115	6000	500	127	G38
4000	CSR4000/HR	200	6000	500	142	G38
CSI (GE)						
400	CSI.990201	100	4000	500	25.5	Special Pin
1000	CSI.990221	77	4000	500	63.5	G22
CID (GE) ***Hot Restrike***						
200	CID.990211	70	5500	150	36.5	Special Pin
300	CID.990413	100	5500	350	36.5	Special Pin
575	CID.990415	95	5500	500	52.0	G22
1000	CID.990222	77	5500	500	63.5	G22
2500	CID.990431	100	5500	350	127.0	G38

Table E.7 European lamps (*continued*)

Par sealed beam discharge lamps

Wattage	*Code*	*Lamp volts*	*Correlated colour K*	*Life hrs*	*Par (1/8″ units)*	*Base*
HMI (OSRAM) ***Hot Restrike***						
1200	HMI1200WPAR	100	6000	1000	64	G38
CSI (GE)						
100	CSI.991222	77	3800	3500	64	G38
CSI (GE) ***Hot Restrike***						
1000	CSI.991422/HR	77	3800	3500	64	G38
CID (GE)						
1000	CID.991225	77	5500	1500	64	G38
CID (GE) ***Hot Restrike***						
1000	CID.991425/HR	77	5500	1000	64	G38
1200	CID.991435/HR	100	5500	1000	64	G38

Appendix F

Gels and diffusions

Table F.1 Kelvin conversion: Lee colour correction gel

Kelvin	0	100	200	300	400	500	600	700	800	900
2000	500	476	455	435	417	400	385	370	357	345
3000	333	323	313	303	294	286	278	270	263	256
4000	250	244	238	233	227	222	217	213	208	204
5000	200	196	192	189	185	182	179	175	172	169
6000	167	164	161	159	156	154	152	149	147	145
7000	143	141	139	137	135	133	132	130	128	127
8000	125	123	122	120	119	118	116	115	114	112
9000	111	110	109	108	106	105	104	103	102	101

Example: To find the MIRED value for a 6500 Kelvin source, look across from 6000, and down from 500. The MIRED value is 154.

Table F.2 Kelvin conversion: Rosco colour correction gel

Light source colour (K)	*CTO (Orange)*				*CTB (Blue)*			
	Lee 223 Eighth	*Lee 206 Quarter*	*Lee 205 Half*	*Lee 204 Full*	*Lee 218 Eighth*	*Lee 203 Quarter*	*Lee 205 Half*	*Lee 201 Full*
2000	1901	1773	1642	1517	2075	2151	2370	2755
2300	1786	1672	1555	1443	1938	2004	2193	2519
2600	2433	2227	2024	1838	2725	2857	3257	4032
2900	2695	2445	2203	1984	3058	3226	3745	4808
3200	2959	2660	2375	2123	3401	3610	4274	5714
3500	3205	2857	2532	2247	3731	3984	4808	6711
3800	3460	3058	2688	2370	4082	4386	5405	7937
4400	3953	3436	2976	2591	4785	5208	6711	11111
5000	4425	3788	3236	2786	5495	6061	8197	15873
5600	4878	4115	3472	2959	6211	6944	9901	23810
6200	5348	4444	3704	3125	6993	7937	12048	41667
6800	5780	4739	3906	3268	7752	8929	14493	100000
7400	6211	5025	4098	3401	8547	10000	17544	
8000	6623	5291	4274	3521	9346	11111	21277	
9000	7299	5714	4545	3704	10753	13158	30303	

Table F.3 Kelvin conversion: GAM colour correction gel

Light source colour (K)	CTO (Orange)						CTB (Blue)						
	R-3410 Eighth	*R-3409 Quarter*	*R-3408 Half*	*R-3411 3/4*	*R-3401 Sun 85*	*R-3407 Full*	*R-3216 Eighth*	*R-3208 Quarter*	*R-3206 Third*	*R-3204 Half*	*R-3203 3/4*	*R-3202 Full*	*R-3220 2 × CTB*
2000	1923	1845	1721	1585	1585	1499	2049	2128	2217	2315	2500	2710	4115
2300	1805	1736	1626	1504	1504	1427	1916	1984	2062	2146	2304	2481	3610
2600	2469	2342	2146	1938	1938	1812	2681	2817	2976	3155	3509	3937	7813
2900	2740	2584	2347	2101	2101	1953	3003	3175	3378	3610	4082	4673	11364
3200	3012	2825	2545	2257	2257	2088	3333	3546	3802	4098	4717	5525	18182
3500	3268	3049	2725	2398	2398	2208	3650	3906	4219	4587	5376	6452	34483
3800	3534	3279	2907	2538	2538	2326	3984	4292	4673	5128	6135	7576	166667
4400	4049	3717	3247	2793	2793	2538	4651	5076	5618	6289	7874	10417	
5000	4545	4132	3559	3021	3021	2725	5319	5882	6623	7576	10000	14493	
5600	5025	4525	3846	3226	3226	2890	5988	6711	7692	9009	12658	20833	
6200	5525	4926	4132	3425	3425	3049	6711	7634	8929	10753	16393	33333	
6800	5988	5291	4386	3597	3597	3185	7407	8547	10204	12658	21277	62500	
7400	6452	5650	4630	3759	3759	3311	8130	9524	11628	14925	28571		
8000	6897	5988	4854	3906	3906	3425	8850	10526	13158	17544	40000		
9000	7634	6536	5208	4132	4132	3597	10101	12346	16129	23256	90909		

Table F.4 Kelvin/MIRED conversion table

Light source colour (K)	CTO (Orange)						CTB (Blue)					
	1555 Eighth	*1552 Quarter*	*1549 Half*	*1546 3/4 CTO*	*1543 Full*	*1540 Extra CTO*	*1535 Eighth*	*1532 Quarter*	*1529 Half*	*1526 3/4 Blue*	*1523 Full*	*1520 Extra CTB*
2000	1916	1852	1721	1585	1520	1294	2037	2110	2315	2577	2703	2817
2300	1799	1742	1626	1504	1445	1239	1905	1969	2146	2370	2475	2571
2600	2457	2353	2146	1938	1842	1520	2660	2786	3155	3663	3922	4167
2900	2725	2597	2347	2101	1988	1618	2976	3135	3610	4292	4651	5000
3200	2994	2841	2545	2257	2128	1709	3300	3497	4098	5000	5495	5988
3500	3247	3067	2725	2398	2252	1789	3610	3846	4587	5747	6410	7092
3800	3509	3300	2907	2538	2375	1866	3937	4219	5128	6623	7519	8475
4400	4016	3745	3247	2793	2597	2000	4587	4975	6289	8696	10309	12195
5000	4505	4167	3559	3021	2793	2114	5236	5747	7576	11364	14286	18182
5600	4975	4566	3846	3226	2967	2212	5882	6536	9009	14925	20408	29412
6200	5464	4975	4132	3425	3135	2304	6579	7407	10753	20408	32258	62500
6800	5917	5348	4386	3597	3279	2381	7246	8264	12658	28571	58824	500000
7400	6369	5714	4630	3759	3413	2451	7937	9174	14925	43478	200000	
8000	6803	6061	4854	3906	3534	2513	8621	10101	17544	76923		
9000	7519	6623	5208	4132	3717	2604	9804	11765	23256			

Table F.5 Daylight colour correction gels (CTO)

Name	*Rosco Cinegel*	*MIRED shift*	*Lee*	*MIRED shift*	*GAM*	*MIRED shift*	*K shift*	*Light reduction (stops)*
Extra CTO	—	—	—	—	1540	+273	20,000K to 3200K	1
							5500K to 2200K	
Full CTO	3407	+167	204*	+159	1543	+163	6500K to 3200K	
Full Straw	3441		441				5500K to 2900K	2/3
Sun 85	3401	+131	—	—	—	—	5500K to 3200K	2/3
85 Acrylic	3761							
3/4 CTO	3411	+130	285	—	1546	+130	5500K to 3200K	2/3
1/2 CTO	3408	+81	205*	+109	1549	+81	5500K to 3800K	1/2
1/2 Straw	3442		441					
12 CTO Acrylic	3751							
1/4 CTO	3409	+42	206*	+64	1552	+40	5500K to 4500K	1/3
1/4 Straw	3443		441					
1/8 CTO	3410	+20	223*	+26	1555	+22	5500K to 4900K	1/4
1/8 Straw	3444		441					

*Also available in 60-in. rolls.

Table F.6 Neutral density and neutral density daylight correction gels (CTO ND)

Gel	*Rosco Cinegel*	*MIRED shift*	*Lee*	*MIRED shift*	*GAM*	*K shift*	*Light reduction (stops)*
.15 ND	3415	0	298	0	1514	0	1/2
.3 ND Acrylic	3402 3762	0	209*	0	1515	0	1
.6 ND Acrylic	3403 3763	0	210*	0	1516	0	2
.9 ND Acrylic	3404 3764	0	211*	0	1517	0	3
1.2 ND	—	—	299	0	1518	0	4
CTO .3 ND	3405	+131	207	+159	1556	5500K to 3200K	1
CTO .6 ND	3406	+131	208	+159	1557	5500K to 3200K	2
CTO .9 ND	—	—	—	—	1558	5500K to 3200K	3

*Also available in 60-in. rolls.
Cinemills Corporation makes gels that share the same product numbers as Lee.

Table F.7 Tungsten correction gels (CTB)

Name	*Rosco Cinegel*	*MIRED shift*	*Lee*	*MIRED shift*	*GAM*	*K shift*	*Light reduction (stops)*
Double Blue	3220	–257	200	—	—	2800K to 10,000K	4
Extra CTB	—	–150	—	—	1520	3200K to 6200K	1 3/4
Full CTB	3202	–131	201	–137	1523	3200K to 5700K	1 1/3
3/4 CTB	3203	—	281	—	1526		1 1/4
1/2 CTB	3204	–68	205	–78	1529	3200K to 4300K	1
1/3 CTB	3206	–49	—	—	—	3200K to 3800K	2/3
1/4 CTB	3208	–30	203	–35	1532	3200K to 3600K	2/3
1/8 CTB	3216	–12	218	–18	1535	3200K to 3400K	1/3

Cinemills Corporation makes gels that share the same product numbers as Lee.

Table F.8 Blue/Orange correction: colourmeter LB Index (MIREDs) and corresponding camera filters and colour correction gels

Colourmeter LB reading (MIREDs)	*Kodak Wratten Filter*		*Light loss due to filter*	*Approximate equivalent gel*	*Kelvin shift*	
	Amber	*Blue*			*from*	*to*
–257	—	—	4	Double CTB	3200	10,000
–133	—	80A	2	Full CTB	3200	5500
–112	—	80B	1 2/3	—	3400	5500
–100	—	80C+82A	—	3/4 CTB	3200	4700
–90	—	82C+82C	1 1/3	—	2490	3200
–81	—	80C	1	1/2 CTB	3800	5500
–77	—	82C+82B	1 1/3	—	2570	3200
–66	—	82C+82A	1	—	2650	3200
–56	—	80D	1/3	—	4200	5500
–55	—	82C+82	1	1/3 CTB	2720	3200
–45	—	82C	2/3	—	2800	3200
–32	—	82B	2/3	1/4 CTB	2900	3200
–21	—	82A	1/3	1/8 CTB	3000	3200
–10	—	82	1/3	—	3100	3200
+9	81	—	1/3	—	3300	3200
+18	81A	—	1/3	—	3400	3200
+27	81B	—	1/3	1/8 CTO	3500	3200
+35	81C	—	1/3	—	3600	3200
+42	81D	—	2/3	1/4 CTO	3700	3200
+52	81EF	—	2/3	—	3850	3200
+81	85C	—	1/3	1/2 CTO	5500	3800
+112	85	—	2/3	—	5500	3400
+133	85B	—	2/3	3/4 CTO or Sun 85	5500	3200
+167	85B+81C	—	2/3	Full CTO	5600	2900

Table F.9 Green/Magenta correction: colourmeter CC index and corresponding gels and filters

Colourmeter II colour compensation	Colourmeter III CC filter Magenta	CC filter Green	Gel source with Gel name	Rosco Cinegel no.	Lee Gel no.	CAM Gel no.	Compensation in f-stops	Conversion
+18	40M	—	—	—	—	—	2/3	Removes Green
+13	30M	—	Full Minus Green	3308	247	1580	2/3	"
+8	20M	—	—	—	—	—	1/3	"
+6	15M	—	Half Minus Green	3313	248	1582	1/3	"
+4	10M	—	—	—	—	—	1/3	"
+3	7.5M	—	1/4 Minus Green	3314	249	1583	1/3	"
+2	5M	—	—	—	—	—	1/3	"
+1	3.5M	—	1/8 Minus Green	3318	279	1584	1/4	"
–1	—	3.5G	1/8 Plus Green	3317	278	—	1/4	Adds Green
–2	—	7.5G	1/4 Plus Green	3316	246	—	1/3	"
–4	—	10G	—	—	—	—	1/3	"
–5	—	15G	1/2 Plus Green	3315	245	1587	1/3	"
–7	—	20G	—	—	—	—	1/3	"
–10	—	30G	Full Plus Green	3304	244	1585	2/3	"
–13	—	40G	—	—	—	—	2/3	"
—	30M	—	Fluoro-Filter	3310	—	1590	1 2/3	Converts cool whites to 3200K
—	—	30G	Plus-green 50	3306	—	—	1 1/4	Converts 3200K source to match cool whites
—	—	30G	Fluorescent 5700	—	241	—	1 2/3	Converts 3200K source to 5700K (cool white fluorescents)
—	—	30G	Fluorescent 4300	—	242	—	1 1/2	Converts 3200K source to 4300K (white fluorescents)
—	—	30G	Fluorescent 3600	—	243	—	1 1/4	Converts 3200K source to 3600K (warm white fluorescents)

Table F.10 Theatrical gels

Gamcolor Gels		440	Very Light Straw	950	Purple
The Great American Market		450	Saffron	960	Medium Lavender
105	Antique Rose	460	Mellow Yellow	970	Special Lavender
	(Minusgreen)	470	Pale Gold	980	Surprise Pink
106	1/2 Antique Rose	480	Medium Lemon	995	Orchid
	(1/2 Minusgreen)	510	No Color Straw		
107	1/4 Antique Rose	520	New Straw	**Lee Gels**	
	(1/4 Minusgreen)	535	Lime (1/2 Plusgreen)	*Cosmetic Range*	
108	1/8 Antique Rose	540	Pale Green (Plusgreen)	184	Cosmetic Peach
	(1/8 Minusgreen)	570	Light Green Yellow	185	Cosmetic Burgundy
110	Dark Rose	650	Grass Green	186	Cosmetic Silver Rose
120	Bright Pink	655	Rich Green	187	Cosmetic Rouge
130	Rose	660	Medium Green	188	Cosmetic Highlight
140	Dark Magenta	680	Kelly Green	189	Cosmetic Silver Moss
150	Pink Punch	685	Pistachio	190	Cosmetic Emerald
155	Light Pink	690	Bluegrass	191	Cosmetic Aqua Blue
160	Chorus Pink	710	Blue Green		
170	Dark Flesh Pink	720	Light Steel Green	*Theatrical Colours*	
180	Cherry	725	Princess Blue	002	Rose Pink
190	Cold Pink	730	Azure Blue	003	Lavender Tint
195	Nymph Pink	740	Off Blue	004	Medium Bastard
220	Pink Magenta	750	Nile Blue		Amber (HT)
235	Pink Red	760	Aqua Blue	007	Pale Yellow (HT)
245	Light Red	770	Christel Blue	008	Dark Salmon (HT)
250	Medium Red XT	780	Shark Blue	009	Pale Amber Gold (HT)
260	Rosy Amber	790	Electric Blue	010	Medium Yellow (HT)
270	Red Orange	810	Moon Blue	013	Straw Tint (HT)
280	Fire Red	820	Full Light Blue	015	Deep Straw (HT)
290	Fire Orange	830	North Sky Blue	019	Fire (HT)
305	French Rose	835	Aztec Blue	020	Medium Amber (HT)
315	Autumn Glory	840	Steel Blue	021	Gold Amber (HT)
320	Peach	842	Whisper Blue (1/2 CTB)	022	Dark Amber (HT)
323	Indian Summer	845	Cobalt	024	Scarlet (HT)
325	Bastard Amber	847	City Blue (Extra CTB)	026	Bright Red (HT)
330	Sepia	848	Bonus Blue	027	Medium Red (HT)
335	Coral (Extra CTO)	850	Primary Blue	035	Light Pink (HT)
340	Light Bastard Amber	860	Sky Blue	036	Medium Pink (HT)
343	Honey (Full CTO)	870	Whinter White (1/8 CTB)	046	Dark Magenta (HT)
345	Deep Amber	880	Daylight Blue	048	Rose Pink
350	Dark Amber	882	Southern Sky (Full CTB)	052	Light Lavender (HT)
360	Amber Blush (1/2 CTO)	885	Blue Ice (1/4 CTB)	053	Paler Lavender (HT)
363	Sand	888	Blue Bell (3/4 CTB)	058	Lavender (HT)
364	Pale Honey (1/4 CTO)	890	Dark Sky Blue	061	Mist Blue (HT)
365	Warm Straw	905	Dark Blue	063	Pale Blue (HT)
370	Spice (CTO/N.6)	910	Alice Blue	068	Sky Blue
375	Flame	920	Pale Lavender	079	Just Blue (HT)
380	Golden Tan (CTO/N.3)	930	Real Congo Blue	085	Deeper Blue (HT)
385	Light Amber	940	Light Purple	089	Moss Green (HT)
390	Walnut (CTO/N.9)	945	Royal Purple	090	Dark Yellow Green (HT)
420	Medium Amber	948	African Violet	101	Yellow

HT = High temperature polycarbonate base.

Table F.10 Theatrical gels (*continued*)

102	Light Amber	174	Dark Steel Blue	21	Golden Amber
103	Straw	176	Loving Amber	321	Soft Golden Amber
104	Deep Amber	179	Chroma Orange	22	Deep Amber
105	Orange	180	Dark Lavender	23	Orange
106	Primary Red	181	Congo Blue (HT)	24	Scarlet
107	Light Rose	182	Light Red	25	Orange Red
109	Light Salmon	183	Moonlight Blue	26	Light Red
110	Middle Rose	192	Flesh Pink	27	Medium Red
111	Dark Pink	193	Rosy Amber	30	Light Salmon Pink
113	Magenta	194	Surprise Pink	31	Salmon Pink
115	Peacock Blue (HT)	195	Zenith Blue (HT)	32	Medium Salmon Pink
116	Medium Green Blue (HT)	196	True Blue	332	Cherry Rose
117	Steel Blue	197	Alice Blue (HT)	33	No Colour Pink
118	Light Blue (HT)	332	Follies Pink	333	Blush Pink
119	Dark Blue (HT)	332	Special Rose Pink	34	Flesh Pink
120	Deep Blue (HT)	343	Special Medium Lavender	35	Light Pink
121	Lee Green (HT)	344	Violet	36	Medium Pink
122	Fern Green (HT)	353	Lighter Blue	37	Pale Rose Pink
124	Dark Green (HT)	354	Special Steel Blue	337	True Pink
126	Mauve	363	Special Medium Blue	38	Light Rose
127	Smoky Pink		(HT)	39	Skelton Exotic Sangria
128	Bright Pink			339	Broadway Pink
129	Heavy Frost	**Roscolux Gel**		40	Light Salmon
130	Clear	*(in sheets and 24 in. rolls)*		41	Salmon
132	Medium Blue (HT)	00	Clear	42	Deep Salmon
134	Golden Amber	01	Light Bastard Amber	342	Rose Pink
135	Deep Golden Amber	02	Bastard Amber	43	Deep Pink
136	Pale Lavender	03	Dark Bastard Amber	44	Middle Rose
137	Special Lavender	04	Medium Bastard Amber	344	Follies Pink
138	Pale Green	304	Pale Apricot	45	Rose
139	Primary Green (HT)	05	Rose Tint	46	Magenta
141	Bright Blue (HT)	305	Rose Gold	47	Light Rose Purple
142	Pale Violet	06	No Colour Straw	48	Rose Purple
143	Pale Navy Blue	07	Pale Yellow	49	Medium Purple
144	No Colour Blue	08	Pale Gold	349	Fisher Fuchsia
147	Apricot	09	Pale Amber Gold	50	Mauve
148	Bright Rose	10	Medium Yellow	51	Surprise Pink
151	Golt Tint	310	Daffodil	52	Light Lavender
152	Pale Gold	11	Light Straw	53	Pale Lavender
153	Pale Salmon	12	Straw	54	Special Lavender
154	Pale Rose	312	Canary	55	Lilac
156	Chocolate	13	Straw Tint	355	Pale Violet
157	Pink	14	Medium Straw	56	Middle Lavender
158	Deep Orange	15	Deep Straw	57	Lavender
159	No Colour Straw	16	Light Amber	357	Royal Lavender
161	Slate Blue	316	Gallo Gold	58	Deep Lavender
162	Bastard Amber	17	Light Flame	358	Rose Indigo
164	Flame Red	317	Apricot	59	Indigo
165	Daylight Blue	18	Flame	359	Medium Violet
166	Pale Red	318	Mayan Sun	60	No Colour Blue
170	Deep Lavender	19	Fire	360	Clearwater
172	Lagoon Blue (HT)	20	Medium Amber	61	Mist Blue

Table F.10 Theatrical gels (*continued*)

62	Booster Blue	89	Moss Green	623	Light Pink
63	Pale Blue	389	Chroma Green	624	Pink
363	Aquamarine	90	Dark Yellow Green	625	Pale Rose Pink
64	Light Steel Blue	91	Primary Green	626	Flesh Pink
364	Blue Bell	92	Turquoise	627	Rose Pink
65	Daylight Blue	93	Blue Green	631	Middle Rose
365	Cool Blue	94	Kelly Green	632	Salmon
66	Cool Blue	95	Medium Blue Green	638	Light Rose Purple
67	Light Sky Blue	395	Teal Green	639	Lilac
68	Sky Blue	96	Lime	641	Lavender
69	Brilliant Blue	97	Light Grey	642	Surprise Pink
70	Nile Blue	397	Pale Grey	644	Deep Lilac
71	Sea Blue	98	Medium Grey	645	Indigo
72	Azure Blue	99	Chocolate	647	Pale Blue
73	Peacock Blue			648	No Colour Blue
74	Night Blue	**Rosco Cinecolor Gel**		649	Booster Blue
76	Light Green Blue	*(in 48 in. rolls)*		651	Light Steel Blue
376	Bermuda Blue	602	Bastard Amber	652	Azure Blue
77	Green Blue	603	Warm Rose	654	Daylight Blue
78	Trudy Blue	604	No Color Straw	657	Primary Blue
378	Alice Blue	605	Pale Gold	658	Medium Green Blue
79	Bright Blue	608	Warm Straw	659	Green Blue
80	Primary Blue	609	Straw	661	Medium Blue
81	Urban Blue	610	Light Flame	669	Pale Yellow Green
82	Surprise Blue	611	Rose Amber	671	Light Green
83	Medium Blue	612	Golden Amber	672	Moss Green
383	Sapphire Blue	613	Light Amber	673	Turquoise
84	Zephyr Blue	614	Flame	674	Primary Green
85	Deep Blue	615	Deep Straw	675	Light Blue Green
385	Royal Blue	617	Peach	676	Blue Green
86	Pea Green	618	Orange	677	Medium Blue Green
87	Pale Yellow Green	620	Deep Salmon	680	Light Grey
88	Light Green	621	Light Red	681	Medium Grey
388	Gaslight Green	622	Pink Tint	682	Chocolate

Table F.11 Diffusion

Types of diffusion	*Product no.*	*Light reduction*	*Notes*
Lee			
Full Tough Spun	214	2 1/2	Slight softening of field and beam edge.
Half Tough Spun	215	1 1/2	Slight softening of field and beam edge.
Quarer Tough Spun	229	3/4	Slight softening of field and beam edge.
Full Tough Spun	261	2	Flame retardant. Slight softening of field and beam edge.
3/4 Tough Spun	262	1 2/3	Flame retardant.
1/2 Tough Spun	263	1 1/3	Flame retardant.
3/8 Tough Spun	264	1	Flame retardant.
1/4 Tough Spun	265	3/4	Flame retardant.
216 White Diffusion	216	1 1/2	Very popular moderate/heavy diffusion. Available in 60″ width.
1/2 216	250	3/4	Moderate beam spread and softening.
1/4 216	251	1/3	Moderate beam spread and softening.
1/8 216	252	1/8	Moderate beam spread and softening.
Blue Diffusion	217	1 1/2	Increases colour temperature very slighty.
Daylight Blue Frost	224	2 1/4	CTB frost.
Neutral Density Frost	225	2	ND 0.6 frost.
Brushed Silk	228	3/4	Diffuses light in one direction only.
Hampshire Frost	253	1/4	Very light frost.
New Hampshire Frost	254	—	High-temperature polycarbonate base
Hollywood Frost	255	—	—
Half Hampshire	256	—	—
Quarter Hampshire	257	—	—
Heavy Frost	129	1 1/3	Flame retardant.
White Frost	220	1 1/3	Flame retardant.
Blue Frost	221	1 1/3	Flame retardant. Increases colour temperature very slightly.
Grid Cloth	430	—	Heavy white fabric 52-in.width.
Light Grid Cloth	432	—	Lighter white fabric in 52-in. width.
Rosco			
Tough Spun	3006	2 1/2	Slight softening of field and beam edge.
Light Tough Spun	3007	1 2/3	Slight softening of field and beam edge.
1/4 Tough Spun	3022	1	Slight softening of field and beam edge.
Tough Frost	3008	2	Slight to moderate softening, moderate beam spread but with discernible beam centre.
Light Tough Frost	3009	1 1/2	Slight to moderate softening, moderate beam spread but with discernible beam centre.
Opal Tough Frost	3010	1	Popular light diffusion with slight to moderate softening, moderate beam spread but with discernible beam centre.
Light Opal	3020	1/2	Slight to moderatc softening, moderate beam spread but with discernible beam centre.
Tough White Diffusion	3026	3 1/2	Like Lee 216. Dense diffusion with wide beam spread creating even field of shadowless light.
1/2 White Diffusion	3027	2 1/2	Like Lee 250. Moderately dense diffusion with wide beam spread.
1/4 White Diffusion	3028	1 1/2	Like Lee 251. Moderate diffusion with wide beam spread.
Tough Rolux	3000	2 1/2	Moderately dense diffusion with wide beam spread.

Table F.11 Diffusion (*continued*)

Types of diffusion	*Product no.*	*Light reduction*	*Notes*
Light Tough Rolux	3001	—	Moderate diffusion with wide beam spread.
Grid Cloth	3030	5	Comes in 54 in. rolls. Very dense diffusion with very wide beam spread which creates soft shadowless light. Ideal for large area diffusion. Not tolerant of high heat.
Light Grid Cloth	3032	3 1/2	Smaller weave than grid cloth. Considerable softening. Comes in 54 in. rolls.
1/4 Grid Cloth	3034	2 1/2	Considerable softening. Comes in 54 in. rolls.
Silent Frost	3029	3	Diffusion made of a rubbery plastic that does not crinkle and rattle in the wind.
Hilite	3014	1	Quiet like silent frost. Comes in 54 in. rolls.
Soft Frost	3002	2	Quite like silent frost, denser than Hilite.
Wide Soft Frost	3023	2	In 72 in. width.
1/2 Soft Frost	3004	1/2	Quiet, light diffuser
Tough Silk	3011	1 1/2	Considerable softening in one direction only.
Light Tough Silk	3015	1	Considerable softening in one direction only.
Tough Booster Silk	3012	—	Raises colour temperature from 3200K to 3500K with silk softening characteristics.
Tough Booster Frost	3013	—	Raises colour temperature from 3200K to 3800K with frost softening characteristics.
Full Blue Frost	3017	—	Raises colour temperature from 3200K to daylight with frost softening characteristics.
GAM—The Great American Market			
Medium GAM Frost	10	—	Soft light, warm centre, diffuse edge.
Light GAM Frost	15	—	Soft light, warm centre, diffuse edge.
Full GAM Spun	32	2 1/2	Textural, warm centre defined edge.
Medium GAM Spun	35	1 2/3	Textural, warm centre defined edge.
Light GAM Spun	38	1	Textural, warm centre defined edge.
Gamvel	45	3	Soft light with diffuse shadow line.
216 GAM White	55	—	Shadowless, white light. Heavy diffusion with no centre or edge visible.
Medium GAM Silk	65	—	Spreads light predominantly in one direction.
Light GAM Silk	68	—	Spreads light predominantly in one direction.
Gam Fusion	10-10	1/4	Almost clear with no colour shift.
Gam Fusion	10-20	1/4	Very light diffusion with no colour shift.
Gam Fusion	10-30	1/2	Light diffusion with no colour shift.
Gam Fusion	10-40	1/2	Medium-light diffusion with no colour shift.
Gam Fusion	10-50	1	Medium diffusion with no colour shift.
Gam Fusion	10-60	2	Medium-heavy diffusion with no colour shift.
Gam Fusion	10-70	5	Heavy diffusion with no colour shift.
Gam Fusion	10-75	5	Heavy diffusion with no colour shift.
Gam Fusion	10-80	6	Very heavy diffusion with no colour shift.
Gam Fusion	10-90	6	Fully diffuse with no colour shift.

Note: Light reduction values given here are manufacturers' approximate figures. The actual transmission will depend on the beam angle of the light and the distance from the diffusion.

Appendix G

Equipment manufacturers and distributors

Abbott and Co., 1611 Cascada Dr., Marion, OH 43302. Electrical connectors.

ADB UK, ADB House, 15 Woking Business Park, Albert Drive, Woking, Surrey, GU21 5JY, UK. Lighting controls systems, dimmers, luminaires, suspension, systems.

Airstar, Lenix helium balloons. Contact Industrial Wholesale Electric Co., 1500 S. Griffith Ave., Los Angeles, CA 90021.

Altman Stage Lighting Company, Inc. 57 Alexander St., Yonkers, NY 10701. Tungsten and HMI fixtures, ellipsoidal and theatrical fixtures.

American Studio Equipment, 8922 Norris Ave., Sun Valley, CA 91352. Studio and grip equipment.

Arri, 617 Route 303, Blauvelt, NY 10913; 600 N. Victory Blvd., Burbank, CA 91502. Tungsten and HMI lights.

Arri (GB) Ltd, 1–3 Airlinks, Spitfire Way, Heston, TW5 9NR, England. www.arri.com

Automated Entertainment, P.O. Box 7309, Burbank, CA 91510-7309. Range of dichroic filters, backlights, fully stocked theatrical rental house.

Avolites Limited, 184 Park Avenue, Park Royal, London, NW10 7XL, UK. Lighting consoles and dimming systems.

Backstage Studio Equipment, 8010 Wheatland Ave., Unit D, Sun Valley, CA 91352. Studio equipment.

Benjamin Electric Co., 1615 Staunton Ave., Los Angeles, CA 90021. Distribution boxes, deuce boards, studio distribution equipment.

Cam-Lok, 531 Fifth St., Unit E, San Fernando, CA 91340. Electrical connectors.

Carol Cable Co., Inc. Pawtucket, RI 02862. Cable.

CCT Lighting Ltd, 4 Turdor Court, Brighton Road, Sutton, Surrey, SM2 5AE, UK. Luminaires and accessories; control systems.

Chimera Photographic Lighting, 1812 Valtec La., Boulder, CO 80301. Soft boxes.

Cinemills Corp., 3500 W. Magnolia Blvd., Burbank, CA 91505. HMI bulbs and lights, gel.

Clairmont Camera. 4040 Vineland Ave., Studio City, CA 91604. Synchronous strobe system, camera rental.

Dedotec USA Inc., 410 Garibaldi Ave., Lodi, NJ 07644. Tungsten lights.

DeSisti, Desmar Corp., 1109 Grand Ave., North Bergen, NJ 07147. Tungsten HMI lights.

DeSisti Lighting Ltd, 15 Old Market Street, Thetford, Norfolk, IP24 2EQ, UK. Luminaires.

Di-Lite (Koto Luminous Corp.), Fujita Estate Building, 5th Floor, 4–8 Ueno 1-Chrome, Taito-ku, Tokyo, Japan 110. HMI bulbs.

DN Labs, 1430 Willamette St., Suite 18, Eugene, OR 97401. HMI lights.

Doughty Engineering Ltd, Crow Arch Lane, Ringwood, Hampshire BH24 1NZ, UK. Grip equipment.

Electronic Theatre Controls (ETC) 3030 Laura Ln., Middleton, WI 53562. Dimmer systems, ellipsoidal and par fixtures.

Electronic Theatre Controls Europe Ltd, Unit 5, Victoria Industrial Estate, Victoria Road, London, W3 6UU. Lighting, control and dimmers.

ExCel Wire and Cable Co., 180 Elm Ave., Tiffin, OH 44883. Cable.

Fisher lights. 5528 Vineland Ave. North Hollywood, CA 91601. Large soft boxes for car photography, soft light crane light.

John Fluke Mfg. Co., Inc., P.O. Box 9090 Everett, WA 98206. Electrical meters.

General Electric, Nela Park, E. Cleveland, OH 44112. Tungsten and HMI bulbs.

Genie USA, 18340 N.E. 76th St., P.O. Box 69, Redmond, WA 98073-0069. Man lift.

Giddings Pace, Inc., 8001 Capwell Dr., Oakland, CA 94621. Underwater HMI lights.

Great American Market, 826 N. Cole Ave., Hollywood, CA 90038. Stick-up lights, flicker boxes, GAM gels, colour changers.

Group 5 Engineering, 11620 Exposition Blvd., Los Angeles, CA 90064. Bates connectors.

High End Systems, 2217 West Braker Lane, Austin, TX 78758. Automated lights.

Hydro Image, Inc., 4121 Redwood Ave., Los Angeles, CA 90066. SeaPar underwater lights and cameras.

ILC Technology Inc., 399 Java Dr., Sunnyvale, CA 94089. HMI bulbs.

Innovision Optics. Santa Monica, CA. Fibre-optics lighting systems.

K 5600, 10434 Burbank Blvd., North Hollywood, CA 91601. HMI Joker fixtures and 200W Bug light and 200W inverter.

Kino Flo, Inc., 8824 Lankershim Blvd., Sun Valley, CA 91352. Fluorescent lights.

Lee Filters, Central Way, Walworth Industrial Estate, Andover, Hampshire, SP10 5AN, UK.

Leonetti (Sunray), 5609 Sunset Blvd., Hollywood, CA 90028. HMI and fluorescent fixtures.

Lightmaker, 28145 Ave. Crocker, Valencia, CA 91355. AC/DC and AC lightweight flicker-free ballasts.

Lightning Strikes, 6571 Santa Monica Blvd., Hollywood, CA 90038. Lightning effects lights.

Lowel-Light Manfacturing, Inc., 140 58th St., Brooklyn, NY 11220. Tungsten fixtures.

L.P. Associates, 6650 Lexington Ave., Hollywood, CA 90038. DCI lights and globes.

LTM Corp. of America, 11646 Pendleton St., Sun Valley, CA 91352-2501. Tungsten and HMI fixtures.

Magic Gadgets/William A. McIntire Enterprises, Box 4244, Portland, OR 97208. Dimmers, flicker effects boxes, various gadgets.

Matthews Studio Equipment, Inc., 2405 Empire Ave., Burbank, CA 91504. Studio equipment.

Meltric Corp., 6212 Ace Industrial Dr., Cundahy, WI 53110. Electrical connectors.

Minolta, 11150 Hope St., Cypress, CA 90630. Light meters.

Mole-Richardson Co., 937 N. Sycamore Ave., Hollywood, CA 90038-2384. Tungsten and HMI fixtures, studio equipment, distribution equipment, carbon arc lights.

Musco Mobile Lighting Ltd., Hwy. 63 S., P.O. Box 73, Oskaloosa, IA 52577. Mobile lighting trucks.

Norms, 5219 Craner Ave., North Hollywood, CA 91601. Studio equipment.

Osram Corp., 110 Bracken Rd., Montgomery, NY 12549-9700; 7658 Haskell Ave., Van Nuys, CA 91406. HMI bulbs.

Peterson Systems International, 2350 E. Central Ave., Duarte, CA 91010. Cable crossovers.

Philips Lighting Co., 200 Franklin Square Dr., P.O. Box 6800, Somerset, NJ 08875-6800. Bulbs.

Phoebus Manufacturing, 200 Third Street, San Francisco, CA 94107. Xenon follow spots and searchlights, electronic shutters, xenon projector and other speciality items.

Power Gems Corporation, 8010 Weatland Ave. G, Sun Valley, CA 91352.

Power Gems Ltd., Sherrington House, Clifton Road, Monton, Eccles M30 9QS, England. Electronic HMI ballasts.

Rosco Laboratories, Inc., 36 Bush Ave., Port Chester, NY 10573. Gel.

Roscolab Ltd, Blanchard Works, Kangley Bridge Road, Sydenham, London, SE26 5AQ, UK. Gels/filters, dimmers.

Royal Electric, Inc., 95 Grand Ave., Pawtucket, RI 02862. Cable.

Sachtler, 55 N. Main St., Freeport, NY 11520. Tungsten and HMI fixtures.

Shotmaker, 28145 Ave. Crocker, Valencia, CA 91355. Custom tow vehicles.

Snorkelift, P.O. Box 4065, St. Joseph, MO 64504-4065. Telescoping boom platforms.

SpectraCine, Inc., 820 N. Hollywood Way, Burbank, CA 91505. Light meters.

Strand Lighting, Inc., 18111 S. Santa Fe Ave., P.O. Box 9004, Rancho Dominguez, CA 90021. Tungsten and HMI fixtures, ellipsoidal and theatrical fixtures, dimmer packs.

Strand Lighting Ltd, North Hyde House, North Hyde Wharf, Hayes Road, Heston, Middlesex, UB25 5NL. Lighting equipment, controls, etc.

Strong International, Inc., 4350 McKinley St., Omaha, NE 68112. Xenon, HMI, and tungsten follow spots.

Studio Lighting, Inc., 13831 Herrick Ave., Sylmar, CA 91342. Space lights.

Sylvania, 500 N. State College Blvd., P.O. Box 14154, Orange, CA 92613-1554; 6505 E. Gayhart St., P.O. Box 2795, Los Angeles, CA 90051; 630 Fifth Ave., Suite 2670, New York, NY 10111. Tungsten and HMI bulbs.

Teatronics, 3100 McMillan Rd., San Luis Obispo, CA 93401. Dimmers.

Ultra Light Manufacturing Co., 6590 S. Bermuda Rd., Las Vegas, NV 89119. Tungsten lights and grip equipment.

Unilux, Inc., 290 Lodi St., Hackensack, NJ 07601. Strobe lighting system.

Union Connector, 300 Babylon Tnpk., Roosevelt, NY 11575. Distribution boxes, electrical connectors.

Ushio America, Inc., 20101 S. Vermont Ave., Torrance, CA 90502. Tungsten bulbs.

Vari-Lite Europe Ltd, 20–22 Fairway Drive, Greenford, Middlesex, UB6 8PW, UK. Automated lighting systems.

VEAM (a division of Litton Systems, Inc.), 100 New Wood Rd., Watertown, CT 06795. Electrical connectors.

Wildfire Inc. 11250 Playa Court, Culver City, CA 90230-6150. Ultraviolet light technology. Black light fresnel and theatrical fixtures, paints and accessories.

Wolfram, 30 Janis Way, Scotts Valley, CA 95066. HMI bulbs.

Xenotech, Inc., 11229 Vinedale Ave., Sun Valley, CA 91352. Xenon lights.

Young Generators, Inc., 6605 Cat Canyon La., Arroyo Grande, CA 93420. Generators.

Appendix H

World power and television systems

Table H.1 World power and television systems

Country	*Language*	*Television standard*	*Line voltage*	*Line frequency*
Afghanistan	Pashtu/Persian	PAL	220/380	50
Algeria	Arabic/French	PAL	220/380	50
Angola	French/Portuguese	PAL	220/380	50
Antigua & Barbuda	English	NTSC	230	60
Argentina	Spanish/Castellano	PAL	220/380	50
Australia	English	PAL	240/415	50
Austria	German	PAL	220/380	50
Bahamas	English	NTSC	120/240	60
Bahrain	Arabic/English	PAL	230/400	50/60
Bangladesh	Bengali	PAL	230/400	50
Barbados	English	NTSC	115/200/230	50
Belgium	Dutch/French	PAL	220/380	50
Benin	French	PAL	220	50
Bermuda	English	NTSC	115/230	60
Bolivia	Spanish	NTSC	220/380	50
Botswana	English/Sitswana	PAL	220/380	50
Brazil	Portuguese	PAL	127/220	60
Brunei	Malay/English	PAL	230	50
Bulgaria	Bulgarian	SECAM	220/380	50
Burma	Burmese	NTSC	220/240	50
Burundi	French	Mono	220	50
Cameroon	English/French	PAL	220/380	50
Canada	English/French	NTSC	120/240	60
Canary Islands	Spanish	PAL	127/220	50
Central African Rep.	French/Sango	Mono	220/380	50
Chile	Spanish Castellano	NTSC	220/380	50
China	Chinese — regional	PAL	220/380	50
Colombia	Spanish	NTSC	110/220	60
Congo	French	SECAM	220/380	50
Costa Rica	Spanish	NTSC	120/240	60
Cuba	Spanish	NTSC	115/120	60
Curacao & Aruba	Dutch	NTSC	127/220	50
Cyprus	Greek/Turkish/English	PAL	240/415	50
Czechoslovakia	English/Czechoslovak	SECAM	220/380	50
Denmark	Danish	PAL	220/380	50
Djibouti	French/Arabic	SECAM	220	50
Dominican Rep.	Spanish	NTSC	110/220	60
Ecuador	Spanish	NTSC	110/120/127	60

Table H.1 World power and television systems (*continued*)

Country	*Language*	*Television standard*	*Line voltage*	*Line frequency*
Egypt	Arabic/English	SECAM	220/380	50
El Salvador	Spanish/English	NTSC	115/230	60
Ethiopia	Amharic/English	Mono	220/380	50
Fiji	—	—	220/415	50
Finland	Finnish	PAL	220/380	50
France	French	SECAM	220/380	50
Gabon	French/Fang	SECAM	230	50
Gambia	English	Mono	230	50
Germany	German	PAL/SECAM	220/380	50
Ghana	English/Acan	PAL	220/400	50
Gibraltar	English	PAL	240/415	50
Greece	Greek	SECAM	220/380	50
Greenland	—	—	220/380	50
Grenada	English	NTSC	230	50
Guadeloupe	French	SECAM	220	50/60
Guatemala	Spanish	NTSC	120/240	60
Guinea Rep.	French	SECAM	220/380	50
Haiti	French/Creole	SECAM	115/220/230	60
Honduras	Spanish	NTSC	110/220	60
Hong Kong	Cantonese/English	PAL	200/346	50
Hungary	Hungarian	SECAM	220/380	50
Iceland	Icelandic	PAL	220/380	50
India	Hindi/Urdu	PAL	230/400	50
Indonesia	Indonesian	PAL	127/220	50
Iran	Farsi/Kurdish/Arabic	PAL/SECAM	220/380	50
Iraq	Arabic/Kurdish	SECAM	220/380	50
Ireland	English	PAL	220/380	50
Israel	Hebrew/Yiddish/Arabic	PAL	230/400	50
Italy	Italian	PAL	220/380	50
Ivory Coast	French	SECAM	220	50
Jamaica	English/Spanish	NTSC	110/220	50
Japan	Japanese	NTSC	100/200/210	50/60
Jordan	Arabic/English	PAL	220	50
Kampuchea	—	—	120/208	50
Kenya	English/Swahili	PAL	240/415	50
Korea (N)	Korean	SECAM/NTSC	220	60
Korea (S)	Korean	NTSC	100/200	60
Kuwait	Arabic/English	PAL	240/415	50
Laos	Lao	PAL	220/380	50
Lebanon	Arabic/French	SECAM	110/190	50
Lesotho	English	Mono	220	50
Liberia	English	PAL	120/240	60
Libya	Arabic/Italian/English	PAL	127/220	50
Luxembourg	French	PAL/SECAM	220/380	50
Macau	Portuguese/Cantonese/ English	PAL	110/220	50
Madagascar	Malagsy/French	PAL	127/220	50
Madeira	Portuguese	PAL	220	50
Malaysia	Malay	PAL	240/415	50

Table H.1 World power and television systems (*continued*)

Country	*Language*	*Television standard*	*Line voltage*	*Line frequency*
Mali	French	Mono	127/220	50
Malta	English	PAL	240/415	50
Mauretania	Hassaniya Arabic/French	SECAM	230	50
Mauritius	English/Creole	SECAM	230	50
Mexico	Spanish	NTSC	120/127/220	60
Mongolia	Mongol	SECAM	127/220	50
Morocco	Arabic/French	SECAM	115/127/220	50
Mozambique	Portuguese	PAL	220/380	50
Nepal	Nepali	PAL	230/380	50
Netherlands	Dutch	PAL	220/380	50
New Zealand	English	PAL	230/400	50
Nicaragua	Spanish	NTSC	120/240	60
Niger	French	Mono	220/380	50
Nigeria	English	PAL	230/415	50
Norway	Norwegian	PAL	230	50
Oman	Arabic/English	PAL	220/440	50
Pakistan	Urdu/English/Punjabi	PAL	230/400	50
Panama	Spanish/English	NTSC	120/240	60
Papua New Guinea	English	PAL	240	50
Paraguay	Spanish	PAL	220	50
Peru	Spanish	NTSC	110/220	60
Philippines	Filipino	NTSC	120/220/240	60
Poland	Polish	SECAM	220/380	50
Portugal	Portuguese	PAL	220/380	50
Puerto Rico	Spanish	NTSC	120/240	60
Qatar	Arabic/Farsi	PAL	240	50
Reunion	French	SECAM	220	50
Romania	Romanian	SECAM	220/380	50
Saudi Arabia	Arabic	SECAM	127/220	50
Senegal	French	SECAM	110/220	50
Seychelles	English/French	Mono	230	50
Sierra Leone	English	PAL	220/440	50
Singapore	Mandarin/English	PAL	230	50
Somalia	Arabic/Italian/English	Mono	220/440	50
South Africa	English/Afrikaans	PAL	220/380	50
Spain	Spanish	PAL	220/380	50
Sri Lanka	English/Sinhala/Tamil	PAL	230/400	50
St Vincent	English	NTSC	230	50
Sudan	Arabic	PAL	240/415	50
Suriname	Dutch/English	NTSC	115/230	50/60
Swaziland	English	PAL	230/380	50
Sweden	Swedish	PAL	220/380	50
Switzerland	French/German/Italian	PAL	220/380	50
Syria	Arabic/Kurdish	SECAM	115/220	50
Taiwan	Mandarin	NTSC	110/220	60
Tanzania	Swahili/English	PAL	230/400	50
Thailand	English/Thai	PAL	220/380	50
Togo	French	SECAM	220/380	50
Trinidad & Tobago	English	NTSC	115/230	60

Table H.1 World power and television systems (*continued*)

Country	*Language*	*Television standard*	*Line voltage*	*Line frequency*
Tunisia	Arabic/French	SECAM	220/380	50
Turkey	Turkish	PAL	220/380	50
Uganda	English	PAL	240/415	50
United Arab Emirates	Arabic/Farsi	PAL	220/240	50
United Kingdom	English	PAL	240/415	50
Upper Volta	—	—	220/380	50
Uruguay	Spanish	PAL	220	50
USA	English	NTSC	120/208/240	60
USSR	Russian	SECAM	127/220	50
Venezuela	Spanish	NTSC	120/208/240	60
Vietnam	Vietnamese	SECAM	220/380	60
Virgin Islands	English	NTSC	110/220	60
Yemen Arab Rep.	Arabic	PAL	220	50
Yemen Dem. Rep.	Arabic	NTSC	250	50
Yugoslavia	Croatian	PAL	220	50
Zaire	French/English	SECAM	220/380	50
Zambia	English	PAL	230	50
Zimbabwe	English	PAL	220/380	50

Appendix I

Lighting equipment order checklist

HMI Fresnels

To include: barn doors, 5-piece scrim set, gel frame, scrim box, magnetic ballast, two 50-ft head cables, ballast feeder cable

24 kW Fresnel
____ 18 kW Fresnel
____ 12 kW Fresnel
6 kW Fresnel
____ 4 kW Fresnel
2500 Fresnel
____ 1200 Fresnel
575 Fresnel
____ 200 Fresnel
Electronic ballasts
____ 12 kW Clear glass lens

HMI PARs

To include: barn doors, 3 piece scrim set, gel frame, scrim box, 4 or 5-piece lens set, magnetic ballast, two 50-ft head cables, ballast feeder

12 kW PAR
6 kW PAR
4 kW PAR
2500 W PAR
____ 1200 W PAR (Sealed Beam)
____ 1200 W PAR (SE)
____ 575 W PAR
____ 400 W Joker
____ 200 W PAR
____ Electronic ballasts

Battery Kits

____ 200 W or 400 W Daylight Sun Gun
____ 250 W 30 V Tungsten Kit
____ 30 V Nicad Belt-Battery
____ AC Power Supply

HMI Soft lights

To include: egg crate, magnetic ballast, two 50-ft head cables, ballast feeder

____ 6000 Soft
2500 Soft
1200 Soft
575 Soft
Electronic ballasts

Tungsten Fresnels

To include: 5-piece scrim set, gel frame, scrim box or bag, 4-leaf barn doors, power feeder

____ 20 kW Fresnel w/Ramp-up dimmer
12 kW Studio Fresnel
____ 10 kW Big Eye Fresnel
____ 10 kW Baby Tenner
5 kW Studio Fresnel
____ 5 kW Baby Senior
2 kW 8″ Junior Fresnel
____ 2 kW Baby Junior Fresnel
2 kW Studio Junior Fresnel
____ 1 kW Studio Fresnel (407)
____ 1 kW Baby Baby Fresnel
650 W Fresnel
____ 420 Pepper

____ 300 Pepper
____ 200 Pepper
____ 200 W Midget
____ 100 W Pepper

Dedos

____ 150 W Dedo Kit
____ 100 W Dedo Kit
____ 250 W Dedo Cool Kit

Fresnel Accessories

____ Snoots
____ Focal Spots
____ Shutters
____ Chimera Banks
____ Chimera Speed Rings

Tungsten Softlights

To include: egg crate, power feeder

____ 8 kW Softlight
____ 4 kW Softlight
____ 4 kW Zip Soft
____ 2 kW Super Soft
____ 2 kW Zip Soft
____ 1 kW Zip Soft
____ 750 Zip Soft
400 Soft

Tungsten Open-Face

To include: 5-piece scrim set, gel frame, scrim box or bag, 4-leaf barn doors

____ 2 kW Mighty Mole
____ 2 kW Blonde
____ 1 kW Mickey Mole
1 kW Red Head
____ 650 W Open Face
____ 2 kW Nook
____ 1 kW Nook
____ 650 W Nook
____ 1 kW Molette
____ 2 kW Molette
____ Pinza (Med Screw Base)

Kits

R-40 Kit
____ Lowel Tape-up Kit
____ Stick-up Kit

Tungsten PARs

____ 1 kW Mole PAR (w/ 3-piece scrim set, barn doors)
____ 1 kW PAR Cans (w/ gel frame, bail block)
____ 6-lite PAR (6 PAR 64s)
____ Maxi-brute (9 PAR 64s)
____ Dino (24 PAR 64s) Bulb:
____ Ultra Dino (36 PAR 64s) Bulb:
VNSP PAR 64
NSP PAR 64
MFL PAR 64
WFL PAR 64
____ 9-light FAY
____ 6-light FAY 'mini-brute'
____ 4-light FAY
____ 2-light FAY
____ 1-light FAY
PAR 36 Dichroic
____ PAR 36 Tungsten MFL
____ PAR 36 Tungsten WFL

Tungsten Area Lights

____ Sky Pan (5 kW or 2 kW)
____ Chicken Coop 6 kW
____ Space Light 6 kW
____ 2 kW Scoop Light
____ 1 kW Scoop Light

Ellipsoidal Spotlights

____ 50° 1 kW 4.5 × 6 equivalent
____ 36° 1 kW 6 × 9 equivalent
____ 26° 1 kW 6 × 12 equivalent
____ 19° 1 kW 6 × 16 equivalent
____ 10° 1 kW 6 × 22 equivalent
____ 5° 1 kW 10 × 23 equivalent
____ Bail Blocks

Other Theatrical Lights

____ Cyc Strip
____ Follow Spot
____ Beam Projector

____ Scene Machine

Fluorescents

____ Wall-o-light (10 bank)
____ 4-ft, Four bank
____ 4-ft, Double Bank
____ 4-ft, Single
____ 2-ft, Four bank
____ 2-ft, Double bank
____ 2-ft, Single
____ 15-in., Four bank
____ 15-in., Double bank
____ 15-in., Single
____ 8-ft tubes w/Slimline Ballast
6-ft tubes w/Slimline Ballast
____ 12-Volt Single 15-in. Kit
12-Volt Mini Flo 9-in. Kit
12-Volt Micro Flo 6-in. Kit
____ 12-Volt Micro Flo 4-in. Kit

Xenons

____ 10 kW Xenon
7 kW Xenon
4 kW Xenon
2 kW Xenon
1 kW Xenon
____ 750 W Xenon
____ 500 W Xenon
____ 150 W Xenon
____ 75 W Xenon Flashlight

Stands

____ Easilift 3/4/5 section
____ Gladiator
____ Cinevator, Mole-o-vator, Hydrovator
____ Arri Supercrank (5, 4, 3 or 2 section)
____ Crank-o-vator
____ Low Crank Stand
____ Mombo Combo 4-riser Stand
____ Steal 3-Riser Junior Stand
____ Steal 2-riser Junior Stand
____ Aluminum 3-riser Junior
____ Aluminum 2-riser Junior
____ Junior Rolling Stand 3-riser
____ Junior Rolling Stand 2-riser
____ Low Boy Junior Stand
____ Steal Three-Riser Baby Stand
____ Steal Two-Riser Baby Stand
____ Baby Rolling Stand 3-riser
____ Baby Rolling Stand 2 riser
____ Low baby Stand
____ Preemie Stand
____ Blade Stand
____ Low Blade Stand
____ Runway Base
Turtle Stand
____ T-bone
____ Wheel Set (3 pc)

Accessories

____ Skate
____ Floor Plate
____ Base Plate
____ Table Stand and Exension
____ Hi Lift
____ Lo Lift Set
____ Side Arm/Low Level Bracket
____ Offset Arm
____ Magic Arm
____ Swan Neck Set
____ T bar Heavy/Light
____ Boom Arm – Heavy/Light
____ Big Ben (pair)
____ Scaffolding Tube
____ Wall Spreaders
____ Pole Cats/Barracudas/Autopole (S, M, L)
____ Extensions
____ Lightbem Kit
____ Barrel Clamp
____ Hook Clamp
____ Set Clamp
____ Prop Arms
____ Universal Clamp
____ Funiture Clamp
____ G Clamp (S, M, L)
____ Italian Clamp
____ Gaffer Clamp
____ Limpet Mount

____ Car Mounting Kit
____ Spigot Adaptor
____ Safety Bond
____ Stage Weight
____ Sand Bag
____ 246'
____ Rain cover
____ A-frame Ladders
Extension Ladder
____ Scissor Clamp
____ Gainsbrough/Candles
____ Frame Holders
Pole Holders

Trollies, Trucks, Barrows

____ Cable Cart
____ Doorway Dolly
____ Head Cart
____ Milk-crate Cart
____ Work box

Dimmers

____ Control Console
____ CD80 (6 × 10 kW)
____ 3 × 10 kW
____ CD80 (6 × 5 kW)
____ 3 × 5kW
____ CD80 (12 × 2.5 kW)
____ 20 kW In-line Dimmer
____ 10 kW In-line Dimmer
____ 5 kW In-line Dimmer
____ 5 kW Variac
____ 2 kW Variac
____ 1 kW Variac
____ 1 kW Triac
____ Transformer 240 V–12 V
____ Transformer 240 V– 110 V

Distribution

____ 400 A ISU (Intake Switch Unit)
____ 400 A CC (Control Centre) 12 × 63
____ 400 A CC 6 × 63 + 3 × 125
____ 400 MCC
____ 400 CSU
____ 400 3-phase 12 × 125
____ 400 CU 3 × 150 A/125 A
____ 400 Changeover Switch
____ 150 ISU
____ 150 CC
____ 150 CSU
____ 125/63 ISU
____ 125/63 3-phase to single-phase
____ 125 Distro Box 3/63 A
____ 125 Distro Box 8/32 A
____ 125 Distro Box 5/16 A + 3/32 A
____ 125 Distro Box 10/16 A
____ 63 Distro Box 5/16 or 3/32
____ 63 Distro Box 10/16
____ 63 A Final Distribution Unit with ELCB 6/32
____ 63 A FDU (Final Distribution Unit) with ELCB 3/32 + 4/16
____ K9 (32 A – 4/16)
____ 125 A Splitter/Y-cord/125 – 2 × 63
____ 63 A Spliter Y-cord 2 × 32
32 A Y-card 32 – 2 × 16
____ 16 A Asterix /4-way block/2-way block
16 A Y-cord
____ 125 A ELCB
____ 63 A ELCB
____ 32 A ELCB
____ 16 A ELCB

Cable

____ 400 A Jumper BAC to spade/tec
____ 150 A Jumper BAC to spade/tec
____ 125 A Jumper tec to spade/tec
____ 63 A Jumper 63 – 32 tec/spade/bare end
____ Jumper other ________________
____ 400 A BAC 100 ft
____ 400A BAC 75 ft
400 A BAC 50 ft
____ 400 A BAC 25 ft
400 A BAC tail
150 A BAC 100 ft
150 A BAC 75 ft
150 A BAC 50 ft
150 A BAC 25 ft

150 A BAC tail
____ 125 A 3-phase 100 ft
____ 125 A 3-phase 75 ft
____ 125 A 3-phase 50 ft
____ 125 A 3-phase 25 ft
____ 125 A 3-phase tail
____ 63 A 3-phase 100 ft
____ 63 A 3-phase 75 ft
____ 63 A 3-phase 50 ft
____ 63 A 3-phase 25 ft
____ 63 A 3-phase tail
125 A 100 ft
125 A 75 ft
125 A 50 ft
125 A 25 ft
125 A tail
63 A 100-ft Extensions
63 A 50-ft Extensions
63 A 25-ft Extensions
32 A 100 ft Extensions
32 A 50-ft Extensions
32 A 25-ft Extensions
16 A 100-ft Extensions
16 A 50-ft Extensions
16 A 25-ft Extensions
____ Socapex 100 ft (6 circuits)
____ Socapex 50 ft
____ Socapex fan-out
____ Socapex fan-in
____ Cable ramps

Generator

____ 5 kW Honda
____ 20 kW
____ 25 kW
30 kW
40 kW
____ 50 kW
____ 60 kW
____ 95 kW
____ 100 kW
____ 130 kW
____ 150 kW
____ 160 kW
____ 200 kW

Carrier or Mobile

Appendix J

Consumables checklist

Gel and Diffusion

Orange

____ roll Extra CTO
____ roll full CTO
____ roll Sun 85
____ roll 3/4 CTO
____ roll half CTO
____ roll quarter CTO
____ roll eighth CTO
____ roll full Straw
roll half Straw
____ roll quarter Straw
____ roll eighth Straw

Blue

roll Extra CTB
roll full CTB
roll 3/4 CTB
roll half CTB
____ roll quarter CTB
____ roll eighth CTB

Magenta

____ roll full minus-green
____ roll half minus-green
____ roll quarter minus-green
____ roll eighth minus-green

Green

____ roll full plus-green
____ roll half plus-green
____ roll quarter plus-green
____ roll eighth plus-green

Neutral Density and ND CTO

ND .3
ND .6
ND .9
____ ND 1.2
85 ND .3
85 ND .6
85 ND .9

Diffusion

roll 216
roll 250
____ roll opal
____ roll Grid Cloth
____ roll Light Grid
____ 1000H Velum

Other Gels

____ Other Colour Correction (e.g. CID, SCI, Y1, Fluorofilter)
____ Heat Shield
____ Cosmetic Colours
____ Party Colours
____ Party Gel Sheets

Bulbs

3,200 K

____ Photoflood No. 1 BC

____ Photoflood No. 1 ES
____ Photoflood No 2 BC
____ Photoflood No. 2 ES
____ 150 W Clear BC
____ 100 W Clear BC
____ 60 W Clear BC
40 W Clear BC
____ 25 W Clear BC 1
____ 100 W Pearl BC
____ 60 W Pearl BC
____ 50 W Pearl BC
____ 150 W Clear ES
100 W Clear ES
____ 60 W Clear ES
____ 40 W Clear ES
____ 25 W Clear ES
____ 150 W Pearl ES
____ 100 W Pearl ES
60 W Pearl ES
____ 40 W Pearl ES
____ 25 W Pearl ES
____ ____________________
____ ____________________

Daylight
____ 100 W BC
____ 60 W BC
____ 100 W ES
60 W ES
____ ____________________
____ ____________________
____ ____________________
____ ____________________

Coloured
60 W Blue
____ 60 W Red
____ 60 W Yellow
____ ____________________

Other Bulbs
____ Argo Blue 500 W
____ Argo White 500 W
____ Golf Ball 25 W BC Clear
____ Golf Ball 40 W BC Clear
____ Golf Ball 25 W SBC Clear
____ Golf Ball 40 W SBC Clear
____ Golf Ball 25 W BC Pearl
____ Golf Ball 40 W BC Pearl
____ Golf Ball 25 W SBC Pearl
Golf Ball 40 W SBC Pearl
____ ____________________

____ ____________________
____ ____________________

Fluorescents
____ Ge Nat Delux 2′ 20 W (3,600 K)
____ Ge Nat Delux 4′ 40 W (3,600 K)
____ Ge Nat Delux 5′ 65 W (3,600 K)
____ Ge Nat Delux 6′ 75 W (3,600 K)
____ Ge Nat Delux 8′ 125 W (3,600 K)
____ GE Northlite 2′ 20 W (5,500 K)
____ GE Northlite 4′ 40 W (5,500 K)
____ GE Northlite 5′ 65 W (5,500 K)
____ GE Northlite 6′ 75 W (5,500 K)
____ GE Northlite 8′ 125 W (5,500 K)
____ Philips Col/93 2′ (3,200 K)
____ Philips Col/93 3′ (3,200 K)
____ Philips Col/93 4′ (3,200 K)
____ Philips Col/93 5′ (3,200 K)
____ Philips Col/95 2′ (5,600 K)
Philips Col/95 3′ (5,600 K)
____ Philips Col/95 4′ (5,600 K)
____ Philips Col/95 5′ (5,600 K)
____ Thorn 8′ Nat Delux
____ Thorn 8′ Northlite
____ Terry Clips
____ End Caps (Slim TLD)
____ End Caps (Standard T12)
____ ____________________
____ ____________________
____ ____________________
____ ____________________

Tape
____ 2″ Gaffers tape (grey)
____ 2″ Gaffers tape (black)
____ 2″ Gaffers tape (white)
____ Black 2″ paper tape

____ Photo Black 2″ paper tape (matt black)
____ White 1″ camera tape
____ Phase tape (Bk, Bl, Rd, Gr/Yl, Yl)
____ 1/2″ Snot tape
____ 3/4″ Snot tape
____ Double Sided tape 1″
____ Double Sided Tape 2″
____ Sellotape 1″
____ Sellotape 2″
____ Hazard Tape

Hardware

____ Crocodile Clips
____ Drawing Pins
____ Nylon Cord
____ Trick line (black) #4
____ Grip Gloves (L, M, S)
____ Mason line (white) #4
____ Hanks Sash cord #6
____ Hank Sash cord #8
____ Hank Sash cord #10
____ Box Large garbage bags
____ 12″ rolls blackwrap
____ 24″ rolls blackwrap
____ 36″ rolls blackwrap
____ Poly Black/White 1″
____ Poly Black/White 2″
____ Poly on a roll
____ Poly White 1″
____ Poly White 2″
____ Card
____ Chinese Lanterns
____ Elbow Grease
____ Bottle Pure isopropyl alcohol
____ Clean lint-free rags
____ Roll Bailing Wire
____ Box Cotter pins
____ Box Sharpie Markers
____ Box Pens
____ Rubber matting (by the metre)
____ Roll Visqueen
____ Refracil (by the yard)
____ Crutch Tips 1 1/4″
____ Crutch Tips 3/4″
____ Bungy Cords (36″, 24″, 18″, 12″)
S-hooks
Mirror Tiles
____ Spray Mount
____ Staple Gun
____ Staples (per pack)
____ Swiss Clips
WD-40
____ Windowlite (by the metre)
____ Windowlite (Roll)

Electrical

AA Batteries
6 V meter Batteries
A-76 meter Batteries
9 V Batteries
____ Spare Mag Light Bulbs
Fuses 13A
____ ES-BC Adaptor
____ Plugs
Sockets
____ Lamp Sockets
____ Connector Strips × 15 A
____ Connector Strips × 30 A
____ Connector Strips × 5 A
____ Cable (Practical Soft Wire Black) (metre)
____ Cable (Practical Soft Wire White) (metre)
Cable Flex
Cable 3-core
In-line Dimmers 1,000 W
In-line Dimmers 600 W

Glossary

Abbie Singer The second to last shot of the day. The shot before the Martini.

Abbott (USA) A manufacturer of single-conductor connectors used on feeder cable.

Above-the-line costs Production costs of the producer, director, writer and principal actors.

Absorption filter A filter which transmits selected wavelengths. The absorbed energy is converted to heat which raises the temperature of the filter.

AC (1) Alternating current. (2) Camera assistant.

Ace (USA) A 1 kW Fresnel luminaire.

Acting area That portion of a stage used by the actors during a performance.

AD See **Assistant director**.

Adaptor A device used to convert from one type of connector to another.

Additive colour mixing The superimposition of light beams, usually consisting of the primary colours, whereby the resultant light is the *addition* of the various wavelengths concerned. See **Subtractive colour mixing**.

Alternating Current (AC) Electric current whose flow alternates in direction. The time of flow in one direction is a half period and the length of all half periods is the same. The normal waveform of AC is sinusoidal.

Ambient light Base light level created by existing light and reflection.

American National Standards Institute (ANSI) An independent association that establishes standards to promote consistency and interchangeability among manufacturers. This organization was formerly known as the United States of America Standards Institute (USASI or ASI) and previously as the American Standards Association (ASA). Three-letter ANSI codes are used to identify lamps (e.g., EGT is a 1 kW bulb).

Ammeter A meter for measuring current (see **Amperage**).

Ampacity Amperage capacity of cable, connectors, etc.

Amperage (I) A unit of current. One ampere will flow through a resistance of 1 ohm under a pressure of 1 volt.

Ampere Measurement of current. One volt applied to a resistance of one ohm produces a current of one ampere.

Ampere-hour A measure of a battery capacity equal to the number of amperes times the number of hours of charge that a battery can deliver.

AMPTP Association of Motion Picture and Television Producers.

Anode A positive electrode.

Apple box A reinforced plywood box used on the set for many purposes, including to raise an actor who is too short or to raise furniture. Apple boxes come in four sizes: full, half, quarter and pancake.

Arc light Usually a luminaire using a carbon arc discharge as the source of illumination. Also describes modern discharge sources such as 'MSR, HMI, CSI', etc.

ASA (1) American Standards Association (now the ANSI). (2) The exposure index (EI) rating of a film emulsion, also referred to as 'ISO'.

Aspect ratio The ratio of the width to the height of any imaging system. The standard aspect ratios are 1.33:1 (television), 1.66:1 (high-definition television and European theatrical film standard), 1.85:1 (American theatrical film standard) and 2.36:1 (Anamorphic 35 mm).

Assistant Director (AD) The person who runs the set. The AD is responsible for co-ordinating the actions of the many departments so that everyone is ready when the time comes to roll cameras.

Automation The ability of a piece of equipment to go to predetermined operational points by means of a closed loop servo system without the need for human intervention. Often confused with 'power assisted systems'.

AWG American wire gauge.

Baby 1 kW Fresnel luminaire manufactured by the Mole-Richardson Co.

Baby stand A ⅝ in. stud.

Baby stud A ⅝ in. mounting stud that mates with a ⅝ in. receptacle.

Back light A luminaire used to light the subject from the rear to help separation from backings and to increase the three-dimensional effect.

Backdrop (Backing) A scenic painting or enlarged photograph transparency used to limit the view of the audience or a camera through openings such as doorways or windows.

Backing lighting The illumination provided for scenery and backdrops.

Bail (Yoke) U-shaped part of a luminaire that is fitted with a spigot which allows the luminaire to be attached to a 'C' clamp or stand. The yoke acts as the pivoting point for the luminaire for pan and tilt.

Ballast The electrical device, required for all discharge lamps, that limits current through the lamp. There are two types: (1) a magnetic choke; (2) an electronic unit. Additional functions may be incorporated in the basic unit such as starting circuits and dimming control.

Banded cable Several single-conductor cables banded together at intervals, forming one bundle.

Barndoors Movable flaps attached to a Fresnel or PC luminaire to shape the light beam.

Barrel (colloq. Bar) A metal tube, generally 48 mm diameter, for suspending luminaires or scenery. Usually manufactured from steel or aluminium.

Base (1) The basket on the underside of a luminaire. (2) The part of a lamp used for the electrical connection to the power supply is called the 'base' (also known as the 'cap'). (3) The lamp socket is also sometimes called the 'base'.

Base light The basic intensity of 'soft' lighting required to satisfy the minimum viewing or technical requirements.

Basher A small luminaire of around 500 W used as a kicker.

Bates A common name for three-pin connectors (20 A, 30 A, 60 A, 100 A and 100 A/220 V).

Batten (1) Horizontal pipe on which luminaires or scenery can be hung. (2) Compartmented multi-colour floodlight unit for theatrical lighting. (3) Refers to 3 in. × 1 in. timber.

Battery belt A battery pack mounted on a belt that can be worn around the waist during location shooting.

Bazooka An adjustable extension tube with a 1⅛ in. spigot for mounting luminaires on catwalks. It is similar to a small stand minus its legs.

Bead board (USA) Polystyrene used to make soft bounce light.

Beam angle Those points on the light output curve which are 50 per cent of maximum output. The included angle between these two points is the beam angle.

Beam light (Beam projector) Lens-less luminaire with a parabolic reflector to give a parallel light beam.

Beam The unidirectional flow of total light output from a source, usually a luminaire.

Beaver board A nail-on plate mounted to a pancake.

Below-the-line costs The production costs of all members of the crew, but not the producer, director, writer and principal actors.

Best boy The assistant chief lighting technician or second electrician. The best boy is the gaffer's chief assistant.

Big eye A 10 kW incandescent luminaire with an extra large lens (Mole-Richardson).

Black wrap Thick matt black aluminium foil to control spill light from luminaires.

Blackbody A body which completely absorbs any heat or light radiation falling upon it.

Blackbody radiation Radiation that comes from an ideal blackbody. The distribution of energy is dependent only on the temperature of the blackbody and is governed by Planck's radiation law.

Blackout switch A master on/off switch used for controlling the overall production lighting for either stage or studios.

Blackout To switch all channels to 'off' on a lighting console. Also refers to switching off all illumination, except the exit lights.

Blind Refers to changes made on a lighting console which do not effect the 'live' console output (usually called Blind Plotting).

Blonde A 2 kW open faced luminaire.

Board A name for a control desk (derived from 'switchboard').

Boom operator The sound person who operates the microphone boom and affixes microphones to the talent.

Bounce lighting Directing light on to a large diffuse surface to produce a soft reflected light.

Brail To pull a lighting suspension device or piece of scenery out of its normal hanging position by means of attached rope lines.

Branch circuit As defined by the American NEC, circuits that are downstream of the last overcurrent protection.

Branchaloris A branch of a tree or bush held in front of a luminaire to create a moving or stationary foliage pattern.

Bridge A narrow platform suspended over the acting area. Luminaires and projection devices mounted on the bridge are accessible during performance.

Brightness ratio The ratio of maximum-to-minimum luminance occurring within a scene.

Brightness See **Luminance**.

British Standards Institute (BSI) Produces technical specifications and other documents which are made generally available. The main aim of the BSI is to maintain standards, quality and safety in goods and products.

Broad A wide angle floodlight.

Brute A 225 ampere DC high-intensity carbon arc spotlight with a 24-in. diameter Fresnel lens.

Bubble Slang term used in the television and film industries to describe lamps of any type.

Build A gradual increase in light level or in the number of light sources used.

Bulb An old term describing the bulbous glass envelope of an electric lamp.

Bull switch (USA) also called an 'isolation switch' or 'main disconnect'. A main switch used on the main feeder or on sub-feeder lines. They come in 60, 100, 200 and 300 A sizes.

Bump To briefly flash lighting channels 'up' or 'down'.

Bus bar Copper bars (¼ in. thick) to which lug connectors are attached.

Butterfly set A large frame used to support a net or silk over the top of the action. The silk reduces and softens direct sunlight.

C-47 A common, wooden spring-type clothes peg.

C-74 A clothes peg inverted to be used as a scrim-puller.

C-clamp See **Hook clamp**

C-stand A multipurpose stand used for setting flags and nets. Short for Century stand.

Cable crossover A special rubber ramp used to protect cable from being damaged by being run over and to protect pedestrians from tripping over cable.

Call sheet A sheet distributed by the production department before the end of each day that indicates the scenes that are to be shot on the following day, the call time of all cast and crew members, special travel instructions, special equipment that will be used and general notices to the cast and crew.

Cam-Lok A type of single pole connector used for feeder cables.

Camera light A luminaire mounted on a camera for lighting along or near the optical axis, usually to provide catch lights for the subjects' eyes.

Can Permanently installed switch gear containing bus bars on a sound stage.

Candela (cd) Unit of luminous intensity.

Candlepower A term that was used for intensity but has been replaced by the candela.

Carbon arc A DC arc source in which the arc is produced in air between a pair of carbon electrodes. These electrodes burn away and must be advanced during operation.

Cathode A negative electrode.

Catwalk A metal or wooden walkway usually used in the film industry to provide access and additional suspension points for luminaires.

Celo cuke A wire mesh painted with a random pattern and placed in front of a luminaire to throw a subtle pattern.

Chain vice grip A mounting device that uses a bicycle chain and vice grip to create a tight clamp around pipes, poles or tree limbs.

Channel number Reference number entered by a key pad; or used by dedicated faders.

Channel The circuit from the lighting control console to its associated dimmer.

Chase A series of programmed sequential steps activating channels from a lighting console.

Chaser lights A linear string of lamps wired and controlled so that the lights appear to be following in sequence.

Chiaroscuro A strongly contrasting treatment of light and shade in drawing and painting. Translated from the Italian, the word means 'half-revealed'.

Chicken coop An overhead suspended light box that provides general downward ambient or fill light. Also called a coop.

Chimera A specially designed, lightweight, collapsible soft box manufactured by Chimera Photographic Lighting.

Chroma In television, the information which gives the colour of the image as distinct from its luminance (brightness).

Chroma key A television special effect which uses a monochromatic coloured background to allow electronic switching to another picture. Deep blue is commonly used for the background when the foreground involves people.

Chromaticity The colour of light, as defined by its chromaticity co-ordinates, generally using the CIE diagram.

Cinevator stand A heavy-duty stand used for the largest types of luminaires. The mechanism that raises and lowers the luminaire is driven by an electric motor.

Circuit breaker An electrical switch positioned in the circuit that will automatically operate to break the flow of current under abnormal conditions.

Circuit The electrical path from a dimmer to the luminaire.

Clothes line cable (USA colloq.) A too-short cable hanging above floor level waiting for someone to trip over it.

Cmils Cross-sectional area of cable in thousandths of an inch, e.g. one square inch (1,000 × 1,000) is equal to 1 million circular mils.

Cold mirror A dichroic coated glass surface which reflects visible light but allows infrared energy to pass through the reflector so that the reflected light contains less heat.

Colour A sensation of light induced in the eye by electromagnetic waves of a certain frequency – the colour being determined by that frequency.

Colour chart A chart of standard colours filmed at the head of a roll of film as a colour reference for the laboratory.

Colour compensation (CC) A reading obtained from a colour meter indicating the amount of green or magenta gel needed to neutralize off-colour hues, usually present in fluorescent lights.

Colour frame A frame used to support colour media at the front of the luminaire.

Colour media Any coloured transparent material that can be placed in front of a luminaire. These are often referred to as 'gels' (for gelatine). Glass and other plastic materials are also used.

Colour Rendering Index (Ra) The evaluation of the effect of a light source on a set of coloured test pieces representing portions of the visible spectrum. The higher the Index towards its maximum of 100 the better the colour reproduction. Sources in general require an Index greater than 90 to prevent noticeable colour distortion.

Colour temperature A method of specifying the colour of a source which emits light in a continuous spectrum. Expressed in Kelvin units, the range used in media lighting is from 2,600 K (white lights with a high red content) to 6,000 K (white light with a high blue content). *Note*: Cannot be used with discharge sources, although sometimes used as a guide to approximation of colour. (See **Correlated colour temperature**.)

Colour wheel A circular mechanism holding several different colours mounted in front of a luminaire which can be rotated by hand or by a motor drive.

Combo stand A junior stand with a 1⅛ in. receptacle used to hold reflector boards and larger luminaires.

Complementary colours Pair of colours which combine to make white light, e.g. Cyan + Red, Yellow + Blue.

Condenser A lens or mirror used in an optical system to collect the light being radiated from a source, which is then directed on to the gate of the projection system.

Condor A vehicle with a telescoping boom arm used as a platform to position luminaires 30 to 120 ft in the air.

Console Name for a control desk (derived from 'organ console').

Consumables (expendables) Supplies such as tape, that are used during the course of a production.

Contactor An electrical switch used within an electrical system to control the on/off state of the supply. Usually operated by an electromagnetic coil.

Continuity (1) Script continuity (the job of the script supervisor): the task of making sure that all the details of the scene remain consistent from take to take and from angle to angle. Shots may be filmed hours and even weeks apart, but they will be cut back to back in the final film. (2) Electrical continuity: the unbroken flow of electricity through various conductors.

Continuity tester A device that runs a small amount of voltage through a conductor and lights a small bulb or makes a sound if the conductor is continuous.

Contrast range This is the ratio of the brightness between the lightest and darkest areas in a subject. In a video system, it is the range between the maximum signal which can be satisfactorily handled without distortion and the acceptable electronic noise level of the system.

Contrast ratio The ratio of the intensity of the key light plus the fill light to the intensity of the fill light alone.

Converter A device for converting AC to DC or vice versa. Can also be used to change the frequency of supply as well.

Cookie See **Cucaloris**.

Cool the lights To turn the luminaires off.

Correlated colour temperature (CCT) Many sources of light energy do not have the same characteristics as black body radiators, but sources which have a mainly white light output can be given a correlated colour temperature. This is defined as that temperature of the black body radiator which *most closely* matches that of the light source in question. It therefore gives a rough guide to the blueness or redness of the source.

Cosine law The equation which allows the calculation of illumination on a surface which is at an angle to the incident light.

Counterweight system Mechanical system for flying scenery in which the weight of the pieces of scenery is balanced by adjustable weights in a cradle running up and down in guides in a frame normally at the side of the stage. The system is also used for lighting bars.

Crank-up stand A heavy duty stand provided with gears and a cranked lever to raise and lower heavy luminaires.

Cribbing Blocks of wood used to level camera dolly tracks.

Croney cone A cone-shaped attachment fitted with diffusion that fits on the front of a luminaire to soften and control the beam.

Cross-lighting Illumination from two luminaires at approximately 180° to each other on opposite sides of the subject. They are generally hard sources.

Crossbarrel Used between barrels to allow accurate positioning of luminaires.

Crossfade A gradual change in the lighting where one lighting set-up *completely* replaces another. Obviously, only one crossfade can occur at a time. (See **Move fade**.)

Crowder hanger A luminaire mount that fastens to the top of a set wall and provides two spigot holders (studs).

Crystal-controlled A crystal-based circuit that maintains a camera's frame rate very precisely. A wild camera has no crystal control.

CSI A discharge lamp which approximates to sunlight for colour balance (CCT 4,000 K).

CTB gel A blue gel that corrects a tungsten source to daylight.

CTO gel An orange gel that corrects a daylight source to tungsten.

Cube tap (USA) A device that allows three Edison plugs to plug into one Edison socket.

Cucaloris A wooden cut-out pattern placed in front of a luminaire to create a pattern.

Cue (1) A signal, which may be written, verbal or by action, that causes motivation of artists or technical staff. (2) Refers to changes in the lighting (e.g. dimmer cue).

Cue light To activate the performer at a specified moment.

Cue number The reference number given to control system memories which contain the lighting set-up information.

Cup blocks Wooden blocks with concave indents. They are placed under the wheels of lighting stands to prevent them from rolling.

Current The rate of flow of electricity measured in amperes.

Cutter A long, thin flag used to make cuts in the light beam.

Cyclorama (cyc) lights (cyc strip) A set of open-face luminaires used to light a cyclorama. The luminaires are often wired from two, three or four separate circuits to provide individual control of different colours.

Cyclorama A backing, mounted in the studio, to provide a continuous surface and an illusion of infinity.

Daylight filter (1) A blue filter used to change the colour of a light source from tungsten at 3,200 K to approximately 5,600 K. (2) A blue filter used on a camera to allow daylight balanced film stock to be used with tungsten lighting.

Daylight Light commonly considered to have a colour temperature of between 5,500 K to 6,000 K. Daylight-balanced film renders colours naturally when lit with 5,600 K light.

DC Direct current.

Dead-man pedal A floor pedal that must be pressed by the operator's foot in order to operate or drive a Snorkelift. The dead-man pedal is a safety device to prevent runaways.

Dedolight A small, special lightweight luminaire with a wide range of beam angle adjustment.

Delta-connected system A system that provides a three phase supply where the coils are connected to form the Greek letter delta (Δ).

Depth of field The depth of the scene that will appear to be in focus on the screen. Depth of field varies with the camera's aperture, focal length and distance from the subject and the film format.

Deuce (USA colloq.) A 2 kW Fresnel.

Deuce board A fused AC/DC distribution box having two high-amperage contactors that can be controlled from remote switches.

Devitrification The process which causes a change from a 'glassy' state to a crystalline state.

Dichroic glass A filter or reflector which acts as a filter. Usually for converting 3,200 K to (approximately) 5,600 K.

Diffuser Sheets of frosted plastic or spun glass fibre used to soften the shadows produced by the light beam.

Dikes (USA colloq.) Wire cutters.

Dimmer An electronic device used to reduce current flow to a lamp and therefore allow its light intensity to be adjusted.

Dimmer curve A graph which shows the light output or voltage output of a dimmer against the channel control setting.

Dimmer room The area which has been allocated for the equipment racks which contain the dimmers and associated equipment.

Dip-less crossfade When channels with the same level in different lighting set-ups do not vary in intensity during a crossfade.

Direct Current (DC) Current that does not alternate in polarity.

Director of Photography (DP) The person in charge of the lighting and camera departments. The DP has direct creative control of the image.

Discharge sources Light produced by the passage of electricity, through a gas, across two electrodes enclosed in a quartz envelope, e.g.: Xenon, CSI, HMI, MSR lamps. (See **Arc light**.)

Discontinuous spectrum A light source with a discontinuous spectrum, such as a fluorescent lamp, that does not emit light evenly across the colour spectrum, but instead has spikes at particular wavelengths and emits little or no light at others, resulting in poor colour rendering.

Distribution box An electrical box with circuit protection used to change cable and connector sizing and provide assorted outlets. Usually called a 'distro box'.

DMX Multiplex protocol for transmitting digital information from control consoles to dimmers and automated luminaires.

Dog collar (USA colloq.) A short length of aircraft cable used as a safety bond to secure luminaires hung above the set. The collar is fitted with a loop at one end and a clip or karabiner at the other.

Dolly grip The grip in charge of laying dolly track and executing dolly moves and crane moves.

Dot A very small, circular flag, net or silk used to alter only a small portion of the beam of light.

Double broad This is a twin lamp floodlight generally used on studio floors as a local filler.

Double purchase A suspension system used on counterweight bars which gears the movement of the counterweight bucket to half that of the bar itself. (See **Single purchase**.)

Douser (Dowser) A small metal flag used in follow spots to cut off the light beam without having to switch off the electrical supply to the source.

Down-fade The portion of a fade that involves only channels that are decreasing in level.

Downlighter Usually refers to small ceiling mounted luminaires in control areas.

Downstage The stage or studio area which is nearest the audience.

Dress a light To tidy up the luminaire and/or its cable.

Drop arm (Trombone) A device used to hang a luminaire lower than the normal suspension system permits.

Duck bill A vice grip with a baby stud on the handle and two 6 sq. in. plates welded to the jaws. Used to mount foamcore and bead board on a C-stand.

Dummy load See **Ghost load**.

Duvetyne Thick, black cloth used to block unwanted light.

Ears The metal brackets on the front of a luminaire that hold the barn doors and scrims.

Earth (Earth continuity conductor) A conductor bonded to earth, other than the neutral, to provide a safety connection for metal components which are not in the electrical circuit. It is accepted to be the point of zero potential.

Edison plug and socket A typical American household plug and socket with two parallel blades and a U-shaped grounding pin. Also called a U-ground parallel-blade plug.

Effects projector A focusing luminaire used to project slides or shapes. The effects can also be motor driven.

Effects Sequence of lighting, usually preprogrammed to give a visual effect (chasers etc.).

Efficacy This is the efficiency of a light source in converting the electrical input power to light and is expressed in 'lumens per watt'.

Efficiency This is a measure of the *useful* light output in lumens against the total lumens generated by the light source.

Egg crate A device consisting of small cross baffle plates to restrict the spread of the light beam on a soft light.

Electrician Common name for a lighting technician.

Electronic ballast A solid-state ballast. The term electronic ballast is synonymous with flicker-free square-wave ballasts (discharge sources), or high frequency (fluorescent sources).

Ellipsoidal spotlight (Profile projector) A luminaire which uses an ellipsoidal reflector and a reasonable quality optical system to project shapes and patterns with a hard edge. Also called a Leko.

Elvis (USA colloq.) Gold lamé stretched on a frame and used to bounce light.

Emulsion The photochemical coating on a piece of film that captures the image.

Equipment grounding The earthing of conductive parts of equipment, such as the outer metal casing, via a earthing wire. (Europe: Green/Yellow stripes; USA: Green.)

Ethernet Data transmission system for computer networks; also used for interconnection of lighting consoles, dimmers and VDUs in remote locations.

Expendables (Consumables) Supplies, such as tape, that are used up during the course of a production.

Extension bar This is used to extend lighting barrels for accurate positioning of luminaires.

Eye light Used to create a twinkle in the eye of the subject.

F-number (F-stop) A set of numbers used to express the aperture of a lens which represents its light transmission. It is worked out by dividing the focal length of the lens by the diameter of the opening in the lens diaphragm. It is also known colloquially as the 'stop'.

Fade A gradual change in light levels from one set of intensities to another.

Fade time The time between the start and end of a lighting change.

Fader A control device for indirectly setting the current output of a dimmer and thus varying the light intensity. Originally were levers, but are often 'wheels' in modern lighting control systems.

Fall-off (1) The diminishing intensity of light across the beam of a luminaire. (2) The diminishing intensity of light anywhere else.

FAR cyc A luminaire that lights a cyclorama.

FAY An incandescent PAR lamp with dichroic coating that creates daylight-coloured light.

Feeder cable Large single-conductor cable used to run power from the power source to distribution boxes on the set.

Field angle Those points on the light output curve which are 10 per cent of maximum output. The included angle between these two points is the field angle.

Filament The tungsten coil inside a lamp that glows when voltage is applied to it creating light.

Filler (Fill light) Light used to control shade areas. Usually a soft light but can be controlled hard light.

Film speed (1) A measure of the film's sensitivity to light expressed in numerical terms to given an 'exposure index' which is used in the ISO and ASA system on light meters. (2) The velocity of film passing through movie cameras or projectors and is measured in frames per second or in metres per minute.

Filter A translucent material used to change the colour, and quantity of light, passing through it.

Finger A very small rectangular flag, net or silk, used to make minute cuts off the beam of light.

First team The director and actors.

Five K A colloquial term for a 5 kW spotlight.

Fixture General term for a luminaire, light or lantern.

Flag A sheet of metal or card mounted a short distance in front of the luminaire to give a sharp cut off to the light beam. Also black duvetyne cloth stretched over a metal frame.

Flag box A wooden box in which flags, nets and silks are stored.

FLB filter A filter used to remove the green hue of fluorescents.

Flex arm A small jointed arm used to hold fingers and dots.

Flicker box An electrical circuit box used to simulate the flickering of a flame or television screen. A flicker box randomly increases and decreases the intensity of the light output of the luminaires.

Flicker-free ballast A solid state ballast that provides square-waves of around 100 Hz to eliminate variations in the light output of discharge sources, thus avoiding problems with synchronization of film shutters and television field frequencies.

Flood By focusing a lamp close to a lens, the diameter of the light beam is enlarged and thus gives the widest field of illumination.

Floodlight A luminaire which has only a reflector to control the beam and has wide angle distribution. (See **Softlight** and **Cyclorama lights**.)

Fluorescence The ability of some materials to convert ultraviolet energy into visible light.

Fly gallery The gallery which extends around the side walls of the stage area approximately 30 ft above the stage floor. It is used for operating the ropes which adjust the counterweight system and hence the height of the bars above the stage.

Fly To suspend scenery or equipment above a stage or studio floor by means of a suspension system which can be manually operated or driven by motorized units.

Fly tower The upper part of the stage area which is formed as a tower, usually with galleries, to suspend scenery out of sight of the audience.

Foamcore A white, glossy card material reinforced with ¼ in. Styrofoam and used to bounce light.

Focal length The distance of the focal point from the lens is called the focal length of the lens. For camera lenses, it is usually expressed in millimetres. A long lens has a very narrow angle of view and a short depth of field. A short lens has a wide angle of view and greater depth of field.

Focal point The point where the incident parallel rays, which are bent by a lens, meet in focus.

Focal spot An accessory that mounts on a Fresnel luminaire, essentially changing the luminaire into an ellipsoidal spotlight.

Focus In optics, the adjustment to give a clearly defined image. Originally used in the lighting industry to indicate the process of 'spotting' or 'flooding' the light beam of a luminaire, but is now used to indicate the general setting of a luminaire on the stage or in a 'pop' rig.

Follow spot A narrow angle, focusing hard edged spotlight used to follow moving artists.

Foot-candle (FC) A unit of illumination still used by the film industry in the UK and Hollywood. One foot-candle equals one lumen per square foot. In some areas (television) foot-candles have now been superseded by 'lux'.

Foot-lambert One foot-lambert equals the uniform brightness of a perfectly diffusing surface emitting or reflecting light at a rate of one lumen per sq. ft. It is the old unit for luminance (brightness) which has been officially replaced by the 'nit'.

Footlights Lights mounted along the edge of a stage to provide uplighting.

FPS Frames per second.

Frequency The number of cycles per second of AC, measured in hertz (Hz).

Fresnel lens A convex lens built with concentric steps to enable its thickness to be reduced.

Fresnel spotlight (colloq. Fresnel) Luminaires fitted with Fresnel lenses of varying sizes, the width of the beam can be changed by varying the spacing between the lens and the lamp/reflector assembly.

Front of house lights (FOH) Luminaires usually mounted on barrels, and generally concealed, above the audience seats.

Frost Translucent gel or plastic used to diffuse light sources.

Furniture clamp An adjustable clamp used for mounting luminaires.

Furniture pad A packing blanket used to protect floors, deaden sound, soften a fall and so on.

Fuse A protective device for electrical circuits; originally a piece of special wire but nowadays nearly always a metal link contained in a ceramic cartridge.

Gaffer's tape Heavy, fabric-based tape that rips cleanly in the direction of the weave.

Gaffer clamp See **Mafer clamp**.

Gaffer Term used in the film industry to describe the chief lighting technician. The gaffer works directly under the Director of Photography.

Gamma A measure of the contrast in image reproduction. (1) In television, overall gamma relates to the receiver screen luminance and the brightness of the original scene. (2) A graph that describes a film emulsion's reaction to tonal gradation and its innate *contrast.* Also called D log E curve or characteristic curve.

Gang box (USA) An outlet box that provides Edison outlets and plugs into a larger connector, such as a 60 A Bates or a 100 A stage box.

Gate The optical centre of a profile projector where the shutters are positioned and an iris or 'gobo' can be inserted.

Gator grip A baby stud on a spring-loaded clamp with rubber jaws, used for mounting lightweight luminaires to doors, poles, furniture and so on.

Gel frame A metal frame that holds gels or diffusion material which slides into the bracket at the front of a luminaire.

Gel See **Colour media**.

Generators A diesel powered unit used to generate power. They are sound baffled and provide either bus bars or other feeder connectors. Also called a 'genny'.

GFI (USA) Ground fault interrupter. See **Residual current device**.

Ghost load A load that is not used to light the set and is placed on a circuit to balance the various legs of power or to bring the load on a resistance-type dimmer up to its minimum operating wattage. Also called 'dummy load' and 'phantom load'.

Globe A lamp or bulb.

Gnats (Gnats whisker) Slang term used in the UK to describe a very small amount. (See **Scosh**.)

Gobo A mask placed in the gate of a profile spot to shape the beam. It is a simple form of outline projection.

Gobo arm The arm of a C-stand.

Gobo head The metal knuckle that attaches the gobo arm to a C-stand.

Grandmaster The device (wheel or fader) which has overall control of the output of a lighting console.

Greens The wooden catwalk suspended above the set in a sound stage.

Grey scale Chart showing gradations from white to black.

Grid (1) A transformer unit used with a carbon arc light. (2) The structure of metal pipes suspended above the stage floor for hanging luminaires. (See **Lighting grid**.)

Grid clamp A clamp that attaches to grid pipe.

Grid cloth A white nylon diffusion fabric with a grid-like weave.

Griffolyn Trade name for plastic material. Griffolyn sheets come in $6' \times 6'$, $12' \times 12'$ and $20' \times 20'$ available in black/white, white/white and clear. They are used as a bounce for fill. Also called griff.

Grip A crew member responsible for the non-electrical aspects of lighting and rigging, and for the camera dolly and other camera platforms.

Grip clip A metal spring clamp.

Grip helper A metal arm that mounts to a junior stand. A gobo head angles down and out from the stand to which a 4-by frame can be attached in front of the luminaire.

Grip truck The lighting truck that houses the luminaires and grip equipment during location shooting.

Ground Fault Interrupter (GFI) See **Residual current device**.

Grounded wire The grounded, white, current-carrying wire (neutral) of an American AC circuit. (*Note*: Do not confuse this term with the green grounding wire.)

Grounding star (USA) A mole-pin connector to which a number of grounding leads can be attached.

Grounding wire The equipment grounding wire of an AC circuit. (See **Earth**.)

Groundrow Compartmented lighting units usually arranged in linear fashion for lighting from the base of cyclorama. A mask normally hides the luminaires from view.

Half-scrim A semi-circular scrim used to attenuate part of the light beam. (See **Scrim**.)

Halogen cycle The cycle by which halogen in a lamp returns tungsten deposits back to the filament thereby preventing blackening of the inner lamp wall.

Hard glass halogen lamp A tungsten halogen lamp with an envelope of boro-silicate glass.

Hard light A luminaire that produces well-defined shadows, normally a spotlight.

Head A luminaire.

Head cable The power and control cable running from the ballast to a discharge source luminaire.

Heat filter A light filter which removes infrared from the beam to reduce heat from the source of illumination.

Hertz (Hz) The unit of frequency which is measured in cycles per second. Other units are kilohertz (kHz) and megahertz (MHz).

Hi boy An extra tall stand.

High key Describes a scene containing mainly light tones well illuminated without large areas of strong shadow.

High leg The 208 V leg of a delta-connected three-phase system.

High roller An extra tall rolling stand, often used to fly an overhead frame.

Highest takes precedence (HTP) On a lighting control system, where the highest setting will win, when two or more pre-set levels are simultaneously selected for that channel. For example, if '7' then '5' is selected for a particular channel, '7' will win. (See also **Latest takes precedence**.)

HMI (also CID and MSR) Discharge lamps which have a daylight colour balance (5,600 K).

Hoist Old term used to describe either manual or motorized lifting equipment. (See **Winch**.)

Honey wagon The trailer that houses the lavatories used when shooting on location.

Hook clamp A clamp used for suspending luminaires from lighting bars.

Hot spot (1) The beam centre. (2) A shiny spot or glare reflection that is distracting to the eye.

House electrician An electrician permanently employed by a theatre or concert hall to maintain and operate the electrical equipment in the premises.
House lights A lighting system permanently installed to either illuminate an audience area or provide work lights in studios.
Housing The metal casing that surrounds the bulb and reflector of a luminaire.
Hue The quality by which one colour is distinguished from another as a result of their wavelengths. It does not take into account the brightness or intensity of the colour.
Hz Hertz (cycles per second).

Illumination The luminous flux falling on unit area of a surface. The unit of illumination is the lux (1 lumen per square metre) and it is the measure of the quantity of incident light.
Impedance (Z) A measure, in ohms, of the opposition to current flow in an AC circuit. Impedance includes resistance, capacitive reactance and inductive reactance.
Incandescence The emission of light by raising a material to a high temperature.
Incident light meter A light meter that reads the light falling on to the face of the meter.
Independent Channels in a control system which only respond to one master and are 'independent' of the rest of the console.
Inductance Opposition to current changing in an AC circuit, which causes the current to lag behind the applied voltage. Inductance is created by turns of wire with or without an iron core.
Infrared (IR) Wavelengths below the visible wavelength of light, felt as heat.
Inky A 100 W or 200 W Fresnel luminaire manufactured by Mole-Richardson Co.
Instrument Name used in the theatre for a lighting fixture (luminaire).
Internal reflector An integral reflector formed on the inner rear surface of the envelope of a lamp and is usually parabolic or elliptic in shape.
Inverse square law The equation which is used to calculate the illumination at a given distance from a source of light.
Iris A series of adjustable metal plates arranged to give a variable circular aperture. Used in lighting projectors to alter the size of the light beam.
ISO See **ASA.**

J-box A junction box. The term usually refers to an Socapex discharge source head cable junction box used to connect an extension head cable to the existing head cable.
Jockey boxes Metal storage containers on the underside of a truck. Jockey boxes usually store sandbags, cable and so on.
Juicer A set lighting technician.
Junior A 2 kW Fresnel.
Junior stand A stand with a 1⅛ in. spigot holder.
Junior stud A 1⅛ in. spigot.

Kelvin The SI unit of thermodynamic temperature. It uses the same size of degree as the Celsius scale. (Zero K = –273 °C.)

Key light The principle modelling luminaire, usually a spotlight.
Kick-out The accidental unplugging of a luminaire.
Kicker Generally a hard light source used to provide obvious highlights.
Kilowatt (kW or k) Electrical power term for 1,000 watts.
Knuckle The part of a C-stand gobo head that grips the flag.

Ladder A metal ladder-like structure, suspended from above or mounted to a wall, that provides a position from which to hang luminaires. Ladders are often used in theatres to position a stack of luminaires in the wings.
Lamp A glass or quartz envelope which contains filaments or electrodes. The term lamp is often used to describe a luminaire, which is to be avoided as it can cause confusion. (Colloq. terms include 'globe', 'bubble', 'source'.)
Lantern See **Luminaire**.
Latest takes precedence (LTP) On a lighting control system, where the last selected level for a particular channel will win. For example, if '7' then '5' is selected for a particular channel, '5' will win. (See also **Highest takes precedence**.)
Layout board Hardboard sheets, 4 × 8 ft, commonly used to protect floors.
LD Abbreviation for Lighting Designer or Lighting Director.
Leko (USA) Ellipsoidal spotlight.
Life Usually refers to the manufacturer's rated life in hours of a lamp at its normal voltage and is based on the average life of a number of lamps which have been tested.
Light centre length (LCL) The distance from the centre of the filament to a standard point at the base of the lamp.
Light meter A device for measuring reflected or incident light. Many modern meters also measure the colour of the source.
Light-balancing (LB) scale. Scale used on Minolta colour meters.
Lighting batten A barrel assembly with integral power feeders for luminaires.
Lighting control console A unit which contains the controls for adjusting the channel levels and thus the dimmer outputs, 'group channel' control, memory control, playback system and special effects.
Lighting Designer (Director) The person who creates and implements the lighting design for a production.
Lighting grid (1) In *television* a structure mounted at high level above the operational area, usually made from steel or aluminium or a combination of the two, for the purposes of suspending luminaires and ancillary lighting equipment. (2) In *theatre*, it is the framework above the stage in a close gridiron formation to allow operators access for positioning luminaires and scenery.
Lighting plot The instructions and drawings of the various lighting set-ups for a production, used by the LD and electricians. (Sometimes simply known as the 'plot'.)
Limbo Describes a state of lighting where the background details are suppressed. In television this is usually created by 'blackness' whereas the film industry tends to use a white background.

Linnebach projector A lighting unit, basically a box without a lens, which contains a small point source of illumination to project soft diffused images of cut-outs or glass slides.

Louvres Thin black metallic strips located on a luminaire to reduce spill light. (**See Egg crates**.) When fitted in front of a luminaire may also be adjustable at various angles to provide dimming without colour change. (See also **Shutters**.)

Low boy A very short stand.

Low key Describes a scene containing mostly dark tones with large areas of shadow and is often used to create a dramatic mood.

Lug A very heavy-duty connector for attaching feeder cables to bus bars, deuce boards and spiders. Also called sister lugs.

Lumen The lumen is the unit of 'luminous flux' and is defined as the amount of light which falls on one square metre of a surface at a *constant* distance of one metre from a source of one candela.

Lumens per watt The light output in lumens produced by a source for each watt of electrical power supplied to the source.

Luminaire A general term for a complete lighting unit. It includes the housing, the reflector, lens and lamps. (Colloq. light, lantern, fixture, unit, instrument, fitting.)

Luminance The measure of brightness of a surface, it is measured in 'nits'. The old unit was the 'foot lambert'.

Luminous intensity A measure of the energy from a light source emitted in a particular direction. It is measured in candelas.

Lux The unit of illuminance (illumination). It is the unit of measurement for the incident light arriving at a surface. The old measuring system used foot-candles. (One foot-candle equals 10.76 lux.)

MacBeth A blue glass filter used on some open faced luminaires which converts tungsten sources to daylight.

Mafer clamp All purpose grip clamp which can utilize different mounting attachments.

Magic hour The hour of light after sunset, during which the western sky creates a warm-coloured soft light.

Martini The last shot of the day.

Master/group master Usually refers to a lighting control system fader which overrides by electrical means a group of individual faders.

Matth pole A pole that braces against two opposite walls to provide a structure from which to hang a lightweight luminaire.

Maximum overall length (MOL) The overall physical length of a lamp including all electrical contacts.

MCB Miniature circuit breaker.

MCCB Moulded case circuit breaker.

Meat axe An arm mounted to the pipe of a catwalk or to the basket of a boom platform that provides a way to place a flag in front of a luminaire.

Meltric A five-pin, heavy-duty connector used in some power distribution systems.

Memory The term used to denote electronically recorded information which contains the lighting set-ups.

Mickey A 1 kW open-face luminaire manufactured by Mole-Richardson.

Microphony The interference caused by the mechanical vibration of any electrode system. Particularly troublesome on the older type of camera pick up tube, such as the Image Orthicon and the Plumbicon tubes used in colour cameras.

Midget A 200 W wide-beam Fresnel luminaire manufactured by Mole-Richardson.

MIDI (Musical Instrument Digital Interface) A communication protocol used to link control consoles for both lighting and automated luminaire systems.

Mini A 100 W or 200 W Fresnel luminaire manufactured by Mole-Richardson, or a miniature soft light manufactured by LTM.

Minus green gel A magenta gel used to take the green out of fluorescent light.

MIRED A figure is obtained by one million times the reciprocal of the Kelvin rating of a given light source. The MIRED (**mi**cro-**re**ciprocal **d**egree) scale is used to determine the colour shift of a given gel when used with any source.

Mirror ball A motor driven ball with its surface covered in small mirrors. When rotated, with spotlights shining to it, it produces moving points of light.

Modelling light The term is used to describe any luminaire, generally a hard source, that reveals the depth, shade and texture of subjects.

Mole-pin A 0.5 in. slip pin used as a distribution system connector.

MolFay A lighting unit consisting of a number of 650 W FAY lamps manufactured by Mole-Richardson.

MOS A scene filmed without recording sound.

Mountain leg The leg of a three-leg stand that extends to allow the stand to remain upright on uneven ground.

Move fade A fade from one lighting set-up to another where *only those channels with a new intensity* change; the other channels remaining static. Several 'Move' fades can occur at the same time. (See **Crossfade**.)

MR-16 A small projector lamp with a self contained reflector.

MT-2 A colour-correction gel used on carbon arc lights with a Y-1 gel to correct the colour temperature of a white flame arc to 3,200 K.

Multi-line spectrum The spectral energy distribution graph of a discharge source such as a HMI luminaire. Instead of a continuous line across the colour spectrum, the colour make-up is created by numerous single spikes.

Musco light A very powerful mobile lighting truck.

Nanometre (nm) A unit of metric measurement equal to one billionth of a metre, which is used to measure light wavelengths.

ND See neutral-density.

NEC (American) National Electrical Code.

Net A black honeycomb netting material sewn on to a rod frame that is used to reduce the intensity of part or all of a light's beam.

Neutral density filter A filter which attenuates the light passing through it without affecting the colour of that light.

Nine-light A luminaire comprising 9 PAR lamps used on exterior lighting.

Nit The unit of luminance, which is one candela per square metre of surface radiation. It is therefore the measure of the *brightness* of a surface.

Non-dim Describes the circuit which replaces the normal dimmer function, where the circuit is switched 'on' or 'off' *only*, either by a switch or relay system.

Nook light A small light-weight open-face luminaire using a double-ended lamp and a V-shaped reflector.

O-zone (USA) The open spaces between the permanent catwalks at high level above film stages. Only rigging grips are allowed to work in the o-zone using safety lines.

Objective lens See projection lens.

Offset A piece of grip hardware used to hang a luminaire out to the side of a stand.

Offstage Areas that are out of the eyeline of an audience.

Ohm (Ω) A unit of electrical resistance equal to the resistance through which 1 V will force 1 A.

On-stage In view of the audience.

Opal A popular, thin diffusion.

Opaque Absorbance of electro-magnetic radiation at specific wavelengths, generally refers to the fact that light is not transmitted.

Open faced luminaire Describes luminaires with no lens system, such as the 'Redhead' and 'Blonde'.

Overcurrent device A circuit breaker or fuse.

Overhead set A large frame with one of several types of material stretched across it, including a solid, single net, double net, silk or griffolyn.

PA See **Production assistant**.

Paddle (USA) The male plug that is inserted into a stage box.

Pan Term describing the horizontal movement, about a point, of luminaires or equipment.

Pancake A ¾ in. piece of plywood matching the dimensions of the large side of an apple box.

Pantograph A mechanical cross-armed device for varying the height of luminaires or other fittings. It is generally spring balanced but can be operated by a motor or manually driven gear system.

PAR A sealed beam lamp with an integral parabolic reflector, similar to a car headlight. PAR lamps are available in a wide variety of sizes and beam shaping lenses.

Par-can A simple luminaire, basically a metal tube, with a PAR lamp mounted in it. The type of lamp determines the beam spread.

Parabolic reflector A reflector shaped like a parabola, giving it a focal point from which all light rays will be reflected outward in a parallel beam.

Parallel circuit Connection of two or more devices or loads so that the current flowing through each one follows a separate path.

Parallels A small, easy-to-assemble scaffold platform, on wheels.

Party gel Coloured gels, also called effects gel or theatrical gel.

Patch panel A system rather like an old telephone operators' interconnection system (switchboard) to connect low voltage circuits or high voltage circuits. (Known as 'hard patching'.)

Patching A term describing the connections made between channels on lighting consoles and dimming systems. (Usually accomplished by software – known as 'soft patching'.)

PCB Printed circuit board.

Peppers A line of relatively small, lightweight tungsten luminaires manufactured by LTM in sizes of 100 W, 200 W, 300 W, 420 W, 500 W, 660 W, 1,000 W and 20 kW.

Perms Permanent catwalks at high level above film stages, used for access and rigging.

Phantom load See **Ghost load**.

Phase (1) An energized single conductor. (2) The positioning of an AC cycle in time, relative to the other two phases. Most electrical services are either single-phase or three-phase.

Photoflood A large standard pear-shaped lamp that has a colour temperature of 3,200 K or 3,400 K.

Piano board originally, a portable dimmer switchboard or road board. This term has come to be used for many types of portable dimmer switchboards.

Pigeon plate (USA) A baby nail-on plate.

Pin matrix A method of coupling control channels into groups by the insertion of special pins into a 'x' and 'y' matrix, where the 'x' axis may represent channels and the 'y' represent groups.

Pins Any of several types of connectors. Mole-pins and .515 pins are single-conductor slip pins used on feeder cable. Three-pin connectors, commonly called Bates connectors, are also sometimes called pins.

Pipe clamp See **Hook clamp**.

Pixel A picture element. The smallest element of a CCD array. The definition is governed by the number of 'pixels per area', the higher the amount the better the definition.

Plano-convex lens A lens which has one flat side and one convex side.

Plano-convex spotlight (PC spot) A luminaire that gives a reasonably even beam with a very sharp edge.

Plate dimmer A resistance-type dimmer commonly used with DC circuits.

Playback (1) That part of a lighting control system where the lighting memories and/or other lighting states are combined and controlled by output master faders or switches. (2) Music playback (commonly used on music videos) to allow the artists to lipsink to the music.

Plugging box (USA) A stage box. May also refer more generally to any outlet box.

Plus green gel A gel used to add green to luminaires to match their colour to that of fluorescent bulbs.

Pocket (USA) Outlets for stage circuits, often located under a protective trapdoor; for example, floor pockets, wall pockets and fly pockets.

Polarity The orientation of the positive and negative wires of a DC circuit or the phase and neutral wires of AC circuits.

Pole cat Lighting support system consisting of sprung metal tubes capable of extension on to which luminaires can be mounted. Used between two surfaces, floor and ceiling or two walls. Also called 'pogo stick' and 'Matth pole'.

Pole operation (Colloq. pole op) The control of electrical and mechanical functions on luminaires and suspension equipment by means of a long metal pole.

Power assisted systems Luminaires and suspension equipment that are under the direct control of an operator, e.g. winch control motor systems.

Power factor In AC, the ratio of the actual or effective power in watts to the apparent power in volt-amperes, expressed as a percentage. Inductive loads cause the current to lag behind the voltage, resulting in a power factor of less than 100 per cent.

Power The total amount of work, measured in watts. The term is also generally understood as 'electricity', or 'juice'.

Practical lamp A luminaire or any fixture that is shown in a scene, e.g. table lamp, that can be effectively switched on and off by an actor or remotely switched (in television from the lighting control console).

Prefocus Denotes special lamp caps so that the filament lines up precisely to the optics of a luminaire.

Prelight or prerig To rig in advance. During production, the grip and electrical crew may form a second crew or bring in a second crew to work ahead, rigging the sets that are to be shot during the following days.

Pre-set A group of faders on a manual desk which are connected to the dimmers and controlled by a 'master fader'. As there are usually two pre-sets or more on manual lighting control systems it is possible for a lighting plot to be set up in one pre-set without affecting the active pre-set. (This is known as 'blind plotting'.)

Primary colours The primary *additive* colours are red, green and blue. The primary *subtractive* colours are cyan, magenta and yellow. When the primary additive colours of light are projected on to a white surface, the area where all three colours overlap should theoretically make white light.

Prime fixture A focusing, open-face luminaire such as a Redhead or Blonde.

Priscilla (USA colloq.) A silver lamé stretched on a frame and used to bounce light.

Producer The person who oversees the production of the film or television show from the very beginning. Obtaining the script, raising money, finding the backing to produce the show to the very end, selling the finished film in domestic and world markets, trying to maximize its sales and profit making potential. The producer is the ultimate authority on all money-related decisions and most others. Everyone on the production works for the producer.

Production assistant (PA) An assistant in the production department who performs any number of menial and administrative tasks.

Profile spot A luminaire used to project shapes or patterns.

Projection lens A lens specially designed to project slides or shapes on to a surface with considerable enlargement of the slide or original material.

Proscenium arch (Opening) The surround to the stage area and through which the audience views the performance.

Pup A colloquial term for a one kilowatt spotlight.

Quartz Crystalline silica which is glass like and used to make envelopes for lamps. It is generally transparent to ultraviolet radiation.

Quick-on plugs and sockets Low-amperage, parallel-blade, no-ground Edison plugs and sockets that are designed to be quick and convenient to wire.

Rag (USA colloq.) The cloth part of an overhead set.

Rain tent A tent to cover luminaires and electrical equipment in case of precipitation.

Reactance (X) A measure, in ohms, of the opposition to AC due to capacitance (X_C) or inductance (X_L).

Receptacle A female connector or female mounting hardware.

Record The action of recording a lighting set-up on a control system.

Rectifier An electrical unit that converts AC to DC.

Redhead A 800 W open-face luminaire.

Reflectance (reflection factor) The ratio of the reflected light to the incident light falling on a surface, measured in lumens.

Reflected light meter A light meter that reads the amount of light reflected by the scene into the meter. A standard reflected meter has a relatively wide angle of view and averages the areas of light and dark to give the reading. See also **Spot meter**.

Reflector boards Silver-covered boards typically used to bounce light, usually sunlight. Also called 'shiny boards'.

Reflector The component in luminaires that focuses the light rays towards the lens. In a Fresnel it will be a spherical reflector whereas PAR lamps use parabolic reflectors. Effects projectors (Leko) generally use ellipsoidal reflectors.

Remainder dim A lighting console instruction which maintains the levels of selected channels, while forcing all other active channels to zero.

Remote A method of controlling the lighting from a position away from the main control system.

Residual current device (RCD) A special type of circuit protection. There are a number of different types, one type compares the outgoing current of a circuit to the returning current. If it detects a difference in the two (indicating a ground fault), it trips a switch to disconnect the circuit. Termed 'ground fault interupters' (GFI) or 'ground fault circuit interupter' (GFCI) in the USA, and 'earth leakage detectors' in Australia.

Resistance (R) A measure, in ohms, of the opposition to current flow in a conductor or device. In DC, volts ÷ amperes = ohms of resistance. For AC see **Impedance**.

Rheostat A resistance dimmer.

Rig (1) The overhead system designed to support luminaire and associated equipment. (2) To set up scenery equipment and lighting.

Riggers control A remote portable hand held control unit for controlling either luminaires or winch systems.

Rigging bible A set of diagrams showing the power layout of a studio's sound stages.

Rigging Collective term for suspension equipment.

Rigging gaffer The gaffer in charge of designing and installing the cabling and electrical distribution for a large set.

Rim A back light that makes a rim around the head and shoulders of the subject from the perspective of the camera.

Riser (1) An extension tube to add height to a lighting stand. (2) A wooden platform used to raise the set, luminaires or the camera.

Risers The flat surfaces on the Fresnel lens rings that form the division between segments.

Ritter fan A large effects fan used to blow snow and rain and to give the appearance of wind or speed.

rms Abbreviation of: Root-Mean-Square. The rms value of the current is a measure of its effectiveness in producing the same heating effect in a resistance as a direct current. It therefore allows for various wave shapes and directly relates to the power in watts.

Safety A wire, chain, cable, or rope looped around the bail (yoke) of a luminaire to prevent it from falling should it come loose from its fixing point.

Safety bond (also Safety chain) A short length of wire rope or chain formed into a loop around a suspension point, to act as a secondary means of suspension in the event of failure of the primary system.

Sandbag A sand-filled bag used to stabilize stands and equipment by adding dead weight or counterweight.

Saturated rig A lighting installation where luminaires are installed in sufficient numbers to cover the total acting area without rigging and de-rigging.

Saturation A term used to describe the density of a colour between the pure colour concerned and white, i.e. a deep red or pink.

Scene machine A lighting unit that projects an image on a screen, usually from the back. The image can be made to move by scrolling through the machine or to rotate by using adjustable-speed motors. Scene machines are often used to create moving clouds across the cyclorama in theatrical productions.

Scissor clamp A device that provides a means of hanging luminaires from a false ceiling such as those found in many modern commercial buildings.

Scissor lift A self-propelled electric lift.

Scissors arc A special carbon arc device used to create a lightning effect.

Scoop A simple elliptical shaped floodlight usually fitted with a large GLS lamp giving a soft light output.

Scosh (USA colloq.) A very small amount, as in 'Flood it out a scosh'. (See **Gnats**.)

SCR A silicon controlled rectifier. A solid state current switching device, used in dimmers for lighting systems. It comes from the *thyristor* family.

Scrim A fine mesh used in front of a luminaire to attenuate the light beam. They are made with various meshes to give different attenuation characteristics. A single dims the light about a half-stop. A double dims it about one stop. A half-single or double affects only half of the beam. (See **Half-scrim**.)

Second team The stand-ins used as models during lighting.

Secondary colours Those colours produced by mixing either two additive primary colours or two subtractive primary colours.

Senior A 5 kW incandescent Fresnel luminaire manufactured by Mole-Richardson Co.

Series circuit Connection of two or more devices or loads in tandem so that the current flowing through one also flows through all the others.

Service (Electrical service) This term refers to the types of circuits installed, for example, single-phase, three-wire service.

Service entrance The main switchboard into which the power lines running to a building terminate.

Shock The nervous sensation imparted to a body by the passage of an electric current.

Short A film of 30 minutes or less. Directors and students often shoot a short as a résumé or promotional piece to demonstrate their abilities or to help them move into a new area.

Short circuit Unwanted current flow of low impedance between conductors.

Shotmaker (USA) A customized tow vehicle for shooting moving car scenes.

Show card (USA) Thick card stock, usually white on one side and black on the other, used to bounce light.

Shutter (1) Metal flags of varying shapes used within a luminaire to block light. They are used to shape the light beam from effects spotlights and follow spots. (2) In a motion picture camera, a butterfly shaped device that spins in front of the film.

Shutters Venetian blind type metal slats mounted in front of a luminaire as a black-out device or dimmer.

Silicone spray A dry lubricant used on dolly track.

Silk Silk fabric used to soften and cut the intensity of light. It is used in all sizes, from very small dots and fingers to very large 20 × 20 ft overheads.

Silver bullet (USA) A 12 kW or 18 kW discharge luminaire manufactured by Cinemills Corp.

Single purchase A suspension system for counterweight bars where no gearing is used. The distance of travel of the counterweight bucket will be the same as the barrel. (See **Double purchase**.)

Sister lugs (USA) See **Lug**.

Sky-cloth A scenery unit used to convey the impression of an open sky. (See **Cyclorama**.)

Sky-pan A very shallow scoop used in the film industry, which is rather like a metal dustbin lid with a bare lamp in the middle. Used for general fill, using either 2 kW, 5 kW or 10 kW bulbs.

Snoot A conical metal tube fitted to the front of the luminaire to enable a reduction in beam size.

Snorkelift A telescoping-boom vehicle similar to the Condor.

Snot tape Sticky adhesive substance used to attach gel to a frame.

Socapex Multi-wire cable connector used (1) on discharge source head feeder cables, and (2) on multi-core cable for dimmer circuits.

Soft box A device used to create very soft, diffuse light.

Softlight A luminaire designed to produce virtually shadowless light and is generally used to control contrast.

Solid A black 'rag' stretched on a frame and used to cut light.

Sound mixer The person who operates the audio recording machine, usually a DAT or Nagra tape recorder.

Space-light A large cylinder consisting of a diffuser with an array of lamps inside to give soft ambient illumination.

Spark A nickname for set lighting technician.

SPD Spectral power distribution (graph).

Specular Describes a mirror like surface. Highly reflective.

Spider box (USA) A cable splicing box used to join lug feeder cables. The cable's lug connectors bolt to copper bus bar plates.

Spigot The male member attached to a yoke used for the suspension of the luminaire and also for insertion into a floor stand. Colloq. 'spud'. (See **Stud**.)

Spill light Extraneous uncontrolled light from a luminaire.

Spot meter A type of reflected meter having a very narrow angle of acceptance (1° to 20°) used to determine the light value of a specific point on the set.

Spot To focus a luminaire by moving the lamp/reflector away from the lens, giving a narrow beam.

Spotlight A luminaire with a focusing system to concentrate the light beam and thus giving greater operational control.

Square wave A type of AC created by an electronic ballast that renders discharge sources flicker-free.

Stage box (USA) A distribution box with sockets that accept male connectors. Stage boxes are normally referred to by the number of sockets they have: one-hole, two-hole, four-hole, or six-hole boxes.

Stage extension (USA) A high-amperage extension cable; it has a paddle on one end and a one-hole or two-hole box at the other.

Stage left/right The performers left and right as they face the audience.

Staging area The area on the sound stage or location selected as a temporary place to keep the lighting equipment and technical equipment trolleys.

Stand A telescopic floor mounted tripod device which provides a means of adjusting the height of luminaires above floor level. Can be manual lift, or by a geared wind-up system.

Stick-up An extremely small, lightweight luminaire that can be taped to the wall.

Stinger (USA) An extension cord; officially, a hot extension cord.

Stop An f-stop or a t-stop.

Strain relief A rope tie used to reduce strain at the point at which a cable attaches to its connector.

Streaks and Tips (Trade name) Cans of hair spray that are often handy for darkening reflective surfaces.

Strike (1) To dismantle a set or to take down and put away a piece of equipment. (2) When referring to an arc or a discharge source, to strike the light means 'turn it on'.

Strobe light A light that creates short, bright, regular flashes of light at an adjustable speed.

Stud Term for shaped piece of cylindrical metal which is attached to the bail (yoke) and used for mounting luminaires on to stands, etc. (See **Spigot**.)

Studio area The total floor area contained within the walls of a studio which may not always be used as the acting area, due to fire lanes, etc.

Sub-master A controller (usually a linear slider) on a dimmer board that allows manual control of groups, effects, cues or channels.

Subtractive colour mixing The removal of light of various wavelengths, by filtering or reflection, e.g. a magenta filter *subtracts* the green from the light path, whereas the pigment of yellow paint reflects the red and green components of the incident light but absorbs (*subtracts*) the blue. (See **Additive colour mixing**.)

Suicide pin (USA) An adaptor with two male ends.

Swing (USA) A crew member who performs the tasks of both grip and electrician, as needed.

System grounding (Neutral) The grounding of the electrical system by the neutral wire to the main power transformer and to earth.

T-bone A metal T-shaped base with a junior receptacle, used to place larger luminaires at ground level.

T-stop The aperture setting of a zoom lens after compensation for light lost in the numerous optical elements of the lens.

Taco cart (Equipment trolley) A special cart that carries grip equipment, such as C-stands, apple boxes, wedges, mounting hardware and grip expendables.

Tag line A line dropped from aloft and used to hoist equipment into a catwalk, green beds or Condor.

Talent On-camera people and animals, usually actors, not necessarily talented ones.

Telescope A grid mounted device made from retractable sets of tubes that is used to suspend luminaires at varying heights in the studio. Older types of telescopes were driven by portable power tools, modern systems are generally equipped with integral electric motors.

Three-fer A connector that provides three female connectors from one male connector

Three-phase A type of alternating current that has three legs. The alternating voltage cycle of each leg is a third of a cycle apart (120°).

Three-riser A stand that has three extensions.

Throw Generally describes the direction of light from a luminaire and also the effective distance between the luminaire and the area being lit.

Tie-in The connection of temporary distribution cables to a facility's electrical service panel.

Tilt Term describing the vertical movement, about a point, of luminaires or equipment.

Titan A 350 A carbon arc luminaire manufactured by Mole-Richardson.

Tower A temporary platform usually made from scaffolding, on which to mount luminaires.

Tracing paper ('brass rubbing paper') Thin, translucent paper used to white out windows.

Transformer A device with no moving parts, consisting of a set of insulated windings on a laminated steel core that is used to increase or reduce AC voltage by inductive coupling.

Tree A tall stand or tower that has horizontal pipes on which luminaires can be hung. Used a great deal in theatre and concert lighting.

Trombone American term for an adjustable drop arm. (See also **Drop arm**.)

Truss A framework, generally made from alloy bars together with cross bracing, to provide lightweight rigging structures. Trusses are used largely in TV temporary lighting rigs and concert lighting to support luminaires and other equipment at high level.

Tungsten halogen Describes a family of lamps with either hard glass or quartz envelopes, tungsten filaments and halogen (usually iodine or bromine) fillings.

Tungsten halogen lamp A lamp designed to maintain an almost constant colour temperature and a high lumen output throughout its life. The halogen cycle is a regenerative process that prevents the blackening of the inside of the bulb.

Turtle stand A very low stand with either three or four feet to position luminaires at ground level.

Tweco clamp An electrical clamp consisting of two saw-tooth jaws that clamp together by turning the threaded screw base.

Tweenie A 650 W Fresnel luminaire manufactured by Mole-Richardson Co.

Twist-lock A connector for which the plug inserts into the socket and then twists, locking the plug to the socket.

Two K A colloquial term for a 2 kW spotlight.

Type W cable Cable that is manufactured to meet the requirements of NEC Articles 520 and 530 regarding portable entertainment cable. It is abrasion, oil, solvent, and ozone resistant and flame tested.

U-ground A standard Edison plug with a U-shaped grounding pin.

Ultraviolet (UV) The band of short wave radiation from 400 nm to 10 nm, although invisible to the eye the energy is extremely powerful and produces reddening of the skin (sunburn). UV-A is black light. UV-B radiation can cause skin burns and eye damage as well as skin cancer if not filtered.

Underwriters Laboratory (UL) An American independent test laboratory that ensures minimum safety standards of equipment.

Undo A memory system feature for cancelling the last instruction and returning the console to its previous set-up.

Unilux A manufacturer of strobe lighting equipment that can be synchronized to a motion picture camera shutter.

Up-fade The portion of a fade that involves only channels that are increasing in level.

Variac An auto-transformer dimmer.

VEAM connector VEAM Litton is a manufacturer of connectors, including multi-pin discharge source head feeder connectors and single conductor feeder cable connectors.

Velum See **Tracing paper**.

Visqueen Plastic material used to protect equipment from precipitation.

Volt (V) A unit of electrical force. One volt is required to force one ampere of electricity though a resistance of one ohm.

Volt-ampere (VA) Voltage times amperage. In DC, volts × amps = watts, but in AC, inductance and capacitance in the circuit may introduce reactance, causing a discrepancy between watts and volt-amperes.

Voltage drop That loss of volts which occurs through energy wastage when a current passes through a cable or electronic device.

Voltmeter A meter used to measure voltage potential between two points in a circuit.

Wall sled A luminaire-mounting device that hangs from the top of the set wall and rests against the wall.

Wall spreader Hardware that mounts to either end of a piece of lumber, creating a span from one wall to another from which luminaires can be hung.

Wash General ambient light on the acting area.

Watt (W) A unit of electrical power, the product of voltage and amperage.

Wedge A triangular wooden block used to level dolly track.

Welding cable (USA) A flexible electrical cable once widely used for power distribution. Welding cable can no longer be used legally, except as a grounding wire.

Western dolly A large flatbed camera platform with large inflated tyres that steer at one end. A western dolly can be useful for moving luminaires and cable.

Wet cell battery A car battery.

Wiggy (USA) A continuity or resistance-testing device.

Winch Term used to describe either manual or motorized lifting equipment.

Wind-up stand See **Crank-up stand**.

Wire rope Ropes formed from fine wires woven in complex patterns to give great strength.

Working lights See **House lights**.

Wrap The process of taking down luminaires and coiling cable that begins after the last shot of the day has been completed successfully.

Wye-connected system A common type of three-phase transformer arrangement. Voltage reads 208 V (415 V) between any two of the phases and 120 V (240 V) between a phase and the neutral.

Xenon luminaires An extremely bright type of arc discharge luminaire that has a colour temperature of 5,600 K. Because the arc is very small, the light can be channelled into a very narrow shaft of extremely bright light.

Y-1 A type of gel that converts a white carbon arc to normal daylight colour balance, by reducing the UV output.

Y-connected system See **Wye-connected system**.

Yoke The suspension frame of a luminaire; possibly containing the drive mechanism for pan and tilt (also fork, stirrup, trunnion, bail).

Zip cord Two-wire, 18 AWG electric lamp cord.

Zip light A small soft luminaire.

Zone system Ansel Adams's system of eleven gradations of grey from pure black to pure white. The zones are numbered in Roman numerals from 0 to X. There is a one-stop difference from zone to zone.

Zoom (1) The movement of a series of elements within a lens to change the focal length of the lens, allowing wide to fairly narrow coverage. To maintain a good aperture the front elements are often fairly large and therefore zoom lenses are quite heavy. (2) Used in profile spots and scenic projectors, consisting of the relative movement of two simple lens elements to change beam width and focus.

Bibliography

The following publications were consulted in the writing of this book. Each is an excellent reference for further reading in specific areas.

Carlson, Verne and Carlson, Sylvia E. *Professional Lighting Handbook.* 2nd ed. Boston: Focal Press, 1991.

Carter, Paul. *Backstage Handbook: An Illustrated Almanac of Technical Information.* New York: Broadway Press, 1988.

Detmers, F. (ed.) *American Cinematographer Manual.* Hollywood: American Society of Cinematographers Press, 1989.

Fitt, B. and Thornley, J. *Lighting Technology*. Oxford: Focal Press, 1997.

Goodell, Gregory. *Independent Feature Film Production: A Complete Guide from Concept to Distribution.* New York: St Martin's Press, 1982.

Johnson, Gordon S. *On-Site Power Generation: A Reference Book*, 2nd ed. Coral Springs, Florida: Electrical Generating Systems Association, 1993.

Local 728, International Alliance of Theatrical and Stage Employees. *Working Manual for Studio Electrical Technicians.* Hollywood: IATSE.

Maikiewicz, Kris. *Cinematography.* New York: Prentice Hall, 1973.

Matthews Studio Equipment Inc. *Matthews 1992 Product Catalog.* Burbarnk, CA, 1992.

Mole-Richardson Co. *Mole-Richardson Co. Catalog.* Hollywood, 1990.

Moody, James L. *Concert Lighting: Technique, Art and Business.* Boston: Focal Press, 1989.

National Fire Protection Association. *National Electrical Code.* Cuincy, MA: NEPA, 1991.

Pilbrow, Richard. *Stage Lighting.* New York: Drama Book Publishers, 1970.

Richter, Herbert P. and Schwan, Creighton W. *Practical Electrical Wiring.* New York: McGraw-Hill, 1990.

Samuelson, David W. *The 'Hands on' Manual for Cinematographers.* 2nd ed. Oxford: Focal Press, 1998.

Samuelson, David W. *Motion Picture Camera and Lighting Equipment: Choice and Technique.* 2nd ed. Boston: Focal Press, 1986.

Schaefer, John P. *An Ansel Adams Guide: Basic Techniques of Photography.* Boston: Little Brown, 1992.
Strand Lighting. *CD80 Digital Pack, Users Manual.* Rancho Domingues, CA, Revision Date 28 September 1992.
Sylvania GTE. *Lighting Handbook for Television, Theatre and Professional Photography.* 8th ed. Danvers, MA: Sylvania, 1989.

Additional references for further reading

Periodicals

American Cinematographer
ASC Holding Corporation
1782 N. Orange Drive, Hollywood, California 90028
Lighting Dimensions
Lighting Dimensions Associates
135 Fifth Ave.
New York, NY 10010-7193

Books

Brown, Blain. *Motion Picture and Video Lighting.* Boston: Focal Press, 1992.
Glerum, Jay. *Stage Rigging Handbook.* Carbondale, Ill: Southern Illinois University Press, 1989.
Hirshfeld, Gerald. *Image Control.* Boston: Focal Press, 1993.
Lowell, Ross. *Matters of Light and Depth.* Philadelphia, PA: Broad Street Books, 1992.
McCandles, Stanley. *A Method of Lighting the Stage.* New York: Theatre Arts Books, 1958.
Schaefer, Dennis and Salvato, Larry. *Masters of Light: Conversations with Contemporary Cinematographers.* Berkley and Los Angeles, California: University of California Press, 1984.
Uva, Michael and Uva, Sabrina. *The Grip Book.* Boston: Focal Press, 1997.
Wilson, Anton. *Cinema Workshop.* Hollywood, CA: ASC Holding Co., 1983.

Index